ROMAN PALESTINE 200–400
MONEY AND PRICES

by

DANIEL SPERBER

מחקרי בר־אילן במזרח התיכון ובתרבותו

BAR-ILAN STUDIES IN NEAR EASTERN
LANGUAGES AND CULTURE

ROMAN PALESTINE
200 – 400
MONEY AND PRICES

DANIEL SPERBER

Second Edition with Supplement

BAR-ILAN UNIVERSITY PRESS

First Edition — 1974
Second Edition with Supplement — 1991

ISBN 965-226-147-5

©

Copyright Bar-Ilan University, Ramat-Gan
Printed in Israel
by "Daf-Noy" Press, Jerusalem

CONTENTS

PART THREE: PRICES

NOTES

INDICES

SUPPLEMENT TO SECOND EDITION

ILLUSTRATIONS

PLATES

The capital letters A to AY appearing in the text and notes refer to the
Hebrew sources on pages 299-309

The numbers 1 to 24 appearing in square brackets in the text and notes refer
to the coins illustrated in the plates

ACKNOWLEDGEMENTS

The following study was almost a decade in the making. From its inception as a London University doctoral thesis under the guidance of Professor S. Stein (of the department for Hebrew Studies at University College London), and Professor A.D. Momigliano (of the department of Ancient History at the same institution) until its present-day form, it has undergone a number of incarnations. No doubt something of the stratification in this work will be discernible to the sensitive reader. Over these years I have enjoyed the help and encouragement of a number of individuals and institutions, and it is both a duty and a pleasure to remember them with gratitude.

During the year 1965 I was granted a research fellowship by the Institute of Jewish Studies, London, under the directorship of the late Professor J.G. Weiss. It was he who gave me the initial incentive to work in this direction, and this study is an expression of my thanks to him. During the years 1966–68 I benefited from scholarships granted by London University, and supplementary stipends from the Memorial Foundation for Jewish Culture. In 1968 I came to Israel, joining the academic staff of Bar-Ilan University. The University's research committee has always proved to be generous in granting any research facilities required.

Of individuals, I have already mentioned Professors Stein and Momigliano, both of whom I recall with pleasure and gratitude. Professor Momigliano, whose peripheral knowledge is proverbial, called my attention to a number of important studies which I would otherwise have probably missed. He also directed my attention to several new avenues of approach and method.

I should like to express my especial appreciation of the late Professor F.M. Heichelheim. Fired with youthful ardour and juvenile zeal, I criticized (in print) his great pioneer studies with unabashed aggressiveness. He, with a gentle wisdom of maturity, accepted my

11

critique with refined grace, acknowledging its measure of justice — where he agreed — and encouraged my further endeavours in these directions with a genuine warmth. May his example serve as a lesson to us all.

While in London I had the honour and good fortune to make the acquaintance of two people, acknowledged to be among the leading authorities in Roman numismatics, Dr. R.A.G. Carson, and Dr. J.P.C. Kent, both of the Department of Coins and Medals at the British Museum. They were unsparing with their time and unstinting of their knowledge, and were always willing to help in any way possible. I also enjoyed frequent use of that department, and was thus able to examine coins at first hand, as well as to find the necessary numismatic literature. Subsequently, I sent a manuscript of this study to Mssrs. Carson and Kent, who did me the great kindness of looking it over and of making a number of important comments. Other comments have been included in the body of the notes with full acknowledgements.

The coin plates at the back of this book are by courtesy of the same department of the British Museum. They were arranged through the good offices of Dr. Carson, who also did me the kindness of supplying the descriptive captions. The specimens themselves are all from the British Museum collection, and were selected by Dr. Carson for their quality and condition. Mr. A. Gardner of the same department produced the excellent pictures. For all this, my own, and I trust the readers' very sincere thanks.

Again, through the personal aid of Dr. Carson, I was able to make (postal) contact with Mr. L. Cope, an expert in numismatic metallurgy of the Roman period. He too very generously agreed to look the manuscript over, and sent me his comments. These have been similarly incorporated in the notes.

At this point I should also like to thank Dr. M. Crawford, of Christ College Cambridge, for sending me copies of his very significant contributions, and to Dr. R.P. Duncan-Jones, of Caius College Cambridge, whose epigraphic surveys serve as models of their kind, for his valued remarks and references. I should also like to thank Dr. Joseph Gary, Prof. Kenan T. Erim and Joyce Reynolds for permission to reproduce the photographs of the Aphrodisias inscriptions, first published in *JRS*, 61 (1971), plate XII.

More recently, I have had the honour of making contact with Professor J.P. Callu, of Paris. He, with great generosity, sent me a copy of his magnificent *La Politique Monétaire*. This monumental work, which combines prodigious labour with painstaking scholarship, opens up manifold new vistas both to historians of the period as well as to numismatists. He has subsequently kept me abreast of his researches, sending me copies of his various publications. His openhandedness and encouraging appreciation of my own endeavours make me deeply indebted to him.

TO THE SECOND EDITION

This book was first published in 1974, and went out of print within about five years. In that edition I acknowledged the help of various friends and colleagues, and these acknowledgements need not be repeated here. More then a decade has passed since the book went out of print, and though requests for the volume were constant, I resisted the temptation to have it reprinted, knowing full well that, in the light of more recent discoveries and further research, many points put forward here require correcting, rethinking and reformulating. But I was not in the position to rewrite, or even to update my work.

However, as inquiries over the book have not ceased coming in, I realized that certain sectors of the scholarly community felt a need for it, and its absence was troublesome to them. In addition I believe that the basic thesis presented, and the inflationary pattern reconstructed, are still tenable, even though many details may be subject to argumentation. Furthermore, it would appear to me that the methodology employed is instructive, and scholars may learn to utilize it in other areas of Talmudic research.

It is to this end, and at the request of many colleagues, that I have included an appendix consisting of the basic text on Palestinian Talmudic monetary theory. This text (in translation), with its commentary, should give the reader a good idea of what the raw material for this kind of research is like; how one goes about interpreting it, dating it and deriving from it all kinds of historical information. In addition I have included two later studies that supplement the data in the original work. Hopefully, the reprinting of this volume, with its additional material, will encourage further research in what is a very fascinating, but extremely complex, field.

In the first edition I thanked my wife and three small daughters who helped "each in her own individual style and manner." I should now like to thank my nine children, ranging from four to twenty, and my wife even more, for their constant forbearance and encouragement. A special debt of gratitude goes to my late father, teacher and mentor, from whom I probably learned more than anyone else, both in the field of Talmudic studies and in the field of historical research. My mother, a pillar of strength and fortitude, is a special source of inspiration to the whole family. An author in her own right, we wish her many more years of literary productivity. The late Professor Saul Lieberman, the doyen of Judaic studies in his generation, with whom I was closely associated during his latter years, appreciated this book, in his own inimicably critical fashion. I remember him with pleasure and awe, and with all students of Judaica deeply regret his loss. May a new generation grow up, steeped in Torah and scholarship, to fulfil the expectations of their seniors.

October 1991   *Daniel Sperber*

*

Tables G and H on pp. 84 and 138–39 are taken from L.C. West, *Gold and Silver Standards in the Roman Empire* (New York, 1941), pp. 83, 192–93.

Table I on pp. 143–44 is based on Carson, INCP, p. 242.

The illustration on p. 171 of B.M. Add. 17148 fol. 67b is reproduced by kind permission of the British Library Board, through the good offices of Dr. Joseph Rosenwasser.

The illustration opposite p. 99 is reproduced from *JRS*, vol. LXI (1971), by kind permission of Prof. Kenan T. Erim, Dr. Joyce Reynolds and Dr. Michael Crawford, through the good offices of Prof. Joseph Gary.

The coin illustrations in the plates opposite pp. 82, 83, 98 are reproduced by kind permission of the Department of Coins and Medals of the British Museum.

INTRODUCTION

The last fifty years have seen a significant change in historiographic emphasis. Ever more is attention being paid to social and economic factors rather than mere political events. In the case of Roman history this tendency has been given added impetus by the great papyrological finds of the last century or so (beginning with Arsinoe in 1877). For these finds revealed to us for the first time a new class of evidence, more intimate, more personal, more banal and everyday, than almost any previously known manner of source-material—bar graffiti, perhaps. One would hardly expect this kind of source-material to survive the stern challenges of time, the countless painstaking transcriptions of fading manuscripts, the secondary and tertiary translations of cherished texts. Nothing less than the classics, the ecclesiastical histories, the great codices, or the hallowed writings of the revered doctors of the church, and other works of such class, would have come to be reverently placed in state libraries and preserved in national archives. Yet somehow or other papyri did survive this challenge, being preserved in the hot dry Egyptian sands for many a century, finally to be rediscovered and yield up their secrets.

Now it is something of an accident of nature—a happy combination of factors both climatic and geological—that such papyrological evidence survives almost exclusively in Egypt. In the last hundred odd years, the Egyptian sands and ancient rubbish heaps have yielded untold papyrological treasures, tens of thousands of fragments, casting light on almost every aspect of Egyptian life. These have been published in numerous volumes and journals, and after analysis it has been possible to build up a remarkably vivid and rounded picture of Egyptian life in Hellenistic and Roman times. Furthermore, scholars have laboriously compared this evidence with the relatively meagre epigraphic and literary material surviving from other provinces, and in this way sought to infer from

15

Egypt to the rest of the Empire, to construct a more complete picture of the times.

This method, though without doubt invaluable, has at times led to somewhat curious results. Thus, for example, a comparison of mid-third century Egyptian prices with those (maximum) prices recorded in Diocletian's edict of 301 appears to reveal that the latter are above the general contemporary price-levels, even though the *Edict's* prologue clearly suggests the reverse, namely that these maximum prices constituted a ceiling below the general price-level. Or again, fourth century Egyptian papyri seem to present incontrovertible evidence of a most phenomenal inflation, while scanty contemporary sources from other provinces suggest distinctly rising costs, but not on a scale remotely comparable with those of Egypt. As a result some scholars have suggested that in Egypt there was a "local devaluation of a coinage, which under the system of Diocletian was current throughout the Empire, and which had not depreciated anything like the same extent in other provinces. . ." (J.G. Milne, *JRS,* 17, 1927, p.10). And yet it is equally an incontestible fact that the same marks of value occur on coins from the mint of Alexandria as do from the mints of Rome, Antioch, Cyzicus, etc.

This must immediately give cause to doubt the methodological soundness of such inferences from Egypt to the rest of the Empire. For Egypt was a particularly independent province, having her own peculiar agricultural system (until the time of Diocletian), and so forth.[1] That is not to say that no inferences are valid, but rather that a class of inference must first in some manner and degree be proven to be valid by reference to unambiguous material before it further be applied conjecturally.

As a result of the enormous preponderance of Egyptian evidence over that of any other province we now have a picture of the Empire which is distinctly Egypt-oriented, and perhaps lopsidedly biased in this direction. The evidence from other provinces has been thus far too scanty to offset this lack of balance (except for an occasional attempt, such as that of the Hungarian scholar Szilági, in *AAH* 11, 1963, pp.325-89).

And yet there remains a whole body of contemporary and highly relevant source-material that is still largely *terra incognita* to the classicist. I refer to the great corpus of Rabbinic literature, the Talmud and Midrash. The degree to which this remarkably rich and informative field has been neglected is somewhat astonishing. Even the amazingly erudite Rostovtzeff in his great *Social and Economic History of the Roman Empire* (=*SEHRE*) never once cites the Talmud or Midrash. And this not only in 1926 (1st edition), but as late as 1933 (Italian edition) by which time almost the whole of the Babylonian Talmud was available in a very fine German translation (by L. Goldschmidt, Berlin, 1925-34), not to mention the Palestinian Talmud, long available in (an inferior) French translation (by M. Schwab, Paris, 1871-89). Likewise the major part of Midrashic material had by then been translated into German by Wunsche. (For bibliographical details, see relevant sections in H.L. Strack's *Introduction to the Talmud and Midrash*, Philadelphia, 1931.)

But more remarkable still, not only do the primary sources remain shrouded in mystery and never utilized by classicists, but even secondary analyses of this material seem to have made no impact upon Roman historians. Thus, for example, Rostovtzeff can write in a note on social and economic conditions in Palestine (*SEHRE*,[2] p.664, note 32) that: "It might be worth while to collect the whole evidence *including that of the Talmud*, on this subject", being apparently completely unaware of a whole body of literature on the subject, such as A. Büchler's classic *The Economic Conditions of Judaea After the Destruction of the Second Temple*, published in London in 1912! (Jews' College Publications, No. 4), or L. Herzfeld's *Handelsgeschichte der Juden des Altertums*[2] (Brunswick, 1894), L. Goldschmidt: "Les impôts et droits de duane Judée sous les Romaine", (*REJ, XXXIV*, 1897, p.192 et seq.), or S. Krauss' invaluable *Talmudische Archäologie*, 1-3, (Leipzig, 1910-12), etc. And yet Rabbinic sources are particularly useful in that they abound in material from the middle and later third century, a period about which Roman sources are lamentably fragmentary and silent.

The first scholar to make any serious attempt to utilize these sources was Fritz Heichelheim, in his section on Syria, in Tenney Frank's *An Economic Survey of Ancient Rome*, vol. 4, pp.121-257 (Baltimore, 1938), his great *Wirtschaftgeschichte des Altertums* (of the same year), and in several other of his studies. However, his were no more than brave pioneering attempts to point out new directions which more painstaking and accurate research would have to follow up and develop.

The aim of this study is to bring to bear upon Roman history a selection of significant Rabbinic texts, and with their aid to re-examine certain aspects of third and fourth century Palestinian economic life. This material may serve to introduce a non-Egyptian dimension into our picture of Roman economic history, and a comparison of the resultant image with that yielded by Egyptian papyrological sources may put the Egyptian evidence into a new perspective. Once fitted into a new frame of reference, the field of inference may be legitimately extended.

17

This volume (the first in a projected series) approaches the subject of economic history from a very specific aspect, the aspect of currency and prices. In so doing it attempts to set up a spare and skeletal framework into which other aspects of social and economic life may be fitted. (These other aspects will be treated in subsequent volumes.)

A clear notion as to the cost of living in a given period is basic to a real understanding, not only of economic, but also social conditions in that period. One method of building up a picture of the cost of living during a given period is to compile a price-list of basic commodities, and a table of wages (standard and otherwise) tabulated chronologically and thus mutually comparable, and comparable with cognate material. Clearly, the data must be fairly unambiguous in meaning, approximately datable, and as far as possible representative of the real conditions obtaining at the time. Thus, abstruse theoretico-legal examples, literary archaisms, etc., when not borne out be "real" independent evidence are to be treated with great reserve (for example, the case in M. Bava Kama 4.5 where the prices for male and female slaves are said to vary from 1 to 10,000 *denarii*).

The first systematic attempt to compile such price-lists for Roman Palestine (and/or Syria) was that of F. Heichelheim, in his section on Syria (in volume 4 of *An Economic Survey of Ancient Rome,* Baltimore, 1938, pp.155-56, 163-66, 184-88). Unfortunately, his work is deficient in several respects. In many cases his dating of the texts is wrong, his readings incorrect, and even the references are inaccurate. (See my examples in *JESHO,* 8, 1965, pp.248-49.) Moreover, monetary terms occuring in the sources cited are not quoted as they appear in the original, but are translated into some kind of standard terminology (eg. "Syrian *ass*", "Imperial *ass*") according to Heichelheim's own personal theories (outlined ibid., pp.211-227). Elsewhere (*JQR,* 56, 1966, pp.273-301), I have endeavoured to show that Heichelheim's views on this subject are problematic to say the least, and perhaps even wholly untenable, and thus many of the prices in his price-list are questionable, if not actually misleading.

He further confused the issue by including prices pertaining to Babylonia. It can be demonstrated (and even a cursory comparison of the Babylonian prices assembled below, Chapter XV, with the Palestinian ones will make it quite clear) that the economic situation in Babylonia was very different from that of Syria, and that a separation of the two sets of material would have been far more valuable. Thus, for example, during the years 320-50 C.E., when the Empire was apparently going through the throes of extreme inflation, in Babylonia one could get a barrel of wine for four *denarii*, a slave for 100 *denarii*, a mansion ("*apadna*") for 500 *zuz*. At the same period in Palestine a pint of wine cost from 75-100 *denarii*, and not so long after, a single pound of meat cost fifty *denarii*. (See Chapter XX.) Whether these enormous differences represent actual differences in prices (in terms of gold, for example), or whether they merely reflect a varying usage in monetary terminology is a problem that will be discussed below, Chapter XXIV. Nonetheless, whichever the case may be, an initial separation of the material is undoubtedly preferable.

My first task, therefore, was to correct and enlarge Heichelheim's price-lists, separating the Babylonian from the Palestinian material, adding brief notes discussing the accuracy and datability of the sources.[2] Our interest is primarily with the third and fourth centuries, the Amoraic period; however, the lists cover the first four centuries. For only in this way can some sort of relative norm be established, a background of the first two comparatively stable centuries, against which may be seen and with which may be compared the fluid and inconstant inflationary prices of the following two centuries. These lists are by no means complete, and can serve as no more than some kind of roughly representative guide.

In order to understand the price-lists one must, of course, understand the monetary terms in which they are expressed. However, the understanding of monetary terminology may do far more than merely give clarity and definition to prices listed. It gives one the opportunity to infer and reconstruct the whole currency system within which the individual terms functioned as units. A knowledge of the structure, and of the changes within it, gives further insight into the monetary conditions posited by it, and the economic forces motivating it.[3]

Purely legal texts may also be utilized for the light they cast upon monetary developments during the period. But here too, the full picture of the third and fourth century pattern only emerges with clarity when seen against the backdrop of the second century legal position.

By now the reader will probably have guessed that in this study a number of very different kinds of approaches and types of source-material have been used in conjunction with one another to help build up the picture of economic development during the Amoraic period. For example, metrological evidence (based on both numismatic and literary sources) has been coupled with Talmudic legal material, coupled and compared both to complement and to countercheck.

19

And here, I think, some further introductory remarks should be made, firstly regarding the use of the numismatic evidence and secondly regarding the treatment of the Rabbinic source-material.

(a) Numismatic research has advanced by leaps and bounds during the last few years. The appearance of the two latest volumes of *RIC*, dealing with the periods of Diocletian and Constantine, fill a significant historical gap, one in which some crucial economic and monetary changes took place. Chronological problems, problems of mint-organization, coinage distribution, etc., have all been subjected to a fine scrutiny yielding very positive results.

Furthermore, the whole discipline of numismatics has become more rigorous and exact. Hoard analysis is no longer a random affair, and statistical methods of appraisal have been carefully applied with telling results (see P. Grierson's Presidential addresses in the *Numismatic Chronicle* of 1965 and 1966). Furthermore, recently there have been most significant developments in methods of metallurgical analysis—by which is meant the analysis of the metallic contents of a coin. Thus, a comparison of the results yielded by two different methods of analysis, that of X-ray on the one hand, and that of wet chemical analysis on the other, has now proved conclusively that the *follis* was an argentiferous bronze silver-coated coin. (See *Archeometry*, 4, 1961, pp.56-60, and see bibliography in Chapter V.) Since the time when Mickwitz's key works were written, i.e. 1923-24, many more coin-analyses have been made, many more coin weights recorded, and this too must affect and modify his findings. Without accurate classification, both chronological and by mints, one cannot hope to use numismatic evidence with trustworthy effect. Thus, Bolin's most important work, *State and Currency in the Roman Empire to 300 A.D.*, is often numismatically weak and hence, sometimes leads to rather strange conclusions, as when he classed under one category many varying types of Gallienus' coins, which in fact belong to different periods and mints. (See Chapter IV.)

(b) The treatment of the source-material requires somewhat more preliminary comment.

Considerable progress has been made in the last few decades in our knowledge of how to tackle Rabbinic sources. The most significant advances are in the field of Yerushalmi studies and have been spearheaded by one of the world's foremost Talmudists, Saul Lieberman, the appearance of whose small booklet *On the Yerushalmi* (Hebrew, Jerusalem, 1929) constituted a turning point for this area of research. The basic studies of J.N. Epstein (and Abraham Weiss) have shown us methods whereby one may disentangle differing historical and regional strata in a single Talmudic discussion (*sugya*). For it is an all-too-common phenomenon in the Babylonian Talmud to find fourth and even fifth century Babylonian Amoraim interpreting statements of first and second century Palestinian Tannaim in terms of their own contemporary Babylonian socio-economic and political situation. Thus, Palestinian Tannaitic and early Amoraic statements, where found in the Bavli, must be carefully separated from the later Babylonian strata of discussion and reinterpretation that surround (and sometimes obscure) them. At times these Babylonian strata of reinterpretation may even radically affect the form of the original Palestinian statement, so as completely to change its meaning. Or that a text may be altered in the process of transmission from one country to another, undergoing translation (from Hebrew to Aramaic) and reformulation. A common pitfall lurks in the fact that what may, on the face of it, appear to be a purely Tannaitic text, may really be an Amoraic rewording of the original model. Or, conversely, statements of fourth century Babylonian authorities may be stylistically dependent on archaic Tannaitic models.

Thus, in a discussion of specific terminology, for example, it is crucial to distinguish the original authentic form of a statement (as far as is possible) from its re-edited or reworded form. Likewise, it must be seen whether a term belongs historically to its own chronological stratum, or whether it is merely being used as a literary device, an archaism, etc. (Work of this kind has been greatly facilitated by the appearance of a series of splendid new concordances on the Mishna, Tosefta, Tannaitic Midrashim, and Bavli [in progress] by the Kasovsky family.)

In the field of Talmudic law, it is perhaps even more essential to be able to differentiate the varying strata in a *sugya* (discussion), and to disentangle an early Palestinian legal view on a problem from a later Babylonian discussion of it. Even now, one cannot help but feel that students of Jewish legal history place too little emphasis on the socio-economic forces acting on the *halacha* and shaping its development.

The state of Rabbinic source-material from a text-critical point of view is better now than ever before, though it still has far to go. We have a number of significant new critical editions, e.g. B. Mandelbaum's *Pesikta de R. Kahana* (which however cannot be used without the old Buber edition), M. Margulies' edition of *Leviticus Rabba*, Epstein-Melamed edition of the *Mechilta* of R. Simeon b. Yochai, S. Lieberman's publication of a new Ms. of *Deuteronomy Rabba*, Finkelstein's publication of a new Ms. of the *Sifra*, etc. S. Abramson's publication of a very early Spanish Ms. of (Bavli) Avoda Zara is also of particular significance, for this Ms. gives for the first time an indication of the text of one complete tractate of the Babylonian Talmud *not* according to the Franco-Germanic literary tradition (see his introduction).[4]

Furthermore, the last decade has seen the publication of well over three hundred new books of early mediaeval commentaries or responsa, philosophic treatises, etc., either critical editions, or publications of texts published from Mss. for the first time (see Sinai, 61, 1967, p.316. A partial list of these publications appeared in a pamphlet entitled *Sifré Rishonim*, by Israel Ta-Shema, Jerusalem, 1967). These numerous texts include many citations (or paraphrases) of passages from the Talmud and Midrashim, and may at times contribute significant variants which help in the correction of corrupt and incomprehensible passages.

Finally, the establishment in Jerusalem of a microfilm collection of all Hebrew Mss. throughout the world (of which to date some 70% are represented there) is of inestimable help to all who work in the field of Jewish studies.

It goes without saying that chronological exactitude is essential to the economic historian, just as is the establishment of a correct text to one who wishes to examine closely terminological (and semantic) developments. All this new material and these new methods now make it more possible than ever before to achieve greater accuracy in the dating of texts and the establishment of their correct reading.

In the following study I have attempted to bring together the legal and textual disciplines of Rabbinics together with up-to-date views in specialized fields of metrology and numismatics, and to put the whole into the contemporary historiographic focus of an economic historian.

However, while I take full responsibility for my treatment and interpretation of Rabbinic sources, in dealing with papyrological evidence I have been content to base myself almost completely on secondary sources, such as the works of West and Johnson (and to a lesser extent those of Mickwitz and Segrè). These works, though between twenty and thirty years old, remain to this day the only systematic examination and comprehensive presentation of the material, and have generally been accepted as sound and authoritative. Thus, my aim in this study has been, not to reappraise the classical and papyrological evidence for this period, a task which I am not qualified to undertake, but rather to present new Palestinian material, and to see whether these hitherto unexploited texts may not serve to clarify some of the puzzles and make some sense of apparent anomalies of third and fourth century Roman economic history.

Finally, I conclude these explanatory remarks with a word on the chronological scope of this work. Talmudic history is traditionally divided up into two major periods: the Tannaitic period, from the destruction of the Second Temple (70 C.E.) until the death of R. Judah ha-Nasi (about 220), and the Amoraic period, from the early third century until about 425 C.E. in Palestine and about 500 in Babylonia. To each of these periods may be assigned certain major literary sources: *Mishna, Tosefta, Mechilta, Sifra (= Torat Kohanim), Sifré, Sifré Zuta,* (and *Seder Olam Zuta)* to the Tannaitic period; the Palestinian and Babylonian Talmudim and much of the Midrashim to the later period. The literary remains of the Tannaim (teachers of the Tannaitic period) differ in style (brevity), genre (codex, brief legal exegesis, etc.) and language (primarily Hebrew), from that of the Amoraim (teachers of the Amoraic period, whose discursive legal disquisitions, and elaborate homiletic structures are in mixed Hebrew and Aramaic). Much Tannaitic material, especially the *beraitot* (Tannaitic *halachot*—legal rulings —not included in the Mishna and Tosefta compilations), is contained in Amoraic sources, but, as already mentioned above, frequently has undergone reworking, restyling, and even radical reformulation.

Of the two centuries of the Amoraic period, the third century is undoubtedly that of more intensive and formative halachic (legal) and Midrashic (homiletic) creativity, while the following century is considerably more derivative. As a consequence there is in Talmudic sources somewhat more material from the third century than from the fourth. This will account, to some extent, for any unevenness of historical treatment that may be felt in this volume.

I have chosen here to deal with the Amoraic period because these two centuries, the third and fourth, are so crucial to an understanding of Roman and Byzantine history. From the fifth century onwards, Palestinian Rabbinic sources are almost completely silenced, or what may survive is not closely datable. Thus the nature of the treatment and its compass has been determined largely by the character of the source-material. Fragmentary, problematic, unbalanced, and limited though it be, this material still contains a wealth of information which, when fully unearthed, may enrich our knowledge of the social, economic and legal history of this period.

PART ONE

CURRENCY TERMINOLOGY

CHAPTER 1

BACKGROUND SURVEY

We open with an examination of third and fourth century monetary terminology as found in Rabbinic literature. We shall attempt to analyse and define certain terms and, basing ourselves on numismatic evidence, to identify them with contemporary denominations. In this way we may reconstruct the systems within which they acted as units. We shall see that some of these terms underwent radical semantic changes, indicative of alterations in the structure within which they had functioned. Throughout, we shall have carefully to distinguish between names of denominations actually current, and terms denoting units of value which may not necessarily have corresponded to currently existing monetary units, but which were archaic survivals of earlier metrological systems (such as the terms *guinea* or *crown* in England today).

However, before we actually begin with the third century, we must briefly set out the earlier Palestinian metrological systems. For their terms survive late into the Talmudic period as theoretical halachic units. Furthermore, frequently these archaic terms are identified or interchanged with the contemporary denominations, so that the two types of terminology are found alongside one another. Thus, in order to distinguish between the real historical and the archaic theoretical terms, or to unravel the various chronological layers of a Rabbinic text, a knowledge of both sets of terms and the system within which they operated is essential.

Briefly, then, we may summarize the developments of the period from about 140 B.C.E. to about 200 C.E. as follows:

Antiochus VII (Sidetes) first granted the Jews the right to autonomous bronze coinage around 139 B.C.E. (I Maccabees 15.7). At first they only minted small bronze denominations and employed a monetary system that was Syro-Greek in form. This means that it was based on the *drachma-obol* system and was dependent upon the standard of the Tyrian *tetradrachma* (Table A).

Later, during the reign of Mattathias Antigonus (40-37 B.C.E.), there was a reorganization of the currency system (perhaps due partly to the incipient inflation) in which larger denominations were introduced and an attempt was made to bring it further in line with the Roman *denarius-as* system (Tables B and C). It appears that at this stage the halachic value of the *pruta* was fixed. For a variety of reasons, both internal and external, this system remained in use for only a short period. Nevertheless, the terminology applied to it continued to be used in subsequent generations, notwithstanding the many changes which took place. However, this now purely Halachic (and theoretical) terminology sounded very similar to actual current Roman monetary terms while having quite different values from the Roman equivalents. There had therefore to be created a completely new system of names for the Roman currency currently in use (Table D).[1]

This, then, briefly is the background against which we may begin our examination of third century Palestinian monetary terminology. We shall start with an examination of two central terms, significant in that they change their meanings at a definite stage in their history.

TABLE A

	Bronze			Silver	
Pruta	Shamin	Hanez Niz	Darosa Hadris	Ma'ah	Dinar
144	72	36	18	6	1
24	12	6	3	1	
8	4	2	1		
4	2	1			
2	1				

TABLE B

Metal	Bronze				Silver	
R. P. Pruta	Quadrans Kardionts Kuntrun(k)	Semis Musmis	As Issar	Dupondius Pundion	Ma'ah	Denarius Dinar
192	96	48	24	12	6	1
32	16	8	4	2	1	
16	8	4	2	1		
8	4	2	1			
4	2	1				
2	1					

R. Roman name.
P. Palestinian name.

TABLE C

Copper (or Orichalcum)			Orichalcum		Silver		Gold	
Quadrans	Semis	As	Dupondius	Sestertius	Quinarius Argenteus	Denarius	Quinarius Aureus	Aureus
1600	800	400	200	100	50	25	2	1
800	400	200	100	50	25	12½	1	
64	32	16	8	4	2	1		
32	16	8	4	2	1			
16	8	4	2	1				
8	4	2	1					
4	2	1						
2	1							
1								

TABLE D

METAL	Orichalcum				Silver			Gold
R	As	Dupondius	Sestertius	Quinarius	Denarius	Didrachm	Tridrachm	Aureus
P	Termissis	Tressis	Riv'a	Tarapik Rova	Dinar	Tiba	Ragia	Dinar-Zahav
	16	8	4	2	1	½	⅓	1/24 or 1/25
	8	4	2	1				
	4	2	1					
	2	1						

R. Roman name
P. Palestinaian name.

CHAPTER II

DINAR

Probably the most common and important monetary term in Rabbinic literature is the *dinar*. In Tannaitic times (i.e. up to about 220) the *dinar* when unqualified almost always refers to the *silver denarius*, whereas the *aureus* is called a *dinar zahav*, *gold dinar*. However, some time during the second half of the third century, we find a change in the usage of the word, and the unqualified *dinar* comes to refer to the *aureus* (or later, the *solidus*), the gold *dinar*, while the silver *denarius* is specifically so called. The new usage of the term *dinar* meaning a gold coin may be demonstrated in the following four examples:

(1) In Yerushalmi Ketubot[A] 4.13 we hear of a *ketuba* of twenty *dinars*, and of a house for ten *dinars*. Now the minimum size of a *ketuba* is two hundred *zuzim* (=*denarii*) for a virgin and on hundred *zuzim* for a widow (Mishna Ketubot 2.1; 5.1,2, etc.). Therefore, *dinars* here cannot mean silver *denarii*, but must mean gold ones. The text is of R. Ḥanina and R. Ḥama who were active from about 350 to 375; hence, they must have been referring to *solidi*.[1]

(2) In Yerushalmi Bava Kama[B] 9.5[2] :

> R. Jona said: "We may learn from this [the previous statement] that a man who gave his friend eight *dinars* to buy him wheat from Tiberias, and he bought it from Sepphoris, may say to him [the purchasing agent]: 'Had you bought it in Tiberias, you would have got 25 *modii*, but since you bought it in Sepphoris and you got only 20 *modii*, you must make up the difference...' "[3]

R. Jona was one of the foremost Amoraim of the fourth generation, and was still alive in 351, though by then he must have been a very old man indeed.[4] Yet from the period after (and even shortly after) the *Edict of Diocletian* (301) onwards, the modius could hardly have cost so little as 1/3 to 2/5 *denarius*.[5] Clearly then, *dinar* here means *aureus* or

31

solidus, and the price was 1/3 to 2/5 *aureus* or *solidus* per *modius.* As the text is probably from well in the first half of the fourth century, the *dinar* would be a *solidus* rather than an *aureus.*[6]

However, such a price now presents the difficulty of being far too high. For Ammianus Marcellinus[7] relates that during a famine at Carthage in the reign of Valentinian I (371-72), the proconsul Hymetius sold wheat from the public stocks at ten *modii* to the *solidus*—a very high price, but evidently below the famine market rate; the next year he was able to replace the wheat he had sold, buying on the open market at thirty *modii* to the *solidus.*[8] Thus in Carthage, ten *modii* per *solidus* was considered a very high price, and thirty *modii* per *solidus* more reasonable.

Furthermore, according to *Vita S. Pachomii* 33-4,[9] in the second quarter of the fourth century, during a year of shortage, in Egypt for one *solidus* one could purchase from 16 *modii* wheat (at a very high price) to 43 *modii* wheat (a more reasonable price). (Below, Chapter XXV, see a discussion of this text in the section on fourth century prices.)

Finally, in his *Misopogon*[10] Julian tells us that when he came to Antioch he found the price of wheat ten *metra* per *argurion.* He decreed that for this same sum of money, i.e. one *argurion,* one should be able to purchase 15 *metra.* He further adds that one would in fact be lucky to get five *metra* for an *argurion,* with a severe winter well under way.[11]

Now the most common silver coin of this period and the most likely to be called ἀργύριον (literally, silver) was the *siliqua* (1=1/24 *solidus).*[12] We shall see below (Chapter XVI) that a *modius castrensis* produced 24 two-pound loaves of bread, each loaf being one man's ration for one day. It seems therefore likely that the *metron* (literally: measure)[13] was the daily ration of wheat *per capita,*[14] and ten such measures cost 1/24 *solidus* (=*siliqua*= ἀργύριον) meaning that 10-15 *modii castrensis* (=20-30 *modii Italici*) cost one *solidus.* Julian apparently reckoned the dole bread in terms of daily ration *per capita,*[15] a system of calculation found also in Rabbinic sources.

From all the above it is quite clear that in the second and early third quarters of the fourth century one *modius castrensis* of wheat cost between 1/8 and 1/20 *solidus,* not 1/3 to 1/5, and the *modius Italicus* cost 1/16 to 1/40 *solidus.*[16]

However, in the *Shita Mekubezet* to Bava Kama 100b, our Yerushalmi passage is quoted with some slight changes,[17] the significant one for our purpose being: he gave his friend *o n e dinar*—not eight *dinars.*

חד (as it is there written) meaning "one" was probably abbreviated to
'ח and then mistakenly taken as ",ח-eight".[18] (The numerical value of
the letter ח is eight and such is a common way of writing numbers in
Hebrew and Aramaic.) Copyists of the Yerushalmi then wrote שמנה,
eight, in full.[19] The new correct reading gives us a price of 1/20 to 1/24
solidus per *modius (Italicus)* and thus compares very well with that of
Julian of the 360's; once again, the *dinar* clearly refers to a gold coin,
the *solidus*.

(3) In Yerushalmi Ma'aser Sheni 4.1 (see below for text, page
91), we read that "a *dinar* here (Tiberias?) is worth 2000 and in
Arbael (a nearby town) 2000 and a *leukon*..."[20] The *leukon* appears to be
a small silver coin of unknown value, the word deriving from the Greek
λευκόν meaning white, and it has therefore been suggested that it is
equal to the *asper* (Greek ἄσπρος meaning the same), a coin that makes
its appearance in the Mishna.[21] (But see pages 91-93.) The meaning of
the passage is that the *dinar*, here clearly an *aureus*, is worth 2000
[*denarii*] "here", and a little more in Arbael. *PSI*. 310 *describes an*
identical situation in Egypt for the year 307 by also giving us the
equation of one *aureus*[22] = 2000 *denarii*. It is interesting to note that
the debased *denarii* are here left unnamed. But what is of yet greater
interest is that the exchange-rate of the *aureus* varied (if only slightly)
from one place to another.[23] This is indeed confirmed by the ruling
found in *Codex Theodosianus* 9.23.1 (of 352), according to which it
was forbidden to transport money, over a certain amount, from one
area to another, in order to benefit from the differences in exchange
rates. (See below, page 153.)

(4) In Yerushalmi Bava Batra 8.4 we read that 100 small *"garbin"*
of wine(?) cost ten *dinars,* and the same number of large ones cost
twenty *dinars.* From a comparison with Yerushalmi Bava Mezia 4.2
we may further learn that the so-called "small *garbin*" were in fact the
standard size ones.[24] The large *garbin* were presumably double the standard size. *Gerev* (plural, *garbin*) means bottle,[25] and thus we see that
one standard bottle of wine(?) cost 1/10 *dinar.* As both R. Jeremiah
and R. Zeira [I] figure in the text, it may be dated around the last quarter of the third century.

There were many kinds of *garbin* of varying sizes, as may be gathered
from the above and from other Talmudic passages (e.g. Mishna Terumot
10.8). But in each case the *gerev* must have corresponded, if only approximately, to some kind of recognised measure. The minimum possible
size we could attribute to the *gerev* would be that of a *xestes*, or pint.

Yet according to the *Edict of Diocletian* of 301, ordinary wine costs as much as ten *denarii* per Italian pint.[28] And looking back to the beginning of the third century, we have an inscription from Zarai, from which it is computed that one *amphora* cost ten *denarii*; hence one *sextarius* (=1/48 *amphora*) cost about 1/5 *denarius*. It is hardly conceivable that over half a century later a *gerev* (a *sextarius* only at the absolute minimum) should have cost as little as 1/10 *denarius*. Clearly then, the *dinar* here means a gold *dinar*, an *aureus*.[27]

From the above four examples we may learn that some time during the third century, and probably in the second half of it, the term "*dinar*" came to refer to a gold coin, the *aureus*, and later in the fourth century it was also applied to the *solidus*, the heir of the *aureus*.[28]

CHAPTER III

MANEH

Another term in which we find a significant semantic change is the term *"maneh"*.[1] During the Tannaitic and early Amoraic times this term meant exclusively 100 *denarii*.[2] However, from the third century onwards we find it being used in the sense of a single *denarius*.[3] Thus, for example, while the Greek Eusebius (in *Historia Ecclesiastica* 9.8.4)[4] relates that during the famine of 312-13 a ϰϱιϑη̃ϱο (=*modius*, in this case) of wheat cost 2500 Attic *drachmae* (=*denarii*),[5] the Syriac version reads: one *modius* of wheat [cost] 250 מגיא *maniah* (=*maneh*).[6] Thus *maneh* equals *denarius* (Attic *drachma*).[7]

Examples of the use of the *maneh* as *denarius* can also cast much light on economic conditions of this period.

(1) In Yerushalmi Berachot[C] 2.8 we read of a butcher charging R. Zeira (II) fifty *maneh* for a pound of meat. We have shown elsewhere[8] that this event must have taken place between the years 317 and 325 (in Tiberias). Now *P. Rylands* 637, line 403 (*Archives of Theophanes*) of much the same period (around 317-24) records the cost of one pound of meat in Betar as (200 *drachmae* =) fifty *denarii*. It seems quite clear that the Yerushalmi price of fifty *maneh* and that of *P. Rylands*—fifty *denarii*—are equal. Hence *maneh* equals *denarius*.

(2) In *Tanhuma Balak*[D] 15,[9] a text that may be dated about 303-304,[10] we read of a pound of kosher meat (probably beef) costing eight *maneh*, while the same amount of pork costs ten *maneh*. According to the *Edict of Diocletian* of only two years earlier (301), one Italian pound of beef costs eight *denarii* and of pork twelve *denarii* (4, 1a and 2). Here again the equation of *maneh* and *denarius* seems to suggest itself.

(3) In *Ecclesiastes Rabba*[E] 5.10, a text from between 290 to 320, the price of a cucumber is given as one to two *maneh*. According to the *Edict of Diocletian* (4.28 and 29) a cucumber costs 1/5 to 2/5 *denarius*. Here is seems more reasonable ot translate *maneh* as one *denarius* than as one hundred *denarii*.

(4)   Likewise in *Esther Rabba*[F] 2.3 (to chapter one, verse 4), not a clearly datable text, we read of endives costing one-half to one *maneh* each, while the *Edict of Diocletian* (6, 3 and 4) gives the price as 2/5 to one *denarius* each.[11]

Thus far our examples for the usage of *maneh* as *denarius* have been taken from fourth century (or very late third century) texts.[12] The following example, however, furnishes evidence that this usage was already present in the early third century.

(5)   For in *Yerushalmi Megila*[G] 4.1 we read that R. Ḥiyya Rabba said that with only two *manii* (=*maneh*, a very small sum), he could buy enough flax-reed to plant, grow, and produce quite a number of ropes (enough with which to make nets and catch deer).[13] During R. Ḥiyya Rabba's period (early part of the third century), 200 *denarii* (the only other possible meaning for two *manii*) was a considerable sum of money, so much so that one who possessed that much was legally regarded as not a poor person and therefore had no rights upon the poor man's gifts (Mishna Pe'a 8.8). Furthermore, in *Yerushalmi Bava Mezia*[H] 5.6 we read of forty *kor* of flax costing forty *aurei* (*"dinars"* in the text, see above). As R. Kahana and Rav are mentioned in the context, this text must be dated from between 219 and 247. A *kor* equals thirty *se'ah*; thus between 219 to 247[14] one *se'ah* of flax cost less than one to two *denarii*. (During this period there were between 25 and 50 *denarii* to the *aureus*.)[15] For two *denarii* one could apparently buy a goodly amount of flax—certainly enough with which to produce several ropes. Hence, it seems likely that two *manii* here are two *denarii*.[16] Of course, in this case one cannot be certain that the Talmud is quoting R. Ḥiyya's statement word for word. Therefore it remains possible, and even likely, that a Talmudic redactor introduced this later term in place of an earlier (to him perhaps less meaningful) one.

(6)   Our final example is perhaps the most important of all, since it casts light on a crucial and vexing problem on which hinges much late third and early fourth century metrology, the problem of Diocletian's monetary reform.[17] In *Deuteronomy Rabba Ki-Tezé*[I] 2 we read as follows:

> R. Aba bar Kahana said: . . ."It is like unto a king who hired for himself workers and put them into his orchard, without revealing to them the wages for looking after the orchard, so that they should not pay no attention to that for which they would be paid little and concern themselves only with that for which they would be paid much. In the evening he called for each of them. He said

36

to the first: 'Under which tree did you work?' [He said to him:] 'It is a pepper-tree.' 'The wage for it is one gold piece.' He called the other and asked him: 'Under which tree did you work?' 'Under that one,' he replied. He (the king) said: 'It is a *perach lavan* tree [literally: a white-flower tree: λευϰόϊνος][19] and the rate for it is half a gold piece.' He called the last one and said to him: 'Under which tree did you work?' 'Under this one,' he answered. 'It is an olive tree, and its rate is 200 *manehs*.' "[20]

Since in this parable we begin with one gold piece, and then go down to half a gold piece, it would appear likely that the final sum mentioned is a quarter gold piece, i.e. ¼ *aureus* (or *solidus*? a unit that did not exist as a coin; hence the change to the smaller denomination). Thus one *aureus* (or *solidus*?) equalled 800 *maneh*, which equalled 800 *denarii* during the period of R. Aba bar Kahana, *floruit circa* 290-320.[21]

Now this was certainly true of the period of Diocletian's monetary reforms and *Edict of Prices* (about 295-301), as has been recently re-affirmed by R.A.G. Carson.[22] According to the *Edict of Diocletian* (Chapter 30, line 1), one *libra aurei* equals 50,000 *denarii*, hence one *aureus* equals 833 2/3 *denarii*. Such was the price of one *aureus*-weight of gold bullion. The minted *aureus*, however, was itself worth some 4% less. (One *aureus* equals 800 *denarii*.)[23] For there was at this time a strange situation, where unminted gold was worth more than minted gold, as has been shown by Bolin, basing himself on papyrological evidence.[24] In the light of the above, the sudden increased usage of gold bullion at this time, frequently referred to in Rabbinic literature, becomes very understandable. (See also below, page 85.)

But returning to our text in *Deuteronomy Rabba*, we may learn from it at least two facts of considerable importance: (a) that the price-levels in Diocletian's *Edict* were dependent upon his currency reform of a few years earlier,[25] and (b) that this currency reform was not merely a theoretical affair, but an effective step whose effect was immediately felt (presumably throughout the Empire and certainly in Palestine). It appears that it was not merely the currency reform and the new rate of the *denarius* that was known in Palestine, but indeed in the whole *Edict of Maximum Prices*. Hence, the remarkable similarity between the prices recorded in the above texts, all of this period, and the prices fixed in the *Edict*. Presumably, after its publication, the *Edict* became one of the main topics of everyday conversation. The homilists incorporated such issues of the day into their public sermons. We shall return below to the question of how long the currency reform continued to have effect.

CHAPTER IV

ANTONINIANUS

Above we have shown that in the beginning of the fourth century the relationship between the *denarius* and the *aureus* was 800:1. A century earlier the relationship had been 25:1![1] [2 and 4} Thus, between approximately 200 and 300 the *denarius*, and indeed the *aureus*, underwent some very erratic vicissitudes, which we shall now attempt to trace. There are few fixed points in the anarchic confusion of third century monetary history, and, as a consequence, one must make use of every kind of method available to construct a logically coherent development. The sources are numismatic, epigraphic, metrological, and literary, and when put together, a vaguely acceptable pattern appears to emerge out of the welter of apparent contradictions.

One of the few given points in this whole period is Caracalla's introduction of a new denomination in the year 215. This denomination is generally called the "*antoninianus*" [3], and at the time of its introduction weighed about one and a half times a *denarius*.[1a] [2] However, there are differing opinions as to its precise value. Because of the dearth of literary evidence from the early third century, there is no direct means to clarify this basic point. Therefore, we shall first have to look at evidence dealing with a later stage in the development of the *antoninianus*, and then backtrack, as it were, to the year 215.

Our point of departure is a text in Yerushalmi Ketubot[M] 11.2, where R. Abbahu in the name of R. Johanan, in order to illustrate a certain legal point, gives the example of a (Jewish) man who borrowed (from a Jewish woman) 12,000[2] on condition that he pay it back within one year in installments of one gold *dinar* (=*aureus*) per month.[3] Now Jewish law does not permit a Jew to take interest on a loan from a fellow-Jew; hence, the sum paid back cannot be more than the one borrowed, nor is it likely to be less. It follows, then, that in this example 12,000 *denarii* equal twelve *aurei*, or 1000 *denarii* equal one *aureus*. Since

R. Johanan died in 279,[4] this must be the *terminus ante quem* for this text.[5] During the period of Diocletian there were 800 *denarii*[6] in an *aureus*. [20] Yet it is known that from the time of Aurelian's monetary reform (about 274) until that of Diocletian the inflation had increased,[7] so that at Aurelian's reform there must have been less than 800 *denarii* in an *aureus*. However, prior to the reform there may well have been many more *denarii* to the *aureus*. Hence, R. Johanan's example is pre-274. During the reign of Aurelian and Claudius II[7a] (approximately 268-72) the so-called silver coinage seems to have reached its highest point of debasement, and the *antoninianus* had a silver content of only 2 to 2.5% (see Table E).[8] [13] It seems likely, therefore, that this text of R. Johanan is evidence for the relationship of the *denarius* to the *aureus* during the years from about 268 to 274.

Now, at that time there were no *denarii* actually being struck, only *antoniniani*. (The *denarius* had finally ceased to be minted some thirty years earlier, and was now merely a unit of reckoning.[8a] See Table E.)

TABLE E

Date	Emperor	Weight of Denarius	Weight of Anton.	Fineness of Denar. in %	Fineness of Anton. in %	Weight of Aureus
215–17	Caracalla	3.10	5.02	50	48	6.5
219–22	Elagabalus	2.98	5.31	40	40	7.14
222–35	Severus Alex.	2.48	—	41	—	6.16 or 6.39
235–38	Maximinus	3.06	—	45	—	6.13
238	Gordiani	3.16	—	—	—	6.35
238	Balbinus & Pupienus	3.09	—	—	44	5.75
238–44	Gordian III	—	4.38	—	40	4.86
244–9	Philip I	—	4.16	—	40	4.5
249–51	Trajan Decius	—	4.05	—	38	4.3
253–60	Valerian	—	3.67	—	} 25–13	3
253–66	Gallienus (joint)	—	3.37	—		3.62
266	Gallienus (sole)	—	2.81	—	1	4.5
268–70	Claudius II	—	2.88	—	2	5.4
270–74	Aurelian (pre-reform)	—	2.81	—	—	5.4
274–5	Aurelian (post-reform)	—	3.77	—	4–4.5	6.5
295	Diocletian (post-reform)	—	4	—	4.18	5.4

The relationship of *antoniniani* to *aurei* must have been expressable in a simple round-numbered equation. We have already mentioned that there has been considerable argument as to the value of the *antoninianus* (see below, this chapter), but the only two suggestions that really deserve to be considered are (a) $1\frac{1}{2}$ *denarii* $= 1$ *antoninianus* or (b) 2 *denarii* $= 1$ *antoninianus*.[9] If from about 268 to 272 there were $1\frac{1}{2}$ *denarii* in an antoninianus, the relationship between the *antoninianus* and the *aureus* would have been 666 2/3 to one. This seems highly unlikely as so complex a number would cause innumerable difficulties even in everyday transactions. If, on the other hand, two *denarii* equalled one *antoninianus*, then there were 500 *antoniniani* in the *aureus* between approximately 268 and 272. This seems to be a far more plausible equation.

According to this argument, the *antoninianus* was certainly equal to two *denarii* during the period of Aurelian {14 and 15}, and it seems most likely that this was its value right from its very introduction by Caracalla in 215. [3 and 4] Its being a double *denarius* is borne out by the fact that it is a radiate coin—a radiate coin is usually the double of a laureate coin[10] (a *denarius*). Furthermore, if it were really to have been worth only one and one-half *denarii*, and its purpose was to take the place of the old *denarius* (as has been recently reaffirmed by Carson),[11] then one can see little point in the introduction of this new piece (or denomination).[12] The *denarius* could as easily have been restruck, and repriced (at 1/36 *aureus* according to Carson's system[13] or) at whatever tariff were fixed. But, the introduction of a coin weighing about $1\frac{1}{2}$ *denarii*—his *denarius* weight is on an average 3.17 grammes, his *antoninianus* weight about 5.02 grammes (see Table E)—but valued at two *denarii*, would mean that in the *antoninianus* the silver was now overpriced by 25%, so that it bore a relationship to gold of about 9:1,[14] while in the *denarius* the silver-gold ratio was about 12:1.[15] The outcome of such monetary policy would be a saving of some 25% silver, which could be used by Caracalla for increased currency output.[16]

In fact, then, Caracalla's *antoninianus* was a *didrachm*, [6] insofar as the *denarius* was identified with the *drachm* (except of course, that it was worth only 1/25 *aureus*, not 2/25). The relative weights of these two sets of coins bear this hypothesis out well. Thus:

Average *denarius*: 3.17 grammes
Average *antoninianus*: 5.02 grammes [3]
              (heaviest: 5.72)
Average *drachm*: 3.11 grammes
Average *didrachm*: 5.5 grammes[17] [6]

From this it seems most likely that the *antoninianus* equalled two *denarii*, and as the *denarius* was originally 1/25 *aureus*,[18] and the *antoninianus* apparently came to take its place, Caracalla's new system would appear to be as follows:

200 *sestertii* = 50 *denarii* = 25 *antoniniani* = 1 *aureus*.

It has already been mentioned above that there have been a number of suggestions as to what exactly Caracalla's system was. These may be set out in tabular form as follows:[19]

	A	B	C	D	E
Aureus	1	1	1	1	1
Antoninianus	20	15	25	24	25
Denarius	30	30	37½	36	50
Sestertius	120	120	150	144	200

Now in a recent article Richard Duncan-Jones has set out a long and exhaustive list of dedication prices found on monuments, buildings, etc., in Roman Africa.[20] These dedications are almost always reckoned in *sestertii*,[21] but by and large they make up a round number of *aurei* (in which denomination they were no doubt paid). Thus, out of some 402 sums listed (dated) before 215, only 27 do not give round numbers of *aurei*.[22] Of these, eleven are undated and some are special cases,[23] while other again are too small to make up round sums of *aurei*;[24] so that there are in fact only fifteen (some undated) sums out of 402 which do not constitute round sums of *aurei*, or four percent.

Now in Table F a list of twelve inscriptions is set out, dated from about 213 to 237, recording donations of various kinds of magnitude.[25] It is highly improbable that sums such as 104,000 *sestertii* (= 26,000 *denarii*) or 82,000 *sestertii* (=20,500 *denarii*) would be paid up in anything less than *aurei*. Thus, these sums too should be translatable into round numbers of *aurei*. Yet according to systems A and B only 33.3% can be translated into such round numbers; according to system C only 25%; and according to system D 00%. According to our system E 100% of the sums may be translated into round numbers of *aurei*. This is a strong argument in favour of the *antoninianus'* being a double-*denarius* and part of system E. It is further borne out by the evidence frequently cited from Ulpianus[26] who states, writing about 225, that a certain fine, known from the second century lawyer Gaius to be 10,000 *sestertii*,[27] is fifty *aurei*. This too suggests that about 225 there were 200 *sestertii* (=50 denarii) in an *aureus*.[28]

TABLE F

at 50 d. per aureus.

No.	Sum in Sestertii	Date	Source	Sum in Denarii
102	1,200	213–17	1 LAlg II i 570	6
373	2,200	After 217	C.19122	11
94	30,000	217–22?	1 LAlg II i 10	150
325	82,000	217–22	1 LAlg II i 10	410
393	400	After 217	1 LAlg II v 186	2
400	60,000 and 30,000	225–35	C.2645B	300 150
221	12,000	222–37	C.2764	60
74	4,000	225	1 LAlg II i 37	20
58	12,000	225	C.15497	60
30	104,000	226–8	AE, 1908, 244–5	520
378	10,000	230–1	IRT 43	50
265	10,000	post 230	C.26275	50

AE	Anneé Epigraphic
C.	Corpus Inscriptionum Latinarum, vol. VIII
1 LAlg II	S. Gael & H. C. Pflaum, Inscriptions latines de l'Algerie, 1957
IRT	J. M. Reynolds & J. B. Ward Perkins, Inscriptions of Roman Tripolitania, 1952

We must now try to bridge the gap between about 225 and 270, tracing the course of the *antoninianus* from both epigraphic and numismatic material. Carson calculates the *antoninianus* of 238 (Gordian III) as 1/20 *aureus*,[29] while Bolin[30] has interpreted two inscriptions from Nubia[31] as showing that during the reign of Philip the Arab (244-9), the relationship of *denarius* to *aureus* was 42-45:1. We would suggest 40:1 as being a more workable equation, divisible by 2 (which 45 is not) and thus easily reckoned in *antoniniani*. Thus Philip kept the same relationship as had been (re)introduced by Gordian III (see below, this chapter).

On the basis of the above information we may now reckon (for those periods for which we know the number of *antoniniani* per *aureus*) the actual ratio of silver to gold (actual though probably not official, see note 16 above).[32] But here it must not be forgotten that the value of the copper in the coin (however small) should also be taken into account,[33] reckoned as it was at 1/100 the value of silver.[34] The formula for this computation may be expressed as follows:[35]

42

$$\frac{N(100\ PQ + PR)}{10,000Y} : 1 \quad \text{where} :$$

where : N = number of *antoniniani* in an *aureus*

P = weight[36] of an *antoninianus*

Q = % of silver in an antoninianus

R = % of copper[37] in an *antoninianus*

Y = weight of an *aureus*[38]

The weights of *antoniniani* and *aureii* and the fineness of the *antoniniani* are given in Table E. According to this data, during the reign of Caracalla the actual ratio (in the *antoninianus*) was 9:1 (see above). Assuming that there were fifty *denarii* to the *aureus* during the reign of Severus Alexander (222-35),[39] the ratio was 9.2:1 (or 9:1, at an *aureus* of 6.4 grammes [=1/50 *libra aurei*]), while Elagabalus' ratios at the same tariff are 7.5:1 for the *antoninianus* and 7:1 for the *denarius*!

Maximinus' ratio at 50 *denarii* per *aureus* is 11.2:1, or, if the *aureus* was 1/50 *libra aurei* (= 6.4 grammes), the ratio would be 10.9:1. If however, there were in his system only forty *denarii* per *aureus* (as in that of Gordian and Philipp I), then, at an *aureus* of 6.13 grammes, the ratio is 9:1 (at an *aureus* of 6.4 grammes, 8.7:1). The latter alternative seems the more likely, namely that already in Maximinus' time the relationship between the *denarius* and *aureus* had been changed from 50:1 to 40:1. However, this would surely suggest that Balbinus and Pupienus also employed the same system (which continued under Gordian III and Philip I). But in the case of Balbinus and Pupienus, such a relationship yields a silver-gold relationship of 6.6:1, which is, to say the least, highly unlikely. A relationship of fifty *denarii* per *aureus*, on the other hand, yields the more probable silver-gold ratio of 8.27:1 (at an *aureus* of 6.35 grammes). Thus, we must assume either that Maximinus improved the situation somewhat, or that he changed the official tariff, but that the old system was subsequently reverted to, until the time when Gordian III brought back the forty *denarii* = one *aureus* system (about 238). Gordian's own system yields a ratio of 7.3:1; (or if the *aureus* was 1/70 *libra aurei* {=4.6 grammes}, then the ratio was 7.7:1). At forty *denarii* per *aureus*[40] in the reign of Philip the Arab (244-49) the ratio was 7.5:1 (or 8.2:1 at a fineness of 44%—Mickwitz's data). Thus far, we note a tendency to progressive overvaluation of silver.[41]

There is some (rather ambiguous) evidence suggesting that Trajan Decius altered the relation of the *antoninianus* to the *aureus* to 50 or 60:1 (perhaps even 80:1), giving a silver-gold ratio lying somewhere between 8 and 9:1.[42] [7]

As to Gallienus' gold coinage, Dr. J. Kent points out to me that it cannot be classed together under one category (as Bolin apparently did).[43] He distinguished four definite periods:

(1) Early laurels, weighing around 3 grammes (with radiates of about 5.2 grammes), 261. These derive directly from the joint reign *aurei*. [8]

(2) Radiates of around 4.6 grammes; going down to 4.1, 261-62. [9]

(3) Late laurels of around 1.3 grammes (ranging from 2.6 to .8 grammes), 263-66. [10 and 12]

(4) *Schufkranz* (reed-crowned) type. Around 3.3, 6 grammes, in several groups. 266 onwards. [11]

He suggests that the diminution in the size of the *aureus* was, so to say, in sympathy with the debasement of the *antoninianus,* in order to keep a fixed and unchanging ratio between them. Thus, if in his early reign, about 261, there were fifty *denarii* (=25 *antoniniani*) to the *aureus,* with an *aureus* of three grammes and an *antoninianus* of 2.8 grammes with 25% fineness, the resultant silver-gold ratio is 6:1. When the *antoninianus* dropped to 20% fineness, the *aureus* dropped in sympathy to 2.6 grammes, keeping a ratio of 6:1 (or at two grammes, 7:1). And when the *antoninianus* dropped to 10% fineness, the *aureus* likewise drops to .85 gramme, giving a ratio of 7:1 (at fifty *denarii* to the *aureus*).[44]

Then came the great collapse: a three-gramme *antoninianus* at four percent fineness, 250 of which make an *aureus* (i.e. 500 *denarii* equal an *aureus*) of 5.4 *grammes* (= 1/60 *libra aurei*), gives a ratio of 7:1. Five hundred three-gramme *antoniniani* at 2% fineness to an *aureus* of 6.5 grammes (=1/50 *libra aurei—Schufkranz* type) gives a silver-gold ratio of 7:1.[44a]

From this time, then (about 266 onwards), no longer was an attempt made to keep a constant relationship between the denominations. No doubt these values were fixed by official decree. Thus, in Claudius' reign the possibilities are (for an *antoninianus* of 2.88 grammes at two percent fineness, and an *aureus* of 5.4 grammes = 1/60 *libra aurei*):

800 d. = 1 *aureus*. Ratio 6.4:1   (48,000 d. = 1 *libra aurei*)
850 d. = 1 *aureus*. Ratio 7 :1   (51,000 d. = 1 *libra aurei*)
900 d. = 1 *aureus*. Ratio 7.5:1   (54,000 d. = 1 *libra aurei*)
1000 d. = 1 *aureus*. Ratio 8.3:1   (60,000 d. = 1 *libra aurei*)[45]

At some time such as this, post-266, R. Johanan made his statement giving the equation of 1000 *denarii* [15] equal one *aureus*. Dr. Kent further points out that hoard analysis bears out this suggestion that the major break came about 266 and that Claudius and the *"Schufkranz"* Gallienus *aurei* are part of a new system.[46]

We now come to the problems posed by Aurelian's coinage. We have seen that in Aurelian's pre-reform period, there were 500 *antoniniani* [13 and 14] to the *aureus* (about 268 to 274). If we assume that the aureus was struck at 1/60 *libra aurei* ($=5.4$ grammes [$325 \div 60$]),[47] the ratio would be about 8 : 1 at $2\frac{1}{2}\%$. However, if we assume that the *aureus* was struck at 65 to the *libra aurei* ($= 5$ grammes), the ratio (at $2\frac{1}{2}\%$) would be $8.58 : 1$.[48] Let us now examine Diocletian's system, which may help clarify the problems posed by Aurelian's reform.

According to Diocletian's reformed system (post 295) the *aureus* was struck at 1/60 *libra aurei*, and hence had a (theoretical ideal) weight of 5.4 grammes.[49] In his time there were 800 *denarii* per *aureus*. He struck a coin marked XXI [16] (or XX.1, or KA, or K.A.) weighing ten grammes,[50] with a fineness of 4.18%.[51] It is now generally held that this coin was a five-*denarius* piece and that XXI (or XX.1, etc.) means that twenty ($=$XX) *sestertii* ($=\frac{1}{4}$ *denarius*) equals one of these, i.e. equals five *denarii*.[52] For the *sestertius* as a unit of reckoning can be found as late as 297.[53] Further evidence for this interpretation is to be found on the *folles* of Antioch (from about 300-301), bearing the notation K/V [18], which Sutherland convincingly argues means twenty (*sestertii*) [$=$] five (*denarii*).[54] According to this, Diocletian's post-reform silver-gold ratio was $14.7 : 1$.[55] Thus part of Diocletian's reform consisted of restoring the silver-gold ratio (actual and official) to a more reasonable balance.[56] This means that now silver was worth only half as much as it had been around 268-72. Prices in the time of Diocletian should have gone up to at least double what they had been in the preceding few decades, in order to maintain the same price-level. In fact, Mickwitz, basing himself primarily on Egyptian papyrological evidence, has shown that this was indeed the case.[57] However, he thought that this indicated a rise of prices in the time of Diocletian, whereas according to the above interpretation they, quite to the contrary, no more than maintain their level (in terms of gold).[58]

We must now return to the problems posed by Aurelian's reform: what was the new system he introduced? Here we may do little more than suggest the various possibilities, and state what seems to us to be the most likely one. If we assume that his reform did not change the silver-gold ratio, then (bearing in mind that his *antoninianus*—i.e. his XXI [13] coin which equalled two *denarii*[59]—weighed 3.77 grammes and had a fineness of about 4.5%), we arrive at the equation of 300

45

antoniniani=one *aureus* (or at a fineness of 40%: 350 *antoniniani*=one *aureus*). However, the rather more likely relationship of 250 *antoniniani* (=500 *denarii*)=one *aureus*, gives the very reasonable result of a silver-gold ratio of 7.2:1 (at 4%, or 7.9:1 at 4.5%). The possibilities for Aurelian's reformed system (post-274) may then be expressed as follows:

    (a) 500 d. = 250 *ant.* = 1 *aureus.*   1 *libra aurei* = 25,000 d.
    (b) 600 d. = 300 *ant* = 1 *aureus.*   1 *libra aurei* = 30,000 d.
    (c) 700 d. = 350 *ant.* = 1 *aureus.*   1 *libra aurei* = 35,000 d.

In *CIL* 1489[60] there is a dedication dated 276-82 of 28,000 *HS* = 7000 *denarii*. This makes ten *aurei*, at 700 *denarii* to the *aureus*, or fourteen *aurei* at 500 *denarii* per *aureus*. But it does not make up a round number of *aurei* (11.6) at 600 *denarii* per *aureus*, and this fact argues perhaps against system (b). Of the remaining two systems (a) seems to be a little more likely, as it would make it very easy for people to reckon the old currency in terms of the new (see below, Chapter VII).[61] From the period of Aurelian's reform to that of Diocletian's reform the value of the *denarius* must again have dropped very considerably, but the details of this phase remain highly uncertain.[62]

CHAPTER V

FOLLIS

Now it is during this period, the last quarter of the third century, that a completely new term begins to make its first appearance in the sources. It is a term that undergoes, in its early life, a rather complex semantic development. An examination of both the development of this term and the vicissitudes of the actual unit it describes is particularly instructive for an understanding of the next half century or so of monetary history. The term we are referring to is the *follis*, well known as a Byzantine monetary unit, which was incorporated into the Islamic system as the *fels*.[1] When is this term found for the first time?

A.H.M. Jones, in an essay on "The Origin and Early History of the *Follis*", stated that the *follis*[2]

> is first attested in 308-9[3] but (that it) was probably introduced at an earlier date, somewhere between the great debasement of the *antoninianus* by Gallienus and the reform of the coinage by Diocletian (about 260-95) when the *antoninianus* or Aurelian's piece XXI were the only coins in circulation and their value had sunk so low that some higher denomination was essential.[4]

Therefore, the *"follis"* was introduced, being a bag or purse containing a certain set sum of money,[5] not in *denarii*, as these were no longer being struck. Around 301 it contained 25,000 *denarii* or 1000 *nummi* κατα τόν ἀργυρισμόν (hereafter: *KTA*) or 250 denarii κατα τόν δηναρισμόν (hereafter: *KTD*). Shortly afterwards, the government cut the value of the *nummus* to $12\frac{1}{2}$ *denarii*, so that the *follis* was worth 12,500 *denarii*.[6]

Briefly then, the *follis* begins its numismatic career as a purse or sack full of coins(?), being derived from the Latin *"follis"*, meaning a pair of bellows, and subsequently acquiring a second derivative meaning: "a leather money bag", presumably because these bags were made in the form of a pair of bellows.[7]

Jones' surmise that the *follis* was introduced sometime in the later third century is borne out by Talmudic evidence. For in Bavli Bava Meziaᴺᵃ 47b we read :

> *Asemon* acquires coined [metal]. What is *asemon*? Said Rav (died in 247): "Coins that are presented as tokens at the baths." An objection is raised: The second tithe may not be redeemed by *asemon*, nor by coins that are presented as tokens at the baths; proving that *asemon* is not [the same as] coins that are presented as tokens at the baths, (Mishna Ma'aser Sheni 1.2). And should you answer that it is a definition (i.e. 'coins that are presented, etc.', is not a separate clause, but a definition of *asemon*), surely the *Tanna* (=teacher) does not teach us thus; [for we learned:] The second tithe may be redeemed by *asemon*, this is R. Dosa's view. The Sages maintain: It may not. Yet both agree that it may not be redeemed with coins that are presented as tokens at the baths, (Mishna Eduyot 3.2). But said R. Johanan (died in 279), "What is *asemon*? פולסא = *folsa*".[8] Now R. Johanan follows his views [expressed elsewhere]. For R. Johanan said: "R. Dosa and R. Ishmael both taught the same thing". R. Dosa: the statement just quoted. And what is R. Ishmael's dictum? That which has been taught: 'And thou shalt bind up the money in thine hand', (Deuteronomy 14.25); this is to include everything that can be bound up in one's hand—that is R. Ishmael's view. R. Akiva said: "It is to include anything that bears a figure" (i.e. a stamped image, וּתְצָר—'and thou shalt bind up'— is connected with the root צוּר 'to form a figure'. By contrast then R. Ishmael must refer to metal not stamped with a figure, i.e. unstruck metal, and R. Johanan equates that with R. Dosa's dictum. This agrees with his interpretation of *asemon* as *folsa*).[9]

That is to say R. Johanan regards *folsa* as money insofar as it is "bound up in the hand", despite the fact that it was not stamped (uncoined). In that it is uncoined it is less money-like than coined metal, and could therefore acquire it (see Mishna Bava Mezia 4.1). There is no doubt of the identification of *folsa* with *follis*, as in the Syriac version of Epiphanius' *Treatise on Weights and Measures* (written in 392) the term *folsa* appears several times,[10] translating the Greek φόλλις, Latin *follis*, and explained there as meaning a purse or bag. From the context, one may see that R. Johanan's statement was made after Rav's death (and obviously before his own—in fact a few years before his death, as he died after an illness of at least three and a half years);[11] hence it may be dated about 247-75. Add to this the numismatic evidence (Jones' suggestion) and the dates are further narrowed down to about 260-75. According to R. Johanan's statement, the *folsa* consisted of a bag (='bound up in the hand') of blanks (hence equatable with ἄσημον of either bronze or silver—this point is not altogether clear.[12] As it did not consist of actual coins it must have been reckoned by its weight or the number of standard-size pieces in it. As long as the official relationship between silver and gold (and that of bronze to both of them) did not change, the value of the *follis* would not change, and would so remain unaffected by fluctuation in the value of coins.[13] Its value would only be affected by a change in the official silver-gold ratio.

There is, apparently, yet another reference in the Talmud relating to the *follis*, also from this period. This time, however, it is not the actual "sack" that is being referred to, but the "blanks" contained therein. In Bavli Bava Mezia 45b we find the following discussion:[14]

> It has been stated: Rav and Levi—one maintains: Coins can effect a barter; the other rules that they cannot. Said R. Papa: "What is the reason of the one who maintains that a coin cannot effect a barter?" Because his [the recipient's] mind is set upon the legend thereof, and the legend is liable to cancellation (i.e. the figure which is stamped on the coin, and which gives it its value). Now, when an ordinary object is used as *halifin*,[15] the recipient accepts its own intrinsic value as symbolic of the whole. But when a man receives a coin, he does not think of the intrinsic value of the metal, but merely of its worth on account of the legend it bears...[16]

And on the next page,º 46a, the discussion continues: [to revert to the original discussion:]

> And Ulla said likewise: "Coin cannot effect a barter", and R. Asi said likewise: "Coin cannot effect a barter"; and Rabba bar bar Ḥanah said likewise in R. Johanan's name: "Coin cannot effect a barter". R. Aba raised an objection against Ulla: "If his carters or labourers demanded [their wages] from a man in the market place, and he said to the money-changer: 'Give me [copper] coins for a *dinar*, and I will pay them, whilst I return you a *dinar*-and-a-*tressis* worth out of the money which I have at home':

then if he has money at home, it is permitted; otherwise, it is not permitted. Now, should you think that coin cannot effect a barter, it is a loan and hence forbidden". (It was assumed that the reason is this: If he has money at home, immediately when he takes possession of the coins, the money-exchanger acquires the owner-ship of the money at home by a process of barter; hence there is no usury, since theoretically the banker does not wait for his money.[16a] But this cannot be upheld if he has no money, in which case it is a pure loan, upon which the *tressis* is interest.) There-upon he was silent. Said he (R. Aba) to him (Ulla): "Perhaps both [that which is given by the banker and that which is returned] refer to פרוטטות (coins of copper) that are as yet without an imprint (like of silver, Rashi ad loc.)[18]—so that they rank as produce, and therefore may be acquired by barter".

The *terminus ante quem* for this discussion is sometime shortly before 279 when Ulla died.[19] As for R. Aba, he was a Babylonian scholar who came to Palestine about 275.[20] I would suggest, though without any definite proof, that this discussion took place in Palestine,[21] sometime between 275 and 279. In it are mentioned unstruck copper disks (coins) which are regarded nevertheless as money in some respects and hence to which the term מעות (money or coins) can be applied. Surely, here too, we may see a reference to the institution of the *follis,* probably dur-ing the post-Aurelianic period, approximately 275-79.

We have seen that the term *folsa* originally referred to a *b a g o f b l a n k* coins (probably, but not certainly, of silver). There is evidence that in the course of time the term *follis* came to be applied to the single metal units that went to make up the *follis*-bags (a standard semantic development). We may learn this from a passage in Epiphanius' *Treatise on Weights and Measures* (written in Palestine at the end of the fourth century), where we find the following statement:[22]

In accordance with another explanation (of the *folsa)* among the Hebrews the term *sala* is used; this[23] coin is entirely of silver the weight of half an ounce... And the *sala* is interpreted as *follis* be-*cause* of the roundness of the form of the coin. The round scales of reptiles are also called *folides* φολιδες, singular φολίς ... It has the name of bag[25] among the Romans but among the Hebrews and Greeks that of snake scales.

This passage is a delightful confusion of mistaken etymologies. סלע *(sela)* has been transliterated into Greek as σαλα and then back into

Syriac as סלעא (sal'a'a), meaning 'basket', and hence identifiable in some measure with *follis* bag. But at this stage it seems to have been realised that a single *sela* could hardly have made up a basket or bag (of coins), and therefore an etymological jump was made to identify the *follis* with the Greek word φολίς,[26] of quite unrelated origin, meaning snake-scale. This is how the "Greeks" relate the *follis* to a snake-scale. The Hebrews would find yet another connection, since in Palestinian usage of the Talmudic period, a snake-scale was called a *sela*.[27] Hence, says Epiphanius, "It has the name of bag among the Romans, but among the Hebrews and Greeks that of snake-scales".[28]

Now in order to re-establish a connection between the point of departure *(sela)* and the stage so curiously arrived at *(φολίς)*, it is stated that the identification of a *sela* with a φολίς is due to the 'roundness of form' of both. As all normal coins are more or less round, this hardly constitutes a distinguishing feature. However, if we are talking of a blank disk which is not a normal coin, then its roundness might be considered as a point of comparison with the scale of a snake.[29]

What seems to emerge out of all this muddle is that the term *"follis"* can also refer to a *s i n g l e* unit (thus comparable with a single *sela* and etymologically falsely derived from the singular *φολίς*), perhaps of silver[30] (thus comparable with the *sela*, silver *tetradrachm*), and probably with a round blank face (thus comparable with a snake-scale). We know that there were two kinds of *follis* bags, one *KTD* and one *KTA*. Presumably the latter consisted of silver blanks and the former of copper ones. Epiphanius' statement seems to suggest that the single units of silver that went to make up the *follis* bag *KTA* were also called *folles*. Presumably the copper units were likewise called *folles (aeris)*.

There is further, if oblique, evidence of this semantic stage in a cryptic passage in the Yerushalmi (Shabbat 6.5). The Mishna[P] (Shabbat 6.6) teaches that one may go out (into a public domain) on the Sabbath with a *sela* (=*tetradrachm*) which is on the *zinit*; (the *sela* served as a cure for the *zinit*, a sore on the foot). R. Aḥa bar R. (A)ba bar Memel (in the same Yerushalmi passage[P]) comments on this as follows: אפילו טס —even a *tas*. Now normally *tas* means a thin plate of metal. As such, it would be almost exactly synonymous with פולסא which also means a circular disk or plate.[31] (It would also translate the Greek φάλαρον, meaning, inter alia, disk.[32]) Furthermore, the Syriac טסא translates the Hebrew קשקשים (literally: scales!) in I Samuel 17.5, while also meaning an amulet (hence, cure).[33] All these chance associations make it very likely that R. Aḥa, living in the first half of the fourth century, may have been referring to a single blank unit (of currency), otherwise known as a *follis*. However, he used the term *tas* here, since by this time *follis* had yet another meaning, namely that of a real coin.

This further stage in the semantic development of the *follis* may be seen in the parallel text to the one we have just seen, which appears in the Babylonian Talmud. For in Bavli Shabbat[P] 65a we read :

> ...What is a *zinit*? A growth caused by the soil. And why particularly [can one go out on a Sabbath with] a *sela* [if one suffers from a *zinit*]? Shall we say anything hard is beneficial thereto? Then let a shard be prepared for it? Again, if it is on account of the rust [of silver][34] (which softens the callus), let a [silver] plate (טסא) be used? But if it is on account of the figure (stamped on the coin which may protect the growth) let him use a *folsa*? (which is apparently not of silver, else it would be identified with a *sela*).[35] Said Abbaye (*floruit* 280-338/9): "This proves that all [these things] are beneficial for it", (viz: the hardness, silver-rust, and the figure, and only a coin possesses all three).[36]

It would appear that the whole text is of Palestinian origin, with the exception of the final section of the Babylonian scholar Abbaye, which merely comes to sum up the argument. Abbaye died in 339; hence, the Palestinian stratum is probably from the first quarter of the fourth century. From this text we may learn that some time early in the fourth century, the term *"folsa"* was being used to describe a copper struck coin.[37] (Once again the connections between the *folsa* and the *sela* are not wholly fortuitous, but probably the result of a continuous tradition.) The usage is amply attested in classical sources throughout the whole of the fourth century.[38]

The philological development of the term *"follis"* (in Palestine, at any rate) seems, then, to have been in three stages: (a) *follis*, a bag containing a set number of blank metal (copper or silver) pieces (about 274 onwards); (b) *follis*, the individual blank units, either of copper or silver (about 280-300); (c) *follis*, a copper struck coin (from about 300 onwards).[39]

CHAPTER VI

FOLLARION

The issue of the *follis*, however, is further complicated by the fact that there appears in Rabbinic literature yet another monetary term, which is similar in form to *follis* and indeed often confused with it, namely the *follar* or *follarion*. At first examination, this term appears to be mentioned considerably earlier than the *follis*. Thus in *Canticles Rabbah*Q to Canticles 1.1 (Chapter 1, section 9)[1] we read :

> R. Pinḥas ben Yair opened his exposition with the text 'If thou seek her as silver', (Proverbs 11.4): "If you seek after words of Torah (=the Law) as other hidden treasures, the Holy One, blessed be He, will not withhold your reward. If a man loses a *sela* or a *follarin*[2] in his house he lights lamp after lamp, wick after wick, till he finds it...."

The *follarin* here is of silver ('If thou seek her as silver') and presumably less than a *tetradrachm* (=*sela*). Presumably, it is either a *tridachm* or a *didrachm*.[3] And as the homily is brought by R. Pinḥas ben Yair, who flourished about 170-200, the text would appear to be from this period, when both *tridachms* and *didrachms* were being struck.

However, elsewhere I have shown in a detailed analysis of this text[4] that Bacher was correct when, on form-critical grounds, he corrected the reading from R. Pinḥas (ben Yair) to R. Pinḥas (bar Ḥama).[5] What probably happened is that the original text read R. Pinḥas, which usually refers to R. Pinḥas bar Ḥama. The words "ben Yair" were added in under the influence of a passage of a few lines further along in the same section, where a famous *beraita* of R. Pinḥas ben Yair is quoted under his (full) name. Our text is then, not of the late second century, but of the first half of the fourth century. The *follarin* that R. Pinḥas is referring to is some kind of silver coin. (Once again the chance(?) connections between the *follis-follarin* and the *sela*!)

Yet another source in which the *follarion* is mentioned is Yerushalmi Pe'a[R] 1.1.[6] Here we are told that "our Teacher Rabbi (=R. Judah the Prince) sent Artabanus a *mezuza* worth (only) one *follar*". Jacob Neusner has argued that the historical background to this story took place about 215-16, the year in which Caracalla introduced his so-called *"antoninianus"* [3], which we have shown above to have been equal to a *didrachm* (except of course that it was worth only 1/25 *aureus*). However, we do not know just when this story or version of events was actually formulated, but most likely in the early fourth century. The author probably applied terminology current in his own period when describing events that took place in Caracalla's reign. It may be that the *follar* here mentioned is intended to refer to Caracalla's new double *denarius*, the *antoninianus;* however, this remains as yet pure conjecture. All one can learn from this text is that the *follarin* was a small coin and may have been of silver.

The *follarin* also appears in several texts from between 290 and 350. Thus according to *Genesis Rabba*[S] 70.14,[8] a man's daily wage was from six to ten *follarin*, while in *Genesis Rabba*[T] 49.4[9] R. Azaria in the name of R. Judah [ben R. Simeon ben Pazi] (*floruit* 290-350) tells us that one *xestes* of wine, one loaf of bread, and one pound of meat cost ten *follarin* each.[10] Here it is clear that the *follarin* is a small single coin, and not a silver one. According to Diocletian's *Edict of Maximum Prices* of 301,[11] prices of daily wages fall between about thirty *denarii* and fifty *denarii*. About 320 to 330, a *xestes* of wine cost approximately fifty *denarii*.[12] Thus it seems likely that ten *follarin* equalled fifty *denarii*, and that a *follar* was a five-*denarius* piece. Now it is known that the five-*denarius* piece of the early fourth century was evolved out of the *antoninianus*. This fact is borne out by numismatic evidence, since Diocletian's XXI coin [16] (=five *denarii*) appears to have developed out of Aurelian's *antoninianus* [13] (=two *denarii*) which bore the same XXI mark.[13] Hence it would be understandable if the *antoninianus* were in later times retrospectively called a *follar*, as we have tentatively suggested above.[14] The five-*denarius* piece of Diocletian's reformed coinage, hitherto called *"follis"*, might more properly be termed *"follar"* or *"follarion"*.

CHAPTER VII

SUMMARY

Let us summarize the conclusions (at least tentatively reached) at this stage: In the first place we have tried to demonstrate that the *antoninianus* was a double-*denarius,* and to show the part it played in the third century monetary system. We also tried to reckon the relative values of silver and gold throughout this century. Here we set out what appears to be the most probable pattern of these ratios:

Caracalla	9:1
Elagabalus	7.5:1
Severus Alexander	9.2:1
Maximinus	11:1 or 9:1
Balbinus and Pupienus	8.3:1
Gordian III	7.7:1
Philip I	7.5:1
Trajan Decius	8.3:1 or 9:1
Aurelian, pre-reform	8:1 or 8.5:1
Aurelian, post-reform	7.2:1
Diocletian, post-reform	14.4:1

The period between Aurelian and Diocletian remains highly problematic, but provisionally (and in the absence of further analysed material), we would suggest that Aurelian's post-reform ratio remained the official one until the time of Diocletian's reform when silver was reduced to half its former value (in terms of gold). This reduction had considerable effects upon prices, wages, taxes, etc.

In the second place we have tried to show that the *follis* was introduced as a bag of blanks as part of Aurelian's reform. Its value was fixed (by weight and/or tally) at half an *aureus (KTD)* or one *libra aurei (KTA).* Later this same term came to denote a single one of these blanks and later still (early fourth century), it was identified with a coin, a five-*denarius* piece. The derivative term *"follar"* was applied to a silver coin at the beginning of the fourth century, and maybe to a copper one too.

55

Now we know that during Diocletian's post-reform period there were 25,000 *denarii* in a *follis (KTA)*, and that then the silver-gold ratio was about 14.7 : 1 (or more probably 14.4 : 1—see above). Thus it was worth one-half *libra aurei*. According to one of our suggestions, (a), in Aurelian's reformed system there were 500 *denarii* in a *libra aurei*, and the silver-gold ratio stood at about 7.2 : 1; that is to say, silver was worth about twice as much in Aurelian's time than it was in Diocletian's time. If we assume for the moment that Aurelian introduced the *follis* as part of his monetary reform, and that its weight was then the same as in Diocletian's time, the *follis* would have been worth twice as much as in Diocletian's time, though still 25,000 *denarii (KTA)* or 250 *denarii (KTD)*.[1] As according to this same system (a) there were 500 *denarii* in an *aureus* and 25,000 *denarii* in a *libra aurei*, the *follis* would have been *KTD* exactly equal to half an *aureus*, and *KTA* exactly equal to one *libra aurei*.[2] It stands to reason that the *follis* at its introduction must have fitted neatly and simply into the monetary system then operating. The above suggestion would appear to satisfy this requirement particularly well. The *follis* would have served as a kind of "stable currency" other than gold (the excessive use of which the government would not be keen on encouraging), easily reckonable in terms of *aurei* and *libra aurei*. Such an interpretation of the purpose of *follis* bears out the suggestion that it formed part of a programme of currency reform.[3]

Here, the numismatic, metrological and literary evidence lead to one and the same conclusion, namely that Aurelian introduced the *follis* bag as part of, or alongside, his monetary reform, and as such, it fitted in as an integral part of his metrological system. Furthermore, it should be noted that it fits into no other metrological system of the third and fourth centuries with such symmetry and logical ease.

CHAPTER VIII

LUMMA-NUMMUS (COPPER)

Thus far we have seen that about 274, after the great crisis in the debasement of the *denarius* and the *antoninianus,* Aurelian not only instituted a very significant currency reform, but also introduced a new idea into the money market, namely the *"follis"*-bag.

In a Talmudic text, which we shall show dates to approximately this same period, we find yet another monetary term, the *lumma.* The history of this term, in all its various meanings, is inextricably bound up with the monetary developments of the period. Therefore, we shall now give it close attention, attempting to date its use and define its usage. In Bavli Avoda Zara[V] 34b[1] we find the following episode :

> Once a shipload of *muries* reached the port of Akko and R. Aba of Akko placed a guard by it (to watch it, lest wine be mixed in with the brine).[2] Said Rava (רבא) to him: "And who watched the ship till now?" "Till now", he replied, "what cause for suspicion? As to mixing the brine with wine, a *xestes* of *muries* costs a *lumma* (in the place from which the cargo came), while a *xestes* of wine costs four *lumma.*" Said R. Jeremiah to R. Zera: "Might they (the ship) not have come by way of Tyre where wine is cheap?" He replied: "There are narrow bays and shallow waters"[3] (on that route, and the pilot would not risk taking that course).[4]

All the printed editions and manuscripts read Rava— רבא in this text.[5] However, it is clear that the correct reading should be R. Aba— ר׳ אבא as Hyman already noted.[6] For (the Babylonian) Rava never left Babylonia[7] throughout his whole life.[8] R. Aba,[9] however, did come from Babylonia to Palestine, perhaps partly by way of the sea,[10] and his first point of arrival in Palestine was Akko.[11] When he arrived, R. Johanan was still alive and so indeed was Resh (=R. Simeon ben) Lakish, who died slightly before R. Johanan.[12] Thus he arrived before 276 (the approximate date of Resh Lakish's death).[13] It would appear that when he arrived, R. Johanan was already very old, and could not see him (at first?) directly;[14] he did, however, come into some, albeit slight, contact with R. Johanan,[15] then in Tiberias. Thus, he seems to have arrived during the reign of Aurelian (270-76). He first arrived at Akko, but soon moved to Tiberias where he took up permanent residence.[16]

To date R. Aba's arrival in Palestine more closely still, one should note that he arrived after his close friend R. Zera I came from Babylonia.[17] Isaac Halevy, in *Dorot Harischonim,*[18] suggests that R. Zera I arrived in Palestine about 280. His dating depends in a great measure upon his emendation of the reading in R. Sherira Gaon's *Iggeret* of the crucial date in Amoraic chronology, R. Johanan's death, which he takes to be 289,[19] and not 279 (599 Seleucid area, instead of 590 as stated).[20] However, there is no textual basis for this emendation,[21] nor indeed any internal chronological necessity, as we have indicated elsewhere.[22] Therefore, following the logic of Halevy's otherwise sound argument, one would put R. Zera's arrival in Palestine some ten years earlier than did Halevy, i.e. about 270.[23] R. Aba, as we have stated above, came some short time after R. Zera, probably around 274-75. But as we have seen above, he very soon moved to Tiberias where he took up permanent residence. Thus, this episode must have taken place almost immediately upon his arrival, i.e. sometime around 275.

The *lumma* of our text is undoubtedly a νοῦμμος *(nummus)* as has long been (at least partly) recognised.[24] (The change from N to L is by no means uncommon in Aramaic and Syriac, etc.)[25] Now according to a number of metrological authorities, the νοῦμμος was a *sestertius Romanus, quarto pars denarii.*[26] As there had been 25 *denarii* in the *aureus* in the classical system, the *sestertius* was 1/100 *aureus,*[27] and as such, was a convenient unit for reckoning. In fact, it was long used as the standard unit for reckoning.[28]

We have stated above that in Aurelian's reform system there were 500 *denarii,* which equalled 250 *antoniniani* [14 and 15], in the *aureus.* If the *lumma-nummus* (=*sestertius*) was 1/100 *aureus* in Aurelian's reform system, its value would have been five *denarii.* This was, however, a five *denarii* unit of value, not a coin of five *denarii,* and not the XXI coin, which according to our calculations (above) was worth only two *denarii* (=twenty *libellae,* etc.). Nonetheless, the appearance of this unit of value was probably bound up in some way with Aurelian's monetary reform of approximately one year earlier.

Now we have seen above that Diocletian's reform currency included two main types of copper (debased silver) denominations: (a) a four gramme piece [17][29]—the weight of an Aurelian *antoninianus* with the same obverse design and radiate bust as the *antoninianus* [14], but without the XXI legend; and (b) a new denomination weighing ten grammes with a different design, but with several features borrowed from the old *antoninianus* [16], most especially its legend XXI.[30] We have also mentioned above that the former was worth two *denarii* (as had been the Aurelian *antoninianus* of the same weight), and the latter five *denarii*. This piece was equal in value to Aurelian's (theoretical) *nummus unit*, and bore the legend XXI, which now meant: twenty *sestertii* (one *sestertius* equalled $\frac{1}{4}$ *denarius*), equalled one of these pieces (new *sestertius*, or *nummus*), which equalled five *denarii*.

That νοῦμμος during the early fourth century meant a debased copper coin is borne out by several papyri. Thus:[31]

Wessely *Pal. St.* XX.85 (c.305/6) line 9:

> ἐν νούμμοις ἰταλικοῖς (ταλ.)
> ἐν ἰταλικῷ νομίσματι (ταλ.) ν

P. Grenf. II 75 (308) line 7:

> ἀργυρίου Σεβαστῶν νομίσματος
> ἐν ν(ο)ύμμο(ι)ς τάλαντα εἴκοσι.

SB. 5676 (307) line 8:

> ἀργορίου Σεβαστῶν καινοῦ νομμίσματος
> τάλαντα δυο και γ' δραγμάι.

According to our suggestion, *nummus* in these cases refers to the ten-gramme coin worth five *denarii*.[32]

CHAPTER IX

NUMMUS (SILVER)

At this point, however, a difficulty arises. For this same term "*num-mus*" occurs in a group of papyri, where it appears to denote a piece worth, not five *denarii*, but 25 *denarii*! The evidence has been best summed up by Jones:[1]

> As the question is important and controversial, it may be well to outline the evidence. *P. Ryl.* 607 is a letter dated on various grounds to A.D. 300, from an official (who is evidently "in the know") to a subordinate, instructing him urgently to buy goods at any price with all his (the writer's) Italian money Ἰταλικὸν ἀργύριον, the reason being that the emperors have ordered the Italian coin to be reduced to half a *nummus* π οσέταξεν ἡ θεία τύχη τῶν δεσποτῶν ἡμῶν το Ἰταλικὸν νόμισμα εἰς ἥμισυ νούμμου καταβιβασθῆναι.[2] It is generally agreed that το Ἰταλιλὸν νόμισμα ἀργύριον means the normal imperial coinage by contrast with the local Alexandrine *tetradrachms* which ceased to be issued in A.D. 296, that is the Aurelianic XX.I pieces. The most natural interpretation of phraseology would be that these pieces had hitherto been known as *nummi*, but were henceforth to be tariffed at half *nummi*.

> *P. Oslo* III.83, also dated to about 300, is unfortunately fragmentary. It contains portions of three official letters, of which the third one alone concerns us. It is clearly concerned with the regulation of the currency, and alludes to the καθολόςιχ or *rationalis*, the imperial minister who controlled the mints or his local representative in Egypt, and to a πρόγραμμα or public notice issued by some high authority παρὰ τῆς μεγαλειστη(τος). The first line speaks of something having reached a 25 *denarii* ἕως εἰς εἴκοσι πέντε Ἀττικάς and the third of *nummi* (being reduced?) to 12½ *denarii* (τ)ῶν δε νούμμων εἰς δώδεκα ἥμισυ Ἀττικάς.

60

It is hard to resist the conclusion that this document refers to the same operation as *P. Ryl.* 607, and states that the *nummus*, which had previously been raised to 25 *denarii*, is now reduced to 12½.[3]

PSI. 965 is also fragmentary. The opening four lines state that the emperors have issued the *Edictum de Pretiis*, lines 5 and 6 are concerned with currency changes. Line 5 alludes to *"denarii"* (Ἀττικὲς), line 6 τὸ δὲ μέχρι τῆς δεῦρο ἀντὶ τοῦ δύο καὶ δέκα (καὶ ἥμισου) may indicate that the coin hitherto current is to be valued at twelve (and a half *denarii*?).

It may be added that some half *nummi* of Licinius are marked XIIS.[3a]

Thus, the νούμμος of these papyri can hardly be the XXI coins of about 301. And yet, the evidence of *P. Oslo* III.83 is surely inescapable; there must have been a coin —on the evidence of *PSI*.965, post 301— worth 25 *ATTIKES* (=*denarii*). *P. Ryl.* 607 must also be post 301, as before then imperial denarii were, on the evidence of hoards, not circulating in Egypt.[4]

Jones' explanation is as follows:[5]

Three papyri documents between them strongly suggest that at the end of the III or the beginning of the IV cent., the imperial government first raised the face value of the *nummus,* i.e. the Aurelianic piece and the similar radiate coins which succeeded it, by stages to 25 d., and then cut its value by half to 12½ d.

However, this explanation, attractive though it be, takes absolutely no account of the gold-silver ratio. For if Diocletian's XXI coin of about ten grammes, and with a silver content of some four percent, had been worth 25 *denarii* (which equalled 1/32 *aureus*, at 800 *denarii* per *aureus*), the resultant gold-silver ratio would be something like 1 : 2.85, clearly an impossible result. Even at 12½ *denarii* per XXI piece, we get the most unlikely gold-silver ratio of 1 :5.7.[6] Thus, we must seek some other explanation for these papyri.

Now the only (non-gold) denominations actually current at that time were the two copper pieces [16 and 17] worth two and five *denarii* respectively,[7] and a good silver coin [19], ranging in weight from 2.4 to 4.4 grammes[8] with a silver content of around 90%[9] and averaging around 3.09 grammes.[10] It is marked XCVI and so was probably struck (*al marco*) at the theoretical weight of 3.4 grammes (= 1/96 *libra*).[11]

This piece, called the *argenteus*, was probably worth 32 *denarii*, which equalled 1/25 *aureus* (at 800 *denarii* per *aureus*), and as such equal to an old *denarius*. This yields a gold-silver ratio 1 : 14.4 (see above).[12] It seems, then, very likely that it is to this silver coin that the papyri refer when speaking of the *nummus*.[13]

It may be that shortly after 301 the value of silver, for some reason or other, dropped (or the value of gold went up) so that the relationship between the two metals stood at 1 : 18. For there is evidence of such a ratio in a papyrological source of the early fourth century (*SB*. 6086 V).[14] The *argenteus* itself had not changed weight, neither apparently had the *official* number of *denarii* in the *aureus*. Hence there were now 25 *denarii* to the *argenteus* (3.4 grammes of 90% at 18 : 1 = 1/32 *aureus* of 800 *denarii*).

This suggestion seems further to be borne out by the fact that

> in 325[15] we find "*siliqua*" as a name of a coin, and the only such coin we know is this 96th of Diocletian. Now a *siliqua* is 1/1728 *libra aurei*, as a name of a silver coin representing that part of a pound of gold. This would give a ratio of gold to silver of 1 : 18.[16]

We have suggested that *nummus* was the name, not only of the copper five-*denarius* piece, but also for a silver coin (cf. *Codex Theodosianus* 15.9.1, of 387) worth, sometime after 301, 25 *denarii*[17] (much as in Palestine the *dinar* could refer to a silver or a gold coin).

There is some evidence, in a difficult passage in Epiphanius, albeit of a tenuous nature, for this identification of the *nummus* with a silver coin worth 25 *denarii*. For there we read:[18] "[Concerning the *nummus*] ... but the ancients called half of the silver (*denarius*) the *dichryson*. And the silver (*denarius*) is what the Romans call the *miliarision*." Now the *miliarense* (=*miliarision*) was so called because it was 1/1000 *libra aurei*.[19] Therefore, the silver (*denarius*) was equal to 1/1000 *libra aurei*, which in 301, according to the *Edict of Diocletian*, was worth 50,000 *denarii*. Hence, one silver (*denarius*) equalled fifty *denarii*, and one *nummus* equalled half the silver (*denarius*), i.e. 25 *denarii*.[20]

According to the above, then, some time after 301, the silver *argenteus*, which was officially tariffed at a *nummus* (25 *ATTIKES*) was halved in value so that it was now worth 12½ *denarii* (*P. Oslo* 3.83). We understand this to mean that if a person handed in an old *nummus* formerly worth 25 *denarii*, he would receive for it only 12½ *denarii*. In other words, in order to get a *nummus*—a unit of value meaning 25 *denarii*—he would have to give in two old *nummi* (fifty *denarii*). Thus, in actual fact, there were now fifty *denarii* in the new *nummus,* and (50 × 32 =) 16,000 *denarii* in an *aureus.* This latter equation is borne out by an undated papyrus, *P.O.* 2106, of the early fourth century, which Segrè dates to about 304.[21] There it is stated that one *libra aurei* equals 100,000 *denarii.* As this is exactly twice the sum mentioned in the *Edict of Diocletian* (of 301), one may assume (approximately) twice the number of *denarii* per *aureus,* i.e. 1600.[22]

CHAPTER X

FOLLIS AGAIN

With the devaluation of the *denarius* (and *nummus*) to half its former value, there also came a devaluation of the *follis* (=sack). We have calculated that according to Diocletian's reform system, the *follis* was worth 25,000 *denarii* ($\frac{1}{2}$ *libra aurei*). Now it would be worth only 12,500 *denarii*. This suggestion is borne out by the evidence first called to our attention by Jones,[1] namely that in one of the mosaics of the villa at Piazza Armerina (early fourth century), which depicts a table on which are prizes, crowns and palms, there are also bags labelled * XII Ⅎ, i.e. 12,500 *denarii*.[2] These then are the "reduced *folles*". Futher confirmation of this has been found recently in *P. Beatty Panop.* 2, line 302, where four *folles* are equated with 33 *talents* (=49,500 *denarii*) plus 500 *denarii*.[3] Hence, one *follis* equalled 12,500 *denarii*. Jones also sees this stage of the *follis'* devaluation reflected in Epiphanius' varying statements. For in one passage he states that the *follis KTD*, equals $2\frac{1}{2}$ silver coins, which are again equated with 250 *denarii*,[4] whereas in another, he states that "the *follis* has 125 silver coins, and it is called among the Romans 'a sack' ".[5] These "silver coins" were surely *miliarensia*[6] (=100 *denarii*, see below, this chapter), hence the *follis* equalled 12,500 *denarii*. The *follis* was now worth 1/8 *libra aurei* (100,000 *denarii* equalled one *libra aurei*).

The fact that the *follis* declined in value with the fall of the *denarius* is evidence of yet another stage of its development, namely that it was no longer a bag of blank metal disks, a specific weight of metal according to a fixed unit of value—one or one-half pound of gold—but a bag of actual coins, whose value sinks with the devaluation of the coins it contains. This agrees with our findings above, that by this stage the *follis* already denoted a coin, and presumably a bag of actual coins.

The metrological history of the following years is somewhat confusing. The fluctuations in the price of silver must have been rather erratic during this period; but they were soon more or less balanced by the introduction of a new denomination called the *miliarense*, struck at 1/72 *libra aurei*,[7] and valued at 1/16 *aureus* (at a gold-silver ratio of 1 : 14.4, with about 90% fineness). No doubt it was tariffed at 100 *denarii*, and as such as 1/1000 *libra aurei*; hence its name *miliarense* (see above, Chapter IX, note 19). The *argenteus* would be worth 64 *denarii*, which was equal to 1/24 *aureus* at the restored gold-silver ratio.

In 307 the ten-gramme piece fell in weight by approximately one-third to 6.64 grammes.[8] As is to be expected, its value fell by slightly less than a quarter, so that there were now 2000 *denarii* per *aureus*. The gold-silver ratio continued to stand at 1 : 14.4. This may be seen from *PSI*.310 (dated 307) (discussed below, Chapter XIV), according to which three ounces 22½ *grammata* are valued at 10930½ *drachmae*, each ounce being worth 2776 *drachmae*. Segrè and Mickwitz both suggest that the three onces 22½ *grammata* are silver and not gold. Thus, the *aureus* was worth either 7992 or 9590 *drachmae*, depending on whether the gold-silver ratio is 18 : 1 or 14.4 : 1. Probably these figures indicate values of 8000 *drachmae* (=2000 *denarii*) and 9,600 *drachmae* (=2400 *denarii*) respectively.[9]

And in Yerushalmi Ma'aser Sheni 4.1 (see below, Chapter XIV), (a text of the early fourth century, discussed above, Chapter II), we read that: "a [gold] *dinar* (=*aureus*) here (Tiberias?) is worth 2000 [*denarii*], and in Arbael (nearby) 2000 [*denarii*] and a *leukon*, (a silver [?] coin or unit whose value will be discussed below, Chapter XIV)".[10] This seems to bear out the former interpretation of *PSI*. 310, which, as we have seen, also gives the equation 2000 *denarii* = one *aureus*.[11]

Now, as stated by Jones,[12] "a papyrus of 308-9[13] appears to indicate (its language is very obscure) that a fine of 5 *folles*, equivalent at that date to ½ lb. gold, was levied on villagers who left their own villages". We have seen that in 307 the *aureus* equalled 2000 *denarii* (1/60 *libra aurei*), and one pound gold equalled 120,000 *denarii*. If five *folles* were *exactly* one-half pound gold, and the *follis* was worth 12,500 *denarii* (as suggested above, this chapter), then there were 125,000 *denarii* per *libra aurei* around 308-9; this is a very reasonable result.[14] At this time ten *folles* equalled 14.4 pounds silver and one *follis* equalled 1.44 pounds silver.

Not long after, early in 312,[14a] the copper piece was again reduced in weight to 3.57/3.36 grammes,[15] i.e. half again. (See Table J, on page 162.) The value of the *denarius* dropped likewise, and it would seem that one could reckon approximately how much. For in

Codex Theodosianus 11.36.2,3, of 315, we find a fine of thirty *folles*, while a law of 341 (*Codex Theodosianus* 11.36.5) fixes the penalty for the same offence at thirty pounds of silver. This implies (though no more than that) that about 315, one pound silver equalled one *follis*.[17] If the *follis* were still equal to 12,500 *denarii*, then one *libra aurei* (12,500 × 14.4) equalled 180,000 *denarii*, and the *aureus* (180,000 ÷ 60) equalled 3000 *denarii*, again a very attractive result.[18]

However, *P. Roll. Princ.* 4.13, of 313-14, yields an equation: one aureus = 7116 *denarii*, and an analysis of the metallic contents of the contemporary coinage bears out this equation (see below, page 158).[19] Shortly afterwards, the situation of the copper coins grew a little better (see below, page 158) and it is possible that in 315 there were only about 6000 *denarii* per *aureus*. In that case, the *follis* was worth approximately one-half pound silver, and by 341 the fine had been doubled.

There are several other sources usually quoted in discussions of these terms *"nummi"* and *"follis"*. However, they are too ambiguous and problematic to be able to draw from them any clear conclusions.[20] Therefore, let us leave for a while the fortunes of the *follis* and examine the problems of gold and silver standards during this period.

PART TWO

GOLD AND SILVER

CHAPTER XI

GOLD AND SILVER "STANDARDS"
(SECOND AND THIRD CENTURIES)

We now turn to some purely legal texts which may cast further light on the pattern of third century monetary development, thus giving added body to the skeletal framework outlined in the preceding chapters.

The key text in this discussion is the Mishna Bava Mezia 4.1, which has been the subject of numerous Talmudic discourses.[1] More recently, however, it has been studied by a number of scholars who have tried to explain it and the difficulties arising out of it on the basis of historico-economic arguments. While this approach was undoubtedly correct, the detailed reasoning was rather less so. Let us then first set out the Mishnaic text(s) and the Talmudic discussions on it in the two recensions which have come down to us—in the Babylonian and in the Palestinian (=Yerushalmi) Talmuds.[w]

Yerushalmi Bava Mezia 4.1 (9b-c)
Mishna: Silver acquires gold but gold does not acquire silver; copper acquires silver; cancelled coins acquire current ones, but current ones do not acquire cancelled coins; uncoined metal acquires coined, but coined metal does not acquire uncoined; movables acquire coins, but coins do not acquire movables. . .

Gemara [9c]: This is the principle of the matter: all which is lower in value acquires its coun-

Bavli Bava Mezia 44a-b Mishna:
Gold acquires silver, but silver does not acquire gold; copper acquires silver, but silver does not acquire copper; cancelled coins acquire current ones, but current ones do not acquire cancelled coins; uncoined metal acquires coined, but coined metal does not acquire uncoined; movables acquire coins, but coins do not acquire movables. . .

Gemara: Rabbi taught his son R. Simeon: Gold acquires silver. Said he to him: Master, in your

terpart [which is higher in value].[2] Said R. Ḥiyya bar Ashi: Who formulated our Mishna? R. Simeon the son of Rabbi. His father said to him (to R. Simeon): Retract and declare that gold acquires silver. He (R. Simeon) replied to him (Rabbi): I cannot retract, for you yourself, whilst you were [young and] strong stated that silver purchases gold. According to Rabbi, gold is produce. But the Mishna states that silver is like produce.

youth you did teach us, Silver acquires gold; now, advanced in age, you reverse it and teach gold acquires silver. Now, how did he reason in his youth, and how did he reason in his old age? In his youth he reasoned: Since gold is more valuable, it ranks as money;[2] whilst silver, which is of lesser value is regarded as produce; hence [delivery of] produce effects a title to the money. But at a later age he reasoned: Since silver [coin] [44b] is current, it ranks as money; whilst gold which is not current is accounted as produce, and so the produce effects a title to the money...

The daughter of R. Ḥiyya Raba lent Rav [gold] *denarii*. She came and asked her father [how he should repay]. He answered her "Receive from him current and full-weight [gold] *denarii*."[3] From [the story of] the daughter of R. Ḥiyya one can learn (that gold is money).[4] R. Idi said: Abba, the father of Samuel, also asked of Rabbi, "May one borrow [gold] *denarii* for [gold] *denarii*?" He replied one may. (Hence, gold *denarii* are money.) R. Jacob bar Aḥa said: "Both R. Johanan and Resh Lakish *also* stated that one may borrow [gold] *denarii* for [gold] *denarii*, a *karat*[5] for a *karat*, but it is forbidden [to borrow] a *leukon*[6] for a *leukon*...

Now, R. Ḥiyya too regards gold [coin] as money. For Rav once borrowed [gold] *denarii* (=*aurei*) from R. Ḥiyya's daughter. Subsequently the [gold] *denarii* having appreciated, he went before R. Ḥiyya. "Go and repay her current and full-weight coin",[3] he ordered. Now if you agree that gold ranks as money, it is well. (Notwithstanding its appreciation, he would be returning money of the same nominal value as that which he borrowed.) But should you maintain it is produce, it is the equivalent of [borrowing] a *se'ah* (=a certain measure) for a *se'ah* (to be repaid later), which is forbidden (lest it appreciate in the meantime, and he would be infringing the pro-

70

hibition of interest). [That[7] does not prove it. For] Rav himself possessed [gold] *denarii* [when he incurred the debt], and that being so, it is just as though he had said to her "lend me until my son comes", or "until I find the key". (cf. Bavli Bava Mezia 75a.)

Now, even the most cursory perusal of these versions clearly reveals that Rabbi (=Rabbi Judah the Prince I) in his youth stated that silver acquires gold, while in his old age he said that gold acquires silver. There must have been some reason for him to change his mind, and it is with this problem that we shall occupy ourselves. But before doing so, let us note a few further points. Not only did Rabbi in his youth consider that silver acquires gold, but so too did his son (Bavli and Yerushalmi), even while he (Rabbi) was old and held the reverse opinion. Furthermore, this was also the opinion of R. Ḥiyya, when Rav borrowed money from his daughter (Bavli and Yerushalmi), and this opinion was likewise held by R. Johanan and Resh Lakish (Yerushalmi).

The chronology of these opinions may be calculated approximately thus: Rabbi was born about 135,[8] so that any time around 170 would probably qualify to be called the period of his youth. He changed his mind when "advanced in age", i.e. probably between the age of sixty and seventy.[9] Thus he probably revised his opinions about 195. At this time, however, his son R. Simeon disagrees with him; presumably then the issue was not clear-cut and hence disputable. And Rabbi himself apparently comes to agree with his son and revert to his earlier opinion. For when Samuel's father (probably sometime early in the third century)[10] asks him whether one can borrow gold *denarii* for gold *denarii*, he answers that one can, meaning that gold coin is "money" (Yerushalmi). Furthermore, by the time Rav borrows money from R. Ḥiyya's daughter, there appears to be no argument. Certainly Rav is not said to have disputed the decision of R. Ḥiyya, though it would have been in his financial interest to do so. Rav left Palestine (where R. Ḥiyya spent his remaining years)[11] in 219, hence this incident took place pre-219.

In fact this incident is well understandable in terms of the monetary developments during this period. Thus, the *aurei* of Caracalla [2] from 211-215 weigh around 7.20 grammes, while those of 215-217 weigh

71

significantly less, between 6.42 and 6.77 grammes. Macrinus' *aurei* (of 217-218) weigh between 6.39 and 6.54 grammes. Only after Rav's departure from Palestine to Babylonia do Elagabalus' Antiochene *aurei* (of 219-20) have their weights restored to 7.11-7.34 grammes, while the Roman ones continue around 6.32 grammes.[12] Thus, in 215 the *aureus'* weight was decreased (Bavli). We have already shown that this incident took place prior to 219.[13] If we assume that Rav borrowed the money some time before 215, and had to pay some time after this date, then the question of what sort of *aurei* to pay with becomes very understandable. R. Ḥiyya ruled that he had to pay back with good *full-weight*, i.e. pre-215 *aurei*, thus demonstrating that he held the view that gold is coin.

The same opinion, namely that silver acquires gold, persists through the period of R. Johanan and Resh Lakish, i.e. from 230 onwards. There is no change of opinion recorded for either of these authorities who lived on until late in the third century—R. Johanan died in 279—so that, in effect then, throughout the period 170 to 280 the opinion was that silver acquires gold, with the exception of a presumably brief spell around 195, when Rabbi held the view that gold acquires silver. Our first question may now be restated and elaborated, thus: What were the specific causes around 195 that made Rabbi change his mind? Why did his son then not accept this reversed opinion? Indeed why did no one (recorded, at any rate) subsequently take up this view?

Scholars who have hitherto dealt with this question have suggested the following explanations:

(a) Heichelheim[14] proves from a Palmyrene inscription (dated, April, 193)[15] that after the time of Commodus the *denarius*—the commonest silver coin—fell into disrepute.[16] He goes on to state that:

> In the light of these inscriptions it is clear that it was not by chance that the famous Talmudic authority Rabbi in his old age, which was contemporary with the inscription mentioned above, reversed his earlier principle "silver buys gold" into "gold buys silver".

Heichelheim here seems to have missed the basic legal principle upon which this whole ruling is based, else he would have seen that this Talmudic reference is actually closer to refuting his statement than to corroborating it. For the principle (clearly expressed in both Talmuds)[17] is as follows: "Coin" is more current than "produce". "Coin" cannot acquire, i.e. actually effect a legal purchase or transfer to property; only "produce" can.[18] Coin can at most commit a person morally to go through with the transaction. Thus, if gold is said to acquire silver, it follows that gold is produce while silver constitutes coin and has the user's confidence. Therefore, when Rabbi said "gold acquires silver", silver must have been *more* current than gold, and not less current, in greater use, and presumably confidently used.

Heichelheim cites further Talmudic evidence to support his contention. He writes: "and in addition, the Talmud (Yerushalmi Ketubot 1.2) states expressly that the silver coins of Septimus Severus had less value". However, this is recorded as being the opinion of R. Johanan. What he implies there—he does not "state expressly"—is that סלעים סביריניות —Severan *tetradrachms*—were already considerably debased.[19] Yet R. Johanan himself (in the Yerushalmi) is of the opinion that gold is coin, or in other words that "silver acquires gold" despite its (silver's) debasement.

(b) A. Marmorstein[20] offers a different solution to the problems presented by our texts. He writes that "according to the ancient law before Caracalla 'silver acquires gold'. But in the period of Rabbi, according to his son, 'gold acquired silver' ". The reason he offers for this change is as follows:

> As long as gold was the current currency it served as money and silver served only as merchandise (=produce). It was after 211 that gold was taken out of circulation and replaced by silver, then gold became merchandise and silver served as money. This confirms the date of Rabbi's death as given by Sherira Gaon, 219. The modification of the Mishna only makes sense after Caracalla's time.

This explanation, convincing though it appears to be, is open to a number of objections: (1) Already in 193 we see that the merchants of Palmyra were refusing debased silver *denarii* and demanding payment in "old gold *denarii*" (see above, this chapter). Some twenty years later with the debasement still further advanced,[21] one would expect less confidence in silver making it less "coin-like". (2) Already before 219, i.e. (according to Marmorstein) less than eight years after 211, R. Ḥiyya and Rav regarded gold money as "coin". (3) There was indeed plenty of gold coin circulating both from the mint of Rome and the Eastern mints (Antioch, etc.).[22] (4) It should also be noted, though this point has no bearing on Marmorstein's argument, that Sherira Gaon does not *explicitly* give Rabbi's date of death as 219. All we may say is that he was probably alive about 219.[23]

(c) Finally, Louis Jacobs, approaching the problem from a completely different angle writes the following:[24]

> There can be little doubt that the two Talmuds were influenced by the currency conditions of their respective lands. In Palestine silver money had long been adulterated and after the reform of Diocletian, the standard was gold. Consequently silver was in the nature of a commodity (=produce) in relation to gold. In Babylon, where silver coins were far more current than gold, the latter would be the commodity.

In this way he wishes to explain the very interesting problem of why two Talmuds adopted varying Mishnas, the Bavli that of Rabbi, the Yerushalmi that of his son. But according to this argument, there should have been a gold-standard in Palestine during Rabbi's youth (about 170), R. Ḥiyya's later years (pre-214), R. Johanan's life (about 250), etc., as they all held the opinion that "silver acquires gold", (meaning that gold is coin). Yet, as he himself says, there was not a gold standard in Palestine until the reign of Diocletian.

Jacob's incorrent explanation of why the two Talmuds chose their respective Mishna versions, has the positive effect of clarifying for us a point of cardinal importance, namely that the criterion here involved is not whether there was a gold or silver *standard*. For it is quite certain that "the Roman Empire was *not* on a gold standard; in it gold was a commodity whose price expressed in normal currency, the *denarius*, might vary like that of wheat".[25] That metallic standard (alone) cannot be the criterion here is most clearly evident from the Mishna version of the Yerushalmi, i.e. that of R. Simeon son of Rabbi. For in this version we read that "silver acquires gold" and also that "copper acquires silver". If it were only a matter of metallic standards, the first statement would suggest a gold standard (for if "silver acquires gold", gold is coin), whilst the following one, of the same period, would suggest a silver standard—an absurd conclusion.[26]

However, there is a sense in which there was a "gold standard" during this period. Thus, Bolin writes[27] that

> from the time of Nero onwards the value of the *denarius* was not determined by its metallic content, but by the fact that it corresponded nominally to a definite part of a gold coin, the *aureus*, which from this time onwards was the only full metallic value coin.

74

Thus, while it is true that gold as such may have been valued in terms of silver, or even silver coins (debased though they were), silver money was expressed in fractions of pure (stable) gold coins. Hence, gold in this sense is coin, and cannot effect a purchase. This indeed is precisely what the Babylonian scholar Rava (early fourth century) says in Bavli Bava Mezia^W 44b:

> This *Tanna* (=Mishnaic authority) [too] is of the opinion that gold is coin, for we have learned in a Mishna (Mishna Eduyot 4.7): A *pruta* (=small bronze coin) that they spoke of is 1/8 Italian *issar*... (Tosefta Bava Batra 5.12), the *issar* 1/24 silver *dinar* (=*denarius*), the silver *dinar* 1/25 gold *dinar* (=*aureus*)... This is understandable if you say that [gold *dinar*] is coin, for then the *Tanna* is reckoning [the silver *dinar*] as part of something fixed; but if you were to say that gold is produce, then the *Tanna* would be reckoning against something unstable [which is impossible]... from here then you may certainly deduce that [gold] is coin.

On the other hand, it could not be denied that there was officially a silver standard (at least when compared with copper); hence, silver as opposed to copper was coin and not commodity or produce. In practice, then, the cheaper metal acquired the dearer one, and this is indeed exactly what the Yerushalmi says: "This is the principle of the matter: all which is lower in value acquires its counterpart [which is higher in value]". (Compare also the Bavli's explanation for the opinion of Rabbi in his youth.)

The question that still remains is why should Rabbi have held the opinion around the year 195 that silver is more "coin" than gold. The answer is surely supplied by the Babylonian Talmud: silver was far more current than gold, hence Rabbi thought that from this point of view it qualified to be considered as "coin". The fact that Rabbi suddenly reversed a former opinion suggests that silver suddenly became far more current than it had been before. Numismatic evidence shows this to have been precisely the case. For, according to Pekári's calculations, between 193 and 196, 529 types were struck, meaning an average of about 176 types per year. This is a most remarkable increase over, for example, the average for the twenty-three years of Antoninus Pius' reign (138-61) of some seventeen types per annum.[28] (See also Table G.) This circulation was so widespread that *denarii* circulated even in Egypt (which had its own currency and limited and discouraged the circulation of foreign coinage)[29] during the reign of Septimius Severus.[30] *Aurei,* on the other hand, may have been slightly less plentiful than usual, as Commodus had struck them less freely than had emperors in preceding reigns.[31] This tremendous boom in the circulation of *denarii* is surely the background and cause of Rabbi's reversed decision.

At one and the same time, however, this flood of silver had an immediate inflationary effect. The Palmyra inscription of 193 (see above, this chapter) may possibly be an indication of this, as the caravan leaders there demand payment specifically in gold. On the other hand, in view of the earliness of the date of this inscription (April, 193), it may be that the caravaneers' attitude reflects earlier conditions, which possibly the silver boom was meant to have combatted.[32]

But if Palmyra does not offer any clear evidence of the immediate inflationary effect of this policy, Egypt does. For in *P. Columbia* 123 (Inventory 516) lines 43-4, dated 199-200 (Alexandria), we read the following ruling:[33] αργυριον αντι πυρου καταβαλλιν υμας εκωλυσαμεν "We have forbidden that you pay money in place of grain". People were apparently only too willing to pay in debased *denarii* (or *tetradrachms*). The government, on the other hand, was unwilling to accept them. The government, it would appear, preferred to keep the coins at their (unreal) nominal value, but receive payment in (full-value of) grain.[34]

This widespread lack of confidence in the silver coinage was apparently appreciated by R. Simeon, son of Rabbi, and for this reason he opposed his father' view, considering silver as no more than a (very unstable) commodity compared with the stable gold coinage.

We see, then, that there were several (alternative) factors governing the Jewish legal concept of "coin" (as opposed to "produce"), such as stability, currentness, and perhaps even value. Thus Rava (above, Bavli Bava Mezia 44b) quotes that "a silver *dinar* is one twenty-fifth of a gold *dinar*", thereby wishing to prove that the *denarius* was reckoned as a fraction of the (stable) *aureus,* and not that the *aureus* was reckoned as worth a certain number of *denarii.* His Tannaitic source is unknown other than from this reference to it. However, in Yerushalmi, Kiddushin 1.1 we read that "a *dinar* of silver is one twenty-fourth of a *dinar* of gold". Furthermore, a Mishna in Me'ila 4.7, dating probably from the early second century implies a ratio of 24 *denarii* to the *aureus,*[35] as does a later statement in Bavli Bechorot 50a.[36] Rava presumably knew of a Tannaitic statement similar to that of Yerushalmi Kiddushin 1.1, but reading "one twenty-fifth" instead of "one twenty-fourth".

Heichelheim has already noted this difference in the value of the *aureus* according to Tannaitic statements, and has argued very plausibly that it reflects the drop in the value of gold following Trajan's gaining possession of the Dacian gold mines in 106.[37] For in 97 a *mneion* was worth 88 *denarii* in Egyptian money, while in 127, it cost only 84½. That is to say, pure gold had dropped some four percent in value. Hence, the *aureus*, formerly worth 25 *denarii* would now be worth only 24 *denarii*.

In point of fact then, a statement of the form "a silver *dinar* is worth one twenty-fifth or one twenty-fourth of a gold *dinar*" is no real proof of the stability of gold. Rava's statement is, however, evidence of his own attitude towards gold.

The story (cited above, this chapter) in which Rav borrows gold money from R. Ḥiyya's daughter is an interesting case in point. For there it is stated (by the editor or reporter) that "the coins went up in value"—implying the instability of gold. R. Ḥiyya, however, declared gold as "coin", and not "commodity" (or "produce"). On the basis of which criterion did he declare gold "coin"? Certainly not because it was more *current* than silver. (Were that to have been the case, it would have gone down in value in relation to silver, not up!) Was it then because he considered gold more stable? If so, he must have considered that silver had depreciated, while gold had kept its fixed standard.

We have already shown that this "appreciation of gold" refers to Caracalla's currency reforms of 215,[38] when he reduced the weight of the *aureus*. At the same time he introduced a new denomination, the *antoninianus*, establishing a new ratio of 50 *denarii*=25 *antoniniani*= one aureus. Clearly the reduction in the weight of the *aureus* was made in sympathy, as it were, with the devaluation of the *denarius* and *antoninianus*. We have shown above that *officially* silver was probably overvalued to a new relationship with gold (of 9 : 1, instead of the earlier 12 : 1), but in actual fact this was a simple inflationary ruse to slow up the rapid depreciation of silver coinage. People must have realised this (just as had the Palmyrene caravaneers some twenty years earlier) and therefore tended to see in the gold coinage (which was never actually debased) the real stable standard. They would seem to have disregarded, or at any rate mistrusted, the official explanations, and were no doubt very confused at the erratic and peculiar course of the inflation, and at the irregular over-valuations of silver that took place throughout most of the third century.

In later generations scholars learning (Talmudically formulated) tradi-tions concerning this revaluation of silver in relationship to gold found sources of considerable puzzlement and offered different possible inter-pretations for them. Thus, in Yerushalmi Kiddushin[X] 1.1 we read that the *ma'ah* (=silver *obol*, 1/6 *denarius*) was first reckoned as 32 *prutas* (the smallest Palestinian bronze denomination)...

> R. Zeira (*floruit* end of third and beginning of fourth centuries) said: "In the days of R. Simai (*floruit circa* 210-40) they declared them (*prutas*) one twenty-fourth of a *ma'ah*". R. Ḥanina [of Sepphoris] and R. Mana II (both *floreunt circa* 350-75): R. Ḥanina [of Sepphoris] said, "Copper stayed in its place; silver went down in price, silver went up in price". And R. Mana said, "Silver stopped in its place, copper went up in price, copper went down in price".[39]

And in a parallel version in the Bavli we read (Bavli Kiddushin[X] 12a):

> When Rav Dimi came (from Palestine to Babylonia in the early fourth century), he said, "R. Simai in his generation calculated that the *pruta* is one-eighth of an Italian *issar*". When Ravin came (from Palestine to Babylonia, shortly after R. Dimi), he said, "R. Dostai, R. Yannai and R. Oshaya (all *floreunt circa* 220-40) calculated that the *pruta* is one-sixth of an Italian *issar*". Said Abbaye (died 339) to Rav Dimi, "Could one say that you and Ravin differ with one another in accordance with the conflict between these [the following] two Tannaim? For we have learned that the *pruta* which the Sages spoke of is one-eighth of an Italian *issar*... R. Simeon ben Gamliel says,... 'Hence the *pruta* is one-sixth of the Italian *issar*'. May one say then, that you, Sir, follow the first opinion, while Ravin follows that of R. Simeon ben Gamliel?" He replied to him, "Both I and Ravin may follow the first opinion, and there is no difficulty in this. The one case is when the *issar* went up in value, the other when it went down in value. When it went up there were 24 to the *zuz* (=*denarius*), when it went down there were 32 of them to the *zuz*".

Thus, according to both the Palestinian and Babylonian tradition, some-time early in the third century the Rabbis reckoned a new value for the *pruta*. And though the pattern of calculation may have its precedents and parallels in early Tannaitic times,[40] the establishment of a new value for the *pruta* in the early third century must have been motivated by some current changes in the monetary system.

This revaluation of the *pruta* in the days of R. Simai—a purely theo-retico-legal procedure, as *prutas* were by now long non-existent as actual monetary units—must surely be a reflection of Caracalla's monetary reform of 215. Now we have seen that part of this monetary reform was the introduction of the *antoninianus* [3] as a denomination to be valued as one twenty-fifth of an *aureus*. Clearly it was meant to take the place of the *denarius* [4], which was now officially valued at one-fiftieth of an *aureus*. However, even in the *antoninianus* silver was con-siderably overvalued, so that it now stood in relationship to gold at 9:1, whereas the classic relationship of silver to gold throughout the previous two centuries had been 12:1.[41] The Rabbis, when calculating the value of the *pruta*—to them an absolute value—would undoubtedly have con-tinued to recognise the classic silver-gold ratio of 12:1. Hence, for them the *antoninianus*, which they regarded as a new kind of *denarius*,[42] was really worth only one thirty-second of an *aureus*. As a consequence, while formerly the *pruta* had been worth 1/192 *denarius* (or one thirty-second of a *ma'ah*, which in turn is a unit of value worth one-sixth of a *denarius*), it was now worth only 1/144 *denarius* (or one twenty-fourth of a *ma'ah*). And this indeed is how the Rabbis ruled when they de-clared that the *pruta* was now worth one-sixth of an Italian *issar*, and not one-eighth as formerly, or (differently expressed but with the same meaning) one twenty-fourth of a *ma'ah*, and not one thirty-second.

Such calculations demonstrate a refusal to recognise the official over-valuation of silver (which theoretically posits a fall in the value of gold) and an insistence upon a constant copper-silver-gold ratio. This in turn implies the stability of the gold standard. The Rabbis saw through the transparent ruse of the government, and were fully aware of the fact that really (silver) coin was going down in value (through debasement and subsequent lack of confidence). Thus, they calculated at a rate of a 25% drop in the value of the new silver *denarius*, i.e. the *antoninianus*.[43]

It appears then that at least among certain early authorities (R. Simeon the son of Rabbi, R. Simai, etc.) there was a keen awareness and appreciation of current economic developments. If their rulings seem to run counter to the principle of a silver standard, it is only because they saw the weakness in it. At a time of economic stability when there *really* was a silver standard, it was recognised and legisla-tion was based on this principle. Thus, for example, in Tosefta Bava Mezia[Y] 3 dating from around 135-70, we read the following:

17. How defective should a *sela* (=*tetradrachm*=four *denarii*) be and not fall within the rule of defrauding? Four *issars* to the *sela* [that is] one *issar* per *dinar* (i.e. 1/24), according to R. Meir (*floruit circa* 135-70). R. Judah (*floruit circa* 135-70) says: "[in] a *sela* four *pundions*", [meaning] a *pundion* per *dinar* (i.e. 1/12). R. Simeon says: "[to] a *sela* eight *pundions*", [that is] two *pundions* per *dinar (i.e.* 1/6). If there is more than this [measure of defectiveness] he may use it according to its [weight] value.

18. [He may use it according to its weight value from] a *sela* to *shekel* (i.e. up to 50% defectiveness, *shekel*=½ *sela*=two *dinars*) and a dinar to a *rova* (=¼ *shekel*=½ *dinar*). [But if] it is worth less than this even by an *issar*, he may not make use of it at all. (Presumably he should melt it down, or flatten it so that it should no longer be a "coin".)

19. He should sell it neither to a peddler nor to a murderer[44] nor to a robber, because they will cheat others with it, but rather he should pierce and hang it round his son's neck... Which case are we dealing with?... That of *dinars* and *selas* (i.e. silver *tetradrachms*). But gold *dinars* (=*aurei*) and coins of copper they would (=can) [always] use [them] at their weight value.[45]

Without going into an analysis of the complexity of legal detail here involved, we may see immediately that a clear distinction is made between silver coins, on the one hand, and gold and copper ones, on the other hand. The former keep their value despite their defectiveness within certain limits. Thereafter, again within certain circumscribed limits, they may be valued according to their weight. However, gold and copper coins are always valued by weight, persumably according to current bullion prices reckoned in *denarii*. This is a clear exposition of the principle of a silver standard in Talmudico-legal terms.

The same principles seem to govern yet another text of approximately the same period, dealing with a completely different subject. In Tosefta Ketubot[Z] 6.5: "(With regard to the laws of a marriage-settlement, gold *dinars* are like silver coins.) R. Simeon ben Gamliel [II] (*floruit circa* 135-70) says: 'The matter is so: [in] a place where they are accustomed not to change gold *dinars* into smaller coins (silver, etc.), but to leave them as they are, <and> gold *dinars* are as vessels'." The principle is as follows: Money brought in as a dowry is assessed at one and a half times its value, and vessels at a fifth below their value (Mishna Ketubot 6.3). The reason given in the Yerushalmi (on Mishna Ketubot 6.3) is that we judge that a woman wishes to wear down (read: לבלות — through use) her "vessels" (including clothes, ornaments, etc.), so that their value decreases by one-fifth. We judge that a man wishes to do business with his money and to increase its value by one-half.[46] In the above *halacha*, the Tosefta teaches us that gold coins were only regarded as coins (with regard to the marriage settlement laws) if they were readily convertible into silver. If not, they were goods, and would presumably be judged according to their bullion value. This is indeed how the Bavli quotes our Tosefta (Bavli Ketubot 67a): "Gold *dinars* are like silver coins; R. Simeon ben Gamliel says: 'In a place where they are accustomed not to change them into smaller money, they assess them and they are value according to their value'."[47] The text speaks, presumably, of bullion value measured in terms of *denarii*. Here again, then, the gold coin is clearly secondary in importance to the silver ones, and is actually valued in terms of its silver equivalent.

From the above texts it becomes evident that we cannot automatically assign any text stating that "gold acquires silver... copper acquires silver" to Rabbi in his old age, as it might just as well come from the period around 135-70 and be a recognition of the principle of a silver standard. Perhaps Tosefta Bava Mezia 3.23 is a case in point, and belongs to the same group of *beraitot* quoted above (nos. 17-19). It reads thus:[48]

> Gold acquires´silver. How so? He gave him a gold *dinar* for 25 silver [*dinars*], then he has acquired [the silver *dinars*] wherever he be (i.e. without his actually having taken possession of them). But if he gave him 25 silver [*dinars*] for one gold *dinar*, he has not acquired the [gold *dinar*] until such time as he shall take hold [of it]. Copper acquires silver. How so? He gave him 30 (copper *issars*) for a [silver] *dinar*, then he acquires them wherever he be (i.e. without actually having taken possession of them)...[49]

We have already pointed out that there are several different consideration in the definition of the legal concept "coin", such as currentness, stability, etc. In some cases the emphasis upon these various considerations could be so manipulated as to permit of apparently contradictory results. A case in point is the very complicated Tosefta in *Ma'aser Sheni*[AA] 2.7 :[50]

> ... Because they (Rabbi) said that copper [coins] may be substituted by silver [coins], and silver [coins] by gold [ones], and silver [ones] by copper [ones] at need, but not gold [ones] by

silver [ones]. R. Eleazer ben R. Simeon says: "Just as one may substitute silver [coins] by copper [ones], so one may substitute gold [coins] by silver [ones]." Rabbi said to him: "And why can one substitute silver [coins] by copper [ones]? Because one can [also] substitute silver [coins] by gold [ones]. [But then] one should not be able to substitute gold [coins] by silver [ones], because one may not substitute gold [coins] by copper [ones]." R. Eleazer ben R. Simeon says: "The Second Tithe consisting of gold [coins] may be substituted by [copper][51] coins that are in Jerusalem."

The basic legal principle here is that one may substitute "produce" for "coin", and not *vice-versa* (cf. Bavli Bava Mezia 44b-45a). Perhaps we may clarify the matter somewhat by tabulating the opinions in the above Tosefta in the following manner:

Rabbi (1)

A. Copper is produce compared to silver which is coin.
B. Silver is produce compared to gold which is coin.
C. Silver is produce compared to copper which is coin [at need].
D. Gold is *never* produce compared to silver.
E. Gold is *never* produce compared to copper.

R. Eleazar ben R. Simeon (2)

C. Silver is produce compared to copper which is coin.
D. Gold is produce compared to silver which is coin.
E. Gold is produce compared to copper which is coin [in Jerusalem].

$C^1 = C^2$. D^1 is the opposite of D^2. Rabbi's argument against R. Eleazar ben R. Simeon runs as follows: C^1 is possible because B^1 is possible; but D^1 should not be possible, because E^1 is not possible. R. Eleazar ben Simeon's very cryptic reply is that it is not correct in his own opinion that E^1 is *never* possible. It is possible in Jerusalem, just as C^1 is possible *at need*.[52] This argument appears to be very formalistic. Furthermore, how is it that C^1 may contradict A^1—"at need", and what is "at need"?

The principles underlying A^1 and B^1 are simple, as these are the views of Rabbi in his youth. Copper is "produce" compared to silver (A^1), because there was an official silver standard. Silver is "produce" compared with gold (B^1), because it is measured as a part of the gold coin (see above, this chapter). But why should silver ever be "produce"

PLATE I

1. AUREUS of Septimius Severus. Reverse: INDULGENTIA AUGG IN CARTH. Dea Caelestis seated right, on lion, holding thunderbolt and drum. RIC IV. 1, p.125, no. 267b. Mint of Rome, 202-210.   2. AUREUS of Caracalla. Reverse: PM TR P XVIII COS IIII PP. Caracalla standing left, sacrificing over altar in front of tetrastyle temple on which stands Aesculapius. RIV IV. 1, p.251. no. 270a. Mint of Rome, 215.   3. ANTONINIANUS of Caracalla. Reverse: PM TRP XVIII COS IIII PP. Pluto standing left, extending right hand to Cerberus. RIC IV. 1, p.249, no. 261d. Mint of Rome, 215.   4. DENARIUS of Caracalla. Reverse: PM TRP XVI COS IIII PP. Serapis standing left, raising right hand and holding sceptre. RIC IV. 1, p.241, no. 208, Mint of Rome, 213. 5. TETRADRACHM of Caracalla, Reverse: DHMARX E Ξ YΠATO Γ. Eagle facing. Mint of Antioch, 208-212.   6. DIDRACHM of Caracalla. Reverse: MHTPO KAICAPIA NEΩK . Mount Argaeus; on summit figure of emperor crowned by Victory ; below ET IZ. Mint of Caesarea Cappadociae, 214.   7. ANTONINIANUS of Trajan Decius. Reverse: ABUNDANTIA AUG. Abundantia standing right, emptying cornucopiae. RIC IV. 3, p.121, no. 20b. Mint of Rome, 249-51. Reverse shows remains of observe inscription ...EV PERT... of denarius of Septimius Severus.   8. AUREUS of Gallienus, (Laureate head). Reverse: OB LIBERTAT REC. Libertas standing left, holding pileus and sceptre. RIC V. 1, p.135, no. 61. Mint of Rome, c.261.

PLATE II

9. AUREUS of Gallienus, (Radiate head). Reverse : FIDES MILIT. Fides standing left, holding two standards. RIC V. 1, p.134, no. 39. Mint of Rome. c.261. 10. AUREUS of Gallienus, (Laureate head). Reverse : VICTORIA AET. Victory standing left, holding wreath and garland. RIC V. 1, p.136, no. 76, Mint of Rome, c.263+. 11. AUREUS of Gallienus, (Reed crown). Reverse : VBIQVE PAX. Victory ambiga, right. RIC V. 1, p.136, no. 72. Mint of Rome. c.266. 12. AUREUS of Gallienus, (Laureate). Reverse : FORTVNA REDUX. Fortuna standing left, holding rudder and cornucopiae. RIC V. 1, p.138, no.103. Mint of Rome. Late sole reign. 13. ANTONINIANUS of Aurelian. Reverse : ORIENS AUG. Sol. walking right, holding branch and bow and treading down enemy. Mint mark.[1] RIC V. 1, p.272, no. 64. Mint of Rome, c.274. 14. ANTONINIANUS of Aurelian. Reverse : SOLI INVICTO. Sol standing left, raising right hand and holding globe : at foot captive. Mint mark.[2] RIC V. 1, p.309, no. 390. Mint of Tripolis ? c.274. 15. DENARIUS of Aurelian. Reverse : VICTORIA AUG. Victory advancing left, holding wreath and garland. Mint mark[3] RIC V. 1, p.273, no. 72, Mint of Rome, c.274. 16. ANTONINIANUS of Diocletian. Reverse : IOVI CONSERVAT AUG. Jupiter standing left, hold thunderbolt and sceptre. Mint mark.[4] RIC V. 2, p.236, no. 160. Mint of Rome, c.285.

compared to copper (C[1] & [2]).[53] Neither of the principles hitherto mentioned are applicable here. The criterion must be that of currentness: because copper is more current than silver, it may "at need" be considered "coin" as opposed to silver, when there is a notable dearth of silver coin. This principle of currentness is here used only "at need", but later on, as we have seen above, it becomes a factor of major importance, making gold (less current than silver, but against which silver is measured) "produce" compared to booming silver. Here two principles are used against each other, as it were.[54]

R. Eleazar ben R. Simeon apparently finds currentness of prime importance. Thus, the lower denomination, always more current, is "coin" compared to the higher denomination, which being less current is "produce"—exactly the opposite to Rabbi's opinion. According to this, copper should be "coin" compared to gold at all times, outside Jerusalem too. (cf. E[2].) Yet, from Rabbi's argument, it is clear that he knew that R. Eleazar ben R. Simeon agreed with him on this point, that at least outside Jerusalem one could not substitute gold by copper. Here too then, it is clear that there are other considerations to be taken into account, such as the fact that copper coins deteriorate more quickly than those of other metals, so that when one collects enough of them one changes them into gold.[55]

However, for Rabbi E[1] always held good, even "at need". Hence, it follows that at this stage he considered stability (meaning gold as a fixed point by which other metals are valued) the principle of primary importance, even more than that of currentness. Later, however (about 195), as we have seen above, he revised his views and it appears that the currentness of silver, coupled with the fact of there being officially a silver standard, became a consideration of greater moment than that of gold's stability, now that gold was relatively scarce. Thus, Rabbi's reversal of opinion was due to a shift of emphasis within a complex interplay of contradictory principles.[56]

TABLE G

Issuer \ Hoard	Augustus	Tiberius	Claudius	Nero	Vespasian	Domitian	Trajan	Hadrian	Pius	Marcus	Commodus	Septimius	Caracalla	Elagabalus	Alexander
Alexander															249
Elagabalus															394
Macrinus															96
Caracalla													91	332	739
Septimius												626			2078
Didius												17	3		5
Pertinax												132	633	102	463
Commodus											1142	1232	2031	313	1186
Marcus										47	1550	1327	1990	301	1120
Pius									484	184	1535	951	1088	231	498
Hadrian								204	641	216	1539	893	721	237	371
Trajan							61	74	19	129	82	61	29		26
Nerva							26	259	250	87	529	239	114	77	108
Domitian						13	107	42	18	200	68	61	11		71
Titus															
Vespasian					88	95	151	197	115	1220	469	407	99		429
Vitellius					23	15	7	11	4	62	25	21	5		21
Otho					9	3	4	6	3	45	11	7	5		7
Galba					22	11	13	9	6	38	19	11	6		31
Nero				1	22	31	13	15	12	106	39	23	8		15
Claudius			1	7	3	3	14	15							
Caligula			3	2	4	1	3	14							
Tiberius		354	46	80	13	41	3	16	1						
Augustus	936	349	13	38	23	46	35		1	1	2				
Republic	326	662	57	300	272	393	419	51	62	579	181	89	12		24

CHAPTER XII

CHANGING ATTITUDES
TOWARDS GOLD AND SILVER

When viewed historically, there emerges out of this mass of very confusing material one remarkable and significant fact, namely, that despite the many precedents in the second century for the view that silver is "coin" and gold is "produce", R. Ḥiyya, Rav, R. Johanan, and Resh Lakish, and even Rabbi himself in later years—that is, all the (foremost) authorities of the third century—hold the view that "silver acquires gold". In other words, despite the fact that officially silver continued to be the standard until the reforms of Diocletian, these Rabbinic authorities held that gold, not silver, is "coin". Here then is evidence of a very radical change of attitude towards silver coinage: a progressive loss of confidence from the end of the second century onwards, to be understood against the background of a creeping inflation. The confidence has shifted to gold, which has become "money" *par-excellence*. While just a century earlier R. Simeon ben Gamliel had stated that gold coins were not always easily translated into readily negotiable currency (i.e. silver),[1] now debts calculated in *denarii* have (by agreement) to be repaid in *aurei*,[2] or else only *aurei* are borrowed.[3] Securities are given in gold *aurei* or even gold ornaments.[4] The use of gold bullion becomes increasingly evident during this period.[5] Likewise, there is some evidence of gold hoarding. For in Yerusalmi Shabbat 13.6 R. Jose bar R. Bun in the name of R. Ḥuna *(floruit circa* 320-50) tells of a case where a man clearing away a pile of rubble finds a צרור של זהובים bundle of gold coins. These gold coins had probably been buried towards the end of the previous century. (See Table G on page 84.)

It appears that earlier gold hoards were opened up and a variety of different kinds of gold coins went back into some kind of circulation, including early second century *aurei*. Against such a background we may understand the statement of R. Johanan (died 279) in Bavli

85

Bechorot 49b-50a. For when he wishes to express the value of the five *shekels* for which the first-born is redeemed (Numbers 18.16), he says that they are worth five-sixths of a "worn Hadrianic-Trajanic *aureus*".[6]

We have already noted that in this period loans are given against gold securities and on condition that they will be repaid in *aurei*. Bearing this in mind, we may now understand a difficult Yerushalmi text, hitherto insufficiently understood. The question under discussion is whether a certain kind of fine should be imposed on poor people. In Yerushalmi Pe'a[AB] 1.6 ad fin, a discussion on the reasons for the different opinions, we find the following statement:

> ... What is Rabbi's reason? [He is of the opinion that] a rich man can borrow [money (i.e. can get credit), whereas] a poor man cannot borrow (i.e. cannot get credit). For Rabbi Judah the Prince is of the opinion that a poor man can always borrow (i.e. can always find credit), while Rabbi says he cannot borrow (i.e. cannot get credit).

This statement as it stands would seem to make little sense, since "Rabbi" almost invariably refers to Rabbi Judah the Prince.[7] However, there seems to be a simple explanation. The "Rabbi" mentioned in this text refers to R. Judah Nesiah, R. Judah the Prince's grandson (a contemporary of R. Johanan and Resh Lakish). We frequently find R. Judah Nesiah called by the title "Rabbi". Thus understood, our text makes good economic sense. For in Rabbi's time conditions were fairly good, and it is far more likely that a poor man would get credit then than in the middle of the third century, a period of economic decline, when creditors were demanding securities and repayment of loans in gold coin or bullion.[8] We learn from this text that R. Judah the Prince, at the end of the second or the beginning of the third century, stated that a poor man, even if he has very little money (i.e. less than 200 *dinars*), can always find someone who will lend him money. In R. Judah Nesiah's time, however, later on in the third century, this was no longer the case. People were very loathe to lend out money, except against the maximum assurances that they receive back its full value, either in gold coin or gold bullion. Obviously, in such a situation the poor man could never hope to find a loan, and this indeed is what R. Judah Nesiah says.

In fact, we find this almost explicitly expressed in a parable of R. Levi, a contemporary of R. Judah Nesiah. For in *Deuteronomy Rabba* 4.10[9] we read:

Said R. Levi: Just as one who said to his friend: "Lend me a gold piece." He said to him: "I do not know your account" (*heshbonecha*). He said: "Check on me." And he checked on him, lent him, and he repaid immediately. On a different occasion he said to him: "If you require even thirty gold pieces, take whatever you want... since you made a good account with me."

A poor man could hardly be expected to have a good account, and would be most unlikely to repay immediately. Repayment in debased silver would obviously be easier for him, but his creditors would no doubt refuse such coin, and insist on *aurei* or bullion. Under such circumstances, the poor people, with their pocketfuls of debased *antoniniani*, would indeed find difficulty in getting loans (except at the highest rates of interest), and would suffer all that the depressed class suffers in a credit squeeze. Such then was the situation around the middle of the third century.

In Egypt by 260 the situation had reached such a state that the banks did not wish to accept the official silver coin—"divine money of the Emperors"—and had to be forced to do so by edict. The instructions were issued not only to the bankers, but also informed all who entered into contractual obligations in any form[10] that if they did not obey this injunction they would experience the penalties which the magnificence of the prefect imposed on them even before this.[11]

At the same time we noted changes in terminological usage that must be seen as part of a parallel development. Thus, *"maneh"* becomes a single *denarius,* and not 100 *denarii,* some time around the middle of the third century.[12] *"Dinar"* by itself comes to denote an *aureus,*[13] where previously it had meant *denarius.* *"Denarii"* from the latter part of the third century onwards may be (little) unspecified units.[14] Then, mainly from the end of the third century onwards, new terms such as *follis, gramma, argurion, karat,* etc. gradually replace the traditional terms.[15]

And yet if one examines price-lists (below, pages 101-111) for the period, one finds no evidence of startling rises in costs until perhaps the last quarter of the third century. While it is true that the major crisis came about towards the end of the 260's, there had been a continuous fall in the value of the *denarius* from the 220's onwards. However, the scale in the rise in costs does not seem comparable to that of the fall of the *denarius* as we have outlined it above. The same seems to be true of Egypt.[16] (But see below, page 131.)

May this not be further indication that people were thinking and reckoning in terms of *aurei* and not *denarii*, and in terms of *aurei* prices did not necessarily change so radically?[17] This may also be a reason for the surprising lack of evidence for an increase in barter-trading during this period, though increase in barter is usually a logical outcome and characteristic result of serious inflation.[18] (But see below, page 178.)

Seen in this light, Diocletian's introduction of a gold standard was perhaps little more than an official recognition *(de jure)* of what was already the economic situation *de facto.*

CHAPTER XIII

RABBINIC ATTITUDES TO GOLD

The great virtue of gold coin as a stabilising element in personal economy was both recognised and appreciated by the Rabbis of this period.[1] Thus in *Genesis Rabba*[AC] 16.3[2] we find R. Isaac *(floruit circa* 250-320) commenting on the Biblical verse (Genesis 2.12) 'And the gold of that land is good': "Good to have in the house, good to take on a journey", i.e. good not only for local purchasing, but acceptable wherever one might go.

The real significance of this statement can only be appreciated when seen against the contrasting background of a second century text. For example, in the *Sifré* to Deuteronomy[AD] 32.2 we read the following : [3]

It is like a man who goes to Caesarea and needs a hundred *dinars* (=*denarii*) or two hundred in cash. If he takes them in single [*denarius*] units, they will tire him with their weight and he will not know what to do (he cannot endure them, *MT* [=*Midrash Tannaim*]). But if he changes them into *tetradrachms* (=four *denarius* pieces), he can change them back into smaller money and spend them wherever he wishes. Similarly, he who goes to the market (to Beit Ilanim, *MT*) and he needs ten or twenty thousand [*denarii*],[4] if he takes them in *tetradrachms* (small coins, *MT*),[5] they will tire him and he will not know what to do (and he cannot endure them, *MT*). But if (But rather, *MT*) he should exchange them for gold *dinars* (=*aurei*), he can (and *MT*) change them for small money and spend [it] wherever he may wish.

From here it is quite clear that in the second century one did not need (or even find convenient) *aurei* for local household consumption. Even when one went to shop in town, one would be quite satisfied to take *tetradrachms*. Only when one needed a very large sum of money for an annual visit to a far-off (?)[6] market did one use *aurei*.[7] A single *aureus* was after all, something like a month's wages[8] concentrated into one unit, and one would certainly have to change it with the local money-changers, and pay him his banker's fee before one could normally use it.[9] From the second half of the third century onwards, however, gold was not only useful but also essential even in ordinary household use.

The same passage in *Genesis Rabba* continues with a statement of R. Abbahu[AC] (who lived in Tiberias and Caesarea around 229-309):[10] "The Lord did his world a good service [in giving gold to man]. A man changes one gold coin and may use it for many purchases". A. Marmorstein[11] sees in this a reference to Caracalla's introduction of a gold piece worth 3125 *sestertii*. However, זהב or זהוב seems almost always to refer to the *aureus*[12] or (later) the *solidus*[13] and there is little reason why it should not do so here too. This statement, as it stands, makes very good sense seen against the background of the silver coinage system in the later third century. For while in the second century one could buy a dozen two-pound loaves of bread with a single *denarius*,[14] by the 270's one could get almost nothing with a single debased *denarius*. An *aureus*, on the other hand, could indeed make several purchases.[15]

Finally, R. Simeon ben Lakish[AC] *(floruit circa* 240-75) states *(Genesis Rabba* ibid.): "This world was not fit to make use of gold. Why then was gold created? For [use in] the Temple. . ." Here, too, we may best understand this somewhat surprising near-adulation of gold as an expression of Resh Lakish's deep appreciation of gold coinage in its crucially important role[16] (certainly) from the 250's onwards.[17]

CHAPTER XIV

GOLD AND SILVER "STANDARDS"
(FOURTH CENTURY)

So far we have examined attitudes towards gold and silver in the second and third centuries. There is, however, some very significant evidence on this subject relating to the fourth century. However, in order to understand it, we must first analyse yet another monetary term, namely לקן. This term לקן occurs only twice in Rabbinic literature, both times in the Yerushalmi and in both cases in difficult and problematic texts. In Yerushalmi Ma'aser Sheni 4.1 we read:[2]

תני משתכר הוא אדם עד שקל משתכר הוא אדם עד רביעית. היך עבידא ?
דינרא הכא בתרין אלפין ובאדבאל[3] בתרין אלפין ולקן,[4] והוא בעי מיתן חמישין[5]
ריבוא ומיסוק, דיהב[6] ליה הכא בתרין אלפין [ובארבלין[7] בתרין /אלפין/[8] ולקן][9]
וחמישין ריבוא.

The text states clearly that one [gold][10] *dinar* (=*aureus*) was worth 2000 [*denarii*] here (probably in Tiberias), and in Arbael (not very far from Tiberias)[11] it was worth 2000 [*denarii*] plus one לקן. As *PSI.* 310, of the year 307, also gives the equation one *aureus* = 2000 *denarii*, this text would appear to be of about 307. The לקן must (from the context) be a coin (or unit of value) and the explanation that לקן = λευκόν is very convincing.[12] It would appear to be a silver-washed coin rather than a pure silver piece,[13] which would probably have been called ארגרין ἀργύριον (see below, pages 154-155), קרט (see below, this chapter), or something similar.

Now at the time there were, as we have seen above, only two kinds of silver-washed pieces, the one (in Diocletian's reform system, around 301, and probably still around 307) worth five *denarii* [16], and the other two *denarii* [17]. I would tentatively suggest the above text to mean the following:

A person is permitted to earn up to a *shekel* (= two *denarii)* [on an *aureus* = 25 *denarii* or 24 *denarii*] or up to a quarter [of a

91

sela[14] (=*tetradrachm*) = one *denarius*] (without transgressing the laws of usury—רבית).[15]How can one do it? (i.e. how can one gain *any* sum of money on such a contract, not necessarily 1/12 or 1/24, as above). [e.g.:] A [gold]*dinar* here (in Tiberias?)[16] is worth 2000 [*denarii*] and in Arbael [it is worth] 2000 [*denarii*] and a *leukon* (=two *denarii*?), and he needs to transfer (literally = give) fifty *myriads* (=500,000) [*denarii*] (to Arbael) and go up (? or go away?)[17]... Then he gives (i.e. lends) him (i.e. another person, who needs to borrow 500,000 *denarii*) here (in Tiberias?) [fifty myriad *denarii*] at a rate of 2000[18] [*denarii* per *aureus*], and in Arbael [he receives back] <and> fifty *myriad* [*denarii*][20] at a rate of two [thousand *denarii*] and a *leukon*. (In this way he would receive 500 *denarii* at two *denarii* per *aureus*, = ¼ *aureus* clear profit.)[21]

The other text in which we find the לקן, and the more important one for us at the moment, is in Yerushalmi Bava Mezia 4.1. There we read :

> R. Jacob ben Aḥa *(floruit circa* 290-350) said: "R. Johanan and Resh Lakish both stated that one is permitted to lend out [gold] *dinars* (=*aurei*) for [gold] *dinars* (=*aurei*)".[22] [He (R. Jacob ben Aḥa) adds:][23] "A *karat* for a *karat* is [likewise] *permitted;* a *leukon* for a *leukon* is forbidden".

Now קרט (*karat*) can be one of two words, and have one of three meanings. It can either come from the Greek κεράτιον,[24] or be like the Syriac קרטא The former can mean one of two things, either a certain weight of gold, a fraction of the gold pound, i.e. 1/1728 *libra aurei*,[25] or its silver equivalent as a coin, the *siliqua* = 1/24 *solidus*,[26] (see above, page 62). The קרטא on the other hand, is, in the words of Brockelmann,[27] "*quarta (pars sicli)*" (=¼ *tetradrachm*=one *denarius*).[28]

We have already seen above that in Yerushalmi Ma'aser Sheni the לקן is a coin. *Dinar* is certainly a coin. *Karat*, therefore, is probably also a coin in this context and not a weight of gold.[29] As such it would be of the same generic type as the [gold] *dinar* (=*aureus*) and the *leukon*.[30]

The halachic context would also seem to point to the *karat's* being a coin rather than a gold weight. For if *karat* here meant *keration*, a specific weight of gold, what would R. Jacob ben Aḥa be teaching us now that we could not have known from the rulings of R. Johanan and Resh Lakish? Surely the reason why one can lend out a gold *dinar* for a gold *dinar* is because its value is (considered to be) constant or stable, in that it is valued as a specific weight of gold (1/60 *libra aurei*, or at whatever fraction it was *officially* struck in R. Johanan's time). And this even when, in point of fact, it may have weighed less! It is thus patently obvious that a (real full) weight of gold may thus be lent out without infringement of the laws of usury. R. Jacob ben Aḥa would hardly have to teach us this.[31]

It follows then that *karat* here must either be the silver equivalent of the *keration* as a coin, i.e. the *siliqua*, or "a quarter (of a *shekel*)", i.e. a *denarius*. The *shekel* by now, however, was no more than a mere theoretical unit of value, a survival of a much earlier system. Therefore, it seems strange and unlikely that when referring to contemporary monetary units, in order to teach a legal ruling of practical topical significance, that such a term would be used. This seems to indicate that the *karat* here refers to the *siliqua*.

Now we have stated above that the *siliqua* was 1/24 *solidus*,[32] and also that earlier in its career this term was applied to the *argenteus* [19] whose value was 1/25 *aureus*,[33] (see above, page 62). Thus, it was in actual fact equal to the old *denarius* which equalled 1/25 *aureus* (as pointed out above). Hence, the application of the term קרט to the *siliqua* was based on a two-fold association: (a) the phonological similarity to κερἀτιον,[34] and (b) to the fact that the *siliqua* was equal to the old *denarius*, which equalled 1/4 *shekel* and had originally been called *quarta-karta*.[35]

According to our interpretation then, in the early(?) fourth century[36] both gold *(aureus* or *solidus)* and silver *(siliqua)* pieces were considered by the Rabbis as "coin" and could therefore be lent out דינר בדינר קרט בקרט without any transgression of the laws of *ribit* (usury).

The לקן *(leukon)*, on the other hand, may not be thus lent out. Now it is clear from the context that the *leukon* is a smaller denomination that the *karat* (just as the *karat* is smaller than the [gold] *dinar*). It cannot be a *siliqua*, as that is called a קרט (see above, note 13). There was in fact a coin current that was only half the size of the *siliqua*, but this too was of good silver, and there is little reason why its halachic status *(vis-à-vis* the laws of "*ribit*") should differ from that of the *siliqua*—קרט. Hence, the inevitable conclusion seems again to be that the *leukon* (=white) is the silver-washed piece [16 and 17],[37] rather than a pure silver one. Since these were, as we have seen above, subject to considerable changes in value—inflation, devaluation, deterioration of silver content—it is understandable that they should not be recognised halachically as "coin".

93

If our interpretation be correct, we have here a very interesting and revealing halachic decision, according to which *both gold and silver* are regarded (in respect of this law of usury) as "coin", while the silver-washed pieces, because of their lack of stability, are regarded merely as "produce".

Thus, while we have seen that in the third century silver was completely discredited[38] and *only* gold was regarded as "coin", it would appear that in the early fourth century, with Diocletian's establishment of a relatively stable system of good (pure) silver coins in addition to the gold ones, silver was reinstated as "coin" alongside with gold. However, because Diocletian's silver-washed *leukons* rapidly declined in value and status, the *halacha* denied these pieces the legal standing of "coins".[39]

There may be yet another reference to Diocletian's silver-washed reform currency in a difficult halachic text in Yerushalmi Ma'aser Sheni[AV] 1.1. There we read:

> If he had DISGNIM (variants: DISCNIM, LSGNIM)[40] coins, R. Jacob ben Zavdi in the name of Rabbi Abbahu *(floruit circa 260-309)*[41] said "He substitutes [the Second Tithe by them] at their value with the money-exchangers.[42] If he wished to use them (the coins) again, he substitutes them at the rate at which he [first] substituted them".

The halachic background to this text is as follows. A person who has Second-Tithe fruits has to take them to Jerusalem and eat them there. If he does not wish to take them there—it may be inconvenient for him to transport them—he may substitute them with money at the going rate. This money now takes on the legal status of the Second Tithe. When later he reaches Jerusalem with the money, he buys with it fruit, or buys fruit to the value of this money. The money now loses its Second Tithe status which in turn passes over to the fruit. Now during all these various exchanges and transactions the rule is that no loss may be incurred to the Second Tithe. With this basic information in mind we may now turn to interpreting the text before us.

In the case described here, the situation is as follows: A man has Second Tithe fruit which he wishes to substitute with certain coins called DISGNIM. We are told that he may do so, but only at their rate with the money-exchanger. From this we may deduce two facts concerning this money: (a) that there is a difference between its official rate and its market rate, and (b) that the market rate of these coins is *lower* than the official rate. Thus, if he substituted at the official rate, when he later came to use this money to purchase fruit in Jerusalem, he would get less for it than he had had at the outset, since its purchasing-power is far lower than the official rate would suggest. This would constitute incurring a loss to the Second Tithe, and for this reason he may only substitute at the market rate. We are further told that when he comes to remove from these coins the status of Second Tithe by substituting for them fruit in Jerusalem, he must do so reckoning their value at the market rate as it was during the first substitution. Now, if these coins had gone up in value between the times of the first and second substitutions, it would be to the advantage of the Second Tithe to substitute at the later (higher) rate. For in this way he would receive *more* fruit for the Second Tithe. The tendency of the halacha is always to seek the interest, and even gain, of the Second Tithe. If R. Abbahu ruled that one must *always* reckon at the earlier rate, it follows that these coins are *always* declining in value. Hence, if he now substituted them for fruit at the present (lower) market rate, he would receive *less* fruit than he had had at the outset, and thus incur loss to the Second Tithe.

In brief, then, from this text we may infer the following situation some time between the years circa 260 and 309: There are coins current called DISGNIM with a market rate lower than their official one, and whose purchasing power (i.e. value) is constantly on the decline.

Now the term DISGNIM (with its different variants listed above) has long been something of a lexical puzzle, and many suggestions have been made to explain its etymology and meaning.[43] However, in the year 1970, during excavations at Aphrodisias in Caria, fragments of an inscription were discovered,[44] beginning with the words BICHARACTA MI [———, which the editors suggest should be read: BICHARACTA MONETA.[45] These words, *"bicharacta moneta"*, are the precise parallel of the words מעות של דיסגנים. *"Bicharacta"* is Greek, meaning "twice-stamped", while DISGNIM is a Latin loan-word, *dusignum* (or, maybe, *dusignatum*), meaning exactly the same thing. The inscription may be dated to the year 301,[46] and is part of an Edict of Diocletian dealing with his monetary reforms. The editors suggest that *"Bicharacta moneta"* perhaps refers to "the new coinage of A.D. 294 [17 and 18], created by a grand recoinage (i.e. second striking) of old pieces".[47]

If we accept the editors' interpretation, adding just one more point, namely that *"moneta bicharacta—disignim"* refers specifically to Diocletian's copper (or silver-washed) coins, our text becomes completely clear. R. Abbahu was referring to Diocletian's reform currency. He was speaking some time after circa 301 and before 309, the year of his decease. He used a term which probably came into use from an edict similar to that found at Aphrodisias. He knew full-well that this coinage had been assigned an official rate which was totally unreal and over-valued,[47a] and was witness to its rapid devaluation on the open market. With a clear awareness of these factors he ruled as he did in the (by now wholly theoretical) case of the Second Tithe.

Finally, we shall examine a text reflecting monetary conditions during the second half of the fourth century. In Yerushalmi Horayot[AE] 3.5 we read:

> R. Samuel bar R. Jose bar R. Bun (=Avin) *(floruit circa 350-75)* said. . .[48] "It is just as when two people enter a city, the one with bars (עשתות) of gold, and the other with units [of currency] (פרוטות).[49] The one who has bars of gold does not [have to] spend [them], and he [nevertheless] can live. [But] the one who has [only] units [of currency] must spend [them] in order to live".

This statement teaches us that a person who had a stock of gold bullion could live on credit, whereas one who had (even the equivalent amount in) units of currency could not, but had to pay in cash for anything he might want.

Now in this text the comparison is made between "units of currency" on the one hand, and gold ingots, on the other, and not, for example, copper coins (פרוטות) and gold *dinars*, the more usual terms of comparison. This appears to mean that even gold coins (=units of currency) were regarded with less confidence than bars of pure gold.[50] For we know from both numismatic and literary evidence that from the early fourth century onwards there was considerable adulteration (and counterfeiting) of *solidi*. Thus, for example, in *Exodus Rabba*[AF] 5.10 we find R. Samuel ben Naḥman giving the following parable:

> Like unto a goldsmith who was brought a *moneta* (coin) and he saw that it was pottery (i.e. clay) inside, and only outside was it of gold. Some time later he was brought a *moneta* which was all gold. He said: "The first one was of pottery and [only] plated with gold, but this is all gold".[51]

This text is most probably of the first quarter of the fourth century.[52] By the middle of the fourth century the extent and scale of forgery was so great that we find the Codes legislating to counteract it. For example, in *Codex Theodosianus* 9.21.4 (Antioch, 343) we read as follows:

96

A reward is offered to the accusers of any persons who can be found to be counterfeiters of *solidi* or who are brought before the public authorities by anyone for this crime. Such criminals shall be delivered to the consuming flames immediately and without delay.

And in *Codex Theodosianus* 12.6.13 of some twenty-four years later (367) we read:

Whenever *solidi* must be paid to the account of the imperial largesses, the actual *solidi* shall not be delivered, because adulterated coins are often substituted for such *solidi*, but either the *solidi* should be reduced to a mass, or if the taxpayer is able to have such material from any other source, the mass of fine gold should be despatched for that part of the tax, of course, which each person pays. (Translation by Pharr.)[53]

And a reflection of this practice may be seen in an anonymous Midrash on Numbers[AG] 6.24, probably to be dated to the latter part of the fourth century: "May the Lord bless thee, and keep thee... that a *zemia*[54] (a kind of tax) should not come to town and say to you, 'Give gold'."

Thus, it appears that in the third quarter of the fourth century the advent of large-scale forgery and adulteration caused confidence even in the *solidus* to be somewhat shaken. Only pure gold ingots continued to have the people's complete confidence to the extent that its holder could be certain of absolute credit.[55] It was to reinstate that confidence in the solidus that the marks OB (standing for 72 and OBRUZOS—pure [gold]) and COM were put on it, testifying its mintage from accredited bullion received by the treasury, and concentrated at the imperial residence (*comitatus* = COM).[56]

PLATE III

17. RADIATE FRACTION of Diocletian. Reverse : Emperor standing left
receiving Victory and globe from Jupiter standing right, holding sceptre. Mint
Mark.[5] RIC VI, p.621, no. 60a. Mint of Antioch, c.296.   18. FOLLIS of
Diocletian. Reverse : Genius standing left holding patera and cornucopiae. Mint
mark.[6] RIC VI, p.620, no. 54a. Mint of Antioch, c.300-01.   19. ARGEN-
TEUS of DIOCLETIAN.[7] Reverse : XCVI/T in two lines in wreath. RIC VI,
p. 282, no. 20a. Mint of Ticinum, c.300.   20. AUREUS of Diocletian.
Reverse : IOVI CONSERVATORI. Jupiter standing left, holding thunderbolt and
sceptre. Mint Mark.[8] RIC V. 2, p.255, no. 315. Mint of Antioch, c.290-92.
21. FOLLIS of Licinius I. Reverse : IOVI CONSERVATORI. Jupiter standing
left holding Victory on globe and sceptre ; to left eagle ; to right, captive. Mint
mark.[9] RIC VII, p.682, no.35. c.321-23.   22. FOLLIS of Constantine I.
Reverse : GLORIA EXERCITUS. Two standards between two soldiers. Mint
Mark SMANΓ. RIC VII, p. 693, no. 86. Mint of Antioch, c.335.   23. FOLLIS
of Constans. Reverse : VICTORIAE DD AV GGQNN. Two Victories. Mint
mark.[10] LRBC I, 140. 341-48.   24. FOLLIS of Constans. Reverse : FEL
TEMP REPARATIO. Warrior spearing falling horseman. Mint mark PLG *.
LRBC II, 197. c.348-50.

1. $\dfrac{\varDelta I}{XIR}$ 2. $\dfrac{*I}{KA}$ 3. $\dfrac{BI}{VSV}$ 4. $\dfrac{}{XXI\varDelta}$ 5. $\dfrac{\varGamma *}{ANT}$ 6. $\dfrac{K/Vs}{ANT}$ 7. $\dfrac{(1\ )}{(96)}$ 8. $\dfrac{Kz}{SMA}$ 9. $\dfrac{/\,III\varGamma *}{SMANT\varDelta}$ 10. $\dfrac{\smile}{TRP}$

PLATE IV

FRAGMENTS OF DIOCLETIAN'S MONETARY EDICT
FROM APHRODISIAS

PART THREE

PRICES

CHAPTER XV

PRICE LISTS

We next turn to an examination of the effect of monetary developments, outlined above, upon costs and prices during this period. First,
however, we shall set out various lists of prices and wages, arranged
in chronological order, later examine them, compare them, and discuss
some of their implications.

PALESTINE PRICE LISTS

Wages

early I cent. C.E.	B. Yoma 35b	Hillel's daily wage: 1 *tarapik* (= ½d.):
"	Ibid.	½ *tarapik* (= ¼d.) given to doorkeeper of academy as entrance fee.
"	Avot de R. Nathan ed. Schechter 27b 2nd version	Daily wages: 1–2d.[2]
"	Mat. 20.2	Daily wage of vineyard workers: 1d.
"	Luk. 10.35	Expenses for looking after sick man: 2d. (or more).
"	B. Yoma 38a	Jerusalem. Daily (!) wages of spe-cialized temple craftsmen (a whole family): 1,200d. before a "strike", and 2,400d. after a "strike".[3]
"	Ibid.	Different estimate of the above: 2,400d. and 4,800 d.
"	Eccles. Rab. begin-ning. Cf. Cant. Rab. 1.4	Porters' fee (5 men) to carry stone from Arab (= Arbat-el-Batuf, N. of Beit Netufa, lower Galilee) to Jeru-salem: 5 *sela'im* (= 20 d.).
40–80 or 135–70	T. Bava Mezia 5.13	Wages for working a field of 10 *kor* of wheat: 200 d.
I–II cent.	M. Shevi'it 8.4	Daily wage: 1 *issar*.[5]
"	B. Avoda Zara 62a	Daily wage: 1 d.[6]
"	T. Bava Mezia 7.1	Wages for weaving a tallit: 2 *sela'im* (= 8 d.).

101

?	Mechilta of R. Simeon b. Yoḥai p. 175	Daily wages: 1–2 *sela'im* (= 8–8d.).
135–70	T. Bava Mezia 6.15	Daily wage: 1–4d. (harvest or threshing).
,,	Eccles. Rab. 2.17	R. Meir, a good scribe, earned 12d. per week (4 *sela'im*); thus 2d. per day. He ate and drank for 4d. per week, and paid for his clothing with 4d. per week.
early II cent	M. Bechorot 4.5	Jamnia. Ritual examination of cattle: 6 *issars* (= ¼d.).
,,	Ibid.	Same of sheep or goats: 4 *issars* (1/6d.).
II–III cent.	B. Bava Mezia 16b	(Palestine and Babylonia) Scribe's wages per document: a few *prutas*.[7]
220–50	Y. Bava Mezia 6.6	Akbara (lower Galilee) daily wage: less than 1d.
*290–320(?)	B. Ketubot 105b	Judges wages: 99 *maneh* (*per annum*).[8]
early IV cent.?	Gen Rab. 70.15	Wages (daily?): 6–7 *follarin*.

Wheat

early I cent. C.E.	Avot de R. Nathan Schechter ed. p. 55 1st version	1 *se'ah*[9]: 2 or 3d.[10]
*I–II cent.	M. Bava Mezia 5.1	1 *se'ah*: 5/6–1d.
,,	M. Ma'aser Sheni 4.6	1 *se'ah*(?): 4–8d.
*100–140	M. Pe'a 8.7 & M. Eruvin 8.2 & M. Kelim 17.11	1 *se'ah*: 1d.
135–70	B. Bava Batra 91a	1 *se'ah*: 2–4d. (expensive).
late II cent.	B. Ta'anit 19b	1 *se'ah*: 1d.[11]
,,	B. Bava Batra 86b	1 *se'ah* (wheat?): 1 *sela* (= 4d.).
,,	Ibid.	1 *kor* (= 30 *se'ahs*): 30 *sela'im* (= 120d.).
220–50	B. Ta'anit 19b	1 *se'ah*: 1d. (cheap) or 4d. (expensive).
*312–13	Eusebius. Hist. Eccles. 9.8.4	Syria/Palestine. 2500 Attic *drachmae* (= 2,500d.)[12]
*c.362–63	Misopogon 369a–d	Antioch. 30 *modii*: 1 *solidus*.[13]
*late IV cent.	Y. Bava Kama 9.5	Sepphoris. 20 *modii*: 8 *solidi*.[14] Tiberias. 25 *modii*: 8 *solidi*.[14]

---

* An asterisk denotes that the price is cited and discussed below in the text. This list cannot be understood or appreciated without reference to those chapters of this study, where the meaning of monetary terms, comparative measures, exact readings, etc. are discussed.

Clothing

I cent. C.E. (pre 70)	B. Yoma 35b	Suits of high-priests: 10,000–20,000d. Jerusalem.
"	Ibid. (& cf. T. Yoma 1.21 22)	Clothing (*kutonet*) of Simeon ben Pavi (High-Priest): 100 *maneh* (= 10,000d.).[15]
80–110(?)	Avot de R. Nathan Schechter ed. p. 85 1st version	Clothing of sacking to last 4 or 5 years: 4d.
110–135	B. Shabbat 128a	Mention made of cloak (*itztela*) and girdle of 100 *maneh* (= 10,000d.).
135–70	Mechilta ed. Friedman 96b	Cloak (*ksut*) of (a rich) man: 100–200d.[16]
"	M. Me'ila 6.4	*Tallit*: 12d.
"	B. Bava Mezia 86b	*Ḥaluk* or *tallit*: 1d. (very cheap).[17]
"	M. Me'ila 6.4	*Ḥaluk*: 12–25d.
I–II cent.	M. Arachin 6.5	Slave-suit: 30d. (a good one)
"	T. Arachin 4.3 & T. Bechorot 6.13	*Tallit*: 5 *sela'im* (= 20d)
"	T. Me'ila 2.10	*Tallit* (small one): 8d.[17]
"	T. Bava Mezia 3.14	*Tallit*: 1 gold *denarius* (= 25d.).
"	T. Shekalim 2.8 & T. Me'ila 1.23	*Tallit*: 50 *zuz* (= 50d.)
"	T. Me'ila 2.10	*Ḥaluk* (small one): 8d.[17]
"	T. Bava Mezia 3.16	*Ḥaluk*: 5–6 *sela'im* (= 20–24d.)
"	T. Me'ila 2.10	*Ḥaluk* (big one): 24d.
220–50	Y. Bava Mezia 4.3	Cloak: 5d.[18]
*early IV cent.	Y. Bava Kama 9.5	Suit (?) 20–25 *maneh*.[19]
*350–75	Y. Kila'im 9.1	Expensive suit of (I and II cent.). Rabbis: 300,000d.[19]]

Bread, Flour

*pre 70 C.E.	M. Shekalim 4.9	1–1 1/3 *se'ah*: 1d.
*I–II cent. C.E.	M. Shevi'it 8.4	1 loaf of bread: 1 *pundion* (= 1/12d.).
"	T. Demai 5.11	1 *gluska* (= large round bread): 1 *issar* (= 1/24 d.)
80–110	M. Eruvin 7.10	1 small loaf: 1 *issar* (= 1/24d.).
135–70	M. Pe'a 8.7 & M. Eruvin 8.2 & M. Kelim 17.11	1 loaf: 1 *pundion* (= 1/12d.) 1 *se'ah* (flour): 1d.
"	T. Shevi'it 6.21	1 loaf: 1 *pundion* (= 1/21d.).
*c.290–320	Gen. Rab. 49.4	1 loaf: 10 *follarin*.

Wine

*end III cent. C.E.	Y. Bava Batra 8.4 & Y. Bava Mezia 4.2	100 ordinary bottles ("*garbin*") of wine (?): 10 *aurei*. 100 big bottles of wine (?): 20 *aurei*.

*290–320	B. Avoda Zara 34b	1 *xestes*: 4 *lumma* (= *nummi*). Akko.
*IV cent.(?)	Lev. Rab. 37.2	1 *xestes*(?): 10 *follarin*.

Olive Oil

66–67 C.E.	Jos. Wars 2.21.2	1 *amphora*: 1 Tyrian *drachma* (= 1d.) Galilee.
110–35	M. Bava Kama 8.6	1 *kad* (= jug): 1 *issar* (= 1/24d.)[20]
135–70	M. Bava Batra 5.9	1 *tzelohit* (= glass jar): 1 *issar* (= 1/24d.)[21]

Meat

*290–350 C.E.	Gen. Rab. 49.4	1 *litra* (= *libra*): 10 *follarin*.
*III–IV cent.	Y. Berachot 2.8	1 *litra*: 50 *maneh*[22].
*early IV cent.(?)	Tanḥuma Numbers ed. Buber, p. 145	1 litra pork: 10 *maneh*[22]. 1 litra kosher beef: 8 *maneh*.[22]

Fruit

I–II cent. C.E.	M. Ma'asrot 2.6	10 figs, 1 pomegranate, 1 cluster of grapes: 1 *issar* (= 1/24d.) each.[23]
,,	T. Demai 5.11	Several pomegranates: 1 *issar* (= 1/24d.).[24]
80–135	T. Bava Mezia 8.8	1 cucumber (expensive): 1d.
135–70	M. Me'ila 6.4	1 pomegranate: 1 *pruta*
,,	Ibid.	1 pomegitron (ordinary size): 1 *pruta* 1 pomecitron (large size): 2 *pruta*.
,,	T. Ma'aser Rishon 2.11 & M. Ma'asrot 2.5	5 figs: 1 *issar* (= 1/24d.).
,,	Ibid.	3–4 figs: 1 *issar* (= 1/24d.)
*290–320	Eccles. Rab. 5.10	1 cucumber: 2 *maneh*.[25]
,,	Esther Rab. 2.3	1 endive: ½–1 *maneh*.[25]

Slaves

late II cent. C.E.	B. Kiddushin 20a & B. Arachin 30b	Prices (ransom) of Jewish slaves to be freed: 100–200d.[26]
320–50	B. Kiddushin 8b	Slave women: a few bronze *prutot* (very little).
359	BGU. 316.	Ascalon. Sale of slave: 18 *solidi*.[27]

Cattle

I–II cent C.E.	M. Menaḥot 13.8	Ox: 100d.
,,	M. Ḥulin 5.4 & Sifra Emor 8 (ed. Weiss 99c)	Ox: 1000d.[28]
,,	M. Bava Kama 3.9	Ox: 100 or 200d.[28]
,,	M. Menaḥot 13.8 & T. Bechorot 6.13	Calf: 5 *sela'im* (= 20d.)

"	T. Bava Mezia 5.1	100 calves: 100 *aurei* (i.e. 1 calf: 25d.).[29]
?	Y. Kiddushin 1.6	Cow: 100–200d.
*135–70	M. Bava Kama 4.1	Ox: 200d.[30]
first half of IV cent.	Pesikta Rabbati 14, ed. Fridmann 56a	Cow (young, red): 3–4 gold [*solidi*].
*second half of IV cent.	Y. Bava Mezia 4.1	Cow: 8 (gold) d. (probably *solidi*).

Asses

80–110 C.E.	B. Bechorot 11a	New born donkey foal: 2–4d. (redemption price).
I–II cent.	M. Bava Kama 10.4	1 ass: 1–2 *maneh* (= 100–200d.)
*late IV cent.	Y. Bava Mezia 4.1	Donkey: 8 *aurei*.

Sheep

80–110 C.E.	M. Keritot 5.2	Ram: 2 *sela'im* (= 8d.).
I–II cent.	M. Menaḥot 13.8	Ram: 2 *sela'im* (= 8d.).
"	M. Keritot 6.6	Rams: 4d. 8d. 10d.
"	M. Menaḥot 13.8	Lamb: 1 *sela* (= 4d.).
"	T. Bava Mezia 5.2	100 Cheep: 100 *aurei* (i.e. 1 sheep = 25d.)[31]
"	M. Shekalim 2.4	1 sheep: 1–3 *sela'im* (= 4–12d.).

Birds

before 70 C.E.	M. Keritot 1.7	Jerusalem. 2 pigeons: 1 *aureus*. Then reduced to 1d.[32]
"	Matt. 10.29	2 sparrows: 1 *ass* (= 1/16d.).
"	Luk. 12.6	5 sparrows: 2 *asses* (= 1/8d.).

Misc. Foodstuffs

before 70 C.E.	B. Ketubot 105a	Plant, 1 year old: 2 *ma'ah* (= 1/3d.). 2 years old: 4 *ma'ah* (= 2/3d.).[33]
70	Jos. Wars 6.3.3	Jerusalem. a trifling quantity of stalks (of grass): 4 Attic *drachmae* (= 4d.).[34]
I–II cent.	M. Bava Batra 9.5	Cheapest meal of bridegroom: 1d.
*290–320	B. Avoda Zara 34b	Akko. 1 *xestes muries*: 1 *lumma* (= *nummus*?).
[350–75	Gen. Rab. 11.4	Fish for 12d. (of gold) considered very expensive in Rome.][35]
?	Midrash Psalms 4.13 ed. Buber, p. 49	Small roll of bread and plate of lentils and 2 pieces of meat and 2 glasses of wine: 2 *issars* (= 1/12d.).[36]

Houses

I cent. C.E.	T. Arachin 4.11	Value of *beit homer* barley in Jubilee year: 50 *shekels* (= 200d.).
I–II cent.	M. Bava Mezia 5.2	Rent of courtyard: 10 *sela'im per annum* (= 40d.).
,,	T. Bava Mezia 4.5	Rent for house 1 *sela* per month (= 48d. *per annum*).
,,	T. Bava Mezia 8.31	Rent for house: 12 *zehuvim* (= *aurei*) *per annum* (= 288d.).
II cent.	M. Bava Mezia 8.8	Lease of bath-house: 12 *aurei per annum* (= 288d.) Sepphoris.
134	DJD, 2, p. 145 line 4	5 *beit seah*: 88d. (= 3,500 sq. metres approx.).
135–70	Y. Ketubot 4.14	Cost of house: 10 *aurei*.
,,	Y. Bava Mezia 4.2	Rent of house: 100d.
c.158–80	Eusebius, Hist. Eccles. 3.10.1	39 *plethra*: 9,000d. (= 34,000 sq. metres).
250–90	Y. Ketubot 8.3	Field unsown: 2 *aurei;* same field sown: 3 *aurei*.
,,	Deut. Rab. 4.8	Half a field: 5 *aurei*.

Palestine Miscellanea

I cent. B.C.E.	B. Rosh Hashana 22b	Boethusians gave bribes of 400d.
10–50 C.E.	T. Ketubot 5.9	Jerusalem. Cosmetics per day: 500 *aurei* (of a very wealthy lady)
80–110	B. Kiddushin 31a	Ascalon. Jewels (estimate): 600,000d. And a new or alternative estimate of the same jewels in 220–50: 800,000d.
9C–135	B. Sukka 41b	1 *lulav*: 1000d. (very expensive indeed, on a sea voyage).[37]
" (?)	T. Sukka 2.11	1 *lulav*: 1 *aureus* (very expensive).[38]
135–70	M. Me'ila 6.3	Several lamps and wicks: 1 *pruta*.
*170–200	Y. Pe'a 1.1 & Gen. Rab. 35.3	1 *mezuza*: 1 *follar*.
200–220	B. Nedarim 38a	Lease of ship: up to 400 *aurei*.
*219–47	Y. Bava Mezia 5.10	1 *kor* (= 30 *s'eah*) flax: 1 *aureus*.
220–50 (?)	B. Gittin 35a–b	Book of Psalms, Job, Eccles., and a thick woolen coat: 5 *maneh* (= 500d.).
pre 250–90	B. Yoma 11a	R. Judah (ben Ezekiel) tells that Artabin was an examiner of *Mezuzot* in the upper market of Sepphoris, and a *quaestor* one took 1000d. from him.
c.250	Y. Sukka 5.1	R. Judah bar Naḥman and R. Levi used to receive 2 *sela'im* each (= 8d. each) for convening the public to attend R. Johanan's lectures.

FROM THE ARCHIVES OF THEOPHANES[39] c.317–323 C.E.[40]

Ascalon
*P. Rylands + 637 line 428 (p. 144)   1 *xest.* fish-sauce: 200 dr. = 50d.

Betar (= *Allage*)
*P. Rylands + 637 line 403 (p. 143)   6 *litra* meat: 1200 dr. i.e. 1 *litra* 50d.

Antioch

*P. Rylands 629 line 44 (p. 126)	9 *litra* meat for salting: 2800 dr. i.e. 1 *litra*: 88d.	
* ,, 629 line 24	4 *litra* meat: 1200 dr. i.e. 1 *litra*: 75d.	
* ,, 629 line 91	½ *kab* (= 2 *sextarii*) sweet wine: 600 dr. i.e. 1 *sext.*: 75d.	
* ,, 630 col. ii line 85	7 *litra* meat for salting: 2800 dr. i.e. 1 *litra*: 100d.	
* ,, + 631 col. ii line 91	1 *kab* wine: 1800dr. i.e. 1 *sext.*: 112½d.	
* ,, + 631 lne 104	1 *xestes* ordinary wine: 700 dr. i.e. 1 *sext.*: 175d.	
* ,, + 636 col. i. line 205	meat (Αἰγ)αιον(?) 3 *litra*: 1200 dr. i.e. 1 *litra*: 100dr.	
* ,, 636 only line 265	2 *litra* meat: 800 dr. i.e. 1 *litra*: 100d.	
* ,, 636 line 267	1 *xest.* wine (for breakfast): 400 dr. i.e. 1 *xest.*: 100d.	
* ,, 630 col. ii lines 36, 51 & + 631 col. ii lines 112, etc.	1 roll: 25d.	

Antipatris
P. Rylands + 637 line 403   1 roll: 25d.

Average *litra* meat: 75–100d.
Average *xestes* wine: 75–100d.

SOME BABYLONIAN PRICES[41]

220–50 C.E.	Kiddushin 12a	1 *kor* (= 30 *se'ah*) dates: 1 drm. (cheap).[42]
* ,,	Bava Mezia 102b	1 *se'ah* (wheat): 1 *selah* (= 4d. = 4 drm.).[43]
,,	Bava Kama 113b	1 bronze vessel: 4–5 drm.
,,	Shabbat 129b	100 pumpkins: 1 drm.
* ,,	Pesaḥim 113a	1 bunch grapes: 1 drm. (expensive).
,,	Ibid.	1 date (*kotevet*): 1 drm.
* ,,	Ibid.	100 cucumbers: 1 drm. (cheap).
230–50(?)	Bava Kama 113a	100 barrels (wine?): 1 drm.[44]
250–90	Bava Mezia 40a	1 barrel (*dana*)[45] wine (containing 48 *kuzé*)[46]: 6 drm. (wholesale).
* ,,	Ibid.	6 *kuzé* wine: 1 drm. (retail).
* ,,	Bava Mezia 115a	Cloak (*glima*): 4 drm.
,,	Bava Mezia 114b	Expensive coat: 12,000 drm.

250–97	Sota 48a	100 *se'ah* wheat: 1d. 100 geese: 1 drm. (very cheap). Then 1 goose: 1 drm. (expensive).[47]
250–309	Bava Mezia 51a	Jewels: 50–60 drm.[48]
*250–320	Pesaḥim 88a	3 baskets of dates: 1 drm.
* ʺ	Gittin 52a	1 barrel wine: 4–6 drm.
*290–320	Pesaḥim 32a & Eruvin 29a	1 *griva*[49] dried figs: 1 drm.[50]
* ʺ51	Pesaḥim 32a	1 *griva* dates: 4 drm.
* ʺ	Ibid.[52]	1 *griva* wheat: 1–4 drm.
ʺ	Bechorot 11a	Young lamb: 1 *danka* (= 1/6 drm.)[53]
* ʺ	Kiddushin 7b	Bundle of silk: 50 drm.
290–320 or 320–350	Bava Mezia 41a	1 barrel wine: 1–4 drm.[54]
c.320	Ketubot 91b	Small field: 50 drm.
320–338/9	Bava Mezia 65a	4 *griva* wheat: 1 drm.[55]
ʺ	Bava Mezia 115a	Book: 80–120 drm.[56]
ʺ	Bava Batra 127b	1 slave (male): 100 drm.
ʺ	Bava Kama 11a	Ox corpse: 1–4 drm.[56]
ʺ	Bava Mezia 65a	1 cloak (*glima*): 4 drm.[57]
* ʺ	Temurah 6b	1 cloak (*glima*): 4–5 drm.
* ʺ	Ḥulin 49a	A cooked goose: 4 drm. (because spiced). The goose (by itself): 1 drm.[58]
320–50	Bava Mezia 51a	Silk-strain: 5–6 drm.[59]
ʺ	Bava Mezia 64a	1 barrel wine: 4 drm.
ʺ	Ketubot 91b	Mansion (*apadna*): 500 drm.
ʺ	Bava Batra 155b	Scribe's wages for writing *Megilat Esther*: 1 drm.
[ʺ	Nedarim 55a	Rava inherited 13,000 drm.[60]
ʺ	Yevamot 63a	100 drm. in business means meat and wine every day. 100 drm. in land, only salt and vegetables. Furthermore, it embroils him in strife and causes him to sleep on the ground.]
350–70	Mo'ed Katan 27b	Cheapest shroud: 1 drm.
[ʺ	Bava Kama 104b & Bava Batra 77b, 150b	Bé Ḥozai owed R. Papa 12,000 drm.][61]
370–425	Bava Mezia 75b	Mansion (*apadna*): 10 drm.
ʺ	Ibid.	Small field: 10 drm.
* ʺ	Bava Kama 115a	Cloak: 4 drm.
* ?	Bava Mezia 76a	Wage of worker per day: 3–4 drm.
?	Sanhedrin 109b	Crossing by ferry: 4 drm.[62]

SOME DURA-EUROPOS PRICES

Dura, Preliminary Report IV, p. 141[63]

Article		Text	Price per article
ἀναβόλαιον	(cloak)	No. 227, I, 4	23d.
		" " 13	23d.
ἀνίκλιον	(trousers)	No· 227, I, 2	23½d.
		" " " 3	23d.
		" " " 6	23d.
βαλανάριον	(cloak or robe)	No. 227, I, 12	27½d.
		" " " 17	17½d.
		No. 243, 2	24d.
δελματική	(robe)	No. 221, 2	60d.
		No. 222, 3	40d.
		No. 227, I, 14	30d.
		" " II, 8	17½d.
ἐπικάρσιον	(unknown garment)	No. 227, I, 7	26 3/4d.
καλίγα	(boots, pair)	No. 243, I	22d.
κολόβιον	(robe)	No. 227, II, 3	17½d.
κολόβιον δελματικόν	(robe)	No. 227, II, 2	22d.
λωδίκον	(blanket)	No. 243, 3	32d.
		" " 4	36d.
		" " 5	36d.
μακρόχειρον	(robe)	No. 227, I, 8	16d.
παιδικόν	(tunic)	No. 222, I	13d.
		No. 227, I, 16	3 or 13d.
παιδικον ψεγόμενον	(tunic, damaged)	No. 227, I, 18	2 3/4d.
πάλλιον	(robe)	No. 222, 9	90d.
σουδάριον	(kerchief)	No. 227, I, 5	6d.
		" " " 9	3 3/4d.
στιχάριον	(tunic)	No. 227, II, 7	10d .
τολάριον	(blanket?)	No. 227, I, 10	25d.
φακιάλιον	(kerchief)	No. 227, II, 4	12d.
χλανίδιον	(tunic)	No. 199	3d.
φέρι . . . μυράψιν ὑδρίας γʹ	(3 jars of myrrh)	No. 256	300d.

Dura Final Report V

No. 30, 232 C. E.

A white robe	(πάλλιον)	125(?)d.
Another white robe	(πάλλιον)	50d.
A tunic (colour unknown)	(στιχάριον)	40d.
An undyed robe	(δελματίκον)	30(?)d.
A crimson robe with purple veil	(μαφόριον)	75d.
A white robe		50d.
(An unknown item of purple)		25d.

109

Persian and striped stuffs(?)	50d.
Crockery and bronze utensils	25d.
Gold earrings and bracelets	50d.

No. 33, 240–50 C.E.[64]

1 linen robe	32d.
1 striped garment of 700(?)	50d.
3 mitres	50d.
2 mattresses, one with fleeces	100d.
1 bedspread[?]	100d.
1 stool	47d.
1 goats hair cloak	75d.

No. 56A, C, 208 C.E.

Horse, four years old, reddish "masked" unbranded	125d.

No. 28, 243 C.E.

Female slave aged twenty-eight	700d.

No. 25, 180 C.E.

Male slave, aged about twenty plus half a vineyard	500dr.

Dura Final Report, V, Part I, p. 8

Date	Text	Amount	Circumstances
121 C.E.	20	400dr.	Loan with personal *antichresis*
133	23	100dr.	Loan with *antichresis*
180	25	500dr.	Price of slave plus half a vineyard
c.189	17A	1000dr.	Loan
c.180	17D	780dr.	Loan with personal *antichresis*
227	26	175d.	Price of land
232	30	2500d.	Approximate amount of dowery plus paraphernalia
?	27	500d.	Incomplete list of unknown items
?	33	459d.	Partial value of list of goods
243	28	700d.	Price of slave
251	29	100d.	Deposit
Penalties for breach of contract:			
88/9 C.E.	19	1000dr. and same to crown	Distribution of inherited property
121	20	400dr. and same to crown	The amount of the loan also was 400dr.
204	31	1000dr. or 3000dr. and same to *fiscus*	Divorce
227	26	Double the price and damages in addition	Sale of land at 175d.
?	27	Double the price and damages in addition	Sale of unknown item at over 500d.
245	32	1000d. and same to crown	Divorce

Dura Preliminary Report II, p. 204

121 C.E.   Work to crown valued at 1 *dr.* per day

Dura Preliminary Report VII and VIII

Hypothetical menus:
No. 861 (p. 125)

δάννα [—]	a jar of wine,	[*denarii*—]
κρέας [—]	meat,	[*denarii*—]
ἔλεν* [—]	oil,	[*denarii*—]
ξύλα* β′	wood,	*denarii* 2
ῥαφενίδια νε′	radishes,	*assaria*(?) 5
κάρτα υβ′	paper,	*assaria* 2
ἐλλύχνιν νε′	lamp-wicks,	*assaria* 5

No. 862 (p. 125)

κρέας* α [θ′ υ ʽη ?]	meat,	*denarii* 19, *assaria* 17
γαρέλεν* α′	sauce,	*denarius* 1
χάρτα υα′	paper,	*assarion* 1
ὕδωρ *α′	water,	*denarius* 1
χύλα *(ξύλα,* Latin χ for ξ*) *α′*	wood	*denarius* 1
δάνα *κη′	υικ′ jar of wine	d. 28, *assaria* 11
*να	υια′ total	d. 51, *assaria* 11

CHAPTER XVI

PRICE RELATIONSHIPS

Wheat—Barley—Spelt:

In Mishna Pe'a 8.5 we read: "One may not give to the poor from the threshing-floor (as the poorman's tithe) less than half a *kav* of wheat or a *kav* of barley".

And in Mishna Ketubot 5.8 we read: "If a husband supports his wife through a third person, he may not grant her less than two *kavs* of wheat or four *kavs* of barley".

From these two texts we learn that wheat costs (in the second century, the approximate date of both texts) twice as much as barley.[1]

According to the *Edict of Diocletian* of 301 C.E. (Chapter 1, lines 1, 2; ed. Graser p. 318):

> 1 *modius castrensis* wheat: 100 *denarii*
> 1 *modius castrensis* barley: 60 *denarii*

Thus in Diocletian's time, too, wheat was almost twice as dear as barley.[2]

In Egypt there are some indications of a comparable kind of ratio:

> *SB*. 7621 316 C.E. Philadelphia Barley: 1000 *drachmae* per *artab*
> *SB*. 7621 315 C.E. Wheat: 3000 *drachmae* per *artab*[3]

And moving forward to the sixth century C.E. and East to Edessa, we have clear indication once again of a similar relationship. In the *Chronicle of Joshua Stylites* XLVI[4] we read that in the year 501-02 wheat was sold at 12 *modii* per *denarius*, and barley at 22 *modii* per *denarius*. In 504-05 (ibid.) LXXXVII[5] the prices were 6 *modii* wheat per *denarius*, and ten *modii* barley per *denarius*.[6]

Nonetheless, the relationship is by no means constant, and is obviously subject to specific seasonal, as well as geographic, conditions. Thus in Egypt for the year 314 C.E. we find in *PER. E.* 2000 Hermopolis: Wheat: 10,000 *drachmae* per *artab*; barley: 10,000 *drachmae* per *artab*.[7]

The Mishna in Pe'a continues: "... or a *kav* and a half of spelt..."
That is to say, wheat costs three times as much as spelt. Once again the
Edict of Diocletian (ibid., line 8) is evidence of the same relationship:
one *modius castrensis* spelt at 30 *denarii*, just a little under one-third of
the cost of one *modius castrensis* wheat (supra).

Wheat—Bread—Wine—Meat:

Mishna Eruvin 8.2:

> And what is the prescribed amount [for a *shittuf*]? Food for two
> meals for each one... R. Johanan ben Beroka says: "... [not less
> than] one loaf worth a *pundion* (=1/12 *denarius*) from wheat
> costing one *sela* [= 4 *denarii*) for four *se'ahs*" (1 *se'ah* = 1
> *modius*).[8] R. Simeon says: "Two-thirds of a loaf of [a size] three
> to a *kav*".

Yerushalmi Eruvin 8.2

> And we have learned in a *beraita* (cf. Bavli Eruvin 82b, Ketubot
> 64b): Their statements (those of R. Johanan ben Beroka and
> R. Simeon) are almost identical in meaning. Come see [in what
> manner are they almost identical in meaning]. Surely the one
> R. Johanan ben Beroka) takes a loaf to be twelve eggs? (For
> there are four *se'ahs* to the *sela*, i.e. 4 *se'ah* at 4 *denarii*. One *se'ah*
> equals six *kav*. Therefore, one loaf of a *pundion* is twelve eggs.)
> The other (R. Simeon) takes a loaf to be eight eggs (= one-third
> *kav*, Mishna above). And yet you say that their statements are
> almost identical! Rav Huna (Palestine, middle of the fourth cen-
> tury), answered: "Subtract (from R. Johanan ben Beroka's one-
> half *kav* = 12 eggs) one-third as expenses" (i.e. on 8 eggs = one-
> third *kav*, he earns one-third more, and therefore the weight of
> one-third *kav* costs 1/12 *denarius* = one *pundion*). R. Jose ben
> R. Bun (Palestine, late fourth century) went [and preached] to
> the bakers [that they should not charge more than one-third more],
> in accordance with the opinion of Rav Huna.

Thus, according to the Palestinian Talmud's explanation, both R.
Johanan ben Beroka and R. Simeon are dealing with a loaf of the same
size, namely of eight eggs (= 1/3 *kav* = 1/18 *se'ah*). But R. Johanan
ben Beroka gives the price of such a loaf (one *pundion*), and R. Simeon
the weight (1/3 *kav*). The Talmud's difficulty was that it first identified

the price of wheat—four *se'ah* at one *sela*—with the price of a finished loaf, and hence R. Johanan ben Beroka's loaf, which costs one-third more than 1/18 *se'ah* of wheat, was thought to weigh one-third more (i.e. 1/12 *se'ah*). The answer given is that the difference between the price of the amount of wheat in the bread and the loaf itself is one-third, and that includes all the costs of labour and profits involved.

In Rav Huna's time (320-50) the net profits did not exceed one-third and in the next generation (350-75) the bakers had to be told not to charge at a higher rate than this.

From the above we may learn two things:

(a) The average loaf was about 1/18 *se'ah*. It is likely that the *se'ah* produced about 22 loaves (of 1/18 *se'ah* each) or even more, as on an average 100 pounds of flour produce over 120 pound-loaves.[9]

(b) Such a loaf cost 1/12 *denarius*. Other Mishnaic sources giving approximately) the same relationship are as follows:

Mishna Shekalim 4.9	I–II century	1–1 2/3 *se'ah* (flour): 1d.
Mishna Bava Mezia 5.1	I–II century	1 *se'ah* (wheat): 5/6 — 1d.
Mishna Pe'a 8.7 &	100–140	1 *se'ah* (wheat): 1d.
Mishna Kelim 17.11		1 loaf (bread): 1 *pundion* (= 1/12d.)
Mishna Shevi'it 8.7	I–II century	1 loaf (bread): 1 *pundion* (= 1/12d.)
Tosefta Shevi'it 6.21	II century	1 loaf (bread): 1 *pundion* (= 1/12d.)

Conclusion (a) would seem to be borne out by a statement in *Pliny, Historia Naturalis* 18,89-90 (about 79 C.E.). There he writes: "*panis vero e modio similaginis p. XXII...*" (...the finest wheat flour will yield 22 pounds of bread to the *modius* of grain...).[10]

Further evidence may be cited from a sixth century Egyptian papyrus, *P.O.* 1920, according to which one *artab* of wheat yields eighty pounds of bread (for the military *annona*).[11] An *artab* equals approximately 3 1/3 *modii*;[12] hence, one *modius* yields approximately 23 pounds of bread.

Assuming for the moment that the average yield of one *modius* wheat is about twenty pounds of bread, and knowing from the *Edict of Diocletian* (ibid. 1, 1; p. 318) that one *modius castrensis* wheat costs 100 *denarii*, we may reckon that two pounds contains five *denarii* worth of wheat. The average loaf weighs about two pounds, or a little more perhaps,[13] and as the difference between the cost of wheat and the loaf is about one-third (see above), the cost of such a loaf would be 5 to 5½ *denarii* + 5 to 5½ = 6 2/3 to 7 1/3 *denarii*.

3

Now in *Genesis Rabba*ᵀ 49.4, R. Azaria in the name of R. Judah [ben R. Simeon ben Pazi] states (around 290-350) that:

one *xestes* (=approximately one pint) of wine costs ten *follarin*,
one pound of meat   costs ten *follarin*,
one loaf of bread (probably fairly large)   costs ten *follarin*.

Thus, one pound of meat costs as much as one pint of wine and one loaf of bread.

According to the Edict of Diocletian:
one pound of meat costs eight *denarii* (ibid., 4, 2, p. 324), one bottle of ordinary wine costs eight *denarii* (ibid., 2, 10, p. 332). Thus, one loaf of bread would cost about eight *denarii* (very little more than our assumed 6 2/3 to 7 1/3 *denarii* above. As one *modius castrensis* wheat costs 100 *denarii*, the relationship between a loaf of bread and a *modius* wheat is 12:1. This is completely in accordance with conclusion (b) above.

We have stated above that one pound of meat costs approximately the same as one pint of wine. This is borne out by a mid-fourth century Egyptian papyrus, *P. London* 985,[14] according to which:

one pound of meat costs 33,000 *denarii*,
one pint of wine costs 33,000 *denarii* (inflationary prices).

This holds good not only for Palestine *(Genesis Rabba)* and Egypt *(P. London)*, but also for Antioch of approximately the same time. For in *P. Rylands* 629[15] (dating from about 317-23) we find the following:

Line 24. 4 lbs. meat: 1200 dr. = 300 d. Therefore, 1 b. meat: 75d.
Line 91. ½ *kab* (= 2 *sext.*) wine: 600 dr. = 150d. 1 *sext.* wine: 75d.

Hence, one *sextarius* (= one pint) of wine costs the same as one pound of meat.[16]

Wine-Honey:

In Mishna Bava Kama 10.4 we read of the following case:

If one man came with his barrel of wine, and another with his jar of honey, and the barrel (read: jar) of honey cracked, and the other poured out his wine and saved the honey [by receiving it] into his [barrel], he can claim no more than his hire. But if he said, "I will save yours [if] you will give me the value of mine", then the other must pay [it] to him.

From the above text it is quite apparent that honey was more expensive than wine. (Palestine, first or second century.) But here there is no precise relationship indicated. When we then refer to the *Edict of Diocletian*, Chapter 2 (dealing with wines), and compare it with Chapter 3, lines 10 and 11 (prices of honey), we find the same thing, namely that wine is less expensive than honey.[17]

Good wine, according to the *Edict,* costs 30 *denarii* per Italian pint (ibid., lines 2-7, 13), while ordinary wine (line 10) costs as little as 8 *denarii* per pint. Honey of the best quality, on the other hand, costs 40 *denarii* per pint, and of the second quality, 24 *denarii* per pint (ibid., Chapter 3, 10, 11). Thus, comparing the ordinary types of honey and wine, we may say that the former is at least three times as expensive as the latter.[18]

Wine—Oil:

Mishna Pe'a 8.5: "...half a *log* of wine or a quarter of a *log* of oil..." From here we learn that oil was approximately twice the price of wine (during the Mishnaic period, and the Amoraic one, Yerushalmi Pe'a 8.5).

According to the *Edict of Diocletian*:

ordinary wine: one Italian pint costs *eight denarii* (2, 10, p. 322), ordinary oil: one Italian pint costs twelve *denarii* (3, 3, p. 323).

Here then the difference in price is far less extreme.[19]

Thus far we have arrived at the following relationships, which may be thus tabulated in terms of units (the unit being approximately eight *denarii* according to the *Edict of Diocletian,* and one *pundion* (= 1/12 *denarius*) in the Mishna):[20]

one *modius castrensis* wheat:	six units
one *modius castrensis* barley:	four units
one *modius castrensis* spelt:	three units
one pint bees honey:	twelve units
one pint oil:	$1\frac{1}{2}$ to two units
one pint wine:	one to two units
one loaf bread (two-pound loaf):	one unit
one pound meat:	one unit

The following items cost one unit each:

Bavli Eruvin 29a (in the name of R. Simeon ben Eleazar, *floruit* 170-200)	Yerushalmi Pe'a 8.5 (anonymous)
	Rice, 1 *Rova*[21]
Spices, 1 *ukla*[22]	Spices, 1 *ukla*[22]
Greens, 1 *litra*	Greens, 1 *litra*
	Carobs, 3 *kav*
Mishna Pe'a 8.5 $= \begin{cases} \text{Wine, } \frac{1}{2} \text{ } log \\ \text{Oil, } \frac{1}{4} \text{ } log \end{cases}$	
Nuts, 10	Nuts, 10
Peaches, 5	Peaches, 5
Pomegranates, 2[22a]	
Pomecitron, 1	Pomecitron, 1

Wheat—Rice:

Combining both Yerushalmi Pe'a 8.5 and Mishna Pe'a 8.5, we find that one *rova* $(= \frac{1}{4} \text{ } kav)$ rice $= \frac{1}{2} \text{ } kav$ wheat. Therefore rice is twice as expensive as wheat.

According to the *Edict of Diocletian*:

one *modius castrensis* wheat:	100 *denarii* (1, 1, p. 318).
one *modius castrensis* rice, cleaned[23]:	200 *denarii* (1, 23, p. 319).

Thus in Italy, too, rice (cleaned) cost twice as much as wheat.

Peaches—Pomegranates:

According to Bavli Eruvin 29a, five peaches cost as much as two pomegranates, or in other words pomegranates cost $2\frac{1}{2}$ times as much as peaches. According to the *Edict of Diocletian*, Chapter 6:[24]

Line 61	peaches, largest size	10: 4d.
Line 62	peaches, smaller size	20: 4d.
Line 71	pomegranates, largest size	10: 8d.
Line 72	pomegranates, smaller size	20: 8d.

Thus in Rome, pomegranates cost only twice as much as peaches, as opposed to $2\frac{1}{2}$ times as much in late second century Palestine. In the Mishna there are five peaches to the unit, and two pomegranates to the unit, while, according to the *Edict of Diocletian*, there are twenty (large) peaches to the unit and ten (large) pomegranates to the unit. Hence, it appears that in Palestine peaches cost four times as much and pomegranates five times as much as in Rome.[25]

Cost of Wheat per Modius[26] in Egypt

c. 18 B.C.E.	P. Fay. 101	Euhemeria	¼d.
13	O. Strassb. 46	Upper Egypt	3/10d.
10	O. Strassb. 48	Thebes	3/16d.
9	O. Strassb. 51	Upper Egypt	3/16d.
5	P. Tebt. 459	Tebtynis	3/20d.
4	Tait OP. 197, 199, 201	Coptos	¼d.
3 C.E.	SB. 7341	Philadelphia	9/40d.
45/6	P. Mich. 127	Tebtynis	1/3d. (Sebastos 10)
			3/7d. (Sebastos 20)
			3/5d. (Sebastos 27)
			6/11d. (Sebastos 29)
			3/5d. (Phaophi 4)
			4/9d. (Phaophi 4)
46/7	P. Mich. 132 V.XI	Tebtynis	2/3d.
56	WO. 1558	Thebes	1/3d.
65	Tait OP. 210	Coptos	1/6d.
100	P. Amh. 133		¼d.
125	BGU. 834 Soc. Nes.		¼d.
138	PSI. 281		3/7d.
153	WO. 1587	Thebes	9/10d.
155	P. Col. 1.4 & Frisk, Bankakten 1	Theadelphia	3/5d.
138/61	P. Baden 79	Heracleopolite nome	9/10d.
162	P. Ryl. 197		5/8d. (exported wheat)
191	P. Goodsp. 30	Caranis	1½d. (Col. XV), 1 1/3d. (Mechir, col. XX)
254	P. Lond. 1226	Theadelphia	9/10d.
255	BGU. 14	Memphis	1 1/5d.
256	P. Flor. 321	Theadelphia	9/10d.
294	P. Rend. Harr. 93	Oxyrhynchus	16½–17 2/5 or 66–69 3/5d.
312	Harv. St. LI.	Caranis	1½ or 50 (emmer) d.
314	PER. E. 2000	Hermopolis	750 or 3000d.
315	SB. 7621	Theadelphia	225 or 900d.
355	P. Lond. 1914	Alexandria	6300d.

Cost of Bread in Egypt

1 C.E.	P.O. 736	Oxyrhynchus	fine loaf: 1/48d. grinding a *modius* of wheat: 1/8–1/6d.
45/6	P. Mich. 123	Tebtynis	one loaf: 1/24d.
46/7	P. Mich. 128	Tebtynis	one loaf: 1/24d.
II cent.	O. Brüssels 71		allowance to builder per day for bread: 1/12d.

118

117	P.O. 1454	Oxyrhynchus	Agreement of bakers to deliver baked loaves each weighing 2 lbs. 9 loaves per *modius*. Bakers receive 1/8 *modius* for milling, selling, and other expenses.
220	SB. 7181	Oxyrhynchus	Military requisition for 3141 loaves at 1/24d. per loaf.
258	P. Flor. 322	Theadelphia	26 2/3 *modii* per 320 double loaves (= 640 single loaves). Rations of labourers: 2 single loaves per day (2½ *modii* per month) or 4 single loaves (5 *modii* per month). If wheat was worth 9/10d. per *modius* (P. Flor. 321) the double loaf was worth approximately 1/12d.
III cent.	SPP. XXII 56 Soc. Nes.		1¼d. per *modius*
III cent.	P.O. 1655	Oxyrhynchus	1 measure fine flour: 3d. 1 loaf: 1d. 20 pairs of dry loaves: 3d. 40 variegated loaves 11d. 40 loaves: 5½d. 20 small cakes: 3d.

Cost of Livestock in Egypt

6 B.C.E.	P. Lond. 890		15d. (balance of price of 5 cows).
110 C.E.	P. Baden II, 19	Hermopolite nome	30d. for cow.
118/38	BGU. 986	Bacchias	75d. (plus) for steer.
123	P. Lond. 839	Hermopolis	15½d. for cow and calf.
136	P.O. 707		2 pair oxen valued at 115d.
139	P.O. 729	Oxyrhynchus	8 cattle (5 fully grown and 3 young cattle(?) valued at 625d.
191/2	P. Goodsp. 30	Caranis	47½d. (at least) paid for cow [col. XL, XLI]
II/III cent.	P. Iand. 35	Philadelphia	30½d. for black cow.
239	P. Flor. 16	Euhemeria	Ox valued at 25d., furnished by lessor for irrigation.

119

III cent.	P. Tebt. 404	Tebtynis	Cow furnished for annona: 15d.
"	P. Lond. 965	Theadelphia	100d. for ox, unbroken for work.
346	P. Gen. 48		Team of full grown oxen 180,000d. (= 1200 *talents*).

Cost of Fowl in Egypt

1 C.E.	P.O. 736	Oxyrhynchus	Pigeon: 1/24d.
42	P. Mich. 121	Tebtynis	2 choice cocks: 1d.
151	PSI. 1124	Tebtynis	Fowl: ½d.
169 or 199	P. Lond. 335	Heraclia	2 chickens at 1d. each
II cent.	P. Ross. Georg.		4 fowls at 1½d. each
	II. 41		2 fowls at 2d. each
II/III cent.	P.O. 2129	Oxyrhynchus	4 fowls at 5/8d. each

Bread and Wheat Costs (*cont.*):[27]

According to *P. Flor.* 332, 26 2/3 *modii* of wheat produced 320 double loaves, or 640 single loaves. Therefore, one *modius* produced twelve double or 24 single loaves. This bears out well our earlier calculations, where we showed that one *se'ah* (= 2 *modii*) produced about 22 double loaves.

About 1 C.E. one *modius* of wheat cost ¼ *denarius* and could produce 24 single loaves. Therefore, one single loaf had 1/96 *denarius* worth of wheat in it. At that time a loaf of fine bread actually cost 1/48 *denarius*, i.e. twice as much as the worth of its wheat content. But the cost of grinding a *modius* of wheat was 1/8 to 1/6 *denarius*. Therefore, the cost of wheat plus the cost of grinding was ¼ + 1/8 to 1/6 = 3/8 to 5/12 *denarius*. Therefore, the cost of a loaf was 3/8 to 5/12 ÷ 24 = 1/64 to about 1/58 *denarius*. As a single loaf of fine bread cost 1/48 *denarius*, the bakers made approximately 20 to 33% profit.

Some added support for this may perhaps be found in *P.O.* 1454. For there bakers are stated to have agreed to deliver nine baked loaves to the *modius*, each weighing two pounds. They received 1/8 *denarius* per *modius* for the milling, selling and other expenses, a *modius* itself costing about ½ *denarius*. Normally a modius produces twelve double (= 2 lb.) loaves, and thus in this case it appears that three double-loaves were left to the bakers as payment in kind, while all expenses were paid for. They thus got a clear profit (a kind of wage) of three out of twelve loaves, or in other words, 25%.[28]

Looking back now on the Mishnaic material that we analysed above, we may perhaps modify our statements slightly. One *se'ah* probably yielded 24 (and not 22) double-loaves. One *se'ah* of wheat cost one *denarius*, and one loaf cost one *pundion* (= 1/12 *denarius*). Yet, the loaf contained in itself only 1/24 *denarius*-worth of wheat, while we know that the bakers made no more than 33% profit. Thus, approximately 17% of the cost of the loaf must be put down to milling, selling, and other expenses (i.e. 1/6 total expense).

Again, looking back at the *Edict of Diocletian*, we may state that one *modius castrensis* of wheat produced 24 double-loaves. As one *modius castrensis* cost 100 *denarii*, a loaf had four *denarii* worth of wheat in it. We have seen that a loaf cost about twice as much as the value of its wheat-content, and hence the price of a loaf would be eight *denarii*. This is equal to the cost of one pound of meat or one bottle of wine in the *Edict*, again bearing out our calculation of the price-relationships of these various commodities (see above, this chapter).

We may then say that in a Palestinian loaf of bread during the Talmudic period:

Approximately 50% = cost of wheat
17% = cost of milling, etc.
33% = clear profit (maximum)
Total 100%

Thus both in Egypt and in Palestine the ratio between the cost of one *modius* of wheat and one single-loaf of bread is 1 : 12.[29]

From *P.O.* 1454 (117 C.E.) we have learned that the bakers got about 25% profit and 1/8 *denarius* expenses. As the cost of wheat accounts for 50% of the price of the bread, and in this case the profit was 25%, the expenses must have been 25% per loaf. Therefore, 1/8 *denarius* (= expenses) ÷ 9 = 25% of the cost of the loaf = 1/72 *denarius*. Thus, the cost of the total loaf equals 1/72 × 4 = 1/18 *denarius*. One *modius* (= one loaf × 12), then, costs 2/3 *denarius*. According to this calculation, in Oxyhynchus in 117 C.E. one *modius* cost 2/3 *denarius*. This is only a little higher price (1/6 in fact) than those recorded in *P. Amh.* 133, for 100 C.E., and in *BGU.* 834, 125 C.E., both of which give ½ *denarius* per *modius*.

From *P. Flor.* 332 we learn that the ration of labourers was usually two single loaves per day. This no doubt was for two meals, and thus corresponds to our Mishna, cited above, where we are told that the poor man is to be given "food for two meals" (ibid.), which amount we have shown to be a double-loaf.

Thus, the undated *P. Brussels* 71, where an allowance of 1/12 *denarius* of bread per day is made to a builder, presupposes a current price for the *modius* of one *denarius*. (The allowance is for one double loaf, i.e. 1/12 *modius*.) It would thus appear to be from the end of the second century, when the prices of wheat in Egypt were approaching this kind of level.[30]

Egyptian Wages[31]

approximate daily wages, unless otherwise stated

28/3 B.C.E.	P. Corn. 25	Philadelphia	1/8d. for harvesters.
c.18	P. Fay 101	Euhemeria	Harvesters receive 1/3 *modius* daily (1/12d.)
13	BGU. 1123	Alexandria	Contract to cultivate 2 *arourae* for 3 years for 112½d.
8	P. Lond. 1171	?	Shepherds and foreman: 6d. per month. Assistant shepherd: 3d. per month.
1 C.E.	P.O. 737	Oxyrhynchus	*Conductei*: 1/6d. weavers: 1/7d. magister: ¼d. (*As* = *obol* here, c.f. P. Teb. 686.)
c.1	P.O. 736	Oxyrhynchus	Household servant: 1/10d.
46	P. Mich. 123	Tebtynis	Contract to harvest 52½ *arourae*: 52½d. Fee for writing document: 1/24— 7/24d. (cf. ibid. 128). *Grammatikon*: 1/24 to 10d.
78	P. Lond. 131*	Hermopolis	Pruning: 5/24 — 7/24d. (Pharmouthi). Boys weeding and gathering leaves: 1/12d. Irrigation: 5/24d.
c.79	P. Lond. 131	Hermopolis	Thoth. Men on farm work: 1/8d. 1/7d. 1/6d. Boys. 1/10d. Plasterer's assistant: 1/5d. Phaophi. Water-guard: 5d. per month. Bricklayer: 1/4d. Pruners: 1/6d. Plough- men: 1/5d. Digging sebakh: 1/6d. Pachon. Harvesting 1/12d. Thre- shing: 1/8d. Cutting

			straw: 1/12d. Cleaning water-channels: 1/8d.
92	P. Grenf. II. 43	Arsine	Guard at metropolis: 10d. per month.
104	SB. 7365	Fayum	Arab guard at customs: 4d. per month.
113	P. Lond. 1177	Arsinoe	Foreman and labourers at waterworks: 10d. per month. (Pachon-Epiph.) 9d.(Thoth-*Phaophi*).5/12d. per day on daily wage. Ox-drivers' foreman: 8d. per month. Others, 3d., 4d per month. Others, 3d., 4d., 6d., per month. On daily contract: 1/6d.
126	P. Fay. 331	Theadelphia	Form-work: 3/8d.
145	P. Lond. 306	Caranis	Deputy tax-collector: 63d. per year.
150	P.O. 1654	Oxyrhynchus	Fee for writing memoranda: 2/3d.
155	P. Col. I.4 and Frisk Bankakten 1	Theadelphia	Tower guards: 6d. and 10d. per month.
156	P. Ryl. 88	Arsinoe	Salary of guard: 4½d. per month.
172	P. Tebt. 42	Tebtynis	Bricklayer laying 10,000 bricks: 10d.
191	P. Goodsp. 30	Caranis	Guard, 6d. per month(?). Ox-drivers, 7d. per month(?). Mason, 7d. per month (?).
214	BGU. 362	Arsinoe	Temple guards: 4 3/4d. and 7d. per month. Keeper of records: 7½d. per month. Clerk: 10d. per month. Fee for advocate pleading before prefect: 15d.
229	P.O. 1500	Oxyrhynchus	Bath-attendant: 2d. for half a month(?)
254	P. Lond. 1226	Theadelphia	Steward: 10d. per month. Cowherds: 12d. and 15d. per month. Donkey drivers: 2d. and 4d. per month.
255	BGU. 14	Memphis	Guard of vineyard: 20d. per month (salary may be for longer than one month).

256	P. Flor. 321	Philadelphia	Steward: 10d. per month. Cowherd: 1 3/4 and 12d. per month. Ox-drivers: 8½ and 12d. per month. Donkey-drivers: 2d. and 4½d. per month. (Probably allowances of wheat and wine to regular workers.)
258	P. Flor. 322	Euhemeria	Steward: 10d. per month. Ox-driver: 1d. and 2d. per month. Cow-herders: 2d. and 3d. per month. Donkey-drivers: 1d. and 4d. per month. Wood-cutter: 1d. per month. Other workmen on monthly basis: 1d. and 2d. Cutting hay: ½d. Cutting hay on contract: ½ and 3/4d. per *aroura*. Harvesting: 5/6d. (Men regularly employed receive 3½ *modii* wheat per month. Others, an allowance of bread from 2–4 loaves per day.)
259	P. Lond. 1170	Theadelphia	Men gathering olives, sowing wheat and performing other farm duties: ½d. Ox-drivers: ½d. (Wine distributed to workmen in varying quantities.)
c.260(?)	PSI. 811	Theadelphia(?)	Worker: 3/4d.
c.270	BGU. 952	Heracleopolis	Pieceworkers: 3d. or 12d.
295	PSI. 712	Oxyrhynchus	8000 (or 2000)d. for making 40,000 bricks.
297	SB. 7676	Caranis	200d. or 50d. for work on Trajan's canal.
299	PSI. 873	Theadelphia	Worker: 240d. or 60d.
301	PSI. 1037	Oxyrhynchus	400d. or 100d. per day for *rhabduchus*.
308	Gr. Pap. II. 75	Oasis	30,000d. (= 20 *talents*) of Augustan silver paid in *nummi*, food and clothing for a fourth part of a nurse's service.
309	P.O. 1499		500d. per month, for bath attendant.

314	PER. E. 2000	Hermopolis	Cutting weeds, clearing ground, dykeing and building home: 100d. Irrigation and builders: 125d. Labour: 162½d.
c.325	P.O. 1626		500d. for *rhabduchus*.
340	BGU. 21		Worker (Payni): 37,500d. (= 25 *talents*); (Epiph.): 22,500d. (= 15 *talents*); (Epiph.): 18,000d. (= 12 *talents*); (Mesori): 22,500d. (= 15 *talents*).
377	PSI. VI. 287	Oxyrhynchus	Apprentice to 300,000d.

On the basis of the above information West and Johnson come to the following conclusions:[32]

	Wheat: *denarii per modius*	Labour: *per day in denarii*
I century C.E.	1/6 — 6/5	1/6 — 2/3
II century	1/2 — 1 2/3	1/2 — 1 1/3
Mid–III century	1	1 — 1 1/3

CHAPTER XVII

COMPARATIVE PRICE-LEVELS

Palestine, Egypt, Rome

Even the most cursory comparison of these results with Palestinian costs of wheat and wages demonstrates that life in Egypt was considerably cheaper than in Palestine. Wheat appears to have cost half as much in Egypt as in Palestine, and Palestinian wages are more than twice as high as Egyptian ones. Our tables further show that cattle were cheaper in Egypt than in Palestine.

In Rome however, prices of wheat appear to have been as much as twice as high as those of Palestine. Thus, N. Jasny[1] very convincingly argues that the price of *triticum* (cheaper type of wheat) per *modius* about 70 C.E. was two *denarii*, and that of *siligo* (more expensive type) was $2\frac{1}{2}$ *denarii*.[2]

In Tosefta Machshirim 3.4[3] we read: "Joshua ben Perahia (latter part of the second century B.C.E.) says: 'Wheat that comes from Alexandria is impure becaues of the (the Alexandrians') *antlia*.'" (= ἀντλία —pumps with wheels and buckets).[4] This seems to mean that when being transported by boat from Alexandria to Palestine, the hold might be sprinkled with water from the bilge-pumps. R. Joshua ben Perahia suspects lest some water may have been sprinkled onto the wheat, thus making it liable to become defiled, if touched by anyone not ritually pure—a highly likely eventuality.[5] "The Sages replied: 'If so, it is impure for Joshua ben Perahia, but it is pure for all [the rest] of Israel'."

L. Ginzberg explains this otherwise rather surprising view of Joshua ben Perahia as being an attempt to legally enforce an economic "boycott" (or sanctions) on Alexandrian wheat, as it was seriously challenging the home market. To protect the local produce, he tried to declare it ritually impure, and hence virtually unusable to at least a certain section of the population.[6] This method had been used to the same ends in the preceding generation by the great Jose ben Jo'ezer who took measures to limit the use of glassware (then predominantly non-Palestinian), and in the following generation by Simeon ben Sheṭaḥ (first half of the first century B.C.E.) who did the same to non-Palestinian metalware.[7]

In the light of the above evidence, we may see that Ginzberg's suggestion has a sound economic basis. If wheat in Palestine cost twice as much as it did in Egypt, it could be brought from Alexandria to Ascalon or any other of the ports by sea at relatively little cost, and sold at considerably less than the price of Palestinian wheat, still making a clear margin of profit. Thus, for example, even if the cost of transport, loading and unloading, etc., came to as much as 10% of the cost of the wheat itself, Alexandrian traders could still under-cut Palestinian prices by 30% and be left with a clear profit of almost 30%.[8] In 363 Julian the Apostate still found it an economic proposition to bring wheat from Alexandria to the famine-ridden Antioch, (see page 193, note 15).

CHAPTER XVIII

THIRD CENTURY PRICES

In the light of the above, we may also point a way to answering the very puzzling problem first presented by Gunnar Mickwitz. On p. 73 of his great *Geld und Wirtschaft im römischen Reich des IV Jahrh. n. Chr.* he sets out a chart which purports to show that prices shortly before 301 were considerably lower than those of the *Edict*,[1] whereas from the prologue to the *Edict* one would expect the exact opposite.[2] But in point of fact all his sources for this period are from Egyptian papyri. On an average, these papyrological prices are half as high as those of the *Edict*. However, if Roman prices were as much as four times as high as Egyptian ones (as we have suggested above, previous chapter), then the *Edict's* prices show in every case a reduction of about 50% on Roman prices (or on those of Constantinople),[3] and this would be well in keeping with its avowed aims.[4]

We may find further evidence for this in the text of Yerushalmi Bava Batra 8.4, discussed above. There we saw that 100 *garbin* of wine cost twenty *dinars*. We dated the text to the last quarter of the third century, and demonstrated that *dinar* then means *aureus*. We may thus state that sometime during the last quarter of the third century, one (ordinary) *gerev* cost 1/5 *dinar* = aureus. Now the ordinary *gerev* must have corresponded to some kind of recognized measure, and we should like here to suggest that in this case the measure was a *chous*, a liquid measure well-known in Palestine, and mentioned for example by Josephus *(Antiquities* 3.8.3).[5] If this suggestion be accepted, then one *xestes* (= 1/6 *chous*) wine (?) cost 1/60 *aureus*. In terms of *Diocletian's Edict* this means then, that one *xestes* wine cost 13 1/3 *denarii*, a very reasonable estimate.[6]

It seems very likely that our Yerushalmi text is from before 301, and thus the *Edict's* price of ten *denarii* per Italian pint of ordinary wine would appear to be a slight reduction on that of our text. We would

128

indeed expect this, going by the prologue to the *Edict*, where it is clearly stated that the whole purpose of the fixing of maximum prices was in order to reduce costs, thus preventing the profiteer from extorting exhorbitant sums of money for various commodities.[7] In Rome the price may well have been even higher, hence the reduction even greater. In Egypt, however, there is a record of wine costing four to five *denarii* per *chous*.[8] This is about one-third of the Palestinian price.[9] And though, of course, wine-costs range very considerably (varying as they do from place to place, and subject to seasonal changes),[10] this seems to be consistent with the general trend we have noted above (with regard to wheat and wages), that Egyptian prices are approximately half that of Palestinian ones, or, at any rate, considerably lower. It seems likely that the reduction in prices, which was the primary purpose of Diocletian's *Edict*, was reckoned mainly from a Roman standpoint and according to Roman price-levels, or from that of one of the major centres of the Eastern Empire (Constantinople, Antioch?), which would have been even higher than Palestinian ones.[11]

Further confirmation of this may be found in the text of Bavli Avoda Zara 34b, which we discussed above (pages 57-59) in some detail. We showed that the episode recorded must have taken place around 275. In discussing its metrological implications, we suggested that the term *"lumma"* which appears there was a unit of reckoning meaning five *denarii*. Let us now examine the economic implications of this text.

Firstly, we learn from it that in Palestine *muries* was more expensive than wine, though we do not know by how much. We only know that it would pay to dilute it with wine.[12] In the place from which the *muries* came, on the other hand, wine was four times more expensive than was *muries*. From R. Zera's question we may deduce that the ship probably came from the North, past Tyre, rather than from Egypt, for example. If R. Zera could automatically suggest that the ship's route had been past Tyre, he must have assumed that the ship had come from a certain place in the North famous for its *muries*. Moreover, it probably came from a place known to export kosher fish primarily, as *muries* was a fish product. Now in Bavli Avoda Zara 39a, we read that R. Abbahu (*floruit* second half of the third century in Caesarea) announced: "The oil of fish and fish may be bought from anyone (i.e. Jew or non-Jew, even though in this state there can be no indication as to whether they come from kosher or non-kosher fish), for they are certain to come from either Aspamia or Plusa".

Plusa is Pelusium in Egypt,[13] south of Akko and therefore excluded from being the source of our *muries*. Aspamia, on the other hand, is almost certainly Apamaea in Syria, as may be seen from a careful examination of Mss. variants.[14]

The "Sea of Apamaea" in Syria was both in Roman times,[15] and even during the Islamic period,[16] famous as a centre of fisheries. But even more than that, in Talmudic times it was the most famous *muries*-producing district. Thus in *Exodus Rabba* 9.6[17] we read: "Normally one brings merchandise to a place where there is a demand for it. Would one bring *muries* to Aspamia (= Apamaea) or fish to Akko?"[18] The sea of Apamaea was an inland lake 45 kilometres east of Laodicea,[19] its nearest major port, which was in turn some 270 kilometres north of Tyre, and a further 40 kilometres from Akko.

Surely our *muries* came from there, and R. Zera's reasonable question was: could not the boat have put into Tyre on its way down to Akko? To which the reply was that this was unlikely in view of the "narrow bays and shoal water"—(of a major port?).[20]

With this information we may now reckon the approximate prices of wine and *muries* in Akko and Apamaea about 275. In Apamaea we have seen that *muries* cost one *lumma* per *xestes* (= 5 *denarii* per *pint*). In Palestine, taking into account the cost of transport (45 kilometres overland, loading, unloading, 310 kilometres of sea journey, etc.)[21] and a good margin of profit,[22] it would probably have to be sold at not less than $2\frac{1}{2}$-3 *lummas* (= $12\frac{1}{2}$-15 *denarii*) per *xestes*. The price of *muries* in Akko must have been very cheap as it had to undercut the local *muries* trade in *Tiberias* (note 22), not so far from Akko, and well-connected by a major road.[23] Wine must have cost less—hence the danger of admixture—perhaps even less than two *lummas* (= ten *denarii*) per *xestes*. In Apamaea on the other hand, it cost four *lummas* (= twenty *denarii*) per *xestes*. These price variations are in themselves very revealing, but let us see whether we can place them into any kind of historical context.

Starting from a (conjectural) point of departure that *muries* in Akko cost $12\frac{1}{2}$-15 *denarii* per *xestes* around 275, wine probably cost around ten *denarii* or less at this time, and *muries* a little more than fifteen *denarii*. (This is very close to the conclusions we drew above from the Yerushalmi Bava Batra 8.4 text). We may now compare these prices with those recorded in the *Edict of Diocletian*. However, as the value of the *denarius* changes so radically during the intervening quarter century, it would perhaps be sounder to translate these prices into fractions of the *aureus* (even though this too is an ever-shifting point of uncertainty). If we accept our suggestion that the *lumma* here (= νοῦμμος) equals a *sestertius* in that it is 1/100 of Aurelian's reformed *aureus* of 500 *denarii*,[24] then we may state that *muries* cost approximately 1/33-1/40 *aureus* per *xestes*, and wine about 1/50 *aureus*. (The Yerushalmi Bava Batra text gave us a price of 1/60 *aureus* per *xestes*.)[25]

When we now compare these necessarily very approximate and conjectural results with prices recorded in the *Edict of Diocletian* (of 301), we find that ordinary wine (probably of the sort of quality one might mix in with *muries*) there costs eight *denarii* per *xestes*,[26] i.e. 1/100 *aureus*, while *garum* (fish-sauce, the nearest thing to *muries* there recorded)[27] of the first quality costs sixteen *denarii* per pint, and of the second quality twelve *denarii* per pint,[28] i.e. 1/50 to 1/66 *aureus*. Thus, Palestinian prices of some 25 years earlier are slightly higher than those of Diocletian's *Edict*.[29] No doubt prices continued to rise rapidly in Palestine—we know them to have done so in Egypt—so that Diocletian's *Edict* would have indeed reduced considerably the *"licentiam pretiorum"* mentioned in his prologue (contra-Mickwitz, as above). Furthermore, we should also bear in mind the change in the gold-silver ratio between Aurelian (7.2:1) and Diocletian's time (14.4:1), which in a way makes for even greater reductions than a comparison of the plain figures themselves might suggest (see above page 55).

Looking back to the Zarai inscription of the beginning of the century, 202,[30] we may reckon that wine and *garum* both cost forty *sestertii* (= ten *denarii*) per *amphora* (= 48 *sextarii*), i.e. about 1/5 *denarius* per pint. This is an African price. One from Egypt, however, probably from the early third century,[31] records that one jar (= *xestes*? or *chous*? = 2.9 litres) of pickled fish cost one *drachma* 1½ *obols* (= 5/12 *denarius*).[32] The Zarai tariff price reduced to a fraction of the *aureus* comes to 1/123 *aureus*. Thus, the so-called enormous price-revolution of the (later?) third century when reduced to gold values is seen to be little more than a doubling or trebling of prices until the beginning of the last quarter of the century. Then it would appear that prices climbed quite steeply.[33] Still, the difference between the price 1/5 *denarius* per pint of wine recorded at Zarai in 202, and about eight *denarii* per pint of 301 *(Edict of Diocletian)* is not a forty-fold rise in cost, but almost an identical price (1/500 *aureus* difference), when reckoned in terms of gold (1/123 *aureus*, Zarai, 1/100 *aureus*, Edict of Diocletian). In fact, it corresponds exactly to the fall in value of the *denarius* in relation to the *aureus*: 25:1, about 200; 800:1 about 300; 25:800 = 1:40.[34]

CHAPTER XIX

CIRCULATION

Out of our examination of third century prices, two points of significance have emerged, both of which require some further consideration.
(a) We noted that though the actual currency started depreciating already
early in the century, prices did not rise radically until some time around
the 270's.[1] (b) When these prices did rise, they did so primarily in terms
of debased silver. In terms of gold, however, prices did *not* change
radically.[2]

The first observation poses something of a problem. The second, left
as it stands, gives a one-sided view of the situation. To complete this part
of the picture, we must first know more as to the relative amounts of
copper, debased silver and gold circulating. Thus, if neither gold nor
pure silver were actually available, people would have to buy and pay in
debased silver and copper, or whatever else was in circulation, so that
even if prices had not radically changed in terms of gold, they would
still be paying out more coins for their purchases. This, in turn, would
not necessarily have any serious adverse effect on the "man in the
street" so long as the government and the banks were willing to exchange silver and gold for the right number of debased units—at the
market-values[3]—and that his wages went up[4] in a ratio equal to the fall
in value of the coins in which he was being paid. Or, as West puts it:[5]

As long as conversion into coins of some more valuable metal
was readily possible, it made no difference in the value of the
subsidiary coinage whether it was pure silver, or a piece of paper
with no intrinsic value. Subsidiary coinages acquired a value of
their own only when their value as bullion exceeded the value
assigned to them by the mint; and under such conditions, they
would not be minted.

Bearing in mind these considerations, we may now reconsider our first point, and the question it appears to pose. Here, a number of factors are of importance. These we shall discuss in the following pages.

(1) We have tried to demonstrate above that until the end of Gallienus' reign, the relationship between the *antoninianus* and the *aureus* was kept more or less steady (at about 25:1). Only towards the end of his reign are we witness to the complete collapse of this "classical" system ,and the extreme debasement of the *antoninianus*.

(2) At the same time, it is clear that already in the earlier part of the century there was a strong desire for a stable currency in plentiful amounts. This is surely the meaning of the tremendous boom in the production of copper coins by the local mints. A few examples of this should suffice to delineate the main tendency. Caesarea Maritima minted in the last nine years of its 186 years of minting history (244-53) 53% of all its production.[6] 41% of all coins issued at Akko Ptolemais during 207 years were struck from 224-68.[7] In Aelia Capitolina[8] 94 out of a total 207 types (from Hadrian onwards) were produced between the years 218-60. Carson[9] estimates the following proportions of second and third century coinage (and here it should be borne in mind that minting in the third century continued for no more than 60 odd years):

Syria	Antioch	1:5
	Emesa	1:2
	Gabala	1:3
Phoenicia	Berytus	1:3
	Byblus	1:10
	Ptolemais Ace	1:10
	Sidon	1:8
	Tripolis	1:3

For Asia Minor, C. Bosch[10] calculates the following ratios for relative quantities of coinage circulating in the second and third centuries:

Ephesus	3:14
Smyrna	5:10
Nicaea	5:14
Ancyra	1:14
Tarsus	5:58
Perge	2:34

Probably more detailed analysis would reveal that in all these cases the major rise in mint production came during the last two or three decades before the mints closed.

It is no mere coincidence that this tremendous boom in the production of copper came just at the time when the *antoninianus* was rapidly depreciating in value. It surely reflects a rising demand for a stable currency, which indeed the copper coinage was.[11]

Why then did this local production come to an end around the middle of the third century? (See Table I end of chapter.) It is clear that there was no imperial edict ordering the closure of these local mints,[12] for they do not all stop their activities at the same time. There are in fact some half a dozen instances of cities in Pamphylia and Pisidia issuing local bronze coins as late as Claudius II (268-70), Aurelian (270-75), and in one case Tacitus (275-76).[13] It seems probable that it gradually became less economic for the cities to produce the local bronze pieces as the *antoninianus* dropped in value. Or, in other words, "their value as bullion (now) exceeded the value assigned to them by the mint, and under such conditions they would not be minted". The fact that the modules tend to get larger in the middle of the third century (see below, Chapter XXII) may well be a sign of copper inflation and not of prosperity.[14] Certainly by the end of Aurelian's reign it would hardly have been worthwhile issuing local bronze denominations.[15] For if, as we have suggested, his pre-reform *antoninianus* was worth 1/500 *aureus*, it was equal to 1/20 of an old *denarius*, i.e. less than an *as* (= 1/16 *denarius*). Even in his post-reform system the *antoninianus* (= 1/250 *aureus*) would have been 1/10 of an old *denarius*, i.e. less than a *dupondius* (a piece of about $8\frac{1}{2}$ grammes—Elagabalus, or 12 grammes—Caracalla).[16]

Furthermore, there was by now no real need for locally produced small change, since the imperial mints were producing what, in effect, served as small change. Formerly the local mints had gained a regular income on the exchange between local and imperial currency, as their rates were always calculated to be to their advantage.[17] The cessation of a need for this exchange brought about a real loss to the income of the cities. Why some cities did, nevertheless, continue issuing bronze is still something of a puzzle, but there may have been localized reasons for this—perhaps strong conservative traditions.

This local copper coinage had undoubtedly acted as a (partially) stabilizing influence (at least) during the earlier part of the century, and the extent of its increase, most especially in the 240's, is clearly indicative of the strong demand for a stable currency. Thus, confidence in the *antoninianus* must have been wavering very considerably. (Hence, the premium on gold noted above.) When this source of "stable currency" dried up, it should have been matched by comparable emissions of some equally stable currency—in gold. The fact that there is no evidence of an "absolute shortage of gold during Gallienus' period" is not enough.[18] In order to satisfy the obvious demand for stable currency, there should have been a significant rise in gold emission and circulation, relatively comparable to the bronze boom. But there is no evidence that this was the case.

(3) Furthermore, yet another potentially stabilizing element had been taken off the market. For up to the middle of the third century, alongside the official debased currency, earlier, fuller-value *denarii* were used. How extensive was this use is not clear. However, the effects of the government policy of about 250, to demonetize and buy up all such earlier silver in circulation, must have been felt on the market.

In order to prove this last point we shall have to make something of a side-excursion into the realms of hoard-evidence, and to examine certain legal texts from which this phenomenon of demonetization during the 250's may be deduced.

First of all, it should be noted that while we have literary evidence that early Imperial, and even Republican, coins were called in by Trajan in the beginning of the second century, early silver coins survived in quite a number of hoards all over Europe until as late as the third century.[19] There are three possible interpretations of this phenomenon: (a) the coins were officially demonetized (declared no longer legal tender) with their withdrawal in the early second century—and hoarded for their bullion value; (b) they were bought up by the government, but not demonetized until the third century—and hoarded as legal tender; or (c) they were gathered in by the government in the second century and never demonetized—and went out of circulation by the later third century.

Now it is known that Trajan introduced certain monetary reforms, probably some time around 100, minting new *denarii* of a slightly lower standard than those of Domitian and Nerva, and debasing them a further 15% (so that they vary from 88%-79% in purity).[20] It is also known from Dio Cassius (*Roman History* 68.15.3) that in the year 107 Trajan had his mint gather in coins of (full weight and?) good silver for profitable recoining. These coins were, however, badly worn: τὸ νόμισματα τα πάν το ἐξίτηλον ἐξεχώνευσε (Dio Cassius, ibid.). Analysis of a considerable number of hoards led West to further define this "ingathering" of the old worn coins in the following manner:

135

It seems clear that what Trajan did in 107 was to call in all the silver coins issued by Augustus, Tiberius, Caligula and Claudius. . . The *denarii* issued by Nero before 63 were also called in(?). . . the inference from twenty-seven hoards is that gold struck before the reform of Nero was likewise called in.[21] (See Table H, pages 138-139.)

However, the question that still remains is whether or not Trajan officially demonetized the earlier coins. Mattingly states:

It seems clear that in 107 the pre-Neronian coinage of gold and silver, so far as it survived Nero, was definitely withdrawn—probably demonetized by an Edict or at least treated as invalid.[22]

Hoard analysis, on the other hand, suggests otherwise: that they were indeed withdrawn, but *not* officially demonetized.

Roman sources appear to be silent on this whole issue of demonetization.

However, some hitherto unexploited Talmudic texts may cast further light upon this problem. For in Jewish law it was important to know what constituted legal-tender ("coin") and what constituted that which was no longer legal-tender and merely bullion ("produce"),[23] since one might substitute the Second Tithe by "coin" alone, and not by "produce". Now in Tosefta Ma'aser Sheni[AH] 1.6 we read:

If he had coins of [Bar-] Koziba (i.e. of the Bar-Kochba uprising)[24] or coins of Jerusalem (i.e. coins of the first Jewish revolt of 66-70 bearing the legend "Jerusalem the holy") he may not substitute [the Second Tithe] by them. . . but coins of the first kings which are current (i.e. not too worn, etc.), one may substitute [the Second Tithe] by them.[25]

We learn from this text that revolt money, though of pure silver, could not be used for substitution, as it was obviously not legal tender (i.e. it was not "coin", but "produce"). However, coins of the "first kings" could be used for substitution as long as they were current and acceptable (i.e. not too worn to be marketable);[26] hence they must have been considered legal tender. It seems most likely that these "first kings" are those late Republican rulers (especially Anthony) and Augustus, who are represented in post-Trajanic hoards.[27] At this stage then, sometime after 135, there had not been any official demonetization of early Imperial coinage. The reference to the ill-fated Bar-Kochba uprising of 132-35, is further evidence that the text post-dates 135. In other words,

136

this text, formulated after Trajan's reign and monetary reform, suggests that Trajan made no edict declaring early Imperial money invalid.

We may see a further stage of a natural development reflected in another Talmudic text, Yerushalmi Ma'aser Sheni[AI] 1.1:

> A coin that has gone out of use (she-nifsal)[28] and the government accepts it—R. Jose in the name of R. Jonathan (floruit circa 135-70) [says]: "It is like asemon" (i.e. bullion, and one may not substitute by it, as it is no longer coin). R. Ḥiyya in the name of (the same) R. Jonathan [says]: "It is like the coin of the first kings" (and one may substitute by it).[29]

It follows from the fact that one may substitute by coins of the "first kings" that they are still legal tender. They are, however, likened to coins "that have gone out of use". This, then, appears to have been the situation during the middle or later second century; namely, that late Republican and early Imperial currency had partially gone out of circulation (partly due to government withdrawal, partly to hoarding, no doubt), but that the government would still accept surviving coins as money.[30]

A final stage in this development may be deduced from a text in the Babylonian Talmud discussing the same topic. In Bavli Bava Kama[AJ] 97b we read:

> Rava asked R. Naḥman (both are early fourth-century Babylonian personalities): "[We have learned]: One may not substitute [the Second Tithe] by coins that are not current (énan yotz'ot). How so? If he had money of [Bar]-Koziba, of Jerusalem, or of the first kings, one (= he) may not substitute [the Second Tithe] by them. . ."

Here the criterion for "currentness' is the coins' acceptability as legal tender. The coinage of both "Jerusalem" and "[Bar]-Koziba" was not "current" because it was illegal revolt-issue. And here, in this last text, the coins of the "first kings" are equated with those of the first and the second revolts. Evidently, by this time Republican and early Imperial coinage had been completely and officially demonetized.

Now this text presents certain difficulties. For it is in its literary form a beraita (i.e. a Tannaitic text), and should therefore have a terminus ante quem of about 220. Yet hoard-analysis betrays no evidence of a sudden absence or withdrawal of Republic and early Imperial coinage until the reign of Valerian (253-60).[31] (See below Table H.) The answer

137

TABLE H

	Maximinus	Gordian III	Philip	Decius	Trebonianus Volusianus	Valerian	Gallienus	Claudius	Aurelian	Tacitus	Probus	Carus	Diocletian
Diocletian													6700
British													903
Carinus												1	3809
Carus													1322
Probus													13499
Florianus										1	5		576
Tacitus									659	1	62		2937
Aurelian									11334	1037	4276	26	11791
Tetricus								137	8075	236	2789	23	16955
Claudius							3900	2631	2783	1055	686	10	13453
Victorinus							1665	1348	7030	107	2627	36	5633
Gallienus						109	1820	1652	2426	1229	52	11	12796
Postumus						1	124	841	281	23	1	2	472
Valerian						33	1643	5		16			86
Aemilianus					32	33	2614	188		2			1
Volusianus					80	73	5712	269	3				5
Trebonianus				1671	1143	229	12334	220	2			3	13
Decius				522	813	278	15473	368	2				15
Philip			267	1025	925	3	108	371	5			1	29
Gordian III		60	332	28	2		3						47
Balbinus etc.		4	7	2									
Gordian I, II		2											

Maximinus	122	115	16	1867	55	26	86	3					5
Alexander	574	269	460	9033	101	853	378	39					30
Elagabalus	458	142	283	6344	128	216	471	11	1				28
Macrinus	115	14	8	440	38	58	13	4					1
Caracalla	813	182	97	6525	63	2233	245						13
Septimius	1061	361	233	13640		3089	197						12
Albinus	7	5	2	200		5	4						
Didius	2			16		1							
Pertinax	6	2		57	6		6	9					
Commodus	125	175	10	3749	4	8		8				1	1
Marcus	231	354	8	13838	3	2	1	5					
Pius	220	271	2	12200				1					
Hadrian	113	140		6689									
Trajan	62	66		5234	1								
Nerva	6	7		323	1								
Domitian	33	6		633									
Titus	22	5		445									
Vespasian	48	35	1	1731									
Vitellius	4	1		134									
Otho		1		47									
Galba	1	2		50									
Nero	6	2		102									
Republic				29									
Totals	4029	2221	1726	86574	3395	7251	46797	8111	32601	3707	10498	113	91132

Grand Total 298155

139

to this apparent anomaly lies in the complex history of the literary transmission of Palestinian texts to Babylonia. For it has long been demonstrated that when Palestinian traditions were transmitted to Babylonia, the Babylonian recipients were often uncertain as to whether the text received was of Tannaitic or Amoraic authority (i.e. pre- or post- 220).[32] Furthermore, it is known that there are late *beraitot*, i.e. texts that are cast in a Tannaitic style, but are of Amoraic composition.[33] Finally, it has been amply demonstrated that the professional memorisers of Tannaitic texts during the Amoraic period frequently embellished, or altered, the original texts to suit their time, changed conditions, or perhaps for harmonistic reasons.[34] Much of this "editing", "composition" and "alteration" went on during the later third century when Palestinian material was brought over to Babylonia by the *"Neḥuté"* (=professional emissaries), like Ulla (*floruit* second half of the third century) and others.[35]

In our own case, Rava (299-352), a Babylonian, is citing an obviously Palestinian text, and not the text we know from the Tosefta (the first text we cited above). Furthermore, the anonymity of this text suggests that it is one of the "later type".[36] It seems likely that Rava was drawing (unwittingly, no doubt) upon a post-Tosefta (i.e. post-220) text, a modification of the original Tosefta made to suit the newly changed circumstances of the middle third century. By this time the coins of the "first kings" were no longer legal tender.

To sum up: Talmudic sources suggest that Trajan did not demonetize by edict pre-Neronian coinage (although he did gather it in, see above), and that though it became ever scarcer during the course of the second century, the government was always willing to accept it as legal tender. It apparently continued to have this status throughout the first half of the third century until some time around 250-60, when it was officially demonetized, and thus ceased to be regarded as "coin" in Jewish law.[38] The government probably bought them up and presumably set some kind of premium on them, else they would all have been melted down to bullion. Whatever actually happened, the effect must have been to take out of circulation completely a (perhaps small, but surely significant) monetary element which could otherwise have served as a stable (and stabilizing) currency-core.[39]

Thus, by the end of Gallienus' reign, several factors combined together to destroy all possible vestiges of confidence in the *antoninianus*, the only coin, practically speaking, in circulation. And though it is true that there may have been a theoretical right to change *antoniniani* into *aurei*, the fact that "in comparison with the issues of subsidiary silver during the third century, the issues of gold seem infinitesimal"[40] meant "the resultant loss of any practical possibility of conversion from silver to gold".[41] This and other factors "brought about a commercial valuation of this subsidiary coinage that differed from the governmental valuation".[42]

The cessation of the activities of local mints, the extreme debasement of the *antoninianus*, coupled with the practical inability of the majority of the population to lay its hands upon stable gold currency, meant the virtual breakdown of the money economy from the later 260's onwards. The socio-economic effects of this breakdown were of deep and widespread significance. In several sectors of economic activity there was a partial reversion to natural economy. For example, the patterns of taxation change during this time from money taxation to taxation in kind. And this in turn has serious sociological repercussions, bringing about alterations in the structure of the rural agrarian community.

It was to remedy these problems that Diocletian instituted his currency reforms and his "prices and incomes" policy. And he had a certain measure of success. For, as we have seen above (page 94), he did restore a relatively stable money economy with his abundant issues of good silver and gold. His handling of the prices problem is somewhat more problematic; we shall return to this issue below.

The pattern of monetary development during the third century that emerges from this chapter is one of an initial expansion of the money market (mainly) with local copper coinage, followed by a sudden contraction of this same market (due to the cessation of the local mints' activities, plus the demonetization of earlier silver still circulating). This same pattern may be seen reflected in a contemporary halachic statement. Tannaitic law (Bavli Bava Batra 91a, Bavli Ta'anit 19b) teaches that: "One may not leave Palestine for abroad except when [wheat] reaches [the price of] two *se'ahs* for a *sela*" (a very high price). Upon this ruling R. Johanan (died in 279) makes the following comment (Bavli Bava Batra 91b, Bavli Ta'anit ibid.):

> This is so when money is cheap and produce is expensive. But when money is expensive, even if [the price of wheat] stood at [as little as] four *se'ahs* for a *sela*, one may leave [Palestine].

Now R. Johanan is here describing two situations: (a) when money is cheap and (food) prices are high, and (b) when money is dear and (food) prices low. The first situation is a result of the expansion of the money market (a flood of new currency), which in turn pushes down the value of the coins (inflation). This has the further effect of forcing up prices, since the increased volume of currency circulating creates a greater demand for consumer goods. The second situation is the result of a reduction in the volume of coin circulating, which conversely forces up the value of money, and at the same time brings down prices.

R. Johanan, in describing these situations, was undoubtedly basing himself upon personal experience. For he himself says (ibid.):

> I recall when [wheat] was four *se'ahs* for a *sela,* and yet in *Tiberias* many people were swollen with hunger for lack of money (literally: an *issar*).

The end of Tiberias' copper coinage came during the reign of Elagabalus (218-22, see Table I).[43] The consequent sudden absence of coin brought a decrease in demand for goods, causing a drop in prices. Nonetheless, people could still not afford to buy bread for lack of money. The sight of the throngs of starving people with their swollen bellies unable to buy the cheap bread readily available in the market-place, must have made a strong impact upon the young Johanan. For these memories of the post-twenties were still vivid in his mind when he reported them, probably some time during the 260's.[44]

Situations such as this, coupled with the ever-increasing burdens of taxation, form the background against which we may more fully understand yet another statement of this same period, i.e. the third quarter of the third century. For in *Canticles Rabba* 2.5[45] R. Levi somewhat sadly recalls:

> In the past, when money (literally: the *pruta*) was to be found, people were eager to listen to lessons in Mishna, Halacha and Talmud. But now that money (literally: the *pruta*) is no longer to be found, and they suffer so much from the affliction (=taxation), they wish only to hear words of blessing and comfort.

Inflation, taxation, and poverty, these elements form the key-notes in the mood of the third century.[46]

TABLE I

End of City Coinage in Palestine

	(a) Galilee	
Diocaesarea	Elagabalus	218–22
Tiberias	,,	,,
	(b) Samaria	
Casesarea	Trebonianus Gallus	251–53
Neopolis	,, ,,	,,
Nysa-Scythopolis	Gordian III	238–44
Sebaste	Elagabalus	218–22
	(c) Judaea	
Aelia Capitolina	Valerian	253–60
Ascalon	Maximinus	235–38
Gaza	Elagabalus	218–22
Raphia	Philip I	244–49

End of City Coinage in Syria

	(a) Commagene	
Samosata	Philip I	244–49
Zeugma	,,	,,
	(b) Cyrrhestica	
Beroea	Macrinus	217–18
Cyrrhus	Philip I	244–49
Hieropolis	,,	,,
	(c) Seleucis and Pieria	
Antioch	Uranius Antoninus	253–54
Emesa	,,	,,
Gabala	Macrinus	217–18
Laodicea ad Mare	Trebonius Gallus	251–53
Nicopolis	Philip I	244–49
Seleucia Pieria	Severus Alexander	222–35
	(d) Coele Syria	
Damascus	Valerian I	253–60
Helipolis	Gallienus	253–69
Leucas	Gordian III	238–44
	(e) Trachonitis	
Casarea Panias	Diadumenian	218

End of City Coinage in Phoenicia

Aradus	Gordian III	238–44
Berytus	Gallienus	253–68
Botrys	"	"
Byblus	Elagabalus	218–22
Caesarea ad Libanum	"	"
Plolemais Ace	Gallienus	253–68
Sidon	Severus Alexander	222–35
Tripolis	" "	"
Tyre	Gallienus	253–68

CHAPTER XX

BABYLONIAN PRICE-LEVELS

It may be of interest briefly to compare our price-lists with comparable material coming from an area outside the confines of the Roman Empire, and yet, geographically near at hand. The Babylonian Talmud affords us information which fulfils just these requirements, namely, prices from the Persian Empire of the third and fourth centuries.

We now, therefore, turn our attention to the East, to take a very cursory glance at the Babylonian material assembled above. However, to compare Palestinian or Roman prices of the third or fourth century with contemporary (or near contemporary) ones from Babylonia introduces added complications. We have some Babylonian prices from the mid-third century onwards, that is, from the period of the Sasanian dynasty. These prices are usually reckoned in *"zuzim"* which were Sasanian *drachms*.[1] We do not know the ratio of silver to gold in the Persian Empire,[2] so that all comparisons with Roman prices must be in terms of silver.

Now the Sasanian *drachm* was a relatively stable coin, of very high (almost completely pure) silver content. Its average weight from about 211 to 420 was around 3.8 grammes.[3] In the time of Diocletian, the Roman *denarius*, on the other hand, had only about .08 grammes silver. (The *follis*, worth five *denarii* [18] weighed ten grammes and had a silver content of around 8%.) Thus we may say that a Sasanian *drachm* equalled approximately 40 Diocletian *denarii* (42.5, more exactly). With this information, we may now try to compare some of our Babylonian prices[4] with those of the *Edict of Diocletian*, but here again—and it cannot be too often stressed—we are comparing two different classes of prices (that is, Diocletian's are *maximum* prices; our equivalences of measures of capacity—*se'ah* = *griva* = *modius castrensis*[5]—cannot be more than very approximate, etc.). Given these reservations, we may nonetheless reach certain general (and tentative) conclusions.

145

Wheat

According to the *Edict of Diocletian* 1.1,[6] one *modius castrensis* wheat cost 100 *denarii*. This in terms of pure silver would be about eight grammes, or a little over two *drachms*. The Babylonian prices that we have for wheat are as follows:

A. 220/50 Bavli Bava Mezia 102b
    1 *se'ah* (=*mod. castr.*):   1 *sela* (=4 d.)

B. 250/97 Bavli Sota 48a
    1 *se'ah* wheat: 1 *drachm*
    100 geese: 1 *drachm* (very cheap)
    Then 1 goose: 1 *drachm* (very expensive)
    (Presumably, 1 *se'ah* wheat: 1 *drachm*, example
    of exaggerated extremes also)[6a]

C. 290/320 Bavli Pesaḥim 32a
    1 griva (=*se'ah*) wheat: 1-4 *drachms*
                                      (perhaps theoretical)

D. 320/339 Bavli Bava Mezia 65a
    4 *griva* wheat: 1 *drachm*

Unfortunately, this information is not susceptible of very satisfactory analysis. Two prices (A and C), spaced well apart in time (but we do not know from which season they come), suggest prices higher than that of the *Edict of Diocletian*. The first price (A) is suspect as it uses Palestinian terminology (*sela*), and is probably merely following the Palestinian (Mishnaic) formulation. The other two prices (B and D), on the other hand, suggest prices lower than that of the *Edict of Diocletian*.

Silk

According to the *Edict of Diocletian* 23.1[7] silk costs 1200 *denarii*. That, in terms of grammes of silver is 960 grammes silver, which is roughly 250 *drachms*. This may perhaps be compared with the price given in Bavli Kiddushin 7b about (290-320), according to which a bundle of silk costs 50 *drachms*. We do not unfortunately, know how large this bundle was, but it is unlikely to have been less than half a pound in weight—a minimum. So that however we take this evidence, it seems clear that the Babylonian price is considerably lower than the Roman one.[8]

Clothing

The evidence for clothing is similarly ambiguous. According to several fourth century Babylonian sources, a cloak cost about four *drachms*.[9] That translated into Diocletian *denarii* is about 160 *denarii*. In chapter 19[10] of the *Edict* (of those where the prices survive), there is not a single item of clothing, and certainly no cloaks of so low a price. In fact, all the cloaks, bar the African ones (line 61, costing 500 *denarii*) cost well over 1000 *denarii*.[11] Thus, the Babylonian prices undoubtedly represent a far lower price-level.

Geese

The price of a goose by itself is given in Bavli Ḥulin 49a as one *drachm* (= 40 Diocletian *denarii*), while according to the *Edict* 4. 21, 22[12] a goose, fattened, cost 200 *denarii*; not fattened, 100 *denarii*. Here again, the Babylonian price is considerably lower.

Figs

The evidence for figs is highly ambiguous. According to the *Edict of Diocletian* 6.85[13] one pint of pressed Carian figs cost four *denarii*. There are 32 *sextarii* in a *modius castrensis*, so that one *modius castrensis* of these pressed figs would cost 128 *denarii*. According to Bavli Pesaḥim 2a and Bavli Eruvin 29a, one *griva* (=*modius castrensis*) of dried figs cost (about 290-320) one *drachm* (=40 Diocletian *denarii*)— again much less than the Roman price.

Grapes

On the other hand, grapes seem to have cost far more in Babylonia than in the West. The *Edict of Diocletian* 6.80[14] gives the price of table grapes, hard-fleshed or long, as four *denarii* for four pounds, while according to Bavli Pesaḥim 113a (about 220-50), an admittedly expensive bunch of grapes cost one *drachm* (=40 Diocletian *denarii)*. And a bunch of grapes would hardly weigh forty pounds!

Wine

The evidence for wine is so unclear as not to permit even of these tentative conclusions. The prices we have listed in our price-lists above vary from one to six *drachms* per barrel. In one case (Bavli Bava Mezia 40a) we know that a barrel (*danna*) containing 48 *kuzé* cost six *drachms*. The *danna* was large. (The Dura *danna* of wine, quoted above,[15] costing 28 *denarii* 11 *assaria,* is evidence of the large size.) If

147

the *kuzé* was a pint, then each *kuza*-pint would have cost about five Diocletian *denarii*. In fact, the cheapest wine recorded in the *Edict* costs eight *denarii* per pint.[16] However, there are too many points of uncertainty in this conjectural calculation for it to be of any real value.[17]

Cucumbers

The price of cucumbers in Babylonia and the West seems to be very similar. Bavli Pesaḥim 113a states that 100 cucumbers cost one *drachm* (cheap) (40 Diocletian *denarii*). Thus ten cucumbers cost four *denarii*. According to the *Edict of Diocletian* 6.28, 29, ten cucumbers of the first size cost four *denarii*, and twenty of a smaller size cost four *denarii*.

Wages

A text in Bavli Bava Mezia 76a, unfortunately undated (also, ibid. 75b) informs us that the wage of a worker per day was three to four *drachms* (=120-160 Diocletian *denarii*). This represents a considerably lower level than that suggested by the *Edict*, chapter 7,[19] where the average is nearer to fifty *denarii* per day (lines 1b-5, 7, 10-12, 14, 30, 49, 64-66, 69, etc.).[20]

Dates

There is some information on dates (e.g. Bavli Pesaḥim 32a, one *griva* of dates cost four *drachms;* Bavli Pesaḥim 88a, three baskets of dates cost one *drachm*), but it is difficult to compare it with that of the *Edict*, chapter 6.81-83,[21] where we are told that 25 (ordinary) dates cost four *denarii*. However, it is clear from Bavli Pesaḥim, ibid. (and Bavli Ta'anit 29b) that dates were far cheaper in Babylonia than they were in Palestine.[22] It is also known from Rabbinic sources (Yerushalmi Ma'aser Sheni 4.1, and concerning figs Bavli Berachot 62b) that dates were cheaper in Palestine than in Rome.

The general upshot of what we have seen above seems to be that, on the whole, Babylonian price-levels were considerably lower than those of the *Edict*. If we are correct in suggesting that Diocletian's *Edict* (of *Maximum* prices) did, in fact, (attempt to) bring down (even) current (Palestinian) prices, then these Babylonian prices will have been even lower than contemporary Palestinian ónes. However, as we have seen, the material is by no means clear and our conclusions therefore are full of uncertainties.

CHAPTER XXI

FOURTH CENTURY: REASONABLE PRICES

The preceding chapters dealt primarily with third century price-levels. Let us now turn to a consideration of fourth century prices and price-levels.

In Yerushalmi Bava Mezia[AK] 5.6 we read that :

> R. Aba ben Zemina gave one [gold] *dinar* (=*aureus* or *solidus*) to a baker, and received from him [bread] the whole year round at a cheap rate (literally: at the cheap[est?] hour of the whole year),[1] ולא מודי רב (literally:) and Rav did not agree.

We know little of R. Aba ben Zemina's biography.[2] But we do know that he was a pupil of R. Zera I, and never once quotes R. Johanan or Resh Lakish directly. When he does quote R. Eleazer, it is via the medium of the traditionary R. Oshiah.[3] Thus he probably was born after 270, and functioned about 310 to 350.

It is clear that the reading ולא מודי לרב cannot be correct, as Rav (died 248) could hardly be said not to agree with the opinions of someone living about a century later. Thus, though no variant reading is recorded for this text either in manuscripts or printed editions,[4] we feel that Z.W. Rabinowitz's[5] correction ולא מודי לרב —and [in this] he did not agree with Rav's opinion (earlier in the same section)—is absolutely necessary and correct.

In the East, the *aureus* (1/60 *libra aurei*) continued to be struck until 324, and only after that date was the *solidus* (1/72 *libra aurei*) introduced. Hence, in our case it is difficult to know whether *"dinar"* refers to the *solidus* (the text being post-324) or the *aureus* (the text being pre-324).

In Mishnaic times a loaf of bread had cost around 1/12 *denarius*, and there had been 25 *denarii* to the *aureus*, so that, at a loaf of bread per day, a year's[6] bread would come to around 1 1/5 *aureus*. Thus, if

R. Aba ben Zemina paid an *aureus* for a year's bread at a cheap rate, or even a *solidus*—one-sixth less—this would presuppose an average (higher) rate of about 1 1/3 *aurei* or 1½ *solidi*, or a little more. (See above, page 113 that the maximum profit that the bakers made was one-third. The price variation throughout the year would probably not be much greater.)

Thus, in the first half of the fourth century the price of bread, when paid (or reckoned) in gold, was not much different to that of the first or second centuries.[7]

Similarly, we have seen above that around 340-60, one *modius Italicus* of wheat cost around 1/25 *solidus*, and one *modius castrensis* about 1/12 *solidus*. This, in terms of first and second century money would be equal to about 1/10 *aureus*, or approximately 2½ *denarii* per *modius castrensis* (= *se'ah*). Here again the price of wheat in terms of gold is fairly similar to that of the second century. Furthermore, it is somewhat below the *maximum* price given in the *Edict of Diocletian*, of 301 (1.1), according to which one *modius castrensis* of wheat cost 100 *denarii* (= 1/8 *aureus*).

At this point we should attempt to assess the abnormally high famine price of wheat recorded by Eusebius (*Historia Ecclesiastica* 9.8.4) for the year 312-13.[8] According to this source, 2500 Attic *drachmas* (= *denarii*)[9] were given for ἑνὸς μέτρου πυρῶν which the Syriac text more explicitly states to have been חד מודיא (one *modius*).[10] In the year 313-14 there were about 7116 *denarii* to the *aureus*,[11] so that Eusebius' famine price was approximately 1/3 *aureus* per *modius* [*castrensis*?], not even three times as high as the maximum price given in the *Edict of Diocletian*. The Talmud speaks on more than one occasion of famines that raised the price of wheat to some four times the normal cost.[12] This was a particularly bad famine, and during that year

> some, indeed, did not hesitate to barter their dearest possessions for the scantiest supply of food with those better provided ; others sold off their goods little by little and were driven to the last extremity of want... and as for the women, some well-born ladies in cities were driven by their want to shameless necessity, and went forth to beg in the market-places, displaying a proof of their noble upbringing in their shamefacedness, and the decency of their apparel.[13]

Had this been a normal year, the prices may well have been at least four times as low, i.e. 600 *denarii* per *modius* [*castrensis*] of wheat, and perhaps even lower, which is a little more than twice as much as the current wheat price in Egypt.[14] We have shown above that the price-relationship between one *modius castrensis* of wheat and one loaf of bread is approximately 12:1. If we further accept (as suggested above, page 121) that one pound of meat cost as much as one loaf of bread during this period too, then about 312 one pound of meat would have cost approximately forty *denarii*. This is very close to both the Yerushalmi's price and that of *P. Rylands* which we have seen above was fifty *denarii* per pound.

But again, returning to prices in gold, in Yerushalmi Bava Mezia[AL] 4.1 we read:

> R. Mana said: "... A man who said to his neighbour, 'I wish to sell my cow'. He said to him, 'For how much?' 'For eight [gold] *dinars*', he replied. He went and deposited it with a money-changer.[15] In the morning he was passing by when he found him standing there. 'What are you doing here?' he asked him. 'I want to take my money (literally: *dinars)* which I deposited [here, yesterday]'. 'What do you want to buy yourself with them?' he asked. 'A donkey', he replied. 'Your donkey is with me',[16] he responded (meaning I have just the donkey you require. Buy yourself my donkey...)".[17]

According to the correction of the *Pnei Moshe*,[18] the beginning of this passage should read: א"ר מנא: אית הכי מילי דיודי ר' בא לר' יוסי ;our text has: א"ר מנא: אית הכי מילי דיודי בה רבי יוסי. Thus, the R. Mana mentioned in this text must be R. Mana II, who lived after R. Ba.[19] Once again, we know little of the exact chronology of his life, but he was the son of R. Jona, who was certainly alive in the 350's,[20] and thus, R. Mana II probably functioned around 350-70.[21] According to this text, thus dated around 350-70, a cow (and a donkey) cost eight *solidi*, which was quite a reasonable price to pay for a cow (see price lists above). Once again, therefore, we find that in terms of gold, a fourth century price is very comparable with that of the two preceding centuries.

In *Codex Theodosianus* 8.4.17 of 389(?), in an order to Cynegius Praetorian Prefect of the Orient, we find that eighty pounds of pork are valued at one *solidus* (one pound of pork cost 1/80 *solidus*).[22] In second century terms that was about ¼ *denarius* per pound. Pork was slightly more expensive than beef,[23] and the price of beef may have been as much as one third less, i.e. about 1/6 *denarius* (one pound of beef cost 1/100-1/120 *solidus*). This is about twice as much as in the second century, but here again we must bear in mind (a) that prices of pork varied from year to year,[24] and (b) that in the *Codex* we are dealing with official government rates of payment to soldiers (to the border militia in this case) and we do not as yet know the relationship between this kind of price and ordinary civilian market rates.[25]

So far, these few sources seem to indicate that prices, when reckoned in terms of gold, had not gone up radically in comparison with second century costs. We turn now to the few sources we have (some of which we have analysed above) recording fourth century prices in terms of debased bronze currency.

According to the *Edict of Diocletian* of 301 (4.1a, 2), beef cost eight *denarii* per pound and pork twelve *denarii* per pound, i.e. 1/100 and 1/66 *aureus* (at 800 *denarii* per *aureus*), or 1/88 and 1/55 *solidus* (at 666 *denarii* per *solidus*), which is a little more expensive than the price of 389 (above).

We have seen above that around 290-350 (probably about 320), one loaf of bread, one pint of wine and one pound of meat cost ten *follarin* each.[26] We have also suggested that one *follarin* or *follis* equals five *denarii* there,[27] and that the price of these commodities was fifty *denarii*. This agrees with the price of one pound of meat recorded in Yerushalmi Berachot 2.8 (fifty *maneh*)—of about 324—which we have shown to be fifty *denarii*. Furthermore, according to R. *Rylands* (see above) the average costs of one *xestes* (=pint) of wine and one pound of meat (perhaps pork?) was 75-100 *denarii*, around 317-24 (nearer to 324, as we have suggested).

Now according to P. *Oxyrhynchus* 1430, one pound of gold was valued at somewhat more than 300,000 *denarii* in 324. This gives a *solidus* of (more than?) 4166 *denarii*, or 4320 *denarii* according to another reckoning, (and an *aureus* of about 5000 *denarii*).[28] According to this, the price of one pound of meat (pork?) about 324 would appear to have been around 1/42-1/56 *solidus*, and perhaps even 1/84 *solidus* (if the *Genesis Rabba* text is of the same date).

We have seen that about 363 bread cost about 1/150 *solidus* for a two-pound loaf (=12 × 1/12½ *solidi*) = 1/124 *aureus*, which is about 6½ *denarii* in Diocletian terms of 800 *denarii* per *aureus*. We have reckoned above that in Diocletian's time a loaf would cost about eight *denarii*. Once again, the Diocletian price is a little higher than those of half a century or more later.

According to *Codex Theodosianus* 14.4.3, in 363 Julian fixed the maximum price of pork at Antioch at six *folles* per pound. Beef, therefore, probably cost around five *folles* per pound (see above). As this price is probably fairly similar to that of bread (a two-pound loaf—see above), five *folles* equalled 1/150 *solidus*, and one *follis* equalled 1/750 *solidus* approximately, around 363.[29]

This is borne out to a certain extent by *Codex Theodosianus* 9.23.1, dated 356. Here, an attempt is made to check speculation in copper coin by prohibiting its transport from place to place, but allowing merchants to carry on their own animals not more than 1000 *folles* for their expenses. Jones writes:[30]

> In this context 1000 *folles* is evidently a very small sum equivalent to 1 or 2 *solidi*; the annual rations of a soldier were commuted for 4 *solidi* (*Nov. Val.* 13.3, of 445), and a merchant even if he had several pack animals and a slave or two, would not have needed half that sum for the expenses of a single journey.

According to our suggestion, 1000 *folles* equals approximately 1½ *solidi*.

In *Codex Theodosianus* 14.4.10 (419, Ravenna) we are told that twenty pounds of pork cost 1000 *denarii*, and that one pound of pork cost fifty *denarii*. We do not know exactly what the *"denarius"* of this text refers to. However, if we assume that here too the pork cost 1/150 *solidus* per pound, then there are 7500 *denarii* per *solidus*, and the *denarius* was 1/10 *follis* in 363. (This is easier than six *follis* = fifty *denarii*, and one *follis* = 8 1/3 *denarii*.)[31]

Maybe the *denarius* here is the same as the *nummus* of *Codex Theodosianus* 14.19.1 (Milan 398). For there we read of Ostian and fiscal bread—we do not know how much—being sold for one *nummus*.[32] Now, according to Valentian's *Novella* 16 (of 445), the banker was required to pay 7000 *nummi* for a *solidus* which he could sell for 7200.[33] It suggests itself that this *nummus* is the same as the *denarius* of 419. This is by no means unlikely as the identification of the *nummus* with the *denarius*[34] is found in papyrological sources, e.g. *PER. E.* 1014, where a pint of relish costs 3T. 150 νοῦμμοι, and *PER. NN.* 117, where the rent of a room is given as χιλίων νουμμίων κέρματος.

CHAPTER XXII

THE BEGGAR'S PENCE: ARGURION

The above evidence shows that prices when reckoned in terms of gold did not rise radically above the levels of the second century, for example. Only when they are expressed in terms of debased currency do they sound so much higher. This means that someone who could afford to pay out in gold currency was less affected by rising costs and inflation that someone who had to pay out in *aes* currency. It was to R. Aba ben Zemina's advantage to pay in *solidi* as it was to the baker's to receive *solidi*. A poor man, however, who had every day to buy his bread with little debased bronze coins would find himself ever more hard-pressed to do so, as his money lost its value. Expressed somewhat differently, we may say that a successful prices policy would have necessitated a strict control over the *aes* currency, and this was in fact lacking throughout much of the fourth century.

This fact, that the man handling *aes* currency was far more adversely affected than someone with silver or gold in his hands, may explain to us certain developments in the Talmudic law of charity. As a point of departure, we shall examine a fourth century Palestinian legal text dealing with this issue, and containing yet another problematic term. In Tosefta Pe'a[AM] 4.8[1] we read:

> One does not give a beggar who is passing from place to place less than one loaf worth a *pundion* (= 1/12 *denarius*) at the rate of four *se'ahs* for a *sela* (see above). If [however] he is wont to go begging from door to door, one gives him nothing (i.e. no money from the קופה של צדקה—Poor-Fund, a communal charity).

The Yerushalmi[AN] (Pe'a 8.7) modifies this latter statement thus:

> All [beggars] that wander from door to door [begging], we do not give them anything (i.e. any charity from the Poor Fund). Said R. Jona (*floruit circa* 320-60): ובלחוד דלא יפחות ליה מן ארגרון[2] דיליה[3]

The meaning of this latter phrase is somewhat uncertain, but most scholars interpret it to mean: "So long as one does not give him less than his ἀργύριον.4 They understand the word *"argurion"* to denote a small coin, and the general burden of R. Jona's statement is that such a beggar should still receive some small charity.

In reaching this interpretation, the commentators were influenced by the BavliᴬᴹÞ (Bava Batra 9a) where we find the following :

> If he goes from door to door [begging], one gives him nothing. A certain poor man, who used to go [begging] from door to door, came before R. Papa (to receive charity from him, as he was in charge of the Poor Fund). He gave him nothing. Said R. Sama bar R. Yeva to R. Papa. "If you, sir, will give him nothing, no one else will give him anything, [and] he will die [of hunger, etc.]". "But", [asked R. Papa in reply,] "have we not learned in a *beraita:* 'If he is a poor man who goes [begging] from door to door, we give him nothing'?" He replied to him, "We do not give him a big present (i.e. a *pundion's* worth of bread), but we do give him a small one."⁵

If this interpretation (that he should receive [from the Poor Fund]⁶ at least an *argurion*) were correct, it would follows that an *argurion* would be worth less than a loaf worth a *pundion* (i.e. the cost of a two-pound loaf, see above). Thus, he may not get the value of a two-pound loaf of bread, but he should at least get an *argurion*. From this it would appear than an *argurion* was worth *less* than the cost of a two-pound loaf of bread.

This can hardly be correct, for we have seen above (page 32) that in the 360's, in Antioch an ἀργύριον (=*siliqua*, 1/24 *solidus*)⁶ would purchase ten two-pound measures μετρα of wheat, equal in price to about five two-pound loaves (see above, page 121). R. Jona lived in Tiberias throughout the first half of the fourth century, and we have seen above (page 33) that around 340 one could (probably) buy, there in Tiberias, 25 *modii (Italici)* of wheat for one *solidus*, and in Sepphoris twenty *modii* per *solidus*. An *argurion*, if it is a *siliqua*, would have purchased about one *modius (Italicus)* of wheat, which would in turn produce about twelve two-pound loaves of bread, but would be equal in value to about six such loaves (taking into account cost of milling, bakers' profits, etc., see above, page 121). Thus an *"argurion"* can hardly be said to be a "small present", and even if this term refers to the smallest silver coin current,[7] it would still be worth much more than one single two-pound loaf of bread.

We would, therefore, like to suggest a different interpretation for R. Jona's statement. The Mishna in Pe'a there (8.7) discusses the question of who is eligible to receive money from the קופה של צדקה —the Poor Fund, or other words: how poor does one have to be to receive such charity. The Mishna answers: "He who has food for fourteen meals (i.e. a week, at two meals per day, or its value in money) may not receive from the [Poor] Fund". Now, we have shown above that a כיבר בפונדיון —a loaf for a *pundion* was a day's ration, i.e. was equal in value to two meals. Therefore, fourteen meals were seven two-pound loaves, or seven *pundions'* (worth of bread). An *argurion*, however, was only worth four to six two-pounds loaves, at the most, (or about 5/6 *pundion*, in Tannaitic terminology), so that a person possessing no more than one *argurion* would certainly have the right to receive charity from the Poor Fund. However, if he wanders from door to door making a living by begging, according to the Tosefta he may not receive anything.[8] But even such a beggar should be entitled to some help, if he cannot by himself earn enough to live on. This, then, is what R. Jona wishes to say, and we would translate his statement thus: such a beggar does not receive charity from the Poor Fund "as long as he does not have (i.e. at the end of a day's work) less than an *argurion*". But if he does have less than this amount, he may claim from the Poor-Fund charity to supplement his earnings. It would appear that R. Jona, who had many dealings with the poor, knew that at times a beggar could barely eke out a living by begging alone.

The question that immediately calls itself to mind is: why this qualification of R. Jona, which is so clearly absent from the Tosefta (cf. Bavli, ibid.), does not appear earlier in Amoraic *halacha*? Or again, expressed slightly differently, why is it that only in the fourth century, in the time of R. Jona, such a(n obvious) proviso had to be made, and not in the third century? We would suggest that the solution may lie in the evolution and change of the monetary situation during this period.

Let us consider for a moment what sort of money (coins) a beggar would probably receive during these various periods. Assuming that each person would give him the smallest coin then current,[9] we may make an approximate reckoning of how many coins he would need to make up the measure of money that would disallow him any right to the Poor-Fund, i.e. seven *pundions* = 7/12 *denarius*, or 7/300 *aureus*. Let us call this latter sum Q.

According to early Mishnaic reckoning there were 192 *prutas* in a *dinar* (=*denarius*), so that he would need about 100 *prutas* to make up Q.[10] However, elsewhere we have shown that this system refers back to Hasmonean currency, in which the *pruta* was a bronze coin of about two grammes.[11] In the Roman Imperial period, however, the smallest denomination was considerably larger,[12] and though almost nothing is known about local currency systems at this time,[13] it is possible that the minimum denomination current was (approximately) equal to a Roman *quadrans*, i.e. 1/64 *denarius*. Q would then be equal to about 35 coins of minimum size during the second and early third centuries.

Carson notes that towards the middle of the third century and approaching the height of the inflation, the city coinage not only of Asia Minor but also of Syria, Phoenicia and Palestine, too, have larger modules.[14] He argues that it can hardly be a coincidence that these developments take place in a period of inflation. He writes:

> These local bronze coins were originally fiduciary, but while the imperial silver was debased to a point at which it was little better than bronze, the city coinages maintained their metallic value and from the Severan period in many cases increased it by using larger coins.

This suggestion is perhaps borne out in some measure by R. Mana's statement (cited and discussed above, page 78)[15] that "silver stopped in its place, copper went up in price, copper went down in price", which in its context suggests that copper coins went up in value (and were therefore a greater fraction of the *denarius*, rather than that the silver *denarius* went down in value with the same effect). It would appear that some attempt was made to keep a steady relationship between bronze and gold, bypassing the silver currency, as it were (cf. above, page 79). Thus, this stage of the inflation would not necessarily have much affected the number of coins in Q.

When the local bronze issues finally come to an end during the 260's,[16] the *antoninianus* became the smallest denomination current, and there may have been as many as 500 of them to the *aureus* (see above, page 40). But even then it would have taken little more than ten such *antoniniani* to make up Q (=1/43 *aureus*).

Around 301, when there were 800 *denarii* to the *aureus*, even if the smallest denomination were to have been a one-*denarius* piece[17] (and not a two-*denarius* piece as suggested above, page 61), Q would still have been no more than twenty of them.

In the year following 301, on the other hand, there was a rapid decline of the copper coinage, as we have seen above (Chapter X and XIV), so that around 304 there were 1600 *denarii* per *aureus* (*P.O.* 2106) and around 307, the *aureus* equalled 2000 denarii (*PSI.* 310).

We can, in fact, check our findings to a certain extent. For given the approximate weight and metallic contents of the silver-washed copper coins, we may reckon the number of them that went to make up the *aureus* (assuming the constancy of the gold-silver ratio). Thus, starting with our formula N(100 PQ + PR): (see above, Chapter IV), we may

modify it thus: $\dfrac{N(100PQ + PR)}{10,000Y} = 14.4$, giving N as $\dfrac{14.4(10,000Y)}{100\ PQ + PR}$.

When Y is an *aureus*, it equals 1/60 *libra aurei* = 5.4, when a *solidus* it equals 1/72 *libra aurei*, 4.65. Where Y is an *aureus*, $Q = \dfrac{7}{300}$ N; where

Y is a *solidus*, Q = approximately $\dfrac{7}{350}$ N. (For the following see Tables J and K and end of chapter.)

Thus,[18] around 307, ten-gramme pieces at about one percent silver, yields a result of N = 390. If each unit equalled five *denarii* (as it had in about 301), then the *aureus* equalled 5 × 390 = 1950 *denarii*.[19] This result is very close to the 2000 *denarii* of *PSI.* 310. If this were to have been the minimum coin, Q would be about nine. In fact, we know that there was a coin worth two *denarii*. Thus, Q is about 21.

Around 313-14, the 3.5 gramme piece at one percent gives a result of N = 1303. If this too was a five-*denarius* piece—and this seems likely in view of its evolution from the ten-gramme piece—then the *aureus* was worth 6515 *denarii*.[20] This is a fairly close result to the equation yielded by *P. Rol. Princ.* 4.13, of 313-14, one *aureus* = 7116 *denarii*. Q would then be equal to 30.4 of these pieces.

Around 317, the situation is a little better, and the three-gramme piece, with a two percent silver content, yields a result: N = 864. Again, if each unit equalled five *denarii*, then one *aureus* = 4320 *denarii*. This too is a fairly close approximation to the equation given by *P. Rol. Princ.* 7.6, of 316, one *aureus* = 4166 *denarii*. Q then equals twenty of these pieces.

P.O. 1430, of 324 (discussed above, page 152), yields an approximate equation of one *aureus* = 5760 *denarii*, one *solidus* = 4800 *denarii*,[21] (or more exactly 4354 *denarii*). Q, therefore, is about 130

denarii, and if the minimum denomination was still the five-*denarius* piece, Q = 26 such pieces. An analysis of the *GLORIA EXERCITUS* pieces [22] of around 330, weighing $2\frac{1}{2}$ grammes and containing about two percent silver (or less), suggests that N = 880 such coins (or more), and if they were five-*denarius* pieces, then one *aureus* = 4440 *denarii* (or more).

By 341, the unit *VICTORIAE DD AUGG Q NN* [23] has become greatly reduced in size (to two grammes) and in silver content (to one percent), yielding a result: N = 1680 (per *solidus*) and if these coins were again five-*denarius* pieces, one *solidus* = 8400 *denarii*; Q = 48 such pieces.

Around 348[22] the *FEL(ICUM) TEMP(ORUM) REPARATIO* piece [24] was introduced, weighing up to five grammes and with (in the East) at least two percent silver. According to this, N = 448. Q then equals a little less than thirteen such pieces. It seems likely that this piece, which was twice the weight of its predecessor, was valued as double its predecessor. Thus, it would be worth ten *denarii*, and the *solidus* worth 4480 *denarii*.

Around 354, the coin weight dropped by half again (to $2\frac{1}{2}$ grammes), with a little less silver perhaps (slightly less than two percent). This gives N as about 880 (maybe nearer to 850), and if these coins were meant to be equal to the *FEL(ICIUM) TEMP(ORUM)REPARATIO* type [24] (i.e. were worth ten *denarii*), the *solidus* equalled around 8500 *denarii*, and Q = 25.

In 361, Julian appears to have made a conscious attempt to improve the coinage, striking a piece of five grammes with around 2.9% silver.[23] N = about 337, according to this, and Q under ten such pieces. Again, as this coin weighed twice as much as the preceding one, it was probably worth twice as much, i.e. 20 *denarii*.[24] Thus, one *solidus* = 6740 *denarii*.

Valentinian's copper coins of 364 onwards have virtually no silver content, and it appears that from then on, copper coinage becomes token coinage.[25] Reduction in the weight of a coin from this date onwards does not necessarily mean a reduction in value, and certainly not a reduction in value in a ratio to the reduction in weight. It is, in fact, probable that after 364, the *solidus* held a fairly steady value of around 7000 *denarii*, fluctuating only to a slight degree. For we have seen above that on the basis of *Codex Theodosianus* 14.4.4 of 419 and Valentinian's *Novella*, 16, of 445, the *solidus* was valued at between 7000 *denarii* and 7500 *denarii*. Slightly earlier, at the end of the fourth century, there were 6800 *denarii* per *solidus*.[26] Cassiodorus, *Variae* 1.10, states that: *veteres... sex milia denarionum solidum esse voluement.*[27] (For the above see Table K and L at end of chapter.)

Of course, there were far smaller denominations than those in which we have reckoned Q thus far. Thus, there are a number of "quarter-*folles*" in Constantinian coinage.[28] In the period 350-63, coins seem to have been struck in at least three denominations (sometimes struck concurrently, but almost certainly circulating concurrently for a while at least), AE 1, AE 2, AE 3 (see above, note 24). Unfortunately, virtually nothing is known of the precise relationships between these various units of the subsidiary copper coinage. Nonetheless, we would probably be safe to multiply our results for Q by 3 in most cases to give us some approximate notion of what Q constituted in terms of the smallest (often very minute) units of copper currency. Thus around 313-14, Q was probably approaching 100. Thereafter it seems to fluctuate between around 60 (about 316) and over 140 (about 341), being perhaps 75 around 354.

Some corroboration of this may perhaps be found in a text in *Leviticus Rabba*AO 34.2[29] where R. Pinḥas in the name of R. Reuben says, on the verse in Proverbs 10.17, 'He that is gracious with the poor lendeth unto the Lord':

> He who gives a *pruta* to a poor man, the Holy One blessed be He gives him a *pruta*. And does he, then, give him [merely] a *pruta*? Does he not give him his life. How so? A loaf of bread costs ten *prutas*, and the poor man stands [there] wishing to buy it and he has only nine, and someone comes and gives him a *pruta* and he buys the loaf and eats it, and his life-strength returns to him. So said to him the Holy one blessed be He: "You too, when your soul is urging to leave your body, I will return it to your body".

The text in this version is probably R. Pinḥas' formulation, therefore of about 325-35.[30] A loaf costs approximately ten minimum-size coins. (Alternatively, the text is indeed R. Reuben's formulation, in which case it is of around 300. The *pruta* here equals the debased *denarius*. As the minimum monetary unit was two *denarii*, Q = 70 denarii.)

Whatever the precise details of this story be, the overall effect is quite clear; as the minimum denomination became progressively (if varyingly) smaller in relationship to the *aureus* or *solidus*, it became more and more difficult for the poor man to achieve this most basic subsistence-level, Q.

It is even likely that the purchasing power of the copper pieces dropped even more than did their *official* value, and since we are actually interested in the cost of fourteen meals (or seven two-pound loaves of bread), and not merely an abstract sum of money, we may reckon Q from certain surviving prices. Thus, as around 324, one loaf of bread (one pint of wine and one pound of meat all) cost ten *follarin*, which we have suggested above (Chapter VI) equals fifty *denarii* (for one *follaris* = one *follis* = five *denarii*), Q would be seventy *folles*, if the *follis* were the smallest denomination. This makes Q equal 350 *denarii* rather than 130 *denarii*, as suggested above, and simply demonstrates (what one would expect to find) that prices had risen considerably higher than would be expected from the extent of the depreciation of the coins.[31] When, and indeed, whether, the purchasing power of the copper coinage caught up with its official value, as a fraction of the gold or silver denominations, we do not know. However, once again it is clear that it must have become increasingly difficult for the poor man to make up his Q.

We have a reflection of what popular opinion thought of this debased coinage in an undated (anonymous) text which must, it appears, be of the mid-fourth century.[32] For in *Tanḥuma Exodus*[AP33] we read :

> Our Sages said: This evil government[34] is (destined to, or) going to use coin[s] of pottery (i.e. clay).[35]

Anyone who has handled the miserable specimens that abound in the mid-fourth century "copper" hoards will appreciate the true sharpness of this criticism.

R. Jona, who was probably negotiating these halachic changes some time during the 340's, must have been well aware of the severity of the situation. He, who had many dealings with the poor,[36] would have been well placed to realise that a man could go begging all day long, and still not end up with an *argurion's* worth (*siliqua?, miliarense?*) of copper coins, or enough for a week's supply of food—a situation almost inconceivable in earlier times. It was to cope with this new situation that he modified the Tosefta's ruling in the manner described above.

TABLE J

Changes of Weight and Size of the *Follis* in the Mint of Alexandria

Date	Weight	NS	Size	Weight	NS	Size
296/307	9.93	(54)	25/8	3.31	(28)	19/21
308/11	6.64	(354)	23/5			
311/12	6.12	(13)	21/3			
312/13	4.92	(93)				
313/14	3.57	(21)	19/21			
314/17	3.36	(12)				
317/18	3.24	(16)				
318/24	3.14	(29)	17/20			
324/27	3.24	(18)				
Mint Closed: 327/55						
335/7	2.65	(20)	17/18	1.70	(30)	14/17

NS = No. of specimens

From West and Johnson, *Currency in Roman and Byzantine Egypt*, p. 97. cf. *RIC*, 6, pp. 101–3, for evidence from other mints.

TABLE K

Date	Weight of Coin Unit	% of Silver
Early Diocletian reform coinage		5½%
Later Diocletian coinage		1 %
317	3 gramme pieces	2–2½%
330 (GLORIA EXERCITUS)	2½ grammes	2 % or less
341 (VICTORIAE DD AUGG a NN)	2 grammes	1%
348 (FEL[ICIUM] TEM [ORUM] REPARATIO)	up to 5 grammes	2½–3½% (2% in Eastern mints)
c.354	2½ grammes	less than 2%
355 (Julian)	3 grammes	2.9%
364 (Valentinian)	2½ grammes	little or no silver

Based on the "Fourth Century Inflation", by Alison Ravetz, *Num. Chron.*, 1964· pp. 215–6. Cf. idem, in *Archeometry* 6, 1963, pp. 46–55, especially p. 54, fig. 2 ibid, For the Julian coin analysis, see *Archeometry*, 6, no. 75. Cf. *Archeometry*, 4, pp. 56–61. See also "An Introduction to the Coinage of Julian the Apostate" (360–3), by J.P.C. Kent, in *Num. Chron.*, 1959, pp. 108–117, especially p. 109; idem, in *Num. Chron.*, 1957, on Constantinian coinage.

TABLE L

Approximate Relationship of *Denarius* to *Aureus* in IV (and V) Cent.
Based on Literary and Numismatic Evidence

c.30I.	800 d.	= 1 *aureus*
307	2,000 d.	= 1 *aureus*
c.313/7	6,500/7,000 d.	= 1 *aureus*
c.316/7	4150/4300 d.	= 1 *aureus*
324	4350/4800 d.	= 1 *solidus*
330	4400 d.	= 1 *sol.*
341	8400 d.	= 1 *sol.*
348	4480 d.	= 1 *sol.*
c.354	8500 d.	= 1 *sol.*
c.355	6740 d.	= 1 *sol.*
end of IV cent.	6800 d.	= 1 *sol.*
419/45	7000/7500 d.	= 1 *sol.*
V cent.	6000 d.	= 1 *sol.*

CHAPTER XXIII

FOURTH CENTURY: PRODIGIOUS PRICES
Palestine, Egypt, Syria

All the above evidence presents the same overall view of the fourth century, one in which prices may have fluctuated to a certain extent (as indeed they did in the first and second centuries), but, when reckoned in terms of gold, did not radically rise above the general price-levels of the second century. Even when reckoned in *aes* coinage, in *folles* or *nummi*, etc., they do not sound impossibly high. However, we do find whole groups of prices, in Palestine, Egypt, and Syria, which, though expressed apparently in terms of debased bronze denominations, sound completely astronomical. Their scale is so vast that they bear no logical relationship to other known prices of the period. There are two famous examples of these prodigious prices, which were first noted by S. Lieberman in one of his characteristically enlightening footnotes,[1] and which we have discussed in some detail eslewhere.[2]

The first is in Yerushalmi Ma'aser Sheni[AQ] 1.1. There we find R. Jona asking what would be the case if someone's purse containing 100 myriad [of debased *denarii*] fell into a pit, and it would cost him fifty myriad to hire someone to get it out. As this example is given by R. Jona, it belongs to some time between about 320 and 355, perhaps around 350. At that time it was apparently conceivable for a person to have one million (!) "*denarii*" in a purse, and for it to cost him half a million (!) *denarii* for the relatively simple task of retrieving it.

And some time between about 320 and 350, R. Mana II speaks of an expensive garment worth thirty myriad *denarii*.[3] To be truly appreciated this astronomical figure should be compared with the second and third century concept of a fabulous price, namely 100 *maneh* (=10,000 *denarii*).[4] This fourth century figure, perhaps from the 340's, is some thirty times higher than the "highest" second century price!

This latter text is perhaps not so completely inexplicable. For if it is also of the mid-fourth century when there were approximately 5000

164

denarii per *solidus*[5] see below, this chapter), in gold currency this very expensive suit would have cost only sixty *solidi* or thereabouts. This price is, in fact, far cheaper than the "10,000 *denarii*" (מאה מנה) of the second centur, which equalled 400 *aurei*.[6]

However, the first text cannot be explained away to simply. For is it possible to imagine a person carrying one million units of any kind in a purse? And would he pay half a million such units to get a simple job done? Even if the smallest coin then current had weighed only half a gramme, the purse would still have contained almost five tons of bronze (one ton = 1016 kilogrammes)! Even translated into *solidi* (200), this sum is somewhat incredible.

We shall now cite further examples of this phenomenon that have hitherto escaped notice. In a *derasha* (homily) probably of R. Pinḥas (ha-Kohen) bar Ḥama (*floruit circa* 330-70), recorded in *Tanḥuma Exodus*[AS] (*Mishpatim*, paragraph 15), we read of a man who has lent his friend מאתי' או רבוא שלש מאות—200 or a myriad 300.[7] (The fact that the name of the monetary denomination is not mentioned further points to this being a fourth century text.) The text as it stands clearly needs some alteration to make good sense (and style) of it, and has therefore been variously corrected to read "200 or a myriad or 300",[8] or "200, or 300, or a myriad",[9] or—a radical emendation with no basis—"100, or 200, or 300".[10] However, these emendations are both forced and unsatisfactory. We would therefore suggest shifting the single "or" of the editio princeps text one word forward, which would leave us with a loan of "two hundred myriad, or three hundred..." According to this, it would appear that probably around the middle of the fourth century ordinary men—the context shows that ordinary people are being spoken of—could lend out two to three million (*denarii*)!

We find further evidence of these astronomical sums in a(n anonymous) *derasha* in *Midrash Tillim*[AT] (Psalms) to Psalms 34.1.[11] There we are told that King David acted as though he were mad:

> ...as it is stated (I Samuel 21.14), 'And he changed his demeanour [before them and feigned himself mad in their hands], and scribbled on the doors of the gate,[and let his spittle fall down upon his beard]'. He would write on the doors saying: "Achish the King of Gath owes me one hundred myriad, and his wife fifty myriad..."[12]

The fact that he claimed that Achish and his wife owed him money may have made him appear to be a lunatic, but the sums he claimed they owed him were, apparently, quite reasonable.

And finally, in *Exodus Rabba* 20.9[AU] we read of a man who enters into a jewelry shop and asks: "How much does this small stone cost?" The answer given is "100 myriad". "The large one for how much?" "100 myriad". "The medium one for home much?" "800"—but probably one should read ‏ת‎, instead of ‏ה‎ thus 500 myriad. Though this is an anonymous passage and thus difficult to date closely, it would appear to be from around the middle of the fourth century.[13] Thus we find that loans range from about one to three million, and that a large precious stone can come to as much as ten million.

With the above sums in mind, we may now better understand a hitherto puzzling text recorded (inter alia) in Yerushalmi Kiddushin[AW] 1.3:[14]

> R. Ḥanina (*floruit circa* 280-330)[15] said: "All the *shekalim* mentioned in the Pentateuch are *sela'im* (*tetradrachms*), and in the Prophets are *litra[s]* (= *librae* = 100 *denarii*) and in the Hagiographa are *kintarin*". Said R. Judah ben Pazi (= R. Judah ben Simon ben Pazi, *floruit circa* 300-350): "Except for the *shekalim* of Ephron the Hittite, which are *kintarin*". "Why so?" "For the full price let him give to me. . ." (Genesis 23.9). ("The *full* price" suggesting the largest monetary unit.)

Now *kintarin* here is undoubtedly the κεντηνάριον (= *centenarius*), whose value during this period was reckoned at 10,000 *denarii*.[16] In other words, a myriad! Thus, the field and the cave of Machpelah cost, according to R. Judah (ben Simon) ben Pazi, 400 myriad *denarii*. The aggadist was apparently translating the Biblical price—400 *shekalim*—into his own contemporary terminology. In explaining the word *shekalim* as referring in this case to *kintarin*—basing himself on an established tradition—he reached a reasonable estimate, 400 myriads, which was intended to denote a high price. Presumably this text, which suggests that four million *denarii* is a large sum of money,[17] is somewhat earlier than R. Jona's text (above), where a single purse could contain one million *denarii*.

Not only in Palestine, but also in Egypt of the fourth century, do we find this same phenomenon of extraordinary high prices. Thus, in 362 the price of a hide is given as 7,500,000 silver *denarii*.[18] West and Johnson write:[19]

> "If these coins were even the poorest of all Egyptian *tetradrachms*, namely those issued by Diocletian before A.D. 296, then a single hide was equivalent to more than 130,000 lbs. of copper, even when one forgets the small amount of silver in *tetradrachm*

(8 gr. is taken as the average weight of the *tetradrachm*, and a kilogram as 2.2046 lbs.). It is obvious that a hide was not worth 65 tons of copper and equally obvious that 7,500,000 silver *denarii* of A.D. 362 were not the actual *tetradrachms* of the late third century".

From Egyptian sources one can multiply these examples very considerably.[20]

P.O. 85	338	wheat	24 talents (= 144,000dr.) per *art.*
BGU. 21	341	sale (or rent)	34 talents (= 204,000dr.) + 1 *cnidion* wine
P. Princeton 188v	c.345	wheat	334 talents (1,904,000dr.) per *art.*
			50 talents (= 300,000dr.) per *art.*
P. London 984	c.360	1 lb. wine	330,000 *denarii* each
		1 lb. meat	
PSI 287	377	daily wage of apprentice to ταρσικάριος	3000,000 *denarii*
P.O. 1753	390	3½ lbs. meat	105 myriad *denarii*
P. Ross Georg. V.61	—	6 military cloaks	200,000,000 *denarii*

Even if the smallest current unit were called a *denarius* or *tetradrachm*, the resultant prices in terms of copper would still be well-nigh impossible. Thus, in the case of the hide, the cost would be equal to over 10,000 pounds of copper, also a rather unlikely relationship.[21]

The paradox is somewhat heightened when, turning now to Syria, one takes note of certain surviving Syrian epigraphic evidence. For example:

(1) inscriptions of about 345[22]
    Monument of two *centuriones ordinarii*   130,000 *denarii*[23]
    Cost of raising a tomb   71,000 *denarii*[24]
    Mothana monument, of 342   15,000 *denarii*[25]
(2) an inscription of 350
    Actuaries *vexillationis*   11,000 Syrian *drachmae*[26]
(3) a tomb from SALKHAD of 325(?)   12,000 Syrian *drachmae*[27]
(4) a tower in IL-MESHKUK of 350   15,000(?) *denarii*[28]
(5) a building of DJEDIL of 352   100,000 *denarii*[29]

Now these may seem to be high figures compared to the first to third centuries,[30] yet the cost of a building is still only one-tenth of what R. Jona's theoretical personage kept in his purse.

On the other hand, there are two undated Syrian inscriptions, which may well belong to the fourth century, which seem to record abnormally high figures. The first (fig. 1), a (tomb) memorial from MJEDIL reads[31] *μ(υρίων), ασ which ought to mean 12,000,000 *denarii,* and the other (fig. 2), on a building from KHARSAH reading[32*] μ(ύρια) φ' (=5,000,000). The editors,[33] considering these sums too vast to be plausible, suggest that the numbers be interpreted to mean 11,200 and 10,500 respectively. However, there is no real basis for such interpretations, and in view of our Palestinian and Egyptian evidence their plain meaning should be seriously considered.

787[14]. BLOCK. Built into the wall supporting the stairway of a house in the eastern part of the northern sections of the village. Length 85 cm.; height 37 cm. The inscription was within a raised dovetailed frame; this frame has been carefully chipped off. Length of the frame, excluding the dovetails, 49 cm.; height 27 cm. Height of letters 3-5½ cm. Copied by Butler.

Aὐρ(ήλιος) Zηνόβιος
Σαγιου ᾠκοδό-
μησε τὸ μνημεῖ-
ον ✳ μ(υρίων) ͵ασ ἐξ ἰδίω[ν,
κὲ Νασεαύ γυνή μου.

Inscr. 787[14]. Scale 1 : 10.

Figure 1

790[4]. FRAGMENT. Found in the southern part of the town a few yards northeast of the courtyard in which no. 790[3] was found. The stone is in the east wall of a tower and is close to the ground. Height 34 cm.; width 9½-14 cm. Height of letters 4½-6 cm. Copied by Magie.

Inscr. 790[4].
Scale 1 : 10.

. . . . ϛλε
. . . . ε
. . . . ἐλ-
τίσθη (?) . . . .]ἐξ
ἰδίων (?) . . . . ✳]μ(ύρια) φ'.

Figure 2

Chapter XXIV

METROLOGY: INFLATED TERMINOLOGY

Now all the above evidence seems to indicate that prices, even in terms of copper coinage, did not rise so phenomenally that a simple job of getting a purse out of a pit should have cost half a million *denarii*, or indeed that a person could walk about with a million *denarii* in his pocket. Nor does it seem likely that a large gem should have cost ten million *denarii*, a memorial twelve million *denarii*, nor a building five million—if these are fourth century inscriptions.

To solve the problem posed by the cases of the phenomenal Egyptian prices, West and Johnson[1] suggest that

> The Egyptian transferred to the new bronze coins of the post-Diocletian period the names of the pre-Diocletian monetary system but instead of calling the smallest bronze an *obol* or a *drachma*, he seems to have called it so many talents or myriads.[2]

In Table M we have set out a conjectural list of such "meanings" arranged in chronological order.

Surely we have a similar situation in our Palestinian text. We have already seen such a phenomenon in that a *denarius* was called a *"maneh"* (formerly 100 *denarii*) from some time during the third century onwards. Now in R. Jona's case of the purse falling into the pit, it is true that he is obviously using round numbers to simplify the legal exposition (hence, one million, one-half million, 2:1, a pattern found throughout Rabbinic literature).[3] Yet, here again these theoretical and simplified numbers must bear some relationship to contemporary conditions.

Let us assume that R. Jona's statement was made about 346, and that he reckoned a *solidus* at around 5000 *denarii*; it would not be unreasonable for a person to have two *solidi* in his purse, or for a job to cost him one *solidus* (partly, of course, for expositional simplification). R. Jona could have said "a man who had 10,000 *manehs* (= 2 *solidi*) in his pocket," but, as a *maneh* (still) meant 100 *denarii*,[4] it would be equally reasonable for him to say 100 myriads (= 10,000 × 100 = two *solidi*).

We have seen an example of this in a passage (cited above, Chapter XIII, text AD) in the *Sifré* to Deuteronomy, which appears to be a third century gloss. There we read, "and he needs 100 *manehs* or two myriads; if he takes them in small coins[6] they will tire him. But he should exchange them for gold *dinars*. . ." Thus, rather than saying 200 *manehs*, one could say two myriads. Two myriad *denarii* in the beginning of the fourth century (when 2000 *denarii* equalled one *aureus*), equalled ten *aurei*.

Perhaps the Syrian inscriptions cited above reflect the same terminological tendency (just as from the Syriac Eusebius we saw the Syriac usage of the *maneh*), and their figures should be likewise divided by one hundred, giving the more reasonable sums of 120,000 and 500,000, a more plausible number of *solidi*,[7] whatever the exact valuation of the *solidus* at the time these inscriptions were carved.

It should further be noted that δηνάριον (certainly in the fourth century if not earlier) had two distinct meanings; one of them was equated with the *mina*— μνᾶ etc. (= 100 *denarii*). This has been convincingly demonstrated by Oskar Viedebantt[8] from his analyses of certain texts in Epiphanius' *Treatise on Weights and Measures*, of 392.[9] Thus, the Syriac there[10] reads: "Sixty *assaria*, however, are a *denarion*, and a hundred *denaria* are a silver [coin] (= ארגוריוס). On this latter word there is a very interesting marginal gloss,[11] headed [12] ארגריוס : *APΓIPYC* / מתפשק דכספא / איתוהי דין אנש נאמר'/ [13] / אכננא דזוזא או מדם אחרא / דאיך היא -*argurius*, translated "of silver", is that of which a man [might] say that it is, for example, a *zuza*, or something like that. (See fig. 3.) The manuscript itself is dated 65-,[14] and the glosses are in a fine estranglela hand of not much later, if not almost contemporary.[15] In any case, whatever its exact date may be, this gloss may well reflect the same fourth century tradition noted above. For according to it, the *zuza* (*zuz*, usually equal to the *denarius*) is equal to the *argurius*, which is 100 *denarii*. Here again, we have a *denarius-zuz-argurius* of 100 *denarii*, and thus equal to a *maneh*, just as we saw earlier that the *maneh* in Talmudic literature came to mean an ordinary debased *denarius*. It is difficult to know whether the third century Talmudic development is in any way dependent upon the *denarion-mina* relationship, which is first clearly attested only in the late fourth century.

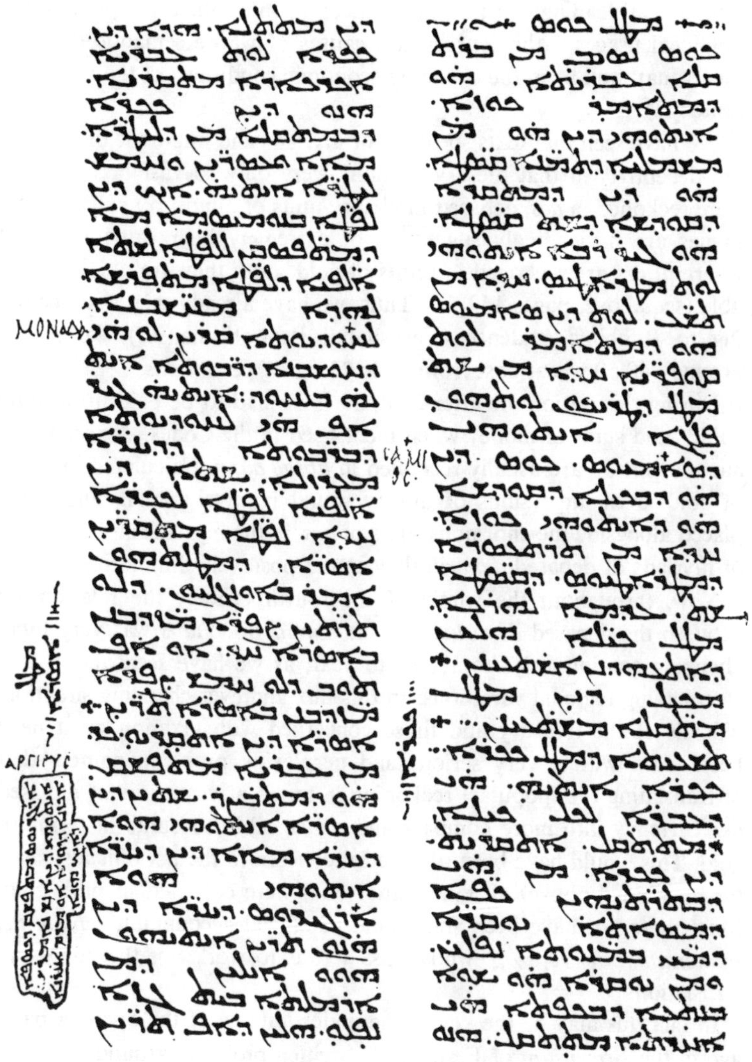

Figure 3

A Page from Epiphanius' Treatise on Weights and Measures

However, the above observation may perhaps serve to add some credence (and rationally explicable basis) to our suggestion that certain fourth century texts apparently suggestive of enormous degrees of inflation, are misleading[16] in that they reflect no more than deceptive terminological usages,[17] the sources and causes of whose semantic developments may well lie in the changing economic conditions of the preceding century.[18]

We have seen that texts speaking of myriads and hundreds of myriads are deceptive, in that these valuations were only so vast because they were reckoned in *aes*, debased monetary units of almost no value, whose names are misleadingly suggestive of extremely high valuations. But where prices are reckoned in terms of gold *solidi* they are quite reasonable (see above, pages 149-52). Thus, we have already seen that according to Rabbinic evidence (Yerushalmi Bava Kama 9.5), some time around 340-50 wheat cost from 20 to 25 *modii* per *solidus*.

During this period (or after 366), all taxes had to be paid up in pure gold,[19] and sums of money when mentioned in the Codes—taxes, allowances or fines—are usually reckoned in *librae aurei*. Calculated in terms of gold, even large sums of money sound relatively small, and when placed alongside the enormous sums of *aes*, in the myriads and hundreds of myriads of debased *denarii*, they sound positively diminutive.

Now, throughout the whole of the fourth century the relationship between the debased *denarius* and the *aureus* or *solidus* was very fluid, changing continuously from year to year, as we have seen above, and even having regional variations. In this flux and ever-changing situation, officials of the treasury and those concerned with taxation must have been faced with a very serious and perplexing problem, namely that of translating the (popular) reckoning in terms of vast sums of debased *aes* currency into more compact and manageable accounts in terms of gold. This would have been of especial concern to the tax officials, since (as mentioned above) all taxes (after 366) were collected in pure gold. Must there not have been some kind of official accountant, *tabularius, numerarius,* or λογιστής whose task it was to work out the confusing translations?

In fact this may be the key to the understanding of the opening passage in the *Brevarium* of Festus (1.1), written probably around 360-70.[20] It reads as follows:

> ...ac morem secutus *calculonum*, qui ingentas summas aeris breuioribus exprimunt, res gestas signabo, non eloquar. Accepe ergo quod breuiter dictis conputetur...

172

It seems clear that the *calculo* Festus had in mind was none other than our suggested accountant. In all probability his official title was $λογιστής$. and Festus translated this literally into the Latin *calculo*. It was indeed the purpose of such *calculones* to reckon these complex accounts, *qui ingentes summas aeris breuioribus exprimunt.*[21]

TABLE M

Relationship of *Denarius* to *Solidus* in Egypt During the Fourth Century

P. Lond. 1259	1 *sol.* = 32T = 48,000d.	If each unit	= 10d., 1 *sol.* = 4,800d.
PER. 187	1 *sol.* = 36T = 54,000d.	" " "	= 10d., 1 *sol.* = 5400d.
PER. 37	1 *sol.* = 100T = 150,000d.	" " "	= 20d., 1 *sol.* = 7500d.
PER. 310	1 *sol.* = 120T = 180,000d.	" " "	= 30d., 1 *sol.* = 6000d.
(cf. SPP xx.96)			
PER. 225 pre–361	1 *sol.* = 183⅓ = 275,000d.	" " "	= 50d., 1 *sol.* = 5500d.
P.O. 2267	1 *sol.* = 4,571, 428d.	" " "	= 750d. (= ½T), 1 *sol.* = 6,095 d.
SB. 7034 c.360	1 *sol.* = 5,760,000d.	" " "	= 750d. (=½T), 1 *sol.* = 7680 d.
P.O. 1056	1 *sol.* = 2000M = 20,000,000d.	"	= 3000 (=2T), 1 *sol.* = 6,666 d.
(cf. PSI. IV. 287, of 377, and P.O. 1223).			
c.380 PSI. VII. 961.	1 *sol.* = 4050M = 40,500,000d.	"	= 6000 (=4T), 1 *sol.* = 6,750 d.
(Cf. P.O. 960).			
P.O. 1917	1 *sol.* = 60,000,000d.	" " "	= 7500 (5T), 1 *sol.* = 8,000 d.

See Segrè, *Metrologia*, pp. 454–6, 489–490; Jones, Inflation, *Econ. His. Rev.*, 5/3, 1953, pp. 308–11; Segrè, *Byzantion*, 15, p. 263; Ruggini, p. 311. Cf. *Currency*, p. 170; Johnson, *Egypt and the Roman Empire*, p. 59; Jones, *The Later Roman Empire*, 3, p. 114 note 74. See also Rémondon in *Chronique d'Égypte*, 31, 1956, p. 146.

CHAPTER XXV

EGYPTIAN PRICES

We have suggested above that the situation in Egypt was not significantly different from that in Palestine. Accordingly, Egyptian fourth century prices, despite their phenomenal size, should show some sort of approximate scale-relationship comparable to those of the first, second (and third) centuries, most especially when expressed in gold terms. That is to say, wheat or meat prices, for example, even when given in *"denarii"*, should be reduceable to a scale where they will be approximately comparable to (perhaps twice as cheap as—see price relationships above, page 126) Palestinian prices, and prices of such commodities recorded in *solidi* should bear an obvious parity to contemporary Palestinian ones.

There is indeed some, if scanty, evidence to show that this is the case. For in the *Vita S. Pachomii* 33-34, we read that during a year of shortage in Egypt, when

> wheat stood at 5 *art.* (= about 16 *modii*) to the *solidus*, Pachomius sent out a monk to buy wheat for his monastery. Eventually he found an obliging tax-collector who sold him corn from his public stocks at 13 *art.* (= about 43 *modii*) per *solidus*, in the expectation of postponing delivery of the tax to the government until after the harvest, when he hoped to replace wheat he had illicitly sold at the cheap rate that would then prevail. Pachomius repudiated this risky transaction, and had to buy at 5½ *art.* (= about 18 *modii*) to the *solidus*.[1]

Clearly the tax-collector had reckoned on making some sort of a profit on this deal, and we may safely conjecture that he had been hoping to replace his wheat at a minimum of about fifty *modii* (= 15 *art.*) per *solidus*, thus making a clear profit of only seven *modii* (=about 2 *art.*) per *solidus*.[2] (In the reign of Valentinian I, a speculator named

174

Hymetius made as much as 200% clear profit during a famine at Carthage.)[3]

This event took place some time between 320 and 346[4]—unfortunately it cannot be dated with greater accuracy. Now, though this text gives us no certain figures for a *normal* Egyptian wheat price, it does give us some idea of the scale of prices. The famine price (which may have been three to four times a normal price, see above, page 150) was 16 *modii* per *solidus*. The tax-collector was willing to sell at 43 *modii* per *solidus*, and would still have been able to make a profit on the deal (at least 7 *modii* per *solidus* we suggested, meaning that the famine had pushed up the price to some three times its normal level). Thus, however we interpret the details of the evidence, the general conclusion seems to be clear, namely, that a normal Egyptian wheat-price during the second quarter of the fourth century was considerably lower than a Palestinian one. In fact, the Egyptian price was at least twice as low, since the Palestinian price for this period was around 20 *modii* per *solidus* (see above, Chapter II). This agrees well with our conclusions for the third century and the first quarter of the fourth century.[5]

Around the year 350 according to *P. Lond.* 427 (Hermopolis), one *art.* of wheat cost fifty talents, i.e. one *modius* cost fifteen talents (= 225,000 *denarii*). We do not know the precise cost of wheat in terms of *solidi* in that year, but if we assume that it was again around 40 *modii* per *solidus*, we get a *solidus* of 9,000,000 *denarii*. Again, if the minimum unit in that time was one talent (= 1500 *denarii*), (cf. Table M above), the *solidus* was worth approximately 6000 *denarii*. Now these are necessarily very conjectural calculations, but the conclusions, though not necessarily accurate—they do not aim for exactitude—are reasonable in their scale. Thus we have reckoned that around 355-61 (see above page 163) there were some 6740 *denarii* per *solidus*. By about 360 (*P.O.* 1056) there were already 20,000,000 *denarii* in the *solidus*, so that nine million *denarii* per *solidus* for around 350 is a *r e a s o n a b l e* conclusion. Again, forty *modii* per *solidus* is probably about half the contemporary Palestinian price.

According to *P.O.* 85 of 338, thirteen *art.* barley cost 500 *denarii*;[6] therefore, one *modius* of barley cost 12.8 *denarii*. Wheat would have cost somewhat more, perhaps 21 *denarii* per *modius*.[7] *P.O.* 85 also informs us that wheat cost 24 talents per *art.*[8] i.e. about seven talents per *modius*. Thus, seven talents = 21 *denarii*, or one *denarius* = 1/3 talent (= 500 *denarii*). If there were some 6,000 *denarii* per *solidus*, the *solidus* would have been equal to three million *denarii* in Egyptian terminology.

175

This seems to be a rather high valuation for the *solidus* at such a date. Furthermore, according to *PSI*. 202 of 338 (? Oxyrhynchus), 1000 pounds of pork cost 900 *denarii*, i.e. each pound of pork cost just under one *denarius*. It seems most unlikely that one pound of pork should have cost under 1/6000 *solidus*, when according to the *Edict of Diocletian* and Palestinian sources pork prices of the first half of the fourth century ranged from 1/175 to 1/150 *solidus* (see above, page 153). However, the reading of the wheat price in *P.O.* 85 is uncertain,[9] and we should therefore not base ourselves on it too much. But what is apparently clear from *P.O.* 85 and from *PSI*. 202 is that the *denarius* was equal to many *denarii*, though how many we do not know.

According to *P. Lond.* 247 of 346, four Babylonian hides cost 120 myriad *denarii*; therefore, one hide cost thirty myriad *denarii*. And according to *P.O.* 1057 of 362, one Babylonian hide cost 750 myriad *denarii*. In the *Edict of Diocletian* (8.1a, 2) the prices for Babylonian hides are given as 500 *denarii* each, for the first quality, and 400 *denarii* for the second quality (i.e. very approximately 3/5 *solidus* or a little more each). According to this, around 346, one *solidus* equalled 500,000 *denarii*, and about 362, one *solidus* equalled 12,500,000 *denarii* approximately. Again, these calculations have no pretensions to accuracy, but the scale of our highly conjectural results seems to be reasonable. As we have calculated that the *solidus* stood at 4480 *denarii* in 348 (above page 159), the minimum unit must have been about 100 *denarii*. Again, as we calculated the *solidus* at about 6800 *denarii* from about 360 onwards, the minimum unit would be about 1750 *denarii* which equalled 1/6 talents, a slightly unlikely figure. A unit of one talent would be more easily acceptable, giving a *solidus* valuation of some 10,200,000 *denarii*; alternatively, there may have been a regional difference in the price of the *solidus* of up to one-sixth, though this again seems a little excessive.[10]

is a text of considerable ambiguity. It reads:

PSI. 781 of 341 seems also to be relevant to our argument, though it

ἐσθητος τιρώνων τη(·)α *ροε δ τέω(ς) ἀργυρίου τάλ(αντα) τετρακόσια εἴκοσι ὀκτὼ καὶ δραχ(μὰς) δισχίλιας.

If this means, as has been suggested, that 175 *denarii* are now worth 428 talents and 2000 *drachmae*, or one *denarius* equals 14,685 5/7 *drachmae*, and the [silver] *denarius* is the *siliqua*,[11] then one *solidus* equals 98,104 *denarii*, or approximately 100,000 *denarii* in 341. If there were 8400 *denarii* per *solidus* in this year, as we have calculated, the minimum unit in Egypt must have been twelve *denarii*. It may however be that this unusual figure contains a hidden charge for exchange,[12] in which case 84,000 *denarii* per *solidus* (meaning a minimum unit of ten *denarii*) might be a more acceptable ratio.[13]

All the above demonstrates that one may generally (and very conjecturally) calculate a roughly comparable price-scale and system of *solidus*-valuations for Egypt as for the rest of the Eastern Empire. This is indeed no more than one would have expected, and for our purposes it bears out our calculations of prices in Palestine, and the values of the *solidus* as calculated from non-Egyptian sources. The precise cause of the singular terminological development in fourth century Egypt, the phenomenon of constantly renaming the minimum unit of value (or the standard unit of reckoning), remains, however, puzzling and unexplained. One can only point out that it was a development apparently equal throughout the whole of Egypt, and not limited to one district, and therefore may be dependent upon official government edicts as opposed to local accounting practices. However, this point is also unclear, and for the moment the problem remains unsolved.[14]

The above analysis of Palestinian and Egyptian prices, etc., seems to bear out the opinion of West and Johnson that

> in spite of the almost universal opinion that there was (an actual money inflation in Egypt), the evidence does not wholly support this view. Egyptian prices, it is true, are expressed in figures of astronomical size but only when the monetary unit is the *denarius* or *drachma,* never apparently when prices or tax-rates are given in gold[15]... The apparent increase of prices expressed in terms of *denarii* and *drachmae* at a time when no rise can be discerned in the prices which are expressed in terms of the *solidus, siliqua* or *follis* is not inflation in the proper meaning of that term.[16]

That is not to say that prices did not rise at all. In so far as the *denarius* depreciated in value at some stages of its career, to as much as one-tenth of its value of 301, prices in terms of copper coinages must have fluctuated accordingly. (Again, the poor man would have been most seriously affected.) It is the scale of these price-increases and their meaning in terms of actual money (coins paid out to the vendor) that we have attempted to reconsider in the preceding sections. By disentangling prices in terms of actual monetary units from prices expressed in terms of units of value, we have tried to show that the situation in Egypt was not radically different from that in Palestine, and indeed in the rest of the Eastern Empire.[17]

CHAPTER XXVI

EPILOGUE

In the preceding pages, we have attempted to trace the course of monetary history during the two centuries of Amoraic Palestine, and to examine its effects upon prices and price-levels. We saw how the double-*denarius*, called the *antoninianus*, was introduced in the early third century. We followed the complex meanderings of its devaluation, culminating in a headlong fall during the later 260's. We noted Aurelian's brave, but short-lived, attempts to patch up the situation with his currency reforms, and his introduction of the *"follis"* concept. However, this was only to be followed by the *antoninianus'* plummeting downwards again in a series of progressive debasements,[1] until the radical reforms of Diocletian and energetic reorganization of so many aspects of social and economic life brought a new relative stability to the Eastern Roman Empire.

Clearly, these monetary changes and crises had their effects not only upon prices and wages, etc., but also, no less directly, upon the whole fabric throughout the Empire. They ran like destructive shudders through the social structure of the community at all its classes and levels. They brought down the wealthy, and impoverished the poor; they cut through society both vertically and horizontally, bringing about an exaggerated stratification in the social structure of the population.

The economic effects were clear and immediate. In the later third century, just as is to be expected, there is a gradual reversion to natural economy in many sectors of economic activity. The pattern of taxation reveals clear changes in governmental policy from one of money taxation to one of taxation in kind.[1a] This well-known fact is perhaps reflected in the late third-century statement of R. Aba bar Kahana[2] that the government says (to the taxpayer): מדד הביא מדד הביא measure out and bring [your taxes], measure out and bring. . .[3]

178

There is also a change of attitude towards land, discernable in Rabbinic texts of this time. For as money lost its stability, people sought frantically to purchase land, thinking it a point of constancy in the economic flux.[4] Even merchandise and trading were considered less "safe" than an investment in land.[5] Thus we find R. Eleazar [ben Pedat] (*floruit* Palestine circa 250-79) declaring that a "man who has no land is not a man",[6] and foretelling that even men with professions will go back to the land.[7] And indeed R. Eleazar's prognostication seems in some measure to have come true, for in the fourth century we find that "many members of the professional classes were also landlords".[8]

This sort of situation led to vicious rivalry and land-grabbing, a struggle out of which the toughest and least scrupulous types emerged on top.[9] These "*ba'alei zero'a*", as they are called in Rabbinic sources, pandered to the officialdom to be "in with the government", and ruthlessly exploited the poor and weak to their own advantage.[10]

Under the pressure of high taxation in kind, the pattern of landholding changed still further. Over-taxation encouraged flight and abandonment of land on the part of the small landowner, and this, of course, helped the "*ba'alei zero'a*" to build up their large new estates.[11] The Yerushalmi[12] relates a colourful tradition which conjures up a vivid picture of the oppressed peasantry and their apparently hopeless plight:

> Diocletian oppressed the people of Paneas.[13] They said to him, "We are going" (i.e. running away from here to escape the burdens of taxation). A wise counsellor (סופיסטא) said to him, "They will not go, and if they do they'll come back. And should you wish to test [this, my statement], take some deer and send them away to a far-off land, and in the end they will return to their place". He (Diocletian) did this. He brought deer and coated their horns with silver and sent them off to Africa, and at the end of thirty years[14] they returned to their place.

Private fortunes invested in land probably incurred relatively little loss of income as the produce could be sold at current prices.[15] The large landholder who marketed a considerable yield was in all probability paid in gold, while the owner of a smallholding may well have been paid only in silver or even in copper. The latter would thus suffer more than the former, and this too would aggravate the trend towards large new estates. Hence "the incident of land tenure on the '*aris* system (colonate) became more strongly marked (during the fourth century)".[16] But clearly, the class depending on salaries must have suffered most of all.[17]

This return to "natural economy" did however not last very long. With Diocletian's re-establishment of a relatively stable gold-based currency system, a confidence in money was re-established, as we have seen above. It was probably during the initial years, when the silver-washed *folles* were rapidly depreciating in value, but gold was standing firm, that R. Isaac [Nappaḥa] counselled[18] that one should divide one's wealth into three parts (i.e. three types of investment), one part land, one part merchandise and one part cash. This would seem to be very sound advice at this period, since too much land would invite the excessively high taxes, and cash was still liable to fluctuate in value (or so people thought). Trade was beginning to pick up again, after its virtual dislocation in the preceding century. If his *Edict of Maximum Prices* was not a complete success, this was in some measure due to his lack of control of the *aes* coinage.

Nonetheless, by the time of Constantine, the currency system with its abundant issues[19] had proven itself, and money was being used by all classes.[20] On the basis of texts from writers such as Libanius, Paul Petit has concluded that large contracts were in gold coinage, small ones in silver or even in copper, and (hoarding and) tax payments in bullion.[21] If this thesis needs any added proof, then the fourth century texts we have cited above can provide this further corroboration. We may even add that not merely large contracts were in gold, but smaller ones too, of the order of one *solidus* as in the case of R. Aba bar Zemina. Furthermore, the absence of any reference to the use of bullion in private contracts during this period (in contradistinction to the late third century, see above, Chapter XII) is surely signficant. It confirms what we have already stated above, that there was a very complete reverting to a money economy.[22]

Clearly the tight control of gold issues was central to the balance of the monetary economy of this time. This problem has recently been the subject of a penetrating study by J. P. C. Kent,[23] who examines the administrative mechanism for this control, its development, and the changing economic theories underlying it. Here we shall quote only his general conclusions :[24]

> In the collapse of the bimetallic system of the early Empire, taxation and wages were reassessed in kind. When from the time of Diocletian onwards a monetary economy was reestablished, the only fixed standard for taxes and payments alike was that of gold, and other coin rose and fell in relative value according to ordinary

economic laws. Since the whole system of imperial finance depended on the maintenance of a satisfactory gold coinage, forgery and mutilation,[25] which tended to reduce the income from taxation, were savagely repressed, and every effort was made to draw in the maximum amount of gold to the treasury.[26] The final steps in perfecting the system were taken by Valentinian I and Valens in 66-7. They decreed that all gold received in taxation was to be melted into ingots and tested before acceptance, and they reorganised the central treasury of the *sacrae largitiones* so that it was able to collect this bullion direct from the provinces and undertake its recoinage.[27] Thus gold coinage became concentrated at the imperial residence (*comitatus*) and. . . the marks OB and COM that appear on it testify its mintage there from the accredited bullion received by the treasury.[28]

This then rounds the picture off, a picture of the transition from a silver to a gold standard,[29] via a short period of "natural economy".[30] Within this period a great many major economic and social changes came about.[31] Patterns of land-holding and taxation altered,[32] as has been noted above. Agricultural changes also took place, and these had serious economic effects. There is evidence in Rabbinic sources that the fertility of the land was diminished, though whether through soil exhaustion or the incidence of less intensive cultivation is not clear.[33] Population movements and the altering patterns of population density also had their social effects,[34] as, of course, did the spread of Christianity.[35]

All these numerous factors (and others too) must be taken into account before a description of any kind of real, round, and living picture of the times can be undertaken. In the above study, we have attempted to do no more than build up a somewhat pale and bloodless (monetary) framework of the period, within which certain primary guidelines are delineated. Into this spare skeletal frame, and following the rough outlines indicated, all the social, economic and political factors will have to be woven, in order to give flesh and colour to our image of the Empire during these two very crucial centuries of its history.

APPENDIX

THE NEW APHRODISIAS FRAGMENTS

Among the many marble panel fragments bearing Latin inscriptions discovered during the 1970 campaign of excavations at Aphrodisias in Caria, a group was found belonging to a monetary edict issued by Diocletian. On closer examination the edict could be dated to the year 301, i.e., the same year in which the *Edict of Maximum Prices* was issued. The fragments were published in 1971 by Kenan T. Erim, Joyce Reynolds and an excellent numismatic commentary by Michael Crawford was included. (*JRS*, 1971, pp. 171-77. My thanks to Dr. Michael Crawford for promptly sending me an offprint of this important article.) The edict begins (fragment a) with the words BICHARACTA MI [. . ., probably *Bicharacta moneta* (*JRS*, ibid., p. 175), already discussed above in Chapter XIV. (See also my comments in *Erchei*, 2 1973, and *Classical Quarterly*, 1973.) Fragment d teaches us that the currency reform took effect on the 1st September in the consulship of Titianus and Nepotianus, i.e., in the year 301, and was thus approximately contemporary with the *Edict* of *Maximum Prices* (ibid., p. 175).

On the provisions of the reform the editors write that from "1st September 301, all new debts and analogous obligations were to be paid in current *pecunia* with a doubled face value. The emperors were at pains to assert that this regulation applied to payments made by the *fiscus* as well as those made by private persons. They were at even greater pains to assert (but without serious justificatory argument) that their associated regulation for payment of debts incurred by 1st September, 301 in *pecunia* at its old face value was perfectly fair—it was of course very much to the advantage of creditors and the interest of the *fiscus* was heavily involved", (ibid., p. 175, based on fragment b, p. 173).

But perhaps even more important for our purposes is the statement in fragment b line 1 : . . .]*rgenteus centum denariis*[. . . which would surely seem to describe the relationship between the *argenteus* and the *denarius* as 1 : 100. Crawford suggests : . . . *ut nummus a]rgenteus centum denariis [ualeat.* . . , adding in a comment : "The relationship involves surprises ; since 1 *argenteus* = 1/96 lb. of silver, 1 lb. of silver = 9,600 *denarii* ; even at a ratio of gold : silver of 1 : 10 the result is that 1 lb. of gold = 96,000 *denarii,* which comes very close to the outside limit of the maximum price for gold specified in the *Price Edict* (99,000 *denarii*) ; the relationship of gold to silver is far lower than had been thought possible" (ibid., p. 175. Cf. above, Chapter III, note 23). This, of course, reopens the whole crucial question of the value of gold in the *Edict of Maximum Prices,* a question which, so we have already seen above (Chapter III, note 23, etc.), is of considerable controversy.

The editors continue their reconstruction of the fragmentary text, restoring it thus : . . . *sed ut nummi radia]ti quinquae denariorum potentia vige[ant],* (p. 176). After discussing the implications of this latter reading (especially *"radia]ti"*), they conclude that, before the reform mentioned in this edict, Diocletian's coins should be identified as follows:

Small radiate bronze	=	2d.
Medium radiate bronze	=	5d.
Large laureate silver-bronze	=	10d.
Argenteus	=	50d.

whereas, after the reform of 301 (*geminata potentia*) the position stood thus :

Small radiate bronze	=	2d.
Medium radiate bronze	=	5d.
Large laureate silve-bronze	=	20d.
Argenteus	=	100d.

It will be noted that according to this suggestion "the face value of the *argenteus* (and with it the large silver-bronze coin) was doubled, while that of the radiate bronze coin (and the small laureate bronze coin) remained unchanged" (ibid., p. 176).

These conclusions, attractive though they be, are by no means certain. They rest primarily upon the restoration of lacunae. Furthermore, they take virtually no account of the papyri discussed above, Chapter IX (with the exception of a brief reference in note 20 on p. 176). Prof. Callu has, however, already demonstrated that quite a number of alternative reconstructions are possible (in *BSFN,* 27/8, 1972, pp. 290-92. My thanks to Prof. Callu for sending me a copy of this very significant communication). The edict may be speaking either of units of reckoning or of real coins. If the former, then a number of possible readings exist :

1. a) sed ut follis centum vigin]ti quinquae. . . (referring to the large *follis*).
   b) et follis vigin]ti quinquae. . . (referring to the small *follis*).
   c) et sestertius [nummus?] vigin]ti quinquae. . .

And if real coins are being discussed, one might read :

2. a) sed ut nummi laurea]ti quinquae. . .
   b) et nummus vigin]ti quinquae. . .

Callu himself rejects the last suggestion (2b) on the basis of metallic relationships, preferring reading 2a. Thus he follows Crawford's suggestion in part, modifying it and reintroducing the papyrological evidence. In reading "*nummi laurea]ti quinquae*", he means that the 2½d. coin became worth 5d., the 10d. coin became worth 20d., and the 12½d. piece mentioned in *P. Oslo* 83 went up to 25d. However he himself, with characteristic modesty, admits that the final solution to this complex set of interrelated problems had not yet been reached.

One key question is whether *PSI*. 965, which mentions the *Edict of Prices* and is therefore generally (though not conclusively) dated to c.301 (and also *P. Oslo* 83, for that matter) is describing a revaluation, (as Callu seems to think) or a devaluation (as Jones suggested; cf. above, Chapter IX). It is surely clear that the Aphrodisias fragments describe a revaluation of coins to double their face value, but this need not necessarily determine our interpretation of the papyrological evidence, which cannot be very closely dated. *P.Ryl.* 607, on the other hand. is certainly speaking of a devaluation (unless, of course, the official got the whole story wrong!). We are in the thick of a period of monetary instability (as papyri amply demonstrate), and there may well have been more than one attempt made to rectify the situation within a relatively short space of time. Indeed, this is the impression given by papyrological sources.

Now what is clear from the Aphrodisias evidence is that after the doubling of the face value of the (some?) coins from the 1st September, 301 onwards, something called "*argenteus*" would be worth 100d. However, whether this *argenteus* corresponds with the "numismatists' convention in relationship to Diocletianic coinage" (*JRS*, ibid., p. 175) to call the 1/96 silver piece an *argenteus* is quite another matter. If, (as Callu suggested as a possibility), the edict is talking of units of reckoning,

"...*]rgenteus*" could stand for "*follis a]rgenteus*", "*denarius a]rgenteus*", just as well as "*nummus a]rgenteus*". "*Denarius argenteus*" might even correspond to Epiphanius' silver *denarius* which equalled two silver *nummi* of 25d. each see above, Chapter IX). It would thus be a unit of reckoning worth 50d., which the edict states would double its value on the 1st September, thus reaching a value of 100d. Seen this way the XCVI (= 1/96) silver coin = 25d., and went up to 50d. The attempt was unsuccessful ; the market did not accept this arbitrary overvaluation, and very soon coin values found their own levels, primarily on the basis of metallic content.

Alternatively, the *argenteus* may be, as Crawford suggested and Callu accepts, the XCVI piece which prior to the reform was worth 50d. If we accept the reading of 50,000d. as the price of gold in the *Edict of Maximum Prices*, it would follow that the gold-silver ratio was somewhat below 1 : 14.4, 1 : 10.4, in fact. An attempt was made to double the face value of these coins, but this attempt was ultimately unsuccessful—the market would not accept what in effect meant a gold-silver ratio of about 1 : 5—and the *argenteus* found itself sinking to a more natural level of 32d., and then 25d., etc.

The above merely demonstrates that the whole issue remains as problematic as ever. The Aphrodisias fragments open up as many problems as they appear at first glance to solve. The crux of the whole edict, the nature of "*bicharata moneta*", remains an unsolved puzzle. This introduces an element of uncertainty into the very nature of the whole document. And this in turn highlights the necessity to examine such a text in the context of related material. Certainly it does not force us to change our opinion as to the price of gold recorded in the *Edict of Maximum Prices*. Until further *lacunae* have been filled in by additional fragments this important document must remain but another unplaced piece in this fragmentary jigsaw puzzle.

      vac.   B. vac. F. [vac.   ]
Imperator Caesar Gai. Aur. Val. Diocletianus p. f. Aug. p[ont. m. Germ.
                    m. VI Sarm. m.]
v. IIII Pers. m. II Brit. m. Carp. m. Aram. m. Med. m. Adiab. m. trib.
              [pot. VXIII(?) cons. VII p. p. procs. et]
Imperator Caesar M. Aur. Val. Maximianus p. f. Aug. pont. m. [Germ.
             m. V Sarm. m. III Pers. m. II Brit. m.]
v Part. m. Arab. m. Med. m. Adiab. m. tri[b. pot.] VXI[I(?) cons. VI
             p.p procs. ? vac. et]

Flabius Valerius Constantius [et G. Val. Maximianu]s Ge[rmm. Sarmm.
Perss. Britt. Carpp. Aramm.(?)]
v. Medd. Adiabb. III conss. nobb. Caess. dicunt(?)]*vac.*[*vac.*   ]

vac. [	*vac.*	]*vac.*[	*vac.*]
Bicharacta MI[	. .*c.* 30. .	]ITIAII[...	
quae in maiore[	. .*c.* 31. .	]riorum[...	
one INVS	. .*c.* 34. .	]CIASAP[...	
Roma[	. .*c.* 36. .	]AIVRV[...	
TVOR[	. .*c.* 37. .	]PGOLI[...	
SIC[	. .*c.* 38. .	]ATTV[...	
		...]EVNIV[...	
		...]ATIONA[...	
		...]VSTRIA[...	
		...]ETDEI[...	
		...]EPREI[...	
		...]REM[...	

cos[. .*c* 17. .]IRE[. . *c.* 8 . .]COIE[. .*c.* 11 . .a]rgenteus centum denariis
[. . *c.* 20. .]
ti quinque den[ari]orum potentia uige[ant? ?cui]us legis obseruantiae
etiam fiscum no[st]rum subiectum
esse scire te comu[. . .]lt ut scilicet ex kal(endis) Se[pte]mbribus Titiano
et Nepotiano cons(ulibus) *v.* hii debitores quicumque
esse noui coeperint etiam fisco geminata p[ote]ntia ea(n)dem tradant
pecuniam parique condicione si usus e
xigat etiam fiscus adnumeret *vac.* Super his autem debitoribus qui ante
kal(endas) Septemb(res) diem uel in fiscalibus
debitis deprehendendum uel in priuatis contractibus monstrantur obnoxii
iustum esse aequissimumque
perspicitur hanc adhiberi obseruantiam ut eandem pecuniam ita
numerent ut ualuisse cognoscitur antequ
am et per prouisionem nostram propter unius obseruantiam leg[is] facta
fuerit adcessio nec iniquitatem ullam
statuti putent quibus ista condicio praescribitur cum in ea potentia
pecuniam repraesentare uideantur in qua
eos suscepisse manifestum est   *vac.*

Aphrodisias fragments of Diocletian's currency reform
Taken from *JRS* 1971, pp. 172, 173.

NOTES

MAIN ABBREVIATIONS

AAH	Acta Antiqua Academia Scientiarum Hungaricae, Budapest
Ant.	Antoninianus
ANS	American Numismatic Society
ANSMN	American Numismatic Society, Museum Notes
B.	Bavli
b.	ben, bar (= son of . . .)
BMC	British Museum Catalogue
BSFN	Bulletin de la Société française de Numismatique
CIG	Corpus Inscriptiones Graecarum
CIL	Corpus Inscriptiones Latinarum
CNP	Corpus Nummorum Palestiniensis
Cod. Theod.	Codex Theodosianus
d.	denarius
Deut. Rab.	Deuteronomy Rabba
DJD	Discoveries in the Judaean Desert
dr.	drachma
drm.	(Sasanian) drachm
EB	Encyclopaedia Britannica
Eccles. Rab.	Ecclesiastes Rabba
Econ. Surv.	Economic Survey of Ancient Rome, ed. Tenney Frank
(or Survey)	
Ed. Diocl.	Edict of Diocletian
Exod. Rab.	Exodus Rabba
Gen. Rab.	Genesis Rabba
gr.	gramme
GRM	Griechische und römische Metrologie
HUCA	Hebrew Union College Annual
ILS	Inscriptiones Latinae Selectae
INCP	International Numismatic Convention Proceedings, ed. A. Kindler
JE	Jewish Encyclopaedia
JESHO	Journal of the Social and Economic History of the Orient
JJP	Journal of Juristic Papyrology
JJS	Journal of Jewish Studies
JQR	Jewish Quarterly Review

JRS	Journal of Roman Studies
JSS	Journal of Semitic Studies
Lev. Rab.	Leviticus Rabba
LRBC	Late Roman Bronze Coinage, by R.A.G. Carson, J.P.C. Kent and P.V. Hill
LW	Lehnwörter
M.	Mishna
MSR	Metrologicorum Scriptorum Reliquiae
NC	Numismatic Chronicle
NNM	Numismatic Notes and Monographs (of ANS)
Nov. Val.	Novellae, Valentinian
Num. Chron.	Numismatic Chronicle
NS	New Series
P.	for Papyrological abbreviations see bibliography, section on papyrology.
PMER	La Politique Monétaire des Empereurs Romains
PG	Patrologia Graeca
PL	Patrologia Latina
QDAP	Quarterly of the Department of Antiquities in Palestine
R	Rabbi, Rav
RE	Real-Encyclopaedia
REJ	Revue des Études Juives
RIC	Roman Imperial Coinage, by Mattingly, Bruun, Sutherland and Carson
sest.	sestertius
sext.	sextarius
SRHJ	Social and Religious History of the Jews
T.	Tosefta
TAPA	Transactions of the American Philological Association
VL	Variae Lectiones
xest.	xestes
Y.	Yerushalmi (= Palestinian Talmud)

PP. 16–31

Notes Introduction

1 Note also that Johnson in *JJP*, 4, 1950, p. 151 writes: "Since more papyri have been preserved from sites above the flood level, the evidence which they present may tend to distort the general picture of economic conditions" (even within Egypt, that is). Furthermore, Milne has suggested that there may be even be distinct differences between the (economic) nature of the evidence coming from Alexandria and that of other parts of Egypt, (*Aegyptus*, 32, 1952, p. 157). This attempt to bring a non-Egyptian perspective was the object of Szilági's article in *AAH*, XI, 1963, pp. 325–89. Basing himself on prices from the Western Provinces, he concluded (p. 325) that Egypt "is an exception in every respect".

2 I have not included any material from late Midrashim, as their accuracy, datability, always raises too many points of uncertainty. For this reason I excluded, for example, the slave price in a text cited in Torat Ḥesed (by Isaac b. Solomon Jabez) as coming from "*Midrash Rabba*". See *Rav Po'alim* by Abraham b. Elija of Wilna (Warsaw, 1894), p. 21. I have also not drawn upon the wealth of interesting material contained in *Seder Eliyahu Rabba* and *Zuta*, despite the fact that M. Margulies regarded it as the work (with later interpolations) of a III cent. Palestinian scholar. See his article in *Sefer Assaf*, pp. 370–90 (Jerusalem, 1953). The dating of this work is still far from being established; see Baron, *SRHJ*², 6, pp. 401–02, note 7, for bibliography.

3 In this discussion I have not made use of the many mediaeval Jewish numismatic and metrological treatises, since they reflect their own current conditions, rather than those of antiquity. See, for example, my remarks in *Sinai*, 58, 1966, pp. 164–68.

4 Hitherto our knowledge of the text of the Bavli has been based almost solely on the (single complete) Munich Ms. (of the Babylonian Talmud). See Rabbinovitz' introduction to this *Variae Lectiones in Mischnam et in Talmud Babylonicum*. This introduction has been re-published separately with additional notes by A. M. Habermann, under the title "*Ma'amar al Hadpasat ha-Talmud*" (Jerusalem, 1952).

Chapter I

1 The above is based upon the conclusions of my article in *JQR*, 56, 1956, pp. 273–301, entitled "Palestinian Currency Systems in the Second Commonwealth". In it I reject the views expressed by Heichelheim in his section of Syria, *Econ. Surv.* 4 (Baltimore, 1938), chap. 3 part 4, pp. 211–213. Add the remarks of Callu in *PMER*, p. 15 and note 2, ibid. However, see most recently A. Ben-David's article in *PEQ*, 103, 1971, pp. 109–129.

Chapter II

1 At the classical ratio of 25d. = 1 *aureus* this *ketuba* would have been worth 500d. Actually it was worth slightly less, as *solidi* were lighter than *aurei*. However, this would be quite a reasonable and usual amount for a *ketuba*; see, eg. Y. Ketubot 6.4.

191

On the halachic issues involved in this Yerushalmi text, see the discussion in the appendix to Nachmanides' *Novellae* to Ketubot (on Ketubot 54a). (These novellae are usually mistakenly attributed to the Rashba = Solomon ben Adret.)

2 See J. N. Epstein, *Prolegomena ad Litteras Amoraiticas* (Jerusalem, 1962), p. 286 (Hebrew).

3 I. S. Horowitz' interpretation of this text, in *Palestine and the Adjacent Countries* (Vienna, 1923, Hebrew), p. 289a and note 57, though clever, is undoubtedly incorrect, as he himself suspected (ibid.).

4 I have discussed the problems of chronology in my article in *Archiv Orientalni*, 31, 1966, pp. 61–2.

5 According to *Ed. Diocl.* 1 *mod. castr.* (= 2 *mod. Ital.*) wheat cost 100 *denarii*.

6 By 324 the *solidus* had completely taken the place of the *aureus*, even in the East.

7 28.1.18, Loeb ed. 3, pp. 98–9.

8 See Jones, *The Later Roman Empire*, 1, p. 445.

9 *Patrologia Orientalis*, 4/5, ed. Bousquet and Nau (Paris, 1907), pp. 445–48. See below, Chapter XXV.

10 369 a–d. Loeb ed. 2, pp. 504–07. See Downey's article in *Studies in Roman Social and Economic History in honour of Allan Chester Johnson* (1951).

11 In 369D Julian writes (loeb ed. p. 506): καιτοι τις μεμνηται παρ' ὑμιν εὐθηνουμενης τῆς πολεως πεντακαιδεκα μετρα σιτον πραθεντα του χρυσου. If *chrusos* here means *solidus*, then the *metron* must be of a different sort to that mentioned above, as fifteen of the first kind of *metron* cost only one *argurion*. If *metra* here can mean *modius castrensis* (as it does in Eusebius, see above), then there is no contradiction between the texts; (see below, where we have shown that 1 *mod. cast.* cost 1/15 *sol.*) Short of actually correcting χρυσου to ἀργυριου or μετρα to μοδιους (*castrenses*), corrections for which there are no manuscript bases, this seems the only possible explanation. See also P. Petit, *Libanius et la Vie Municipale à Antioche au IV siècle après J–C* (Paris 1955), p. 114, notes 2 and 3, and Rostovtzeff in Pauly-Wissowa *RE*, 7, p. 147, s. v. *Frumentum*.

12 Mattingly, *Roman Coins*[2] (London, 1960), p. 220; Segrè in *Byzantion*, 15, 1941, p. 265. *Cod. Just.* 90, 32, end; West and Johnson, *Currency in Roman and Byzantine Egypt*, p. 129, etc. On *argenteus-siliqua*, see Adelson in *Centennial Publication of the American Numismatic Society*, ed. Harald Ingholt (New York, 1958), p. 13.

13 μετρον, here cannot mean *modius*. Misopog. 369 B: οὑς ἐπιχωριον ἐστιν λοιπον ὀνομαξειν μοδιους. See Downey, *Studies in Roman Social and Economic History*, note 48. On the various meanings of *metron*, see above Eusebius, *metron = modius (castrensis)*, *P. O.* 90v. (1 *artab* = 10 *metra*). Hulsch, *MSR*, index, s. v. μετρον.

14 We do find other examples of reckoning in loaves (or *per capita* daily rations). Thus Socrates, *Historia Ecclesiastica* 2, 13 (Migne *P. G.* 67, 209): ἐζημιωσε δε την πολιν ἀφελων του σιτηρεσιου του παρασχεθεντος παρα του πατρος αὐτου ἡμερεσιου, ὑπερ τεσσαρας μυριαδες, while in the Migne ed. note 6, the editor cites Photius' biography of Paul of Constantinople: ἡ δε ὁλον της δωρεας, ἡμερησιον ἀρτοι μυριαδες ὀκτω. (i. e. that 80,000 loaves, rather than merely unspecified units were daily distributed). But see editor's comments, ibid. Cf. Johnson and West, *Byzantine Egypt: Economic Studies*, p. 234. See also *Testament of Job* 5.20 (ed. Kohler), in *Semitic Studies in Memory of Dr. Alexander Kohut* (Berlin, 1897), p. 323.

15 The "dole bread" was also called ἀρτοι πολιτικοι: *panes civilis*, (*Chron. Pasch.* p. 263, Migne 92, 641b, ibid., p. 389, 997a), and was probably reckoned in units of

the ἄρτος as indeed it was served by Julian (*Misopog* 369 B). This is the Rabbinic mode of reckoning too (e. g. M. Eruvin 8.2, see below, Chapter XVI). Such an interpretation of the *metron* makes good sense of other sections of this passage. Thus Julian states (ibid.) that he imported 400,000 *metra* of wheat into Antioch from Alexandria, but they were not sufficient. He therefore brought in a further 22,000 *modii*. This is itself is some indication that the *metron* is a very much smaller measure than the *modius*. According to our interpretation he imported an additional 528,000 *metra*, thus totalling 928,000 *metra* (excluding unspecified amounts from Egypt). As the population of Antioch at this time is reckoned at some 150,000 this amount would suffice to feed the whole population only one week or so. Clearly Julian wished to cater only for the poorer inhabitants, (πνιγομενος ὑπο των πλουσιων — 358c Loeb ed. p. 504). On the population of Antioch, see *Econ. Surv.* 4, p. 158 (references cited). Also Downey in *TAPA*, 89, 1958, pp. 84–91, "The Size and Population of Antioch", and his *A History of Antioch in Syria* (Princeton, 1961), excursus 2, pp. 582–83. On the whole Julian episode, see further P. de Jonge in *Mnemosyne*, 1948, pp. 238–45, and J. Adelson, "Economic Theory and Practice in Antioch, 361–63", *INCP*, pp. 33–40.

16 But see Ammianus Marcellinus 25, 8.15: *ut si usquam modiis farinae fuisset repertus, quod rara contigerat, aureis decem mutaretur ut minus* (363 c. e.). However, these were truly remarkable circumstances.

17 See S. Lieberman's *The Talmud of Caesarea* (Supplement to Tarbiz, 1931), p. 98, note 60. There the reading is R. Josa (a contemporary of R. Jona) which Lieberman prefers. If this reading is accepted the text is probably from not earlier than the 40's. See my remarks in *Talpiot*, 9/3, 1970, p. 610, note 72. See also *Or Zaru'a* by R. Isaac ben Moses of Vienna (c. 1200–70), Bava Kama (102a) sect. 412, pp. 61–62.

18 The Leiden Ms. has דינרין ח', an intermediate stage.

19 A parallel example of חדא being abbreviated to ח' and then the ח' being understood to mean eight may be found in *Leviticus Rabba* 34,16, ed. Margulies, p. 812. There it is related that R. Tarfon gave R. Akiva a certain sum of money to buy himself an estate — חדא אוסיא. However, Ms. Munich 117 (= כ) and Aruch, ed. Pesaro (= ע), which both have ח', instead of חדא, read אסוון and אסוונן respectively, i.e. "estates" in the plural. Apparently, they understood the ח' to mean eight; hence, estates. There are many similar examples of this kind of scribal-error development. I should here like to cite one example. It is explained by Reuben Margaliot in his *Nitsotsei Or* (Jerusalem, 1965), p. 133a, to Kiddushin 76b. In the Talmud there it is related that King David had 400 children, all the sons of captive women. This is not possible, as the law permits one to marry only one captive woman per battle, and David waged no more than 18 battles in all (*Leviticus Rabbah* 1). However, in I Chronicles 3:6–8, nine of David's sons are enumerated, in a separate category from the six born in Hebron (ibid. 6) and the four in Jerusalem (ibid. 5). These nine children whose mothers' names are not given (in contradistinction to the others) were explained by the Talmud to be the children of captive women. The original text presumably read: תשעה nine, which was abbreviated to ת', and subsequently misinterpreted to stand for 400 — the numerical value of the letter ת. (For a parallel development, see *Midrash Shir Ha-Shirim*, ed. Grünhut, 7b note 8, ט = ת and cf. *Yalkut* Exodus, section 195, in the name of Midrash "Avchir".) Finally the scribes wrote out ארבע מאות (= 400) in the full. These examples are evidence of the varying traditions in the writing of numbers. See also

Reuben Margaliot's *Mechkarim be-Darkei ha-Talmud ve-Ḥidotav* (Jerusalem, 1967), study 10, pp. 51–61, for many other examples of this process. Also compare *Lev. Rab.* 21.9 (ed. Margulies p. 488) and Y. Yoma 1.1 with B. Yoma 9a, etc. On number corruptions, see Baron's remarks in *SRHJ*[2], 3, p. 284, note 48, and see my article in *Sinai* 62 (1968), pp. 278–80.

20 I have pointed out some of the difficulties in this very complex text in my article in *Archiv Orientalni*, 1968, p. 63. See also Lieberman, *Tosefta ki-fshutah, Zera'im*, 2, p. 752 (to T. Ma'aser Sheni 3.8). For further discussion see below, chap. XIV.

21 M. Eduyot 1.10. See further Zuckermann, *Talmudische Münzen und Gewichte*, (Breslau, 1862), pp. 30–31, V; Krauss, *LW*, 2, p. 319; Jastrow p. 719b, s.v. לְקָן, who identifies *leken* with *lepton*(?). See also Herzfeld, *Metrologische Voruntersuchungen* (Leipzig, 1863), pp. 165–69. I have suggested in my article in the *JQR*, 56, 1966, that the *asper* was 1/5d. (smaller than a *sestertius* but larger than an *obol*). Note also that in Y. Bava Mezia 4.1 the *leken* is smaller than a *karat* which is 1/4d. But see below Chap. XIV for a fuller discussion of this term. From there it will be seen that the *leken* (*leukon*) and the *asper* were not identical in value, and belong to totally different periods. On the other hand, in their relationship to the *aureus* they are not altogether dissimilar, and the *leukon* may possibly be a derivative (linguistically and metrologically) of the *asper*.

22 Furthermore, a comparison of this passage with the text on which it is based, in Tosefta Ma'aser Sheni 3.4, will demonstrate that it is the *aureus* that is being spoken of.

23 There were (at least) two Arbels. One is about 10 kilometres by road from Tiberias. (see Avi-Yonah's *Map of Roman Palestine*). Hirschensohn, in *Sheva Chochmoth* (London, 1912), p. 43, s.v. אָרְבֵּל, believe that this is the Arbel here referred to. There is, however, yet another Arbela in Transjordan, 39 kilometres S.E. of Tiberias. (See Horowitz, *Palestine and the Adjacent Countries*, Vienna, 1923, pp. 75–77, on both Arbels.) As this was one of the major cities of its area, it is perhaps more likely to be the Arbel of our text.

24 Stated in the name of R. Jose, whom we know transmitted traditions of R. Jeremiah, and also followed his opinions (e.g. Y. Ḥala 1.1). He may then here be transmitting the view of R. Jeremiah, similar to that of Y. Bava Batra 8.4.

25 Jastrow, *Dict.*, pp. 263b–269a, s.v. גרב I–III.

26 The *gerev* was used for containing wine. See Y. Brand, *Klei Ha-ḥeres Besifrut Hatalmud* (Jerusalem, 1953), p. 95.

27 CIL, 8, 4508; *JRS*, 4, 1914, pp. 143–46; *Econ. Surv.*, 4, pp. 80–82. See also Richard Duncan-Jones, *Papers of the British School at Rome*, 30, NS. 27, pp. 74–75, who is of the opinion that these computations are too high.

28 This also explains why the Latin *denarius* and the Greek δηναριον refer to silver coins while (the Syriac *dinar* and) the Arabic *dinar* refer to gold coins. (See Schrötter, *Wörterbuch das Münzkunde*, s.v. *Dinar*, pp. 139b–142b. But see Brockelmann, *Lexicon Syriacum*[2], p. 160.) See also the remark of Sukenik in *Journal of the Palestine Oriental Society*, 15, 1935, p. 142, concerning certain inscriptions found in the synagogue of El Ḥammeh (from the fifth century, probably) that "...contrary to the earlier practice of the Talmud, without further specification (*denarius*) was at this time and place (i.e. El-Ḥammeh) understood to mean a *gold denarius*", (my addition in brackets). He further notes (ibid.) that in the *Syro-Roman Statute Book* the gold *denarius* is simply called *denarius*. However, even in the El-Ḥammeh inscriptions

the use of *dinar* is not wholly consistent, so that while twice (pp. 143, 146, ibid.) it appears unspecified, once (p. 131, ibid.) we find: דהבון הכא חמישה דינרין זהב. (See more recently, Frey, *CIJ*, 2, Rome, 1952, nos. 856, 858, 859, pp. 96, 98.) As to the *Syro-Roman Statute Book*, see, eg., *RI* sect. 33: או דינרא או זוזא, (= E. Sachau, *Syrisch Rechtsbücher*, 1, Berlin, 1907, p. 18.)

Chapter III

1 I have discussed this problem at considerable length in my article in *Talpiot*, 9/3–4, 1970, pp. 591–611, entitled "Al Erko shel Maneh" (hereafter simply — *Talpiot*).

2 See Hultsch *MSR*, index s.v. μνα, μανη, ἀργυρος, etc. See Jastrow, *Dict.*, p. 797ab, s.v. מנה. Also *P.O.* 9v (III cent. C.E.). In *Inscriptions Grecques et Latines da la Syrie*, Jalabert & Mouterde, 3/1 (Paris, 1950), pp. 479–81, no. 867, read: μναϹστατηρων and not μναϛστσηρων (p. 480) to make sense of the inscription. See also my detailed discussion of the use of the term *maneh* in the *Peshitta* to Mark 12.42, in *Novum Testamentum*, 9, 1967, pp. 178–90.'

3 In this we reject the suggestion of Segrè, *JQR*, 34, 1943–44, p. 481. See further S. Lieberman, in his edition of *Deut. Rab.* p. 126, note 2, and in Margulies' ed. of *Lev. Rab.* p. 879. Segrè equates the *maneh* with the *ma'ah*, on the basis of a comparison of the *Targum Onkelos* to Exod. 30.31 with that of the *Targum Ps. Jonathan*. However, here he followed the printed ed., while the Mss. of the *Targum Ps. Jonathan* read מעין as does *Onkelos*. Eg. Brit. Mus. Add. 27,031 fol. 97a, (misread by J. Ginzburger in his edition of this text, Berlin, 1903). So also Ms. Neofiti 1. On possible causes motivating the printed editions' mistaken מנין, see my articles in *Novum Testamentum*, 1967, and *Talpiot*, op.cit. During this same period, however, "*maneh*" still sometimes meant 100d. and *dinar* unqualified, 1 silver *denarius*. See *Talpiot*, 9, 1970, p. 611, note 74. See also Y. Pesaḥim 8.3, (Y. Pe'a 8.8?). There is thus no hard and fast rule for interpreting these terms, and each case must be examined individually. If we discount the example of Y. Megila 4.1 (see below) then this change takes place only in the late III cent. when the *denarius* was very debased and had very little value. Perhaps the old use of *maneh* (= λεπτον) meaning a minute coin (*minuta*, *Vulgate*, Greek and *Peshitta* to Mark 12,42 = Luke 21.2, but not *Peshitta* reading in latter) was adopted to describe the almost worthless devalued *denarius*. The key to the problem hangs to a certain extent on the interpretation of Y. Megila 4.1 (G). See my remarks in *Novum Testamentum*, 9, 1967, pp. 178–90.

4 Migne, *Patrologia Graeca*, 20, 816: ὡς ἑνος μετρου πυρων δισχιλιας και πεντακοσιας 'Αττικας ἀντικαταλλατεσθαι. (Loeb ed. 2, 352).

5 See Callu *PMER*, p. 148 and notes 1 and 13; idem, *BSFN*, 20/8, 1965, pp. 500–1, basing himself on *P. Beatty Panop.* 2.

6 See Payne Smith, *Thesaurus Syriacus*, 2164, s.v. *mana*. But cf. the Syriac version of Eusebius, from the St. Petersburg manuscript (dated 462 C.E.) by W. Wright and N. McLean (Cambridge, 1898), p. 369 and P. Bedjan's ed. (Leipzig, 1897), p. 530, where the reading is "*ma'in*", (= *obols*). Quite clearly this cannot be the correct reading, as an *obol* was never equal to an Attic *drachma*. Furthermore, in Bar

Hebraeus, *Chronography* (ed. Budge, 1, p. 58) we read "God admonished the world with famine and pestilince so severly that a *modius* of wheat was sold from 250 *manin*". See further *Chronique de Michel le Syrien*, ed. Chabot 1 (Paris, 1899), p. 202, who reads 2500 *minas*. (See Lieberman, in *Annuaire de l'Institut de Philologie et d'Histoire Orientales et Slaves*, 7, 1939–44, p. 434, note 4.) In Syriac the difference between an "n" and an "ayin" is hardly noticeable at times. See, for example, the different readings to Syriac Job 21:24 cited in Schulthess, *Lexicon Syro-Palaestinum* (Berlin, 1905), p. 115a, s.v. m'a. (Another example of this change may be found in *The Story of Aḥikar*, ed. Conybeare, Rendel Harris & A. Smith Lewis (Cambridge, 1913), p. xxxi.) The St. Petersburg Ms. is a copy of an earlier one, now lost. The Greek version was first translated into Syriac in the IV cent; See E. Lohmann, *Der textkritische Wert der Syrischen Übersetzung der Kirchengeschichte des Eusebius* (Halle, 1894), pp. 10–12.

7 The *maneh* is used to describe a small coin. Thus in *Deut. Rab.* (K), ed. Lieberman, p. 126 (= *Tanḥuma Ha'azinu* 1, *Tanḥuma Buber* 3, pp. 51–2): "when a man is way-laid by highwaymen while on a journey, he says to them 'Would you wish to kill me for the five *manehs* I have with me?' Later, when they reach the city, they discover he is a rich man, and say to him: 'Yesterday when we caught you, you said you have nothing but five *manehs*, and now you pull out priceless jewels, etc.'" (cf. *Exod. Rab.* 30.24 for another version of this parable.) And in *Esther Rabba* 10.4 (L) we read that in reply to his taunts, Haman was told that the *omer* cost about 10 *manin*. Now the *omer* consists of an *issaron* of barley; $3\frac{1}{2}$ *issaron* = 1 *se'uh*. Therefore, 1 *se'ah* barley costs about 33 *manin*. The *se'ah* (for which there were many different standards; see my remarks in *JESHO*, 8, 1965, pp. 266–71) was probably less than a *modius castrensis*. According to *Ed. Diocl.*, 1,2 (ed. Graser, p. 318), 1 *mod. castr.* barley cost 60d.

8 I first discussed this text in an article in *Archiv Orientalni*, 34, 1966, pp. 54–66, and subsequently in *Talpiot*, 9, 1970, pp. 601–603,, where I considerably revised my opinions. See also L. Bank, *REJ*, 38, 1899, pp. 47–63.

9 ed. Buber, p. 145.

10 The dating of this text is discussed in detail in my article in *Talpiot*, op. cit., pp. 597–98, a modification of what I wrote in *Archiv Orientalni* ibid., p. 63. The sum of 99 *maneh*, as judges' wages, recorded in B. Ketubot 105a, is problematic. If this text belongs to the inflationary period, then it may be recording a daily wage. See note in Chap. XV, section on wages.

11 See also *Levitivus Rabba* 30.1 (ed. Margulies, pp. 680–81) = *Pesikta de R. Kahana*, "U-lekaḥtem" 1, ed. Mandelbaum 2, p. 404 (S) according to which a "bunch of hyssop" (see Exod. 12.22) costs 4 *maneh*. The text is from between c. 290 and 320. Cf. *Ed. Dicol.* chap. 6 in which bunches of vegetables are usually priced at 4d.

12 On the Y. Berachot text, see S. Goren's edition of Yerushalmi Berachot, called *Hayerushalmi Hamephurash*, etc. (Jerusalem, 1961), p. 89. His reference there to Y. Sanhedrin 7.2 seems to be somewhat misguided. See commentators, on this text.

13 cf. parallel in B. Bava Mezia 85b.(G) According to the Yerushalmi this statement of R. Ḥiyya was made during the lifetime of Rabbi [Judah the Prince], i.e. prior to c.220. According to the Bavli, this is not necessarily the case, and the statement could have been made even after Rabbi's death.

14 I have discussed the dating of this text in greater detail in *Talpiot*, 9, p. 604. It seems

likely that this is a Babylonian text. See also Bacher's remarks in *Aggadot ha-Tan-naim*,2/2, pp. 181–82, note 6.

15 See for example Bolin, *State and Currency in the Roman Empire* (Uppsala, 1958) chap. 11, especially p. 281, basing himself on a Nubian inscription *CIG*, 5008 (ed. J. Franzius, 3, 1953, p. 468, et seq.). See also *Zeitschrift für Numismatik*, 15, 1887, p. 325 (Wilcken), and Kubitschek, *Quinquennium*, p. 325. See also below, Chap. IV.

16 I am still not wholly staisfied with this interpretation.What is clear from the context is that 2 *manii* was considerably less than the cost of the whole of the Holy Scriptures. We do however not know the price of books at that time; (B. Gittin 35a is undated and ambiguous). For that matter neither do we know the price of nets. If it could be shown here that a complete Bible cost much more than 200d., then *maneh* here might mean 100d. If it could be shown to have cost less than 200d. then *maneh* must be a small coin, most likely a *denarius*. (cf. B. Bava Mezia 115a.) See further *Masechet Semachot*, chap. 6, section 2, where we read of a *Torah*-scroll being worth 100 *maneh*, c. 60–70 C.E.; (ed. M. Higger, New York, 1931, p. 135, lines 45–47 = *The Tractate Mourning*, Yale Judaica Series, 17, 1966, p. 70, transl. Dov Zlotnik). Although this is not intended as an exact estimate it is clear that a *Torah*-scroll was very expensive — 10,000d. See also Acts 19.19 for magical books to the value of 50,000 silver pieces. See also T. Bava Kama 9.3, and compare Y. Bava Kama 8.3, noting the significant change in order.

17 I have treated this subject very fully in an article published in *JRS*, 56 (1966), pp. 190–95, entitled "Denarii and Aurei in the Time of Diocletian". See also *Talpiot*, 9, pp. 595–97. See also Graser's observations in *TAPA*, 71, 1940, p. 152. However, see Johnson and West's reservations concerning this fragment in *Byzantine Egypt*: *Economic Studies*, (Princeton 1949), pp. 140–1, but cf. ibid., p. 160. Fragments of the Edict have been found in the West too. See Szilági, *AAH*, 11, 1963, p. 333, note 43, for bibliography, and Lauffer's new edition of the *Edict*, (Berlin 1971). On the basis of this evidence I reject much of the argumentation of Bolin, followed recently by Sutherland in *RIC*, 6, 1967, pp. 98–99. For the date of Diocletian's first currency reform see Sutherland *RIC*, 6.

18 ed. Lieberman, p. 103.

19 See M. Margalioth, *Sefer Ha-Razim* (Jerusalem, 1966), p. 103, note 40. See also Lieberman, *Tosefta ki-fshutah*, 2, (New York 1955), p. 551.

20 Standard editions (Wilna, etc.) have "*zuz*" (= d.)!

21 It is however true that there was one R. Aba bar Kohen, who is at least on one occasion confused with R. Aba bar Kahana (B. Bava Mezia 11b, also Y. Halla 2.7, see A. Hyman's *Toldot Tannaim Ve'Amoraim*, p. 48b), and who flourished in Palestine c.350–75. Thus one might argue that our text is of a later date, c.370 for example, and *maneh* is here being used in its traditional meaning of 100d. Hence, we would have an equation of 1 *aureus* = 80,000d., quite a plausible ratio for the later fourth cent. (See eg. Segrè, *Byzantion*, 15, p. 263.) A careful analysis of certain cognate texts (*Yalkut*, 1, 298; 2, 237; *Midrash Tillim* 9, Buber ed. p. 81; *Pesikta Rabbati* 23; Y. Pe'a 1.1) will however demonstrate conclusively that the reading R. Aba bar Kahana in our text is not to be altered. For there we find statements of a similar exegetical nature (based on the same Biblical verse), yet independent in style and form all in the name of R. Aba bar Kahana. The last source cited (Y. Pe'a) is particularly significant as it is wholly independent both exegetically and formally, and similar only in idea and content. These texts may therefore be regarded as in-

dependent corroborations of the reading "Kahana" (as opposed to the suggested "Kohen") in Deuteronomy Rabba. (See also *Tanḥuma Buber*, Deuteronomy pp. 16 and 34.) The equation of 1 *aureus* = 80,000d. could not be prior to c.340 (Segrè, *Byzantion*, ibid.), when R. bar Aba Kahana was no longer alive. Hence "*maneh*" cannot here be taken in its more usual sense of 100d.

22 In a paper read before the International Numismatic Conference in Israel, 1963, published in *INCP*, pp. 231–45. This reference is to p. 237. See also Mattingly, *Roman Coins*[1], (London, 1928), p. 226; West, *Gold and Silver Standards in the Roman Empire* (New York, 1941), p. 187, etc. Contra Bingen, for example, in *Chronique d'Égypte*, 40, 1965, pp. 206–08, 431–34. Further confirmation of this Diocletianic ratio of 800d. = 1 *aureus* may perphaps be found in a difficult text in the *Scriptures Historiae Augustae*. In this very problematic work we find the following equation: 100,000 *sestertii* = 30 silver pounds, (*Elagabalus* 24.3, Loeb ed. 2, p. 152). Mommsen, in *Ges. Schr.* 7, p. 316, states that the *sest.* here is confused with the debased *denarii* of Diocletian. 800d. = 1 *aureus*, in the system of Diocletian, and there are 60 *aurei* to the *libra aurei*. This there were 48,000d. to the *libra aurei*. The relationship between silver and gold during this period was 14.4 : 1. Therefore 30 lbs. silver = (48,000/14.4) × 30 = 99,990. This result is very close to the *Scriptores Historiae Augustae's* 100,000 *sest.* (= *denarii*), and constitutes independent, if oblique, evidence in support of other metrological arguments, outlined below.

23 Ed. E. R. Graser, in *Econ. Survey*, 5, (Baltimore, 1940), p. 412. Although the reading was called into doubt by Mattingly, in his article "Monetary System of the Roman Empire from Diocletian to Theodosian I", (*Num. Chron.* 1946, p. 113), he himself later accepted the reading as correct when new corroborative fragments were discovered. (See Mattingly, *Roman Coins*[2], London, 1960, pp. 217–18.) See also F. Ehrendorfer "Die Münzreform des Diokletian", *Num. Zeitschrift*, 72, 1947, p. 101, and L. C. West "The Coinage of Diocletian and the Edict of Prices" (*Studies in Roman Economic and Social History in Honour of Allan Chester Johnson*, 1951), p. 290 etc. Most recently F. M. Heichelheim, in *JRS*, 55, 1965, p. 251, basing himself on information supplied to him by Klaffenbach, has shown conclusively that the reading in the Elatea Fragment is not to be called into doubt, (contra West, Mattingly, Pareti, Mazzarino, Bernardi, Ruggini, Skeat, cited *JRS*, 55 ibid.). Klaffenbach's epigraphic evidence, however, is in itself not enough to render Heichelheim's thesis irrefutable, as West (1.c.) for example, considered the possibility of a mason's error in the carving of the inscription. But Heichelheim's argument from papyrological sources is very convincing, and the Rabbinic evidence here cited would seem further to bear it out. See also Callu *PMER*, pp. 358–59, note 6, and p. 362. The reading has most recently again been called into doubt, as the result of the discovery of a new inscription which is a fragment of an edict of Diocletian on his currency reforms. See *JRS*, 1971, p. 175. (It is called the Aphrodisias fragment.) However, I am not convinced by the argumentation there. The reading "50,000" has been accepted by S. Lauffer in his critical edition of *Diokletians Preisedikt*, Berlin 1971, (reviewed by A. Chastagnol in *Revue des Études Latines*, 1970, pp. 664–8).

24 *State and Currency*, pp. 332–33, 285. See *P. Mich.* p. 286. For Rabbinic evidence of the use of gold bullion, see e.g. Y. Ketubot 12.7 (290–320 C.E.); *Gen. Rab.* 63.3; *Deut. Rab.* 1.13 (both 290–320); Y. Bava Kama 8.8 (250–60), etc. However, Carson doubts the validity of Bolin's argument. He writes (in a private communication of 15 August, 1972): "Would not a coin, if only as an easily exchangeable object,

carry some bonus over the same weight of unminted metal?" Dr. J. Kent (in a private communication of 23 August, 1972) expresses the same doubts. On Bolin in general, see Buttrey's brilliant review an *American Journal of Archeology*, 65, 1961.

25 Confirmed by the discovery of the new Aphrodisias fragment of Diocletian's edict on his monetary reforms; see *JRS*, 1971, p. 177.

Chapter IV

1 It appears that despite a falling off in the fineness of the *denarius* towards the end of the second century, its official tariffing *vis-à-vis* the *aureus* remained unaltered. Certainly Tannaitic sources suggest no such alteration.

1a See Callu, *PMER*, pp. 164 et seq. See also his remark, ibid., p. 178 on hoarding during this period. For a comprehensive survey of the *antoninanus*, see ibid. chapter 4.

2 The *Korban Ha'edah* (R. David Fraenkel, a commentator on the Yerushalmi) here reads 100 [d.], but has no manuscript basis for this reading. It is merely a hypothetical correction of his own to make the text more "plausible". Likewise, Z. N. Rabinovitz (Jerusalem, 1940), in *Sha'are Torath Eretz Israel*, p. 397.

3 See Y. Ketubot 12.1 where Resh Lakish says: "It is like one who marries a woman on the understanding that he give her twelve gold *dinars* during a year in installments of one gold *dinar* per month."

4 For this date see sources cited in my article in *Archiv Orientalni*, 34, 1966, p. 57, note 11.

5 I have discussed the dating of this text in *JRS*, 56, 1966, pp. 190–95. See the remarks of Callu in *BSFN*, 20/8, 1965, pp. 500–1, who finds further confirmation for my suggestions in *P. Beatty Panop. 2*.

6 See Carson, *Revue Numismatique*, 1965, pp. 233–35, and further bibliography in Callu, *PMER*, pp. 232–24, note 4, Also, I have brought new evidence to prove this in my article in *JRS*, 56.

7 See for e.g. R. A. G. Carson in *INCP*, pp. 231–45. I have drawn frequently upon Carson's study in this section.

7a L. H. Cope, in a private communication of 10 Sept. 1972, informs me on the basis of numerous and accurate analyses he has made that the nadir was in the reign of Claudius II. See also his article in *Num. Chron.* 1969, pp. 145–61.

8 This tale is based in part (weights of d., ant., and their fineness) on the table compiled by Carson at the end of his article, *INCP*, p. 245. *Denarius* and *antoninianus* weights: Caracalla-Septimius Severus from *British Museum Catalogue of Coins in the Roman Empire* (= *BMC*), Gordian III — Gallienus from L. C. West, *Gold and Silver Standards in the Roman Empire* (New York, 1941). (Cf. *RIC*, 5/1, pp. 250–51.) Diocletian: G. Mickwitz, *Geld und Wirtschaft im römischen Reich* etc., (Soc. Scient. Fen. Commentationes Humanarum Litterarum, 4/2, Helsingfors, 1932), pp. 40–41. *Aureus* weights: West, ibid., and S. Bolin, *State and Currency in the Roman Empire* (Uppsala, 1958), pp. 252–54, 260, 293, etc. *Denarius* and *antoninianus* fineness: J. Hammer, "Der Feingehalt der griechischen und römischen Münzen",

Zeitschrift fur Numismatik, 1908, pp. 1, et seq.: P. Le Gentilhomme, "Le jeu des mutations de l'argent en IIIe siècle", in *Métaux et Civilisations* 1, p. 127. See also Gentilhomme in *Revue Numismatique*, 1962, pp. 141–62, on the *antoninianus* in the III cent.; also, Mickwitz, ibid.; (cf. Bolin, ibid., p. 211). Also cf. *BMC*, 6, Carson (London, 1962), pp. 16–21. All weights are given in grammes. See also A. Ravetz, in *Archeometry*, 6, p. 50, for some other III cent. analyses. Caracalla *denarius* 32% silver; Valerian I, SALUS AUGG 17.1%; Gallienus, MARTI PACIFERO 4.9%; Aurelian, ORIENS AUG 4%, Probus, VICTORIA AUG 3.7%; Diocletian, IOVI CONSERVATORI AUGG 1.3%; See also *Num. Chron.*, 1965, pp. 175–76, nos. 7–11 (R. Reece). See most recently Callu, *PMER*, pp. 237 et seq., and pp. 430–43. Concerning the Diocletianic *ant.* L.H. Cope writes, in a private communication of 10 Sept. 1972: "...4.18% silver ... is on the high side. I do have some similar results, but the average is more in keeping with an XX.I alloy identical with that of the post 301 eastern *folles*". With regard Table K (below and of Chapter XXII) he comments: "... Most of Ravetz' n.a. values are on the high side of reality, and I have numerous real analyses which give precision and accuracy to the general trend which she observed in embryo".

8a Mr. Carson points out to me that though in practice this is true, there are "silver" coins with the laureate head, admittedly quite rare, right up to Diocletian's reform.

9 See Heichelheim's interesting comments in *Classical Philology*, 39, 1944, p. 115 (bibliography, ibid.), which is, however, not really convincing. On the other hand, his observation that Caracalla struck Syrian *tetradrachms* with the XX or K notation is very significant (if correct) and still requires a suitable explanation.

10 *BMC*, 6, p. 20, note 5, also *BMC*, 5, p. xviii. See also *JRS*, 51, 1961, C.H.V. Sutherland's article "Denarius and Sestertius in Diocletian's Reform", p. 95, note 16.

11 *INCP*, pp. 234–35, and in *Revue Numismatique*, 1965, p. 228. Carson in a private communication to me (of 15 August 1972) writes: "I am not totally wedded to my view that 1 *ant.* = 1½ d. A ratio of 1 *ant.* = 2 d. is more to be expected and certainly workable. The main obstacle to this solution is the behaviour of hoards. From the list which I put together in BMC, 6, pp. 35 et seq. it emerges that while quite a good many hoards ended at the point (238)when the denarius ceased to be effectively struck, others go on much later and seem to show d. and *ant.* being happily hoarded together, (and this is true of hoards ending in 238 which include *ant.* of Caracalla, Macrinus and Elagabalus). On the face of it, this would only be so if the relationship of the *ant.* and the *denarius* was that indicated by its metrology, i.e. 1 = 1½. To permit the most simple and workable ratio 1 = 2, we have to suppose a widespread acceptance of artificial fiduciary tariffing, i.e. to believe that there was still sufficient confidence in the system for the public to accept the coins at the value placed on them by the State and not the value which the metal content would suggest. Perhaps I have always taken too pessimistic a view about when the crisis of confidence came, and perhaps still early in the third century the State could still impose an artificial relationship between the *ant.*and the *denarius*. All that Duncan-Jones' figures prove is that there were 50 *denarii* to 1 *aureus*."

12 Was a *smaller* denomination needed at that time of inflation?

13 *Revue Numismatique*, op. cit.

14 25 *ant.* of 5.02 at 48% fineness = 1 *aureus* of 6.5. Cf. Bolin, op. cit., pp. 267 et seq. In fact this relationship is already to be found in the coins of Septimius Severus; see Mickwitz, *Geld und Wirtschaft*, p. 40.

15 50 d. of 3.1 at $\pm$ 50% fineness = 1 *aureus* of 6.5.

16 The real problem with this interpretation is why (bearing in mind Gresham's law) should the *denarii* have continued *subsequently* (after the new silver-gold ratio had been established) to be struck at 2/3 the weight of the *ant.* and not $\frac{1}{2}$ its weight. Yet Caracalla continued to strike such *denarii*, so did Macrinus, Elagabalus, Balbinus and Pupienus. Moreover, for the case of Elagabalus, where we have metallic analyses, it appears that both the d. and the *ant.* were struck at around 40% fineness. Why was the silver content of the d. reduced by 25%? While I cannot really answer this question, I should like to point out that the exact application of Gresham's law to Roman economics is by no means clear and straight-forward. Thus the *drachm* was often heavier than half the weight of a *didrachm*, 1/3 *didrachm*, $\frac{1}{4}$ *tetradrachm*. Eg. Commodus' *didrachm*: 4.52; his *tridrachm*: 7.07; (West, *Gold and Silver Standards*, p. 110). See also below, this chapter. It may be that the Emperors did not want to change the *official* silver-gold ratio from 12:1. (For if the price of silver officially went up by 25% they would be gaining relatively little.) In order to support the official standard they had therefore to strike some coins at the old weight and fineness, i.e. at the official standard. The *denarius* was chosen for this for several reasons: (a) not to change a long-established denomination; (b) it was the keystone of the monetary system, hence more exemplary; (c) it was smaller; (d) less *denarii* were struck. See also C. Oman in *Num. Chron.*, 1916, pp. 37 et seq. and Bolin, *State and Currency*, chap. XI. On my whole interpretation, cf. however, L. C. West, in *American Numismatic Society Museum Notes* (= *AMSMN*), 4, 1954, pp. 6–9. That the *ant.* is a double-*denarius* and was introduced as a measure of economy for the treasury has recently been reaffirmed by Callu in *PMER*, p. 242. Cf. Bellinger, *The Syrian Tetradrachms of Caracalla and Macrinus* (New York, 1940), p. 6.

17 His *tetradrachms* weigh 13.15, giving a *dr.* of 3.3. (See our coin no. 5.) Of course, all these are only *average* weights, and therefore by no means necessarily accurate. Weights are from West, *Gold and Silver Standards*.

18 Dio Cassius 55.12 (see W. Kubitschek, *Rundschau über ein Quinquennium der antiken Numismatik* [1896], p. 104; Bolin, *State and Currency*, p. 269, note 2); B. Bava Mezia 44b; T. Bava Mezia 3.13 (377, 5–8); B. Bechorot 50a. See my article in *JQR*, 56, 1966, p. 275, notes 9 and 10. For the earlier period (Augustus) see Suetonius, *Vita Caesarum*, 8.7; (Bolin, ibid., p. 265, note 2). See also T. V. Buttrey in *JRS*, 51, 1961, p. 41, who cites other sources for the I and II cent. and discusses the whole Dio Cassius text. See finally Callu, *PMER*, p. 444.

19 A–C are taken from *Num. Chron.*, 1941, p. 30, (G. C. Haines, "The Decline and Fall of the Monetary System of Augustus"). D is Carson's system. E is my own. For different opinions as to the value of the *ant.*, see also *RIC*, 5/1, p. 6; P. Bastien, *Le Monnayage de Bronze de Postume* (Belgium, 1967), pp. 21–22, citing, *inter alia*, V. Picozzi, *Le Monetazione Imperiale Romana* (Rome, 1966), pp. 7–9; Callu in *PMER*, pp. 242, 325–29.

20 "Costs, Outlays and Summae Honororiae from Roman Africa", *Papers of the British School at Rome*, 30 (New Series, 17), 1962, pp. 79–108.

21 On reckoning in *sestertii* during the III cent. see Sutherland in *JRS*, 51, p. 94.

22 I exclude sums under 100 *sest.* (= 1 *aureus*), nos. 244, 291–305, 389, 396, 425, 426.

23 Eg. nos. 83, 139, 420, 424.

24 Eg. no. 212, 115d.; no. 297, 35d.; nos. 273–77, 60, 62$\frac{1}{2}$, 72d; no. 287, 235d.

25 Taken from R. Duncan-Jones' article, op. cit. The numbering is according to his numbering. See also his article in *Papers of the British School at Rome*, 33 (N.S. 20), "An Epigraphic Survey of Costs in Roman Italy". Nos. 674 and 697, foundations of 50,000 and 8,000 HS from the years 230–40 and 234. See also nos. 1055, 1066, 1151 and 1358, from this period which further bear out our suggestions. I exclude from the discussion reference to the *sportulae*, (nos. 841, 892, 893); concerning these, see the discussion in Duncan-Jones, ibid., pp. 210 et seq. and p. 306. Dr. J. Kent in a private communication (of 23 August, 1972) writes: "These calculations support the relationship between *aureus*, *denarius* and *sestertius* — at least in accountancy — but I do not see why or how it tells anything about the *ant.*" (cf. above note 11, end, Carson's similar remark.) However, if one assumes, as I have throughout, that the *ant.* must fit snugly and comfortably into the system of denominations, having easy accounting relationships to them, then these calculations certainly do tell something about the *ant.*

26 *Digesta*, 2.4.24; *Corpus Iuris Civilis*, 1, 1902, p. 21.

27 Gaius, *Institutionum juris civilis commentarii*, 4.46; ed. Huschke (1886), p. 361.

28 See Mickwitz, *Geld und Wirtschaft*, p. 37; Heichelheim, *Klio*, 26, 1932, p. 104; Bolin, *State and Currency*, p. 269. But see West, *Gold and Silver Standards*, pp. 132–33, 136 et seq. Also Buttrey in *JRS*, 51, p. 41; Callu, *PMER*, p. 444.

29 *BMC*, 6, p. 20, note 5. However, Carson now (in a private communication of 15 August, 1972), has some doubts as to this calculation. He writes that it does not seem logical (as there probably was a falling in fineness) that 1 *aureus* = 50 d. under Severus Alexander, and that 1 *aureus* = 40 d. under Philip. He would expect the movement to be the other way, even allowing for some fall in the average weight of the *aureus*.

30 *State and Currency*, pp. 278–81.

31 *CIG*, 5008, 5010, ed. J. Franzius 3, (1953), pp. 468 ed. seq. For earlier discussions of these inscriptions, see sources cited in Bolin, ibid., p. 278, notes 3 and 4. However, Pekári, in *Syria*, 38 (1961), p. 278, declares these documents as unusuable. See Johnson in *Econ. Surv.*, 2, pp. 426–27; West and Johnson, *Currency in Roman and Byzantine Egypt*, pp. 94–95; Mickwitz, *Geld und Wirtschaft*, p. 51; and Callu, *PMER*, p. 445, note 1, who cites additional bibliography. For further information on this period, see Samuel K. Eddy, *The Minting of Antoniniani A.D. 238–49 and the Smyrna Hoard, NNM*, 156 (New York, 1967), pp. 106–15.

32 According to our suggestion in note 16 above, the purpose of continuing to mint limited amounts of *denarii* was in order to preserve official silver-gold ratio (thereby keeping the price of silver down). Caracalla continued striking d. throughout his reign. Macrinus (217) and Elagabalus (218–19) struck some *ant.* at the beginning of their reigns and then no more. The next four Emperors (Severus Alexander, Maximinus and the Gordiani) struck no *ant.* Balbinus and Pupienus struck both d. and *ant.*, but were the last to strike *denarii* (cf. *BMC*, 6, p. 103). From Gordian III onwards a new *official* standard was established? (See West in *ANSMN*, 1, 1945, p. 62.)

33 Carson in his computations appears not to have taken this admittedly small element into account.

34 Bolin, *State and Currency*, p. 303, note 6.

35 This is a simplification of the more explicit $(PQN/100) + (PRN/100 \times 100) = Y$

36 These are, of course, only *average* weights.

37 More accurately the non-silver remainder of the coin, of whatever combination of metals (primarily copper) that be. See, for example, *RIC*, 5/1, p. 252.

38 These are again only average weights. The result should be a simple fraction of the *libra aurei*, (or possibly as a round number of *scripula*). For the sake of convenience, I have consistently reckoned the *libra aurei* as 325, whereas, in fact, it is closer to 327.45. The *scripulum* is 1/288 *libra* = 1.137; (cf. *RIC*, 5/1, pp. 11–12, note 3). See, however, West in *ANSMN*, 1, 1945, pp. 59–63, article entitled "Determination of gold standards by use of the carat".

39 Buttrey, in *JRS*, 51, p. 45, thinks that Dio Cassius' statement (above note 18) indicates a (theoretical?) relationship of 25 d. to the *aureus* during the reign of Severus Alexander. Whatever the correct interpretation of Caracalla's monetary reform may be, it seems most unlikely that in Severus Alexander's reign the relationship should have been a pre-Caracalla one. Further evidence for our equation may be found in a fragmentary inscription concerned with the damaging of vineyards, *IGRR*, 3, 1341 (from Gerasa, Arabia): . . . if anyone is found plucking or bringing in . . . this person to pay the same twenty-five *denarii*, but if . . . until thirty days concerning . . . this person to pay fifty *denarii*. (Trans. in *Ancient Roman Statutes*, ed. A.C. Chester, P.R. Coleman-Norton, F.C. Bourne, Austin, Texas, 1961, no. 286, p. 230.) This text was first dated to the late third century, but such a dating makes little economic sense. Furthermore, by that time *denarii* were no longer being used. Therefore, more recently, it has very rightly been dated to c.231, *(Ancient Roman Statutes*, ibid.). It seems most likely that we have here fines of an *aureus* and a *quinarius aureus*.

40 If 40 d. = 1 *aureus*, and 3000 d. = 1 *libra aureus*, then 75 *aurei* = 1 *libra aurei*. Therefore, 1 *aureus* weighs 4.33.

41 Note the sudden jump from around 9.1 to around 7.5:1. If Gordian III really recognized a new actual silver-gold ratio, the effect would have been to drive the price of silver up suddenly and sharply. This is what seems to have happened (see above, note 32). Note also West's remark in *ANSMN*, 1, 1945, p. 62, that, with Gordian III there is a complete change in the regulation of standards.

Carson (in *Revue Numismatique*, 1965, p. 230) notes that Trajan Decius' ant. are frequently found overstruck on *denarii* of the period from Septimus Severus to Severus Alexander. [7] (See H. Mattingly, "The Great Dorchester Hoard of 1936", *Num. Chron.*, 1939, pp. 41–43.) He concludes that the ratio of ant. for Decius was now the same as the earlier ratio of *denarii*. Thus if 1 *aureus* = 20 ant. = 40 d. (Philip's equation), there would now be 40 ant. = 80 d. in an *aureus*. This, however, does not necessarily follow. For the earlier *aurei* were far heavier, at least one third more. Thus in Philip's time these earlier *denarii* were probably reckoned at 20d. (=ant.) to the *aureus* of their time, i.e. of 6.5 gr. Hence there were only about 13.4 to an *aureus* of Decius weighing 4.5 grammes. If they were then overstruck and declared to be ant. there would be only about 27 of them to the *aureus*. [Carson, in a private communication to me (15 August 1972), writes that he still thinks his argument is quite strong, and doubts whether weight differences would have much effect.] It is difficult to know exactly what the ratio was meant to be, as the overstriking appears on coins of very different weights. Mattingly records overstrikes on coins of Sept. Sev. weighing 2.5 and 3.4 grammes, of Elagabalus of 2.9, 3.2(?) gr., of Sev. Alex. of 2.4, 3.1 gr. (two specimens of this latter). (Furthermore they all have different degrees silver content.) Thus it may well be that Trajan Decius still kept (or rather reverted to) the ratio, 1 *aureus* = 50 d., or perhaps he set up a new standard, 1:60. He probably considered the metallic contents of these coins equal in a sufficiently approximate degree to his *ant.* to permit such overstriking. (His *ant.* have about 1.62 gr. silver, 40% of 4.05gr. and those which he overstruck had likewise around 1.4–1.5 gr. silver; cf. Mickwitz, *Geld und Wirtschaft*, p. 40.) Depending on what the silver contents of these coins were meant to be, and what was the precise ratio of *ant.* to *aureus*, we get a gold-silver ratio lying somewhere between 8.3:1 and 9:1. Of course, it may be that this was a government ruse to combat the hoarding of these earlier coins, and thus find a relatively cheap way to circulate more currency. People would then have handed in their hoarded *denarii*, being only too pleased to get back what was at least nominally worth twice as much. Now, though all these overstruck coins must have been officially assigned the same value, in point of fact their metallic values varied considerably, as we indicated above. Hence it is likely that on the market they passed at different rates, and each would be individually valued by the money-exchangers. This may be the meaning of a problematic passage in the Yerushalmi. For in Y. Ma'aser Sheni 1.1 AV, we read that R. Jacob ben Zavdi in the name of R. Abbahu (flor. c. 260–309) said that anyone that had DISGNIM money (variants: DISCNIM, LSGNIM) could substitute (the Second Tithe) by them at their value with the banker or money-exchangers, (θερμοσαριος, Lieberman, *Tosefta ki-fshutah, Zera'im*, 1, p. 26; 2, p. 716, notes 25 and 29). DISGNIM is generally taken to be *"dusignum"* — *Dopplezeichen*, (see Krauss, *LW*, 2, p. 208b, and bibliography, ibid.; Jastrow's interpretation of *"dextans"*, in *Dict.* p. 302b, is most unlikely). As *"signo"* can mean "to coin, strike" (Lewis & Short, p. 1697b s.v.), could *dusignum* not mean overstruck, *doublefrappé*; (*duo signatus*; see Krauss, *LW*, 2, p. 605a, s.v. referring to Jost 131 *Noten*, p. 183, who suggests *duo signa (dopplegeprägt)*? See further L. Herzfeld, *Metrologische Voruntersuchungen*, Leipzig, 1863, pp. 181–82). R. Abbahu would then be referring to such coins of Decius, or later overstrikes (West, *ANSMN*, 7, pp. 117–23), and from his statement, thus interpreted, one could learn that these coins did not have a fixed market-rate, but had to be individually valued. But see below chapter XIV for a different interpretation of this text.

43 Bolin, *State and Currency*, p. 254, diagram 20, p. 260, table 21, and pp. 259–61, 286–87.

44 The few available analyses seem to bear out this suggestion. Cf. L.C. West in *ANSMN*, 7 (New York, 1957), pp. 96–101. On p. 106 we find the following material:

253–6	Rome 37%	Western 36%	
257	Cologne 40%	Western 36%	
259	Cologne 20%		

	Rome	Western	Antioch
262	12%	19%	12½%
266	7%	11%	9%
267	2½%	5%	8.7%

cf. *Revue Belge*, 1951, p. 85 et seq.; *Revue Numismatique*, 1945, p. 15 et seq.; *Gallia*, 1947, p. 239. On the instability of the *aureus* during this period, see Callu, *PMER*, p. 445.

44a L.H. Cope, in a private communication of 10 Sept. 1972, writes as follows: "I have 40 or more unpublished assays of the Gallienic *ants.* They show a fineness standard of 2 *unciae* per *libra* (16.7%) at the beginning of the sole reign, then stepwise debasement. I think I have found a mid-reign reform; then debasements continue down to a 6 *scrupula* standard for the Animal issues. My revised figures affect your detailed gold/silver ratios, since the real basic data are different from those you have used." See most recently Kent in NC, 1973, p. 67.

45 For more reliable analyses recently published, see L.H. Cope's article in *Num. Chron.*, 1969, pp. 145–61, where it will be seen that Claudius' *ant.* reached a nadir of 1.08% silver (p. 151). However, note should be taken of J. Guey's pertinent comments in *Revue Numismatique*, 1967, p. 48.

46 Dr. Kent further drew my attention to the fact that in the Gallic Empire this break seems to have come somewhat earlier so that the *aurei* of Postumus are all large, while the state of the *ant.* is more or less the same as in the central empire. Thus, in the West the shifting *denarius-aureus* relationship was probably established c. 260. Note also that it is around this time that the term χαινον νομισμα first begins to appear in Egyptian papyri. See Segrè, *Metrologia*, pp. 433–40 etc.; Segrè, *Chronique d'Égypte*, 40 (No. 79, Jan. 1965), p. 205 note 4. (Cf. *P. Herm.* 86 = Wilcken *Chrest.* 195 etc.) See also, Callu, *PMER*, pp. 186–87, 180–90. See P. O. 2587.

47 See above, note 38.

48 Claudius II's *aurei* weigh 5.02 on an average.

49 Bolin, *State and Currency*. p. 396. In the discussion I reject most of what has been suggested by Hamburger in *Israel Numismatic Journal*, 2/3–4, 1964, pp. 21–25.

50 Mickwitz, *Geld und Wirtschaft*, p. 61. Most recently Sutherland in *RIC*, 6, 1967, p. 98; (contra Bolin, *State and Currency*, p. 247: 10.52).

51 Mickwitz, ibid., p. 83. Cf. *Archeometry*, 4, 1961, pp. 56–61, especially, p. 60.

52 This has again been reaffirmed by Sutherland in *Archeometry*, 4, 1961, p. 59, and in *RIC*, 6 (1967), p. 98, note 2. See also Brambach, *Frankf. Münzzeit*, 1920, p. 204 et seq. Against this view see Pearce in *JRS*, 23, 1933, p. 87. And most recently the suggestions of Cope in *NC*, 1960, pp. 145–49. On Aurelian's coins, however, this marking has a different meaning, see below, Chap. VIII.

53 *Panegyrici Latini*, V (IX), ii, 2.

54 These two observations are made by Sutherland in *RIC*, 6, 1967, p. 98, note 2. The Antioch *folles* are further treated, ibid., p. 603, vii.

55 Cf. Mickwitz, *Geld und Wirtschaft*, p. 62. But note that according to Bolin there are post-reform pieces (= 2 d.) of pure copper (Bolin, *State and Currency*, p. 318). This gives the impossible ratio of 3:1. However, here he is probably mistaken, and the silver-wash in all probablility had come off. (See Adelson in *ANSMN*, 6, 1954, pp. 11–29, article entitled "Bronze alloys of the late Roman Empire", and further sources cited at he end of this note.) The *argenteus* was struck at 1/96 *libra aurei* (= 3 *scripula*, Bolin, ibid., p. 303, and cf. ibid., p. 295; West, *Gold and Silver Standards*, p. 186) = 3.4. At the same silver-gold ratio it was probably 1/25 *aureus*, the old *denarius* (Bolin, ibid., p 303), rather than 23.3 to the *aureus*, which result the equation yields. According to *PSI*, 310 (dated 307), 8328 d. = 1 *libra argentei*, If at this date 1 *libra aurei* = 120,000 d., the silver-gold ratio = 14.4:1. *P.O.* 2106 (which is variously dated 293–308 or 317–24) states that 100,000 d. = 1 *libra aurei*. It would seem that this is pre-307 and post 301, and related to the reduction of the *nummus* to half its value, sometime post 300. See *P. Oslo* III, 63, *P. Ryl*, IV. 607, *PSI.* 965; Jones in *Econ. Hist. Rev.* 5, 1958, pp. 317–18; Segrè, *Byzantion*, 15, pp. 252–55. (But see our detailed discussion of the whole problem below, Chap. IX.) See also Sutherland, in *JRS*, 51, pp. 96–97. Here I follow Mickwitz, ibid. and

P.Strauss (*Revue Numismatique*, 5/8,1944–45, pp. 4–5), and Mattingly (*Roman Coins*[2], pp. 232–33) in regarding these coins as non-fiduciary. See, however, Adelson, referred to above in this note. See also Sutherland and Harold, in *Archeometry*, 4, 1961, pp. 56–61; A. Ravetz, in *Archeometry*, 6, 1964, p. 214, and note 4; E.S. Hedges and Dudley A. Robins, in *Num Chron.*, 1963, p. 237 et. seq. The evidence of Sutherland, Ravetz, Adelson, etc. makes it completely certain that all *folles* originally had a surface layer of silver. See Sutherland, *RIC*, 6, 1967, p. 94, who gives the silver content of *folles* as 4.3 to 3.4%, giving the average of 3.87%. See also Carson in *INCP*, 1967, p. 250; Cope in *NC*, 1968, pp. 144–45, and 340–44.

56 Bolin (*State and Currency*, p. 308, note 1) cites two IV cent. sources that give a ratio of 14.4:1; (Ammianus Marcellinus, 20.4.18; *Cod. Theod.* 13.2.1 of the year 397). This then was probably Diocletian's standard too. *P. Oslo* 162 (IV cent.), *Cod. Theod.* 13.4.27 (422), and *Cod. Just.* 78.1 (VI cent.) give the same ratio. See West and Johnson, *Currency in Roman and Byzantine Egypt*, p. 108. See table below chapter IX, note 14.

57 Mickwitz, *Geld und Wirtschaft*, p. 73. Cf. Bolin, *State and Currency*, pp. 321–25.

58 We shall see below (Chap. XVII) that Roman prices were naturally far higher than Egyptian ones. Thus, their being in this case the same (i.e. papyrological prices equalling those of Diocletian's *Edict of Maximum Prices*) in actual fact constitutes a reduction in the Roman price-levels. See also Helen H. Tanzer's *The Common People of Pompei* (Baltimore, 1934), p. 94, for a I cent. piece of bread, (*Panem libra IS*, "One sest. for 1 lb. bread") and compare our price lists for Palestine and Egypt below chap. XV. See, however, *CIL*, 11, 6117, (Italian II cent.), 1 d. per *mod.* wheat. That Diocletian's *Edict* actually brought prices down is asserted by Szilági in *AAH*, 11 (1963), p. 332, (and note 41).

59 For Sutherland's view that Aurelian's XXI coins are worth 5 d. see *JRS*, 51, p. 95, and Carson in *Revue Numismatique*, 1965, p. 230. See also Mattingly, in *Numismatic Chronicle*, 1972, p. 221 (cited in *JRS*, 51, note 25). Our argument assumes that the XXI coin was equal to 20 *libellae* = 2 d. See Mattingly, *Roman Coins* (1928), p. 130. See also D. Magie, *Roman Rule in Asia Minor* (Princeton, 1950), 2, p. 1576, note 47. For full survey of the various interpretations of this marking see Callu, *PMER*, pp. 324–29. The explanation XX.1 = 5 d., while attractive (in that this seems to be its meaning on Diocletian's coins) leads to an unacceptable gold-silver ratio of about 1:2. Hence, I understand XX.1 to mean (here) 20 *libellae* (= 2 d.) = one of these coins; i.e. that this coin equals 2 d. The VSV̇ coin (*Gallia* 20, 1962, p. 278) [15], which weighs about 2.50 gr. probably equalled 1 d., i.e. ½ *ant.*, and may have meant USUALIS or alternatively 5 + 5 *libellae* (= 10 *libellae* = 1 d.) = ½ (S) of the *ant.* Perhaps even both meanings were alluded to in the one formula, and hence the strange VV rather than a simple X. See Callu, *PMER*, pp. 328–29.

60 Richard Duncan-Jones, *Papers of the Brit. School at Rome*, 30 (New Series, 17), 1962, no. D. 403.

61 Note also that Zosimus (1.61.3) says that Aurelian relieved business transactions from confusion by delivering out good money for bad. This too argues for a simple straightforward exchange rate between the "bad" (pre-reform, I suggest) and "good" (post-reform) money. Cf. Segrè, *Metrologia*, p. 435, note 3, and Percy H. Webb, in *Num. Chron.* 1919, pp. 253–43, and Magie, *Roman Rule in Asia Minor*, p. 1576, note 47. See Callu, *PMER*, p. 324.

62 Contra Johnson, *Egypt and the Roman Empire*, p. 51 who writes: "This statement (of Zosimus) cannot be supported by any numismatic evidence". See Callu's suggestions in *PMER*, pp. 366 et seq. See also Callu in *BFSN*, 20/8, 1965, pp. 500–01, also ibid., 22/3, 1967, pp. 135–36, who believes that there was relatively little change in the last decade or so of the third century. (However, according to his argument, which is based on Y. Ketubot 11.2 (see above, note 5), one must alter the chronology somewhat, so that there was almost no change in the last three decades of the third century.) From *P. Beatty Panop.* 2, of Feb.–March 300, he learns that there were 60,000 d. per *aureus*, and Diocletian altered this ratio slightly in the year 301.

Chapter V

1 See Schrötter, *Wörterbuch des Münzkunde*, s. v. *follis* (pp. 199–200), *fels* (pp. 192–93); West and Johson, *Currency*, pp. 134–37; E. Schilbach, *Byzatinische Metrologie* (München, 1970), p. 185, etc. See also S. Fraenkel, *Die Aramäischen Fremdwörter im Arabischen* (Leiden, 1886), p. 192.

2 *JRS*, 51, 1959, pp. 34–38. See Callu, *PMER*, pp. 360–64.

3 *Scriptores Historiae Augustae, Elagabalus* 22 (Loeb, 2, pp. 148–49); *CIL* 5, 1880, 1973, 2046, (*JRS*, 51, p. 35, note 4). Add: *CIL*, 9, 4215, 338.

4 *JRS*, ibid., p. 34.

5 Ibid., pp. 34–35. See Jones in *Economic History Review*, 5, 1953, pp. 317–18. See also *P. Ryl.* 607; *P. Oslo* 3, 83; *PSI.* 965. Epiphanius in Hultsch, *MSR*, 1, p. 276; cf. p. 144, note 4; 2, pp. 151–2; 1, p. 269. Also P. A. Boetticher (= Lagarde) *Symmicta* 2 (1880), p. 197 and 1 (1887), p. 224.

6 Evidence for these 'purses" is found in N. Lewis' article in *NNM*, 79, pp. 17–21; *P. O.* 1917 (cf. West and Johnson, *Currency*, p. 137); *CIL*, 5, 1880 (? cf. *CIL*, 8, 5333); G. Finlay, *Greece under the Romans* (1906), p. 127, note 1, notes that in Turkey people still speak of a purse of 50 *piastres*. (presumably he is referring to the term كيسة اقجه, Keyssé àkcha; See Redhouse, *Turkish Dictionary*, London, 1880, p. 249a, s. v. purse.) See also S. D. Goitein, *A Mediterranean Society*, 1 (1967), pp. 231–34, on the institution of sealed purses of money in Mediaeval Genizah documents etc. However, this is because "weighing and assaying were tedious and time-consuming procedures. Therefore, money was handled largely in sealed purses of coins the exact values of which were indicated on the outside" (Goitein, ibid., p. 231). The Turkish "purses" are probably derived from this custom, which was already established in Roman times and is to be found in Talmudic sources (see Gulak, *Tarbiz*, 2/2, 1931, pp. 157–48). See Adelson, in *ANSMN*, 6, 1954, pp. 118–19. See also *Studi in Onore di A. Calderini e R. Paribeni* (Milan, 1957), 2, p. 329, and *JRS*, 49, 1959, pp. 34–35, notes 2 and 3. Also my remarks in *Tarbiz*, 40/4, 1971, pp. 444–449. See also F. Pringsheim, *Gesammelte Abhandlungen*, 2, (Heidelberg, 1961), p. 121, = *Vierteljahrschrift für Sozial- und Wirtschaftgeschichte*, 15, 1920, p. 521. Amboroklon in Y. Bava Mezia 4.1 = *involucrum*, a purse, (*Tarbiz* ibid.)

7 See Lewis & Short, p. 765c, s. v. *follis*, and Liddell & Scott[2], p. 1949a, s. v. φολλις. See also Isid. *Etymologia* 16.18.12, cited below, note 25. See Heichelheim in *Econ. Surv.* 4, p. 215, note 19, and p. 223, note 56, *Klio*, 26, p. 98. He cites as parallels of

usage Ulpian and Paulus in *Digesta*, 16, 3,29; 40, 7, 3, where *follis* means a purse filled with a certain number of coins. See also Schrötter, *Wörterbuch der Münzkunde*, p. 199b, s.v. *follis*.

8 Payne Smith, in his *Syriac Dictionary*, 437b states that the Syriac פולסא is derived from the Greek ὀβολός via the Arabic, (cf. Brockelmann, *Lexicon Syriacum*[2] 575a; Sachs, *Beiträge zur Sprach und Alterthumsforschung*, 2, Berlin, 1854, p. 149, note 1). This is clearly not the case since the Syriac *folsa* is found in pre-Islamic times (in the Talmud and in the Syriac Epiphanius, see below, this chapter). Furthermore, in Syriac the *folsa* and the *obol* are not always equated, (e. g. Ḥnana d'Adiabene, *Patrologia Orientalis*, 7, p. 62, line 8, of 540–42).

9 Cf. Soncino translation, (H. Freedman), London, 1935, p. 281–82, and notes there. Cf. also *Sifré Deut.* 107, Ish-Shalom ed., p. 96a. For correct readings, see Rabbinovicz, *VL*, Bava Mezia, p. 133.

10 *Epiphanius on Weights and Measures*, ed. James Elmer Dean (Chicago, 1935), sect. 53, p. 61, fol. 69b, line 22 — fol. 69c, line 16, pp. 109–110. Cf. source cited above in note 5.

11 See Y. Megila 1.11; cf. B. Bava Mezia 84a.

12 *Asemon* can be silver or bronze but never gold. It is most usually silver; see West and Johnson, *Currency*, pp. 119, 139, and Bolin, *State and Currency*, pp. 89–90, note 7. (See also Boak in *JJP*, 1, 1964, p. 10, referring to *P. Thead.* 33, 19, 25–6, 33–5; *P.O.* 1524, 2.) *Sifré Deut.* 107; Y. Ma'aser Sheni 1.1. That *asemon* can only be of bronze may be seen from the fact that Rav identifies it with the "*tessarae*" which are invariably of bronze. Concerning these *tessarae*, see S. Lieberman, *Tosefta ki-fshutah, Zera'im* 2, pp. 715–16, where he shows that they sometimes had a market-value as coins, and were therefore not considered (by R. Johanan, etc.) as *asemon*. See also Mickwitz, in *Num. Chron.* 1937, p. 142, note 2, who states that *asemon* meaning silver is not found before the IV cent. See also the very interesting statement in the Palestinian Byzantine (?) text, *Sefer ha-Ma'asim li-Vnei Eretz Yisrael*, published in *Tarbiz*, 1/1 (Oct. 1929), p. 95 (fol. 30a), according to which *asemon* could be either of silver or gold. (On the dating of this text see below, Chap. XIV.) See the strange Septuagint to Job 42.11. But cf. Lieberman's remark in *Tosefta ki-fshutah, Zera'im* 2, p. 715, note 19. See also Sachs, *Beiträge* 2, p. 80, note 76; Lagarde, *Beitraege zur Baktrischen Lexicographie* (Leipzig, 1868), pp. 13–14. Carson (in a private communication of 15 August, 1972) writes: "It appears from your evidence that the *follis* or *folsa* could contain unstamped metal. I question whether this would necessarily be in the form of blanks, at least in the numismatic understanding of the term. There would be a cost in preparing metal in this form, and I do not know of any evidence of finds of such blanks in quantity. I could accept that the *follis* purse contained unstamped metal, but I think it a long step to describe it formally as a *bag* of blank *coins*." Likewise, Kent (private communication of 23 August, 1972), referring to R. Johanan's regarding the *folsa* as money, despite the fact that it was not stamped writes: "Surely not a bag of *blank* coins, for which there is no independent evidence or finds, but a reference to the anomaly that a bag has no type, though it has a monetary value." Despite the lack of independent evidence and doubts, it still appears to me that the evidence cited below (*protetot*, etc.) suggest far more than merely bits of unstamped metal, and something far closer to real 'blanks'.

13 The existence of such a kind of "stable currency" other than gold at such a time of progressive inflation must have been invaluable. The introduction of the *follis* appears to have been part of a currency-reform programme. See below Chap. VII.

14 This translation is based on that of the Soncino ed. (N. Freedman) with some slight changes. The explanations in brackets are found in the notes of the Soncino ed. L. Herzfeld, in *Metrologische Voruntersuchungen* (Leipzig, 1863), pp. 108–70 already noted this text in connection with the *follis*.

15 *Ḥalifin* = barter, makes the property pass immediately. On the whole issue, see Isaac Herzog, *The Main Institutions of Jewish Law*, 1 (London, 1936), pp. 171–72, 179–84.

16 Cf. Rashi on this text for a slightly different exposition of the argument, and Herzog, ibid., pp. 182–84, especially p. 183, for a penetrating analysis of the problem, and criticism of Rashi's explanation. See also other commentaries on this text, and the *Digest of Commentaries*, complied by Zacharia ben Judah Aghmati (London, 1961), fol. 95b. These differing explanations do not affect our argument. See further Gulak's comment in *Tarbiz*, 2/2, 1931, pp. 163–64.

16a Dr. J. Kent comments (private communication of 23 August, 1972): "This makes good sense, since money-changers were always spoken of as 'buying' and 'selling' *solidi*, and no doubt all other coins — so a man who 'sells' something which he actually owns, even though he has not got it with him, 'borrows' nothing."

17 See Jastrow, *Dict.*, p. 1219b, s.v. פרוטטות, and Kohut, *Aruch Completum*, 6, p. 422b, s.v. פרט. Also cf. *VL*, Bava Mezia, p. 129, note 2, for correct reading.

18 The printed text reads: perhaps both refer to "*protetot*" (which have on them no imprint). However, the bracketed words are a later gloss. See *VL*, ibid., p. 129, note 1.

19 Ulla died in R. Eleazar's lifetime, (B. Ketubot 111a). (The reading in this chronologically problematic text is borne out by the readings in Ms. Munchen, Geniza fragments and other Mss.) R. Eleazar died in the same year as did R. Johanan, i.e. 279. See *Iggeret R. Scherira Gaon*, ed. Benjamin Lewin (Haifa, 1921), pp. 84 and 85, and notes there. Cf. my remarks in *Archiv Orientalni*, 34, 1966, p. 57, note 11. Ulla dies in Babylonia, (B. Ketubot 111a, and Y. Kila'im 9.3 ad fin.)

20 The argument for this is rather complex and has been set out in greater detail elsewhere. Briefly, it is as follows: R. Aba arrived in Palestine some time after his friend R. Zera I had arrived there (also from Babylonia). Isaac Halevy, in his *Dorot Harischonim*, 2, p. 302 (Berlin, & Wien, 1923) argues that R. Zera I arrived in Palestine c. 280. However, while his reasoning is undoubtedly correct, his reckoning depends in a large measure upon his emendation of the reading in *Iggeret R. Scherira Gaon* to read that R. Johanan died 289 and not 279, (see preceding note 19, above). But as we accept the date 279 as correct, and in no need of emendation — no other readings appear in the Mss. cited by Lewin in his adition, p. 79 — we must backdate R. Zera I's arrival to c.270. Thus, R. Aba who came a few years later, probably arrived c.275. See my article in *Archiv Orientalni*, 38, 1970, pp. 3–10, where I have discussed some of these chronological problems in detail.

21 Ulla (ben Ishmael) was a Palestinian scholar who moved backward and forward between Palestine and Babylonia, (see W. Bacher, *Agada der Paläst. Amoräer*, pp. 93–97, *Jewish Encyclopaedia*, 12, p. 340). R. Aba was certainly acquainted with Ulla in Babylonia, and thus there is no proof that this conversation did not take place in Babylonia, i.e. pre c.270. See also A.Hyman, *Toldoth Tannaim Ve-Amoraim* (London, 1910), p. 5a, who suggests that Ulla encouraged R. Aba to immigrate to Palestine.

22 Ed. Dean, pp. 62–63, fol. 69d, (p. 110). See also Lagarde's ed. 2.14, p. 3, lines 37–38.

23 The English translation reads: "*but* this coin is entirely of silver", suggesting that the *follis* is not of silver. But the Syriac does not warrant this "but". All that is stated is that: this coin is entirely of silver (lines 27–29). Cf. Lagarde ed. p. 56, lines 20–21.

24 Note that the spelling of the coin *follis* with a single *lamda* appears in Byzantine Greek texts. E.g. Hultsch, *MSR*, 1, p. 306, line 19, p. 320, lines 6 and 11 (the latter being from *Fragmenta ex Hesychio Exerpta*). Cf. Sophocles, 2, p. 1149a, s.v. φολις.; also Preisigke, *Wörterbuch der Griechischen Papyruskunden*, 2 (Berlin, 1927), p. 700, line 1. This "defective" spelling is even found in some Epiphanius Greek texts, and seems perhaps partly to have led Lagarde (in *Symmicta*, 2, p. 103) to regard the etymology of Epiphanius as well-founded. (His argument is based on the Persian "*pisez*".) It is interesting to find the same mistaken etymology presupposed in a little-known Midrash published in A. J. Wertheimer's *Batei Midrashot* (Jerusalem, 1954). There (1, p. 303) we come across a small coin called a קסקס. The editor (ibid., p. 243) is at a loss to explain this term. And yet it is really very obvious. קסקס[ת] means a fish-scale, and is thus a translation of φολις. See my articles in *Le Muséon*, 80 (1967), pp. 267–68, and in *Leshonenu*, 31, 1967, pp. 185–88.

25 Cf. Isid. *Etymologia*, 16. 18.12: Follis dicuntur a sacculo quo conduntur, a continento id quod continentur appellatum.

26 It can only have been derived from the singular, for the plural is φολιδες. The plural of φολλις is of course φολλεις. Another possible explanation for the statement of "the Hebrews" is as follows: *sela* (a Rabbinic word) equals the "*shekel*" of Biblical Hebrew. In the *Targum* (= Aramaic translation) to Ezekiel 4.10, the Biblical "*shekel*" is translated פילס — *Piles* (= *files*). The word "*shekel*" comes from the Hebrew root שקל (*shakol*) — to weigh. The root פלס (*pales*) means the same thing. Hence the identification of *follis* (= *files*) with *sela* (= *shekel*). I have discussed this whole problem in *Leshonenu*, 31, 1967, pp. 183–88.

27 *Exodus Rabba* 3.13; *Tanḥuma Buber, Lev.*, p. 47; *Genesis Rabba* 20.4, ed. Theodor, p. 184.

28 See Dean's notes in his edition, nos. 440 and 443.

29 Perhaps we should read "smoothness of form" instead of roundess. Note that the root עגל can mean "to smooth" or "make even"; Jastrow, *Dict.*, p. 1041a, s.v. עגל.

30 See above, note 23.

31 Jastrow, *Dict.*, 1142a, s.v. פולסא.

32 Liddel & Scott², 1914a; Lewis & Short, 1367b, s.v. *phalerae*.

33 Brockelmann, *Lexicon Syriacum²*, 281b, s.v. טסא; Payne Smith, *Thesaurus Syriacus*, 1491 s.v. טסא.

34 Here I follow the interpretation of Rashi on this text. See Jastrow, *Dict.*, p. 1534a, s.v. שוכתא, Kohut, *Aruch Completum*, 2, p. 210a–b, s.v. בת ארעא; Levy, *Wörterbuch*, 4, p. 519a, s.v. שוכתא. See also Lieberman, *Tosefta ki-fshutah, Zera'im*, 2, p. 915, note 18, and Brockelmann, *Lexicon Syriacum²*, p. 778a, s.v. שוכתא.

35 On the connections between "*sela*" and "*folsa*" see above, note 26. See also *Otzar Ha-Geonim, Shabbat*, p. 63, and *Beth Ha-beḥira* to Shab. ed. Lange, p. 237.

36 Cf. Soncino translation (H. Freedman), London, 1938, p. 310. For the correct reading see Rabbinovicz, *VL*, Shabbat, p. 138; also B. M. Lewin, *Otzar Ha-Geonim, Shabbat* (Haifa, 1930), p. 63.

37 See Tosafot Rosh to Shabbat, ed. Lange, pp. 156–57, and *Sepher Hayashar* of R. Tam, ed. Schlesinger (Jerusalem, 1959), pp. 324–43. See, however, Adelson's remark in *INCP*, pp. 276–77.

38 See above, note 3, sources from *SHA, Elagab.* 22. In all these cases small single units are meant, Thus: *centum aureos et mille argenteos et centum folles aeris*, where the *folles* are clearly stated as being of copper; *CIL*, 5, 1880: *denariorum folles sexcentos*, where it is stated that the *follis* is a coin and what denomination it is. See also A. Cameron in *Num. Chron.*, 1964, p. 135., citing an Egyptian text of 391 (*Anth. Pal.* 9, 528) which reads: Those who inhabit the halls of Olympus have turned Christian and dwell there unharmed; for not even them will the melting pot which provides the life-giving *follis* put in the fire. From this, Cameron concludes that "there cannot be the slightest doubt that it (the *follis*) meant the sort of coin that could be struck from bronze obtained from melting down bronze coins!"

39 For an identification of this coin, see below, chap. VIII.

Chapter VI

1 Cf. Soncino translation (Maurice Simon), London, 1939, pp. 10–11.

2 The text reads כילרין (kilrin) which should be amended to פולרין (*follarin*). See Jastrow, *Dict.*, pp. 633a, 146b; Kohut, *Aruch Completum* 4, p. 243b, and 2, p. 106b; Levy, *Wörterbuch* 2, p. 343a, and 1, p. 200b. *Follarin = follarion*, according to Jastrow and Kohut, and equals βωλάριον (a nugget) according to Levy. See also Soncino, translator's note on this text, p. 11, note 1. See also Sachs, *Beiträge*, 1 (Berlin, 1852), p. 169. See also Bacher, *Aggadat Amora'ei Eretz-Yisrael*, 3/2 (Tel Aviv, 1936), p. 53 who reads כיטרון, which he explains as meaning a key(?). This reading has no basis.

3 The *didrachm* was also called "*tib'a*" (M. Shekalim 2.4), and the *tridrachm* "*ragia*" (B. Bechorot 49b). See my article in *JQR*, 56, 1966, p. 294.

4 See my article in *Bar-Ilan*, 7–8, 1970, pp. 133–37, xxiv. There I analysed the various readings: Ed. princ., Pesaro 1519: כילרין, followed by subsequent editions (Venice, 1525, 1546, etc.). (Correct what I wrote ibid. p. 133 accordingly.) However, the evidence of manuscripts points in a different direction: Ms. Vatican 76.3 (c. 1350) and Ms. Bodl. 164.2: בולדין; Ms. Vatican 249.9 (c. 1450): בולרין; Ms. Munich 50.2 (1552): בולבין. The correct reading would appear to be בולרין, which is probably φολλερον (rather than βωλάριον). The interchange of ב and פ is not uncommon both in the voiced and the voiceless forms. Eg., הפקר – הבקר; פקיעין – בקיעין, (see Lieberman, *Tosefta ki-fshutah* 1, pp. 50, 158; 4, p. 761. See also H. Yalon, *Pirkei Lashon*, Jerusalem, 1971, p. 315. (I am indebted to Dr. M. Sokolov of Jerusalem for this last reference.) This consonantal change is found not only before a "*qof*", but also before a "*lamed*", as in our case. Eg. פלפל – פלבל, (see Yalon, ibid., p. 92).

5 Bacher, op. cit., p. 53.

6 Parallels in *Genesis Rabba* 35.3, ed. Theodor-Albeck, p. 333 in the apparatus to line 10; *Yalkut Josh.* sect. 31 (ed. Venice 80), Prov. sect. 934. See *Sefer Ha-Eshkol*, ed. Albeck, "*Mezuza*", pp. 188–89, notes, where the Arabic "*fals*" influenced certain readings. (My thanks to Prof. M. Beer for calling my attention to this latter source.)

7 *A History of the Jews in Babylonia,* 1 (Leiden, 1965), pp. 82–83. The identification
of "Our Teacher" with R. Judah the Prince, is not accepted by all (e.g. Kohut in
Aruch Completum 1, p. 280b, s.v. ארטבן; see Neusner, ibid., p. 85. Kohut, on the
other hand, thinks that "Our Teacher" = Rav, in which case this episode would be
of a slightly later date. (Rav comments on Artabanus' death in Avoda Zara 10b.)
The identification of Artaban(?) in *Yalkut Zacharia,* par. 578 is problematic; see
Kohut, ibid., and also Neusner, ibid., p. 86, note 1 for a view (Guttman's) that
"Artaban" is merely a high official we can no longer identify. See my article in
Leshonenu, 34, 1969–70, pp. 61–65. See also below, Chap. XI, note 13.

8 Ed. Theodor-Albeck, p. 814. Cf. *Lekaḥ Tov,* Buber ed., p. 147, an anonymous text,
but maybe of R. Ammi, flor. c. 290–320.

9 Ed. Theodor-Albeck, p. 503, line 3.

10 For a discussion of these prices see below, Chap. XVI. See also *Lev. Rab.* 37.2, ed.
Margulies, pp. 856–57 (U).

11 Chap. 7, lines 37–42.

12 See my article in *JRS,* p. 192, note 31, which should be corrected in the light of what
I have shown below, Chap. XVIII. Cf. *P. Rylands* 629, line 41 (c. 317–23), a *xest.*
wine in Antioch cost 75 d. See also my remarks in *Talpiot,* 9/3–4, 1970, pp. 602–3.

13 Bolin, *State and Currency,* p. 291. See however *JRS,* 51, pp. 95–97, for Sutherland's
view that Aurelian's XXI coin equalled 5 d. [13]. Against this see L.C. West in
ANSMN, 7, 1957, pp. 112–113, who points out that there is a mark of value IA,
which would seem to anticipate the XXI mark of value. He suggests that this is 1 d.
(10 = 1), in which case the XXI coin equals 2 d. (20 = 1). The argument is per-
suasive if not conclusive, especially in view of the apparently resultant AE:AR
ratio and other marks of value there cited. See also above, Chap. IV.

14 A. Souter, *Glossary of Later Latin* (Oxford, 1949), p. 151a, s.v. *follaris,* states that
the *follis* — s.v. *follis* — is a copper coin worth 2 d.! See Marcell. *Chron.,* 2, p. 45,
498.3; Sophocles, 1149, s.v. φολλερον = Joann. Mosch., 2913c, 2941c, 2976a;
Leont. Cypr., 1709, 1936c; Mal. 400.20. See also E. Schilbach, *Byzantinische Metrologie,* p. 128. Alternatively, the *follis* or *follar* was applied to the XXI denomination in or after Aurelian's reign, and was transferred to the Diocletianic *"follis".*
(This is how Dr. J. Kent sees it, according to a private communication of 23 August,
1972.) The form *follaris* may be adjectival, scil. *(nummus) follaris,* (Kent).

Chapter VII

1 Epiphanius speaks also of a unit of 25 *denarii,* called a *kodrantes,* "because it is
bound up in a bag ... for they call a bag of silver a *kodarion"* (= κῳδαριον — a
false etymology, of course), (Epiphanius, Syriac ed. Dean, p. 59 and note 412). It is
tantalising to see this as yet a further unit in this *"follis*-bag" system, a tenth of the
follis KTD, and equal in value to the *nummus,* (see below, Chap. IX). See also
Boetticher (= Lagarde), *Symmicta,* 2, p. 195.

2 Note also that the *gleba,* surtax, imposed by Constantine on senators was levied at
the rate of 8, 4, or 2 *folles,* according to the wealth of the tax-payer, (Zosimus,
11.19; the figures come from Hesychius, (below, this note), but the minimum scale

of 2 *folles* is confirmed by *Cod. Theod.* 6.2.13). However, Hesychius of Miletus, who wrote under Justinian, about a century after the *gleba* had been abolished by Marcian, states that the tax was of 8, 4, and 2 lbs. gold, (Hesychius, fr. 5; *FGH*, IV, 154; see Jones in *JRS*, 1959, p. 35, notes 19 and 20). This leads one to identify the follis with the *libra aurei*; (see Mommsen-Blacas, *Histoire de la monnaie romaine*, 3, Paris, 1873, pp. 162–63; L. Incarnati, *Moneta e Scambio, nell' Antichità e nell' Alto Medioevo*, Rome, 1953, pp. 212–13; P. Petit, "Les Senateurs de Constantinople dans l'Oevre de Libanius", *L'Antiquité Classique*, 26, 1957, pp. 247–48). However Jones (*JRS*, ibid.) followed by Lelia Ruggini (in her basic article, "A proposito del *Follis* nel IV Secolo", *Rendiconti dei Lincei*, 16, Rome, 1961, p. 306 and 317–18) demonstrates convincingly (by a comparison with *Cod, Theod.* 6.2.15, etc.) that Hesychius' statement cannot be correct. Be that as it may, for our purpose it is significant to note that Hesychius (rightly or wrongly, in this particular case), identified the *follis* with the *libra aurei*. Presumably, he did so on the basis of some metrological tradition, now lost to us. According to our calculations this tradition would date from the *follis'* introduction c. 274.

3 This interpretation seems to fit *all* the facts best. Other suggestions are possible, however. (Systems b and c suggested above for Aurelian's reform system yield no satisfactory results in this context, but) if we apply the same method to Aurelian's pre-reform system of 200 d. = 1 *aureus*, assuming the silver-gold relationship of 7.94 : 1 as being twice as high as that of Diocletian, we arrive at a *follis* of 500 or 50,000. While the former equals ½ *aureus*, the latter bears no clear relationship to the *libra aurei* which was then equal to 60,000 d. (5 : 6). Throughout I have assumed a fixed relationship between copper and silver and a fluctuating one between silver and gold as the most likely situation. It is however possible that copper had a fixed relationship to gold and fluctuated in its relationship to silver, or that both copper and silver had fluctuating relationships to one another and to gold, based upon who knows what! See below, Chap. XI.

Chapter VIII

1 Cf. Ms. of the Jewish Theological Seminary (New York), *Tractate 'Avoda Zara*, ed. and annotated by Shraga Abramson, (New York, 1957), (= MS JTS), fol. 30a, line 24 et seq.: R. Zera said to him: "Till now what need one suspect? The mixing in of wine? A *xest.* of *muries* costs 1 *lumma*, a *xest.* of wine 4 *lummas*. And perhaps they came by way of Tyre, where wine is plentiful, and [there] they mixed it in. [That could not be, for] there there are narrow bays and shallow waters". This is a slightly telescoped version of our text. The printed edition's text seems to be the more accurate, (especially in view of B. Ḥulin 57a). For a detailed analysis of this text see my articles in *Archiv Orientalni*, 38, 1970, pp. 1–25, and *ZDMG*, 1969, pp. 265–68.

2 Wine was cheaper than muries in Palestine, hence the danger of admixture, (Rashi on this text). Wine was usually mixed in with muries for different purposes (see *Archiv Orientalni*, ibid., p. 11). See S. Lieberman, *Tosefta ki-fshutah, Zera'im* 1, p. 203. On muries in general see Darenberg et Saglio, *Dict. des Antiquités Romaines*, 3/2, p. 2046, s.v. *muria*, and Pauly-Wissowa *RE*, 16/1, pp. 661–62.

3 Jastrow, *Dict.*, p. 1074a, עיקולי ופשורי — cf. B. Ketubot 107a. I have found no satisfactory explanations for this statement. Tyre continued to be an active and successful port. See M.D. Judlewitsch, "Akko", *Sinai*, 7/3–4 (78–79), 1943, p. 186.

4 Cf. Soncino trans., A. Mishcon (London, 1935), pp. 166–67. (Correct R. Aḥa to R. Aba, and *xestos* to *xestes*.)

5 R. Rabbinovicz, *VL*, Avoda Zara, p. 79; MS JTS, fol. 35a, lines 22–25.

6 A. Hyman, *Toldoth Tannaim Ve'amoraim* (London, 1910), pp. 5b, 55b.

7 Ibid.

8 The mistake of substituting רבא for אבא ר' probably came about in the following manner: Originally the text read אבא ר'. This was copied at some stage as ראבא, which was in turn mistakenly understood to refer to רבא, as this *plena* form of spelling occurs not infrequently in Gaonic writings. (See, for example, *Gaonica* I, S. Assaf, Jerusalem, 1933, p. 310, lines 2, 3; MS JTS fol. 65a, line 10, p. 243, No. 10, etc. See *Sefer Halachot Pesuqot*, ed. S. Sasoon, Jerusalem, 1950, index of names, p. 214, for numerous examples.) Many examples of such parallel changes can be cited. Eg. *Iggeret R. Sherira Gaon*, ed. B. Lewin (Haifa, 1921) [= Iggeret=], p. 21: the French version has Rava bar R. Aba = B. Gittin 49a, etc., where he is called Rava bar Rava, and compare Spanish version of that text, or MS JTS, p. 235, s.v. Raba b. Zutra (= *Sefer Yuḥassin ha-Shalem*, ed. Filipowski, London and Edinburgh, 1857), p. 185a, reading R. Aba b. Zutra = B. Avoda Zara 28b, which in the Munich Ms. reads Rava, etc. (See further MS JTS, p. 237, s.v. Rava b. Shira, p. 238, s.v. Raba b. Zimuna, p. 239, 241–42, 243 line 10 — Raava b. Ada, *Iggeret*, p. 63, French version has Rava — etc. In B. Nidda 11a, we come across R. Aba b. Jeremiah, who elsewhere in the Bavli is called Rava or Rabba b. Jeremiah, e.g. B. Pesaḥim 36b., B. Mo'ed Katan 4a, B. Gittin 74a, etc. See also B. Berachot 34a: Rava in the name of R. Ḥiyya b. Ashi = B. Shabbat 73b: R. Aba in the name of . . . according to Mss. and *Sefer ha-Ittim.* — see Shabbat, *VL*, p. 71, note 80 and p. 156, note 1.) Also see *Seder ha-Dorot* of Y. Heilprin, Jerusalem, 1956, part 3, p. 109a. See also B. Horayot 2a, Rava, where the reading of R. Ḥananel—Horayot 2b— is R. Aba. See further S.K. Mirsky, *Perakim*, 4, 1966, p. 27, note 75; *VL* to Sukka, p. 71, note 300; *Menorat Ha-Maor*, ed. Enelow, 2, (New York, 1930), p. 39 line 2, note.

9 On R. Aba's biography, see Hyman, 3a–8b; W. Jaawitz, *Die Geschichte Israels* (or *Toldot Yisrael*), (Berlin, 1904) (Hebrew), 7, pp. 203–04; *Encyclopedia of Talmudic and Geonic Literature*[4], ed. M. Margalioth (Israel, 5712), (Hebrew), 1–3.

10 B. Rosh Hashana 35a, cf. B. Eruvin 12a. But see Rabbenu Tam's explanation to ימא לטיגנא, B. Kiddushin 44a (Hyman, *Toldoth* 390a). See next note. This may refer to a river journey from Pumbeditha northwards, or to some quite different journey from Palestine. See also *VL* to Rosh Hashana, p. 106, note 200, and *VL* to Eruvin, p. 34, note 9. The printed text would seem to have a good reading. See also Sachs, *Beiträge* 2, p. 7, (τηγανον), and I. Löw, *Fauna und Mineralien der Juden* (Hildesheim, 1969), p. 13, section 46.

11 B. Ketubot 112a. When he arrived he kissed כיפי דעכו. Cf. Y. Shevi'it 4.7, that R. Jose b. R. Ḥanina kissed the כיפתא of Akko as it was the boundary of Palestine. (כיפי = כיפתא, Jastrow, *Dict.* 636a, s.v. כיפתא.) See also Y. Shevi'it 6.1, that in Rabbi's time (c.160–220) above (= north of?) the "kipta" was outside Palestine. The military road from the North from Keziv (= Ekdippa) formed the border, the narrow strip west of the road being outside Palestine, (T. Ohalot 18.14 = Y. Shevi'it

6.1; B. Gittin 7b). But many places east of the road also belonged to the "Land of the heathen", (ibid.). If R. Aba came from the North by land from Tyre or Laodicea or Antioch, he would have first come across the "*kipta*" of Akko, which was traditionally the border, and had been kissed by R. Jose b. R. Ḥanina. But had he come by boat, no sooner would he have stepped ashore than he would have been in Palestine, (Shevi'it 5.2 = Y. Ḥalla 4.5), and we would have expected him to kiss the "shore" or the "dust" — עפרא — or the sands of Akko. This suggests, albeit only slightly, that he did not come down to Akko by sea but by land. On the border situation round Akko, see *Studies in Jewish History* by A. Büchler (Oxford, 1956), pp. 203–06 (= *JQR*, 13, 1901); *Studies in the Geography of Eretz Yisrael*, H. Hildesheimer and S. Klein (Jerusalem, 1965) (Hebrew), p. 153; M. Avi-Yonah in *Quarterly of the Department of Antiquities in Palestine*, 5, 1935, pp. 144, 199.

12 B. Ḥulin 19b; Y. Nedarim 4.2; B. Shabbat 63b; cf. B. Bava Kama 117b.

13 He died shortly before R. Johanan (B. Bava Mezia 84a), who died in 279 (*Iggeret*, p. 84). See below, notes 20, 21.

14 B. Ḥulin 19b.

15 B. Eruvin 46b, etc.; Hyman, p. 5b.

16 B. Ḥulin 57a, etc.

17 For his biography see Jaawitz, *Geschichte*, p. 190–99; Hyman, *Toldoth*, pp. 386b–398b. From B. Ḥulin 57a we learn of his prior arrival.

18 *Dorot Harischonim*, 2, (Berlin & Wien, 1923), p. 302.

19 *Dorot Harischonim* 2, p. 306, etc.

20 *Iggeret*, ed. Lewin, p. 84 and note 3; See Hyman's ed., p. 70 and note 37.

21 *Iggeret*, ed. Lewin, p. 84, *apparatus criticus*.

22 See my article in *Archiv Orientalni*, 34, 1966, p. 57, note 11. For a full bibliography on this discussion see H. Strack, *Introduction to the Talmud and Midrash* (Philadelphia, 1931), p. 319, note 2.

23 The argument is very complex and need not be restated here. However, it should be noted that his main teachers in Babylonia were R. Huna (d. 297) and R. Judah (b. Ezekiel) (d. 299), and that he studied under them for quite awhile. He also received many traditions from R. Ḥisda (d. 309), (Hyman, Toldoth, p. 387b–88a). Also, he cites R. Naḥman (b. Jacob) (d. 329) quite a number of times, (e.g. B. Ketubot 98a, B. Gittin 39b, 43b, B. Bava Batra 11a, 11b, B. Ḥulin 18a, Y. Eruvin 7.5 (?), see Hyman, ibid., p. 388b). See also Jaawitz, *Geschichte*, p. 159, note 2. However, R. Aba must have lived a long time as he appears to have still learned a little directly from Rav (d. 247) and Samuel (d. 254), (Hyman, ibid., p. 3a–b).

24 Krauss, *LW*, 2, p. 311a, and bibliography. Also see L. Herzfeld, *Metrologische Voruntersuchungen* (Leipzig, 1863), p. 180. Most recently, S. Lieberman, in *Tosefta ki-fshutah*, 1, p. 229 (to T. Demai 3.12), though there לומין is probably νουμμιον (see Löw apud Krauss, ibid.). Cf. Brockelmann, *Lexicon Syriacum*2, p. 361b, and 420b; (also Drower and Macuch, *A Mandaic Dictionary* (Oxford, 1963), p. 231a, s.v. LGT; and *JQR*, NS 12, p. 366 et seq.) Cf. Syriac Epiphanius, where נומא (fol. 69a, line 60) = *nummus* = νουμμος.

25 Lieberman, *Tosefta ki-fshutah*, 2, p. 658, note 47; Brockelmann, ibid., p. 367a; *Otzar ha-Geonim* to Berachot, B. Lewin, 1 (Haifa, 1928), p. 112, note 4; Z. Frankel, *Mevo ha-Yerushalmi* (Breslau, 1870), p. 8. See Y. Kila'im 8.3, etc.

26 F. Hultsch, *MSR*, 2, p. 200. index s.v. νουμμος 2. Also see νουμμος 3 = 1½ *obols* (= 1 *sest.*). See also Dessau, *Inscr.* 7313, 8303 ("*sestertio nummo uno*").

27 Hultsch, ibid., p. 20.

28 Sutherland in *JRS*, 51, 1961, p. 94 et seq. Note that the *nummi terentiani* of Anastasius I have been taken to be *"terunciani"*, referring to the old valuation of the *sestertius* at 40 *teruncii*; the M = 40–*nummia* piece, would be in question (Mattingly, *Roman Coins*[2], London, 1960, p. 217; Mommsen, *Chron. Min.* 2, p. 95 — Marcellinus —; cf. *Num. Chron.*, 1927, p. 223; see also P. Grierson in *INCP*, p. 286).

29 This piece was of almost pure copper, as opposed to the 10 gr. piece which had on an average 3.87% silver (*RIC*, 6, p. 94; see above, Chap. IV). It should be noted that the issue of this piece was discontinued after the *Edict* (301). Sutherland suggests that its valuation in relationship to the 10 gr. piece with its silver content proved to be unacceptable and unworkable (*RIC*, 6, pp. 99–100).

30 There was a 1½ gr. piece too. See *ANSMN*, 7, 1967, p. 113, suggesting that in Gallienus' time there was a unit, 3½ of which equalled the *ant*. See also Sutherland in *RIC* 6, p. 98, who suggests that this very rare piece was the *"denarius communis"* of Diocletian's *Edict*.

31 These sources are brought by Segrè, in *Byzantion*, 15, 1941, p. 251, to prove this point. The identification of the νουμμος with the 5d. piece is also accepted by Mickwitz, in his article in *Transactions of the International Numismatic Congress*, 1936 (London, 1938), pp. 219–28 on Dessau 9420. See also his remarks in *Geld und Wirtschaft*, pp. 84–85, notes 21 and 22; (also on Ditt.[2] 900 and 901). See further Callu, *PMER*, pp. 360–64.

32 Above we have stated that this piece was called a *follis*. Hence *follis* = *nummus* (on occasions). In later Byzantine writings one finds such an identification. E. g., Cedrenus 1.801: φολλεις ἤτοι νουμμοι. See Schrötter, *Wörterbuch der Münzkunde*, p. 200b. Cf. Ducange, *Glossarium Mediae et Infimae Latinitatis*, 5/2, p. 623a, s.v. *nummus*. Note further the fine of 20,000 *nummi* in *Cod. Theod.* 8.3.1 of the year 321. It seems clear that in this text the *nummus* is a small coin or unit of account. See also *Cod. Theod.* 14.19.1 (398), Jerome, *Epist.* 43 (Migne, *PL*, 22, 479), *Cod. Just.* 11.29.1. These texts are discussed by Adelson in *INCP*, pp. 274–75.

Chapter IX

1 In *Economic History Revue*, 2/5, 1953, pp. 317–18. See also Callu, *PMER*, pp. 368–69, note 4.

2 Cf. Mickwitz, *Geld und Wirtschaft*, p. 104, note 2.

3 Cf. *Symbolae Osloensis*, 14, p, 85 (Heichelheim); West, *Gold and Silver Standards*, p. 187; Segrè in *Byzantion*, 15, p. 253; and West and Johnson, *Currency*, pp. 131–32, 184–85.

3a Cope's assays of these pieces show them to be void of silver, (private communication of 10 Sept. 1972).

4 See West and Johnson, *Currency*, p. 131; contra Segrè in *Byzantion*, 15, p. 253, and also Sutherland, in *JRS*, 51, 1961, p. 97, note 38. See also R. Taubenschlag, *The Law of Greco-Roman Egypt in the Light of the Papyri*[2], (Warsaw 1955), p. 675, note 95

5 *JRS*, 49, 1959, p. 34.

6 See P. A. Bruun, in *RIC*, 7 (London, 1966), who on p. 11 suggests that some time in the mid second decade, after the *argenteus* had been discontinued, the silver-washed *follis*, formerly worth 5d. was revalued to be worth 25d. This view is quite unacceptable. For even after the minting of *argentei* had been discontinued, such pieces must have continued to circulate. It is difficult to visualize two such radically different coins circulating side by side with the same nominal value even for the briefest of periods. Furthermore, according to Bruun, the law against counterfeiting would have had to be the same for *argentei* (silver) and *folles*. However, this is not the case as has been conclusively demonstrated by P. Grierson in his searching study, "The Roman Law of Counterfeiting", in *Essays in Roman Coinage*, etc., ed. Carson & Sutherland (London, 1956), pp. 241–42, 245, and particularly, p. 248. See also Buttery's remarks in *Gnomon*, 41, 1969, pp. 679–80.

7 Note that the lowest price in Diocletian's *Edict* is 2d. But see Pearce in *JRS*, 23, 1933, p. 87.

8 Pink, *Numismatische Zeitschrift*, 1940, p. 38.

9 Hammer, *Zeitschrift für Numismatik*, 1908, p. 110; West, *Gold and Silver Standards*, p. 186, note 39 — 94%. Cf. Bolin, *State and Currency*, p. 303. But see Howard L. Adelson, in *Centennial Publication of the American Numismatic Society*, ed. Harald Ingholt (New York, 1938), p. 2, note 6 — 98%. See also Sutherland in *RIC*, 6, 1967, pp. 98–99, who gives 90% as the silver content.

10 G. Mickwitz, *Die System des römischen silbergeldes in IV Jahrh.* etc. (Soc. Scient. Fenn. Comm. Hum. Litt. 6, Helsingfors, 1933), p. 42, based on 560 specimens.

11 Adelson in *Centennial Publication of ANS*, p. 7; Mattingly, *Roman Coins*[2], p. 217; Sutherland, *RIC*, 6, pp. 98–99.

12 Contra Sutherland, *RIC*, 6, p. 99, who follows Bollin to a large extent. See also Cope's remarks in *Num. Chron.*, 1968, pp. 147–49.

13 See Ammianus Marcellinus 24.3.3, etc.

14 Cf. *Cod. Theod.* 8.4.27 of 422, yielding the same equation. Also *Cod. Theod.* 11.21.2 of 396, suggesting this equation. Cf. Mickwitz, *Geld und Wirtschaft*, p. 105, etc., Bolin, *State and Currency*, p. 307 and note 7. Mickwitz, *Die System*, p. 7, et seq. thinks that *SB* 608V is post 324. Cf. West and Johnson, *Currency*, pp. 186–86; Adelson in *Centennial Publication of ANS*, p. 9 and note 34. However, see Segrè in *Maia*, 16, 1964, pp. 264–65, and pp. 266–68. See also Sutherland, *RIC*, 6, p. 99, who suggests that such a ratio could have existed during or very shortly after the year of Diocletian's *Edict*. The ratio of 14.4:1 seems to have been used in the '60's of the IV cent., for in Ammianus Marcellinus 20.4.18 we find a donative of 5 *aurei* plus 1 lb. silver, in 360. At this period "*aurei*" are *solidi* and there are 72 of them to the *libra aurei*. If we accept a ratio of 14.4:1 between AR and AV at this time, then 1 lb. silver = 5 *solidi* ($72/5 = 14.4$). Hence the donative consisted of twice five *solidi*, five in gold *solidi*, and five in pure unminted silver. This text was already cited by Mommsen-Blacas (*Histoire de la Monnaie Romaine*, 3, p. 155). See also Jones, *Later Roman Empire*, 3, p. 114, note 73. See, however, Segrè, *Byzantion*, 16, 1943, p. 413, and Adelson's additional comments in *INCP*, p. 268, note 20. (On donatives of 5 *aurei* and 10 *aurei* see *Deut Rab.*, 1.13, *Exod. Rab.* 30.9; cf. Dio Cassius 21.6, 53.13, 54.12. See I. Ziegler, *Die Königsgleichnisse des Midrasch* (Breslau, 1903), p. 66, and and Krauss, *Paras ve-Romi*, p. 232. Furthermore, in Ammianus Marcellinus 24.3.3 of the year 363, we find a donative of 100 silver *nummi*. If we assume that these *nummi* are pieces struck at 1/96 (see Table K at end of chapter XXII), at 96%, and

at a ratio of 14.4:1, then this sum equalled 5 *solidi*. The material is summarised in the following table.

GOLD AND SILVER RATIOS

SB 6086	early IV cent.		1:18
P. Oslo 162	IV cent.		1:14.4
Cod. Theod. 13.2.1	397		1:14.4
CIL V 8734	c.400		1:15
Cod. Theod. 8.4.27	442		1:18
Cod. Just. 10.78.1.	534		1:14.4

From "Silver Currency and Values in the early Byzantine Empire", by Howard L. Adelson, in *Centennial Publication of the American Numismatic Society*, ed. Harald Ingholt (New York, 1958), pp. 7, 10–11. Cf. L.C. West, "The Roman gold standard in ancient sources", *American Journal of Philology*, 62, 1941, pp. 278–301; See also *Currency*, p. 108. *Cod. Theod.* 11.21.2 (396) suggests 1:18; Cf. Mickwitz, *Geld und Wirtschaft* etc., p. 105; Segrè, *Circolazione*, p. 53 et seq.; idem, *Metrologia*, p. 451. Also cf. *Cod. Just.* 10.29 (1:14.4), and *P. Lond.* IV. 1434,5. For the period c.500, see Segrè, *Metrologia*, p. 481; Mickwitz, *Geld und Wirtschaft* etc., evidence of the marks of value on Vandal coins. See also Jones, *The Later Roman Empire*, 3, pp. 113–4, note 73.

15 Dessau, *Inscr.* 9420. Cited by Mattingly, *Roman Coins*[2], p. 218.

16 Mattingly, ibid.; cf. Mommsen, *Römische Münzwesen*, p. 791, citing the Dessau inscription.

17 The *nummus* can also be a gold coin; e.g. *SB.* 6222, *P.O.* 1165, *Cod. Just.* 11.29.1(?); West and Johnson, *Currency*, pp. 131–32. Cf. *P. Giess, Univ. Bible*, 22, lines 3–4; Heichelheim in *Symbolae Osloensis*, 14, 1935, pp. 82–83; Segrè, in *Byzantion*, 15, p. 251, note 11, and in *JEA*, 31, 1945, p. 113, (contra Heichelheim *JEA*, 29, 1943, p. 79).

18 Syriac version, ed. J.E. Dean (Chicago, 1935), par. 52, p. 61. Cf. Hultsch, *MSR*, 2, p. 105, and also Boetticher (= Lagarde), *Symmicta*, 2, pp. 196–97.

19 Syriac version, ed. Dean, note 426 ibid. A.R. Burns, *Money and Monetary Policy in Early Times* (London, 1927), p. 242, note 5; nomic gloss in Dindorff's ed. of Epiphanius, 4/1, p. 128; O. Seeck, in *Zeitschrift für Numismatik*, 17, 1890, pp. 36–89, 113–66; E. Stein's *Geschichte der Spätrömishes Reiches*, 1 (Wien, 1928), p. 178, note 109. But, cf. Jones in *JRS*, 49, 1959, p. 36, note 27. Also Jones in *Essays in Roman Coinage presented to Harold Mattingly* (Oxford, 1956), p. 28, note 1. See further Adelson in *ANSMN*, 7, 1957, p. 130, and note 12, for a discussion of this nomic gloss, also p. 132, note 20.

20 Cf. Hultsch, *MSR*, 2, p. 173, s.v. διχρυσον. Note also that Epiphanius speaks of a unit of 25d., called a *kodrantes*, (see above, Chap. VII, note 1).

21 *Byzantion*, 15, p. 276. See also Adelson in *ANSMN*, 7, 1957, p. 133. See also Segrè, *Journal of Égyptian Archeology*, 26, 1941, pp. 114–15; W. Seston, *Chronique d'Égypte*, 43–4, 1947, pp. 333–37; Callu, *PMER*, p. 291 note 3 and p. 358; idem, *BSFN*, 20 1965, pp. 500–01.

22 As to the Licinius XIIr coin (our coin no. 21), this belongs to a group of coins bearing this mark of value from 318–24, and weighing about 3.14 grammes, (West and Johnson, *Currency*, p. 101). The meaning of this notation is unclear (see Mickwitz, *Geld und Wirtschaft*, pp. 103–04, note 18), as are most other marks of value

on IV cent. currency, (West and Johnson, *Currency*, p. 102). Whatever its meaning, it probably has nothing to do with the reduction of the *nummus* to half its value, an operation which had taken place perhaps more than a decade and a half earlier. (See, however, West in *Studies in Roman Economic and Social History*, etc., ed. Coleman Norton, p. 301, note 13.) If the reduced *nummus* (10 gramme piece) was of pure copper, the bronze-gold ratio would be about 1185 : 1, which is considerably above the more usual 1440 : 1 (West and Johnson, *Currency*, p. 98). It appears therefore that there was (at least in theory) a slight percentage of silver in or (washed) over the coins which affected their value. This is borne out by metallic analyses; cf. for example, Adelson in *ANSMN*, 6, 1954, pp. 111–29, article entitled "Bronze Alloys in the late Roman Empire", with bibliography. Most recently this has been categorically stated to be the case by Sutherland, in *RIC*, 6, 1967, p. 94. (See above, Chap. IV, note 55, for fuller bibliography). See also Carson in *INCP*, 1967, p. 250. If we do wish to see a connection between the mark of value XIIr and the halving of the *nummus*, we may explain it thus: 10 (X) *sests.* = 2½ (IIr) d., i.e. this piece is worth 2½ and not 5 d. (Cf. Pridik, in *Num. Zeitschr.*, 1929, pp. 64–69, article entitled "Miliarense, Follis und Centenionalis".)

Chapter X

1 *JRS*, 49, 1959, p. 35 and note 1.
2 Incorrectly described on p. 42 of G.V. Gentili's *The Imperial Villa of Piazza Armerina*, 1956; cf. the photograph of the mosaic (no. 26); see also Gentili's *La Villa Erculia di Piazza Armerina, I mosaici figurati* (Rome, 1959), pl. XLI.
3 See Jones, *The Later Roman Empire*, 3 (Oxford, 1964), p. 2, note 18. See also Segrè, in *Chronique d'Égypte*, 40, 1965, pp. 198–99; Callu, *BSFN*, 20/8, 1965, pp. 500–01.
4 Since the standard ratio between copper and silver was 100:1, what Epiphanius probably means to say here is that 2½ silver *denarii* (or units) equal 250 copper *denarii* (or units) of the same size, and that this indeed was the value of the *follis KTD*. The *follis KTA* would be 100 times bigger, i.e. worth 25,000 d., which is the value of the *follis* c. 301, before devaluation cut it down to half the price. In this passage we find Epiphanius eclectically collating two different traditions, one from before the devaluation, the other from after it, without his even feeling the contradiction. This gives us some insight into his methods in compiling this work.
5 *JRS*, 49, 1959, p. 35. Hultsch, *MSR*, 1, p. 269, par. 17.
6 See Lellia Ruggini's article in *Atti della Academia Nazionale dei Lincei, Rendiconti*, 16, 1961, entitled "A proposito del *Follis* nel IV secola", p. 306.
7 West and Johnson, *Currency*, p. 106; cf. Adelson, *Centennial Publication of the American Numismatic Society*, p. 7.
8 West and Johnson, ibid., p. 76 — an average based on 353 specimens. For the patterns of the weight reduction of the *follis* in different mints, see Sutherland, *RIC*, 6, 1967, pp. 101–03.
9 See the discussion in West and Johnson, ibid., p. 158; Segrè, *Metrologia*, pp. 438–39; Bolin, *State and Currency*, p. 324. See also *Ianda inv.* 315, of 347, which according to R. Rémondon, in *Chronique d'Égypte*, 31, 1956, p. 146, yields an equation of 115,000 *sol.* to the *libra aurei*.

10 I have discussed this text in greater detail, and examined the difficulties in it, in *Archiv Orientalni*, 34, 1965, p. 63, and in *Num. Chron.*, 1968, pp. 103–09. See also S. Lieberman, *Tosefta ki-fshutah*, 2, p. 752, (to T. Ma'aser Sheni 3.8). See below, Chap. XIV for a further discussion of this text.

11 Of course Y. Ma'aser Sheni may be referring to a stage between 1600d. to the *aureus*, and 2,400d. to the *aureus*. However, such an explanation would necessitate a change of the gold-silver ratio between c.305 and 307; thus I prefer to follow the explanation given in the text here.

12 *JRS*, 49, 1959, p. 35. He compares it with *Cod. Theod.* 5.17.2 (cf. 386), a fine of 6 oz. gold on those who harboured a runaway *colonus* of a private landlord. But cf. the view of the editors of this papyrus, Boak and Youtie, *Studi in onore di A. Calderini e R. Paribeni*, 2 (Milano, 1957), p. 327, who think that 5 *foll.* = 20d.!

13 *Studi in onore*, ibid., p. 329.

14 Actually *PSI*. 310 yields a *libra aurei* of 124,920 d. (at 14.4:1). See Ruggini, op. cit. p. 311, Bolin, *State and Currency*, p. 324. For c. 312, see *P. Ryl.* 616, and Rémondon's remarks in *Chronique d'Éegypt*, 31, 1956, p. 146.

14a Cope, private communication of 10 Sept. 1972. Cf. table J.

15 West and Johnson, *Currency*, p. 97. *RIC*, 6, pp. 101–03.

16 For the dating, see O. Seeck, *Regesten der Kaiser und Paepste* (Stuttgart, 1919), p. 54.

17 Jones, *JRS*, 49, 1959, p. 35.

18 Mickwitz, *Geld und Wirtschaft*, p. 105, thinks that in 315, 1 *libra aurei* = 1,400,000 d.! Ruggini, *Rendiconti dei Lincei*, p. 311, gives for 314–16, 1,500,000 d. per *libra aurei*. Segrè, in *Byzantion*, 15, p. 250 and note 7 derives (from very scanty evidence) an equation for 1 *sol.* = 3500 d., (based on *P.O.* 2113), which is very close to *P. Roll. Princ.* VII. 6., of 316, which yields an equation of 1 *sol.* = 3472 d. See also Mickwitz, in *Transactions of the International Numismatic Congress*, 1936 (London, 1938), p. 221, note 1, who brings (speculative) evidence for 314–16, based on *PER.E.* 2000, *P.O.* 2114, (and *P.O.* 84). Mickwitz' and Ruggini's conclusions are unlikely in view of the evidence of *P.O.* 1430, of 324, yielding the equation: 1 *libra aurei* = 313, 488 d. (Cf. West and Johnson, *Currency*, pp. 158–59.) The pattern, though not a clear curve on a graph does not seem to warrant the conclusions of Ruggini and Mickwitz. The *P. Roll. Princ.* papyri cited (4.31, and 7.6, yielding 437,000 d. and 250,000 d. per *libra aurei* respectively) argue against their conclusions. See P. Bruun's remarks in *RIC*, 7, p. 11, note 2. The high price of *P. Roll. Princ.* 4.31 may be explicable in terms of the very debased coins then current. (See below, Chaps. XXIV and XXV.)

19 It is a great temptation to interpret notations (marks of value?) on the coins of this period. Thus *folles* of Lyons from 308–09 bear the notation CI_S^H (*RIC*, 6, p. 104). One might interpret this as meaning that 1 (*follis*) = 100(C) *sestertii* (HS), i.e. 25 d. This would give an *aureus* of 4000 d. for the years 308–09. However, this does not fit in well with the evidence of the papyrus of 308–09, cited above (note 12), nor of metrological evidence cited below (Chap. XXII). Finally, how would we interpret the notation on the *folles* of Nicomedia of 308–11: CMH (*RIC*, 6, p. 104)? Could the value of the *follis* have varied so radically from Egypt to Asia Minor (and the West)? This seems highly unlikely. In the meantime these notations remain a puzzle.

20 The other sources cited by Jones in *JRS*, 49, 1959, have been thoroughly re-examined by Ruggini in her article in *Rendiconti dei Lincei*, 16. See also Callu, *PMER*, p. 265 et seq. See further: *Cod. Theod.* 11.36.2 (of 315); *Cod. Theod.* 13.3.1 (of

321), (cf. Mickwitz, *Geld und Wirtschaft*, p. 91); *Cod. Theod.* 14.21.1 (of 328); *Cod. Theod.* 6.4.5 (of 340), (cf. Ruggini, ibid., p. 313); *Cod. Theod.* 7.20.3 (cf. ed. Mommsen, p. 351; Segrè, *Metrologia*, p. 462; Ruggini, ibid., p. 311; Mickwitz, ibid., pp. 86–87; Kubitschek in *Num. Zeitschr.*, 1909, p. 60; Santo Mazzarino, *Aspetti sociali del Quarto Secolo* (Roma, 1961), pp. 112–13); Augustin, *Sermo*, 389.3 (cf. Mickwitz, ibid., p. 88, Ruggini, ibid., p. 317). See also Pearce in *JRS*, 23, 1933, p. 87. I have also not discussed the famous Feltre Inscription of 323, (= Dessau 9420) because of its ambiguity, (cf. Segrè, *Metrologia*, p. 461; Mickwitz, ibid., p. 84 and note 21, and his article entitled "Uber die Kupfergeldinflationem in den Jahren der Thronkämpfe nach Diokletians Abdangkung", *Proceedings of the International Numismatic Congress of 1936*, pp. 219–28; Kubitschek in *Num. Zeitschr.*, 1909, pp. 47–66, especially p. 56, note 1; Mommsen in *CIL*, 5, 2987; Mattingly, *Roman Coins*[2], pp. 219–20, etc.). Likewise I have not discussed Ditt.[2], 901 (of 312–15) from Delphi, and 900 (311) from Panamara in Caria, (cf. Mickwitz, ibid., p. 85, note 22; Segrè, *Metrologia*, p. 452, note 2).

Chapter XI

1 I first discussed these texts in an article in *Num. Chron.*, 1968, pp. 83–113.

2 It will be noted that such statements are taken as descriptive of a situation rather than explanatory. Subsequent discussion will demonstrate conclusively that such can hardly have been the complete reason, either legal or economic.

3 The phrase used here by both Talmuds is (דינרין) טבין ותקילין, literally: (*dinars*, Y.) good and of [full] weight. Cf. *TAM*, 2, 334, cited by D. Magie, *Roman Rule in Asia Minor*, 2, p. 1573, note 39: *(δηναρια) βονα*. This phrase continues to be used (or recurs) in much later periods; e.g. in a document from the Cairo Geniza of the year 1052 "... excellent *dinars* of full weight," (cited by Goitein, in *A Mediterranean Society*, 1, 1967, p. 242; cf. ibid., p. 236).

4 The commentators on this text understand this statement thus: And can we learn from the [story of the] daughter of R. Ḥiyya (that the law is) that gold is money? — a rhetorical question. However, it is fairly clear that this indeed was R. Ḥiyya's opinion; cf. Ridbaz on this text. The Bavli's version of this story is slightly expanded.

5 See below, Chap. XIV.

6 See Krauss, *LW*, 2, p. 319a s.v. לקן; Zuckermann, *Talmudische Münzen und Gewichte* (Breslau, 1862), p. 29, and see below, Chap. XIV.

7 This latter part is a typical piece of (Babylonian) Talmudic argumentation and is of no historical importance for us.

8 See *JE*, 7, p. 333b, s.v. Judah I (article by W. Bacher), and see below, note 23.

9 The specific term used in the Babylonian Talmud is בזקנותו — בזקנותך, which usually means between 60 and 70; see M. Avot 5.21; בן ששים לזוקנה — 'sixty years for mature age'.

10 See Hyman, *Toldoth*, pp. 11–15.

11 Hyman, ibid., p. 431.

12 See Callu, *PMER*, pp. 430–31.

13 *JE*, 1, p. 298 (s.v. Abba Arika, article by W. Bacher). Rabbi himself probably changed his mind again when he indicated to Samuel's father that gold is coin. However, this may also have been an event of Rabbi's youth. The chronology is as yet unclear. We know only that Samuel himself died in 254. On this date see recently J. Neusner, *A History of the Jews in Babylonia*, 2, 1966, pp. 45–48 and bibliography. It may here be in place to make a few additional comments on chronological issues: Rav went to Babylonia in 219–20 (*Iggeret*, ed. Lewin, p. 78) during the lifetime of R. Judah ha-Nasi (contra Lewin, ibid., note 3, who suggests that this took took place in the life of R. Judah Nesiah, Rabbi's grandson. See also A. Epstein, *REJ*, 44, 1902, pp. 56–7). R. Judah ha-Nasi is mentioned explicitly in *Sefer ha-Kabbalah* of Abraham ibn Daud (c. 1110–80), (Neubauer, *Mediaeval Jewish Chronicles*, 1, Oxford, 1887, p. 57; G. Cohen's edition, Philadelphia, 1967, Hebrew, p. 24; English, p. 32) cf. Neubauer, ibid., pp. 177, 182). Likewise in *Maḥzor Vitry*, ed. Horowitz (Berlin, 1889–97), p. 482 (see note 400). This same date, stated to be 150 years after the destruction of the Temple, is also found in Nissim Gaon's introduction to the Talmud, (i.e. his introduction to his *Sefer ha-Mafte'aḥ*). Menahem Me'iri (1249–1306) in his introduction to Avot (ed. Prag, Jerusalem, 1964, p. 49) quotes this same tradition as coming from Nissim Gaon's *Sefer ha-Kabbalah*. (It appears that he was confusing the Gaon's introduction to the *Sefer ha-Mafte'aḥ* with a book that he stated he would write, but probably never did, called *Sefer ha-Kabbalah*; see S. Abramson, *R. Nissim Gaon* etc., Jerusalem, 1965, Hebrew, pp. 16–17.) In the latter two sources (Nissim Gaon and the Me'iri) it is stated that the end of the editing of the Mishna was at this time, 150 years after the destruction of the Temple (= 220). Therefore, R. Judah ha-Nasi, who completed the editing of the Mishna, must have still been alive c.220. This tradition, that the Mishna was completed 150 years after the destruction of the Temple, is already found in the *Sefer ha-Galui* of Sa'adiah Gaon, (cited by Baron, *SRHJ*[2], 6, 1958, p. 203; cf. ibid., p. 425 note 63, also p. 428 note 67. See also M. Beer, *Bar-Ilan*, 4–5, 1967, pp. 181–85). The passage in *Yalkut Zachariah* 578 (citing the *Yelamdenu*), which states that Rabbi (Judah ha-Nasi), Antoninus and קרבן מלך פרסי (reading in ed. princeps) — KRBN Persian King — all died in the same month, must be speaking of a Roman emperor and a Persian king who died after 220; (contra S.A. Rappaport, *Erech Milim*, Warsaw, 1914, 2, p. 20; according to him Rabbi died in 192, the year in which Commodus and Volgases III died). Perhaps we may suggest that Rabbi died in 222, the year in which Elagabalus (named M. Aurelius Antoninus) was murdered. In an article in *Leshonenu*, 34, 1969, pp. 61–65, I suggested that KRBN = *Karaban, the Pahlevi for "a general". Can this enigmatic KRBN refer to Papak, King (first of Xir then) of Istaxr, called in the Ka'abah of Zoroaster MLK' 'RY'NSTR — King of Iran (see Chaumont, "Papak, roi de Staxr et sa cour", *Journal Asiatique*, 247, 1959, p. 157 et seq.), who probably died 222, (see R.N. Frye, *The Heritage of Persia*, 1962, p. 320. See also Taqizadeh in *Archiv Orientalni* 18, 1940, p. 260 et seq.)? Finally, Sherira in his *Iggeret* tells us that R. Johanan died in the year 279 (ed. Lewin, p. 84; cf. *Maḥzor Vitry*, p. 483, note 6, Neubauer, ibid., p. 177, 183, etc.). His statement that "R. Johanan reigned for 80 years in Palestine after R. Ḥanina, who was after R. Efes, who was after Rabbenu Ha-Kaddosh", (= R. Judah the Prince) (*Iggeret*, ed. Lewin, pp. 83–84) clearly needs to be emended, (see Lewin's note 6 on p. 83).

14 *Econ. Surv.*, 4 (Baltimore, 1938), p. 221.

15 Ibid., p. 210. Cagnat, *IGRR*, 3, 1050 = *CIS*, 2, 3, 1, no. 3948; also Cooke, *North Semitic Inscriptions* (Oxford, 1903), p. 273, no. 115 (= Vog. 6).

16 Cf. *Econ. Surv.*, (Baltimore, 1940), ed. Tenney Frank, p. 93; Heichelheim, *JRS*, 27, 1937, pp. 286–87. But see West, *Gold and Silver Standards*, p. 118.

17 Cf. also T. Bava Mezia 3.14 (377, 9–13).

18 For further discussion of the problem of *"kinyan kesef"* (= purchase by money), see Isaac Herzog's *The main Institutions of Jewish Law*, 1, *"Law of Property"* (London, 1936), pp. 163–66, 182 etc., also A. Gulak, *Yesod Hamishpat Ha-Ivri*, 1, (Berlin, 1922), para. 36, p. 107 et seq.

19 Does "Severan *tetradrachms*" means *tertradrachms* of Septimius Severus or those of Severus Alexander? If those of Sev. Alex., they are probably Antiochene. The rights of Antioch had been taken away after Niger's defeat by Septimius (*Scriptores Historiae Augustae*, *Sev.* 9. 4, Loeb ed., 1, p. 393). They were restored by Caracalla, probably when he received the *toga virilis* and assumed his first consulship, 202, (ibid., *Sev.* 16, 8, Loeb ed., 1, p. 409; *Caracalla* 1.70, Loeb ed. 2, p. 4, note 1). In Septimius' reign, therefore, relatively few *tetradrachms* could have been struck at Antioch, (cf. *BMC*, 5, Mattingly, London, 1950, p. XVI, note 1). Only very few *tetradrachms* were struck at the beginning of his reign. (*BMC*, 6, Carson, London, 1962, pp. 5, 8; *Dura Final Report*, 6, *Coins*, A. R. Bellinger, 1949, pp. 205–06). Casarea in Cappadocia produced a few (*BMC*, 5, p. XVI), and so did Laodicia and Tyre (ibid., p. 202). Severus Alexander's coins seem the more likely for the comments of R. Johanan, (*BMC*, 5, p. XVI). See also Bellinger's *Syrian Tetradrachms of Caracalla and Macrinus*, *NNM*, 3 (New York, 1940), pp. 21, 30–32, 86. Incidentally the correct interpretation of this Yerushalmi text was realised by Herzfeld (*Metrologische Voruntersuchen*, Leipzig, 1863, p. 63), *Brüll Jahrb.*, 1, 1874, p. 182, and by Zuckermann, *Talmudische Münzen*, p. 15, and was followed by all the dictionaries, (Kohut, Levy, Krauss) except for Jastrow (*Dict.*, p. 519b. s.v. טבריא) whose emendation to טברניות (= Tiberian) is not only unnecessary but impossible, as Tiberias (the city) never produced silver currency. (See e.g. Arie Kindler, *The Coins of Tiberias*, *Tiberias*, 1961.) Similarly unlikely is the suggestion of L. Hamburger, in *Die Münzprägungen Während des letzten Aufstandes der Israeliten gegen Rom* (Berlin, 1892), p. 104. See further Herzfeld, *Metrologische Voruntersuchungen*, pp. 159–60. The *denarii* of Septimius Severus were only 58.3% silver; see Bolin, *State and Currency*, p. 211, Table 17.

20 *REJ*, 98, 1934, pp. 36–37 ("Dioclétian à la lumière de la Litterature rabbinique").

21 See, for example, Mickwitz, *Geld und Wirtschaft*, pp. 40–41. It is interesting to note that according to *CIL*, 6, 29691 of 206 there is already some indication of the mistrust in minted silver and copper. For there we find a record of a distribution of 10 *libra* of silver and 100,000 *sest*. Thus, first the unminted silver is mentioned, and only then the minted coins.

22 Cf. *BMC*, 5, index "gold".

23 See *Iggereth Rav Sherira Gaon*, ed. Hyman, p. 65, note 5, (chap. 3, section 2); ed. Lewin, p. 76, line 15 and p. 78 line 5 (variants and notes); *Dorot Harischonim* of Halevy, 2/3, chap. 24, 5–6. See also A. Guttman's article in *HUCA*, 25, 1964, pp. 244–54 for Rabbi's birth-date, (c.135), and pp. 256–61 for the date of his death, which remains unclear. See Ginzberg, *Ginzei Schechter*, 2, p. 397 and Lewin, *Otzar ha-Gaonim* to Sanhedrin, 97b (Jerusalem, 1966), p. 499, note 1. However, it does seem clear that Rabbi lived till c.220, see above, note 13.

24 *JSS*, 2, 1957, pp. 355–56, note 3. This has to be seen in a wider context of the problems of Mishna editing, Mishnaic sources, etc. See, for example, S. Lieberman, *Greek and Hellenism in Jewish Palestine* (Hebrew ed., Jerusalem, 1962), pp. 217–18, and note 49; E. Schachter, *Ha-Mishna ba-Bavli u-ba-Yerushalmi* (Jerusalem, 1959), p. 305, 734 (to M. Avoda Zara 4.4), (cf. Rappaport in *Kerem Chemed*, 7, letter 9, sect. 4, pp. 157–60); Schachter, ibid., introduction, pp. 17–36, and pp. 1, 42, 171, 305; L. Ginzberg, *A Commentary on the Palestinian Talmud*, 1 (New York, 1941), Hebrew introduction, p. 51; J. N. Epstein, *Mavo le-Nusaḥ Ha-Mishna* (Jerusalem, 1958), pp. 673–726, especially pp. 707–30; Z. Frankel, *Mavo ha-Yerushalmi* (Breslau, 1870), fol. 20a et seq. Dr. J. Kent, in a private communication (of 23 August, 1972) writes as follows: "I can see that the Babylonian and Palestinian solution to the question 'Does gold acquire silver, or *vice-versa*?' might well be different. In the Roman Empire, both metals were used for coinage, and with the attested premium of AV over AR, 'silver would acquire gold'. But among the Parthians, gold coin was a commodity imported from Roman, and its status was goods, not coinage. Therefore, 'gold acquires silver'. . ." This may well explain (in part) why the Babylonian Talmud adopted the Mishna reading that 'Gold acquires silver', but it does not explain developments and changes of attitude *within Palestine itself*.

25 A. H. M. Jones, in *Economic History Review* (New Series), 5, 1952–53, p. 300. Cf. also *P. Mich.* 111 verso 1.6 (42 C. E.) where 11 and 21 gold pieces are referred to, but their value is expressed in silver *(ἀργυριον χρυσων)*. See West and Johnson, *Currency*, p. 70. See also *P. Baden*, 37 (c. 100 C. E.), where the price of gold is given, in *dr.* (?), West and Johnson, ibid., pp. 181 and 90–93.

26 We would be forced to posit different historic strata which were put together without real understanding of the issues involved.

27 Bolin, *State and Currency*, p. 59 and cf. p. 63. See also the comment in West and Johnson, *Currency*, p. 164 that "In the earlier period the gold piece whether *aureus* or *solidus* seems to have been equated with amounts expressed in *drachmae* or *denarii*, in the later period the *solidus* was equated with *myriads* or *talents* but the customary practice was to express sums less than a *solidus* as fractions of that coin or of the *carat*."

28 See Pekári's "Studien zur römischen Währungs und Finanzgeschichte von 161 bis 235", in *Historia*, 8, 1959, pp. 456–57; also T. F. Carney, *Catalogue of Courtauld Collection of Roman Coins* etc., (Salisbury, S. Rhodesia, 1963), p. XXIX. However, sceptical one may be of Pekári's methods in arriving at such precise results — dating and definition of types for this period is extremely complex — the general conclusions are hardly to be doubted, so great is the discrepancy in number. Pekári reckons (including, of course, non-silver cons) as follows: Pertinax 14; Didius Julianus, Manlia Scantilla and Didia Clara 8; Pescinius Niger 155; Clodius Albinus 10; Septimius Severus (till the end of 196) 342. Though these coin-types include AV, AR and AE, it seems clear that there were far more silver coins during these years than earlier. Carson, in a private communication to me (15 August, 1972) comments as follows: "One must be careful . . . not to equate a greater number of issues and changing types with greater amount of coinage. This does not necessarily follow. An analysis of hoard statistics would be necessary for assurance on this point. Your table G bears on this. Though in hoards buried under Severus Alexander coins of Septimius Severus are twice as plentiful as those of Antoninus Pius; if you take coins of Pius from all hoards they are 5000; all coins of Severus only about 3000."

29 West and Johnson, *Currency*, pp. 1–2, 89–90. *Econ. Surv.*, 2 (Baltimore, 1936), pp. 427, 432. Weber, *NNM*, 54, p. 4; A. C. Johnson, *Egypt and the Roman Empire*, 1951, pp. 11, 14.

30 Dattari, *Revista italiana numismatica*, 1903, pp. 285–86; cf. Jones in *Econ. Hist. Rev.*, 1952–53, p. 297.

31 *BMC*, 4, Mattingly (London, 1940), p. XV.

31a This interpretation is borne out by metallurgical analysis discussed by Cope in his article in *Num. Chron.*, 1967, pp. 114–18. (My thanks to him for this reference.)

32 Pekári dates the silver boom as beginning in 194–95 (*Historia*, 8, 1954, p. 443 et seq.) and therefore rejects Heichelheim's interpretation. See his remarks in *Syria*, 38, 1961, p. 283, note 3. Metallurgical analysis shows that there was a change in fineness late in 193, (Cope ibid., pp. 114, 118). Cope (ibid., p. 118) writes: "... As a result of an imperial decision, of which we have no other remaining record than the coinage, the base alloy addition to the *libra* bar of silver was simply trebled from A.D. 194 onwards." For a recent discussion of the whole Palmyra inscription, see J. Guey, *Syria*, 38, 1961, pp. 268–74, who thinks that "old *denarii*" refers to a unit of value. It should also be noted that on long journeys it was easier to take a small amount of gold rather than a large amount of silver. See *Sifré Deut.*, sect. 306, cited below, Chap. XIII. See also Callu, *PMER*, p. 56, on hoarding patterns during this period.

33 *Apocrimata, Decisions of Septimius Severus in Legal Matters*, ed. Williams Linn Westermann, and Arthur Schiller (New York, 1954), pp. 32–34, commentary, p. 89. Westermann and Schiller in *Chronique d'Égypte*, 30, 1955, pp. 327–45, with no significant changes. Note also that hoards were buried during this period; e.g. *Num. Chron.*, 1960, p. 245, hoard buried c. 194–95. For a list of such hoards, see Bolin, *State and Currency*, pp. 351–52 (table 7, nos. 1, 2, 10, 12, 13, 15, all from 193–95). The editors regard this decision as "based on a previous decision ... possibly a general edict applying to the entire Empire", (*Apocrimata*, ibid., p. 32).

34 This interpretation (the editors') is accepted and further borne out by MacMullen in *Aegyptus*, 43, 1962, p. 100. Cf. p. 99 for his graph.

35 "If he gave him a gold *dinar* (= *aureus*) and said to him: 'Buy me a shirt', and he went and bought him a shirt for 3 *selas* (= 12d.) and a cloak for 3 *selas* (= 12d.), they are both guilty of sacrilege" etc. For the context shows that the amounts are meant to be exactly equal. Hence 24 d. = 1 *aureus*.

36 R. Ḥanina (flor. c. 220–40) says that eight Syrian *istiras* (= *staters*) are worth one *aureus*. The Syrian *stater* must surely be a cistophoric *tetradrachm*, worth 3 d. Hence (3 × 8 =) 24 d. = 1 *aureus*.

37 *Klio*, 25, 1932, p. 124 et seq.; *Econ. Surv.*, 5, p. 215; ibid., 2, p. 425; ibid., 5, p. 91. See *P. Baden* 37. See also A. C. Johnson in *American Journal of Archeology*, 38, 1934, p. 53; Mickwitz, *Geld und Wirtschaft*, pp. 32, 42.

38 This would be 4 years before Rav left Palestine (219). Perhaps we may see Rav's need to borrow money against the background set by *OGIS*, 515, (*Econ. Surv.*, 4, p. 897), an inscription of c.210, which mentions poverty and disruption of the markets through lack of currency. (Cf. B. Ta'anit 19b, B. Bava Batra 91b, reflecting such a situation? See below, Chap. XIX.) Such a date, if accepted, is further proof against Marmorstein's explanation (see above, this chapter). Cf. *Num. Chron.*, 16, p. 42; (cited by West, *Gold and Silver Standards*) where it is stated that in the time of Caracalla there was so little gold that it ceased to be readily acceptable for silver. West (ibid.) rejects this statement. Our texts, if correctly interpreted, are also evi-

dence to the contrary, for if such were truly the situation, R. Ḥiyya could hardly have considered such money as "coin".

39 On this text see D. Halivni, *Sources and Traditions*, 1968, pp. 629–31 (Hebrew). There were two other scholars with these same names who flourished early in the III cent. (c.220–50): R. Ḥanina [b. Ḥama] and R. Mana I. However, the structure of this passage in the Yerushalmi makes it quite clear that the comments of R. Ḥanina and R. Mana refer to the statement of R. Zeira (I or II, either later III or early IV cent.). Hence, they must post-date R. Zeira, and must therefore be the later IV cent. personalities by these names. The Bavli version of theis text in B. Kiddushin 12a is somewhat more detailed and the main discussion there is of an earlier date than that of the Yerushalmi, (i.e. pre-339, death of Abbaye). In my article in *NC*, 1968, pp. 93–94, I misdated the Yerushalmi text.

40 See my article in *JQR*, 56, and the recent study of A. Ben-David in *PEQ*, 103, 1971, pp. 115–16. See further tables A and B, at end of Chapter I.

41 See West and Johnson, *Currency*, p. 93, note 18. The famous inscription of 209–11, from Mylasa in Caria (*OGIS*, 515) demonstrates that people were fully aware of the depreciation of the currency, and were expecting a devaluation. As a result a sort of blackmarket grew up, in which, presumably, people tried to buy up earlier silver coins (of purer metallic content) in exchange for local bronze The right to exchange local bronze for imperial silver was normally the prerogative of the city, which always reckoned the exchange rates to its own advantage. The local black-market, in competing with the official exchange, robbed the city of a significant source of income. See further *Econ. Surv.*, 4, pp. 895–97.

42 There is little doubt that the "Gordian *dinar*" mentioned in several Rabbinic sources (e.g. *Canticles Rabba* 3.8.3, = Y. Yoma 4.4) refers to Gordian III's *antoninianus*. See *INCP*, p. 260; Callu, *PMER*, p. 133, note 5.) Gordian III reintroduced the *ant.* after a lapse of some fourteen years, and, moreover, finally did away with the *denarius* completely (see Table E in Chap. IV). It is, thus, understandable that his ant. was regarded by the Rabbis as a new *denarius*, a "*dinar Gordiani*". This term must, however, be distinguished from another earlier one, which appears in pre-Gordianic Rabbinic sources, (e.g. B. Menachot 29a, *Num. Rab.* 12.4 = *Cant. Rab.* 3.8.3, and B. Ḥulin 54b, see *VL*, ibid., 67ab). This similar-sounding term is, in fact, of quite a different nature. It is problematic and merits a study in its own right. See further Krauss, *LW*, 2, pp. 169–70, and 518–19, which needs some modification; also Herzfeld, *Metrologische Voruntersuchungen*, pp. 170–71. As to Y. Ketubot 7.7 = Y. Kiddushin 2.4, see the significant variant in *Hilkhot Terefot li-Vrei Eretz Yisrael*, ed. M. Margalioth, *Talpioth* 8/3–4, 1963, pp. 324–5, (not noted by the editor).

43 Neither R. Ḥanina nor R. Mana, nor Ravin in the Bavli, could come to a correct interpretation of this valuation, since they were basing themselves upon texts in which the gold element is not mentioned. Consequently, all their interpretations are based on the erroneous assumption that only silver and copper changed in their relationship to one another. In a sense, however, R. Ḥanina may be said to be the more correct, except that it was not silver that went down, only silver coin through adulteration. Of course, these interpretations were never intended as accurate historical commentaries to these texts, but were advanced as logical ways of explaining the texts at hand.

44 Or read חרג, instead of הרג, meaning some kind of tax offical; see Lieberman, *Tosefta ki-fshutah*, pp. 418–19.

226

45 There are a number of different interpretations of these texts offered by the commentators. None seem to be as satisfactory as the interpretation here offered. The
difficulties lie in the meaning of the phrases "more than this" (end of 17), "less than
this ... by an *issar*" (18), and the word "value", which we interpret as "weight
value" as opposed to nominal value. Cf. Lieberman, *Tosefta ki-fshutah*, 2, p. 753 to
line 4, (T. Ma'aser Sheni 3.6). Cf. also Y. Bava Mezia 4.4 where the text appears
to require several corrections. Krauss, in *Paras ve-Romi*, p. 261, points out that
these texts are indicative of a silver standard.

46 See Boaz Cohen, *Jewish and Roman Law* (New York, 1966), p. 360.

47 I have here not taken account of the Bavli's reconstruction of this text (B. Ketubot
67a). These texts try to establish the relative "fiduciaryness" of coins in this complex
multi-metallic system. The common feature to coins of all metals is expressed clearly
in M. Shevu'ot 6.3, of B. Shevu'ot 40a. Cf. West in *ANSMN*, 6, 1954, p. 9.

48 See also J.N. Epstein, *Mevo'ot Le-Safrut Ha-Tanna'im* (Jerusalem, 1957), p. 243,
note 10.

49 This text would seem to present a real difficulty of quite a different nature. For it
seems to posit an equation of 30 *issars* = 1 *dinar* (= *denarius*), while we know from
numerous sources that there were only 24 *issars* in a *dinar*, (e.g. T. Bava Batra 5.12,
405, 20). (See above, Table B in Chap. I, and *JQR*, 56). It might have been suggested
that we have here an indication that people who wanted to buy *denarii* with copper
had to pay a premium. This sort of thing certainly went on, as is evident from Hadrian's famous letter to Pergamum. This letter relates the abuses which arose in
connection with a public lease to a group of bankers of a monopoly of exchange
between the *denarius* and the local bronze coinage (*Econ. Surv.*, 4, p. 892; see ibid.,
pp. 892–94; *IGRP*, 4, 352; *OGIS*, 484 and p. 552; cf. West, *Gold and Silver Standards*, pp. 93–94; see also, end of letter). It reads thus:

> For although they (the bankers) should have accepted 18 *asses* per *denarius*
> from the merchants, small dealers, and fish dealers, who are accustomed to
> traffic for small bronze, and should have paid 17 *asses* to those who wished to
> exchange *denarii*, they were not satisfied with the exchanging of *asses*, but even
> in cases where a man bought fish for silver *denarii* exacted an *ass* for each
> *denarius*.

(But cf. Epictetus, *Discourses*, 3.3.) The *denarius* was equal to 16 *asses*, but the bankers were officially permitted to sell them for 18 *asses*. (West, *Gold and Silver
Standards*, pp. 86–87; *BM*, 481, line 245 ff. show 750 d. divided among 1500 persons
with a gift to each stated as 9 *asses*; this gives a denarius of 18 *asses*. But cf. bilingual
inscriptions of 103/4, *CIL*. 3, 14195, 4, 5, 6, 7 (West, ibid., note 140), giving 16 *asses*
to the *denarius*.) According to the *Gnomon of the Idiologus* it was forbidden to exchange money for more than its value; on the *Gnomon of the Idiologus*, see Rostovtzeff, *SEHRE*[2], p. 625, note 53, and West and Johnson, *Currency*, p. 92. However,
see Crawford's observations in *JRS*, 58, 1968, pp. 291–92, that the *denarius* was worth
more than sixteen asses at the outskirts of the Empire. See further his observations
in *JRS*, 60, 1970, p. 43. The key to solving this apparent anomaly may be found in a
text in B. Kiddushin 12a: "... Calculate how many *prutot* are there in two *selaim*
(= *tetradrachms*) ... close to two thousand ..." (cf. *Sifra*, ed. Weiss, 27a). At 30
issars to the *dinar* (= *denarius*), there were 240 *prutot* to a *dinar*, and thus 1920 *prutot*
in two *selaim*. This indeed is "close to two thousand". In other words, there was
some early (?) local (?) system in which there were 30 (local) *issars* to the *dinar*.

However, this system was largely forgotten, remaining recorded only in these two texts. A lack of understanding of this very unusual system led to the misinterpretation (and even alteration) of the text in later (Amoraic) periods. See L. Ginzberg, *Al Halakha ve-Aggada* (Tel-Aviv, 1961), pp. 112, 131, and my article in *Sinai*, 67/1 (405), 1970, pp. 61–62, where I discussed this problem in detail. For a recent suggestion as to when this sytem was in use, see A. Ben-David in *PEQ*, 103, 1971, pp. 109–29.

50 Ed. Lieberman, p. 250–51, lines 30–35.

51 See J.N. Epstein, *Mevo'ot Le-Safrut Ha-Tanna'im*, p. 177.

52 See S. Lieberman, *Tosefta ki-fshutah*, 2, p. 734 and note 16.

53 This proves conclusively that the Bavli and Yerushalmi in Bava Mezia (quoted at the beginning of this section) are oversimplifying matters when they say that *the principle is*: that which is lower in value acquires its more valuable counterpart.

54 The explanation may, however, be slightly different. See Hadrian's letter to Pergamum end, (*Econ. Surv.*, 4, p. 894; West, *Gold and Silver Standards*, pp. 93–94): "In the case of food sold by weight, the price of which is set by the market-masters, I think it is right that even those who purchase several *minas* worth should pay the price in bronze coinage so as to preserve for the city the revenue from the exchange; so too, where several appear together in an agreement to make a purchase in silver *denarii*, and then to divide their purchases, they should pay the dealer in small bronze, so that he might bring it to the banker's table; and they should pay at the rate of 17 *asses*, since the traffic in exchange is supposed to refer to merchants only." (West's transl.) In such a situation one can easily imagine silver being judged (legally) "produce" and not "coin". See also Lieberman, *Tosefta ki-fshutah*, 2, p. 733, line 19 on "at need".

55 Lieberman, ibid., p. 735, note 16. Note also that according to Rabbi's argument, the premises of which would have to be agreed with by R. Eleazar b. R. Simeon, silver is produce compared with gold (B[1]). Yet R. Eleazar b. R. Simeon himself is of the opinion that gold is produce compared to silver (D[2]). This very difficult problem is dealt with by Lieberman, ibid., pp. 734–735 to lines 33–34, 36.

56 The (legal) complications arising out of a bi- or tri-metallic system are remarkably demonstrated in this case.

Chapter XII

1 T. Ketubot 6.5; B. Ketubot 67a. See above, Chap. XI.

2 Y. Ketubot 11.2. See above, Chapter IV.

3 *Deut. Re'e*, 10, ed. Lieberman, p. 95, c.260–320. Cf. Y. Ketubot 12.1.

4 Y. Shevi'it 10.9, cf. Y. Bava Mezia 4.2, c. mid III cent.

5 Y. Ketubot 12.7; *Gen. Rab.* 63.3; *Deut. Rab.* 1.13 — all c.280–320; Y. Bava Kama 8.10, — 250–60. See also *Lev. Rab.* 14.2, ed. Margulies, p. 301, from the latter part of the III cent., and B. Bava Batra 33b, probably early IV cent. Cf. *P. Thead.* 33 (312), and *P.O.* 1653 (307). These conclusions as to the growing importance of gold are, I think, borne out to some extent by those of Mickwitz, in his article "Ein Goldwertindex der römisch-byzantinischen Zeit", *Aegyptus*, 13, 1933, pp. 95–106, especially pp. 105–06. For there he demonstrates that in the late Roman (and

Byzantine) period gold went up in value. *"Diese Steigerung hängt teils damit zusammen, dass die Inanspruchnahme des Goldes als Tauchmittel sich vergrössort hat..."* (ibid., p. 106). See further Callu, *PMER*, p. 297 on the use of *"métal non monnayé"*, citing (note 1) *Scriptores Historiae Augustae*, Claud. 15.4, and *P. Panop.* 2.302, and ibid., pp. 428–30 for gold ornaments, etc. See Y. Ketubot 6.3 (= B. Ketubot 67a) where R. Johanan speaks of a woman bringing in gold bullion as part of a dowry; (cf. T. Ketubot 6.5, ed. Zuckermandel, p. 267). The bullion here is considered a safe investment that will not be speculated in, and should it be made up into ornaments will not lose its value. In Tannaitic times (Tosefta, ibid.) gold bullion was considered something with which to make things. Cf. Yerushalmi, ibid.; *Tosafot* in Bavli, ibid., Rabbenu Ḥananel's view. See also B. Bava Baṭra 165b–66a (= B. Ketubot 110b, = B. Menachot 107a) , R. Eleazar (possibly Palestinian text), suggesting the use of נסכא — bullion. See also Y. Ma'aser Sheni 1.1, silver bullion (R. Johanan) and broken plate (late III cent.?), and *Num. Rab.* 20.18 = *Tanḥuma "Balak"* 12, (?).

6   On gold hoarding during this period see West, *Gold and Silver Standards*, p. 83, Table A. But see L. Kadman's remark in *INCP*, p. 321. The text in B. Bechorot 49b reads thus: "R. Johanan says: A worn Hadrianic Trajanic *dinar*, which is sold for twenty-five *zuz*; subtract from them one sixth, and this (i.e. what is left) is for the redemption of the first-born." The Aramaic reads: *dinra Hadriana Traiana shaifa*, which we have translated "a worn Hadrianic Trajanic *dinar*". Mediaeval Talmudic commentators, recognizing the first two terms as names of prominent emperors, assumed that *"Shaifa"* too was "the name of a king" (Rashi, = Rabbi Solomon b. Issac of Troyes, 1040–1105, to B. Bechorot 50a), while modern scholars (eg. Krauss, *LW*, 1, pp. 288–90) suggested that *"shaifa"* or *"saifa"* is an aramaicized form of "Sabina", Hadrian's wife, or εὐσεβής = Pius, Marcus Antonius' title. (See also M. A. Levy, *Geschichte der Jüdische Münzen*, p. 129.) However, these suggestions are not only far-fetched, but also philologically untenable, (see Löw's remarks in *LW*, 2, p. 581). The simple meaning of *"shaifa"*, "worn", from the Aramaic root *"shuf"*, "to rub", "wear down", (eg. B. Bava Kama 98a; see Jastrow, p. 1539a, s.v. שוף II; but cf. ibid., p. 1565b, s.v. שיפא) was already advanced by Nathan b. Yeḥiel of Rome in the 11 cent., in his *Aruch*, and was accepted by the *Tosafot* (B. Bechorot 49b, s.v. *dinra*; Rashi, B. Avoda Zara 52b). Let us examine the different readings of this text a little more closely. Printed ed. and Ms. Munchen in B. Bechorot, and printed ed. in B. Avoda Zara 52b, Rashi to Bechorot and *Tosafot* to Bechorot and Avoda Zara: *dinra Hadriana Traiana shaifa*. (Cf. Raavad = R. Abraham b. David of Posquieres, 1125–98, to Avoda Zara, ed. A. Sofer-Schreiber, New York, 1960, p. 137: *dinra Hadriana*.) MS JTS of Avoda Zara, Rashi to Avoda Zara, *Yalkut Ezekiel*, 7 (section 346): *dinra Traiana Hadriana shaifa*. Ms. Munchen in Avoda Zara: *dinra Traiana ve-Hadriana shaifa*, (see Rabbinivicz *VL*, Avoda Zara, p. 114. Some of the readings have *"Turiana"* instead of *"Traiana"*). The most significant point to emerge from this comparison is that only one reading (Ms. Munchen to Avoda Zara) has *"ve"* (= and), i.e. worn *dinar* of Trajan *and* Hadrian. All other readings have *"dinar* of Trajan Hadrian" or *vice-versa*. The absence of the *"vav"* — conjunctive (= and) is consistent with the repeated use of the singular *"dinra"* (= *dinar*, as opposed to the plural *"dinrei"* = *dinars*) throughout all the readings. From the above it becomes completely clear that "Trajan — Hadrian" or "Hadrian — Trajan" is one personality, and not two (contra Rashi, *Tosafot*, Zuckermann, *Talmudische Münzen*, p. 19). Trajan's full name was Nerva Traianus,

while Hadrian's was Traianus Hadrianus. Trajan's name fits none of the readings, while Hadrian's is exactly represented in the readings preserved in Ms. JTS to Avoda Zara, Rashi to Avoda Zara, *Yalkut Ezekiel.* The reading in MS Munich to Avoda Zara (with the "and") is to be dismissed as the work of an emendor. The reverse order in the printed editions of the Bavli, etc., probably represents an attempt to clarify the emperor's identity by putting his main name first. Palestinians certainly knew Hadrian's full name from local coins; (eg. *CNP*, 1, Aelia Capitolina, nos. 1,3, 7, 9; *CNP*, 2, Caesarea Maritima, nos. 26–32; *CNP*, 4, Akko Ptolemais, nos. 101–04, 106–08, and of course, the imperial issues). Thus, what R. Johanan is saying is that the five *shekels* one has to give for the redemption of the firstborn equals five-sixths of a worn Hadrianic *aureus* (unspecified *dinar!*), which *aureus* is worth twenty-five *denarii.* This corresponds to the classical ratio of 25 d. = 1 *aureus,* mentioned in Dio Cassius 55.12. By R. Johanan's time these *aurei* were bound to be worn-down, even if they had been hoarded after relatively little use. The above interpretation is of added significance since it contradicts Heichelheim's theory that the reduction of the *aureus'* weight by Trajan brought about a new ratio of 24 d. to the *aureus,* a ratio reflected, according to Heichelheim in certain Rabbinic texts, (e.g. M. Me'ila 6.4, and R. Ḥanina's statement in B. Bechorot 49b). Since Hadrian continued to produce *aurei* at Trajan's reduced standard, according to Heichelheim's assumption, his *aurei* should be worth twenty-four *denarii,* and not twenty-five as R. Johanan states. (See Heichelheim in *Klio*, 25, 1932, pp. 124 et seq.; see further *Econ. Surv.,* 4, p. 215; ibid., 2, pp. 425–26, 443–45; ibid., 5, p. 91; Johnson in *AJA*, 38, 1934, p. 53; Mickwitz, *Geld und Wirtschaft*, pp. 32, 42; Segrè, *Metrologia*, pp. 428–30; Bolin, *State and Currency*, p. 208, note 1; West, *Gold and Silver Standards*, p. 89, Table R. See also *CPR*, 12; *SPP* XX 20; *P. Giss.* 47; Wilcken *Chrest.* 326. On the coins, see *BMC*, 3, 1936, pp. xiv-xv; Bolin, ibid., pp. 191–95.) As to the related statement of R. Oshaya in B. Bechorot (and its citation in B. Avoda Zara) 49b, see Joshua Brand's article in *Sinai*, 53, 1963, pp. 21–30. The remainder of the *sugya* in B. Bechorot 49b is of later Babylonian Amoriac strata with Gaonic glosses, (see my remarks in *Sinai*, 55, 1964, pp. 333–38; ibid., 58, 1966, pp. 164–68; and cf. the briefer version of Ms. Munchen). As to R. Asi's statement on the Mishna in B. Bechorot 49b, it may be that he is referring to the late provincial Tyrian *tetradrachms* struck at around 15,14 grammes, (see G. F. Hill, *Greek Coins of Phoenicia*, London, 1910, p. cxxxix). The Tyrian standard continued to be used long after the mid I cent. C.E., (see A. Ben-David, *Jerusalem und Tyros*, Basel, 1969, pp. 36ff.; A. Ben-David, *PEQ*, 1971, pp. 120, 128, and *Dura, Final Report*, 6, p. 204, note 31; ibid., 5, p. 9, note 14, p. 164, note 20, p. 201, note 22; Kraeling, *Gerasa*, 1938, pp. 374–76, nos. 3–5; *Studi in onore di A. Calderini*, etc., 2, pp. 265–67). R. Ḥanina's statement in B. Bechorot 49b probably refers to cistophoric *tetradrachms,* one ot which equalled three *denarii,* (see Schrötter, *Wörterbuch der Münzkunde*, pp. 308–09, s.v. *Kistophora*). As to R. Ammi's "Arabian *dinar*", this probably refers to the Nabataean standard (see G.F. Hill, *Greek Coins and Arabia, Mesopotamia and Persia*, 1922, pp. xx–xxi) as opposed to the (higher) Himyaritic standard (see ibid., p. lxxix). Finally S. Safrai's remarks, in his article in *INCP*, pp. 256–57, require some modification.

It is for this reason that some commentators (see *Pnei Moshe*, and *Gilion Ha-Shass* of R. Akiba Eiger, on this text) read, instead of הנשיא ר"י (Rabbi Judah ha-Nasi — The Prince), ר"י נשיאה (R. Judah Nesiah), Rabbi's (i. e. Judah the Prince's) grandson.

According to their reading, in the time of Rabbi, i.e. late II and early III cent., a poor man could not get credit and could therefore not borrow money, while in the middle of the III cent. his grandson R. Judah Nesiah is of the opinion that a poor man could always find someone to lend him money. The explanation hardly makes good sense in terms of the relative economic conditions obtaining during the respective periods of Rabbi and his grandson. Furthermore, it seems most unlikely that the opinion of Rabbi's grandson would be given before his own. Note the variant reading ברבי instead of רבי in the Sirilio Ms. But this is clearly Sirilio's own emendation, forced upon him by the difficulty of the text as it stands. See Ratner, Ahavat Zion vi-Yerushalayim, on Pe'a 1.6. Leiden Ms. has 'ר instead of רבי (not noted by Epstein).

8 Furthermore, according to this explanation, the order of the two views is understood: first R. Judah the Prince's view is given, and only afterwards that of his grandson. See my article in Sinai, 67/1-2 (398-99), pp. 101-02, for a full discussion of this issue. See Sha'are Torath Eretz Israel, pp. 274-75, who shows that "Rabbi" can refer to (almost) any of the "Nesi'im". See M. Fogelman, Sinai, 21/1 (251), 1957, pp. 27-30, referring to B. Ta'anit 14b, Judlewitsch, Tiberias (Jerusalem, 1950, Hebrew), pp. 55-56 and note 4, referring to Genesis Rabba, ed. Theodor-Albeck, pp. 689 line 2, 951 line 3. See further Esther Rabba 4.24, but cf. Pesaro ed. (ed. princ.). Cf. parallel in Y. Horayot 3.5, and cf. Liebermann, Hayerushalmi Kipshuto, p. 175, who's interpretation is difficult to accept on chronological grounds.

9 ed. Lieberman, p. 95.

10 See Epictetus, Discourses 3.3.3: "For just as neither the banker nor the greengrocer may legally refuse the coinage of Caesar, but if you present it, whether he will or not, he must turn over to you what you are purchasing with it . . ."

11 P.O. 1411; West and Johnson, Currency, p. 183. However, see West in ANSMN, 7, 1957, p. 114; Callu, PMER, p. 186. Note also that according to the Scriptores Historiae Augustae, Aurelian, 47, officials were being paid in kind not money in the later III cent. Also most taxes were paid in kind, not money, between 260 and 300; Currency, p. 84. See also Johnson's Egypt and the Roman Empire, (Ann Arbor, 1951), pp. 29, 269-79; F.F. Abbott & A.C. Johnson, Municipal Administration in the Roman Empire (Princeton, 1926), No. 199. See R. Taubenschlag, The Law of Greco-Roman Egypt in the Light of the Papyri², (Warsaw 1955), p. 675, for a different interpretation of P.O. 1411.

12 Tanḥuma Buber, Deut. p. 23; Deut. Rab., ed. Liebermann, p. 126 and note 2, where 5 maneh is a small sum of money — c. 200-50. Cf. Exod. Rab., chap. 30 end. And see above, Chap. III, our long discussion on the "maneh".

13 See also Guey's convincing argument in Syria, 38, 1961, pp. 261-67 (supported by Buttrey), that the 500,000 δηναριων of the Naqshi Rustam inscription, of the mid III cent. are aurei. See also Callu, PMER, p. 313. But there this usage may be no more than the result of the influence of the Persian original, (DYNR).

14 Y. Ma'aser Sheni 4.1, see above, Chap. II. Also Y. Ma'aser Sheni 1.2.

15 See West and Johnson, Currency, p. 157 for a parallel development in Egypt.

16 West and Johnson, ibid., p. 84. See also Johnson in JJP, 4, 1950, p. 156.

17 E.g.: If in the II cent. a mod. wheat cost 4 d. — prices range from 1 to 4 d. — in gold this would be about 1/6 aureus. According to Ed. Diocl. 1 mod. wheat: 100 d. = 100/800 = 1/8 aureus. (See below, Chap. XVI.) Of course, I have not taken into account the varying weights of the aureus etc., but this does not affect the general

line of our argument. There was no absolute shortage of gold during Gallienus' period, see below, Chap. XIII, note 1.

18 The same is true of Egypt. Cf. *Econ. Surv.*, 2 (Egypt), p. 437.

Chapter XIII

1 See L. C. West in *ANSMN*, 7, 1957, p. 96, who shows that there is no evidence of an absolute shortage of gold during Gallienus' reign.

2 Ed. Theodor, p. 143, and parallels.

3 Ed. Finkelstein, pp. 338–39; ed. Friedmann 132a, par. 306; = *Midrash Tanna'im* (= MT), ed. Hoffmann, p. 185, with slight variants. I dealt with this text in my article in *Archiv Orientalni*, 34, 1966, pp. 63–64, but there I misdated it completely, and therefore did not see its true significance. It is a part of a text by R. Judah [b. Ilai], and is of the middle or later II cent., probably from the lower Galilee (Usha?). See also J. N. Epstein, *Prolegomena ad Litteras Tannaiticas* (Jerusalem, 1957, Hebrew), pp. 628–30, and Judlewitsch,"Caesarea", *Sinai*, 4/11–12, (49–50), 1941, p. 284, note 9.

4 The Hebrew reads 100 *maneh* or 2 *myriads*. Again we see here that the *maneh* here is parallel to the *dinar* in the first part of the passage. It appears that the second part of the passage is a III cent. gloss, and one should read פרוטרות rather than סלעים (which is a reading influenced by the first part of the passage). See also how this text is cited in *Menorat Ha-Maor*, ed. Enelow, 4 (New York, 1932), p. 501.

5 פרוטרות. So also in *Midrash ha-Gadol*, cited in Finkelstein's apparatus, ibid.

6 I. S. Horowitz, in *Palestine and the Adjacent Countries* (Vienna, 1923, Hebrew), p. 119b states that Beith Ilanin is 14 kilometres S. W. of Tiberias (A-Sadjarah), while Avi-Yonah, in the *Quarterly of the Dept. of Ant. for Palestine*, 5, 1936, p. 167, equates it with Butna, near Hebron in the South. So also in *Sefer ha-Yishuv*, 1, ed. S. Klein (Jerusalem, 1934), pp. 11, 12; Heichelheim in *Econ. Surv.*, 4, p. 210, note 20. However, Horowitz argues very well against this view (ibid., p. 120, note). Butna had an annual market: *Gen. Rab.*, 47 *ad fin.*, ed. Theodor-Albeck, p. 477; Y. Avoda Zara 1.4. See also S. Klein, *Eretz Yehuda* (Tel Aviv, 1939), p. 167. But see G. Allon, *Meḥkarim be-Toldot Yisrael*, 2 (Israel, 1958), pp. 97–98, for his identification of this place with βεθελεα, near Gaza, which had a great annual market.

7 This may be why the Palmyrene caravaneers wanted *aurei*, but why old ones (παλαια)? See above, Chap. XI, and West, *Gold and Silver Standards*, p. 118 (χρυσα παλαια δηναρι[α]) = דינרין די זהב עתיקין, Cooke, *North Semitic Inscriptions*, p. 273 no. 115. See *Syria*, 38, 1961, pp. 268–74, where it is argued that "old gold *denarii*" refers to a unit of value rather than to actual old gold coins. See Callu, *PMER*, p. 187.

8 See price lists in Chap. XV.

9 E. Lambert in *REJ*, 51, 1906, p. 217 et seq. and 52, 1906, p. 25 et seq., article entitled "Les Changeurs et la monnaie en Palestine du I-er au III-e siècle de l'ère vulgaire d'après des textes talmudiques"; Gulak in *Tarbiz*, 2/2 , 1931, pp. 154–57; and note Hadrian's letter to Pergamum, (cited above, Chap. XI, note 54).

10 See Lieberman, *Annuaire de l'institute de Philologie et d'Histoire Orientales et Slaves*, 7, 1939–44, pp. 399–402.

11 *REJ*, 98, 1934, pp. 35–36.

12 Even in the Mediaeval sources. See eg. *Ma'or ha-Afelah* (*Nur al-Z'lam*), ed. J. Kafih (Jerusalem, 1957), p. 116 top (a XIII cent. text).

13 It is interesting to note that the term *solidus* does not appear in Rabbinic literature. סולדיא in *Midrash Tanna'im*, ed. Hoffmann, p. 202, is not *solidus*, as Hoffmann suggested (ibid., note 10), but *salarium*. See *Sifré*, ed. Finkelstein, p. 378, line 11. See various spellings cited in Krauss, *LW*, 397a, s.v. סלרין, especially that of *Yalkut Prov.*, section 947, which reads סודרין, *Lev. Rab.* 34.3, ed. Margulies, p. 776, suggesting an original reading of סולרין; but see Kohut, *Aruch Completum*, 6, p. 66b, s.v. סלתרין. Perhaps the spelling סולרין is the result of the influence on the similar-sounding Latin word *solarium*, meaning a ground-tax, (see Souter, *Glossary of Later Latin*, p. 308b, s.v. *solarium*). However, the specific reading סודרין is the Greek σουδαριον (= Latin *sudarium*) a towel, and is a copyist's emendation of the original word in accordance with the context (of washing statues, etc.).

14 See below, Chap. XVI.

15 However, this text too suggests that prices had risen considerably by this time, and that an *aureus* was good not for, e.g. a month's living expenses or even a fortnight's, but only for "several purchases".

16 But cf. *Gen. Rab.*, ed. Theodor, p. 135. Cf. *Lev. Rab.* 3.1 (ed. Margulies, p. 55), R. Isaac (again) cautioning against unwise speculation and borrowing at interest. Better by far to have 10 *aurei* — note the use of gold coins again — and to do quiet business with them, he advises, than to borrow large sums (at interest) and speculate with them. For, as the proverb goes, "he loses his own and that which is not his own too". Cf. *Eccles. Rab.* 4.6. It should be noted that probably already in 238 gold commanded a premium. For in *CIL*, 13. 3162, of that year, M. Aedinius Julianus on the Marbe de Thorigny boasts of having received his salary in gold. See J.P.C. Kent's article "Gold Coinage in the Later Roman Empire", in *Essays in Roman Coinage presented to Harold Mattingly*, ed. R.A.G. Carson and C.H.V. Sutherland (Oxford, 1964), 1, pp. 27–28. See also the inscription from Asia Minor of 237 discussed by D. Magie in *Roman Rule in Asia Minor*, p. 1573, note 37. Dr. J. Kent writes (private communication of 23 August, 1972): "I think that just as silver commanded a premium over copper much earlier, so gold coin always commanded a *de facto* premium over silver."

17 Note the Palmyrene inscription, cited in Cooke's *North Semitic Inscriptions*, p. 283, No. 123 (= Vog. 17), from the mid III cent. recording a donation of 10,000 d. ('Ατ[τικας] = זוזין). The magnitude of the sum donated is suggestive of inflation (but no more than suggestive). See also the literature on the Polecharmas inscription of Stobi in *Dumbarton Oaks Papers*, 3, Ernst Kitsinger, 1964, pp. 142–43, 159–60, especially Marmorstein in *JQR*, NS 27, 1937, pp. 373–84. However, a fine of 250,000 d. even in the later III cent. (= 250 *aurei*?) seems a little excessive. See, most recently, B. Lifshitz, *Donateurs et Fondateurs dans les Sunagogues Juives*, (Paris, 1967), pp. 18–19.

Chapter XIV

1 See J.M. Sheftel, *Erech Milim*[2] (Berditchev, 1906), pp. 776–80, s.v. לקן.

2 According to the British Museum Ms. Or. 2823, fol. 26a (Sirilio Ms.) add: ר' יהודה

אומר. And cf. Tosefta Ma'aser Sheni 3.4 (ed. Lieberman, p. 257) on which this passage is based.

3 Printed ed.(Krotoschin) has אדבאל; correct to ארבאל, as in Venice ed. The Sirilio Ms. has ארבל. On these two forms, see G. R. Driver, *Aramaic Documents of the Fifth Century B.C.* (Oxford, 1965), p. 58. See also S. Klein, *Beraitha shel 24 Mishnarot (Mechkarim Arzi-Yisraeliim*, 2, Vienna, 1924), p. 19. See also Frey, *CIJ*, 2, no. 857, p. 97.

4 Printed ed. (Krotoschin) has ילקן, correct to ולקן, as in Vilna ed., Sirilio Ms., etc.

5 Leiden Ms. has ששים corrected to חמישים; See J.N. Epstein, *Prolegomena ad Litteras Amoraiticas* (Jerusalem, 1962), p. 473.

6 Rome Ms. has ומיסלוק ויהב. Sirilio Ms. as above.

7 Correct to ובאארבאל or ובארבל, as above, note 3. See also *Pesikta de R. Kahana*, ed. Buber 66b, note 76.

8 Not in any text, but conjecturally restored. See below, this chapter.

9 Missing in all but Rome Ms.

10 Cf. Tosefta, ibid., from which it becomes clear that here the gold *dinar* is being referred to.

11 See above, Chapter XI, note 23.

12 Krauss, *LW*, 2, p. 319a, s.v. לקן; Levy. *Neuhebräisches und Chaldäisches Wörterbuch*, 2, p. 526; Kohut, *Aruch Completum*, 6, p. 58b. This explanation is based on that of Zuckermann, in his *Talmudische Münzen und Gewichte* (Breslau, 1826), pp. 29–30. However, for the Greek λευκον one would have expected something more like לבקן, ליוקן or לפקן, (cf. Krauss, *LW*, 1, pp. 57, 90. Also H.B. Rosen, in *Journal of Semitic Studies*, 8, 1963, p. 65 and note 4). The complete omission of both sets of vowels is rather surprising. I was, therefore, first tempted to identify לקן with the Greek ὁλκη, as the dropping off of the first ὁ is by no means uncommon (eg. מגורסי = ὁμηγυρις, *LW*, 1, p. 123, para. 228. However see Zuntz, in *JSS*, 1, 1956, p. 134: μαγειρος). However, this leaves the final "*nun*" unexplained, and as the form לקן appears identically in both texts (see below, this chapter) and in all Mss. and editions, it seems hardly likely to be a corruption. Also ὁλκη, appears in Syriac as אלקא Epiphanius, ed. Lagarde, p. 52, line 38, ed. Dean fol. 68b, line 7 (= BM.Or. Add. 17148); Brockelmann, *Lexicon Syriacum²*, p. 23b, (not listed in Payne Smith, *Thesaurus or Supplement*). The omission of the final o of *leukon* is easily accepted (eg. cf. readings in *Tosefta ki-fshutah, Zera'im*, 2, p. 229, etc.), and even the falling out of ευ has its precedents (eg. קלסיס = κελευσις, רמטיקוס = ῥευματικος, etc., Krauss, *LW*, 1, p. 24, para. 34). Thus לקן = *leukon*, Horowitz' suggestion (*Eretz Yisrael* etc., p. 76, note 13) that לקן = the Syriac נקון, the *Peshitta* translation of קשיטא (Gen. 33.19, etc.) is quite wrong. נקין is the plural of נקיא, (eg. *Peshitta* to Job 42.11) meaning a lamb (Brockelmann² p. 444b. s.v. נקיא; cf. Jastrow, *Dict.*, p. 932b, s.v. נקי). The *Peshitta* translation of קשיטא parallels that of the *LXX* (ἀμνων etc.), Onkelos. (חורפן, cf. Gen. 21.22, etc.). Cf. *Gen. Rab.* 79.7, ed. Theodor-Albeck, p. 948, notes. Also Levy, *Targumin* (Leipzig, 1881), p. 284a, s.v. חורפא 2. Note reading נקון in *Midrash Ha-Gadol* (ed. Margaliot, p. 585). See also *Midrash ha-Ḥefetz*, apud M.M. Kasher, Gen., *Torah Shelemah*, pp. 1515–16, note 67. See my remarks in *REJ*, 1968, pp. 265–68. (This article, though a strange quirk of circumstances, subsequently reappeared in *Acta Antiqua*, 19, 1–2, 1971, pp. 37–39.) Perhaps in the defective spelling we may see a conscious attempt to differentiate between this *leukon*, and the other which is a disease (a kind

of elephantiasis). See Jastrow, *Dict.*, p. 701a–b, s.v. לוּקן, Kohut, *Aruch Completum*, p. 308, s.v. לווקן, Levy, *Wörterbuch*, 2, p. 490a–b, s.v. לבקן, לווקן, Krauss, *LW*, 2, p. 304a, s.v. לבק. The various spellings are cited in Krauss, ibid. Note that in every case the final o of *leukon* is omitted. In B. Bechorot 45b the word is explained by the Aramaic חוורא (=white), see following note. See also J, Fürst, *Glosssarium Graeco-Hebraeum* (Strassburg, 1890–91), p. 132b. For later parallels, see Schrötter, *Wörterbuch der Münzkunde* (Berlin und Leipzig, 1930), s.v. *blanc, blancu, witten* (pp. 77–78, 748), etc.

13 It is a parallel use to זוזא חיוורא, of B. Shabbat 68b (Abaye). Brockelmann[2], p. 223a, s.v. חור (b) writes: *albus (nummus, i.e. argenteus).* This is certainly the meaning given by Eliya of Nesbis (ed. Lagarde, Gottingaen, 1879), p. 78, line 68, חורא no. 7 — translated into Arabic as a "silver *dirham*". However, חור in Bar-Hebraeus' *Laughable Stories* (ed. E. A. Wallis Budge, London 1897, no. 418, p. 84, line 18) seems to be different from זוזא = כספא, cf. no. 419, ibid. Note also that *La Chemie au moyen âge*, (P. E. M. Berthelot & Duval, Paris, 1873) 34.4 gives חור another meaning, namely tin. Lane: الُورَبِيّ — silver. Cf. Payne Smith, *Thesaurus Syriacus*, 1230, s.v. חוראβ; (*Supplement*, p. 112b). It is parallel to *asperi*, which appears to denote pure silver coins; see Duncange, *Glossarium Mediae et Infinae Latinatis* (Du Fresne, Henschel) 1/2, p. 425a, s.v. *asperi*, citing Suetonius, *in Nerone*, chap. 44, *Aurum obryzum et nummum asperum ingenti fastidio exegit*; Persius, *Sat.* 3: *Quid asper utile nummum habet.* Also *Gloss. Graeco-Lat.* δηναριον, λευκον. In view of the above evidence one might suggest that the *leukon* is the *pure* silver *siliqua* (= 1/24 *sol.*). In that case the Yerushalmi would be exemplifying the earning of 1/24 profit (i.e. a רביעית = 1 d., in the *aureus*) as in the *beraitha* first quoted. However, in view of evidence brought below from the context of another source mentioning the לקן, I feel *leukon* here must be, *not* the pure silver piece, but one that is whitish. Note also that לבן in Hebrew does not always necessarily mean white, but also grey (as opposed to black), (eg. B. Makkot 20b, Jastrow, *Dict.*, p. 690b, s.v. לבן II). According to this, the לקן is not identical (though similar) to the Mishnaic "*asper*" (contrary to what I wrote in *JQR*, 56, 1966, p. 293.) See above, Chap. II, note 21. On the silver wash in the first half of the IV cent. see H. L. Adelson's article "Bronze Alloys of the Late Roman Empire", *ANSMN*, 6, 1954, pp. 111–19, especially p. 112, note 2, and p. 117; E. S. Hedges & Dudley A. Robins, in *Num. Chron.*, 1963, p. 237 et seq.; Sutherland & Harold, *Archeometry*, 4, 1961, pp. 56–61; Cope in *NC*, 1968, pp. 144–45. See also *Leyden Pap.* X.24; χαλκον λευκον ποιησαι, (Berthelot, *Archéologie et histoire des sciences*, Paris, 1906, p. 278). Heichelheim's suggestion in *Econ. Surv.*, 4, p. 229, may be rejected.

14 The Tosefta, Ma'aser Sheni 3.4, mentions the *rova*, which must there equal ¼ *shekel* (= *didrachm*), i.e. ½ d.

15 Cf. first interpretation of *Pnei Moshe* on the Yerushalmi Ma'aser Sheni 4.1 and that of the Gaon Elijah of Wilna, on Yerushalmi Ma'aser Sheni 4.1; contra Lieberman, in *Tosefta ki-fshutah*, 2, p. 751. The same argumentation could quite as well be applied to the case of the substitution of the Second Tithe, (Lieberman, ibid., *Pnei Moshe*, explanation 2, ibid.). The cost of transport would be minimal.

16 This is the usual meaning of "here" in the Palestinian Talmud, see J. N. Epstein, *Mavo le-Sifrut ha-Amoraim* (Jerusalem, 1962), p. 275; but see Liebermann, *Talmuda shel Kisrin* (supplement to *Tarbiz*, 2/4, Jerusalem, 1931), p. 11; Liebermann, *Siphre Zutta* (New York, 1968), p. 131. Here the juxtaposition with Arbel makes it fairly certain that the text is from Tiberias.

17 The commentators (Lieberman, *Pnei Moshe*, note 15) explain that it costs 50 myriad to transport the money. (The *Pnei Moshe* says this number is an exaggeration! See also R. Josef Engel's *Glioné ha-Shas*, on the Yerushalmi text). However, this seems most unlikely at so early a date, c.307. See, for example, Segrè, in *Byzantion*, 16, 1942–43, pp. 404–06. It is more plausible that he wishes to shift his money for business purposes. Cf. *Sifré* to Deut. 32.2, discussed above, Chap. XIII. See *Cod. Theod.* 9.23.1 (356); Jones, *Later Roman Empire* 1, pp. 439, 441. Cf. above Chap. II note 23, and below Chap. XXI note 30.

18 So I understand the ‎ב‎-, in ‎בתרין אלפין‎, etc.

19 Delete. According to all readings this seems to make no sense as it stands.

20 According to Rome Ms. According to other Mss. etc. we must supply the fact that he receives back money at a higher rate.

21 Cf. Zuckermann, *Talmudische Münzen und Gewichte*, pp. 29–30. His interpretation, attractive though it be, takes no account of the other text (below) in which the *leukon* is mentioned. According to our interpretation too, the text remains difficult and problematic.

22 In the Bavli (B. Bava Mezia 45a) we read the opposite, namely that R. Johanan did not permit the lending of a *dinar* for a *dinar*. The Talmud there explains that this refers to a gold *dinar*. However, this is in order that R. Johanan's statement be in accord with the Mishna as it appears in the Bavli. For, as the Mishna of the Bavli reads that "gold purchases silver" (above), gold must be "produce". Hence a gold *dinar* could not be lent for a gold *dinar*, as this would be like lending a measure of "produce" (‎סאה‎) for another, etc. (See *Sdei Yehoshua* on the Yerushalmi, Ma'aser Sheni 4.1.) However, we have shown (above, Chap. XI) that Rabbi's son, R. Ḥiyya, etc., are of the opinion that silver is "produce", hence R. Johanan and Resh Lakish probably would also hold this view. To solve the apparent contradiction between the Bavli and the Yerushalmi, I would suggest that R. Johanan's statement in the Bavli is referring to *silver dinars*, which in his time were regarded as "produce", and therefore could not be lent out for silver *dinars*. (I make this suggestion despite the Bavli's own clear explanation to the contrary.) That the Yerushalmi is talking of gold *dinars* will become even more certain below. Further proof, if any be deemed necessary, that both R. Johanan and Resh (= R. Simeon) b. Lakish are of the view that gold is coin may be found in the very complex *sugya* appearing in various forms and recensions in B. Bava Mezia 44b–45a, and Y. Ma'aser Sheni 2.3. From the first recension in B. Bava Mezia ibid. it emerges clearly that both R. Johanan and Resh Lakish, in explaining an earlier controversy between the Schools of Shammai and Hillel, ascribe to the School of Shammai the view that silver is coin and to that of Hillel the view that gold is coin. Since the rule is that (but for some notable exceptions) one always follows the view of the School of Hillel — a rule already established in early Tannaitic times — it is patent that R. Johanan and Resh Lakish would not have ascribed to this School a view they did themselves not share. A careful examination of the Yerushalmi version of this *sugya* (Ma'aser Sheni ibid.) reveals again that both R. Johanan and Resh Lakish took for granted that gold is coin, (see Z. M. Dor, *Torat Eretz-Yisrael be-Bavel*, Tel-Aviv, 1971, p. 54). On the other hand, the second recension in the Bavli gives quite a different picture of the views of R. Johanan and Resh Lakish. However, Z. M. Dor (ibid., pp. 54–55) has demonstrated convincingly that this recension, though of Palestinian origin, underwent radical editorial revision in Babylonian academies in accordance with the local

view that silver is coin (compare above chap. XI, note 24). Hence, in this recension the Babylonian view has been ascribed to the great Palestinian scholars.

23 I understand this section to be either R. Jacob b. Aḥa's own addition or an addition by an anonymous editor, but not a continuation of R. Johanan and Resh Lakish's statement. The main reason is that such terms — according to the interpretation given below — could hardly be used before the early IV cent. This is borne out by the Yerushalmi's terminology אוף — They *too* hold that gold is coin, and the change from Hebrew to Aramiac.

24 As suggested by Krauss, *LW*, 2, p. 566b, s.v. קרט. However, he corrects himself in *Additamenta ad librnm Aruch Completum*, 7, p. 194a; Levy, *Wörterbuch*, 4, p. 375 b. See also Scheftel, *Erech Milim*, p. 123a–b.

25 Liddell and Scott², p. 941b, s.v. κεϱατιον II.

26 A Souter, *Glossary of Later Latin* (Oxford, 1964), p. 328a, s.v. *siliqua. Cod. Just*, 4.32.26. But cf. Jones in *Essays in Roman Coinage*, ed. Carson and Sutherland (Oxford, 1956), p. 28, note 2, who believes that the *siliqua* is never a coin and only an accounting unit. See also Schrötter, *Wörterbuch der Münzkunde*, p. 638a, s.v. *siliqua*. See further my remarks in *Sinai*, 55/4,1969, pp. 234–35, and ibid., 66, 1970, pp.372–73.

27 *Lexicon Syriacum²*, p. 695; but see below, note 29.

28 See S. Fraenkel, *Die aramäischen Fremdwörter im Arabischen* (Leiden, 1886), p. 200. See also Y. Shekalim 2.4.: דינרין קרטין, and what I wrote in *Sinai*, 66/4–5 (401–02), 1970, pp. 272–74. There is no basis or justification for Krauss' suggested emendation to דינרין קרל[מ]טין (= κϱεματιστης), neither is קרמטין a form the Hebrew loan-word would be likely to have taken on (see Krauss, *Talmudische Archäologie*, 2, Leipzig, 1911, p. 40 and p. 715, note 655). The correct reading seems to be קורטין (as in Sirilio) = *quartus* (Kohut, *Aruch Completum*, 4, p. 11, note 3). See also *Yerushalmi Shekalim*, Sofer edition, p. 22; *Seridei Ha-Yerushalmi*, ed. Ginzberg, p. 125, Ratner, *Shekalim* 2.4, p. 12.

29 It can however mean a weight of gold too, (contra Brockelmann, note 27 above), as in *Acta Martyrum et Sanctorum*, ed. P. Bedjan, 4 (Paris and Leipzig, 1897), p. 311, line 10: דדהבא (קירטא or קרטא) יהב הבת מן חדא הבת דדהבא The *Sdei Yehoshua* in Y. Bava Mezia 4.1 thinks that the *karat* is a gold weight. Elijah of Fulda (on this same text), on the other hand, says it is a silver coin.

30 The פירוש הקצר in the Krotoschin ed. translates לקן a cup, confusing it with לקנא — λεκανη (Krauss, *LW*, 2, p. 319b, s.v. לקנא). However, in view of the context this explanation is hardly acceptable. (The author of the פירוש הקצר is R. David Darshan; See S. Liebermann, *Hayerushalmi Kiphshuto*, Jerusalem, 1934, p. viii, note 1.)

31 Or, conversely, one may argue that since a weight is *asemon*, and *asemon* may not be lent out, the *karat* here cannot be a weight, but must be a coin.

32 Note also that in Galen, 24r, the קרטא — 1/3 *obol*, i.e. 1/24 *denarius*. (Payne Smith, *Thesaurus Syriacus*, 3741, s.v. קרטא). (Can this be a confusion with 1/24 *dinar*, *dinar* being a gold coin in the Islamic monetary systems? Cf. my remarks in *Sinai*, 53, p. 167, also p. 166, note 14.)

33 On the connections between the Constantinian *siliqua* and the Diocletian *argenteus*, see P. Bruun in *RIC*, 7, 1966, p. 7.

34 Note also that in the Siniai palimpsest Gospels (Cambridge, 1894), קרטא, in Luke 15.16, translates the Latin *siliqua* and Greek κεϱατιον (Brockelmann², p. 694b, s.v. קרטא). Normally (*Tetra Ewangalion Kaddisha*, p. 418, *Palestinian Lectionary*,

237

p. 126, etc.) this word is translated חרובא. The *karat* is a carob (*Book of Medicines*, ed. E.A.Wallis Budge, Oxford, 1913, p. 278, line 6; Syriac Epiphanius, ed. Lagarde, p. 57, line 53, ed. Dean, translation p. 64). (Note that in the Arsacid period the *girû* = carob (seed) = 1/24 *shekel*.See A. L. Oppenheim in *Orientalia*, 42/1, 2, 1973, p. 327. My thanks to Prof. M. Beer for referring me to this article.) In this way we may better understand the use of the term חרוב (= חרובא carob) in the Byzantine Palestinian legal text, the *Sefer ha-Ma'asim li-Vnei Eretz Israel*. (On the problem of the date of this text see S. Liebermann, in *Ginzei Kedem*, 5, Jerusalem, 1934, p. 185 et seq.; Contra A. Aptowitzer, in *Tarbiz*, 4, p. 142, and Baron, *SHRJ²*, 6, chap. 27, note 71.) There fol. 20a (*Tarbiz* 1/1, Oct. 1929, p. 95, ed. B. M. Lewin) we read: בכל מקום שאת שונה סלע ארבע חרובין הוא הסלע והכסף / והכסף לשקל שני חרובין והזוז חרוב / אחד ודינרין סתם שני חרובין הן ודינרי / זהב עשרים וארבע חרובין... (See J. N. Epstein's note in Lewin's introduction, *Tarbiz*, ibid., p. 90, note 1.) It is clear that the text is talking of the *siliqua*, which is translated חרוב, and pointing out that it corresponds with the old *zuz* (= *denarius*), which is ¼ *sela* (= *tetradrachm*, Biblical *shekel*), and is 1/24 gold *dinar* (= *solidus*). The כסף (= 2 חרובין) is surely the *miliarense* (= 2 *siliquae*) which Epiphanius (Syriac, ed. Dean, p. 61, para. 52) called ארגוריוס (= כסף) (fol. 69a25). The term חרוב was a common one and turns up in a V cent. (?) Palestinian papyrus letter, (Cowley, *JQR*, 16, p. 1 et seq.; *Sefer ha-Yishuv*, 1, ed. S. Klein, Jerusalem, 1939, pp. 174b–175a). It would seem that this section of the *Sefer ha-Ma'asim* — a composite text of several historical strata — cannot be dated to before the first century of the Islamic era. Note further that in the Cowley papyrus the רביע is also mentioned, surely ¼ חרוב. In the VI cent. the smallest fraction of the *solidus* was 1/96 (= ¼ *karat*, or *siliqua*), (West and Johnson, *Currency*, p. 129). See also the remarks of E. Y. Kutscher, in *Words and their History* (Jerusalem 1961, Hebrew), pp. 28–29, which should be modified slightly in view of the above. See also *Excavations at Nessana*, 3, by C. J. Kraemer (Princeton, 1958), p. 343, index IX, s.v. κεϱάτιον. The ratio in the early IV cent. between AV and AR was 1:18, and as the *karat* weight was ·18 gr. (1 *libra* = 325 gr. ÷ 1728), the *siliqua — karat silver coin* weighed 3.24 gr. (In fact the *siliqua* weighed a theoretical 3.4.) Thus at that time the value of the *karat* weight actually (almost) equalled that of the *siliqua* coin, which in turn was associated with the now archaic *denarius*. Hence, perhaps, the phrase in Y. Shekalim 2.4 "*dinarin karatin*" (or *kartin*), meaning an (archaic) *dinar* equalling a (present-day) *karat* (*siliqua*). Or, more simply still, an early IV cent. personality explaining the dinar would equate its *value* with that of the gold *karat*, either thinking of the classical (Nero to Trajan) *denarius*, of about 3.2 gr. silver (Mickwitz, *Geld und Wirtschaft*, p. 40) — a coin by then very rare — at AV:AR 1:18 (= 3.24 gr. silver), or, more likely, of the later Marcus Aurelius to Septimius Severus *denarius* of about 2.5 gr. silver (Mickwitz, ibid.), at the more usual ratio of 1:14.4, giving 2.6 gr. silver. But the most likely explanation of *karatin* (or *kartin*) here is *quartus*. The *karat* in Y. Sota 3.4 (= Y. Pe'a 8.7 = B. Sota 21b) is an accounting unit, the smallest unit of weight currently in use. The text is post III cent., (see *Tosafot's* reading in B. Sota 21b; Ratner, Pe'a, p. 77; Ginzberg, *Seridei ha-Yerushalmi*, p. 210). "200 *zuz* minus a *dinar*" is an archaic use quoted from the Mishna (Pe.'a 8.8), and in no way indicative of monetary usage during the period when this text was finally edited.

35 This interpretation makes it quite clear that a "*dinar* for a *dinar*" means a "[gold] *dinar* for a [gold] *dinar*". For if the silver *denarius* is being spoken of (as would have

to be the case if the Bavli's interpretation be correct, and the two Talmuds do not contradict one another, why mention the *karat* of the same value? On *dinar* meaning gold *dinar*, see above Chap. II.

36 It is clear that IV cent. authorities followed the III cent. rulings on the status of gold as "coin". R. Jacob b. Aḥa's statement (or that of the anonymous editor) is probably of the third decade of the IV cent. In the first decade silver values fluctuated considerably, while his rulings presuppose some period of stability for silver. The term *siliqua* appears to be a third decade term; see above, Chap. IX.

37 After 307 only one denomination was struck as a rule, probably the larger of the two. See Table J (at end of Chapter XXII).

38 This was, of course, only because it too was greatly debased, and thus very similar in character (and behaviour) to the Diocletianic silver-washed piece.

39 Most recently P. M. Bruun, in *RIC*, 7, p. 2, has reaffirmed the character of the Constantinian *solidus* as money, as opposed to bullion. Both the silver and gold had the same character, and similar degrees of over-valuation (Bruun, ibid., pp. 1–8). Also see his remarks in *Congresso Internazionale di Numismatica* (Rome, 1961), *Atti*, 2 (Rome, 1965), p. 338, on *Cod. Theod.* 12.7. 1, contra Seeck in *Zeitschr. f. Num.* 17, p. 54. It is interesting to compare our results with the conclusions of P. Grierson in his penetrating analysis of "The Roman Law of Counterfeiting", (*Essays in Roman Coinage*, ed. Carson & Sutherland, London, 1956). For there he shows that even during the IV cent. the law of counterfeiting clearly distinguished between gold, and silver, on the one hand, and bronze, on the other hand. Bronze coinage was not "*Caesaris moneta*" or καισαρος νομισμα, as was gold and silver coinage (pp. 241–42, 244–45, 247–48; cf. *CIL* 6, (i), Nos. 42–44 [= *ILS* nos. 1634–35]; Grierson, Counterfeiting, p. 245, note 3). The above argument rejects the interpretation of Sutherland in *RIC*, 6, 1967, pp. 89–90. On the stability of the Constantinian *solidus*, see recently Andreotti, *RIDA*, 3/16, 1969, pp. 242–43.

40 דיסגנים — so in ed. princeps and Ms. Leiden. לסגנים in Ms. Rome. Further variant in Sirilio Ms.

41 R. Abbahu died in the year 309. See Lieberman, *Annuaire de l'institut de Philologie et d'Histoire Orientales et Slaves*, 7, 1939–44, p. 402.

42 Θερμοσαριος, see Lieberman, *Tosefta ki-fshutah*, 1, p. 26; 2, p. 716.

43 See above Chapter IV, note 42. And see Lieberman, *Tosefta ki-fshutah*, 1, p. 716, note 29, who writes that he does not know what "*disignim*" is.

44 See *JRS*, 1971, pp. 171–77, article entitled "Diocletian's Currency Reform: A New Inscription", by Kenan T. Erim, Joyce Reynolds and Michael Crawford.

45 Ibid., pp. 172, 175.

46 Ibid. p. 172.

47 Ibid. p. 175. But see above Chapter IV, note 42, where a different interpretation was tentatively suggested.

47a In the same edict it appears that the authorities wished to double the face-value of the coins!

48 This is part of a Midrash on Proverbs 28.11. There are some problems connected with the Midrashic exegesis of this verse, which cannot be discussed here. Suffice it to say that the interpretation of the *Pnei Moshe* on this text is, in part, refuted by the statement of R. Levi, a few lines below. Cf. *Targum* on this verse; *Midrash Mishlé* (= Proverbs), ed. Buber, p. 102; *Yalkut Machiri* to Proverbs, ed. Grünhut, on Proverbs 28.11. See also *Midrash Shir ha-Shirim*, ed. Grünhut, Jerusalem 1896,

fol. 45b. See my article in *Sinai*, 64/3–4 (388–89), 1969, pp. 185–89. See also A. Marmorstein's remarks in *Ha-Soker*, 4, 1936–7, p. 133.

49 I have found no variants, and therefore accept this reading as correct. The meaning "units (of currency)" is well attested. See Jastrow, *Dict.*, 1220b.

50 Dr. J. Kent (private communication of 23 August, 1972) writes: "your distinction between the 'confidence' felt in bullion and currency seems to me over-subtle. A man with coins does not require credit to live, but pays his way; a man without coins must have instant credit — even with his bars he would otherwise go hungry. A bar — particularly if designed to support credit — could be counterfeited as easily as a solidus." At a pinch one could interpret our text differently; however, such other interpretations would be forced. I understand the text to mean that if a man comes into a strange town flaunting bars of gold, this would make quite an impression on the local population, probably more than had he come with the equivalent in a purse of coins. And should he go to the butcher to buy a pound of meat, or to the baker to buy a loaf of bread, they will not make him change his bar in order to pay these small sums, but will trust him the while, allowing him to run up a small bill. While the man with coins will have to pay his way along, and will indeed have no excuse not to pay out for everything he buys in ready cash.

51 *Zahavi*. In Egypt, *P. Würz.* 15 of the year 341 seems to be the earliest mention of goldsmiths as unofficial buyers of gold from peasants. See further Johnson and West, *Byzantine Egypt: Economic Studies*, p. 174, on goldsmiths as bankers and dealers. (The homily is linked to the verse in Prov. 26.23.) Cf. *Pesikta de R. Kahana*, ed. Buber, 122b, ed. Mandelbaum, pp. 259–60. See also Julian *Or.* II, 91c. Loeb ed., 1, pp. 242–3.

52 In Y. Terumot 8 ad fin. we find R. Samuel b. Naḥman going with R. Ami to Palmyra to speak with Zenobia, i.e. c. 270; (see Bacher, *Aggadat Amora'ei Eretz-Yisrael*, 1/2, p. 248). Therefore, he cannot have lived much after the first quarter of the IV cent. From *Genesis Rabba* 9, 5, ed. Theodor-Albeck, p. 70, it would appear that he was born c. 215. Furthermore we know of a certain, albeit small, amount of gold plated coins from the period of Diocletian and Constantine; see A. R. Burns, *Money and Monetary Policy in Early Times* (London, 1920), p. 438, (citing Mommsen-Blacas, 3, p. 68). On the problem of Roman plated coins in general, see Oeconomides in *ANSMN*, 12, 1966, pp. 71–74; W. Campbell, *NNM*, 57, 1933; L. A. Lawrence in *Num. Chron.*, 1940, pp. 185 ff; M. H. Crawford in *Num. Chron.*, 1968, pp. 55–59. On the Rabbinic attitude to plated coins see *Pesikta de R. Kahana*, ed. Buber, 122b, ed. Mandelbaum, pp. 259–60. Finally, compare *Cod. Theod.*, 9.21.1, of 323–25; and ibid., 2, of 321, 318; and ibid., 3 and 4 of 326.

53 Cf. ibid., 12.6.12 (366), 12.7.3 (367), 10.1.11 (379); on counterfeiting see ibid., 9.21.22, 9.38.6 — 9.38.8, 11.21.1, etc. See below, Chap. XXIV. See also Kent's "Gold Coinage . . ." and Grierson's "Roman Law of Counterfeiting", both in *Mattingly Festschrift*, which bring ample literary and numismatic evidence.

54 See Jastrow, *Dict.*, 394b, s. v. זימיא (= ζημια). See also Amir in *Teva ve-Aretz*, 10/4, 1968, p. 263. Yet another text indicating this may be found in *Aggadat Bereishit* 56, ed. Buber, 57, p. 115, a text of the mid-fourth century (R. Berechia), (AX). See also ibid., 58, ed. Buber, p. 118.

55 This reduction in confidence *vis-à-vis* bullion probably had no direct halachic effect.

56 Kent in *Mattingly Festschrift*, p. 203–04, cited more fully below in Chap. XXIV. More exactly *OB(RIZIATUM)*, Kent, ibid., p. 200, note 2. See also *De rebus bellicis*

III. 1, ed. Thompson, pp. 95, 111; Libanius *Or.* XVIII. 138; and St. Basil, *Epist.* 40, the assumed date of which is 362. (The letter is generally regarded as spurious; see Deferrari's comment in the Loeb ed. 1, p. 231, note 2.) Also St. Basil, *Epist.* 88, probably of early 368, (see Loeb ed. 2, pp. 106–07, note 2, citing *Cod. Theod.* 7.6.3).

Chapter XV

1 Considered very little.

2 As *Avot de R. Nathan*, was edited in the II and III cent., this probably represents a II or III cent. estimate of Hillel's wages, and is no doubt meant to mean a low wage. On the problems of dating texts in Avot de R. Nathan, see L. Finkelstein's *Mabo le-Massektot Abot ve-Avot d'Rabbi Natan* (New York, 1950).

3 Estimate of II cent.

4 Estimate of R. Judah [b. Ilai], c. 135–70.

5 See J.H. Heinemann's remark in his article in *HUCA*, 25, 1954, p. 275, note 21.

6 Beraita based on earlier text with substituted coin.

7 Meaning a small sum.

8 See above, Chap. III. If *maneh* here means one *denarius*, as it can from the end of the III cent. onwards, then this may be a daily wage. (Cf. *Ed. Diocletian* VII, 72–73, ed. Graser, p. 346.) This is a Babylonian statement of the later III cent.: Rav Judah said (in the name of Rav). However, Rav had many accurate traditions of early Palestinian material. He may mean that in the period of the Second Temple, i.e. pre 70 C.E., these judges used to receive around 30 d. per day, (= around 10,000 d. per annum).

9 On the *se'ah* see my remarks in *JESHO*, 8, 1965, pp. 266–71. Jastrow, *Dict.*, 268a–b, s.v. גריוא and Levy, *Wörterbuch*, 1, p. 354a, s.v. גריבא; both state that the *gariba* (*griva*) equals a *modius* or *se'ah*. They further identify the two forms גריוא and גריבא as different spellings of the same word. In Syriac sources the identity of the *geriba* and the *se'ah* is clearly stated. See J.P. Margoliouth's *Supplement* to Payne Smith's *Thesaurus Syriacus* (Oxford, 1927), p. 706, s.v. גרב, citing Bar-Hebraeus on Hos. 3.2, said to be a British Museum Ms., Supplement p. xii. (I have been unable to find it in the British Museum. It is, in fact in Berlin, Orqu. 870, Abs. der zweiter; see Baumstark, *Geschichte der syrische Literatur*, Bonn, 1922, p. 308, note 5.) Add to this *Bar-Bahlul*, ed. Duval, (Paris, 1901), 887, s.v. כילא : סאתא גריבא חד a *sa'ata* (= *se'ah*) is one *gariba* (= *griva*). See G.R. Driver, *Aramaic Documents of the Fifth Century B.C.* (Oxford, 1965), p. 60, where Nyberg cites Sprengling proving from the *Ka'abah-yi-Zaradušt* that one *griv* equals the *modius* which contained ten *hofen* in third century Iran. This is derived from the statement: לחמא חד גריב חופן ||| ||ו which is translated ἄρτων μόδιος εἰς ἥμισος. (See Sprengling in *American Journal of Semitic Languages and Literature*, 57, pp. 287, 390, 416; idem, *Third Century Iran, Sapor and Kartir*, Chicago, 1953, IV, 4, 5, 6, pp. 17–19, and my remarks in *JESHO*, 13, 1970, p. 13–269.) The metrological material in the Armenian Ananias of Širak further bears out this equation. See H.A. Manandian, *The Trade and Cities of Armenia in Relation to the Ancient World Trade*, Lisbon, 1965, pp. 124–27. (See my comments in *JESHO*, 13, 1970, p. 13.)

10 Perhaps II or III cent. estimate.

11 The phrase appears to be a Tannaitic formulation, but is used by R. Johanan who recalls such a situation in Tiberias, probably c. 230. See below, Chap. XIX ad fin.

12 Famine and inflationary price.

13 Julian the apostate sold at this price to alleviate the famine, (see our discussion in Chap. II). The wheat was imported.

14 See above, Chap. II, where we corrected the text to read 1 *solidus*.

15 Considered very expensive. Probably a II cent. estimate. See Krauss, *Kadmoniot ha-Talmud*, 2/2, p. 17 and note 2. The Tosefta version varies slightly.

16 The context is as follows: R. Nathan said "If a man is found owing 100 d. to his neighbour and he is wearing a *ksut* worth 200 d., the claimant may not say to him 'Sell your *ksut* (worth 200 d.) and cover yourself with [one worth] 100 d., and give me 100 d. . . .'" The full context suggests the case of a rich man who has suddenly become impoverished.

17 Price of *tallit* = price of *ḥaluk*. On *ḥaluk*, see Krauss' remark in *Kadminiot ha-Talmud*, 2/2, p. 29. Also Y. Brand in *Sefer ha-Yovel le-Yisrael Elfenbein* (Jerusalem, 1962), pp. 46–55.

18 Considered cheap, but not very respectable.

19 Inflationary prices. In *Pirkei de Rabbenu ha-Kaddosh*, 7.15, ed. Schönblum 37a, we hear of an *itztelit* of 48 *maneh*. This is considered a very high price. See Krauss, *Kadmoniot*, 2/2, p. 18.

20 *Kad* is probably big, comparable with *ḥavit*, a barrel. See M. Bava Kama 2.1.

21 The *tzeloḥit* may not have been full. It is only stated that the vendor served the child an *issar*-worth of oil.

22 Probably early IV cent. inflationary price. See above, Chap. III.

23 Purely theoretical examples.

24 R. Judah said that once in Jerusalem . . .

25 Probably early IV cent. inflationary prices. See above, Chap. III.

26 Both in Palestine and Babylonia.

27 But according to Taubenschlag in *JJP*, 3, 1949, pp. 51–52, basing himself on Arangio-Ruiz's edition, this sould read 22 *denarii* (!). See *Econ. Survey*, 5, p. 235 note 38 that the prevailing price during the first two centuries of the Empire for work-slaves was 500 d. (= 20 *aurei*).

28 Theoretical examples, taking the form of . . . "Even if an ox were worth 100 d." etc., suggesting that in fact this is a more or less impossibly high price.

29 Cf. sheep.

30 Theoretical prices, convenient for reckoning. On the cost of horses in the third cent., 125 d., see R. W. Davies' interesting remarks in *Latomus*, 28, 1969, pp. 438–9, 447–8.

31 Cf. cattle.

32 Report of R. Judah [b. Ilai], c. 135–70, talking of Temple times. See Varro 3.7.10, that a pair of pigeons in austere times cost 1000 *sest.* (= 10 *aurei*); cf. Columella 8.8.9, = 4000 *nummi* (= *as*).

33 Report of R. Jose, c. 135–70.

34 Famine price.

35 *Pesikta Rabbti*, ed. Friedman, 119a. There R. Pinḥas is mentioned, so it may be of the earlier IV cent.

36 This text is probably of a late date and the price unreliable.

37 Perhaps exaggeration. Story told regarding R. Gamliel (II), as is evident from the other scholars mentioned, e. g. R. Akiva.

38 This seems to be the more accurate version, while the Bavli's price is perhaps a later recension. In this version only R. Gamliel and "the elders" are mentioned.

39 Published in the *Catalogue of Greek and Latin Papyri in the John Rylands Library*, 4, ed. by C.H. Roberts and E.C. Turner. (On these texts, see M. Schwabe's remarks in *Eretz-Yisrael*, 3, Jerusalem, 1954, pp. 181–85, Hebrew.)

40 Roberts and Turner, ibid., p. 105.

41 All references are to be the Babylonian Talmud. We have equated the *zuz* with the Sasanaian *drachm* (= drm) throughout.

42 Samuel, d. 254. Wholly theoretical, of the order of: "Even if it were the case that…"

43 (Samuel and) Rav, d.247. Jacobs, in *JSS*, 2, 1957, p. 354, note 1, seems to have misunderstood this text, stating that 1 *kor* costs 1 *sela*.

44 R. Kahana [I?]

45 Jastrow, *Dict*, 515a, s.v. כוז, defines the *dana* as a "cylindrical jar, (*dolium*)". For its etymological root he refers to the word דנא (ibid., p. 22b) — "a leather-bottle, jar (a liquid measure)", etc. A more likely root, however, is the Accadian "*dannu..*, jug, tub, vessel", see eg. Liddell & Scott, *Addenda et Corrigenda*, 2060a, s.v. δανας. See Muss-Arnolt's *Assyrian Dictionary*, 1 (Berlin, 1905), p. 258a, *Chicago Assyrian Dictionary*, 3, pp. 98–99, and W. Von Soden, *Akkadisches Handwörterbuch*, 1, p. 161. (See also Payne Smith, *Thesaurus Syriacus*, 924, s.v. דנא; Latin *tina* — Lewis and Short, s.v. *tina*, p. 1873a.) There is, however, no clear indication as to the size of the *dana*, if indeed it had a standard size. It was quite large, as is evident from an inscription found at Dura Mithraeum, in which the price given for a *dana* (line 6, δανα δανα *κη′ υ′ ια′*) of 28 d. is very high. (See *The Excavations at Dura Europos, Preliminary Report of the Seventh and Eighth Season of Work*, 1933–34, 1934–35, New Haven, 1939, p. 125, no. 862. Of. ibid., no. 861, line 1 δαννα [—]. See also Report IV, no. 245, pp. 122 ff. = *SEG*, VII, 401.)

46 = Jug. Jastrow, p. 618a, s.v. כוז. Cf. Hulin 107a, a *kuza* of ¼ *log*.

47 Exaggerated extremes. But see below Chap. XX note 6a.

48 R. Hisda, d. 309. True value, 50 d.

49 See Jastrow, p. 268a, s.v. גריוא, where he equates it with the *se'ah* and the *modius*. See above, note 9.

50 R. Joseph, d. 333. Theoretical.

51 Perhaps even earlier.

52 By inference. Probably wholly theoretical.

53 Wholly thereotical, of the order of: "Even if a lamb were to cost …"

54 Rabba (d.339) or Rava 299–352).

55 Abbaye, d.338/39.

56 Wholly theoretical. Jacobs, *JSS*, 2, 1957, p. 354, cites this as the price of an ox-hide. Yet the whole corpse including its meat value (as it would be sold to a non-Jew) is being considered.

57 Rava, d.352.

58 Cf. Sota 48a, R. Hisda (d.309), 1 d.

59 See Jastrow, p. 376a, s.v. וורשכא. Other explanations in Jastrow, ibid.: beads, frontlets. (True price: 5 drm.) But see Geiger's remarks in *Additimenta ad Librum Aruch Completum*, ed. Krauss, p. 166b.   60 Rava, d.352.   61 R. Papa, d.375.

62 Legendary Aggada on the people of (Biblical) Sodom.

63 See also *SEG*, 7, nos. 417, 419, 420, 623; Heichelheim in *Econ. Surv.*, 4, pp. 186–87.

64 Cf. *Dura Rep.*, IV, no. 266.

Chapter XVI

1 However, see the somewhat different interpretation in N. Jasny, *The Wheats of Classical Antiquity*, (Baltimore, 1944), p. 143 et seq. His suggestion is not altogether convincing, while ours is borne out by a wealth of comparative material.

2 See further Cicero, *Verr.* 3.188; Wheat 4 *sest.* per *mod.*, barley 2 *sest.* per *mod.*, (*Econ. Surv.*, 1, p. 403); Polybius 2.15.1, wheat 4 *obols* per Sicilian *medimnus*, barley 2, etc. (*Econ. Surv.*, 3, p. 264). In *JESHO*, 8, 1965, pp. 257–58, I misinterpreted the material from Ephesus, cited in *Econ. Surv.*, 4, p. 880. Dr. R. Duncan-Jones, (in a private communication of 31/10/72), calls my attention to N. Jasny's comments on this text in *Agric. Hist.* 21, 1947, p. 190.

3 Johnson and West, *Byzantine Egypt: Economic Studies*, pp. 175–76. See also *P. Tebt.* 520 (15 C.E.), Tebtynis, 574 *art.* barley = 344 *art.* wheat.

4 Ed. W. Wright (Cambridge, 1882), p. 35.

5 Ibid., p. 69.

6 See also ibid., p. 29 (chap. XXXIX), for the year of the great famine, 500 C.E., when wheat was 4 *mod.*: 1 d., and barley 6 *mod.* : 1 d. See also *DJD*, 2, ed. Benoit, Milik and De Vaux (Oxford, 1961), p. 219, from which it is clear that wheat is twice as expensive as barley. *Revelation* 5.6; also *Scriptores Historiae Augustae, Claudius*, 14,3. In Syria and Egypt of the XII–XIV cent. we find a fixed relationship between the cost of wheat and barley of 3:2. See A. Strauss, *Toldot ha-Yehudim be-Mizrayim ve-Suria Taḥat Shilton ha-Mamlukim*, 2 (Israel, 1951), p. 139, and tables on pp. 132–37.

7 It may of course be that these prices are from different times of the years, as Mickwitz thinks. Johnson and West, *Byzantine Egypt: Economic Studies*, p. 175. See also Y. Bava Mezia 9.8. See also *SB.* 7341; *P. Mich.* 127; *SB.* 7365; *PSI.* 281; *P. Grenf.* 11.77. All these Egyptian sources (dating from the I and II cents. C.E.) give the price of wheat as being equal to that of barley. See *Econ. Surv.*, 2, pp. 310–12. On the other hand *P. Col.* 1.4, *Frisk Bankakten*, 1, (Theadelphia, 155 C.E.) gives the price of wheat as 8 *dr.* per *art.*, and that of barley as 4 *dr.* 2 *ob.* or 4 *dr.* 3 *ob.* or 4 8/10 *dr.* per *art.* (*Econ. Surv.*, ibid.). See further Mickwitz, *Geld und Wirtschaft*, p. 100, note 9. See also Boak in *Harvard Studies in Classical Philology*, 51, 1940, p. 45 (article entitled "Some Early Byzantine Tax Records from Egypt").

8 *Peshitta* and *Septuagint* identity the *modius* with the *se'ah*. Mat. 5.15 and Mark 4.21, (see *Old Syriac Gospels*, ed. A. Lewis Smith, 1910, p. 10; *Sinai palimpsest*, p. 9, *Tetraevangalion Kaddisha*). See also above, Chap. XV, note 9, and see Jastrow, *Dict.*, p. 738b, where the two are equated (cf. B. Eruvin 83a). See Syriac Epiphanius, ed. J. E. Dean (Chicago, 1935), pp. 12, 40; 1 *kor* = 30 *mod.* 1 *kor* = 30 *se'ah*. Therefore, *se'ah* = *modius*. Also ibid., p. 142, note *; Segrè, *Metrologia*, p. 342, note 2; Segrè, *Circolazione*, p. 56.

9 See e.g. *Encyclopaedia Britannica*, 9th. ed., 3, p. 254, s.v. baking. According to *P. Flor.* 322, 26 2/3 *mod.* produced 320 double-loaves (or 620 single loaves), therefore 1 *mod.* produced 12 double (or 24 single)-loaves. Thus 1 *se'ah* (= 2 *mod.*) would produce about 24 double-loaves. See below, note 13.

10 See also Pliny, *Hist. Nat.* 18.66: Nunc ex his generibus, quae Romam invehuntur levissimum est Gallicum atque Chersonneso advectum, quippe non excedunt modii vicenas libras, si quis granum ipsum ponderet. ("Of the various kinds of wheat which are imported into Rome, the lightest in weight are those which come from Gaul and

the Chersonese; for, upon weighing them, it will be found that they do not yield more than twenty pounds to the modius.") See *Econ. Surv.*, 5, p. 144. On identifications of different kinds of wheats, see, most recently M.A. Kislev's article in *Leshonenu* 37, 1973, pp. 83–95, 243–52.

11 West and Johnson, *Byzantine Egypt*, p. 183. See also *P. Flor.* 322 (Theadelphia 258 C.E.), from which one may derive the same conclusion. But see *P.O.* 1454 (Oxyrhynchus, 117 C.E.). *Econ. Surv.*, 2, p. 316. See below, note 13.

12 St. Jerome (*Comm. in Daniel.* 11.5), see *Econ. Surv.*, 2, p. 466.

13 See above, note 9, and A. Segrè in *Byzantion*, 15, p. 270, note 86, commenting on *Forschung. in Ephesos*, 1923, Oesterr. p. 101, inscr. 10, according to which loaves were about 1 lb. in weight. The loaves (?) there vary between 10 and 14 ozs. See also *P.O.* 1454 (Oxyrhynchus, 117 C.E.), an agreement of a baker to deliver baked loaves, each weighing 2 lbs., 30 loaves to the *artab*. (See above, notes 9 and 11.) 2 lb. loaves. (or slightly less) are also referred to in *P. Flor.* 322, (above, note 9); also *Scriptores Historiae Augustae, Aurelian* 36.

14 See West and Johnson, *Currency*, p. 125.

15 *Catalogue of Greek and Latin Paypri in John Rylands Library*, ed. Turner & Roberts, 4, p. 126.

16 But cf. Pliny, *Hist. Nat.* 17.4 (line 17). For the identity of costs of 1 lb. meat and 1 *log* (= pint) wine, see also M. Sanhedrin 8.2; Y. Sanhedrin 8.2, B. Sanhedrin 70a.

17 Ed. Graser, pp. 321–23.

18 But see Graser, ibid., line 12, Phoenician (date) honey, 1 Italian pint costs 8 d., i.e. the same as a pint of cheap wine (Chap. II, 10). The Mishna would appear to be talking of bees' honey. See also T. Bava Kama 10. 25, 26. According to *P.O.* 1733 (of 390), bees' honey costs 25 *xest.* per *sol*. Cf. the much later (IV cent.) *P. Nessana* 85, according to which 21 *xest.* honey cost 1 *sol*.

19 In Egypt, however, it would appear that oil was many times more expensive than wine. Thus if we accept Segrè's equation of *ceramion* = *metrates* (*Econ. Surv.*, 2, p. 467), then we may calculate the following price-relationships: According to *P. Amherst* 126/7 (Hermopolis, 110 or 130 C.E.), oil cost 17 times as much as wine. According to *P. Ross Georg.* II, 41 (II cent.) oil costs 4–8 times as much as wine. (*Econ. Surv.*, 2, p. 314–17. (In the above we have reckoned the *drachma* at 6 *obols*; see West and Johnson, *Currency*, p. 43 et seq.)

20 The use of this unit system of price-relationship is demonstrated in the following examples:

Example 1: If 1 *xest.* wine cost 1 unit and 1 *modius* wheat cost 8 units and 1 *ceramion* wine = 72 *xest.* Then 1 *art.* wheat cost 8 × 3 1/3 = 26 units and 1 *xest.* wine cost (1 *ceramion*/72). Therefore, 1 *art.*, wheat cost (1 *ceramion* wine /72) × 26. 1 *ceramion* = 1 *metrates* (Segrè); *Econ. Surv.*, 2, p. 467; (see also *Econ. Surv.*, 4, p. 394). 1 *metrates* = 12 *choes* = 144 *cotylae*, (ibid.). Therefore 1 *xest.* = 2 *cotylae. BGU.* 14 (Memphis, 255 C.E.). (*Econ. Surv.*, 2, pp. 311, 315.) 1 *ceramion* wine: 28, 40, or 52 dr. 1 *art.* wheat cost 16 dr. (28, 40, or 52/72) × 26 = 10 1/9, 14 4/9 or 24 1/7. Average = 16 dr. = cost of 1 *art.* wheat.

Example 2: *P. Lond.* 1226 (Theadelphia 254 C.E.) (ibid.) 1 *art.* wheat cost 12 dr. 1 *monochoron* wine cost 8 dr. 4 *monochoron* = 1 *ceramion* (ibid., p. 467), therefore 1 *ceramion* wine cost 32 dr. (32/72 × 26) = 11 5/9 dr. almost exactly the same as the cost of 1 *art.* wheat (12 dr.). But see *P. Goodsp.* 30 (Caranis 199 C.E.): *BGU.* 1717 (Theadelphia III cent.). *Econ. Surv.*, ibid., pp. 311–12, 314–15, where these methods lead to very different results. See also Mickwitz, *Geld und Wirtschaft*, p. 73. It should, however, again be stressed that this table is no more than a working hypothesis, meant as a rough guide to scale-ratios.

21 *Rova* = ¼ *kav*. See Jastrow, *Dict.*, p. 1456a.

22 *Ulka* = 1/8 *litra* = 1/8 *log*. B. Bava Batra 80a.

22a See A. Goor's remarks in *Economic Botany*, 21/3, 1967, p. 222.

23 But note "cleaned" and cf. *Ed. Diocl.* lines 24, 25. We understand the Mishna to be talking of cleaned rice, since "uncleaned" rice — i.e. with the husks — was not considered proper edible food. See J. Feliks, "Rice in Rabbinic Literature," in *Bar-Ilan*, 1, Jerusalem, 1961, pp. 181–82, (Hebrew).

24 Chap. VI, p. 334.

25 Of course the *Edict of Diocletian* is of a hundred years later. Furthermore, its purpose was to bring down prices to a "normal" standard, perhaps as much as four times cheaper than their actual standard. Thus the Mishnaic prices may well accord with actual prices of c. 301 C.E., but then they would be abnormally high — see Diocletian's introduction to his *Edict*, ed. Graser p. 314 — whereas we take it that the Mishna is speaking in terms of normal price standards.

26 In the above we have reckoned the *artab* as 3 1/3 *modii* (St. Jerome, *Comm. on Dan.* 11.5. See also *The Book of Paradise of Palladius*, ed. E.A. Wallis Budge, London, 1904, 2, p. 582 = 2, p. 428, fol. 195b, ad init.). But there were a number of *artab* measures varying from 57 3/5 *sextarii* to 78 *sextarii*, according to Segrè in *Metrologia*, p. 35; (see also *Econ. Surv.*, 2, p. 466). We have also reckoned the *denarius* as equalling 24 *obols*. (6 *obols* = 1 *drachma*, 4 *drachmae* = 1 *denarius*.) However sometimes *tetradrachms* (= *denarii*) were rated at 28 or 29 *obols*, (West and Johnson, *Currency*, pp. 2, 6, 7, 47, 49–50, 72 etc.). Furthermore, in certain papyri, around 270–290, it appears that the *drachma* and *denarius* were equated, (*P.O.* 1414, *P.O.* 1718, West and Johnson, *Currency*, p. 72). Thus while in the above lists we have translated *obols* into *denarii*, and *artabs* to *modii*, to make comparisons possible, there is no clear guarantee of the accuracy of any individual price listed. However, the total resultant picture is, in all probability, fairly accurate. The material is taken from *Econ. Surv.*, 2, pp. 310–12, etc., and Johnson and West, *Byzantine Egypt*: *Economic Studies*, pp. 176, 183, etc. (See further Callu, *PMER*, pp. 395–402 for additional material on prices.)

27 Continued from above section: "Wheat-Bread-Wine-Meat". On the whole issue of bread wheat and flour, see the excellent study of L.A. Moritz, *Grain Mills and Flour in Antiquity* (Oxford, 1958).

28 They obviously were not given anything for the cost of milling etc. other than their own 25%. Had they been paid for this they would have received 25% more or 1/6 d.

29 E.g. Egypt, c.1 C.E., 1 *mod.* wheat cost 1/4 d.; 1 loaf bread cost 1/48 d. c.45 C.E. 1 *mod.* wheat (average) cost ½ d.; 1 loaf bread cost 1/24 d. etc. For a breakdown of the cost of a loaf of bread in Mamluk Palestine and Egypt, see E. Strauss, *Toldot ha-Yehudim be-Mizrayim ve-Suria*, etc., 2, p. 143.

30 Sometimes the allowances in Egypt were more generous, e.g. 4 single loaves per day, as in *P. Flor.* 322, *P. Flor.* 135, *PSI.* 1050, all from Theadelphia and dating around 250 C.E. See further Richard Duncan-Jones in *Papers of the British School at Rome*, 33, NS 20, 1965, pp. 222–23, for further examples of these higher rates, (and their approximate calorific value). For the whole subject of bread and wheat costs, see Segrè, in *Aegyptus*, 30, 1950, pp. 180–89, and also Szilági in *AAH*, 11, 1963, p. 380.

31 The following information is based upon the material contained in *Econ. Surv.*, 2, pp. 306–10, Johnson and West, *Byzantine Egypt*, p. 194, Segrè, *Circolazione*, pp. 118–21, Mickwitz, *Geld und Wirtschaft*, pp. 226–28.

32 West and Johnson, *Currency*, p. 81. Johnson in *JJP*, 4, 1950, p. 156 gives the following wheat averages: I cent. ½ d. per *mod.*; II cent. 2/3 d. per *mod.*; early III cent. 1 d. per *mod.* For 245–46 he gives prices of 1–1 1/3 per *mod.* For 269 (*P. Erlangen* 101), 2 d. per *mod.*; (but this may be a famine price, *JJP*, ibid., note 24). For 276 the price has risen to 15 d. per *mod.*, (*P. Mich.* 1. 157, corrected by Youtie in *TAPA*, 76, 194–95, pp. 144–47). For 293, add: *P.O.* 2142, 23 d. per *mod.* For Western wages (eg. Pompeii, 5 *asses* per day, *CIL*, 4. 400), see Szilági, *AAH*, 11, 1963, pp. 345–52.

Chapter XVII

1 *In Wheat Studies of the Food Research Institute* (Stanford University, California, 20/4, March, 1944), pp. 137–70, article entitled: "Wheat Prices and Milling Costs in Classical Rome". See further Richard Duncan-Jones in *Papers of the British School at Rome*, 33, NS 20, 1965, pp. 221–22 (with bibliography) and p. 224, where it is shown that land was cheaper in Egypt than elsewhere.

2 Basing himself on Pliny, *Hist. Nat.* 18.20.90. See his extensive bibliography in *Wheat Studies* (note 1), for earlier scholarly opinions, notably that of Rostovtzeff; in Pauly-Wissowa *Real-Encycl.* s.v. Frumentum, etc.

3 Ed. Zuckermandel, p. 675, lines 21–23.

4 Jastrow, *Dict.*, p. 84a, s.v. אונטלייא. See my note in *Jewish Review*, Oct. 30, 1968, p. 7, where I suggested that *antlia* here refers to a type of pump used for bailing water out of the boats which must have been used to transport the wheat from Egypt to Palestine. We find such a meaning for the word in a mediaeval Arabic source, preserved in the Cairo Geniza (TS 8 J19, f. 27, lines 3–8, cited by S.D. Goitein, in his *A Mediterranean Society*, 1, 1967, pp. 320–21, 483): "This is to inform you that I arrived safely . . . after a journey of eight days . . . Water seeped into the ship and I worked the pumps ('ntly') from the day we left *Alexandria*. Each man had to bail fifty buckets of water in a shift, each bucket being the size of half a Byzantine bucket", (Goitein, ibid., p. 321). Thus, the pump used for draining the water out of the ship is called an "*antlia*", (Goitein, p. 483, note 55). This explanation is indeed borne out by classical sources, which use the verb ἀντλέω with the meaning to bale out bilge water from a ship (Liddell & Scott², 166a, s.v. ἀντλέω). ἀντλία itself (just like ἄντλος) means "bilge water" (Liddell & Scott², ibid., s.v. ἄντλος). See *Jewish Review*, ibid. for a discussion of the exact halachic status of sea-water in buckets, etc. For the classical interpretations of this term, see S. Liebermann, *Tosefet Rishonim*, 4 (Jerusalem, 1939), pp. 15, 115, and his remark, ibid., 2 (Jerusalem, 1938), p. 200. The above explanation bears out Krauss' conjectures in *Talmudische Archäologie*, 2 (Leipzig, 1911), pp. 167, 343 (followed by Feliks, *Agriculture in Palestine* etc., p. 336).

5 Louis Ginzberg in his Hebrew University Public Lecture (1st Adar 5689, published afterwards in Jerusalem 1931, and subsequently as a chapter in his book *Al Halacha ve-Aggada*, Tel-Aviv, 1960, pp. 13–40) entitled "Mekomah shel ha-Halacha be-Chochmat Yisrael", p. 37, note 4, basing himself mainly on R. Simeon of Sens,

explains the *antlia* as being a pump with which water was brought from the river (or canals) to the fields for irrigation. In other words, a water-wheel. (See also Z. Frankel, *Darkei ha-Mishna*, p. 36, Krauss, *LW*, 2, s.v. אונטליא and Löw's comments in *LW*, ibid., Zeitlin, *JQR*, 1971, etc.) However, this explanation is not only halachically problematic, but also difficult to accept on both historical and philological grounds. Historically, the water-wheel was not introduced into Egypt until some fifty years later. (See Strabo 17.1.30; Winlock and Crum, *The Monastery of Epiphanius at Thebes*, 1926, 1, pp. 64–65, Rostovzeff, *SEHRE*[2], p. 669, note 44, and his *Social and Economic History of the Hellenistic World*, 3, p. 1645, etc.). Philologically, one would have expected one of the local Coptic terms, *kados* or *tollenos*, (Crum, *Coptic Dictionary*, p. 650b; M. Schnebel, *Die Landwirtschaft im Hellenistischen Ägypten*, 1925, p. 356; Rostovtzeff, *Large Estate* etc., p. 49; Spiegelberg, *Göttingen Abhandlungen*, 1917, p. 77; Reil, *Beiträge* etc., p. 82). See finally, *Econ. Surv.*, 2, pp. 14–15.

6 Ginzberg, *Mekomah shel ha-Halacha*, p. 6.

7 Ibid., pp. 5–6. B. Shabbat 14b. Y. Pesaḥim 1.6.

8 Johnson and West, *Byzantine Egypt*, p. 160. Cost of transport from Alexandria to Rome and Byzantium in *Ed. Diocl.* 16% and 12% respectively. *Edict XIII* of Justinian 10%. Constantine (342) allowed 4% to shipowners as cost of transport from Alexandria to Byzantium. From Alexandria to Ascalon, e.g., is only a fraction of the distance from Alexandria to Rome or Byzantium, although, of course, the fraction of the cost is considerably higher than the fraction of the distance. See also *Giulio Jacopi, Gli scavi della Missione Arachaeologica Italiana ad Afrodisiade nel 1937*, XV–XVI; *Monumenti Antichi*, 1939, XXXVIII. Cf. Jasny, *Wheat Studies*, p. 145b. But cf. Libanius, *Epistles* 549–50 (of 358?) on Julian's journey and the remarks of Liebeshutz, in *Rheinisches Museum für Philologie*, 104/3, 1961, p. 242; also Segrè in *Byzantion*, 16, 1942–43, pp. 400–02.

Chapter XVIII

1 See also Bolin, *State and Currency*, p. 323, and his approach to this problem, and see my remarks on his views in *JRS*, 56, 1966, pp. 194–95.

2 Citing *P. Tebt.* 394, *P. Fay.* 333, *S.B.* 7181, *P.O.* 1753 and 1920, *P. Cairo Masp.* 67330 and 67141. It should be noted that in Egypt price variations are particularly great, see below, note 10.

3 See Segrè's remark in *Byzantion*, 16, 1942–43, p. 395: "The Edict, hastily applied to the provinces of Diocletian..." Cf. Mommsen *Das Edict* etc., p. 50, and see my own conclusions in *JRS*, 56, 1966, p. 195. See also Guarducci, *Rendiconti dei Lincei*, 1963, pp. 43–50, and J. Robert's remarks there on in *Revue des Etudes Grecques*, 77, 1964, pp. 140–41. (My thanks to Dr. R.P. Duncan-Jones for calling my attention to this latter reference.)

4 Note also that according to Y. Ma'aser Sheni 4.1, Nicolaus dates were cheaper in Palestine than in Rome, — such dates are mentioned in *Ed. Dicol.* VI, 81–82, Ed. Graser, p. 336 — and compare Bar Kappara's advice cited in B. Berachot 62b from which it appears that figs were also cheaper in Palestine than in Rome, (at least in certain seasons),so much so that it paid to transport them to Rome and sell them there.

5 This term does not appear in Rabbinic literature, yet its absence is no indication that the measure was not used. Thus the *sestertius* is not mentioned either, yet *sestertii* were certainly known. The *chous* would probably be reckoned in terms of local measures — *logs*. It may of course be that *gerev* here = *kav* (= 4 *log* = 4 *xestes*). In that case each *log* (= *xestes*) would cost approximately 1/40 *aureus*. In terms of *Ed. Diocl.* (800 d. — 1 *aureus*), 1 *xestes* cost 20 d. This seems rather unlikely but not impossible. It only strengthens our following argument. See also *Econ. Surv.*, 4, p. 185. I do not know how Heichelheim reached these conclusions. Epiphanius (Syriac version, ed. J.E. Dean, p. 6, note 383) erroneously equates (philologically) the *chous* with the *kuza*. (See Jastrow, *Dict.*, p. 618a. Cf. Brockelmann, *Lexicon Syriacum²*, p. 320b, and *Additamenta ad Aruch Completum*, ed. S. Krauss, p. 219b.) The *gerev* was larger than a "*kuz*" or "*legin*" (see Y. Mo'ed Katan 2.2, and Y. Megila 1.6). See Y. Brand, *Klei Haheres Besifrut Hatalmud*, pp. 82–96, especially p. 94, notes 39, 40 and 41. Similarly the measures of length *pes*, *gradus* and the fathom, though never mentioned in Rabbinic literature, were clearly known, as they occur in the form of "*shi'urim*" — legal measures — expressed as 4 *tefahim* (= handbreadths), 10 *tefahim*, or 4 *amot* (= cubits). See my remarks in *Journal of Jewish Studies*, 20/1–4, 1969, pp. 81–86.

6 Reckoned at 1/60 d. (= 1 *aureus*).

7 *Ed. Diocl.*, Graser ed., pp. 311–17.

8 *Gr. Pap.* II.27, Oasis, late III cent. See Johnson and West, *Byzantine Egypt: Economic Studies*, p. 178.

9 One cannot be more accurate without knowing the exact date, and the exact ratio of the *drachma* to the *aureus* at that date. Hence this is only a very rough estimate.

10 E.g. compare *P.O.* 1733, 160 dr. per *ceramion* (= 72 *xest.*) and *P. Baden* 26, Hermopolis, dated 293, 5 dr. per *ceramion*. For wine prices from the West, see Szilági, in *AAH*, 11, 1963, pp. 340–42. The price of wine in Pompeii is recorded in *CIL*, 4. 16679 (1 *sext.*: 1–4 *asses*).

11 Compare the prices recorded in *The Archives of Theophanes*, above, Chap. X.

12 Compare the prices recorded in the *The Archives of Theophanes*, above, Chap. XV, where fish-sauce is more expensive than wine.

13 Neubauer, *La Géographie du Talmud* (Paris, 1868), p. 408; Hirschensohn, *Sheva Chochmoth* (London, 1912), p. 196, and cf. p. 231.

14 Neubauer, ibid., pp. 28, 304; Hirschensohn, ibid., p. 40; Kohut, *Aruch Completum*, 1, pp. 188b, 298a, etc.; Buber, *Tanhuma Exod.* p. 28, note 111; I.S. Horowitz, *Palestine and the Adjacent Countries*, pp. 323–34, 66–67, (Hebrew); Bacher, *Aggadat ha-Tannaim*, 1/2, p. 54. It should be noted that both Apamaea and Pelusium produced non-kosher fish too, byt apparently did not export it to Caesarea. As Caesarea was by no means a "Jewish City", it may well be that the fish trade was monopolized by Jews.

15 Aelian 12.29, *Gen. Rab.* 5.8 (ed. Theodor, p. 38, line 2).

16 Abu al-fida (c. 1321) tells us that the "sea of Apamaea" was famous for its "ankalis" fish, which looks like a snake, clearly an eel — ἐγχελυς. See *Palestine Under the Moslems*, Guy le Strange, pp. 70, 420. This was nothing to do with the "Spanish Kolias" (contra Horowitz, *Palestine and the Adjacent Countries*, p. 327a, note 3). See Talmudic dictionaries. For Aelian's σιλουρος (see preceding note), see Löw, "Aramäische Fishnamen", apud *Nöldeke Festschrrift*, ed. Carl Bezold (Giessen, 1906), s.v. שיבוטא, קוליס and σιλουρος. It is clearly a "sheat fish", as in Liddell &

Scott[2], p. 1599a, s.v. *σίλουρος*, as is evident from Syriac sources, eg. Jacob. Edess. *Hex.* 45v (= Bar Kepha, *Hex.* 130r; cf. *Menarat K.* ms. 48b). (Cf. also Athenaeus, 7, 309–22.) The Loeb translation of "large perch" (Aelian, 3, p. 44) appears to be mistaken. See also Ritter, *Syrien*, 2, 1075, (cf. 1004, 1201, 1208, 1617, 1619), cited by Löw, *Aramäische Fischnamen*, ibid. See most recently, my article in *ZDMG*, 1969, pp. 265–69. (Löw's article has been reprinted in his *Fauna und Mineralien der Juden*, Hildesheim, 1969, pp. 3–24.)

17 Cf. *Tanḥuma Buber*, Exod., p. 28, note 111; *Sifré Ekev*, 39, ed. Friedmann, 78a, note 12; *Gen. Rab.*, ed. Theodor, p. 38, line 2.

18 The equivalent of "coals to Newcastle".

19 Horowitz, *Palestine and the Adjacent Countries*, p. 324.

20 Perhaps if one hugged the coastline, as one might when going from Laodicea to Akko, there were these dangers, but not if one came in from the open sea(?). The whole statement is somewhat problematic. Were they confusing Tyre with Antioch(!), past which the ship may also have gone? See Julian, *Or.* I, 41a, Loeb ed., 1, pp. 104–5.

21 Such a journey might take about four days. See Jean Rougé, *Récherches sur l'Organisation du Commerce Maritime en Méditerranée sous l'Empire Romaine* (Paris, 1966), pp. 101–05, especially p. 103, citing durations of journeys (North to South): Antioch to Alexandria (about 800 kilometres) 10 days, (sources ibid.). On the speed of travel in general and difficulties in calculating it, see Rougé, ibid., pp. 99–101. See also L. Casson, "Speed under Sail of Ancient Ships", in *TAPA*, 82, 1951, pp. 136–48; also Johnson and West, *Byzantine Egypt: Economic Studies*, p. 141. For eastern Mediterranean routes in general, Rougé, ibid., pp. 86–87, 91; Johnson and West, ibid., pp. 140–141. For eastern Mediterranean coastal ports, Rougé, ibid., pp. 127–28.

22 It had to compete with a local market round the Sea of Galilee, which was within easy reach of Akko. See Y. Shabbat 8.1 = Y. Pesaḥim 10.1, B. Pesaḥim 109a. For fishing around Tiberias, see Heichelheim in *Econ. Surv.*, 4, p. 154. Note the name Taricheae (dried fish), a place near Tiberias. Cf. S. Krauss, *Kadmoniot ha-Talmud*, 2/2 (Tel-Aviv, 1929), p. 217. Tarichaea is also called Migdal Nunia (= Tower of Fishes) in B. Pesaḥim 56a, and in the Kalir. See *Sefer ha-Yishuv*, 1, ed. S.Klein, p. 136, and M.Avi-Yonah in *QDAP*, 1935, study entitled "A Map of Roman Palestine", p. 36.

23 The distance from Akko to Tiberias is about 50 kilometres. There was a good road connecting these two cities. See Avi-Yonah, *QDAP*, ibid., p. 179 [= p. 41], and also his *Historical Geography of Palestine* etc., (Jerusalem, 1962, Hebrew), pp. 84–86 (no Ia [2]).

24 Note that R.A.G. Carson, in *Revue Numismatique*, 1965, p. 255, has dated Aurelian's monetary reforms, and his introduction of the XXI coin to the beginning of 274. This tallies very well with our dating of this *"lumma"* text. The *"lumma"* was no doubt a new term connected with the reform, useful (as it took the place of the *sestertius* as a unit of reckoning) and likely to be used then.

25 13 ½ d. per *xestes*.

26 II.10, Graser, p. 322.

27 *Muries* is, in fact, inferior to *garum*; see Mart. 13.103; Aur. Vict., *De Vir. Ill.*, 66. On *garum*'s price in Ascalon, c. 317–22, see *P. Ryl.* + 637, 428, and compare Antiochene prices of wine in *P. Ryl.* 629. 44, 363, 267, + 631 ii 91. The material is assembled in the price lists above, Chap. XV.

28 III. 6, 7. Graser, p. 323. L. Casson in *TAPA*, 70, 1939, p. 15, shows that in Byzantine Egypt from the IV to the VII cents., there were three grades of wine, (1) cheap wine costing from 1/500 to 1/792 *sol.* per *sextarius*, (2) medium priced wine costing from 1/150 to 1/336 *sol.* per *sextarius*, and (3) expensive wine costing 1/50 *solidus* per *sextarius*. The cheapest wine in the *Edict of Diocletian* (II, 10) costs 1/100 *aureus* per pint (= *sextarius*) again showing that Egyptian price-levels are consistently lower than those of the *Edict* (and those of Palestine).

29 *Scriptores Historiae Augustae, Severus Alexander*, 22.8 (Loeb ed. 2, p. 220), note 1: price of 1 lb. beef and pork is 8 *minituli*. Mommsen (*Röm. Münzwesen*, p. 783) equates the *minitulus* with the debased *denarius*. According to the *Edict of Diocletian* (IV. 1a–2), 1 lb pork costs 12 d. and 1 lb. beef 8 d. But in *Aurelian* 9.7 (Loeb ed. 3, p. 211, see notes 1 and 2), we read: *argenteos Philippeos minitulos . . . aeris denarios . . .* Thus "*aeris denarius*" = *denarius*; (in Diocletian's time some of the so-called "silver" coins had almost no noticeable silver content). Thus *minitulus arg.* probably refers to the *antoninianus* (= 2 d.). Hence the price of beef and pork was 16 d., and therefore *above* the maximum price. It was subsequently reduced to 2 or 3 *minituli* per pound, (= 4 or 2 d.), (see *Scriptores Historiae Augustae, Severus*, ibid.).

30 *CIL*, 8. 4508; *JRS*, 4, 1914, pp. 143–46; *Econ. Surv.*, 4, pp. 80–82.

31 *P. Lips.*, II, V.

32 Cf. Martial (d.106) 12.76: 20 *asses* per *amphora* wine = 1/30 d. per *xest.*; Columella (c.50) 3.310: ordinary Italian wine, 60 *asses* per *amphora*, = 1/10 d. per *xest.* See *Econ. Surv.*, 5, p. 273, note 1. Of course, wine prices are particularly deceptive as they vary so radically according to place, type and season. Cf. above note 28.

33 Johnson in his article on "Roman Egypt in the Third Century", *JJP*, 4, 1950, writes: "The extraordinary expenditure on public works during the third quarter of the century is clear evidence of prosperity", (p. 151, referring to *P.O.* 1450 of 249–50, *P.O.* 54 of 261, *Archiv f. Papyrusforsch*, 4,115, Antinoopolis 258). "There was no apparent cause in Egyptian internal economy for the sudden rise in prices under Aurelian. Presumably Mediterranean price-levels had risen due to inflation in the imperial currency under Gallienus or Claudius, and this was speedily reflected in the Egyptian open market for grain," (Johnson, ibid., pp. 156–57). See also his remarks in *Aegyptus*, 32, 1952, p. 70, especially note 4.

34 See Callu, *PMER*, p. 187.

Chapter XIX

1 To this we may add that "there is no indication of a significant change in price-levels in the period covered by parchments and papyri from Dura", which extend from the late I cent. to about 254. (See price lists above, Chap. XV.) *Dura, Final Report*, 5/1, ed. Ann Perkins (New Haven, 1959), p. 8. Cf. Johnson in *JJP*, 4, 1950, p. 156: "Inflation in prices quoted in terms of fiduciary currency suddenly became acute (in Egypt) during Aurelian's reign."

2 Cf. D. Magie, *Roman Rule in Asia Minor* (Princeton, 1950), 1, p. 713.

3 See for example, *P.O.* 1411 (referred to above, Chap. XII) according to which the banks did not wish to accept the official "silver" coins.

4 The annual salary of a *trecanarius* fell from 70 lbs. gold to a nominal 1½ lbs. gold (Kent, in *Mattingly Festschrift*, p. 191). Note also that Caracalla halved the value

of the *denarius*, but increased army wages only by a half (from 500 d. to 750 *per annum*). See Jones, *The Later Roman Empire*, 1, p. 29, 3, p. 6, note 25 (*Pan. Lat.* 6.11) etc.

5 *ANSMN*, 4, 1954, p. 9, article entitled "Ancient Money and Modern Commentators". Cf. Johnson in *JJP*, 4, 1950, p. 151.

6 *CNP*, 2, p. 38.

7 *CNP*, 4, pp. 39, 55–58.

8 *CNP*, 1, p. 26.

9 *INCP*, pp. 240–42.

10 "Die Kleinasiatischen Münzen der römischen Kaisarzeit", in *Arch. Anzeiger*, 1931, p. 430. See also D. Magie, Roman Rule in Asia Minor, p. 710; E. Gren, *Kleinasien und der Ostbalkan in der Wirtschaftlichen Entwicklung der römischer Kaizerzeit* (Uppsala Universitets Arsskrift, 9, 1941), p. 5; and recently B. Levick, *Roman Colonies in Asia Minor* (Oxford, 1967), pp. 170–72. But see Magie, *Roman Rule*, 2, p. 1550, note 38. For a survey of the bronze coinage of the III cent. in the eastern Empire, see most recently Callu, *PMER*, chap. 1, a chapter very rich in pertinent material. See also Carson, *BMC*, 6, pp. 10–16, and E. Schönert-Geiss' article entitled "Das Ende der Provinzialprägung in Thrakien und Mösien", *Klio*, 50, 1968, pp. 251–55. See finally *Econ. Surv.*, 4, pp. 912–3.

11 Cf. D. Magie, *Roman Rule in Asia Minor*, 1, p. 713. Above, Chap. XII, we noted the greater emphasis on gold and gold bullion, also part of the same pattern. Likewise, the change from money taxation to taxation in kind reflects the same trend. See particularly *Lev.Rab.* 15.9, ed. Margulies, p. 338 (R. Aba b. Kahana) מדד הביא מדד הביא. See G. Allon, *Toldot ha-Yehudim be-Eretz Yisrael be-Tekufat ha-Mishna ve-ha-Talmud*, 1955, 2, pp. 182 et seq.; Jones,The Later Roman Empire, 1,pp.30–31 etc.

12 Contra West in *ANSMN*, 7, 1957, p. 110. See also West, ibid., p. 109. See Callu, *PMER*, p. 27.

13 Carson, *INCP*, p. 242.

14 *CNP*, 4, p. 55, Akko Ptolemais, metallic content of coins better, size large, post c.225. In Antioch too the coins of this period have a larger module; see B. Levick, *Roman Colonies in Asia Minor*, p. 171. See further Callu, *PMER*, p. 29.

15 See *INCP*, pp. 247–48; Callu, *PMER*, p. 110.

16 *BMC*, 5 (Mattingly, London, 1951), pp. 21–22. See also Jones, *The Later Roman Empire*, 1, p. 27. See further Callu, *PMER*, pp. 57–58 on the value of the local "*assarion*", etc., and p. 109. See also *CNP*, 2, pp. 78–9.

17 See *Econ. Surv.*, 4, p. 892; *OGIS*, 484, etc. See also A.R. Bellinger, in *Mattingly Festschrift*, p. 147.

18 See West in *ANSMN*, 4, 1954, p. 6: "In the fifteen years from 253 to 268, probably the darkest period in Roman history, enough different types of gold coinage are known to average about one every three weeks for the entire period". This is, of course, not a very accurate index of the actual bulk of coinage in circulation.

19 See H. Mattingly, *Roman Coins*[2] (London, 1960), p. 174. *BMC*, 6, (Carson), pp. 36–38 lists such British hoards in Caiter by Yarmouth, Darfield, East Anglia, Falkirk, Kirkhan, Llanarmon, Nuneaton, St. Mary Cray, etc. Also in France, Germany, Italy, Rumania, Bulgaria, Albania, (*BMC*, ibid.). See also *BMC*, 3, p. XXX. Below, note 21, evidence of Dura hoards. West, *Gold and Silver Standards in the Roman Empire*, pp. 192–93, etc. Also Bolin's hoard analyses, *State and Currency* pp. 344 et seq.

20 The early dating of the reform seems to be clear from numismatic evidence. See West, *Gold and Silver Standards*, p. 89, table R ; Bolin, *State and Currency*, p. 208, note 1, and pp. 210–11. This reform and the debasement do not seem to have anything to do with the conquest of Dacia. Contra Heichelheim, *Klio*, 25, 1932, pp. 124 et seq., (cf. West & Johnson, *Currency*, p. 92), who is followed by several other scholars, eg. in Tenney Frank's *Econ. Surv.*, 4, p. 215; ibid., 2, pp. 425, 443–45; 5, p. 91 (cf. *P. Baden* 37; *CPR.* 12; *SPP.* XX.2; *P. Giss.* 47; *Wilcken Chr.* 326). See further A.C. Johnson in *AJA*, 38, 1934, p. 53; Mickwitz, *Geld und Wirtschaft*, pp. 32, 42; Segrè, *Metrologia*, pp. 428–30, etc. Cf. above, Chap. XII, note 6. See most recently Jaques Schwartz, *Annales, Economies, Sociétés, Civilisations*, 15/1, 1961, p. 42.

21 West, *Gold and Silver Standards*, p. 84. Cf. *Dura, Final Report*, A.R. Bellinger (New Haven, 1944), p. 203: "no coins from Augustus to Claudius", but of Anthony and Nero. His new coins were of the Nero-reform standard (about 111 grains). Domitian, Nero and "early Trajan" are of a heavier standard. See *BMC*, 3, pp. XIV–XV; Bolin, *State and Currency*, pp. 191–95. The whole issue gains visual clarity in Table H.

22 In *BMC*, 3, pp. LXXXVIII–LXXXIX.

23 On the distinctions between "coin" and "produce" see above, Chap. XI. For further discussion of the legal aspects of this problem, see Isaac Herzog's *The Main Institutions of Jewish Law* 1, "Law of Property" (London, 1916), pp. 163–66, 182, etc.; also Asher Gulak, *Yesod Ha-Mishpat Ha-Ivri*, 1 (Berlin, 1922), no. 36, pp. 107 et seq. This problem was touched upon by Heichelheim in *Econ. Surv.*, 4, p. 219.

24 On these coins see my article in *Sinai*, 55, pp. 37–41.

25 Ed. Zuckermandel, p. 86, lines 22–24; ed. S. Lieberman (New York, 1955), p. 244, lines 15–16.

26 Jewish legal texts discuss the degree of wear that invalidates a coin from being considered "current"; e.g. M. Bava Mezia 4.5, T. Bava Mezia 3.17 (p. 377, 21, etc.).

27 It is clear that silver coinage is here referred to, as no *aes* coinage of the first revolt bears the name Jerusalem, and it could therefore not be called "Jerusalem money". The "first kings" can therefore not refer to the later (= first?) Herodians, or procurators (= Kings?) as they never struck silver money. The author of this text is of the opinion that silver is "coin" and may therefore be used for substitution (i.e. the later opinion of Rabbi, see above, Chap. XI), if all else is well. Cf. M. Bava Mezia 4.1, etc.

28 A problematic term difficult to translate, usually meaning something like "invalidated".

29 Cf. S. Lieberman, *Tosefta ki-fshuta*, 2, p. 717, line 16 (and p. 716, lines 14–15), who offers different interpretations of these texts.

30 It was, not doubt to the government's advantage to accept such coinage, as legal tender, as it had a higher silver content than their own current coin, of the same nominal value. Had they not done so, it would no doubt have been melted down, and as bullion might possibly have been worth more than its nominal value as coin.

31 See West, *Gold and Silver Standards*, pp. 192–93, (Table AP) (our Table H). In Decius' hoards Republican coins are still represented. After Decius, in the hoards of Trebonius and Volusianus only one Nerva and one Domitian is found, nothing earlier. After Valerian, nothing pre-Hadrianic. The evidence when seen in tabular

form is strikingly convincing, and it appears that c.250–60, this early coinage was withdrawn. Can this evidence be related to Decius' overstriking of earlier (Severan) *denarii* (see H. Mattingly, The Great Dorchester Hoard of 1936, *Num. Chron.*, 1939, pp. 41–43)? See above, Chap. IV, note 42. [7]

32 See eg. Z. Frankel, *Mevo ha-Yerushalmi* (Breslau, 1870), 26a.

33 See e.g. J.N. Epstein, *Prolegomena ad Litteras Tannaitaicas* (ed. E.Z. Melamed, Jerusalem 1957), p. 252; ibid., p. 251–53, for a discussion of late *beraitot* in general. Also, ibid., p. 246, for Palestinian-Babylonian textual transmission, etc.

34 Epstein, *Prolegomena*, pp. 252–53. See also Ch. Albeck, *Mechkarim ba-beraita u-ba-Tosefta* (Jerusalem 1944), pp. 23, 26, 29, 31, 52–54, 88–89, 137–38, etc.

35 Jastrow, *Dict.*, p. 894a, s.v. נחותא. See W. Bacher, *Tradition und Tradenten in den Schulen Palästina und Babyloniens* (Leipzig, 1914), chap. XXXVI.

36 Cf. sources cited above, notes 32–33.

37 *Jewish Encyclopedia*, 12, p. 340a–b, s.v. Ulla; Bacher, *Tradition und Tradenten*, p. 519, etc.

38 See my article in *Num. Chron.*, 1970, pp. 111–15, where I first discussed this issue.

39 See Jones, *The Later Roman Empire*, I, p. 28.

40 West, in *ANSMN*, 4, p. 6; see Callu, *PMER*, p. 428.

41 West, ibid., p. 7.

42 West, ibid., p. 7.

43 See A. Kindler, *The Coins of Tiberias* (Tiberias, 1961), pp. 62–63. See also *Econ. Surv.*, 4, p. 897, referring to *OGIS*, 515.

44 R. Johanan also remembered when workers would not go to the east of the city, as the smell of bread being wafted into their nostrils would kill them, (B. Bava Batra, 91b, see commentators on this text). He himself suffered considerable poverty in his youth and was forced to sell his properties in order to be able to continue his studies, (*Lev. Rab.* 30.1, ed. Margulies, p. 689 and parallels). He almost left Palestine, so dire were his straits, (B. Ta'anit 21a). R. Johanan spent his earlier years in Sepphoris and moved to Tiberias probably during the thirties. (See Y. Beza 1.1, cf. B. Nidda 20b, and on this first text see the remarks of Halevy in *Dorot ha-Rischonim*, 2, p. 307, note 26, Hyman, *Toldoth Tannaim Ve'Amoraim*, p. 493b, and Z.W. Rabinowitz, *Shaare Torath Babel*, p. 432. Rabinowitz's explanation is without doubt the correct one. See Marmorstein in *Tarbiz*, 3/2, 1932, p. 178 (contra Krauss, in *Antoninus und Rabbi*, Wien 1910, p. 129).

45 In a parallel version in *Pesikta de R. Kahana*, ha-Ḥodesh, 3, ed. Mandelbaum, 1, p. 205, this statement is given in the name of R. Isaac, a friend and contemporary of R. Levi. There are a number of variations between the two versions; e.g. instead of "affliction" the *Pesikta* has "Kingdoms" (i.e. authorities), instead of "blessings and comfort", "Scripture and *Aggada*", etc.

46 It should however be noted that with the cessation in the activities of the local mints, there comes a great rise in the output of *antoniniani* by the imperial mints. The following statistics are taken from Callu, *PMER*, p. 198, note 1, (who bases himself on R. Göbl, "Der Aufbau der römischen Münzprägung in der Kaiserzeit", *Numismatische Zeitschrift*, 1951, pp. 8–45, 75, 1953, pp. 5–53). The first number represents the toal number of emissions in the emperor's reign; the second, the minimum number of annual emissions.

Septimius Severus	(193–211)	315	17
Caracalla	(198–217)	98	16
Macrinus	(217–218)	49	24
Elagabalus	(218–222)	61	20
Severus Alexander	(222–235)	105	7
Maximinus	(235–238)	21	7
Gordian III	(238–244)	83	14
Philip	(244–249)	85	17
Decius	(249–251)	40	14
Aemilianus	(253)	25	25
Valerian	(253–260)	366	58
Gallienus	(253–268)	514	64
Probus	(276–282)	1582	264
Carinus, etc.	(283–285)	173	86

Much the same picture emerges from Callu's statistics on *Ateliers* (first number) and *Officinae* (second number), (*PMER* p. 273):

238	1	6	259–268	6	29
238–244	2	9	268–269	7	33
244–249	3	10	269	6	25
249–251	2	12	269–274	9	43
251–253	3	15			
253	2	9			
253–259	4	15			

Chapter XX

1 In our Babylonian price-lists (above, Chap. XV) we have equated the *zuz* with the Sasanian *drachm*.

2 H.A. Manandian, in *The Trade and Cities of Armenia in Relation to Ancient World Trade* (Lisbon, 1965), p. 120, conjecturally suggests a ratio of 10:1, but has no real basis for this suggestion. It would appear that in IV cent. Babylonia the silver-gold ratio was not 12:1. See B. Zevaḥim 115b (and Tosafot *"gava"*; B. Ketubot 96a, Tosafot *"natan"*; *Yefei Einayim* of R. Aryeh Loeb Yellin ad loc.; Shevu'ot 44b, Tosafot *"hitkabalt"*; *Pirkei de R. Eliezer*, chap. 36, etc.) on the apparent contradiction between 2 Sam. 24.24 and 1 Chron. 21.25.

3 For exact weights in terms of maximum and minimum averages see Paruck (Furdoonjee, D.J.), *Sasanian Coins* (Bombay, 1924), pp. 37–38, and Mordtmann in *ZDMG*, 1880, p. 147.

4 See above, Chap. XV, section on Babylonian prices.

5 Cf. Manandian, *Trade and Cities in Armenia*, pp. 124–25, and cf. what I wrote in *JESHO*, 8, 1965, pp. 266–71.

6 Ed. Graser, p. 318.

6a Prof. M. Beer suggests to me that this change in price levels may have been the result of political events. The first price of geese is given by Rav Huna, ed. c. 298, the second by R. Ḥisda, d. c. 310. In the year 298 Diocletian made a treaty with Narseh, king of Persia, after the latter had been vanquished by Galerius, and his wife and children had been taken into captivity. As a result of this treaty Narseh lost Armenia, Meṣopotamia and parts of the left bank of the Tigris. (See Nöldeke, *Aufsätz zur Persischen Geschichte*, Liepzig 1887, p. 97; idem, *Tabari*, Leyden 1879, p. 50, note 3.) These events must surely have brought in their wake a raise in the price of Mesopotamian products. Rav Huna's statement was made before these events. Rav Ḥisda's after them. The Talmudic redactor, unaware of this background, presented the material in a somewhat different light.

7 Ed. Graser, p. 382.

8 This is as we would have expected. Silk was considered fabulously expensive; cf. *Scriptores Historiae Augustae, Aurelian*, 45. See Friendländer, *Roman Life and Manners* (English ed.) 2, p. 179; also F. Hirth, *China and the Roman Orient* (Shanghai and Hong Kong, 1885, reprinted in China, 1939), p. 225, and note 2. Silk was meant to have been weighed up against gold, not only according to Roman sources *Scriptores Historae Augustae*, ibid.), but: "The *Shuo-wen* published in A.D. 100 (see Wylie, p. 8), explains the character *chin*, an old name for the finest ornamental silk textures, as being composed with the radical *chin*, i.e. gold, "because its price was then equal to that of gold." (*Ko-chih-ching-yuan*, chap. 27, p. 4)" (Hirth, ibid.). (But was silk really so dear in China, or gold so cheap?) Cf. *Ed. Diocletian*, XXX.2 (ed. Graser, p. 412), according to which 1 lib. gold, drawn out *(χρυσου ἐνηγμενον)* cost 12,000 d., while the *Edict's* price for 1 lb. silk (XXXII, 1a, Graser p. 382) is also 12,000 d. In this connection it is interesting to note that Talmudic phrase טיריקון של זהב — "*σηρικον* of gold" in B. Kid. 31a, and B. Ḥagiga 16b; (cf. Rabbinowicz, *VL* to Ḥagiga, p. 65, note 10, and Krauss, *LW*, 2, pp. 393b–394a, and also 588b–589a, s.v. תירקי, and other Dictionaries). This may mean silk thread intertwined with gold thread (see Hirth, ibid., pp. 353–54; cf. Ed. Diocletian XX.7 etc.), a more likely explanation than silk material merely embroidered with gold thread; (see Krauss, *Kadmoniot ha-Talmud*, 2/2, p. 74, and Herszberg, *Ḥayyé ha-Tarbut be-Yisrael be-Tekufat ha-Mishna ve-ha-Talmud*, 1, Warsaw, 1924, p. 52). But, in view of the above Chinese source, may it not be that טיריקון של זהב means no more than pure silk (worth its weight in gold)? (See, however, Geiger, *Zeitschrift*, IV; Allon, *Meḥkarim*, 1, pp. 266 — Θωρακες). Note further that according to some Mss. readings in *Gen. Rab.* 40.5, ed. Theodor, p. 384, line 12 (in apparatus), the custom dues on silk were (in Palestine) higher than on gold; (cf. Herszberg, ibid., p. 54). The Babylonian price cited here is highly theoretical. Perhaps these price differences are due not merely to variations in transport costs, but also to the fact that silk was woven in Babylonia (and Syria), i.e. east of Rome and Byzantium. See J. Neusner, *A History of the Jews in Babylonia*, 1 (Leiden, 1965), p. 90, with bibliography; also Krauss, *Kadmoniot*, 2/2, p. 73, and note 4, etc. See also *The Doctrine of Addai, The Apostle*, ed. G. Phillips (London, 1876), p. 33.

9 B. Bava Mezia 65a, 115a; B. Bava Kama 115a; B. Temura 6b.

10 Ed. Graser, pp. 369–77.

11 See *Études de Papyrologie*, 1939, for a price from Caranis, 314; tunic: 4000 dr., cloak 5000 dr. (It is not clear whether the dr. = 1 d., or ¼ d.). See Johnson and West, *Byzantine Egypt: Economic Studies*, pp. 186–87, for Egyptian prices of clothing for the early IV cent. onwards. Due to terminological difficulties in Egyptian prices of this period, it is difficult to compare this material with our own.

256

12 Ed. Graser, p. 325.

13 Ed. Graser, p. 336.

14 Ed. Graser, p. 336.

15 In the note on the Babylonian prices (above, Chap. XV, note 45). Cf. *JESHO*, 9, 1966, p. 198.

16 II.10, ed. Graser, p. 332.

17 Cf. M. D. Judlewitsch, *Meḥoza* (Jerusalem, 1947), p. 21.

18 Ed. Graser, p. 331.

19 Ed. Graser, pp. 336–46.

20 Some of these workers get maintenance (cf. B. Bava Mezia 83a etc.). For Egyptian wages of the IV cent. onwards, see Johnson and West, *Byzantine Egypt: Economic Studies*, p. 194. For Egyptian wages of the I–IV cent. see the material mentioned above, Chap. XVI.

21 Ed. Graser, p. 336.

22 See, for example, J. Newman, *The Agricultural Life of the Jews in Babylonia* (London, 1932), p. 22 and note 6, with bibliography.

Chapter XXI

1 See comentators on this text.

2 See Hyman, *Toldoth Tannaim Ve, Amoraim*, pp. 64b–45b, Margalioth, *Encyclopedia le-Ḥachmei ha-Talmud*, 9, 10. He is called זמינא, זמונא, זבינא, אמינא. There was also a R. Aba b. Avina (Hyman, ibid., pp. 14b–15b), a pupil of Rav who could perhaps at times be confused with our R. Aba b. Zemina (through an interchange of א for י). However, in the Yerushalmi the latter is always called R. Ba (בא), and either b. Avina or b. Mina, but never Amina.

3 Y. Ta'anit 1.3.

4 See also J. N. Epstein, *Prolegomena ad litteras Amoraiticas* (Jerusalem, 1962), p. 592, for Leiden Ms. readings, or the photographic edition, (Jerusalem, 1970).

5 *Sha'are Torath Eretz Yisrael* (Jerusalem, 1940), p. 491. See his explanatory comments on Y. Bava Mezia 5.6.

6 I have reckoned at an average solar year of 365 days, minus the 7 days of Passover. I have also calculated according to the *minimum* amount of bread he would be likely to get. Cf. Richard Duncan-Jones in *Papers of the British School at Rome*, 33 (NS, 20), 1965, pp. 222–23. In the last quarter of the IV cent. the average yearly wage of a *grammaticus* was 1 *sol.* per pupil. See A. Cameron in *Classical Review*, 15, 1965, pp. 257–58, basing himself on *Anth. Pal.* 9.174 (Palladas).

7 I have not compared with III cent. prices, because of the many difficulties involved in evaluating them with any degree of accuracy. (See preceding chapter for the problems involved.) See also Bernardi, in *Studia Ghisleriana*, 3, Pavia, 1961, p. 301.

8 Discussed in detail in my article in *Archiv Orientalni*, 34, 1966, pp. 59–60.

9 Segrè, *Byzantion*, 15, p. 249, note 1, and see above, Chap. III, the discussion on this text.

10 Ed. Wright and McLean (Cambridge, 1898), p. 369; ed. Bedjan (Leipzig, 1897), p. 530. For a discussion of the Syriac version see above, Chap. III. See also S. Lieberman, in *Annuaire de l'Institut de Philologie et de l'histoire Orientales et Slaves*, 7,

1939–44, p. 434, note 4. Lieberman (ibid., p. 434) was right in regarding Eusebius' statement as plausible and indeed accurate, (contra Lawlor and Oulton, etc. See Lieberman, ibid.).

11 *P. Roll. Princ.* 4.31, see below, Chap. XXII.

12 Tosefta Avoda Zara 5.4, ed. Zuckermandel, p. 446, lines 4–9; B. Bava Batra 91a–b (III cent.). See my remarks in *Archiv Orientalni*, 34, p. 60, note 33. (For famine prices in Edessa in the year 501, see *The Chronicle of Joshua the Stylite*, ed. W. Wright Cambridge, 1882, p. 35.) See also the very strange, and as yet not satisfactorily explained, text in *Gen. Rab.* 25 ad fin., ed. Theodor, p. 243, line 2 (= p. 383, line 10 and parallels, etc.), a text from c. 290–320. See Theodor's note, ibid. Here I would very tentatively offer the following explanation: The rule is that prices would have to double before one can leave Palestine, (see ibid.). In the time of Ruth (Ruth 1.1) there was a famine that was bad enough to permit Elimelech to leave the country. Therefore prices must have doubled. The text reads: רעב שבא בימי השופטים ר׳ הונא בשם ר׳ דוסא מ״ב סאין היו ונעשו מ״א. (See also the interesting reading recorded in *VL* to Bava Batra 91a, p. 248, note 9.) However, a number of Mss (Paris, Oxford, Stuttgart, Munich, etc., see apparatus ibid.) read סאה. I would tentatively emend the text to read: מ״כ מאה היה ונעשה מ״א = 1 m[odius] c[astrensis] was (= cost) 100 d. (as in the price of the *Edict of Diocletian*), and that became the price of the m[odius] I[talicus]. (On CK), see Krauss, *LW*, 1, pp. 31–32, para. 43; 2, p. 295a, s.v. כצוצרא = *castra* and p. 317a, s.v. לכיס = λαῖκος, etc.). As the modius Italicus if half the *mod. castr.* the price doubled. However, this explanation is highly conjectural, if somewhat ingenious. Also cf. B. Gittin 57a (Egypt). Prof. Callu, (in a private communication of 5/3/73), calls my attention to an interesting passage in the *Historia Apollonii Regis Tyrii* (of the first half of the III cent.), according to which the price of wheat in Tyre was 8 *sestertii* (*octo aereis*) per *modius*, while at Tarsus during a famine it was 100 *sestertii*.

13 Eusebius, *Hist. Eccles.* 9.8.4, Loeb translation 2, p. 353, et seq.

14 *PER.E.*2000 Hermopolis 10,000 dr. per *art.* (= 750 d. per *mod. castr.*?) of the year 314; *SB.*7621, Philadelphia, 3000 dr. per *art.* (= 225 per *mod.*). See price lists above, Chap. XVI. But see Boak, *Harvard Studies*, 51, 1949, and my remark in *Archiv Orientalni*, 34, p. 60, note 33. Cf. West and Johnson, *Cuurency*, p. 122.

15 Line 55: טרפונוטי, correct to טרפוזוניטי = פריטיי׳ of Y. Kiddushin 1.6, (a parallel text). Cf. S. Liebermann, *The Talmud of Caesarea* (Supplement to *Tarbiz*, 2, Jerusalem, 1931), p. 43. See also Gulak's remark in *Tarbiz*, 2/2, 1931, p. 159.

16 For slight variant in Leiden Ms., cf. Epstein, *Prolegomena ad Litteras Amoraiticas*, p. 592 (line 49).

17 See *Pnei Moshe* (of R. Moses Margulies), on this text, and cf. his comments on Y. Kiddushin 1.6.

18 Ibid., s.v. מנא א״ר. Cf. *Mar'eh ha-Panim* (of R. Moses Margulies) and *Ridbaz* (R. Jacob David of Slutsk) on this text.

19 Hyman, *Toldoth Tannaim Ve'Amoraim*, pp. 885a–888b, Margalioth, *Encyclopedia*, 633–35. Jaawitz, *Toldot Yisrael*, 7, pp. 84–86. For R. Mana I, see Margalioth 633, Hyman, pp. 884a–885b, flor. c. 220–50.

20 I have discussed the chronology of R. Jona in my article in *Archiv Orientalni*, 34, 1966, pp. 61–62. He was alive during the period of Ursicinus' exploits in Palestine, c. 351. On Ursicinus, cf. recently Jones, *The Later Roman Empire* (Oxford, 1964), 1, p. 116, and 3, p. 19, note 8; (Socr. 2.33; Soz. 4.7). Also Graetz, Hebrew ed.

(Warsaw, 1893), 2, pp. 400–01. See also Lieberman in *JQR*, NS 36, 1945–46, p. 352, note 176, on R. Jona's chronology; ibid., pp. 336–41, on Ursicinus.

21 Hyman, *Toldoth Tannaim Ve'Amoraim*, thinks that he died c. 353 (p. 888a); Halevy, *Dorot Harischonim*, 2, pp. 368–72, 375–80, etc. puts him c. 300. Neither of these views can be correct for reasons suggested in the preceding note, namely that R. Mana appears to have outlived his father R. Jona by more than a few years, and R. Jona was alive c. 350. Halevy's main argument (p. 380) is based on Y. Ḥala 4.7, (no variants), where we find R. Bun (= Avin) b. Ḥiyya talking to R. Mana. R. Avin b. Ḥiyya was 3rd generation personality who lived for only 28 years, and who had studied with R. Johanan and Resh Lakish (Halevy, ibid.). (But see Rabinowitz's comment, in *Sha'are Torath Babel*, Jerusalem 1961, p. 333.) This however was probably R. Mana I (above, note 19), a contemporary of R. Johanan, (ibid., pp. 92b–93a, Margalioth, *Encyclopedia*, 784–86). They both (Ravin II and R. Mana II) lived in Sepphoris. See also Frankel, *Mevo-ha-Yerushalmi*, 115a, Lieberman, *JQR*, NS 36, 1945–46, p. 352, note 176.

22 Cf. *Cod. Theod.* 7.4.17 (389); 14.4.10 (419); *Nov. Val.* 13.4 (445); 36.2 (452). On prices in the IV cent. see L. Ruggini, *Economia e Societa nell' Italia Annonaria* (Milan, 1961), pp. 361–79; Bernardi, in *Studia Ghisleriana*, 3, Pavia, 1961, pp. 293, et seq., especially notes 208 and 215; and Adelson in *INCP*, pp. 269–74.

23 See *Tanḥuma Numbers*, ed. Buber, p. 145; *Ed. Diocl.* IV. 1a, 2.

24 See *Cod. Theod.* 14.4.2–4 (324–26; 362; 367).

25 Cf. *Nov. Val.* 32.2, of 452, where 240 lbs. of pork cost 1 *sol*. Cf. Mickwitz, *Geld und Wirtschaft*, p. 87. However, one would have imagined that these would be low prices.

26 *Gen. Rab.* 49.4.

27 Cf. Bolin, *State and Currency*, p. 305.

28 According to West & Johnson, in *Currency*, p. 167.

29 Contra Jones, in *JRS*, 49, 1959, p. 37. Cf. Mickwitz, *Geld und Wirtschaft*, pp. 86–87; Ruggini, *Rendiconti d. Lincei*, 1962, pp. 314–16; and Adelson, in *INCP*, pp 269–70, who discusses this price in detail.

30 *JRS*, 49, p. 37.

31 Contra Segrè, *Byzantion*, 15, p. 268. Note that according to this calculation there are now 10 d. in a *follis*, not 5, as in Diocletian's time, and as late as c. 324. Is this because the *denarius* was halved in value, while the *follis* stayed firm, or that the *follis* doubled in value while the *denarius* stayed firm? Cf. Mickwitz, *Geld und Wirtschaft*, p. 95. According to Casson in *TAPA*, 70, 1939, p. 15, from the IV to the VII cent. the average cost of medium-priced wine was 1/150–1/336 *sol*. per *sextarius*. (See above, Chap. XVIII, note 28.) See Adelson in *INCP*, pp. 270, 278.

32 See Adelson in *INCP*, p. 274.

33 Contra Segrè, *Byzantion*, 15, p. 268. Cf. West and Johnson, *Currency*, p. 164, and Adelson in *INCP*, p. 275.

34 Suggestions of West & Johnson, in *Currency*, p. 131; Segrè, *Metrologia*, p. 479; Ruggini, *Rendiconti dei Lincei*, 1962, p. 312. Cf. Segrè, Maia, 16, 1964, pp. 272–75. See, however, Adelson's discussion in *INCP*, pp. 273–78.

Chapter XXII

1 Ed. Zuckermadnel, p. 23, line 20; ed. Lieberman, p. 57, lines 26–27.

2 The various readings of this word are as follows: (a) ארגרן (regular ed.) or
(b) ארגדן (Krotoschin ed.), (c) ארגולן, Sirilio Ms. (B. M. Or. 2822 fol. 162a),
(d) אגרן (Rome Ms. Cited in Ginzberg, *Yerushalmi Fragments* etc., p. 356a, also
published separately, Jerusalem, 1971). The basic letters are "ARGRON". In (b)
the R has changed to D (ר to ד), a very common occurrence in Hebrew orthogra-
phy. In (c) the R has changed to L, a common dialect change (eg. גלעינים –גרעינים).
(Cf. also *Sefer Halachot Pesuqot*, ed. S. Sasoon, Jerusalem, 1950, pp. 28–29.) In
(d) the first R has been omitted. ארגרן appears to be the Greek ἀργύριον (Krauss,
LW, 2, p. 127, and Dictionaries). Though one would have expected ארגורין, the
omission of the U has numerous precedents, (eg. συνέδριον — סנהדרין, Cf. Krauss,
LW, 1, pp. 85–86, para. 121). Normally –ιον changes into ין (i.e. συνέδριον —
סנהדרין, cf. Krauss, *LW*, 1, p. 92, para. 140. See also Rosen, in *JSS*, 8, 1963, p.
66). The form ארגרן thus suggests the Greek ἀργύρον (rather than ἀργύριον).
Sophocles, p. 245a, s.v. ἀργύρον equates it with the μιλιαρήσιον, on the basis of
Epiphanius, III.289 (= *Patrologia Graeca* 43); τὸ δὲ ἀργύρον, τοῦτο ἐστιν ὅ οἱ
ʿΡωμαίοι μιλιαρήσιον καλοῦσιν, ὅ ἐρμενευεται στρατιωτικόν δομα (= Hultsch,
MSR, I, p. 266, lines 20–22; cf. Lagarde, *Symmicta*, Göttingen, 1877, p. 277, lines
19–21, p. 182, lines 20–21, and cf. p. 197). However, there are cases of –ιον turning
into ין — (eg. γαγγλιον — גלגלון, σπαρτιον — אספריתן; cf. Krauss, *LW*, 1, p. 134),
so that ארגרן could well be ἀργύριον. Below we have adopted the latter suggestion.

3 Rome Ms. has דידיה (cf. Lieberman, *Tosefta ki-fshutah, Zeraʾim*, 1, p. 184).

4 Some commentators following reading (c) interpret ARGALON from רגיל —
that which he is used to (receive by way of charity). However, this interpretation
need not be seriously considered.

5 As to who it is who gives this "small present" (or ἀργύριον) — private individuals,
or the communal charity — see *Tosefta ki-fshutah*, 1, p. 184, who shows that this
is a point of disagreement among the classical commentators.

6 However, here it is probably a coin, and not a unit of measure, and may therefore
be the piece struck at 1/60 *libra*, (from Constantius onwards), not the 1/72 (=
siliqua), which did continue to be struck. In that case, the *argurion* might be 1/20
not 1/24 *solidus*, thus worth about 6 loaves. There was also a small silver piece
struck at 1/192 *libra aurei*, which would be worth approximately 2 loaves of bread.
This too could perhaps have been called an *argurion*. (See table):

Standard	Theoretical Weight in Grammes	292–305	305–337	337–360	360–363	363–393	393–450
192	1.71		x	x			x
144	2.27			x	x	x	
96	3.41	x	x	x			
72	3.55		x	x	x	x	
60	3.46		x	x		x	

[Silver denominations current in the IV cent. based upon their theoretical standards, (as fractions of the *solidus* etc.). Based on Adelson, *Silver Currency and Values in the Early Byzantine Empire*, p. 7; cf. West and Johnson, *Currency*, p. 106.] Or alternatively, since the earlier silver-gold ratio was probably restored by 305 or shortly afterwards, (see supra, Chap. IX), the *argurion* could be the coin struck at 72 to the *libra* and worth about 1/18 *aureus*. There may be a reference to this coin in a statement of R. Asi (flor. c. 270–315) in B. Bava Batra 9a. In a continuation of the text just cited above (AM), the Talmud relates that R. Asi, basing himself on a verse in Nehemiah 10.33, taught that a person should not give less than one-third of a (Biblical) *shekel* (= *tetradrachm*) to charity per annum. This sum must have had some significance on R. Asi's time, and since 1/3 *tetradrachm* is about 1/18 *aureus* (according to the classical system), he may well have been referring to the *miliarense*, which was introduced in 305, (see table above, and West & Johnson, *Currency* p. 106). However, see *VL* to Bava Batra 9a, pp. 36–37, note 90, which records manuscripts reading R. Ashi (Babylonian V cent. scholar) in place of R. Asi. In this case it is difficult to determine which reading is the better.

7 The smallest silver coin recorded in Egypt is worth 1/192 *sol.* (P. Liepzig 87); see preceding note.

8 Presumably because each day he can make enough to live on.

9 Cf. B. Nedarim 33b, the famous (Babylonian, of course) פרוטה דרב יוסף. (Cf. B. Bava Kama 46a: ריפתא.) B. Bava Batra 9a, 10a; *Lev. Rab.* 34.2; Midrash Psalms 17, etc. Often however, people gave much more than the minimum coin: e.g. *Midrash Canticles Zuta* ed. Buber, p. 19: *issar dinar* or *sela* (Tannaitic). Cf. B. Bava Mezia 78b; B. Sota 21a; B. Ḥagiga 5a (all a *denarius* or *zuz* = *denarius*); B. Pesaḥim 8a, *sela*, etc.

10 T. Bava Batra 5.11 (405, 19–24); B. Kiddushin 12a; Y. Kiddushin 1.1 (58d 30–35). Cf. Zuckermann, *Talmudische Münzen und Gewichte* (Breslau, 1865), and my own article in *JQR*, 56, 1966, p. 298.

11 See my article in *JQR*, 56, pp. 273–301.

12 E. g.: The coins of Aelia Capitolina, L. Kadman, *Corpus Nummorum Palestinensium* (= *CNP*) 1 (Jerusalem, 1956), out of 206 types only 4 (nos. 6, 21, 83, 205) weigh under 4 gr.; Caesarea Maritima, *CNP*, 2, 1959, 3 types (nos. 25, 30, 46) out of 230; Akko Ptolemais, *CNP*, 4, 1961, 4 types (nos. 91, 130, 156, 271) out of 189 (from Claudius onwards). In Tiberias (*The Coins of Tiberias* by A. Kindler, Tiberias, 1961) after Antoninus Pius no such small pieces were minted (p. 51).

13 Aelia, *CNP*, 1, p. 27; Caesarea, *CNP*, 2, p. 31; Akko Ptolemais, *CNP*, 4, p. 41.

14 In his paper published in *INCP*, p. 240; Bosch, Die Kleinasiatischen Münzen der römischen Kaiserzeit, *Arch. Anzeiger*, 1931, p. 438; Aelia, *CNP*, 1, p. 27; Caesarea Maritima, *CNP*, 2, nos. 91 et seq.; Akko Ptolemais *CNP*, 4, p. 42; Tiberias, Kindler, *Coins of Tiberias*, p. 51. Cf. West in *ANSMN*, 7, 1957, p. 107; see also E. W. Klimowsky's material set out in *INCP*, pp. 168–69 and compare with the table of the "seventh period", ibid., pp. 166–67. Finally. see B. Levick, "The Coinage of Pisidian Antioch in the Third Century A. D.", *Num. Chron.*, 1966, pp. 51–53.

15 Y. Kiddushin 1.1.

16 The material has been collected and set up by Carson in his article in *INCP*, p. 242. See above, Table I at end of Chap. XIX. Also West in *ANSMN*, 7 (New York, 1957), p. 107.

17 Here we are referring to the little laureate coin of about 1.3 grms., which is almost silverless. Sutherland, in *Archeometry*, 4, 1961, p. 60, thinks that it is a 1 d. piece. But soon the 2 d. piece was the lowest denomination, ibid., p. 59.

18 See Table K at end of Chap. XXII, compiled from A. Ravetz, "The Fourth Cent. Inflation", *Num. Chron.*, 1964, pp. 215–16; Ravetz, *Archeometry*, 6, pp. 56–61, especially, p. 53, fig. 2 and p. 54. As the mints represented are Italian (Rome, Trier) or Eastern (Antioch), and not Egyptian, the results constitute evidence independent of papyri. L.H. Cope writes to me as follows (private communication of 10 Sept. 1972): "The eastern *folles* of 307 still contain about $3\frac{1}{2}\%$ of silver; the most recent analyses which I have just completed show a nadir in the west of nearly 1%. The 1/96 pieces of 313 onwards in the west assay 1.4% — corresponding to 4 *scrupula* of silver per *libra*. In the east Licinius' standard was higher — perhaps 6 *scrupula* per *libra* at this time (317). Despite the apparent acceptability of your calculations I think you should try using the new assay results." He further writes me (ibid.): "I haven't confirmed Ravetz's assays of the VICTORIAE pieces; I find them silver free, except for traces of impurity. Also the FEL TEMP issues present a very complicated picture of change. They start, however, at about $2\frac{1}{2}\%$ silver. The Julian *Apis* issue I find to have about $1\frac{1}{2}\%$ silver (2 assays)." (See below.) "In view of this more accurate data, your figures in the text should be slightly altered. However, the argument is in no ways affected, only strengthened at times."

19 However, see Ravetz's figure in *Archeometry*, 6, p. 48, c. 307 (nos. 1–3 and 6), according to which there was still more like 2% silver in these coins.

20 This suggests that our interpretation of *Cod. Theod.* 11.36.23, of 315, which appeared to yield an equation of 1 *aureus* = 3000 d. is not correct. It would seem then that 1 *follis* = $\frac{1}{2}$ lb. silver, and that the fine was doubled by 341 (*Cod. Theod.* 11.36.5).

21 West and Johnson, *Currency*, pp. 158–59; Segrè, *Metrologia*, p. 439; Segrè, *Byzantion*, 15, pp. 249–50.

22 Dr. Kent's redating of this coin, rather than the usually accepted date of 346. Cf. *Cod. Theod.* 9.21.6 of 349. Dr. J. Kent (in a private communication, 28 August 1972) now sends me the following information:

"VICTORIAE DD etc. averages 1.67 gr. (Our coin no. 23.)

The FEL TEMP coinage (our coin no. 24) starts in three denominations:

(a) c. 5.2 gr. 3% AR; (b) c. 4.5 gr. 1.5% AR; (c) c. 2.6 gr. no AR;

(a) is probably double (b). Julian's AE 1 weighs 9.23 gr."

In view of this new and more accurate information, our calculations should be somewhat modified. However, these modifications in no way effect our argument. On the contrary, if anything they only reinforce it. Thus, for example, Q would equal well over fifty of the VICTORIAE DD coins, and well over fifty of the smallest kind of the FEL TEMP type, (since c must be at least half b).

23 *Archeometry*, 6, no. 75, dated 361–63, mint of Constantinople (no. 2056), not as in *Num. Chron.*, 1964, where it is apparently dated 355.

24 We have seen above that the *follis* was worth approximately 1/750 *sol.* c. 363. Possibly it was worth 10 d. (giving 7500 d. per *sol.*), and was $1\frac{1}{2}$ this older denomination. Julian did in fact strike denominations of AE 1 and AE 3 throughout his reign. Cf. J.P.C. Kent in *Num. Chron.*, 1959, p. 109, ("An Introduction to the Coinage of Julian the Apostate"). See also *Late Roman Coinage*, Carson & Kent (London, 1965), pp. 92–93. Q would be at least 20 such pieces.

25 *Num. Chron.*, 1964, p. 218.

26 Hultsch, *MSR*, 1, pp. 338–40; Symm., *Rel.*, 29; Ruggini, *Rendicondi dei Lincei*, 16, p. 311, note 29; Adelson, *INCP*, p. 277.

27 Ruggini, ibid., p. 311, note 28; Adelson in *Centennial vol. of ANS*, p. 17, note 64. This is in agreement with Ruggini's thesis, ibid., pp. 312, 316–18; but cf. Ruggini, ibid., p. 316, note 57, with bibliography, and Adelson in *INCP*, p. 278.

28 Kent, in *Num. Chron.*, 1957, nos. 175–78, 205–06, 443–47, 485–86, 611.

29 Ed. Margulies, p. 775.

30 Cf. *Tanḥuma Exod.*, *Mishpatim*, sect. 15. *Midrash Ha-Gadol*, *Leviticus* 25.35, ed. Rabinowitz, p. 634.

31 See, for example, Heichelheim, in *Economic History*, 3, p. 11.

32 This seems to be the opinion of S. Lieberman in *Greek and Hellenism in Jewish Palestine* (Hebrew ed.). Jerusalem, 1962), p. 4, note 24. Dr. J. Kent, in a private communication (of 23 August, 1972) suggests a different interpretation: "Coins of pottery? = cast in clay moulds — a very frequent type of third and fourth cent. counterfeit." Attractive though this interpretation may be, it does not really seem to fit the sense of the passage which is suggesting that the authorities will come to produce coins made out of clay. The verse in Daniel 40.42, upon which this exegesis is based suggests the same thing. Furthermore see *Deut. Rab.* 5.10, discussed above Chap. XIV.

33 *Teruma*, para. 7 (Warsaw ed. = printed ed. 1888, p. 178); Buber ed., Exod. *Teruma*, para. 6, p. 92. Cf. *Sefer Ve-Hizhir* (ed. Freimann). 1, p. 155.

34 Referring to the Christianized government(?). But cf. the problematic *Gen. Rab.* 64.8, ed. Theodor-Albeck, pp. 710–12; note variants in p. 710, line 4.

35 Cf. the (very different) remarks of the anonymous author of *De Rebus Bellicis*, ed. E.E. Thompson (*A Roman Reformer and Inventor*, Oxford, 1953), p. 93, line 25; a late IV cent. text (ibid., p. 2). If this text is post-364, it may also mean that since copper coins were token coinage, they might just as well be of clay, and indeed the government might well resort to such means. It may be noted in passing that the Jewish laws of charity and (Palestinian) charitable institutions were so well developed and run that the contemporary Roman Emperor Julian can write: "For it is disgraceful that when no Jew ever has to beg, and the impious Galilaeans (= Christians) support not only their own poor but ours as well, all men see that our people lack aid from us". (*Epistle* 22 in Wright ed., Loeb ed. 3, p. 71, = Hertlein 49, = Bidez-Cumont 84. Note how this passage is quoted in Sozomen, *Hist. Eccles.* 5.16; translation C.D. Hartranft, in H. Wace and P. Schaff, *A Select Library of Nicene and Post-Nicene Fathers*, Second Series, 2, Oxford–New York, 1891, p. 338.)

36 Note his opinion in Y. Bikkurim 3.6 ad fin., where he cites a tradition in the name of R. Ḥiyya b. Aba in the name of R. Simeon b. Gamliel that one may sell a *Torah-scroll* in order to gain a livelihood. In this he differs from his close friend R. Jose, (ibid.). On his dealings with the poor, see Y. Pe'a 5.3; *Lev. Rab.* 34.1, ed. Margulies, p. 733, etc.

Chapter XXIII

1 In *Greek and Hellenism in Jewish Palestine* (Hebrew ed.), p. 4 and note 24. Also cf. his remarks in *Annuaire de l'Institut de Philologie et d'Histoire Orientales et Slaves*, 7, 1939–44, p. 434, note 4. See also *Tosefta ki-fshutah*, *Zera'im*, 2, p. 718,

note 39. Note Herzfeld's attempt to understand these texts by altering ריבוא to ריבעה and explaining that they refer to *sestertii*, (*Metrologische Voruntersuchungen*, Leipzig, 1863, p. 167). Of course, there is no basis for such corrections.

2 In my article in *Archiv Orientalni*, 34, 1966, pp. 61–62, 65.

3 Y. Kilaim 9.1 (AR). See my remarks on the first part of this text in *Archiv Orientalni*, 34, 1966, p. 65. It is, however, possible that the Hillel b. Vales mentioned here is a third generation personality (c. 280–330), and not the R. Hillel b. Vales who was a contemporary of R. Judah the Prince (i.e. c. 180–220). The words "and he gave them to Rabbi" are absent in the Vat. Ms. and are only a marginal gloss in the Leiden Ms. Thus they are no real indications of the dating of this personality. That there was such a person in the third generation becomes clear from a straightfoward reading of Y. Beza 5.2, where he appears in a list of traditions from a group of third generation Rabbis, (R. Samuel b. Isaac, R. Ilai, R. Jeremiah). The reading there is ר' ליל ב"ר אלס. Similarly, in Y. Ḥala he appears with R. Zeira, R. Ḥama b. Ukva, who bring a statement in the name of ר' יהודה דמן הדא. There he is called הלל בן הלס. (See Ratner, *VL*, on this text in Beza, pp. 105–06.) See Frankel, *Mevo ha-Yerushalmi*, 75a; contra Hyman, *Toldoth Tannaim Ve'Amoraim*, p. 375a. As to the second part of this passage, see Krauss, *Kadmoniot*, 2/2, p. 19, note 1, whose interpretation is borne out to some extent by the reading in the Vat. Ms. On prices of clothes, see further Adelson in *INCP*, p. 271. See also A. Brüll's remark, in his *Trachten der Juden*, (Frankfurt A/M, 1873), p. 76 note 4.

4 Eg. B. Yoma 35b; T. Yoma 1.21–22; Y. Gittin 4.7, 8 (46a 56, 69). Cf. B. Shabbat 128a; B. Shavout 31a; B. Pesaḥim 36a top (?); B. Ḥulin 84a; T. Arachin 4.26 (548); *Mechilta de R. Ishmael*, ed. Horowitz & Rabin, p. 86, line 17, etc.

5 Segrè, *Byzantion*, 15, p. 263; *Num. Zeitschr.*, 1913, pp. 161, 219, etc.

6 Cf. *Ed. Diocl.*, chapters XXII–XXIV. Cf. L. Friedländer, *Roman Life and Manners*, etc., 1908, 2, p. 177.

7 Ed. Princeps, Constantinople, 1522, = second ed. Venice, which, however, has the 200 in a non-abbreviated form.

8 Ed. Mantua, 1563, corrected by Menaḥem Azariah of Fano, followed by Verona ed. 1595, etc.

9 In the Warsaw ed. of 1877.

10 Buber, in *Tanḥuma Exod.*, p. 84, note 48, etc.

11 Ed. Buber, p. 246.

12 So also is the reading in *Yalkut ha-Maḥiri* to Psalms 34.1, ed. Buber, p. 214, and *Yalkut Shim'oni* to Samuel, section 131.

13 *Exodus Rabba* II (Chapters 12–40) is of the *Tanḥuma-Yelamdenu* type, and contains much early material. See Zunz-Albeck, *Ha-Derashot be-Yisrael²* (Jerusalem, 1954), p. 125; *Encyclopaedia Judaica* (Jerusalem, 1971), 6, 1068–69. See also *Tanḥuma Exod.*, Mishpatim sect. 9, which mentions a large loan of "10 myriads" (= 1 *maneh* in parallel in *Exod. Rab.* 31.6), worth the equivalent of houses and trees. The text is anonymous and difficult to date. See my articles in *Sinai*, 64, 1969, pp. 185–98; *Sinai*, 66, 1970, pp. 273–74; and *Classical Quarterly*, 9/2, 1969, pp. 374–78. See also *Aggadat Bereishit* 55, ed. Buber, 56, p. 111 (AY), where, in a homily, R. Berechia (second quarter of the fourth century) mentions a person who has two wives, one with a *ketuba* (= marriage settlement) of 4 myriad, and the other with one of 10 myriad. (The numbers four and ten are determined by the context of the homily.) 4 myriad here is most probably worth more than 8 *aurei*

(= 200 d.), the minimum *ketuba* of a virgin bride, and certainly more than 4 *aurei*, the minimum possible *ketuba* (for a non-virgin bride). Cf. *Tanḥuma Buber*, Gen., *Va-Yishlaḥ*, 8, p. 166. See also *Cant. Zuta*, ed. Buber, p. 37, (and see Buber's note 9), = *Aggadath Shir Hashirim*, ed. Schechter, p. 46 line 1377, and p. 95. See also *Midrah Ha-Gadol*, *Deut.* 15.10, ed. Fisch, p. 336 a fourth century text and not a Tannaitic one as Hoffmann thought (in his *Midrash Tannaim*, p. 84).

14 Cf. B. Bechorot 50a; B. Bava Mezia 87b; *Tanḥuma Deut.*, *Re'e* 10; *Tanḥuma Buber*, Deut., p. 20. See also *Pesikta de R. Kahana*, ed. Mandelbaum, p. 160; *Exod. Rabba* 31.17; *Gen. Rabba* 58.7 (ed. Theodor-Albeck, pp. 626–27); *Peskita Rabbati*, ed. Friedman 2a; *Midrash Ha-Gadol, Gen.* 23.14–15 (ed. Margulies, p. 386); Bacher, *Aggadat Amorei Eretz-Yisrael*, 1/1, p. 20, note 1. The reading in the Yerushalmi seems the most correct.

15 See Albeck, *Mavo La-Talmudim*, pp. 241–43. It seems unlikely that the R. Ḥanina here mentioned is R. Ḥanina [b. Ḥama] of the early III cent., contra Bacher, ibid., and Avi-Yonah, *Bimei Romi u-Vizantion*, p. 65, since the term *kintarin* suggests a later date for this text.

16 Liddell & Scott², p. 939a. See *Ed. Diocl.* XVIII.5; Olymp. *Hist.*, p. 469d (V cent.); Men. Prot., p. 100 d. (VI cent.). Likewise, *Targum Ps. Jonathan* to Exod. 25.39, ibid. 37.24 (cf. *Esther Rabba* 10.4). See also Hultsch, *MSR*, 2, index s.v. ταλαντον II, 17.20a; ibid., pp. 115, lines 12–13, p. 140, lines 6–7 (Isidorus); Payne Smith, *Thesaurus Syriacus*, 3664; Epiphanius (Syriac), ed. Dean, chap. 54, p. 57, etc. See also E. Schilbach, *Byzantinische Metrologie* (Munich, 1970), pp. 171, 230–31. All this contra Rashi, Bechorot 50a; Avi-Yonah, *Bimei Romi U-Vizantion* (Jerusalem, 1946), p. 65.

17 The tendency of the Midrash is to depict Ephron as one who extorted a great sum of money for the field and the cave.

18 *P.O.* 1057. Cf. *P. London* 247 (c. 346): 4 Babylonian hides: 120 myriads. Cf. *Ed. Diocl.* VIII. 1a, 2: 1 Babylonian hide, first quality: 500 d., second quality: 400 d. (ed. Graser, pp. 346–47).

19 West and Johnson, *Currency*, p. 169.

20 For numerous sources see Johnson and West, *Byzantine Egypt: Economic Studies*, pp. 179–94, etc.

21 West and Johnson, *Currency*, pp. 169–70.

22 LeBas et Waddington, *Voyage Archéologique en Asie Mineur, Syrie*, section 3/1 (Paris, 1870), *Royaume Nabatéan* (apud Friedländer, *Roman Life and Manners*, 4, p. 283, see his discussion, pp. 283–84). The readings of these inscriptions are at times doubtful.

23 Ibid. 1999.

24 Ibid. 2000.

25 Ibid. 2036.

26 Ibid. 2037.

27 *Syria*, 3a, E. Littman and D. Magie (Leiden, 1921), p. 99, no. 168.

28 Ibid., p. 104, no. 177.

29 Ibid., p. 432, no. 799.

30 For the I cent. see Gerasa inscriptions: nos. 3–6, 17, 49, 52, 92. No. 6 (p. 377) line 5: a donation of 7100 dr. for the construction of a temple, 1500 for *propylon* etc. of the year 70. No. 52 (399): *cuneus* built for 3000 dr., c. 83/96. *Syria*, part 3, *Greek and Latin Inscriptions*, ed. William Kelly Prentice, nos. 104, 352; ibid. 3b (Nor-

thern Syria), no. 1076, (p. 116) of 227(?); a fine of 2000 dr. if someone shares this tomb. (KWARD). For this latter compare *Inscriptions Grecques et Latines de la Syrie* Jalabert et Mouterde, 1–2, no. 102, no. 171 (from KARA MOUGARA): a fine of 10,000 d., and 5, p. 279, no. 2652, (from HAB'ARA); a fine of 1,000 d. for selling the tomb. Both unfortunately are undated. Cf. *Cod. Theod.* 9.17.2 (349), ibid., 4 (356), ibid., 6 (381). See also *Econ. Surv.*, 4, pp. 175–76.

31 *Syria* 3a (Southern), E. Littman and D. Magie, no. 787[14] (p. 392).

32 Ibid., no. 790[4] (p. 401).

33 Ibid. There are two other interesting, but unfortunately undated inscriptions from this area. Cf. ibid., nos. 875[1], a fine of 2500 d. for opening the tomb (NEDJRAN), and no. 787[10], a memorial from MDJEDIL of 80,000 (?) d. (fig. 4). The reading in this latter text is rather uncertain, as there are only two vertical strokes instead of the usual H (= 8). The editors therefore suggest reading $\iota\gamma$ (= 13), comparing such a reading with Waddington 1999 of 345. Both on paleographic grounds and a consideration of the names, in the case of the former, (non-Christian, $A\upsilon\varrho(\eta\lambda\iota o\varsigma)$ $Z\eta\nu o\beta\iota o\varsigma \Sigma\alpha\gamma\iota o\upsilon \ldots \ N\alpha\sigma\varepsilon\alpha\theta \ldots$), 787[14] and 790[4] cannot be later than the IV cent. One may add that in a V or VI cent. inscription one would not expect the term *denarius**, but rather *keration, nummus, follis,* or *nomisma,* (eg. Waddington 2562 + *CIG*, 8944). See, eg. P. Grierson in *JRS*, 49, 1959, pp. 77. (However, even if they were on V or VI cent. inscriptions, this would still be too vast for a straight-forward interpretation. See Grierson, *JRS*, 49, pp. 78–80.) LeBas and Waddington list two more undated fragmentary inscriptions mentioning the "myriad", nos. 1993, donations of seven myriads, and 2341, an interesting fragment (from Kana-tha, Batanea) reading: $\delta(\eta\nu)\alpha\varrho\iota\alpha, \mu\nu\varrho\iota\alpha,$ *M. Finally, can we not understand the puzzling line in Waddington no. 2053 (fig. 5, from Meschgorig) of the year 350 as $'A\nu\varepsilon\lambda o\theta[\eta]\ast\mu\nu\varrho\iota\alpha \ o\varepsilon \ \Sigma\varepsilon o\varsigma \ldots$ meaning an expense of 850,000 d.? (See also, ibid. no. 1963, of 295.)

787[10]. Lintel. Serving as the lintel of a stable in the southern part of the northern section of the village, about fifty yards west of the tower where nos. 787[7] and 787[8] were found. The stone faces north. Length 1.24½ m.; height 27 cm. The right end is irregular, but the stone seems to be intact. The inscription was copied as it was growing dark, and the correctness of the copy cannot be vouched for. Height of letters 2½–4½ cm. Copied by Magie.

$A\upsilon\varrho(\dot{\eta}\lambda\iota o\varsigma) \ K o\varrho\varepsilon\nu o\varsigma \ X\alpha\sigma\varepsilon\tau o(\upsilon) \ \mu\varepsilon\tau' \ \dot{\varepsilon}\pi\iota$-
$\tau\varepsilon\lambda\varepsilon\upsilon\tau\dot{\eta}\nu \ B\alpha\nu\alpha\theta o\sigma\upsilon \ \dot{\alpha}\delta\varepsilon\lambda\phi o\tilde{\upsilon}$
$\dot{\varepsilon}\nu\kappa o\delta\dot{o}\mu\eta\sigma\alpha \ \tau\dot{o} \ \mu\nu\eta\mu\tilde{\iota}o\nu \ \ast \ \dot{\eta} \ \mu(\upsilon\varrho\iota\alpha\delta\tilde{\omega}\nu) \ \varepsilon\xi \ \varepsilon\dot{\iota}$-
$\delta\dot{\iota}o\nu. \ A\nu o\chi\upsilon(\lambda)o\varsigma \ \chi\varrho\dot{\iota}(\sigma\tau\eta\varsigma) \ (?), \ A\upsilon\mu o\varsigma \ o(\dot{\iota})\chi o(\delta\dot{o}\mu o\varsigma).$

.Inscr. 787[10]. Scale 1 : 10.

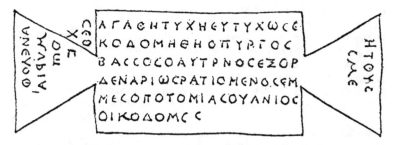

Prof. Callu writes me in a private communication (29.12.73) that he has some doubts as to my interpretation of this material, and most especially of the myriad sign. Since he is working on this problem in conjunction with the prominent French papyrologist J. Schwartz, we eagerly await his conclusions. Meanwhile, I find this the most satisfactory approach.

Chapter XXIV

1 West and Johnson, *Currency*, p. 170. See also Johnson, *Egypt and the Roman Empire* (Ann Arbor, 1951), p. 59; Jones, *The Later Roman Empire*, I, p. 440.

2 Thus according to this argument, e. g.: *SB.* 7034, 1 *sol.* = 5,760,000. If each unit equals 750 d., = $\frac{1}{4}$ talent(= T), 1 *sol.* = 7680 d. c. 360, *P.O.* 1056, 1 *sol.* = 2000 myriad (= M). If each unit = 3000 d. (= 2T), 1 *sol.* = 6,666 d. (Cf. *PSI.* 4, 287, of 377, and *P.O.* 1223.) c. 380, *PSI.* 7, 961, 1 *sol.* = 4050 M. If each unit = 6000 d. (= 4T), 1 *sol.* = 6750 d. (Cf. *P.O.* 960.) *P.O.* 1917, 1 *sol.* = 60,000,000 d. If each unit = 7500 d. (= 5T), 1 *sol.* = 8000 d. Compare our results above. See further, Segrè, *Metrologia*, pp. 454–56, 489; Jones, *Econ. Hist. Rev.*, 5/3, 1953, pp. 308–11, Ruggini, *Rendiconti dei Lincei*, 16, p. 311; Segrè, *Byzantion*, 15, p. 263, etc.

3 Cf., for example, M. Bava Kama 3.9; 4.1, etc.

4 There are certainly some IV cent. text in which the *maneh* retains the primary meaning 100 d. Cf. my examples in my article in *Talpiot*, 1970, p. 611, note 74.

5 Ed. Finkelstein, pp. 338–39.

6 We follow the reading as recorded in *Midrash Tannaim* and *Midrash Ha-Gadol*; see above, Chap. XIII.

7 Possibly around 20 and 100 *solidi*. Compare our price-lists above, Chap. XV, and the Gerasa inscriptions, nos. 3–6, 17, 49, 52 of the I cent. Compare with the dated mid-IV cent. Syrian inscriptions cited above (LeBas & Waddington, *Voy. arch. en Asie Mineur, Syrie* 3, nos. 2000, 2036, 2037, 2053).

8 *Antike Gewichtsnormer und Münzfüsse* (Berlin, 1923), pp. 81–82, especially p. 81, note 3, and p. 97–98. (Note also the variants cited by Swete in the *Septuagint* to Ezra B, 2.69. Swete, 2, p. 165: καθαρος μναι] δραγμας, translating the original דרכמונים. Ezra B is usually attributed to Theodotian who probably lived in the later II cent. C.E.)

9 Cf. *Syriac Epiphanius*, ed. Dean, p. 57, and note 394. See also Lagarde, *Symmicta*, 2, p. 194 (= *MSR*, 1, pp. 265, 267; 2, p. 152, etc.), p. 196, line 12 (= *MSR*, 1, p. 271.4) etc.

10 Translation Dean, p. 57, B.M. Add. 17148, fol. 67b.

11 Ibid. bottom left.

12 Dean, p. 57, note 395 (read, ibid. ארגריוס). The absence of the U (of ἀργυριος) is paralleled in the Rabbinic transformation ארגרון, see above, Chap. XXII.

13 The last letter is obscurred by a mark on the vellum.

14 See W. Wright, *Catalogue of Syriac Manuscripts* etc., (London, 1870), p. 718a.

15 The fact that it is in a different coloured ink does not indicate that it is of a later date. I discussed the matter with Mr. R.F. Hosking of the British Museum, and he too thought the glosses near in date to, if not completely contemporary with, the Ms. itself.

16 As I was mistaken in my article in *Archiv Orientalni*, 34, 1955, especially p. 61.

17 Again we may explain certain Egyptian papyrological texts along these lines. Thus we have suggested above, Chap. XXII, that the *denarius* and the *nummus* were at one time at least (in the late IV cent.) identified with one another. The *nummus* we have shown above was worth 25 d. (in the early IV cent.) Thus: *PER*. 37, 1 sol. = 100 T (= 150,000). If a *denarius* is a *nummus* of 25 d., 1 *sol.* = 7000 d. If the *nummus* was 32 d. (as suggested above, Chap. IX), then in the case of *PER*. 310, where 1 *sol.* = 120 T (= 180,000 d.), 1 sol. = 5626 d. approximately. (Cf. *SPP*.XX.96.) The 50 d. unit is also a unit that we may make use of in this connection. Thus, *PER*.225 gives the equation 1 *sol.* = 183 1/3 T (= 275,000 d.). (Cf. *SPP*.XX.96.) At a unit of 50 d., the *sol.* = 5500 d. This sort of method, as that employed above in note 2, gives us results which are on the whole very favourably comparable with the ratios we arrived at using analyses of metallic contents of coins, etc.

18 Note also the *Itala*, Mark 12,42 (*Didasc. apost.* 33.25): *denarios minutos duos quod est quodrantes.* (λεπτα, Vulg. *dua minuta*) = *Tetra-Ewangalion Kaddisha*, ed. Puseus & Gwilliam (Oxford, 1901). תרין מנין. See my article in *Novum Testamentum*, 9, 1967, pp. 178–90, on Mark 12,42 and its metrological background.

19 See *Cod. Theod.* 12.6, 12–13, of 366–67; 12.7.3 of 367; 12.13.14 of 379; and 7.24.1 of 395.

20 See J.W. Eadie's edition of *Festus* (London, 1967), pp. 1–3.

21 See my article in *Classical Quarterly*, 19/2, 1969, pp. 375–78, where I discussed this problem in detail.

Chapter XXV

1 Jones, *The Later Roman Empire*, 1, p. 445; *Patrologia Orientalis*, 4/5, ed. Bousquet and Nau (Paris, 1907), pp. 445–58; ed. Bedjan, in *Acta Martyrum et Sanctorum*. 5 (Paris, 1895), pp. 148–51 (Syriac version). See above, Chap. II. See also *The Book of Paradise of Palladius*, etc., ed. E.A. Wallis Budge (London, 1904), 1, pp. 455–57 = 2, pp. 321–24.

2 This text is interesting also in that it gives us some idea of the great range of (possible) seasonal price fluctuations.

3 Jones, *Later Roman Empire*, p. 445, citing Ammianus Marcellinus, 27.17–18.

4 See *Evangelisches Kirchenlexikon*, 3 (Göttingen, 1959), p. 1, s.v. Pachomius, with bibliography. Pachomius came to Tabenna (= Thebais) in 320 and died in 346. *P. Princeton* 1834, which is post-345, reflects a period of very high wheat prices, 334 T. per *art.* Cf. *P. Lond.* 1914 of 335, Alexandria, 14 T. per *art.*; *P.O.* 85 of 338,

247 per *art*.(?). (Cf. H.I. Bell's note to *P. Lond.* 1914; *Byzantine Egypt*; *Economic Studies*, p. 177), *P. Lond.* 427, Hermopolis, c. 350, 50 T. per *art*. However, it does not seem likely that the Pachomius incident took place in 346 (i.e. post-345, and before Pachomius' death).

5 Such were our conclusions for c. 313/13 above, Chap. XXI.

6 Cf. West and Johnson, *Currency*, pp. 113, 124–25.

7 See price-relationships above, Chap. XVI. But cf. *PER.E.*200, Hermopolis, 314, etc.

8 So according to Bell, in a note to *P. Lond.* 1914.

9 See Johnson and West, *Byzantine Egypt*: *Economic Studies*, p. 177, where the authors write "24 T. for an *art*. in tenth measure". See note, ibid.: "This is dubious. The reading of the text seems to be 24 *art*. (ἀρταλ) in the tenth measure as the amount left in stock ... etc.".

10 On regional variations in the value of the *solidus*, see *Cod. Theod.* 9.23.1, of 352, and above, Chap. II. See also Procopius, *Hist. Arcan.* 25.12. The value of the *solidus* during the IV cent. must have been approximately the same in Egypt as in other parts of the Eastern Empire, as the same marks of value appear on coins of Egyptian and non-Egyptian mints. E.g., the famous, XIIr of Licinius, which appears on coins from the mints of Cyzicus (SMKA) and Nicodemia (SMNA) as well as those of Alexandria (ALE). Cf. also West and Johnson, *Currency*, p. 101. Contra J.G. Milne, in *JRS*, 17, 1927, p. 10.

11 West and Johnson, *Currency*, p. 125. But cf. ibid., pp. 156–66.

12 Suggested by West and Johnson, in *Currency*, p. 125.

13 See *BGU*.21, of 340, (Hermopolis), according to which 1 *sest*. wine: 3 T. (= 4500 d.). This means that wine cost about 1/20 *sol*. per *sest*., or about 32 d. per pint in terms of the *Ed. of Diocl.* This seems to be a rather high, though not impossible, price for wine. Cf. *P.O.* 2114, of 316, 65 d. per *sest*. of old wine. Cf. also *SPP.XX.*93, for an oil price probably of 334, as oil was generally more expensive than wine. See also *P.O.* 1953, of 390, according to which 40 *sest*. olive oil cost 1 *sol*., which compares well with the price given in the *Edict of Diocl.* (III.3). Also compare meat prices *P.O.* ibid.: 30 myr. d. per lb.

14 See the remarks on the usages in literary sources in West and Johnson, *Currency*, pp. 157, 168.

15 West and Johnson, *Currency*, p. 157; similarly A.H.M. Jones, in *Economic History Revue*, 1953, p. 304, and Adelson, in *INCP*, p. 263.

16 West and Johnson, *Currency*, p. 169.

17 This fact has been appreciated before, though never convincingly demonstrated in any detail. See, for example, Lellia Ruggini's remarks in her article in *Rendiconti dei Lincei*, 16, 1961, p. 315. But see Segrè in *Byzantion*, 15, p. 251, who calls the IV cent. "one of the worst (periods) in the economic and political history of the world", (cf. ibid., p. 275). Obviously he was basing himself primarily on Egyptian papyrological evidence. See also Segrè in *Circolazione monetaria e prezzi nel mondo antico ed in particolare in Egitto* (Roma, 1922), pp. 359–405, etc.; Segrè, *Metrologia*, p. 457; Mickwitz, *Geld und Wirtschaft*, p. 114; E. Petrie, "The Rise of Prices in Roman Egypt, in *Ancient Egypt*", 1922, p. 103; cf. Bernardi in *Studia Ghisleriana*, 3 (Pavia, 1961), p. 303, note 222, etc. See also J.G. Milne, in *JRS*, 17, 1927, p. 10, who writes that in Egypt there was a "local devaluation of a coinage ... which had not depreciated anything like the same extent in other provinces," and idem, *Aegyptus*, 32, 1952, p. 151. See most recently, Heichelheim, *An Ancient Economic*

History, 3 (Leyden, 1970), pp. 281–90. On the other hand, see West and Johnson, *Currency*, pp. 157, 169; Jones, *Economic History Revue*, 1953, p. 304; Adelson, *INCP*, p. 263. See also P. Chanaris in *Byzantion*, 17, 1944–45, p. 409, for an expression of puzzlement at the extreme divergence between scholarly opinions on this subject. See also Jones, Later Roman Empire, I, p. 440.

Chapter XXVI

1 However, L. H. Cope writes me (private communication of 10 Sept. 1972): "My assays do not show any downward plummeting of debasement of the *antoninianus* in this period. From Aurelian to Diocletian the XX.I standard seems to have been fairly well maintained. This would match its valuation at 5d. throughout."

1a See Rostovtzeff, *Social and Economic History of the Roman Empire*[2] (= *SEHRE*), p. 728, note 60; Jones, *Later Roman Empire*, 1, pp. 30–31. On taxation in late III cent. Palestine see G. Allon, *Toldot ha-Yehudim be-Eretz Yisrael bi-Tekufat ha-Mishna ve-ha-Talmud* (Israel, 1955), 2, p. 182 et seq., and p. 253.

2 *Lev. Rab.* 15.19, ed. Margulies, p. 338. In the parallel text in B. Shabbat 149b–150a this statement is recorded in the name of "R. Judah said in the name of Rav", which suggests that this is an early III cent. *derasha*. However, see Rabbinovicz, *VL* to Shabbat, p. 360, note 80, for Ms. (and other) readings of "R. Johanan" instead of "R. Judah", and no mention of Rav. These readings seem very plausible, and would shift the dating of the text to the second half of the III cent. In any case it is significant that R. Aba b. Kahana used, or quoted, this *derasha*.

3 Cf., for example, *Michilta Yitro* 1 (ed. Friedmann 61b, ed. Horowitz-Rabin, p. 221) for the use of the root שקל (relating to money) with regard to taxes, (a late I cent. text). Concerning this text see A. Büchler, *The Economic Conditions of Judaea after the destruction of the Second Temple* (Jews' College Publications, 4, London, 1912), p. 62, and *Econ. Surv.*, 4, p. 235. See also Büchler, *The Political and Social Leaders of the Jewish Community of Sepphoris in the Second and Third Centuries* (Jews' College Publications, 1, London, 1909), p. 42, note 3, who states that שקל seems to be a "technical term for delivering taxes". Cf. *Tanḥuma Shelaḥ* 15, and other sources cited in Büchler ibid., especially T. Demai 6.3. (See also *Lev. Rab.* 34.12.) Here it is the change from שקל to מדד that is significant.

4 *Lev. Rab.* 22.1, ed. Margulis, p. 495, a text in the name of R. Jeremiah (flor. c. 270–320). This is a point made by Walbank in his chapter "Shrinkage, Crisis and The Corporative State", in his *The Decline of the Roman Empire in the West* (London, 1946), pp. 38–57.

5 *Deut. Rab.*, ed. Lieberman, p. 58.

6 B. Yevamot 63a.

7 Ibid.

8 Jones, *Later Roman Empire*, p. 770.

9 B. Sanhedrin 58b, R. Eleazar [b. Pedat]. Cf. Rostovtzeff, *SEHRE*[2], index s.v. "landgrabbing", especially 2, p. 746, note 60.

10 *Pirké Rabbenu ha-Kaddosh*, ed. Shönblum (Lemberg, 1877), p. 12. Cf. B. Sukka 19b, early III cent.; *Tanḥuma Buber, Exod.*, p. 80, section 1, and printed *Tanḥuma*

cited by Buber, ibid., note 2. (See also *Midrash Shemuel* 7.6, ed. Buber, p. 68; Y. Bikkurim 3.3 later III cent. text, etc.). Cf. Oertel in *Cambridge Ancient History*, 12, p. 274. See also *Lev. Rab.* 34.13, ed. Margulies, p. 800 for mentions of impoverished landowners (*ba'alei batim*) by R. Isaac, c. 250–320. See my articles in *JESHO*, 14/3, 1971, pp. 227–52, and *RIDA*, 3/19, 1972, pp. 29–42.

11 *Cod. Just.* 2.59.1; *SEHRE*[2], p. 497, and index s.v. "flight"; Allon, *Toldot ha-Yehudim*, p. 209. On the decline of the small peasant land proprietor, see Jones, *Later Roman Empire*, pp. 778–79, and Allon, ibid., p. 209. See also Jones' article in *Antiquity*, 33, 1959, pp. 39–43, entitled "Over-taxation and the decline of the Roman Empire", where he puts forward the theory that the increase of taxation — evidence of Themistius in 364 that taxes had doubled in preceding 40 years (Jones, ibid., p. 39) — reduced profits so much that it became no longer profitable to farm, and therefore people left the land. Walbank, in his *Decline of the Roman Empire in the West*, calls this building up of large estates "manor economy".

12 Y. Shevi'it 9.3. See Lieberman's remarks in *JQR*, 36, 1946, pp. 350–1.

13 = Banyas = Panias = Caesarea Paneas. See Neubauer, *La Géographie du Talmud*, pp. 236–37; Hirschensohn, *Sheva Chochmoth*, p. 196; Avi-Yonah, *Map of Roman Palestine* (*QDAP*, 5/4), p. 146 [8]. See also Amir, in *Teva ve-Arez*, 10/4, 1968, p. 263.

14 "Thirteen years" according to Leiden Ms. This reading of thirteen seems to be the more correct one. Such was the reading before Nachmanides; see his commentary on Gen. 49.21 (ed. C.B. Chavel, 1, Jerusalem, 1959, p. 272 — Chavel does not note this point). See J.N. Epstein, *Prolegomena ad Litteras Amoraiticas*, p. 437, note 11. See also *Midrash Shir Ha-Shirim*, ed. Grünhut, 48b, section 14, which also has "thirteen", and see Buber's remark in Grünhut's edition, p. 34. As to the identification of Africa, see the interesting comments of M. Wohlmann, *Hikrei Ha-Aretz* (Tel-Aviv, 1939), pp. 19–21.

15 Magie, *Roman Rule in Asia Minor*, p. 714.

16 E.E. Urbach, "The Laws Regarding Slavery", in *Papers of the Institute of Jewish Studies, London*, (ed. J.G. Weiss). 1, (Jerusalem, 1964), p. 87. On the economic background to the colonate see Allon, *Toldot ha-Yehudim*, pp. 207–09. On the lateness of the colonate in Palestine (Cynegius, 383–88, as opposed to the more usual 332), see A. Gulak, *Le-Heker Toldot ha-Mishpat ha-Ivri bi-Tekufat ha-Talmud*, 1, *Dinei Karka'ot* (Jerusalem, 1929), pp. 135–37, with bibliography. On the colonate in general see Jones, *Later Roman Empire*, pp. 795–803.

17 Magie, *Roman Rule in Asia Minor*, p. 714.

18 B. Bava Mezia 42a. R. Isaac. *flor.* c. 260–320. He was a pupil of R. Johanan and a friend of R. Ammi and R. Asi.

19 See Kent in *Mattingly Festschrift*, p. 191; Jones, *Later Roman Empire*, p. 807.

20 See P. Petit, *Libanius et la vie municipale à Antioch en 4e siècle après J.C.* (Paris, 1955, Institut Français d'Archéologie de Beyrouth, Bibliothèque Archéologique et Historique, 62), pp. 298–303. This is especially clear from the Codes: eg. *Cod. Theod.* 9.21; 9.22.1; 9.38. 7–8; 11.21.1; *Serm.* 8; *Cod. Theod.* 9.23. 1; 7.20, 11, etc. See also Grierson in *Mattingly Festschrift*, p. 240 et seq.; Kent, ibid., pp. 203–04; *Libanius' autobiography, First Oration*, ed. and transl. A.F. Norman (Oxford, 1965), p. 161 (to Or. 1.61); Mickwitz, *Geld und Wirtschaft*, pp. 154–64 (basing himself primarily on patristic sources).

21 Petit, *Libanius*, pp. 300, 303.

22 See Petit, ibid., p. 298: *"Les historiens modernes les plus representifs, et parmi eux, en France, M. Piganiol, au premier rang, semblent d'accord aujourd'hui pour nous offrir de L'Empire sur ce point une image à peu près identique; ils constatent le développement des échange monétaire et la triomphe de l'économie ouvert"*, (= *geldwirtschaft*) etc. Bibliography, ibid. See also Santo Mazzarino, *The End of the Ancient World* (London, 1966), p. 153; Passerini, *Studi in Onore di Gino Luzzatto*, 1949, etc. See also *De Rebus Bellicis* III.1, ed. Thompson, pp. 94, 110.

23 "Gold Coinage in the Later Roman Empire", in *Mattingly Festschrift*.

24 Ibid., pp. 203–04.

25 See P. Grierson's essay on "The Roman Law of Counterfeiting", also in *Mattingly Festschrift*, p. 240, et seq. See *Cod. Theod.* 9.23.1 (348) 9.22.1 (317, 343).

26 A discussion of the "cash-producing" taxes is to be found in Kent's article in *Mattingly Festschri t*, pp. 194–96.

27 Kent, ibid., p. 197, states that the "excellent preservation of most surviving later Roman gold [is evidence that] the chance of any individual piece circulating for long was slight. If it escaped recoining, it must have gone quickly to ground."

28 On this whole subject see Jones, *Later Roman Empire*, chap. 13, especially pp. 427–37, 462–69, etc.

29 The acceptance of a full gold standard in the modern sense of the term came about in 367. See *Cod. Just.* 11.11.2 of that year, according to which the variation in the price of the *solidus* is to be accompanied by proportional changes in the prices of other commodities. Cf. also *Cod. Theod.* 9.23.1 (of 359) which states that coinage should be used for purchase and not as merchandise. See Kent in *Mattingly Festschrift*, pp. 191–92.

30 However, see Callu, *PMER*, pp. 309–12.

31 For evidence of these changes in Rabbinic literature see the following: A. Marmorstein, "Ha-Matzav ha-Kalkali ... be-Doro shel R. Johanan etc.", in *Freimann Festschrift* (Berlin, 1937), pp. 1–12; idem, "Doro shel R. Johanan etc.", in *Tarbiz*, 3, 1932, pp. 161–80 (Much of what Marmorstein wrote has to be radically revised. Thus he dated the *Otot ha-Mashiaḥ* c. 260–70, *Tarbiz*, ibid., p. 164, while Yehuda ibn Shemuel, in his *Midreshei Ge'ulah*, Israel, 1957, p. 297, demonstrates that it is mediaeval, and probably post c. 950. Furthermore, many of Marmorstein's arguments are based on undated texts.) S. Lieberman in *JQR*, NS 36, 1945–46, pp. 328–70 contains much valuable information (but is perhaps too kindly disposed towards the Romans?). Cf. Baron's remark in his *SHRJ*[2], 2, chap. 13, p. 398, note 11. Valuable information is also found in Lieberman's *Greek and Hellenism in Jewish Palestine* (Hebrew edition, Jerusalem, 1962), and his article in *Annuaire de l'Institut de Philologie et d'Histoire Orientales et Slaves*, 7, 1939–44, on "The Martyrs of Caesarea". See also S. Krauss, *Paras ve-Romi ba-Talmud u-ba-Midrashim* (Jerusalem, 1948), and, of course, Allon's *Toldot ha-Yehudim*, especially the second volume.

32 See also Allon, ibid., pp. 210–13. See also S. Appelbaum's article in *Zion*, 23–24, 1958–59, "The Province of Syria-Palaestina as a Province of the Severan Empire", pp. 35–45 (English summary, p. III); pp. 94–95, for changes of land-tenure pattern in III cent.; p. 43, note 64 for move away from land because of taxation; pp. 42–43 for attempt to increase agricultural productivity in III cent.; and p. 43 for increase in cattle-raising during III cent. See also A. Gulak's article "The Method of Collecting Roman Taxes in Palestine", in *Magnes Anniversary Book* (Jerusalem

1938), pp. 97–104, (English summary, pp. XXI–III), especially his interpretation of the very interesting passage in Y. Ketubot 10.5, a text that must be dated 350–75, mentioning *"shequi'im"*-lands sunk into debts of unpaid taxes.

33 Allon, *Toldot Ha-Yehudim*, pp. 209, 253. See J. Feliks, *Agriculture in Palestine in the Period of the Mishna and Talmud* (Jerusalem, 1963), p. 159, note 37, (in Hebrew), and my article in *JESHO*, 15/3, 1973, pp. 227–55.

34 Allon, ibid., pp. 252–62. See also M. Avi-Yonah, *IEJ*, 8/1, 1958, pp. 40–41, article entitled "The Economics of Byzantine Palestine".

35 See Avi-Yonah, ibid., p. 41 et seq. who discusses the economic effect of the change of Palestine from being an obscure province (in the period before Christianity became the official religion of the Empire — e.g. Eusebius, *De Martyribus Palaest.* 11.9–11) to being the "Holy Land", a center of tourism and of massive donations (to the Churches, etc.).

36 This is the subject of my next volume, which will deal with problems of flight and taxation (and their effects upon certain halachot), changes in the structure of the agrarian society, agricultural trends, etc. in Amoraic Palestine.

BIBLIOGRAPHY

PRIMARY SOURCES

Hebrew and Aramaic

Aggadat Bereishit, Warsaw 1876, ed. S. Buber (Agadath Bereishith), Cracow, 1902.

Aggadat Esther, ed. S. Buber, Cracow, 1879.

Avot de Rabbi Nathan, ed. S. Schechter, Vienna, 1887.

Babylonian Talmud (= Bavli). Wilna ed.; Codex Munich 95, Jerusalem, 1970; (see also Rabbinovitz and Abramson).

Batei Midrashot, ed. A. Wertheimer[2], Jerusalem, 1954.

Bet ha-Midrasch, ed. Jellinek, Leipzig, 1853–77.

Deuteronomy Rabba, ed. S. Liebermann[2], Jerusalem, 1964. (called "*Midrash Debarim Rabba*").

Discoveries in the Judaean Desert, vols. 1–3; ed. Barthélemy, Milik, De Vaux & Baillet, Oxford, 1955–62.

Gaonica I, ed. S. Assaf, Jerusalem, 1933.

Genesis Rabba, ed. Theodor & Albeck[2], Jerusalem, 1965, (called "*Midrash Bereschit Rabba*").

Ginzei Schechter, ed. L. Ginzberg, vol. 1 and 2, New York, 1928–29.

Halachot Pesuqot, ed. S. Sasoon, Jerusalem, 1950.

Agadath Shir Hashirim, ed. S. Schechter, Cambridge, 1896.

Hilkhot Terefot li-Vnei Eretz Yisrael, ed. M. Margalioth, *Talpioth*, 8/3–4, pp. 307–30.

Igereth Rav Sherira Gaon, ed. A. Hyman, London, 1910.

Iggeret R. Scherira Gaon, ed. B. Lewin, Haifa, 1921.

Lamentations Rabba, ed. S. Buber, Wilna, 1899, (called "*Midrash Echa Rabbati*").

Leviticus Rabba, ed. M. Margulies, Jerusalem, 1953–60, (called "*Midrash Wayyikra Rabba*").

Meor Ha-Afelah (= *Nur al-Z'lam*), by Netanel b. Isaiah (dated 1329), ed. J. Kafih, Jerusalem, 1957.

Masechet Semachot (called "*Treatise Semaḥot*"), ed. M. Higger, New York, 1931; ed. and transl. D. Zlotnick, Yale University Press, 1966 (called "*The Tractate 'Mourning'*", Yale Judaica Series, vol. XVII).

Mechilta de R. Ishmael, ed. M. Friedmann (= Ish-Shalom), Vienna, 1890; ed. Horowitz & Rabin[2], Jerusalem, 1960, ed. J.Z. Lauterbach, Philadelphia, 1933–35.

Mekhilta d'Rabbi Simon b. Jochai, ed. Epstein and Melamed, Jerusalem, 1955.

Menorat Ha-Maor, of R. Israel ibn Al-Nakawa, ed. H.G. Enelow, New York, 1929–32.

Midrash Ha-Gadol, Genesis & Exodus, ed. M. Margulies, Jerusalem, 1947–56.

"   "   Leviticus, ed. E.N. Rabinowitz, New York, 1932.

Midrash Ha-Gadol, Numbers, ed. S. Fisch, vol. 1, London, 1957, vol. 2, Jerusalem 1963; ed. Z. M. Rabbinowitz, Jerusalem, 1967.

" " Deuteronomy, ed. S. Fisch, Jerusalem 1972, and see *Midrash Tanna'im.*

Midrash Lekaḥ Tov (on the Pentateuch), ed. S. Buber, Wilna, 1880. (also called *Pesikta Zutrati).*

Midrash Mishlé, ed. S. Buber, Wilna, 1893.

Midrash Psalms (= *Tehilim),* ed. S. Buber, Vilna, 1891, (called "*Schocher Tob").*

Midrash Shemuel, ed. S. Buber, Cracow, 1893.

Midrash Shir Ha-Shirim, ed. L. Grünhut, Jerusalem, 1896.

Midrash Rabba, Wilna ed.; *Midrash Rabba* to Cant., Ruth ,Esther (called Ahasuerus), Lament., Eccles., ed. princeps, Pesaro, 1619.

Midrash Tanḥuma, ed. S. Buber, Wilna, 1885; printed ed., Wilna, 1833.

Midrash Tanna'im, ed. D. Hoffman, Berlin, 1909.

Midrash Zuta, ed. S. Buber, on Cant., Ruth, Lament., Eccles.; Berlin, 1894.

Midreshei Ge'ula, ed. Judah Even-Shmuel, Jerusalem, 1954.

Mishna, Standard editions, (see also M. Schachter).

Palestinian Talmud (= Yerushalmi), Krotoschin ed., Gilead ed., New York, 1949; editions Venice (ed. pr. 1523?), Zitomir, 1860; L. Ginzberg, *Yerushalmi Fragments from the Genizah,* New York, 1909; Sirilio Ms., British Museum Ms. OR.2823–4 (Zera'im); Codex Vatican 133, (Zera'im and Sota), Jerusalem, 1971; Leiden MS. (whole Yerushalmi), Cod. Scal. 3, Jerusalem, 1970. (See also J. N. Epstein, *Prolegomena ad litteras Tannaiticas,* for Leiden Ms. variants, and S. Lieberman, *On the Yerushalmi,* from Codex Vatican 133, variants to Sota; Ginzberg in *Yerushalmi Fragments,* etc. also cites variants from Codex Vatican 133 to Zera'im.)

Pesikta de R. Kahana, ed. S. Buber, Lyck, 1860; ed. B. Mandelbaum, New York, 1962.

Pesikta Rabbati, ed. M. Friedmann (= Ish-Shalom), Vienna, 1880.

Pesikta Zutrati, see *Midrash Lekaḥ Tov.*

Pirké Rabbenu ha-Kaddosh, ed. Schönblum, Lemberg, 1877.

Seder Eliahu Rabba and *Seder Eliahu Zuta,* ed. M. Friedmann (= Ish-Shalom), Vienna, 1904.

Seder Olam Rabba, ed. D. B. Ratner, Vilna, 1894–97; (see Neubauer, A.).

Seder Olam Zuta, ed. M. Grossberg, London, 1910–11; (see Neubauer, A.).

Sefer ha-Kabbalah of R. Abraham ibn Daud, ed. S. Cohen, Philadelphia, 1967; (see Neubauer, A.).

Sefer ha-Ma'asim li-Vnei Eretz Yisrael, ed. B. M. Lewin, Tarbiz, 1/1, Oct. 1929.

Sefer Ve-Hizhir, ed. Freimann, 1, Leipzig, 1873; 2, Warsaw, 1880.

Sefer Yuḥassim ha-Shalem, ed. Filipowski, London, 1857.

Sifra (= *Torat Kohanim,* on Leviticus), ed. I. H. Weiss, Vienna, 1861; Codex Assemani LXV, ed. L. Finkelstein, New York, 1956.

Sifré, ed. Friedmann (= Ish-Shalom), Vienna, 1963; ed. Horovitz & Rabin[2], Jerusalem, 1966.

Sifré on Deuteronomy, ed. L. Finkelstein, New York, 1969, reprint of Berlin ed. 1939.

Sifré Zuta, ed. Horovitz & Rabin[2], Jerusalem, 1966.

Targum Onkelos, ed. A. Sperber, Leiden, 1959–1968.

Targum Ps. Jonathan, ed. M. Ginzburger, Berlin, 1903, based on British Museum Ms. Add. 27, 031. Also Ms. Neofiti I, Jerusalem, 1971.

Tosefta, ed. S. Lieberman, Zera'im, New York, 1955, Mo'ed, New York, 1962, Nashim, New York, 1967; ed. Zuckermandel, Halberstadt, 1881.

Tractate 'Avodah Zarah (of the Bavli), according to a Ms. of the Jewish Theological Seminary of America, ed. S. Abramson, New York, 1957.

Yalkut Shimoni, Salonica ed., 1521–27; Venice ed., 1566, and Horeb ed., Berlin, 1926.

Yalkut ha-Machiri to Prov., ed. L. Grünhut, Jerusalem, 1902.

Yerushalmi, see Palestinian Talmud.

Syriac

Acta Martyrum et Sanctorum, ed. P. Bedjan, Paris, 1890–97.

The Story of Aḥikar (Syriac version), in the ed. of Conybeare, Rendel Harris & A. Smith Lewis, Cambridge, 1913, second ed.

Bar-Bahlul, ed. R. Duval, Paris, 1910.

Book of Medicines, ed. E. A. W. Budge, Oxford, 1913.

Chronique de Michel de Syrien, ed. Chabot, vol. 1, Paris, 1899.

The Book of Paradise of Palladius etc., ed. E. A. W. Budge, London, 1904.

The Chronicle of Joshua Stylites, ed. W. Wright, Cambridge, 1882.

Chronicon Syriacum Gregorii Barhebraei, ed. P. Bedjan, Paris, 1890.

The Chronography of Gregory Abu'l Faraj . . . etc., ed. E. A. W. Budge, London, 1932.

The Doctrine of Addai, The Apostle, ed. G. Phillips, London, 1876.

Ecclesiastical History of Eusebius, ed. W. Wright and N. Mclean, Cambridge, 1898.

Eliya of Nesbis, ed. Lagarde, Göttingean, 1879.

Epiphanius Treatise on Weights and Measures, ed. J. E. Dean, The Oriental Institute of the University of Chicago, Studies in Ancient Oriental Civilisations, No. 11, Chicago, 1935; ed. Lagarde, in *Veteris Testimenti ab Origine recensit fragmenta apud Syros servata quinque*, pp. 1–76, Göttingae, 1880; from British Museum Mss. Add. 17, 148, and 14, 620.

Four Gospels in Syriac, transcribed from the Sinai Palimpsest, R. C. Bensly, J. Rendel Harris, E. C. Burkitt & A. Smith Lewis, Cambridge, 1894.

Histoire Ecclesiastique de Eusèbe de Césarée, ed. P. Bedjan, Paris and Leipzig, 1897.

Ḥnana d'Adiebene, Patrologia Orientallis, 7, ed. Sher, Paris, 1911.

The Laughable Stories collected by Bar-Hebraeus, ed. E. A. W. Budge, Luzac's Semitic Texts and Translation Series, vol. 1, London, 1897.

Peshitta, ed. Lee, London, 1823; Urmia ed., 1852, and British Museum Mss. Add. 14,425 and 14,427.

Palestinian Syriac Lectionary of the Gospels, ed. A. Smith Lewis & M. Dunlop Gibson, London, 1899.

Syrische Rechtsbücher, ed. Sachau, (= *Leges Constantini Theodosii Leonis*), Berlin, 1907.

Tetra Euangelium Sanctum, Simplex syrorum versio, ed. P. E. Pusey & G. H. Gwilliam, Oxford, 1901.

Other sources in Brokelmann's *Lexicon Syriacum²*, and Payne Smith's *Thesaurus Syriacus* and its *Supplement*. See section on Dictionaries.

Latin and Greek

Aelian, *De Natura Animalium* ed. R. Hercher, Leipzig, 1858–64; ed. A. F. Schofield, 1958–9, Loeb.

Ammianus Marcellinus, *Res Gestae*, ed. C. V. Clark, Berlin, 1910–15; ed. J. C. Rolfe, 1935–39, Loeb.

Ancient Roman Statutes, ed. A.C. Johnson, P.R. Coleman-Norton & F.C. Bourne, Austin Texas, 1961.

Ps. Aurelius Victor, *De Viris Illustribus Urbis Romae*, ed. Pichlmayr, Leipzig, 1911.

Saint Basil, *The Letters*, ed. Roy J. Deferrari, Loeb, ed., London, 1924–34.

Cassiodorus, *Variae, Monumenta Germaniae Historicae, Auctores Antiquissimi*, XII, ed. Mommsen, 1894.

Cicero, *Actio in Verrem*, ed. C.F.W. Mueller, Leipzig, 1886; ed. Greenwood, 1928–35, Loeb ed.

Chronicum Pascale, Migne, *Patrologia Graeca*, 92; *CSHB* 9, ed. Dindorf, Bonn, 1832.

Codex Justinianus, ed. P. Krüger, Berlin, 1877.

Codex Theodosianus, ed. T. Mommsen & P.M. Meyer, Berlin 1895; ed. P. Krüger, Berlin, 1923; transl. C. Pharr, Princeton, 1952.

Corpus Iuris Civilis, ed. T. Mommsen & Krüger, Berlin, 1928–29.

De Rebus Bellicis, ed. E.A. Thompson, Oxford, 1952.

Digesta Justiniani Augusti, ed. Bonfante etc., Milan, 1931, and ed. Mommsen, Berin, 1863–70.

Dio Cassius, ed. V.P. Boissevain, Berlin, 1895–1901; ed. E. Cary, 1914–27, Loeb.

Epictetus, *Dissertationes ab Arriano digestae*, ed. H. Schenkl[2], 1916.

Epiphanius, *De Mensuris et Ponderibus*, Migne, *Patrologia Graeca*, 43, 238–94, and apud F. Hultsch, *Metrologicorum Scriptorum Reliquiae*, and apud Lagard, *Symmicta*.

Eusebius, *Histoia Ecclesiastica*, ed. & transl. Kirsopp Lake, Loeb ed., London, 1929–32, and ed. Lawlor & Oulton, 1927.

Eustatius, *Commentarii ad Homeri Iliadem et Odysseam etc.*, Leipzig, 1825–30.

Festus, *Brevarium of*, ed. J.W. Eadie, London, 1967.

Gaius, *Institutionum iuris civilis commentarii*, in *Collectio librorum juris antejustiniani*, ed. Krüger, Mommsen & Studemund, Berlin, 1878, and in Huschke, 1935.

Hesychius, *FHG*, IV (= *Fragmenta Historicorum Graecorum*), ed. C. Miller, Paris, 1885.

Hieronymous, *Commentarius in Danielem*, Migne, *Patrologia Latina*, 25, 491–584, 1845.

Isidorus Hispalensis (of Seville), *Etymologiae*, ed. W.M. Lindsay, Oxford, 1911.

Joannes Moschus, *Patrologia Graeca*, 87; *Patrologia Latina*, 74.

Julianus Imperator (the Apostate), *Orations* and *Misopogon*, ed. F.C. Hertlein, Leipzig, 1876; ed. Bidez & Cumont, Paris, 1922; ed. W.C. Wright, London, 1913, Loeb ed.

Libanius, *Epistles & Orations*, ed. R. Foerster, Leipzig, 1903–23.

Malalas, *Chronographia ,Corpus Scriptorum Historiae Byzantinae*, ed. Dindorf, 1831, PG, 97.

Marcellinus Comes, *Chronicon*, ed. Mommsen, in *Chronica Minora II*, Berlin, 1894, also Dindorf, *Monumenta Germaniae Historicae, Auctores Antiquissimi*, II, pp. 60–104.

Martial, ed. W.M. Lindsay, Oxford, 1927; ed. Ker, 1919–20, Loeb ed.

Novellae, Valentinian, *Codex Theodosianus*, 2, ed. P. Meyer, Berlin, 1905; translation in *The Theodosian Code*, Clyde Pharr, Princeton, 1952.

Panegyrici Latini, ed. E. Galletier, Paris, 1949–52.

Persius, *Satires*, ed. Owen, transl. G.G. Ramsay, 1918, and J. Tate, 1920.

Photius, *Lexicon*, ed. S.A. Naber, Leiden, 1864–65.

Pliny, *Historia Naturalis*, ed. C. Mayhoff, Leipzig, 1892–1909, and ed. Rackham, Eicholz & Jones, 1938–52, Loeb ed.

Polybius, *Universal History*, ed. T. Büttner-Wobst, Leipzig, 1882–1905; ed. W.R. Paton, 1922–27, Loeb.

Procopius, *Anecdota (Historia Arcana)*, ed. Orelli, 1827, Bonn, 1838; Dindorf, *CSHB*, 10/3; ed. H.B. Dewing, Loeb ed. 6, 1935.

Socrates, *Historia Ecclesiastica*, Migne, *Patrologia Graeca*, 67, pp. 33–841; also in Bohn's *Ecclesiastical Library*, London, 1851–77.

Scriptores Historiae Augustae, ed. Hohl, Leipzig, 1927; ed. D. Magie, London, 1921–32, Loeb ed.

Sozomen, *Ecclesiastical History*, translation C.D. Hartranft, in H. Wace and P. Schaff, *A Select Library of Nicene and Post-Nicene Falthers, Second Series*, vol. 2, Oxford and New York, 1891.

Suetonius, *Vitae Duodecim Caesarum*, ed. M. Ihm, Leipzig, 1923; ed. J.C. Rolfe, 1914, Loeb ed.

Symmachus, *Relationes*, *Monumenta Germaniae Historicae, Auctores Antiquissimi*, VI, ed. Seeck, 1883.

Testament of Job, transl. K. Kohler in *Kohut Memorial Volume, Semitic Studies in Memory of Alexander Kohut*, pp. 264–338, Berlin, 1897; also in James, *Apocrypha Anecdota*, pp. 104–37.

Theodoretus, *Historia Ecclesiastica*, ed. L. Parmentier, *Die Griechischen Christlischen Schriftsteller der Ersten drei Jahruhund.* etc., vol. 84, 1911.

Ulpianus, *Regulae*, in *Collectio librorum juris antejustiniani*, ed. Kruger, Mommsen & Studemund, Berlin, 1878.

Vita S. Pachomii, ed. Bousquet & Nau, Paris, 1908, *Patrologia Orientalis*, 4/5.

Zosimus, *Historia Nova*, ed. L. Mendelssohn, Leipzig, 1887; and *CSMB*, 20, ed. Bekker, Bonn, 1837.

Papyri

Apocrimata, Decisions of Septimius Severus in Legal Matters, ed. W.L. Westermann & A. Schiller, New York, 1954. See also *Chronique d'Égypte*, 30, 1955, pp. 327–45.

BGU., *Aegyptische Urkunden aus der staatlischen Museen zu Berlin, Griechische Urkunden*, Berlin, 1892–1937.

Dura Rep., *The Excavations at Dura Europos, Preliminary (or Final) Report of First (Second...) Seasons of Work*, ed. P.V.C. Bauer, M.I. Rostovtzeff, A.R. Bellinger and others, Yale University Press, 1929.

Frisk, Bankakten, Bankakten aus dem Faijum nebst anderen Berliner Papyri, ed. M. Frisk, Göteborgs Kungl. Vetenskaps-och Vitterhets-Samhälles Handlingar, femte följden, Ser. A. Band 2, No. 2, Göteborg, 1931.

Harv. St., *Havard Studies in Classical Philology*, vol. LI, Boak, "Some Early Byzantine Tax Records from Egypt".

O. Brüss., *Ostraca aus Brüssel und Berlin*, O. Viereck, Berlin, 1922.

P. Amh., *The Amherst Papyri*, B.P. Grenfell & A.S. Hunt, London, 1900–01.

P. Bad., *Veroeffentlichungen aus den badischen Papyrus–Sammlungen*, W. Speigelberg, F. Bilabel and others, Heidelberg, 1923–34.

P. Beatty Panop., *Papyri from Panoplis in the Chester Beatty Library*, T.C. Skeat, Dublin, 1964.

P. Cairo Masp., *Catalogue générale des antiquités égyptiennes du Musée du Cairo*; *Papyrus grecs d'époque byzantine*, J. Maspéro, Cario, 1911–16.

P. Col., *Columbia Papyri*, Greek Series, II, W.L. Westermann & C.W. Keys, New York, 1932.

P. Corn., *Greek Papyri in the Library of Cornell University*, W.L. Westermann & C.J. Kraemer, New York, 1926.

PER., *Mitteilungen aus der Sammlung der Papyrus Erzherzig Rainer*, Vienna, 1887, N.S.I, Vienna, 1932.

P. Erlangen, *Die Papyri der Universitätsbibliothek Erlangen*, W. Schubart, Leipzig, 1942.

P. Fay., *Fayum Tawns and their Papyri*, A.S. Hunt & D.G. Hogarth, London, 1900.

P. Flor., *Papiri greco-egizii*, D. Comparetti & G. Vitelli, Milan, 1906–15.

P. Gen., *Les Papyrus de Genève*, J. Nicole, Geneva, 1896–1900.

P. Giss., *Griechische Papyri im Museum des oberhessischen Gesechichtsvereins zu Giessen*, O. Eger, E. Kornemann and P.M. Meyer etc., Leipzig, 1910–12.

P. Goodsp., *Greek Papyri from the Cairo Museum together with Papyri of Roman Egypt from American collections*, E.J. Goodspeed, Chicago, 1902.

P. Grenf., *New Classical Fragments and other Greek and Latin Papyri*, B.P. Grenfell & A.S. Hunt, Oxford, 1897.

P. Land., *Papyri Iandanae*, cum discipulis edidit C. Kalbfleisch, Leipzig, 1912–28.

P. Lond., *Greek Papyri in the British Museum*, F.G. Kenyon & H.I. Bell, London, 1893–1917.

P. Mich., *Tebtunis Papyri in the University of Michigan Collection*, A.E.R. Boak, University of Michigan Studies, Humanistic Series, vol. XXVII, Ann Arbor, 1933.

P. Nessana, *Excavations at Nessana*, conducted by H.D. Colt, Jr., vol. 3, Non-literary Papyri, C.J. Kraemer, Jr., Princeton, N.J., 1958.

P.O., *The Oxyrhynchus Papyri*, B.P. Grenfell, A.S. Hunt and others, London, 1898–.

P. Rol. Princ., *A papyrus roll in the Princeton Collection*, E.A. Kase, Jr., Baltimore, 1933.

P. Ross. George., *Papyri Russicher und Georgischer Sammlungen*, Zereteli, O. Krüger, P. Jernstedt, Tiflis, 1925–35.

P. Ryl., *Catalogue of Greek Papyri in the John Rylands Library*, Manchester, A.S. Hunt, J. de M. Johnson, V. Martin, C.H. Roberts and E.G. Turner, Manchester, 1911–52.

PSI., *Papiri greci e latini, Pubblicazioni della Società italiana per la ricerca dei Papiri greci e latini in Egitto*, G. Vitelli, M. Norsa and others, Florence, 1912–.

P. Strass., *Griechische Papyrus der kaiserlichen Universitäts-und Landesbibliothek zu Strassburg*, F. Preisigke, Leipzig, 1912, 1920; continued as *Papyrus grecs de la Bibliothèque nationale et Universitaire de Strassburg*, P. Collomp and his pupils, Paris, 1948.

P. Rend. Harr., *The Rendel Harris Papyri of Woodbrooke College, Birnimgham*, J.E. Powell, Cambridge, 1935.

P. Tebt., *The Tebtunis Papyri*, B.P. Grenfell, A.S. Hunt and other, London, 1902–38.

P. Würz., *Mitteilungen aus der Würznurger Papyrussamlung*, U. Wilken, Berlin, 1934.

SB., *Sammelbuch griechische Urkunden aus Ägypten*, Preisigke & Bilabel, Strassburg, then Berlin & Leipzig, then Heidelberg, 1913–34.

SPP. or Stud. Pal., *Studien zur Paläographie und Papyrus Kunde*, Leipzig, 1901–.

Tait OP., *Greek Ostraca in the Bodleian Library at Oxford and various other collections*, Tait, London, 1930.

WO., *Griechische Ostraka aus Ägypten und Nubien*, U. Wilcken, Leipzig & Berlin, 1899.

Epigraphic

Corpus Inscriptionum Graecarum (= *CIG*), A. Boeckh, Berlin, 1828–77.

Corpus Inscriptionum Judaicarum (= *CIJ*), P.J.B. Frey, Rome, 1936, 1952.

Corpus Inscriptionum Latinarum (= *CIL*), Berlin, 1862–.

Edict of Diocletian, ed. E.R. Graser, apud Tenney Frank, *Econ. Survey* 5, pp. 307–421, and in *TAPA*, 71, 1940, pp. 157–74. See also Erim, Kenan T., and Lauffer, S.

Forschungen in Ephesos, veröffentlicht von Oesterreichischer Archäologischen Institut, Vienna, 1912–32, Baden bei Wien, 1937.

Gerasa, City of Decapolis, ed. C.H. Kraeling, New Haven Connecticut, 1938.

Inscriptiones Latinae Selectae (= *ILS*), H. Dessau, Berlin, 1892–1906.

Inscriptions Grecques et Latines de la Syrie, L. Jalabert & R. Mouterde, Paris, 1929–1953.

Inscriptions latines d'Afrique, R. Cagnat, A. Morlin & L. Chatelain, 1923.

Inscriptions latines de l'Algerie, S. Gael & H.G. Pflaum, 1957.

Inscriptions of Roman Tripolitania, J.M. Reynolds & J.B. Ward Perkins, 1952.

North Semitic Inscriptions, G.A. Cooke, London, 1903.

Orientis Graeci Inscriptiones Selectae (= *OGIS*), ed. W. Dittenberger, Leipzig, 1903–1905.

Publications of the Princeton University Archaeological Expeditions to Syria in 1904–05 and 1909, Section III, Greek and Latin Inscriptions, part A, E. Littman, D. Magie, and D.R. Stuart, Leyden, 1921; part B, W.K. Prentice, Leyden, 1922.

Sylloge Inscriptionum Graecarum[2], W. Dittenberger (= Ditt.), Leipzig, 1915–24.

Voyage Archéologique en Grèce et en Asie Mineur, Syrie, III/1, P. Lebas et W.H. Waddington, Paris, 1870.

DICTIONARIES AND ENCYCLOPAEDIAS

Akkadian
The Assyrian Dictionary of the Oriental Institute of the University of Chicago, 1956 onwards.
Muss-Arnolt, *Dictionary of the Assyrian Language*, Berlin, 1905.
von Soden, W., *Akkadische Handwörterbuch*, 1959, onwards.

Arabic
Dozy, R., *Supplement aux Dictionnaires Arabes*, Leiden, 1887.
Lane, E.A., *Arabic English Lexcion*, London, 1863–93.

Aramaic
Fürst, J., *Glossarium Graeco-Hebraeum*, Strasbourg, 1890.
Jastrow, M.A., *A Dictionary of the Targumin, The Talmud Babli and Yerushalmi, and the Midrashic Literature*, London, New York, 1903.
Kohut, A., *Aruch Completum*, Vienna [and New York], 1878–92.
Krauss, S., *Additamenta ad librum Aruch Completum*, Vienna, 1937.
————, (and Löw, I.,), *Griechische und Lateinische Lehnwörter im Talmud, Midrasch and Targum*, Berlin, 1898–99.
Levy, J., *Chaldäisches Wörterbuch über die Targumin*, Leipzig, 1881.
————, *Neuhebräisches und Chaldäisches Wörterbuch über die Talmudim und Midrashim*, Leipzig, 1876–89.
See also in the general bibliography S. Fraenkel and I. Löw.

Coptic
Crum, W.E., *Coptic Dictionary*, Oxford, 1935.

Greek
Hesychius, Iena, 1862.
Liddell & Scott[2], Oxford, 1961. Supplement, Oxford, 1968.
Photius, Leipzig, 1808.
Preisigke, F., *Wörterbuch der Griechischen Papyruskunden*, Berlin, 1925–31.
Sophocles[2], Cambridge Mass., 1887.
Suidas, Leipzig, 1925.

Latin

Ducange, *Glossarium Mediae et Infimae Latinitatis*, Niort, 1883–87.
Lewis & Short, Oxford, 1962.
Souter, A., *A Glossary of Later Latin to 600 A. D.*, Oxford, 1964.

Mandaean

Drower & Macuch, *A Mandaic Dictionary*, Oxford, 1963.

Syriac

Bah-Bahlul, ed. Duval, Paris, 1910.
Brockelmann, C., *Lexicon Syriacum*[2], Göttingae, 1928.
Payne Smith, R., *Thesaurus Syriacus*, Oxford, 1897–1901, and the *Supplement to the Thesaurus Syriacus* of R. Payne Smith, by J. P. Margoliouth, Oxford, 1927.

Turkish

Redhouse, *Turkish Dictionary*, London, 1800.

Encyclopaedias

Encyclopaedia Brittanica[9], London, 1875–79.
Encyclopaedia Judaica, Jerusalem, 1972.
Jewish Encyclopaedia, New York and London, 1925.

GENERAL BIBLIOGRAPHY

Abbott, F.F. & Johnson, A.C., *Municipal Administration in the Roman Empire*, Princeton, 1926.

Abraham, B. Elija of Vilna, *Rav Po'alim*, ed. S.M. Chones, Warsaw, 1894.

Abramson, Shraga, *Rav Nissim Gaon*, Jerusalem, 1965.

————, *Tractate 'Avodah Zara*, New York, 1957.

Adelson, J., "Economic Theory and Practice in Antioch, 361–63", *INCP*, pp. 33–40.

Adelson, Howard L., "Silver Currency and Values in the Early Byzantine Empire", in *Centennial Publication of the American Numismatic Society*, ed. Harald Ingholt, New York, 1938.

————, "The Bronze Alloys of the Coinage of the Later Roman Empire", *ANSMN*, 6, New York, 1954, pp. 111–29.

————, "A Note on the Miliarense from Constantine to Heraclius", *ANSMN*, 7, New York, 1957, pp. 125–35.

————, "The Monetary Deterioration in the Fifth Century", *INCP*, pp. 262–82.

Albeck, Ch., *Meḥkarim be-Beraitha u-ba-Tosefta*, Jerusalem, 1944.

————, *Mavo La-Talmudim*, Tel-Aviv, 1969.

————, See also Zunz, L.

Allon, G., *Toldot ha-Yehudim be-Eretz-Yisrael bi-Tekufat ha-Mishna ve-ha-Talmud*, vol. 2, Israel, 1955.

————, *Meḥkarim be-Toldot Yisrael*, vol. 2, Israel, 1958.

Amir, David, "Mi Panias ha-Hellenistit ve-'ad Banias ha-'Aravit", *Teva ve-Arez*, 10/4, 1968, p. 263.

Andreotti, Roberto, "Politica di sicurezza e controllo del commercio", *RIDA*, 3/16, 1969, pp. 215–57.

Appelbaum, S., "The Province of Syria-Palaestina as a Province of the Severan Empire", *Zion*, XXIII–XXIV, 1958–59, pp. 35–45 and p. III.

Aptowitzer, A., "Sefer ha-Ḥefetz ve-Sefer Metivot", *Tarbiz*, 4, 1933, pp. 127–52.

Ashtor, see Strauss, E.

Assaf, Simcha, *Gaonica*, I, Jerusalem, 1933.

————, *Sefer Assaf*, ed. Cassuto, Klausner & J. Guttman, Jerusalem, 1953.

Avi-Yonah, M., "A Map of Roman Palestine", *Quarterly of the Dept. of Antiquities for Palestine*, 5, 1935, pp. 139–93.

————, "The Economics of Byzantine Palestine", *Israel Exploration Journal*, 8/1, 1958, pp. 39–51.

———— *Historical Geography of Palestine*, Jerusalem, 1962, Hebrew.

————, *Bimei Romi u-Vizantion*, Jerusalem, 1946.

Bacher, W., *Die Agada der palästinischen Amoräer*, Strassburg, 1892–99.

————, *Aggadot ha-Tanna'im ve-ha-Amora'im*, Jaffa & Tel-Aviv, 5780–90.

————, *Tradition und Tradenten in den Schulen Palastinas und Babyloniens, Studien und Materialen zur Entstehungsgeschichte des Talmuds*, Leipzig, 1914.

————, *Jewish Encyclopedia*, I, p. 298, s.v. Aba Arika; VII, p. 333–37, s.v. Judah I; IX, p. 340, s.v. Ulla, etc.

Bank, L., "Rabbi Zeira et Rab Zeira," *REJ*, 38, 1899, pp. 47–63.

Baron, Salo Wittmayer, *A Social and Religous History of the Jews*[2], vol. 2, New York, 1958.

Bastien, Pierre, *La Monnayage de Bronze de Postume*, Belgium, 1967.

Baumstark, A., *Geschichte der Syrische Literature*, Bonn, 1922.

Bedjan, P., *Acta Martyrum et Sanctorum*, Leipzig & Paris, 1890–97.

————, *Eusebius, Histoire Ecclesiastique*, Leipzig & Paris, 1897.

————, *Chronicon Syriacum Gregorii Barhebraei*, ed. P. Bedjan, Paris, 1890.

Beer, M., "Iyyunim be-Iggeret Rav Sherira Gaon", *Bar-Ilan* 4–5, 1967, pp. 181–96.

Bellinger, A.R., *Dura Final Report*, 4, New Haven, 1949.

————, "Greek Mints under the Roman Empire", in *Mattingly Festschrift*.

————, *Syrian tetradrachms of Caracalla and Macrinus*, ANS Numismatic Studies, 3, 1940.

Ben David. A., "Jewish and Roman Bronze and Copper Coins: Their Reciprocal Relations in Mishna and Talmud from Herod the Great to Trajan and Hadrian", *PEQ*, 103, 1971, pp. 109–29.

————, *Jerusalem und Tyros*, Basel, 1969.

Benoit, P., and Milik, J.T., and De Vaux, R., *Les Grottes de Murabba'at (Discoveries in the Judean Desert, II)*, Oxford, 1961.

Bernardi, A., "Tendenze di Fondo nell' economia del tardo impero romano", *Studia Ghisleriana*, 3, Pavia, 1961, pp. 257–321.

Berriman, A.E., *Historical Metrology*, London, 1953.

Berthelot, M., *Archéologie et histoire des sciences*, Paris, 1906.

————, & Duval, R., *La Chemie au moyen âge*, Paris, 1873.

Bingen, J., "Le pris de l'Or dans l'Édit des Maximum", *Chronique d'Égypte*, 40, 1965, pp. 206–08, 431–34.

Boak, A.E.R., "Some Early Tax Records from Egypt", *Harvard Studies in Classical Philology*, 51, 1940.

————, "A Fourth Century Petition for Relief from Extortion", *JJP*, 1, 1946, p. 10.

————, & Youtie, *The Archive of Aurelius Isidorus*, Ann Arbor, 1960.

Boetticher, see Lagarde.

Bolin, Sture, *State and Currency in the Roman Empire to 300 A.D.*, Uppsala, 1958.

Bosch, C., "Die kleinasiatischen Münzen der römischen Kaiserzeit," *Arch. Anzeiger*, 1931.

Brand. Y., *Klei Haḥeres Besifrut Hatalmud*, Jerusalem, 1953.

————, "Tilboshet Me-ha-Tekufa ha-Talmudit", *Sefer ha-Yovel le-Yisrael Elfenbein*, Jerusalem, 1962, ed. Y.L. Maimon, pp. 46–55.

Broughton, T.R.S., *Roman Asia Minor*, in *Economic Survey of Ancient Rome*, vol. 4, pp. 499–918, Baltimore, 1938.

Brüll, Adolf, *Trachten der Juden*, 1, Frankfurt A/M, 1873.

Brüll, N., *Jahrbücher der Jüdische Geschichte und Literatur*, Frankfurt a Main, 1874.

Bruun, P., "Law on tax payment in gold and Constantinian solidi," *Congresso Internazionale de Numismatica*, 1961, *Atti*, vol. 2, Rome, 1965, pp. 387–98.

————, *Roman Imperial Coinage*, 7, London, 1966.

Büchler, A., *The Economic Conditions of Judaea after the Destruction of the Second Temple*, Jews' College Publications, 4, London, 1912.

————, *The Political and Social Leaders of the Jewish Community of Sepphoris in the Second and Third Centuries*, Jews' College Publications, 1, London, 1909.

————, *Studies in Jewish History*, Oxford, 1956.

Budge, E. A. Wallis., *Book of Medicines*, Oxford, 1913.

————, *The Book of Paradise of Palladius*, etc., London, 1904.

————, *The Chronography of Gregory Abu 'I Faraj . . . .*, London, 1932.

————, *The Laughable Stories collected by Bar-Hebraeus*, London, 1907.

Burns, A. R., *Money and Monetary Policy in Early Times*, London, 1927.

Buttrey, T. V., "Dio, Zonaras and the Value of the Roman Aureus", *JRS*, 51, 1961, pp. 40–45.

————, Revue of Bolin, *State and Currency*, etc., *American Journal of Archeology*, 65, 1961.

————, Revue of Sutherland, *Roman Imperial Coinage*, 6, *Gnomon*, 41, 1969, pp. 676–80.

Caley, Earl R., *Orichalchum and related Ancient Alloys*, *NNM*, 151, New York, 1964.

————, "A propos du JRS, 56, 1966, pp. 190–195", *BSFN*, 22/3, 1967, pp. 135–36.

Callu, Jean-Pierre, "A propos de JRS, 56, 1966, pp. 190–195", *BSFN*, 22/3, 1967, pp. 135–36.

————, *La Politique Monétaire des Empereurs Romains de 238 à 311*, Paris, 1969.

————, "P. Beatty Panopl. no. 2", *BSFN*, 20/8, 1965, pp. 500–1.

————, "Remarques sur, JRS, 61, 1971, pp. 171–77", *BSFN*, 27/8, 1972, pp. 290–92.

Cameron, A., "Roman School Fees", *Classical Revue*, XV, 1965, pp. 257–78.

Campbell, W., *Greek and Roman Plated Coins*, *NNM*, 57, New York, 1933.

Carney, Y. E., *Catalogue of the Courtauld Collection of Roman Coins*, etc., Salisbury, 1963.

Carson, R. A. G., *British Museum Catalogue of Coins of the Roman Empire*, 6, London, 1962.

————, "The Inflation of the Third Century and its Monetary Influence in the Near East", *INCP*, pp. 231–45.

————, "The Reform of Aurelian", *Revue Numismatique*, 6/7, 1965, pp. 225–35.

————, & Kent, J. P. C., *Late Roman Bronze Coinage*, part 2, London, 1965.

————, & Sutherland, C. H. V., *Essays in Roman Coinage, presented to Harold Mattingly* (= *Mattingly Festschrift*). Oxford, 1956.

Casson, L., "Speed under Sail of Ancient Ships", *TAPA*, 82, 1951, pp. 136–48.

————, "Wine measures and prices in Byzantine Egypt", *TAPA*, 70, 1939, pp. 1–16.

Chanaris, P., *Byzantion*, 17, 1944–45, p. 409 (review of West & Johnson, *Currency*).

Chastagnol, A., review of S. Lauffer, *Diokletians Preisedikt*, *Revue des Études Latines*, 1970, pp. 664–68.

Chaumont, M. L., "Papak, roi de Staxr et sa cour", *Journal Asiatique*, 247, 1959 pp. 175–92.

Chavel, C.B., Editor of Nachmanides' commentary on the Bible, vol. 1, Jerusalem, 1959.

Cohen, Boaz, *Jewish and Roman Law*, New York, 1966.

Cooke, G.A., *North Semitic Inscriptions*, London, 1903.

Cope, Lawrence H., "Alloys of Large Tetrarchic Folles", *N.C.*, 1968, pp. 115–49.

————, "The Nadir of the Imperial Antoninianus in the reign of Claudius II Gothicus, A.D. 268–70", *N.C.*, 1969, pp. 145–61.

————, "Roman Imperial Silver Coinage Alloy Standards: The Evidence," *N.C.*, 1967, pp. 107–27.

Cowley, "Hebrew and Aramaic Papyri", *JQR*, 16, 1904, pp. 1–8.

Crawford, M.H., *JRS*, 1969, pp. 291–92 (review).

————, "Money and Exchange in the Roman World", *JRS*, 60, 1970, pp. 40–48.

————, "Plated Coins — False Coins", *Num. Chron.*, 1968, pp. 55–59.

————, see also Erim, Kenan T.

Dalman, G., *Arbeit und Sitte in Palästina*, Gütersloh, 1928–35.

Darenberg et Saglio, *Dictionnaire des Antiquités Grecques et Romaines*, Paris, 1877–1919.

Dattari, "Nuova teoria sopra il sistema monetario della riforma di Diocleziano e dell' epoca Constantiniana", in *Revista Italiana Numismatica*, 19, 1906, pp. 375–96.

Davies, R.W., "The Supply of Animals to the Roman Army", *Latomus*, 28, 1969, pp. 428–59.

Dean, J.E., *Epiphanius on Weights and Measures*, The Oriental Institute of the University of Chicago, Studies in Ancient Oriental Civilizations, No. 11, Chicago, 1935.

de Jonge, P., "Scarcity of Corn and corn prices in Ammianus Marcellinus", *Mnemosyne*[4], 1, 1948, pp. 238–45.

Dor, Zwi Moshe, *Torat Erez-Yisrael be-Bavel*, Tel-Aviv, 1971.

Downey, G., "The Economic Crisis at Antioch under Julian the Apostate", in *Studies in Roman Social and Economic History in Honour of Allan Chester Johnson*, ed. P.R. Coleman-Norton, Princeton, 1951, pp. 312–21.

————, *A History of Antioch in Syria*, Princeton, 1961.

————, "The Size and Population of Antioch", *TAPA*, 89, 1958, pp. 84–91.

Driver, G.R., *Aramaic Documents of the Fifth Century B.C.*, Oxford, 1965.

Duncan-Jones, Richard, "Costs Outlays and Summae honororiae from Roman Africa", in *Papers of the British School at Rome*, 30, N.S.27, 1962.

————, "An Epigraphic Survey of Costs in Roman Italy," in *Papers of the British School at Rome*, 33, NS 20, 1965.

Duval, R., see Berthelot.

Eddy, Samuel, K., *The Minting of Antoniniani A.D. 238–49 and the Smyrna Hoard*, *NNM*, 156, New York, 1967.

Ehrendorfer,"Die Münzreform des Diocletianus", *Num. Zeitschrift*, 72, 1947, pp. 101–06.

Epstein, A., "Le retour de Rab en Babylonie d'après M. Isaac Halévy,", *REJ*, 44, 1902, pp. 45–61.

Epstein, J.N., *Mavo le-Nusaḥ ha-Mishna*, Jerusalem, 1948.

————, *Prolegomena ad Litteras Amoraiticas* Jerusalem, 1962.

————, *Prolegomena ad Litteras Tannaticas*, Jerusalem, 1957.

Erim, Kenan I., Joyce Reynolds and Michael Crawford, "Diocletian's Currency Reform: A New Inscription", *JRS*, 1971, pp. 171–77.

Feliks, J., *Agriculture in Palestine in the period of the Mishna and Talmud*, Jerusalem, 1963 (Hebrew).

287

————, "Rice in Rabbinic Literature", *Bar-Ilan*, 1, Jerusalem, 1963, pp. 177–89 (Hebrew).

Finkelstein, Louis, *Mabo le-Massektot Abot ve-Abot d'Rabbi Natan*, Texts and Studies of the Jewish Theological Seminary of America, vol. XVI, New York, 1950.

Finlay, G., *Greece under the Romans*, London, 1906.

Fogelman, M., "Rabbi Tana Hu u-palig", *Sinai*, 21/1 (251), 1957, pp. 25–30.

Fraenkel, S., *Die Aramäischen Fremdwörter im Arabischen*, Leiden, 1886.

Frankel, Z., *Darkei ha-Mishna*, Leipzig, 1859.

————, *Mavo ha-Yerushalmi*, Breslau, 1870.

Frank, Tenney, ed., *An Economic Survey of Ancient Rome*, 5 vols., Baltimore, 1926–1940.

Friedländer, L., *Roman Life and Manners*, London, 1908.

Frye, R.N., *The Heritage of Parsia*, 1962.

Fürst, J. *Glossarium Graeco-Hebraeum*, Strassbourg, 1890–91.

le Gentilhomme, Pierre, "Le jeu des mutations de l'argent en IIIe siècle", *Métaux et Civilisations*, I, 1940, pp. 113–27.

————, "Variations du Titres de l'Antoninianus au IIIe Siècle", *Revue Numismatique*, 1962, pp. 141–66.

Gentili, G.V., *The Imperial Villa of Piazza Armerina*, 1956.

————, *La Villa Erculia di Piazza Armerina*, 1 *mosaici figurati*, Rome, 1959.

————, *La Villa Romana di Piazza Armerina, etc., Itinerari dei musei e monumenti d'Italia*, no. 87, Rome, 1951.

————, *A Commentary to the Palestinian Talmud*, New York, vols. 1–3, 1941, vol. 4, 1961.

Ginzberg, Louis, *Al Halakha ve-Aggada*, Tel-Aviv, 1960.

————, *Ginzei Schechter*, vols. 1–2, New York, 1928–29.

————, *Mekoma shel ha-Halacha be-Ḥochmat Yisrael*, Jerusalem, 1931.

————, *Yerushalmi Fragments from the Genizah*, New York, 1909.

Ginzburger, M., *Targum Jonathan*, Berlin, 1903.

Göbl, R., "Der Aufbau der römischen Münzprägung in der Kaiserzeit", *Numismatische Zeitschrift*, 74, 1951, pp. 8–45, 75, 1953, pp. 5–35.

Goitein, S.D., *A Mediterranean Society*, vol. 1 *Economic Foundation*, Berkeley and Los Angeles, 1967.

Goor, A., "The History of the Pomegranate in the Holy Land", *Economic Botany*, 21/3, 1967, pp. 215–29.

Graetz, H., *Divrei Yemei Yisrael*, vol. 12, Warsaw, 1893, with additional notes by Rabbinowitz, S.P. (called "Shefer").

Graser, E.R. ed., *The Edict of Diocletian on Maximum Prices, Economic Survey of Ancient Rome*, vol. 5, Baltimore, 1940, pp. 307–421.

————, "The significance of the Two New Fragments of the Edict of Diocletian", *TAPA*, 71, 1940, pp. 157–74.

Gren, E., *Kleinasien und Ostbalkan in der Wirtschaftlischen entwicklung der römischer kaiserzeit*, Uppsala Universitets Arsskrift, 9, 1941.

Grierson, P., "The Monetary Reforms of Anastasius and their Economic Consequences", *INCP*, pp. 283–301.

————, "The Roman Law of Counterfeiting", *Essays in Roman Coinage presented to Harold Mattingly*, London, 1956, pp. 240–61.

Guarducci, "La pubbicazione in Italia del calmiere di Diocleziano", *Rendiconti dei Lincei*, 1963, pp. 43–50.

Guey, Julien, "Autour des Res Festae Divi Saporis", *Syria*, 38, 1961, pp. 261–74.

———, "Techniques Romaines III", *Revue Numismatique*, 1967, pp. 33–60.

Gulak, A., "Banking in Talmudic Law", *Tarbiz*, 2/2, 1931, pp. 154–71 (Hebrew).

———, *Le-Ḥeker Toldot ha-Mishpat ha-Ivri bi-Tekufat ha-Talmud, vol.* 1 (*Diné Karka'ot*), Jerusalem, 1929.

———, "The Method of Collecting Roman Taxes in Palestine", *Magnes Aniversary Book*, Jerusalem, 1938, pp. 97–104 (Hebrew), pp. XXI–III, (English Summary).

———, *Yesod Ha-Mishpat Ha-Ivri* I, Berlin, 1922.

Guttman, A., "The Patriarch Judah I, His Birth and Death. A Glimpse into the Chronology of the Talmudic Period", *Hebrew Union College Annual*, 25, 1954, pp. 239–62.

Haines, G.C., "The Decline and Fall of the Monetary System of Augustus", *Num. Chron.*, 1941, pp. 17–47.

Halevy, Isaac, *Dorot Harischonim, Die Geschichte und Literature Israels*, Berlin & Wien, 1923.

Halivni, David, *Sources and Traditions*, Tel-Aviv, 1968 (Hebrew).

Hamburger, H., "A Hoard of Antoniniani of Late Roman Emperors from Tiberias", *Israel Numismatic Journal*, II/3–4, 1964, pp. 19–31.

Hamburger, Leopold, *Die Münzpragungen während des letzten Aufstandes der Israeliten gegen Rom*, Berlin, 1892.

Hammer, J., "Die Feingeld der griechischen und römischen Münzen", *Zeitschrift für Numismatik*, 1908, pp. 1–144.

Harold, M.R., "The Silver Content of Diocletian's Early Post-Reform Copper Coins", part II, *Archeometry*, 4, 1961, pp. 60–61.

Hedges, E.S. & Robins, D.A., "Examination of Some silver-coated Roman Coins", *Num. Chron.*, 1963, pp. 70–61.

Heichelheim, F.M., *An Ancient Economic History*, 3, Leyden, 1970.

———, "New Light on Currency and Inflation", *Economic History*, 1935, pp. 5–11.

———, "Pap. Argent. Gr. 1, Verso, col. 2", *Journal of Egyptian Archaeology*, 29, 1943, pp. 78–79.

———, Review of Jones' *Later Roman Empire*, *JRS*, 15, 1965, pp. 250–51.

———, "*Roman Syria*" in *An Economic Survey of Ancient Rome*, vol. 4, pp. 121–257, Baltimore, 1938.

———, Supply Bases for Caracalla's Parthian Campaign", *Classical Philology*, 39, 1944, pp. 113–15.

———, "Zu Pap. Osl. 83", *Symb. Osloensis*, 14, 1935, pp. 82–85.

———, "Zur Wahrungkrisis des römischen Imperiums in 3 Jahrhundert n. Chr.", *Klio*, 26, 1932, pp. 96–113.

Heilprin, J., *Seder ha-Dorot*, Jerusalem, 1956, reprint of Warsaw ed.

Heinemann, Josef H., "The Status of the Labourer in Jewish Law and Society in the Tannaitic Period", *HUCA*, 25, 1954, pp. 263–325.

Herszberg, A.S., *Ḥayyei ha-Tarbut be-Yisrael be-Tekufat ha-Mishna ve-ha-Talmud*, vol. 1, Warsaw, 1924.

Herzfeld, L., *Metrologische Voruntersuchungen, Jahrbuch für die Gesichte des Juden und des Judenthums*, 3, Leipzig, 1863, pp. 95–191.

Herzog, I., *The Main Institutions of Jewish Law*, vol. 1, London, 1936.

Higger, M., *Masechet Semachot*, New York, 1931.

Hildesheimer, H., & Klein, S., *Studies in the Geography of Eretz Yisrael*, Jerusalem, 1965, (Hebrew).

Hill, G. F., *Catalogue of Greek Coins of Arabia, Mesopotamia and Persia in the British Museum*, London, 1922.

———, *Catalogue of Greek Coins of Phoenicia in the Bristish Museum*, London, 1910.

Hill,P. V. & Kent., J. P. C., *Late Roman Bronze Coinage*, part 1, London, 1965 (see Carson).

Hirschensohn, *Sheva Chochmoth*, London, 1912.

Hirth, F., *China and the Roman Orient*, Shanghai & Hong Kong, 1885.

Horowitz, I. S., *Palestine and the Adjacent Countries*, Vienna, 1923, Hebrew.

Hultsch, F., *Griechische und Römische Metrologie*[2], Berlin, 1882.

———, *Metrologicorum Scriptorum Reliquiae*, Leipzig, 1864–66.

Hyman, A., ed., *Igereth Rav Sherira Gaon*, London, 1910.

———, *Toldoth Tannaim Ve'amoraim*, London, 1910.

Ibn-Shemuel, Y., *Midrash Ge'ulah*[2], Tel-Aviv, 1954.

Incarnati, L., *Moneta e Scambio nell' Antichità' e nell' Álto Medioevo*, Rome, 1953.

Isaac b. Moses of Vienna, *Or Zaru'a*, Zitomir, 1882; Jerusalem, 1968.

Jaawitz, W. (= Jawitz), *Toldoth Yisrael — Die Geschichte Israels*, Tel-Aviv & Berlin, 5669–88.

Jacobi, Guilio, *Gli scavi della Missione Archeologica Italiana ad Afrodisiade nel 1937*, XV–XVI.

Jacobs, L., "The Economic Conditions of the Jews in Babylon in Talmudic Times compared with Palestine", in *Journal of Semitic Studies*, 2, 1957, pp. 349–59.

Jalabert, L. & Mouterde, R., *Inscriptions Grecques et Latines de la Syrie*. Paris, 1929–1953.

Jasny, N., *The Wheats of Classical Antiquity*, Baltimore, 1944.

———, "Wheat Prices and Milling Costs in Classical Rome", *Wheat Studies of the Food Research Institute*, Stanford University, California, 20/4, March, 1944.

Johnson, A. C., *An Economic Survey of Ancient Rome*, vol. 2, Roman Egypt, Baltimore, 1936.

———, *Egypt and the Roman Empire*, Ann Arbor, 1951.

———, "Notes of Egyptian Coinage", *American Journal of Archeology*, 38, 1934, pp. 49–54.

———, "Roman Egypt in the Third Century", *JJP*, 4, 1950, pp. 151–58.

———, "The ἐπιβολή of Land in Roman Egypt", *Aegyptus*, 32, 1952, pp. 61–72.

———, See also West, L. C., and Abbott, F. F.

Johnson, A. C., & West, L. C., *Byzantine Egypt: Economic Studies*, Princeton University Studies in Papyrology, 6, Princeton, 1944.

Jones, A. H. M., "Inflation under the Roman Empire", *Economic History Review*, 2/5, 1953, pp. 293–318.

———, *The Later Roman Empire*, Oxford, 1964.

———, "Numismatics and History", *Mattingly Festschrift*, Oxford, 1956, pp. 13–33.

———, "Overtaxation and the Decline of the Roman Empire", *Antiquity*, 33, 1959, pp. 39–43.

———, "The Origin and Early History of the Follis", *JRS*, 49, 1959, pp. 34–38.

Judlewitsch, M. D., "Akko", *Sinai*, 7/3–4 (78–79), 1943, pp. 183–94.

———, *Meḥoza*, Jerusalem, 1947.

———, *Tiveria*, Jerusalem, 1950.

Kadman, L., *The Coins of Aelia Capitolina*, CNP, I, Jerusalem, 1956.

————, *The Coins of Akko Ptolemais*, CNP, IV, Jerusalem, 1961.

————, *The Coins of Caesarea Maritima*, CNP, II, Jerusalem, 1957.

————, "The Monetary Development of Palestine in the Light of Coin Hoards", *INCP*, pp. 311–21.

Kasher, M. M., *Torah Shelemah*, Jerusalem, 1927–.

Kent, J. P. C., "Gold Coinage in the Later Roman Empire", *Mattingly Festschrift*, Oxford, 1956, pp. 190–204.

————, "An Introduction to the Coinage of Julian the Apostate", *Num. Chron.*, 1959, pp. 108–17.

————, "The Pattern of Bronze Coinage under Constantine I", *Num. Chron.*, 1957, pp. 16–77.

————, See Hill, P. V., and Carson, R. A. G.

Kindler, A., *The Coins of Tiberias*, Tiberias, 1961.

————, ed. *Proceedings of the International Numismatic Convention in Jerusalem*, 1963, ed., (= *INCP*), Tel-Aviv, 1967.

Kislev, M. A., "Le-Zihui ha-Ḥitah ve-ha-Kusemet, 1, Ha-Kusemet", *Leshonenu*, 37, 1973, pp. 83–95.

Kitzinger, E., *Dumbarton Oaks Papers*, 3, 1946, pp. 142–43, 159–60.

Klein, S., *Beraitha shel 24 Mishmarot, Mechkarim Artzi-Yisraeliim*, 2, Vienna, 1924.

————, *Eretz ha-Galil-Galilee*, Jerusalem, 1967.

————, *Eretz Yehuda*, Tel-Aviv, 1939.

————, *Sefer ha-Yishuv*, vol. 1, Tel-Aviv, 1939.

Klimowsky, E. W., "Monetary Function of City Coins", *INCP*, pp. 129–73.

Kraeling, C. H., *Gerasa City of the Decapolis*, New Haven, Connecticut, 1938.

Kraemer, C. J., *Excavations of Nessana*, 3, Princeton, 1958.

Krauss, S., *Antoninus und Rabbi, Jahresberichte Israelitisch-theologische Lehranstalt in Wien*, XVII, Wien, 1910.

————, *Grieschische und Lateinische Lehnwörter*, etc., Berlin, 1898–99.

————, *Kadmoniot ha-Talmud*, Berlin & Vienna, and Tel-Aviv, 1929.

————, *Paras ve-Romi ba-Talmud u-ba-Midrashim*, Jerusalem, 1948.

————, *Talmudische Archäologie*, Leipzig, 1910–12.

Kubitschek, W., "Ein Stiftung aus Feltre", *Num. Zeitschrift*, 1909, pp. 47–66.

Kutscher, E. Y., *Words and their History*, Jerusalem, 1961 (Hebrew).

Lange, Isaak S., ed., *Beth Habeḥira* (on Sabbath) by R. Menahem Hameiri, Jerusalem, 1968.

————, *Tosafot Rosh* (to Sabbat)), Israel, 1969.

Lagarde, Paul A. (= Boetticher), *Beitraege zur Baktrischen Lexicographie*, Leipzig, 1868.

————, *Eliya of Nesibis*, ed., Göttingaen, 1879.

————, *Gasammette Abhandlungen*, Leipzig, 1866.

————, *Symmicta*, Goettingen, 1877, 1880.

Lambert, E., "Les changeurs et le monnaie en Palestine du I–er au III–e siècle de l'ère vulgaire d'après des textes talmudique", *REJ*, 51, 52, 1906.

Larsen, J. A. O., *An Economic Survey of Ancient Rome*, vol. 4, section on Greece, Baltimore, 1938, pp. 259–498.

Lauffer, S., *Diokletians Preisedikt*, Berlin, 1971.

Lawrence, L. A., "Hoard of Plated Roman Denarii", *Num. Chron.*, 1940.

Le Bas, P., et Waddington, W. H., *Voyage Archéologique en Asie Mineur*, Paris, 1847.

Le Strange, Guy, *Palestine under the Moslems*, London, 1890.

Leveen, J., see Margoliouth.

Levick, B., "The Coinage of Pisidian Antioch in the Third Century A.D.", *NC*, 1966, pp. 47–59.

————, *Roman Colonies in Asia Minor*, Oxford, 1967.

Levy, M.A., *Geschichte der Jüdische Münzen*, Leipzig, 1862.

Lewin, B.M., *Iggeret R. Scherira Gaon*, Haifa, 1921.

————, *Otzar Hageonim*, 1928–43, ed.

————, *Sefer ha-Ma'asim*, etc., *Tarbiz*, 1/1, 1929, ed.

Lewis, N., *A Hoard of Folles from Selz,Alsace* . . . etc., *NNM*, 79, New York, 1937.

Libanius, *Autobiography, First Oration*, ed. A.F. Norman, Oxford, 1965.

Lieberman, S. (= Liebermann), "Al Betuim asher be-Seridim mi-Sefer ha-Ma'asim", *Ginzé Kedem*, 5, Jerusalem, 1934, pp. 177–85.

————, *Greek and Hellenism in Jewish Palestine*, Jerusalem, 1962, Hebrew trans. of *Greek in Jewish Palestine*, New York, 1942, and *Hellenism in Jewish Palestine*, New York, 1962.

————, *Hayerushalmi Kipshuto*, Jerusalem, 1934.

————, "The Martyrs of Caesarea", *Annuaire de l'Institut de Philologie et d'Histoire Orientales et Slaves*, 7, 1939–44, pp. 395–446.

————, *On the Yerushalmi*, Jerusalem, 1929.

————, "Palestine in the Third and Fourth Centuries", *JQR*, NS 36, 1945–46, pp. 329–70; 37, 1946, pp. 31–54.

————, *The Talmud of Caesarea*, Supplement to *Tarbiz*, 2/4, 1931, Hebrew.

————, *Tosefeth Rishonim*, 2, Jerusalem, 1938; 4, Jerusalem, 1939.

————, *Tosefta ki-fshutah, Zera'im and Mo'ed and Nashim*, New York, 1955–67.

Liebeschutz, "Money Economy and Taxation in Kind in Syria in the 4 cent. A.D.", *Rheinische Museum für Philologie*, 104/3, 1961, pp. 242–56.

Lifshitz, B., *Donateurs et Fondateurs dans les Synagogues Juives*, Cahiers de la Revue Biblique, 7, Paris, 1967.

Littman & Magie, *Syria III a.*, Leiden, 1921.

Lohmann, E., *Der textkritische Wert der Syrischen Übersetzung der Kirschengeschichte des Eusebius*, Halle, 1894.

Löw, Immanuel, "Aramäische Fischnamen", *Nöldeke Festschrift*, ed. Carl Bezold, Giessen, 1906.

————, *Aramäische Pflanzennamen*, Leipzig, 1881.

————, *Die Flora der Juden*, 4, Vienna, 1934.

————, *Fauna und Mineralien der Juden*, Hildesheim, 1969.

————, notes in Krauss' *Lehnwörter* 2, see Krauss, S.

McLean, see Wright.

MacMullen, R., "Diocletian's Edict and the Castrensis Modius", *Aegyptus*, 41, 1961, pp. 3–5.

————, "Some Tax Statistics from Roman Egypt", *Aegyptus*, 42, 1962, pp. 98–102.

Magie, D., *Roman Rule in Asia Minor*, Princeton, 1950.

————, see also Littman.

Manandian, H.A., *The Trade and Cities of Armenia in Relation to Ancient World Trade*, Lisbon, 1965.

Margalioth, M., *Encyclopaedia of Talmudic and Gaonic Literature*[4], Jerusalem, 1962.

————, "Le Ba'ayat Kadmuto Shel Seder Eliyahu", *Sefer Assaf* (see Assaf), pp. 370–91.

Margaliot, R., *Darkei ha-Talmud ve-Ḥidotav*, Jerusalem, 1967.

————, *Nitzotzei Or*, Jerusalem, 1965.

Margolioth, G., *Catalogue of the Hebrew and Samaritan Manuscripts* (in the British Museum), vol. 1/3 (vol. 4, J. Leveen), London, 1899–1935.

Marmorstein, A., "Dioclétian à la lumière de la litterature rabbinique", *REJ*, 98, 1934, pp. 18–43.

————, "Doro shel R. Johanan", *Tarbiz*, 3, 1932, pp. 161–80.

————, "Ha-Matzav ha-Kalkali... be-Doro shel R. Johanan", *Freimann Festschrift*, Berlin, 1932, pp. 1–12.

————, "Meḥkarim be-Aggada", *Ha-Soker*, 4, 1936–37, pp. 131–45.

————, "The Synagogue of Claudius Tiberias Polymarchus in Stobi", *JQR*, 27, 1937, pp. 378–84.

Mattingly, H., *British Museum Catalogue of Roman Coins*, 1–5, London, 1923–50.

————, "The Clash of the Coinages c. 270–96", *Studies in Roman Economic and Social History presented to Allan Chester Johnson*, ed. P.R., Coleman-Norton, Princeton, 1957, pp. 278–89.

————, "The Great Dorchester Hoard of 1936", *Num. Chron.*, 1939, p. 211.

————, "Monetary System of the Roman Empire from Diocletian to Theodosian I", *Num. Chron.*, 1946, pp. 111–20.

————, *Roman Coins from the Earliest Times to the Fall of the Western Empire*, 1–2, London, 1928, 1960.

Mattingly, H. & Sydenham, *Roman Imperial Coinage*, 1–5, London, 1923–49.

Mazzarino, Santo, *Aspetti sociali del Quarto Secolo*, Rome, 1951.

Mickwitz, Gunnar, *Die System des römischen silbergeldes in IV Jahrhunderts*, Societas Scientarum Fennica, Commentationes Humanarum Litterarum, 6, Helsingfors, 1933.

————, "Ein Goldwertindex der römische-byzantinischen Zeit", *Aegyptus*, 13, 1933, pp. 95–106.

————, *Geld und Wirtschaft im römischen Reich des Vierten Jahrhunderts N. Chr.*, Societas Scientarum Fennica Commentationes Humanarum Litterarum, 4/2, Helsingfors, 1932.

————, "New Papyri of Numismatic Interest", *Num. Chron.*, 4, 1937, pp. 141–43.

————, "Über die kupfergeldinflationen in den Jahren der Thronkämpfe nach Diokletians Abdankung", *Transactions of the International Numismatic Congress of 1936*, London, 1938, pp. 219–28.

Milne, J.G., "The Ruin of Egypt by Roman Mismanagement", *JRS*, 17, 1927, pp. 1–13.

————, "Roman Coinage in Egypt in Relation to the Native Economy", *Aegyptus*, 32, 1952, pp. 143–51.

Mirsky, S.K., *Perakim*, 4, 1966, p. 27, note 75.

Momigliano, A.D., *Studies in Historiography*, London, 1966.

Mommsen, T., *Chronica, Minora* II, Berlin, 1894.

————, *Geschichte des römischen Münzwesens*, Berlin, 1860.

————, *Histoire de la Monnaie Romaine*, 1–4, Paris, 1865–75.

————, *Über das Ed. Diokletians de pretiis rerum venalium"*, Berichte über die *Verhandlungen der Königlich. Sächsischen Gesellschaft der Wissenschaft zu Leipzig*, Phil. Hist. Kl., 3, 1851.

————, & Geyer, P.M., ed. *Codex Theodosianus*, Berlin, 1895.

————, & Kruger, P., ed. *Corpus Iuris Civilis*, Berlin, 1928–29.

Moritz, L.A., *Grain Mills and Flour in Antiquity*, Oxford, 1958.

Neubauer, Adolphe, *La Géographie du Talmud*, Paris, 1868.

————, *Mediaeval Jewish Chronicles* (including Mss. versions of *Seder Olam Rabba and Zuta, Sefer ha-Kabbalah* of Ibn Daud, etc.), Oxford, 1887–95.

Neusner, J., *A History of the Jews in Babylonia*, vol. 1, Leiden, 1965; vol. 2, Leiden, 1966.

Newman, J., *The Agricultural Life of the Jews in Babylonia*, London, 1932.

Nöldeke, Th., *Aufsätze zur Persischen Geschichte*, Leipzig, 1887.

————, *Geschichte der Perser und Araber zur Zeit der Sasaniden aus der Arabische Chronik des Tabari*, Leyden, 1879.

Norman, A.F., *Libanius Autobiography*, ed. and transl., First Oration, Oxford, 1965.

Obermayer, Jacob, *Die Landschaft Babylonien in Zeitalter des Talmud und der Gaonäts*, Schriften des Gesellschaft zur Förderung des Wissenschaft des jüdenthums, Frankfurt am Main, 1929.

Oeconomides, Mando, Caramessini, *On a Hoard of Plated Roman Coins*, *ANSMN*, XII, New York, 1966.

Oertel, F., "The Economic Life of the Empire", *Cambridge Ancient History*, vol. 12, pp. 232–80.

Oman, C., "The Decline and Fall of the Denarius in the Third Century A.D.", *Num. Chron.*, 1916, pp. 37ff.

Oppenheim, A.L., "A new subdivision of the Shekel in the Arsacid Period", *Orientalia*, 41/1–2, 1973, pp. 324–7.

Paruck, Furdoonjee, D.J., *Sasanian Coins*, Bombay, 1924.

Pauly-Wissowa, *Realencyclopaedia der classischen altertumswissenschaft*, Stuttgart, 1894–.

Pearce, Review of Mickwitz's *Geld und Wirtschaft*, *JRS*, 23, 1933, pp. 87–88.

Pekári, Th., "Le Tribut aux Perses et les finances de Philippe L'Arabe", *Syria*, 38, 1961, pp. 275–83.

————, "Studien zur römischen Währungs- und Finanzgeschichte von 161 bis 235 nach Chr.", *Historia*, 8, 1959, pp. 443–89.

Perkins, A., *Dura Final Report*, 5/1, New Haven, 1959.

Petit, P., "Les Senateurs de Constantinople dans l'oeuvre de Libanius", *L'Antiquité Classique*, 26, 1957, pp. 347–82.

————, *Libanius et le vie municipale à Antioch en 4e siècle après J.C.*, Institut Français d'Archéologie de Beyrouth, Bibliothèque Archéologique et Historique, vol. 62, Paris, 1955.

Petrie, W.M.F., "The Rise of Prices in Roman Egypt", *Ancient Egypt*, 1922, pp. 103–07.

————, "Weights and Measures", *Encyclopaedia Britannica⁹*, vol. 24, pp. 480b–489b.

Picozzi, V., *La Monetazione Imperiale Romana*, Rome, 1966.

Pink, K., "Die Silberprägung der Diocletianischen Tetrarchie", *Num. Zeitschrift*, 63, 1930, pp. 9–38.

Pridik, E., "Miliarense Follis und Centenionalis. Zur Münzreform des Diokletians und Konstantins des Grossen", *Num. Zeitschrift*, 1929, 62, pp. 64–68.

Preisigke, *Wörterbuch der Griechischen Papyrus Urkunden*, Berlin, 1913–34.

Pringsheim, F., "Zum römischen Bankwesen", *Vierteliahrschrift für Sozial- und Wirtschaftgeschichte*, 15, 1920, pp .513–21, (reprinted in *Gesammette Abhandlungen*, 1, Heidelberg, 1961.).

Rabbinovicz, R., *Ma'amar al Hadpasat ha-Talmud*, Jerusalem, 1952, ed. and annotated by A.M. Habermann.

————, *Variae Lectiones in Mischnam et in Talmud Babylonicum*, Munich, 1868–86, (called *Dikdukei Soferim*).

Rabinowitz, Z.W., *Sha'are Torath Babel*, Jerusalem, 1961.

————, *Sha'are Torath Eretz Israel*, Jerusalem, 1940.

Rappaport, S.A. (called "Shir"), *Erech Millim*, Warsaw, 1914.

Ratner, Baer, *Ahavat Zion vi-Yerushalaim*, Wilna, 1901–17.

Ravetz, A., "The Fourth Century Inflation", *Num. Chron.*, 7/4, 1964, pp. 201–31.

————, "Neutron Activation Analysis of Silver in some Late Roman Copper Coins", *Archeometry*, 6, 1965, pp. 46–55.

Redhouse, *Turkish Dictionary*, London, 1880.

Reece, R., "Analyses of some Roman Imperial Denarii of the Second and Early Third Centuries", *Num. Chron.*, 1965, pp. 175–76.

Rémondon, A., "A propos du Papyrus d'Antinoé no. 38", *Chronique d'Égypte*, 63–64, 1957, pp. 130–46.

Reynolds, Joyces, see Erim, Kenan T.

Robert, J., review of Guarducci in *Rendiconti dei Lincei*, 1963, pp. 43–50, *Revue des Études Grecques*, 77, 1964, pp. 140–41.

Robins, D.A., see Hedges, E.S.

Rosen, H.B., "Palestinian ϰοινή in Rabbinic Illustration", *Journal of Semitic Studies*, 8, 1963.

Rostovtzeff, M., *RE*, 7, s.v. *Frumentum*.

————, *A Large Estate in Egypt in the Third Century B.C.*, A Study in Economic History, University of Wisconsin, Studies in Social Sciences and History, No. 6, Madison, 1922.

————, *The Social and Economic History of the Hellenistic World*, Oxford, 1941.

————, *The Social and Economic History of the Roman Empire*, revised by P.M. Fraser, Oxford, 1963.

Rougé, J., *Récherches sur l'Organisation du Commerce Maritime en Méditerranée sous l'Empire Romaine*, Paris, 1966.

Ruggini, Lellia, *Economia a Societa nell' Italia Annonaria*, Milan, 1961.

————, "A proposito del Follis nel IV secolo", *Rendiconti dei Lincei*, XVI, Rome, 1961, pp. 306–19.

Sachs, M., *Beiträge zur Sprach- und Alterthumsforschung*, Berlin, 1852–54.

Safrai, Shemuel, "Monetary Development in the Third and Fourth Centuries as Reflected in Talmudic Literature", *INCP*, pp. 251–59.

Sasoon, S., ed. *Sefer Halachot Pesuqot*, Jerusalem, 1950.

Schachter, E., *Ha-Mishna ba-Bavli u-ba-Yerushalmi (The Babylonian and Jerusalem Mishna textually compared)*, Jerusalem, 1959.

Scheftel, J.M., *Erech Milim²*, (BIBLEISKO-TALMUDICHESKII METEROLOGICHESKII LEKSIKON), Berditschev, 1906.

Schilbach, E., *Byzantinische Metrologie*, München, 1970.

Schiller, A., see Westermann.

Schlesinger, S., ed. *Sepher Hayasher* by Rabbenu Tam, Jerusalem, 1959.

Schnebel, M., *Die Landwirtschaft im Hellenistischen Ägypten*, 1, Munich, 1925.

Schönert-Geiss, Edith, "Das Ende der Provinzialprägung in Thrakien und Mösien", *Klio*, 58, 1968, pp. 251–55.

Schrötter, A., *Wörterbuch der Münzkunde*, Berlin & Leipzig, 1930.

Schulthess, F., *Lexicon Syropalaestinum*, Berlin, 1903.

Schwabe, M., "Documents of a Journey through Israel in the Years 317–323 C.E.", *Eretz-Yisrael*, 3, Jerusalem, 1954, (Hebrew).

Schwartz, Jacques, "L'Empire romaine et le commerce orientale", *Annales, Economies, Sociétés, Civilisations*, 15/1, 1960, pp. 18–44.

Seeck, O., "Die münzpolitik Diocletians und seiner Nachfolger", *Zeitschr. F. Num.* 17, 1890, pp. 36–89, 116–42.

————, *Regesten der Kaiser und Paepste*, Stuttgart, 1919.

Segrè, Angelo, *Circolazione Montaria e Prezzi nel Mondo Antico ed in particolare in Egitto*, Rome, 1922.

————, "Essays in Byzantine Economic History I, Annona Civica and Annona Militaris", *Byzantion*, 16, 1942, pp. 393–444.

————, "Inflation and Its Implications in Early Byzantine Times", *Byzantion*, 15, 1941, pp. 249–79.

————, "Maneh-Obolos", *JQR*, 34, 1934–44, pp. 481–82.

————, *Metrologia e Circolazione Monetaria degli Antichi*, Bologna, 1928.

————, "A note on P. Argent. Gr. 1, Verso, col. 1", *Journal of Egyptian Archeology*, 31, 1945, p. 113.

————, "Note sulle Moneta Romane del I sec. d. Chron. All. Età Bizantina", *Maia*, 16, 1965, pp. 259–74.

————, "Note sulla Storia dei Ceriali Nell' Antichità", *Aegyptus*, 30, 1950, pp. 161–97.

————, "On the date and circumstances of the Prefect's letter, P. Oxy. 2016," *Journal of Egyptian Archeology*, 26, 1941, pp. 114–15.

————, "Papirologia e Numismatica, A.I.P. Beatty Panop. a le moneta dell' età Diocleziano e di Constantino", *Chronique d'Égypte*, 40, No. 79, Jan. 1965, pp. 198–205.

Seston, W., "L'anmistie des Vicennalia de Dioclétien", *Chronique d'Égypte*, 43–4, 1947, pp. 333–37.

Souter, A., *A Glossary of Later Latin*, Oxford, 1949.

Sperber, Daniel, "Agricultural Trends in Third Century Palestine," *JESHO*, 15/3, 1972, pp. 227–55.

————, "Al Erko shel Maneh", *Talpiot*, 9/3–4, 1970, pp. 591–611.

————, "Amboroklon", *Tarbiz*, 40/4, 1971, pp. 444–449.

————, "Ani mazui lilvot", *Sinai*, 66/1–2, (398–99), 1969, pp. 101–02.

————, "Calculo Logistes Hashban", *Classical Quarterly*, 19/2, 1969, pp. 375–78.

————, "Costs of Living in Roman Palestine", I, *JESHO*, 8/3, 1965, pp. 248–71; II, *JESHO*, 9/3, 1966, pp. 182–211; III, *JESHO*, 11/3, 1968, pp. 233–74; IV, *JESHO*, 13/1, 1970, pp. 1–15.

————, "Denarii and Aurei in the time of Diocletian", *JRS*, 56, 1966, pp. 190–95.

————, "Dinarin Karatin", *Sinai*, 66/4–5, (401–02), 1970, pp. 272–74.

————, "Files-Follsa-Follis", *Leshonenu*, 31, 1967, pp. 183–88.

————, "Flight and the Talmudic Law of Usucaption," *RIDA*, 3/19, 1972, pp. 29–42.

————, "Gilgulei Misparim", *Sinai*, 62/5–6, (378–79), 1968, pp. 278–80.

————, "Gold and Silver Standards", *NC*, 1968, pp. 83–113.

————, "He'arah le-Tanḥuma Buber", *Sinai*, 63/3–4, (382–83), 1968, p. 189.

————, "The Inflation in Fourth Century Palestine", *Archiv Orientalni*, 34, 1966, pp. 54–66.

————, "Iyunim be-Matbe'ot Bar-Kochba", *Sinai*, 55, 1964, pp. 37–41.

————, "*Karapan", *Leshonenu*, 34/1–2, 1969–70, pp. 61–65.

————, "Karov Le-Alpayim — Li–fshutah shel Beraita", *Sinai*, 67/1, (405), 1970 pp. 61–62.

————, "Le-Ḥeker ha-Kalkala ba-Me'ah ha-Revi'it", *Sinai*, 64/3–4, (388–89), 1969, pp. 185–89.

————, "Mark 12:42 and its metrological background", *Novum Testamentum*, 9, 1967, pp. 178–90.

————, "New Light on the Problem of Demonetization in the Roman Empire", *NC*, 1970, pp. 111–15.

————, "A Note on some shi'urim", *JJS*, 20/1–4, 1969, pp. 81–86.

————, "Notes on the *Kesitah*", *REJ*, 127, 1968, pp. 265–68, (= *Acta Antiqua*, 19, 1–2, 1971, pp. 37–39).

————, "Numismatic Hapax-Legomena", *Le Muséon*, 80, 1967, pp. 265–68.

————, "On Social and Economic Conditions in Third Century Palestine", *Archiv Orientalni*, 38, 1970, pp. 1–25.

————, "Palestinian Currency Systems during the Second Commonwealth", *JQR*, 56/1, 1966, pp. 273–301.

————, "Patronage in Amoraic Palestine", *JESHO*, 14/3, 1971, pp. 227–52.

————, "Some Observations on Fish and Fisheries in Roman Palestine", *ZDMG*, 1969, pp. 265–69.

Sprengling, M., "Shahpur I, The Great, on the Ka'abah of Zoroaster (KZ)", *American Journal of Semitic Languages and Literature*, 57, 1940, pp. 341–420.

————, *Third Century Iran, Sapor and Kartir*, Chicago, 1953.

Stein, E., *Geschichte der Spätrömisches Reiches*, 1, Wien, 1928.

————, *Histoire du bas empire*, 2, Paris, 1949.

Strack, H., *Introduction to the Talmud and Midrash*, Philadelphia, 1931.

Strauss, E., (=Ashtor), *Toldot ha-Yehudim be-Mizrayim ve-Suria taḥat Shilton ha-Mamlukim*, 2, Israel, 1951.

Strauss, P., "Remarques sur la Monnaie de Cuivre Romaine au IVe, siècle", *Revue Numismatique*[5], 8, 1944–45, pp. 1–12.

Sukenik, E.L., "The Ancient Synagogue of el-Ḥammeh", *Journal of the Palestine Oriental Society*, 15, 1935, pp. 101–80.

Sutherland, C.V.H., "Denarius and Sestertius in Diocletian's Coinage Reform", *JRS*, 51, 1961, pp. 94–97.

————, "The Silver Content of Diocletian's Early Post-Reform Copper Coins", part I, *Archeometry*, 4, 1961, pp. 56–60.

————, see Carson, R.A.G.

Sutherland, C.V.H., and Carson, R.A.G., *Roman Imperial Coinage*, 6, London, 1967.

Szilági, J., "Prices and Wages in the Western Provinces of the Roman Empire", *AAH*, XI, 1963, pp. 325–89.

Tanzer, H., *The Common People of Pompei*, Baltimore, 1934.

Taqizadeh, S.H., "The Early Sassanians", *AO*, 18, 1940, pp. 258–317.

Taubenschlag, R., "Papyri and Parchments from the Eastern Provinces of the Roman Empire", *JJP*, 3, 1949, pp. 49–61.

————, *The Law of Greco-Roman Egypt in the Light of the Papyri*[2], Warsaw, 1955.

Taubes, Ch. Z., *Otzar ha-Geonim to Sanhedrin*, Jerusalem, 1966.

Urbach, E.E., "The Laws regarding Slavery as a Source for Social History of the Period of the Second Temple, the Mishna and Talmud", *Papers of the Institute of the Jewish Studies*, vol. 1, ed. J.G. Weiss, Jerusalem, 1964, pp. 1–94.

Viedebannt, Oskar, *Antike Gewichtsnormer und Münzfüsse*, Berlin, 1923,

Waddington, see Lebas.

Walbank, T.W., *The Decline of the Roman Empire in the West*, London, 1946.

Webb, P.H., "The Reform of Aurelian", *Num. Chron.*, 1919, pp. 235–43.

Weber, S.H., *An Egyptian Hoard of the Second Century A.D.*, NNM, 54, New York, 1932.

Wertheimer, A., *Betei Midrashot*, Jerusalem, 1954.

West, L.C., "Ancient Money and Modern Commentators", *ANSMN*, 4, 1954, pp. 6–9.

————, "The Coinage of Diocletian and the Edict of Prices", *Studies in Roman Economic and Social History in honour of Allan Chester Johnson*, ed. P.R. Coleman-Norton, Princeton, 1951, pp. 290–302.

————, "Determination of Roman Gold Coin Standards by Use of the Carat", *ANSMN*, 1, 1945, pp. 59–63.

————, *Gold and Silver Standards in the Roman Empire*, NNM, 96, New York, 1941.

————, "The Relation of Subsidiary Coinage to Gold under Valerian and Gallienus", *ANSMN*, 7, 1957, pp. 95–123.

————, "The Roman Gold Standard and the Ancient Sources", *American Journal of Philology*, 62, 1941, pp. 278–301.

————, see Johnson, A.C.

West, L.C., and Johnson, A.C., *Currency in Roman and Byzantine Egypt*, Princeton, 1944.

Westermann, W.C. & Schiller, A., *Apocrimata. Decisions of Septimius Severus in Legal Matters*, New York, 1954.

————, "Second Thoughts on the Columbia 'Apocrimata'", *Chronique d'Égypte*, 30, 1955, pp. 327–45.

Winlock, H.E. and Crum, W.E., *The Monastery of Epiphanius at Thebes*, Publication of the Metropolitan Museum of Art's Egyptian Expedition, 3, 4, Cambridge, 1926.

White, Peter, "The Authorship of the Historia Augusta", *JRS*, 57, 1967, pp. 115–33.

Wohlmann, M., *Ḥikrei Ha-Aretz*, Tel-Aviv, 1939.

Wright, W., *Catalogue of Syriac Manuscripts in the British Museum*, London, 1870.

————, *Chronicle of Joshua Stylites*, Cambridge, 1882.

Wright, W. & McLean, N., *Eusebius Ecclesiastical History in Syriac*, Cambridge, 1889.

Yalon, Ḥanoch., *Pirkei Lashon*, Jerusalem, 1971.

Youtie, "Graeco Roman Ostraca", *TAPA*, 76, 1945, pp. 144–47.

————, see Boak, A.E.R.

Ziegler, U., *Die Königagleichnisse des Midrasch beleuchtet durch die römische Kaiserzeit*, Breslau, 1903.

Zuckermann, *Talmudische Münzen und Gewichte*, Breslau, 1862.

Zuntz, G., "Greek Words in the Talmud", *JSS*, 1, 1956, pp. 129–40.

Zunz, Leopold & Albeck, Ch., *Ha-Derashot be-Yisrael*[2], Tel-Aviv, 1954, (being a Hebrew translation of Zunz' *Die Gottesdienstlichen vorträge der Juden Historisch entwickelt*[2], 1892, with additional notes by Albeck).

HEBREW SOURCES

A ירושלמי כתובות ד יג

.... חדא איתא הוא פורנא עשרין דינר, והוה תמן חד בית בטב עשרה דינר. אתא עובדא
קומי ר׳ חנניה. אמר: או ייבנין לה ביתא, או יבון לה כ׳ דינר. א״ר מנא: מכיוון דלית ביתא
טב אלא י׳, כמאן דלית לה פורנא אלא עשר. מיכן והילך, היא אומרת קרקע והן אומרין
מעות, הדין עם היתומין.

B ירושלמי בבא קמא ט ה

בר נש דיהב לחבריה חמשה מיני (צ״ל: מנוי) עמר וחמשה מיני (צ״ל: מנוי) סממנין ועשרה מנוי
אגריה. א״ל: ציבעיה סומק, וצבעו אוכם. א״ל: אילו צבעתיה סומק, הוה טב עשרים וחמש
מנוי. וכדן דצבעתיה אוכם, לית הוא טב אלא עשרים מנוי. את אובדת דידך, אנא לא אובד
דידי. אמר רבי יונה. ותשמע מינה: בר נש דיהב לחבריה שמנה (צ״ל: חד) דינרין דזבין ליה
חיטין מטבריה, וזבן ליה מצפורי. א״ל: אילו זבנת לי מטיבריא, הוון עשרין וחמשה מודי. כדן
דזבנת מציפורי, ליתנין אלא עשרין מודיי. את אובדת דידך, אנא לא אובד דידי.

C ירושלמי ברכות ב ח

ר׳ זעירא כד סליק להכא, אזל אקיז דם. אזל בעי מיזבון ליטרא דקופד מן טבחא. א״ל: בכמה
הדין ליטרתא? א״ל: בחמשין מניי, וחד קורסם. א״ל: סב לך שיתין, ולא קביל עילוי. סב לך
ע׳ ולא קביל עילוי. סב לך פ׳, סב לך צ׳, עד דמטה מאה, ולא קביל עילוי. א״ל: עביד
כמנהגך. ברומשא נחית לבית וועדא. אמר לון: רבנן, מה ביש מנהגא דהכא, דלא אכיל בר נש
ליטרא דקופד עד דמחו ליה חד קורסם. אמרין ליה: ומה הוא דין? אמר לון: פלן טבחא.
שלחון. בעיי מייתיתיה, ואשכחון ארוניה נפקא. א״ל: רבי, כל הכין! א״ל: וייתי עליי דלא
כעסית עילוי, מי סברת דמנהגא כן.

D תנחומא בלק טו (תנחומא בובר בלק כד, עמ׳ 145)

ילמדנו רבינו, מי שאכל ולא נטל ידיו מה יהא חייב? כך שנו רבותינו: נטילת ידים לפני המזון
רשות לאחר המזון חובה, (השווה בבלי חולין קה ע״א). מעשה בחנוני מישראל שהיה מבשל
בשר טהור ובשר חזיר ומוכר שלא ירגישו בו שהוא יהודי. וכך היה מנהגו, כל מי שנכנס לחנותו
ולא נטל ידיו, יודע היה שהוא נכרי ונותן לפניו בשר חזיר. וכל מי שנטל ידיו ומברך, יודע
שהוא יהודי ומאכילו בשר טהור. פעם אחת נכנס יהודי לאכול שם ולא נטל ידיו. היה סבור
שהוא נכרי, נתן לפניו בשר חזיר. אכל ולא ברך. בא לעשות חשבון על הפת ועל הבשר, ובשר
חזיר נמכר ביוקר. א״ל: יש לי עליך כך וכך מן בשר שאכלת, שחתיכה נמכר עשרה מנה. א״ל:
אתמול אכלתי אותה בשמנה, היום אתה רוצה ממני עשרה. א״ל: זו שאכלת היום של חזיר היה.
כיוון שאמר לו כך, עמדו שערותיו, נבהל ונחפז. א״ל בצנעה: יהודי אני, ונתת לי בשר חזיר!
א״ל: תיפח רוחך. כשראיתי שאכלת בלא נטילת ידים ובלא ברכה, הייתי סבור שאתה נכרי.
מכאן שנו חכמים: מים הראשונים האכילו בשר חזיר, מים אחרונים הרגו את הנפש ...

E קהלת רבה קהלת ה י

"ברבות הטובה רבו אוכליה" (קהלת שם). ר' חנניה ור' יונתן שאלון למנחם טלמיא. ור' ברכיה
בשם ר' יוסי בן חנניה אמר: שאל לון מנחם טלמיא: מהו דין "יערנך ויריעבך (ויאכלך את המן
אשר לא ידעת ולא ידעו אבותיך" וכו') (דברים ח ג) – וכי מאכל רעבון נתן להם הקב"ה
המן לישראל? מה עשה? הביא לפניו ב' קישואין, אחת שלימה ואחת שבורה. אמר: הדא
שלימתא היא בכמה? א"ל: בתרין מנה. והדא תבירא בכמה? א"ל: בחד מנה. אמר לון: לית
טופא (אולי צ"ל: סופא) דהדיא דהיא מתעביד בהדא? אמר להם: לא דומה, כשם שהוא
מתהנה מן הטעם כך הוא מתהנה מן הראיה.

F אסתר רבה ב ג (לאסתר א ד)

עובדא הוה בגברא חד דהוה שמיה ברבוהי. הלכו רבותינו אצלו על עסק מגבת חכמים.
שמעון לבריה דאמר ליה: במה אנן אכלין יומא דין? אמר ליה: בטרוקסימון. מן חד במנא או
מן תרין במנא? אמר ליה: מן תרין במנא, דאינון כמישין וזלילין. אמרין: היכן אנן אזלין גבי
הדין. ניזיל ונעביד עבדיתן בקרתא, ובתר כן ניתי לגביה. אזלון ועבדון עיבידתהון בקרתא
ואתו לגבי. ואמרין ליה: הב לן מצוותא. אמר לון: אזלון לגבי דא דבייתא והיא יהבה לכן חד
מודיא דדינרין. אזלון לגבי אינתתא. ואמרין לה: אמר ליך בעלך: הב לן מצוותא חד מודיא
דדינרין. אמרה לון: היכי אמר לכון, גדיש או מחיק? אמרין לה: סתם אמר לן. אמרה: אנא
יהבה לכון גדיש. אין אמר לי בעלי: למה? אמינא ליה: חביתין מן פרני. אתון לגביה, אמרון
ליה: בריךך ימלאון חסרונך. אמר לון: היכן יהבתיה לכון, גדיש או מחיק? אמרו ליה: סתם
אמרן לה, ואמרה, אנא יהבה לכון יתיה גדיש. ואין אמר בעלי: למה? אנא יהבה גדראניה מן
פורני. אמר לון: איכן דכן הוית בדעתי למתנא לכון. ולמה לא אתיתון לגבי מריש? אמרון
ליה: שמעינן לעובדך דאמר לך: במה אנן אכלין יומא דין? ואמרת ליה: בטרוקסימון. ואמר
לך: מן חד במנא או מן תרין במנא? ואמרת ליה: מן תרין במנא דאינון כמישין וזלילין. ואמרין:
בר נש דאית ליה כל הדין ממונא, הוא אכיל בטרוקסימון מן תרין במנא! אמר לון: בנפשי אנא
רשיי, ברם במצוותא דברייי לית אנא יכיל ולא רשיי.

G

ירושלמי מגילה ד א

ר' יוסי אומר: יכיל אנא כתב כל קרייא מן
פומי. ר' חייה רבה אומר: יכיל אנא כתב
כל קרייא בתרין מניי. היך עבידא? וזבן
בתרין מניי זרע דכיתן, וזרע ליה, וחצד
ליה, ועבד חבלין, ותפש טביי, וכתב כל
קרייא על משכיהון. שמע רבי ואמר: אשרי
הדור שאתם בתוכו.

בבלי בבא מציעא פה ע"ב

כי הוו מינצו רבי חנינא ורבי חייא, אמר
ליה רבי חנינא לרבי חייא: בהדי דידי קא
מינצית! חס ושלום אי משתכחת תורה
מישראל, מהדרנא לה מפלפולי. אמר ליה
רבי חייא לרבי חנינא: בהדי דידי קא
מינצית! דעבדי לתורה דלא תשתכח
מישראל. מאי עבידנא? אזלינא ושדינא
כיתנא, וגדילנא נישבי, וצאידנא טבי, ומא־
כילנא בשרייהו ליתמי, ואריכנא מגילתא
וכתבנא חמשא חומשי, וסליקנא למתא,
ומקרינא שיתא ינוקי שיתא סדרי, ואמרנא
להו: עד דהדרנא ואתינא אקרו אהדדי
ואתנו אהדדי ועבדי לה לתורה דלא תשתכח
מישראל. היינו דאמר רבי: כמה גדולים
מעשה חייא. אמר ליה רבי ישמעאל ברבי
יוסי: אפילו ממר? אמר ליה: אין. אפילו
מאבא? אמר ליה: חס ושלום, לא תהא
כזאת בישראל.

H ירושלמי בבא מציעא ה ו

כהנא יהב מ׳ דינרין לבר נש מיזבן ליה כיתן. יקרא כיתנא. אתא שאל לרב. אמר ליה איזיל
סב מיניה מ׳ כורין רברבין.

I דברים רבה כי תצא ב (מהדורה ליברמן, עמ׳ 103)

הה״ד ״אורח ימים פן תפלס״ וגו׳ (משלי ד ו), א״ר אבא בר כהנא: אמר הקב״ה: לא תהא
יושב ושוקל במצוותיה של תורה, כענין שנאמר ״ושקל בפלס הרים״ (ישעיה מ יב). לא תהא
אומר: הואיל והמצוה הזו גדולה אני עושה אותה ששכרה מרובה, הואיל וזו מצוה קלה איני
עושה אותה. מה עשה הקב״ה? לא גילה לבריות מהו מתן שכרה של כל מצוה ומצוה, כדי
שיעשו כל המצוות כתום. מנין? שנאמר: ״נעור מעגלותיה לא תדע״ (משלי ה ו). לה״ד? למלך
ששכר לו פועלים והכניס אותן לתוך פרדסו. סתם ולא גילה להם מהו שכר של פרדס, שלא
יניחו דבר ששכרו מועט ויעשו דבר ששכרו מרובה. בערב קרא לכל א׳ וא׳. א״ל: תחת איזה
אילן עשית? א״ל (א״ל:) פלפל הוא. שכרו זהוב אחד. קרא לאחר. א״ל: תחת איזה אילן עשית?
א״ל: שכרו חצי זהוב. פרח לבן הוא. קורא לאחר. א״ל: זית הוא. שכרו מאתיים מנה. א״ל:
לא היית צריך להודיע אותנו איזה אילן שכרו מרובה כדי שנעשה תחתיו? אמ׳ להם המלך:
אילו הודעתי אתכם, היאך היה כל הפרדס נעשה? לא גילה הקב״ה מתן שכרן של מצוות חוץ
משתי מצוות החמורות שבחמורות והקלה שבקלות. החמורה שבחמורות, כיבוד אב ואם, ומתן
שכרה אריכות ימים, שנא׳: ״כבד את אביך ואת אמך (למען יאריכון ימיך וגו׳) (שמות כ יב).
והקלה שבקלות, שילוח הקן, ומתן שכרה אריכות ימים, שנאמר: ״שלח תשלח את האם (ואת
הבנים תקח לך, למען ייטב לך והארכת ימים)״ (דברים כב ז).

J ויקרא רבה ל א (מרגליות תר״צ – תרצ״א). פסיקתא דרב כהנא
״ולקחתם״ א (מנדלבוים ב 404)

א״ר אבא בר כהנא: משכר לקיחה אתה למד שבר לולב. לקיחה במצרים, ״ולקחתם אגודת
אזוב״ (שמות יב כב), ובכמה הות טימי דידיה? בד׳ מיני (בארבעה מני, בחמשה מניי –
פסיקתא), והוא שגרם לישראל לירש ביזת הים, ביזת סיחון ועוג, ביזת ל״א מלך. לולב שעומד
על האדם בכמה בכמה דמים, וכמה מצוות יש בו, על אחת כמה וכמה! לפיכך משה מזהיר את ישראל
ואומר להם: ״ולקחתם לכם ביום הראשון״ (ויקרא כג מ).

K דברים רבה מהדורת ליברמן עמ׳ 126 (=תנחומא העזינו סי׳ א,
תנחומא בובר שם סי׳ ג עמ׳ 1–2)

״יערוף כמטר לקחי״ (דברים לב ב) – אמר רבי יהושע בן לוי: כשעלה משה למרום עמדו
המלאכים להרגו. אמר להם: בשביל שני דברים שנתנו לי בני אדם אתם מבקשים להרגני?
הניחוהו. מלה״ד: לסוחר גדול המהלך במקום סכנת נפשימו. תפסוהו ליסטים, בקשו להרגו.
אמר להם: בשביל ה׳ מנה שיש עמי אתם מבקשים להרגני ולא היו יודעים שיש לו אבנים (טובות)
ומרגליות שאין להם דמים. אמרו לו: אתמול תפשנו אותך
ואמרת לנו: אין עמי אלה ה׳ מנים, ועכשיו אתה מוצא אבנים טובות ומרגליות שאין להם דמים
בעולם. אמר להם: כשאמרתי לכם כך, בשעת הסכנה הייתי אומר. ואף כך אמר משה למלאכי
השרת, שנאמר ״עלית למרום (שבית שבי לקחת מתנות האדם)״ (תהלים סח יט). אמר דוד: ״טוב
לי תורת פיך (מאלפי זהב וכסף)״ (שם קי״ט עב), ואומר ״הנחמדים מזהב (ומפז רב)״ (שם
יט יא), ואמר ״אמרות ה׳ אמרות טהורות״ וגו׳ (שם יב ז). אמרו ישראל למשה: אשריך שלקחת
מתנות. אמר (להם): אילולי שאמרתי למלאכי השרת שהן שני דברים הייתי נשרף מאשם,
והתורה הזאת היא הצלתני מידם. עליהם אמר ״יערוף כמטר לקחי״ וגו׳. אין יערף אלא
הריגה. שנאמר ״וערפו שם את העגלה״ (דברים כא ד), וכן ביהודה הוא אומר ״ידך בעורף
אויבך״ (בראשית מט ח), ואין לקח אלא תורה, שנאמר ״כי לקח טוב נתתי לכם״ וגו׳ (משלי
ד ב).

L אסתר רבה י ד

...אמר לון (המן): והדין עומרא מהו, דדהב או דכסף? אמרי ליה: לא דדהב ולא דכסף ולא
דחיטין, אלא דשעורין. אמר לון: בכמה הוא טימיה דידיה הוה, בעשרה קנטרין? אמרין ליה:
סגין בעשרה מנין. אמר לון: קומו דנצחון עשרה מנכן לעשרה אלפי קנטרין דכסף דילי.

M ירושלמי, כתובות יא ב

כהדא דאמר רבי אבהו בשם רבי יוחנן: לווה ממנו יב אלף לשנה להיות מעלה לה מדינר
זהב לחדש... (השווה ירושלמי כתובות יב א)

N בבלי בבא מציעא מז ע"ב

אסימון קונה את המטבע וכו'. מאי אסימון? אמר רב: מעות הניתנות בסימן לבית המרחץ.
מיתיבי: אין מחללין מעשר שני על אסימון ו(לא) על מעות הניתנות בסימן לבית המרחץ (משנה
מעשר שני א ב), מכלל דאסימון לאו מעות הניתנון בסימן לבית המרחץ. וכי תימא פירושי
קמפרש, והא לא תנא הכי: מחללין מעשר שני על אסימון, דברי ר' דוסא. וחכמים אומרים:
אין מחללין. ושוין שאין מחללין על מעות הניתנות בסימן לבית המרחץ (משנה עדויות ג ב,
תוספתא מעשר שני א ד). אמר ר' יוחנן: מאי אסימו, פולסא. ואזדא רבי יוחנן לטעמיה, דאמר
ר' יוחנן: רבי דוסא ורבי ישמעאל אמרו דבר אחד. רבי דוסא דאמרן. רבי ישמעאל מאי היא?
דתניא: "וצרת הכסף בידך" (דברים יד כה), לרבות כל דבר הנצרר ביד, דברי רבי ישמעאל.
רבי עקיבא אומר: לרבות כל דבר שיש עליו צורה.

O בבלי בבא מציעא מד ע"א

איתבי רבי אבא לעולא: הרי שהיו חמריו ופועליו תובעין אותו בשוק ואמר לשולחני: תן לי
בדינר מעות ואפרנסם, ואני אעלה לך יפה דינר וטריסית ממעות ממעות שיש לי בביתי. אם יש לו
מעות, מותר. ואם לאו, אסור. ואי ס"ד אין מטבע נעשה חליפין, הוא ליה הלואה ואסור.
אשתיק. אמר ליה: דילמא אידי ואידי בפרוטטות שנו, דליכא עליהו טבעא, ואידי ואידי פירא
הוי, ומשום הכי נקנו בחליפין. אמר ליה: אין. דיקא נמי דקתני "יפה דינר וטריסין", ולא קתני
"דינר יפה וטריסין". שמע מינה.

P

ירושלמי שבת ו ה	בבלי שבת סה ע"א
מ ש נ ה : יוצאין בסלע שעל הצינית...	מ ש נ ה : יוצאת בסלע שעל הצינית...
ג מ ר א : יוצאין בסלע שעל הצינית, פודגרה. רבי אחא בר רבי בא בא ממל: אפילו טס.	ג מ ר א : מאי צינית? בת ארעא, ומאי שנא סלע? אילימא כל מידי דאקושא מעלי ליה, ליעבד לה חספא! אלא משום שוכתא, ליעבד לה טסא! אלא משום צורתא, ליעבד לה פולסא! אמר אביי: שמע מינה כולהו מעלין לה.

Q שיר השירים רבה א ט (לפסוק א א)

ר' פנחס בן יאיר (צ"ל: חמה) פתח: "אם תבקשנה ככסף (וכממונים תחפשנה)" (משלי ב ד).
אם אתה מחפש אחר דברי תורה כמטמונים הללו, אין הקב"ה מקפח שכרך. משל לאדם, אם
מאבד סלע או כילרין (נ"א: בולרין) מתוך ביתו, הוא מדליק כמה נרות כמה פתילות עד
שימצא עליהם. והרי דברים קל וחומר. ומה אלו, שהם חיי שעה של עולם הזה, אדם מדליק
כמה נרות וכמה פתילות עד שימצא עליהם. דברי תורה, שהם חיי עולם הזה וחיי עולם
הבא, אין אתה צריך לחפש אחריהם כמטמונים הללו! הוי "אם תבקשנה ככסף" וגו'.

302

R ירושלמי פאה א א (טו ע״ד 54—60)

ארטבן שלח לרבינו הקדוש חד מרגלי טבא אטימיטון. א״ל: שלח לי מילה דטבה דכוותה. שלח שיה חד מזוזה. אמר ליה: מה אנא שלחית לך? מילה דלית ליה טימי. ואת שלחת לי מילה דטבא חד פולר. א״ל: חפציך וחפצי לא ישוו בה. ולא עוד אלא דאת שלחת לי מילה דאנא מנטר לה ואנא שלחית לך מילה דאת דמך לך והיא מנטרא לך, דכתיב ״בהתהלכך תנחה אותך״ (משלי ו כב).

S בראשית רבא ע יד (תיאודור – אלבק עמ׳ 813—814)

״ויאמר לבן ליעקב הרי אחי אתה ועבדתני חנם (הגידה לי מה משכרתך)״ (בראשית כט טו). אפשר כן? אלא אם היה פעלה בעשרה פולרין, הוה יהב ליה חמשה. ואי הות מובלתיה בשיתה פולרין, הוה יהיב ליה בתלתא פולרין. אמר ליה: מה את סבור, ממון אתית בעי? לא אתית אלא מן בגין של תרתין טלייתא.

T בראשית רבא מט ד (תיאודור, אלבק עמ׳ 502—503)

״כי ידעתיו למען אשר יצוה את בניו (ואת ביתו אחריו ושמרו דרך ה׳ לעשות צדקה ומשפט וכו׳) (בראשית יח יט) . . . ר׳ עזריה בשם ר׳ יהודה (בר׳ סימון): בתחילה צדקה ולבסוף משפט. הא כיצד? אברהם היה מקבל את העוברים והשבים. משהיו אוכלין ושותים אמר להון: בריכו. אמרין ליה: מה נאמר? אמר: ברוך קל עולם שאכלנו משלו. אין מקבל עלוי לברך, הוה אכיל ושתי ואזיל ליה. ואין לא יקביל, הוה אמר ליה: מה אית עליי? היה אמר ליה: חד קסיט דחמרא בעשרה פולדי וחד ליטר דקופד בעשרה פולדי וחד איגול דפיתא בעשרה פולדי. מן יהב לך חמר במדברא? מן יהב לך קופד במדברא? מן יהב לך פיתא במדברא? מן דהוה חמי עקתיה עקא הוה אמר: ברוך קל עולם שאכלנו משלו. הה״ד בתחילה צדקה ובסוף משפט.

U ויקרא רבה לז ב (מרגליות עמ׳ תתנ״ו—ז)

״כי פועל ה׳ ישלם לו (וכאורח איש ימצאנו)״ (איוב לד יא). עובדא הוא בחד גבר דהוה ליה תרין בנין. חד הוה עביד מצווין סגין, וחרנא לא הוה עביד כל עיקר. דין דהוה עביד מצווין סגין זבין ביתיה וכל מה דהות ליה בגין מצוותא. חד זמן ביומא דהושענא יהבת ליה איתתיה עשרה פורין (צ״ל: פולרין, או פולסין). אמרה ליה: פוק זבון לבניך כלום מן שוקא. כיוון דנפק מן שוקא, פגעון ביה גבאי צדקה. אמרי: הא מרי מצוותא אתא ליה. אמרי ליה: הב חולקיך בהדין מצוותא, דאנן בעיין מזבון קלוב לחדא יתמא. נסב הלוך פורייא (צ״ל: פלוריא או פולסי) ויהב להון . . .

V בבלי עבודה זרה לד ע״ב

ההוא ארבא דמורייסא דאתי לנימלא דעכו. אותיב רבי אבא דמן עכו נטורי בהדא. א״ל רבא (צ״ל: ר׳ אבא): עד האידנא מאן נטרה? א״ל: עד האידנא למאי ניחוש לה? אי משום דמערבי ביה חמרא, קיסטא דמורייס בלומא, קיסטא דחמרא בד׳ לומי. א״ל ר׳ ירמיה לר׳ זירא: דילמא איידי דצור אתו, דשוי חמרא? א״ל: התם עיקולי ופשורי איכא.

W ירושלמי בבא מציעא ד א

משנה

הכסף קונה את הזהב, והזהב אינו קונה את הכסף. ונחושת קונה את הכסף, והכסף אינו קונה את הנחושת. מעות הרעות קונות את היפות, והיפות אינן קונות את הרעות. אסי־מון קונה את המטבע, והמטבע אינו קונה האסימון. והמטלטלין קונין את המטבע, והמטבע אינו קונין את המטלטלין. זה הכלל: כל המטלטלין קונים זה את זה.

בבלי בבא מציעא מד ע״א—ע״ב

משנה

הזהב קונה את הכסף, הכסף אינו קונה את הזהב. הנחושת קונה את הכסף, והכסף אינו קונה את הנחושת. מעות הרעות קונות את היפות, והיפות אינן קונות את הרעות. אסי־מון קונה את המטבע, והמטבע אינו קונה את האסימון. מטלטלין קונין את המטבע, מטבע אינו קונה את המטלטלין. (זה, הכלל:) כל המטלטלין קונים זה את זה.

גמרא

זה כללו של דבר: כל הירוד מחברו קונה
את חברו. א״ר חייא בר אשי: מאן תניתא?
ר״ש ברבי. א״ל אבוי: חזור בך ותני כהדא:
הזהב קונה את הכסף. א״ל: לינא חוזר בי
דעד דהוה חילך עליך אתניתנו: הכסף
קונה את הזהב. מילתיה דר׳ אמר זהב
כפירות. מתני׳ אמרת כסף כפירות.
ברת ר׳ חייא רובה אוחפה לרב דינרין.
אתת שאלת לאבוה. אמר לה: שקילי מיניה
דינרין טבין ותקילין. מברת ר׳ חייא ילפן.
א״ר אידי: אוף אבא אבוי דשמואל בעא
קומי רבי: מהו ללות דינרין בדינרין? א״ל
מותר. א״ר יעקב בר אחא: אוף ר׳ יוחנן
וריש לקיש תריהון מרין: מותר ללות
דינרין. קרט בקרט שרי. לקן בלקן אסור.
תמן תנינן (קדושין א ו): כל הנעשה
דמים באחר, כיון שזכה זה נתחייב זה
בחליפיו. א״ר יוחנן: לא שנא אלא שור
בפרה או חמור בשור. הא ציבור בציבור
לא קנה. רב ירמיה בשם רב: אפילו ציבור
בציבור קנה. ר׳ אבא בר מינה בשם רב:
המחליף אברוקלון באמבורקלין קנה.

גמרא

מתני ליה רבי לרבי שמעון בריה: הזהב
קונה את הכסף. א״ל: רבי, שנית לנו
בילדותיך: הכסף קונה את הזהב, ותחזור
ותשנה לנו בזקנותיך: הזהב קונה את הכסף?
בילדותיה מאי סבר, ובזקנותיה מאי סבר?
בילדותיה מאי סבר: דהבא דחשיב הוי
טבעא, כספא דלא חשיב הוי פירא, וקני
ליה פירא לטבעא. בזקנותיה סבר: כספא
דחריף הוי טבעא, דהבא דלא חריף הוי
פירא, וקני ליה פירא לטבעא. [אמר רב
אשי: כילדותיה מסתברא, מדקתני: הנחושת
קונה את הכסף. אי אמרת בשלמא כספא
לגבי דהבא פירא הוי היינו דקא תני:
הנחושת קונה את הכסף, דאע״פ דלגבי
דהבא פירא הויא, לגבי נחושת טבעא הוי.
אלא אי אמרת כספא לגבי דהבא טבעא
הוי, השתא לגבי דהבא דחשיב מיניה אמרת
טבעא הוי. לגבי נחושת דאיהו חשיב ואיהו
חריף מבעיא? איצטריך. סלקא דעתך
אמינא הני פריטי באתרא דסגיי אינהו
חריפי טפי מכספא, אימא טבעא הוי.
קמ״ל, כיון דאיכא דוכתא דלא סגי ביה,
פירא הוי.]

ואף רבי הייא סבר דהבא טבעא הוי. דרב
אוזיף דינרי מברתי׳ דר׳ חייא. לסוף איקור
דינרי. אתא לקמיה דרבי חייא. א״ל: זיל
שלים לה טבין ותקילין. אי אמרת בשלמא
דהבא טיבעא הוי, שפיר. אלא אי אמרת
פירא הוי, הוה ליה סאה בסאה ואסור. רב
דינרי הוו ליה, וכיון דהוו ליה דינרי נעשה
כאומר לה: הלויני עד שיבוא בני או עד
שאמצא מפתח (השוה לקמן מ״ו ע״א).
אמר רבא: האי תנא סבר דהבא טבעא הוי,
דתנן (עדויות ד ז): פרוטה שאמרו אחד
משמונה באיסר האיטלקי. למאי נפקא
מינה? לקדושי אשה. איסר אחד מעשרים
וארבע בדינר של כסף. למאי נפקא מינה?
למקח וממכר. דינר של כסף אחד מעשרים
וחמשה בדינר של זהב. למאי נפקא מינה?
לפדיון הבן. אי אמרת בשלמא טבעא הוי,
משער תנא במידי דקיץ. אלא אי אמרת
פירא הוי, משער תנא במידי דאוקיר וזיל.
זימנין דמהדר ליה כהנא וזמנין דמוסיף ליה
איהו לכהנא. אלא שמע מינה טבעא הוי,
ש״מ.

בבלי קדושין יב ע״א

ירושלמי קדושין א א   X

גופא. כי אתא רב דימי אמר: שיער רבי
סימאי בדורו כמה היא פרוטה, אחד
משמנה באיסר האיטלקי. וכי אתא רבין
אמר: שיערו רבי דוסתאי ורבי ינאי ורבי
אושיעא כמה היא פרוטה, אחד ממשה
באיסר האיטלקי. אמר ליה אביי לרב
דימי: נימא את ורבין בפלוגתא דהני תנאי
קא מפלגיתו, דתניא: פרוטה שאמרו חכמים
אחד משמנה באיסר האיטלקי. שש מעה
כסף דינר. מעה שני פונדיונין. פונדיון שני
איסרין. איסר שני מוסמוסין. מסמס שני
קונטרורקין. קונטרורנג שתי פרוטות. נמצא
פרוטה אחת משמנה באיסר האיטלקי.
רשב״ג אומר: שלשה הדרסין למעה. שני
הינצין להדריס. שני שמנין להנג. שתי
פרוטות לשמין. נמצא פרוטה אחת ממשה
באיסר האיטלקי. לימא דמר אמר כת״ק,
ורבין דאמר כרשב״ג. א״ל: בין דידי ובין
רבין אליבא דת״ק, ולא קשיא. הא דאיקור
איסורי, הא דזול איסורי. הא דאיקור
איסורי, קום עשרים וארבע בזוזא. הא
דזול, קום תלתין ותרין בזוזא.

וכמה היא פרוטה? אחד משמונה באיסר
האיטלקי. תני: האיסר אחד מעשרים
וארבע בדינר כסף, דינר כסף אחד
מעשרים וארבע לדינר זהב. תני רבי חייה:
סילעא ארבעה דינרין. שש מעה כסף דינר.
שני פונדיונין מעה. שני איסרין פונדיון. שני
מסומיסין איסר. שני קרדיונטס מסומס. שני
פרוטות קרדיונטס. סלקין אחד משלושים
ושנים למעה. אמר רבי זעירא: בימי רבי
סימאי ורבותינו עשו אותם אחד מעשרים
וארבעה למעה. ותני: רשב״ג אומר: שלושה
דורסים מעה. שני ניצים דרוסה. שני שמין
ניצים. שני פרוטות שמין. סלקין אחא
מעשרים וארבעה למעה. רבי חנינה ורבי
מנא, רבי חנינה אומר: נחשא באתריה קיים
כספא זליל כספא יקיר. רבי מנא אומר:
כספא באתריה קיים, נחשא יקיר נחשא
זליל ...

Y תוספתא בבא מציעא ג יז–יט (מהדורת צוקרמנדל עמ׳ 377)
17. סלע כמה תהא חסירה ויהא בה אונאה? ארבע איסרות, לדינר איסר, דברי ר׳ מאיר. ר׳
יהודה אומר: סלא ארבע פונדיונות, לדינר פונדיון. ר׳ שמעון אומר: שמונה פונדיונות, לדינר
שני פונדיונות. יותר על כך היה מוציאה בשויה.
18. סלע עד שקל ודינר עד רביעית. פחות מכן אפילו איסר אין רשאי להוציאה.
19. לא ימכרנה לא לתגר ולא להרג ולא לחרם מפני שמרמין בהן את אחרים. אבל נוקבה
ותולה בצואר בנו. וכשם שאתה אומר בחולין כך אתה אומר במעשר שני, ובלבד שלא יתכוין
להטיל על השני. במה דברים אמורים? בדינרין ובסילעין. אבל בדינרי זהב ובמטבעות של
נחושת היו מוציאין בשויין.

Z תוספתא כתובות ו ה (צוקרמנדל עמ׳ 267)
פסקה להכניס לו שני סלעים, נעשית משישה דינרים. מה שחתן פוסק פחות חומש חוץ ממאתים
לבתולה ומנה לאלמנה. פסקה להכניס לו זהב הרי זהב ככלים ודינרי זהב הרי הן ככספים.
אמר ר׳ שמעון בן גמליאל: כן הדבר מקום שנהגו שלא לפרוט דינרי זהב אלא מונחים כמות
שהן, ודינרי זהב הרי הן ככלים ...

AA תוספתא מעשר שני ב ז (צוקרמנדל עמ׳ 88–89)
סלע של מעשר שני של חולין ושל הקדש שנתערבו מביא בסלע מעות ואומר: סלע מעשר שני
בכל מקום שהוא מחולל על המעות האילו. בורר את היפה שבהם ואומר: אם הקדש הוא הרי
הוא הקדש, אם לא הקדש בכל מקום שהוא מחולל על זה. נוטל את השנייה ומחלל את המעות
עליה, ושלישית הרי זו מותרת. מפני מה אמרו: מחללין נחושת על כסף וכסף על זהב כסף על
נחושת מדוחק, אבל לא זהב על הכסף? ר׳ אלעזר בר׳ שמעון אומר: כשם שמחללין כסף על

נחשת כך מחללין זהב על הכסף. אמרו לו: מפני מה מחללין כסף על נחשת, כך יחללו כסף
על זהב. לא יחללו זהב על הכסף, שאין מחללין זהב על הנחשת. ר' אלעזר בר' שמעון אומר:
מעשר שני של זהב מחללין אותו על מעות שבירושלים בשל דמאי, אבל ודאי הרי זה אסור.
אבל בדמאי מחללין אתו וארבי עליהן על אוכלין. מעשר שני של זהב שעשאום כלים יש לו פדיון.
ושל כסף הרי זה מותר. מעשר שני של דמאי שנתערב בשל ודאי יאכלו כחמור שבהן.

AB ירושלמי פאה ספ״א

תני: לא נחלקו רבי ור' יהודה הנשיא על הלוקח פירות מחוברים מן הגוי שהן חייבין במעשרות,
ועל של ישראל שנכנס תחתיו, ועל של הלוקח פירות תלושין מן הגוי שהן פטורות מן המעשרות.
על מה נחלקו? על הלוקח פירות תלושין מחבירו בשנת מעשר עני. ר' יהודה הנשיא אומר:
אחד עני ואחד עשיר מוציאין מידו. ורבי אומר: עשיר מוציאין מידו, עני אין מוציאין מידו. מ״ט
דר״י הנשיא? כשם שאין אדם זוכה בלקט שכחה פיאה שלו, כך לא יזכה במעשר עני שלו. ומ״ט
דר'? לקט שכחה ופאה אין טובלין. מעשר עני טובל, וכבר נטבל עד שהוא ברשותו של ראשון.
מ״ט דר״י הנשיא? משום קנס. ומ״ט דר'? עשיר בידו ליקח, עני אין בידו ליקח. ור״י הנשיא
אומר: מצווי הוא ללות, ורבי אומר: אינו מצוי ללות.

AC בראשית רבא טז ג (מהדורת תיאודור – אלבק עמ' 143)

״וזהב הארץ ההיא טוב״ (בראשית ב יב). אמר ר' יצחק: טובו דהוא בביתיה, טובו דהוא
בלוייתיה. אמר ר' אבהו: טובה גדולה חלק הקב״ה לעולמו. אדם פורט של זהב והוא מוציא
ממנו כמה יציאות. אמר ר' שמעון בן לקיש: לא היה העולם ראוי לשתמש בזהב. זהב למה
נברא? בשביל בית המקדש ״וזהב הארץ ההיא טוב״ (שם) – מה דאת אמר ״ההר הטוב הזה
והלבנון״ (דברים ג כה).

AD ספרי דברים פרשת האזינו, פיסקא שי (מהדורת פינקלשטיין 338–339)

דבר אחר, ״יערף כמטר לקחי״ (דברים לב ב). היה רבי מאיר אומר: לעולם הוי כונס דברי
תורה כללים, שאם אתה כונסם פרטים מייגעים אותך ואי אתה יודע מה לעשות. משל לאדם
שהלך לקיסרי וצריך מאה זוז או מאתים זוז הוצאה. אם נוטלם פרט מייגעים אותו ואינו יודע
מה לעשות. אבל מצרפם ועושה אותם סלעים ופורט או מוציא בכל מקום שירצה. וכן מי שהלך
לבית אייליס לשוק וצריך מאה מנה או שתי רבוא הוצאה. אם מצרפם סלעים (פרוטרות, כך
הוא במדרש תנאים ובמדרש הגדול) מייגעים אותו ואינו יודע מה לעשות. אבל מצרפם ועושה
אותם דינרי זהב ופורט ומוציא בכל מקום שירצה.

AE ירושלמי הוריות ג ה

דרש ר' שמואל בריה דרבי יוסי בי ר' בון: ״חכם בעיניו איש עשיר ודל מבין יחקרנו״ (משלי
כח יא) – ״חכם בעיניו איש עשיר״, זה בעל התלמוד; ״ודל מבין יחקרנו״, זה בעל אגדה. לשנים
שנכנסו לעיר, ביד זה עשתות של זהב וביד זה פרוטרות. זה שבידו עשתות של זהב אינו מוציא
וחיה. וזה שבידו פרוטרות מוציא וחיה.

AF שמות רבה י ה

ד״א ״וישק לו״ (שמות ד כז). אמר רבי שמואל בר נחמן: משל לזהבי שהביאו לו מונייתה אחת
וראה אותה מבפנים של חרס ומבחוץ של זהב. לימים הביאו לו מונייטה כולה זהב. אמר להם:
הראשון חרס היה והיא מצופה זהב. אבל זה כולה זהב. כך נשיקה שנשק עשו ליעקב לא היה
אלא לפסולת, שנאמר: ״כסף סיגים מצופה על חרס״ (משלי כד כג). ומה היה סופר שפתים
דולקות ולב רע״ (שם), שלא בקש לנשקו אלא לנשכו, (השווה בראשית לב ד). אבל נשיקה של
אהרן ומשה היתה נשיקה של אמת, ועליהם הוא אומר ״חסד ואמת נפגשו״ (תהלים כה יא).

AG במדבר רבה יא ה (= תנחומא במדבר, נשא פסקה י)

ד״א ״יברכך ה'״ (במדבר ו' כד) – בממון. ״וישמרך״ (שם) – שלא תהא עשוי במדינה פניאם
שלא תבא זימא למדינה, ויאמרו לך: תן זהב. אלא ״יברכך . . . וישמרך״ . . .

AH תוספתא מעשר שני א ו

כיזה צד? היה לו מעות כוזביות ומעות ירושלמיות אין מחללין אותו עליהן, ואם חילל לא קנה
מעשר. אבל מטבע היוצא לשם מלכים ראשונים מחללין אותו עליהן.

AI ירושלמי מעשר שני א א

מטבע שנפסל והמלכות מקבלתו, רבי יוסי בשם רבי יונתן: כאסימון. רבי חייה בשם רבי
יונתן: כמטבע של מלכים ראשונים.

AJ בבלי בבא קמא צז ע״ב

איתיבי רבא לרב נחמן: אין מחללין על מטבעות שאינן יוצאות. כיצד? היו לו מעות כוזביות
ירושלמיות או של מלכים הראשונים אין מחללין.

AK ירושלמי, בבא מציעא ה ו

אבא בר זמינא יהב חד דינר לקפילה ונסב מיניה בשעה זלילה דכל שתא, ולא מודי רב
(צ״ל: לרב).

AL ירושלמי בבא מציעא ד א

א״ר מנא: אית הכא מילי דיודי בה רבי יוסי (צ״ל: דיודי רבי בא לרבי יוסי). אדם שאמר
לחבירו: פרתי אני מבקש למכור. א״ל: בכמה? א״ל: בשמונה דינרין. אזל סמכיה גבי טרפו־
ניטיה (צ״ל: טרפזוניטיה). בצפרא עבר ואשכחיה תמן קאים. א״ל: מה את עביד הכא? א״ל:
אנא בעי מיסב דינרין דאסמיכתני. א״ל: מה את בעי מיזבון לך בהון? א״ל: חמור. א״ל: חמורך
אצלי. משך זה, לא קנה זה. אלא כל אחד ואחד נקנה בגופו.

AM תוספתא פאה ד ח

אין פותחין לעני עובר ממקום למקום מכר בפונדיון מארבע סען בסלע ... והמסבב על
הפתחים, אין נזקקין לו לכל דבר.

AN

ירושלמי פאה ח ה

תני המסבבין על הפתחים אין נזקקין להן
לכל דבר. אמר רבי יונה: ובלחוד דלא
יפחות ליה מן ארגדון (צ״ל: ארגרון)
דיליה.

בבלי בבא בתרא ט ע״א

תנא: אם היה מחזיר על הפתחים אין נזקקין
לו. ההוא ענייא דהוה מחזיר על הפתחים
דאתא לקמיה דרב פפא. לא מזדקק ליה.
א״ל רב סמא בריה דרב ייבא לרב פפא:
אי מר לא מזדקיק ליה, איניש אחרינא לא
מזדקיק ליה, לימות ליה. והא תניא: אם
היה עני המחזיר על הפתחים אין נזקקין
לו? א״ל: אין נזקקין לו למתנה מרובה,
אבל נזקקין לו למתנה מועטת.

AO ויקרא רבה לד ב (מהדורת מרגליות עמ' תשע״ד-ה)

"מלוה ה' חונן דל" (משלי יט יז) ... ר' פינחס בשם ר' ראובן: כל מי שנותן פרוסה לעני הקב״ה
נותן לו פרוטה. וכי פרוטה הוא נותן לו? והלא אינו נותן אלא נפשו. הא כיצד? היתה ככר בעשר
פרוטות, והעני עומד ליקח ואין בידו אלא תשע, ובא אחד ונתן לו פרוטה, ונטל את הכיכר
ואכלה ושבת נפשו עליו. אמר לו הקב״ה: אף כשנפשך מצפצפת לצאת מגופך הרי אני משיבה
לך לתוך גופך ...

AP תנחומא תרומה ז (= תנחומא בובר שמות עמ׳ 92)

״ומלכו רביעא תהוא תקיפה כפרזלא... רגליא מנהון פרזל ומנהון חסף״ (דניאל ב מ־מב), זו
אדום. למה נמשלה בברזל וחרס? אמרו רבותינו: המלכות הרשעה הזו עתידה להשתמש
במטבע של חרס.

AQ ירושלמי מעשר שני א א

יכול אם היה לו מעות בהר המלך ובקצרה, מחללין עליהן? ת״ל, ״וצרת הכסף בידך״ (דברים
יד כה). מהו בידך? ברשותך. ר׳ יונה בעי: נפל כיסו לבור ובו מאה ריבוא, והיה יכול להוציא
חמשין ריבוא להעלותן, אותן ג׳ ריבוא כמו שהן ברשותו? (השווה בבלי בבא קמא צח ע״א).

AR ירושלמי כלאים ט א

רבי הלל בי רבי וולס היה לו בגד בשלושים ריבוא דינר, (ויהביה לרבי – מוסף בגליון כ״י ל׳
וליתא בכ״י ר׳) ומצא בו כלאים ושרפו. רבי מנא היה לו בגד בשלושים ריבוא דינר (ומצא
בו כלאים – כך בכ״י ר׳ וליתא בכ״י ל׳) ויהביה לר׳ חייא בר אדא. א״ל: זבנית למית
(נ״א למיתה). והוה עלוי עד דהוא מברך (והוה קיים עליה עד קרחיה עד דהוה מברך –
כך בכ״י ר׳).

AS תנחומא משפטים טו

ר׳ פנחס הכהן בן חמה בשם ר׳ ראובן... אדם שהיה חייב לחבירו מאתי׳ או ריבוא שלוש
מאות...

AT מדרש תהלים לתהלים לד א (מהדורת בובר עמ׳ 246)

...(דוד) עשה עצמו כשוטה ומשנה את טעמו, שנאמר: ״וישנה את טעמו (בעיניהם ויתהולל
בידם) ויתו על דלתות השער״ (שמואל א כא יד). היה כותב על הדלתות ואמר: אכיש מלך
גת חייב לי מאה ריבוא, ואשתו חמשים ריבוא. ובתו של אכיש היתה היא ואמה שוטות, והיו
צועקות ומשתטות מבפנים ודוד היה צועק ומשתטה בחוץ. אמר להם אכיש לעבדיו: ״חסר
משוגעים אני (כי הבאתם את זה להשתגע עלי)״ (שם טז)! ובאותה שעה שמח דוד שמחה שיצא
לו השטות מתוך השמחה, ועשה את השירה הזאת באלף־א בית־א. אמר להקב״ה: כמה טובה
היא השטות, דכתיב ״אברכה את ה׳ בכל עת תמיד תהילתו בפי״ (תהלים לד ב), בעת
חכמה ובעת שטות. וכן את מוצא בתחילת בראשית ״וירא אלקים את כל אשר עשה והנה
טוב מאוד״ (בראשית א לא).

AU שמות רבה כ ט

ד״א ״ויהי בשלח פרעה״ (שמות יג יז) – משל לאחד שמצא צרור של מרגליות ולא היה יודע
מה בידו. אמר לאחד בדרך: רצונך ליטול הצרור הזה שבידי? אמר לו: למה לי צרור שלך?
אמר לו: טול אותה ואיני עומד בפניך. נטלה הימנו. כיוון שנכנס במדינה ישב וחרז הגדולות
לעצמן והקטנות לעצמן והבינוניות לעצמן. נכנס אותו שמסר ואמר לו: קטנה זו בכמה? אמר לו:
בק׳ ריבוא. והגדולה בכמה? אמר לו: באלף רבוא. והבינוניות בכמה? אמר לו: בח׳ (אולי צ״ל:
בה׳) מאות רבוא. כיוון שראה כך, קרע בגדיו. אמר: כל העושר הזה בידי היה, וחנם הוצאתי
מידי. אוי לי לאותו האיש שכך הוציא הוציא מידי! כך היה פרעה. הצרור של מרגליות, אלו ישראל
שהיו בידו, שנאמר ״צרור המר דודי לי״ (שיר השירים א יג). התחיל צווח: ״קומו צאו״ (שמות
יב לא) התחיל משה מונה אותן שש מאות אלף, חוץ משבטו של לוי שלא מנה אותן. כשראה
פרעה כל האוכלוסין, התחיל צווח: ״ווי! הוי – ״ויהי בשלח פרעה״ (שמות יג יז).

AV ירושלמי מעשר שני א א

מעות של דיסקנים, רבי יעקב בר זבדי בשם רבי אבוה: מחללין כדרך שהן יפות אצל התור־
מוסר. בקש להוציאן, מחללין כדרך שהוא מחלל עליהן.

308

AW ירושלמי קידושין א ג (השווה בבלי בכורות נ ע״א)
...דאמר ר׳ חנינא: כל שקלים שכתוב בתורה סלעים, ובנביאים ליטרא, ובכתובין קינטרין.
א״ר יודה בן פזי: חוץ משקלי עפרון דהוון קינטרין. מאי טעמא? ״בכסף מלא יתננה לי״
(בראשית כג ט) ...וכו׳.

AX אגדת בראשית נו, מהדורת בובר נז, עמ׳ 115
אמר ר׳ ברכיה ...״ואחריו סוסים אדומים שרוקים ולבנים״ (זכריה א ח), אלו המלכים שעמדו
הימנו, ״[אדומים]״, שהן אוהבים את הזהב. ״שרוקים״, שהן מסרקי׳ גפן של ישראל ונוטלין
ממונו. ״לבנים״, כדי להלבין עונותיהם ישראל ...

AY אגדת בראשית נה, מהדורת בובר נו, עמ׳ 111
א״ר ברכיה ...משל לאחד שהיה לו שתי נשים, אחת כתובתה עשר ריבוא, ואחת כתובה בד׳
ריבוא. אמרה לו אותה של ארבע ריבוא: למה אין אתה נוהג בי כבוד כחברתי? אמר לה: את
כתובתך בארבע ריבוא, ושל חברתך בשל עשר. כך אמר איוב: למה אין אתה נוהג בי כבוד
כאברהם? אמר לו: וכי נתנסית כאברהם? ״הנסה דבר אליך תלאה״ (איוב ד ב), ואין ״נסה״
אלא אברהם, שנאמר ״והאלקים נסה את אברהם״ (בראשית כב א). אמר להם: ואני לא הכנסתי
ארבע עטרות, ״תם וישר ירא אלקים וסר מרע״ (איוב א א)? אמר לו: אברהם נתנסה בעשרה
והי׳ לו עשרה עטרות ...

ADDENDA

p. 140: We have tried to demonstrate here that in the '50s or '60s of the third century the authorities demonetized pre-Neronian coinage, and it ceased to be regarded as "coin" in Jewish law. Perhaps we may find a further reference to this fact in a story cited in Y. Kilaim 7.3: A certain person showed his *sela* to R. [E]leazar (died circa 280). He said to him: It is good. And it was cancelled. The case came before R. Simeon b. Lakish (died circa 279), and he fined him (R. Eleazar) on the basis of this text: He who shows a *dinar* to a banker, (and he says it is good), and it is found to be bad, he he has to pay (any damages incurred by reason of his misjudgment) ... A similar version is found in Bavli Bava Kama 100a: Resh Lakish showed a *dinar* to R. Eleazar. He said it was good. "See, I'm relying upon you..." (On the reading R. Ilai, instead of R. Eleazar, see Rabbinovicz, *VL* to Bava Kama, p. 242 note 2; Ratner, Kilaim ad loc., p. 53, Vat. Ms. ad loc., 188b.) It appears then that some time before circa 279 R. Eleazar (or Ilai) was shown a *sela* (Yerushalmi) or *dinar* (Bavli), which he thought was good and in fact it turned out to be cancelled. Could it not be that we are speaking of an old *tetradrachm* (or *dinar*) — hence, the need for it to be checked — which he thought was still legal tender, but in the meanwhile had been demonetized? (See also E. and H. Guggenheimer's remarks in *Leshonenu* 37/2–3, 1973, pp. 105–08.)

pp. 204–05 (*Chapter IV n.* 44–46): On Gallienus' coinage see most recently Kent's article "Gallienae Augustae", in *Num. Chron.*, 1973, pp. 64–68, where he also refers to the relevant literature.

p. 231 (*Chapter XXI n.* 10): See E. and H. Guggenheimer's speculative (!) remarks in *Leshonenu* 37/2–3, 1973, pp. 105–08, where they wish to find a reference to bad coinage in a Rabbinic statement of the third quarter of the III century.

p. 210 (*Chapter V n.* 34): See also J. Preuss, *Biblisch-Talmudische Medizin–Beiträge zur Geschichte der Heilkunde und der Kultur überhaupt,*[2] (Berlin, 1921), p. 192, and compare further Celsus, *De Medicina*, 4.31.7. For a further discussion of the disease "*podgara*" see W.G .Spenser's note in the Loeb edition of Celsus, 1, 1935, pp. 463–65.

p. 231 (*Chapter XII n.* 11): See further H. MacLennan, *Oxyrhynchus — An Economic and Social Study* (Princeton, 1935), pp. 31–32. For an arrangement whereby the creditor would be paid back in "old coin" ("Ptolemaic coin"), or according to an old coin standard, see *P.O.* 2587, from 289, and editor's comments ibid., pp. 145–

46, and Segrè's remarks in *Chronique d'Égypte*, 40, no. 79, Jan. 1965, pp. 204–05. For an example of payment in kind in the early IV century, see *Leviticus Rabba* 24.8, ed. Margulies, pp. 562–63, (R. Avin).

p. 244 (*Chapter XVI n.* 3): See also *P.O.* 2796, (304/5), 1 *art.* wheat: 1,200 dr. See editor's comments, ibid., p. 91.

p. 245 (*Chapter XVI n.* 16): For an Egyptian meat price from the year 338, see *P.O.* 2571, (and see editor's comments p. 123, line 12).

p. 252 (*Chapter XIX n.* 6): See also L. Levine's discussion in his article "Some Observations on the Coins of Caesarea Maritima", *IEJ*, 22, 1972, pp. 136–40.

p. 261 (*Chapter XXII n.* 9): The change between פרוטה and ריפתא may be related to the common interchange between פרוטה and פרוסה. See, e. g., Lieberman, *Tosefta ki-fshutah*, 1, p. 184 line 30, and idem, *Yerushalmi ki-fshuto*, pp. 320–21.

p. 267 (*Chapter XXIV n.* 2): See also *P.O.* 2730, 1 sol. = 730 myr. dr., (undated' from IV century).

INDICES

A. SOURCES*

Rabbinic Sources

---

* For the main part only sources discussed are brought in this index, and not incidental references. Likewise, sources cited in the price-lists on pp. 101–11, 118–20, 122–25 are not brought in this index unless they are discussed elsewhere.

24.3– 198
Sev. Alex. 22.8– 251
Socrates, Hist. Eccles. 2.13– 192
Syro-Roman Statute Book– 194–95
Val. Nov.– 153, 156

Vita S. Pachomius 33–34– 32, 174, 268
Zozimus 1.61.3– 206
11.19– 212

B. ROMAN EMPERORS

Aemilianus (253)– 255
Albinus (193–97)– 139, 224
Anastasius I (491–518)– 216
Anthony (b. 83–d.30B.C.E.)– 139
Antoninus Pius (138–61)– 75, 84, 139, 224, 229, 261
Augustus (27B.C.E.–14C.E.)– 84, 136, 201, 253
Aurelian (270–75)– 45–46, 54–55, 57, 59, 134, 138, 200, 206, 212–13, 231, 251, 270
Balbinus (238)– 39, 43, 55, 138, 201–02
Caligula (37–41)– 84, 136
Caracalla (198–217)– 38, 40, 71, 73, 77, 79, 84, 134, 139, 199–203, 223, 225, 251, 255
Carinus (283–85)– 138, 255
Carus (282–83)– 138
Claudius I (41–54)– 84, 136, 253
Claudius II (268–70)– 39, 45, 134, 138, 205, 251
Commodus (176–92)– 84, 139, 201, 222
Constantine I (306–37)– 160, 180, 237, 239–40
Constantius I (305–06)– 260
Diadumenian (218)– 143
Didius (Julianus) (193)– 84, 139, 224
Domitian (81–96)– 84, 135, 139, 253
Diocletian (284–305)– 55–56, 59–61, 63–64, 85, 93–95, 112–17, pass.
Elagabalus (218–22)– 39, 55, 72, 84, 134, 139, 142–44, 201–02, 223, 255
Florianus (276)– 138
Galba (68–69)– 84, 139

Galerius (Maximianus) (305–11)– 256
Gallienus (253–68)– 39, 44, 47, 135, 138, 140, 143–44, 199–200, 216, 232, 251, 255
Gordianus I & II (238)– 39, 138, 202
Gordianus III (238–44)– 39, 42–43, 55, 138, 143, 199, 202–03, 226, 255
Hadrian (117–38)– 84, 86, 133, 139, 227–30, 232, 253
Julian (361–63)– 32, 159, 162, 192–93, 242, 248, 250, 262–63
Licinius (307–24)– 262, 269
Macrinus (217–18)– 72, 84, 139, 143, 200–02, 223, 255
Marcus (Aurelius) (161–80)– 84, 139, 239
Maximinus (235–38)– 39, 43, 55, 139, 143, 202, 255
Nero (54–68)– 84, 136, 139, 253
Nerva (96–98)– 84, 135, 139, 253
Otho (69)– 84, 139
Pertinax (193)– 84, 139, 224
Pescinius Niger (193)– 223–24
Philip I (244–49)– 39, 43, 55, 138, 143, 202, 255
Postumus (258–67)– 138
Probus (276–82)– 138, 200, 255
Pupienus (238)– 39, 42–43, 55, 201–02
Septimius Severus (193–211)– 76, 84, 139, 199–200, 203, 223–24, 238, 255
Severans (general)– 73
(Severus) Alexander (222–35)– 39, 55, 84, 139, 143–44, 202–03, 223–24, 255
Tacitus (275–76)– 134, 138
Tetricus (267–74)– 138

319

C. OTHER AUTHORITIES ETC.

D. NUMISMATIC TERMS

* For the dating (July to December 253), see H.R. Baldus, *Uranius Antoninus*:
Münzpragüng und Geschichte (Bonn, 1971), and M. Jessop Price's review in *Num.*
Chron., 1973, p. 231.

E. MINT-MARKS, LEGENDS, ETC.

F. WEIGHTS AND MEASURES

G. INDEX OF AUTHORS

H. GENERAL INDEX

SUPPLEMENT TO
SECOND EDITION

INTRODUCTION

Chapter Four of the Palestinian Talmudic Tractate Bava Mezia (called in the Yerushalmi *Ha-Kesef*) contains much material directly pertinent to Talmudic monetary and economic theory. Here I have presented a translation and commentary of this chapter, hoping it will give the reader some idea of the nature of the material we deal with when analysing Rabbinic legal texts to extract from them historical data.

The text on which the translation is based is the *editio princeps* (Venice, 1523), which is based on an edited and emended version derived from Ms. Leiden, Codex Scaliger 3. More recently, an additional text (of Tractate Nezikin) was discovered by the late Prof. E.S. Rosenthal, called Ms. Escorial G1-3, and published by him, with a commentary by the late Prof. Saul Lieberman (Jerusalem, 1983). In all cases where I refer to Lieberman, in an unqualified fashion, I am referring to his commentary to Ms. Escorial. I have also made use of S. Lieberman(n)'s *The Talmud of Caesarea (Talmudah shel Kisrin)*: Yerushalmi Tractate Nezikin (Supplement to *Tarbiz* II, 4) (Jerusalem, 1931), and to his final publication, *Tosefta ki-fshutah,* vol. 9 (New York, 1988), which contains his extended commentary to Tosefta Bava Mezia.

For the main part, I have not discussed in detail the Mishnayot, numerous commentaries for which exist in a number of languages. I have made constant reference to the Bavli, and, where Bavli-unqualified is cited, it refers to Bavli Bava Mezia, Chapter IV (*Ha-Zahav*).

TRANSLATION

Mishna 1   Silver acquires gold but gold does not acquire silver; copper acquires silver, but silver does not acquire copper. Bad money acquires good, but good does not acquire bad. An *asemon* (blank, unminted piece of metal, like a token) acquires coin, but coin does not acquire *asemon*. Chattels acquire coin; but coin does not acquire chattels. This is the rule: All chattels acquire each other.

Gemara 1   This is the principle of the matter: all that which is lower [in value] than its counterpart acquires its counterpart.

Said R. Hiyya b. Ashi: "Who taught our Mishna? R. Simeon the son of Rabbi [Judah ha-Nasi]." His father said to him (to R. Simeon): "Retract and teach thus: 'Gold acquires silver'." He replied to him: "I shall not retract; for you yourself, while you were [young and] strong taught me: 'Silver acquires gold'."

The statement of Rabbi posits that gold is like "fruit". Our Mishna posits that silver is like "fruit". The *beraitha* of R. Hiyya posits that gold is like fruit. His statement posits that silver is like fruit. The daughter of R. Hiyya Rabbah lent Rav [gold] *denarii*. She came and asked her father [how should Rav repay her]. He answered her: "Go, receive from him good and full-weight [gold] *denarii*." From [the story of] R. Hiyya Rabbah's daughter we may learn [that gold is "coin"].

R. Idi said: "Also Aba, the father of Samuel, asked of Rabbi: 'May one borrow [gold] *denarii* for [gold] *denarii*?' He replied: 'One may borrow [Gold] *denarii* for [Gold] *denarii*'."

R. Jacob b. Aha said: "Both R. Johanan and R. Simeon b. Lakish also state [that] one may borrow [gold] *denarii* for [gold] *denarii*. [To loan out] a *karat* for a *karat* is permitted, a *leukon* for a *leukon* is forbidden."

We have learned there (Mishna Kiddushin 1.6): Everything which is assessed at full value in exchange for another thing, as soon as one party has acquired the one thing, the other party becomes answerable for what is given in exchange.

Said R. Johanan: "They did not teach [in the Mishna] but [the case of]

336

an ox [being exchanged] for a cow, or a donkey for an ox." Surely then [the exchange of] one pile for another pile would not constitute an acquisition?

R. Jeremiah in the name of Rav: "Even a pile for a pile is an acquisition."

R. Ba b. Bina in the name of Rav: "He who exchanges one money-bag (*involucrum*) for another money-bag acquired [the other]."

R. Zeura-<Zera> [Ba] [in the name of] Rav Judah in the name of Samuel: "One man had a cow and the other a donkey, and they exchanged the one for the other. The owner of the donkey 'drew' (i.e. took possession of) the cow, and [then] the owner of the cow was about to 'draw' the donkey when he found it was broken [in limb]. — It is incumbent upon the owner of the donkey to bring evidence that the donkey was whole at the hour when he 'drew'." "He who is not of this opinion", [says R. <Zera> [Ba], "understands nothing in matters of damages (or in the tractate 'Nezikin')."

Said R. Zera: "I am not of this opinion, and do I understand nothing in matters of damages? [Surely] we have learned there (Mishna Ketubot 7.8): If defects were found in her while she was yet in her father's house, the father must bring proof that these defects arose in her after she was betrothed, [and that] his field was laid waste."

R. Huna, R. Pinhas [and] R. Hezekiah went to R. Josa at Gadfa (?). They said before him that, [and] he said to them: "Say the last part [of the Mishna]: If she entered into the control of the husband, the husband must bring proof. — And is it not the father who has to bring proof?.... And [so just as] you say the husband must bring proof, so also here it is the owner [of the cow] who must bring proof"...

<R. Ba [in the name of] Rav Judah in the name of Samuel:> "The one has a cow and the other a donkey, and they exchanged [them] one to the other. If the owner of the <donkey> [cow] 'drew' the <cow> [donkey], he did not acquire it. The donkey — can it cause acquisition"? R. Ba said: "He acquired"; R. Josa said: "He did not acquire."

Said R. Mana: "There is here a case in which <R. Josa> [R. Ba] would agree [with R. Josa. For example:] A man who said to his friend: 'I wish to sell my cow'. He said to him: 'For how much?' 'For five [gold] *denarii*', he replied. He (the vendor) went and pressured him and he (the purchaser) deposited [the money] with a banker. In the morning he was passing by, when he found him (the vendor) standing there (at the banker's). He said to him: 'What are you doing here?' 'I wish to bring these *denarii* you placed here for me', he replied. 'What do you want to buy with them?' he asked. 'A donkey', he replied. 'Your donkey is with me'. (I.e. the donkey at my house

= my donkey, is as though it were yours. That is to say: Buy my donkey.) If the one 'drew' [the cow], the other did not acquire [the donkey], [and] if the one 'drew' [the donkey], the other did not acquire [the cow]. Rather each one must be acquired [by an act of acquisition] individually."

Mishna 2 How so? He drew produce from him, but did not give him money; one cannot go back on it. He gave him money, but did not draw produce from him; one can go back on it. But they said: He who punished the men of the generation of the flood and of the generation of the dispersion, He will surely exact punishment from him who does not stand by his word. R. Simeon said: Whoever holds the money, he has the upper hand.

Gemara 2 R. Aha said: "It is written [in the Scriptures] (Gen. 6.13): ['The end of all flesh is come before Me;] for the earth is filled with violence through them'. What was their 'violence'? A man would go in the street carrying a basket of lupines, and they would wilfully take [from him] less than a *peruta*-worth, an amount that cannot be reclaimed before the judges (i.e. in Court)."

Said R. Hiyya b. Ba[1]: "Great" (see Gen. 6.5), "Great" (see Gen. 18.20). The behaviour of these [people of the Flood-generation] was like the behaviour of these [people of Sodom and Gomorrah]."

Said R. Hanina: "The law is according to R. Simeon. But we do not say so in all cases."

Rav Jeremiah in the name of Rav: "A case came up and Rav ruled like R. Simeon."

R. Hiyya b. Josef gave a [gold] *denarius* for salt. The other (i.e. the seller) changed his mind. He (R. Hiyya b. Josef) said: "Does he not know that they have already wielded the sickle across that man's legs? He that exacted punishment from the generation of the Flood will exact punishment from him that does not abide by his spoken word."

A certain person gave [gold] *denarii* for silk. He (i.e. the vendor) changed his mind. The case came before R. Hiyya b. Josef and R. Johanan. R. Hiyya b. Josef said: "He should either give him [silk] against the value of the pledge,[2] or hand him over for [the procedure of pronouncing

---

1 XII in the printed editions = בא in Ms. Escorial = אבא, Aba.
2 Ms. Escorial has here not כדי עירבונו as Ms. Leiden and the printed edd., but כל ערבונו, the whole pledge, which more closely parallels the following statement of R. Yohanan.

against him the] 'He who exacted...' [formula]." R. Johanan said: "He should either give him his complete purchase, or hand him over for [the procedure of pronouncing against him] the 'He who exacted...' [formula]."

R. La (= Ila, Ilai) said: "It was a pledge." R. Zera said: "He gave him a part payment."

R. Hiyya bar Josef would agree with R. Johanan in [the case of] a purchase which is not bought by halves, such as a cow or a cloak.

R. Jacob b. Idi, R. Abahu in the name of R. Johanan: "A ring is not [regarded] as a pledge."

Anyone who has [only] verbally negotiated [a sale and then changed his mind and cancelled the sale], one does not hand him over for [the procedure of pronouncing against him] the "He who has exacted" [formula].

R. Jacob b. Zavdi, R. Abahu in the name of R. Johanan: "He said he would give a present to his friend, and [then] wished to change his mind, he may do so"... He said: "At the time he said [he would give it], he has to say so with whole-hearted intentions. After that, if he changed his mind, he may <not>[3] do so."

This you [can] say [is true] of a poor man; but with a rich man, [his word] becomes a vow.

Rav ordered his servant: "Whenever I tell you: 'Give a present to someone', if he is a poor man, give him [it] immediately, but if he is a rich man, I will consider [the matter] a second time."

R. Johanan gave his relatives [gold] *denarii* for oil. The oil went up in price. He came and inquired of R. Jannai [what should be done]. He replied to him: "According to Biblical law, [payment of] money makes acquisition. And why [did the Sages] say it does not make acquisition? Lest he (the vendor) say to him (the purchaser): 'Your wheat (i.e. which you bought from me) was burned up in [my] attic'."

R. Samuel b. Sosartai [said] in the name of R. Abahu: "If he said to him: 'Your wheat was burned up in [my] attic', he is believed."

[Against this] R. Isaac raised [the following] objection: "What do we hold? If his money has bought him [the wheat], it is his own [wheat] that has been burned up; and if his money has not bought [it] for him, it is the other's (i.e. vendor's) which has been burned up?"

R. Simeon [said] in the name of R. Joshua b. Levi: "A man who gave his

---

3 Deleted by commentators, and absent in Ms. Escorial. See commentary below.

friend ten [gold] *denarii*. He said to him: 'I have with you (= you owe me) one hundred <*denarii*> [bottles of wine][4] out of this house,' — [that is] 'Out of this vineyard'. — [that is] forbidden. What is [the difference] between a vineyard and a house. A house is unlikely to fall; a vineyard is likely to <fall> [be burned down]."[5]

Said R. Jose: "You may learn from it [the following]: A man who gave his friend ten [gold] *denarii*, saying to him: 'On one condition that you supply me with one hundred bottles [of wine]'. As soon as he starts using them (i.e. the *denarii*), he is obliged to supply him his purchase."

R. Simeon b. Lakish said: "['If thou sell aught unto thy neighbour,] or buy from thy neighbour's hand...' (Lev. 25.14) — from the hand of 'your neighbour' you require 'drawing', but you do not require 'drawing out of the hand of a non-Jew'." According to the view of Resh Lakish, for what do you [not][6] hand him over for the "He who exacted" [procedure]?

Said R. Jose b. R. Bun: "It follows that Tanna who teaches: 'He who negotiated [only] verbally [and changed his mind], one does not hand him over for the 'He who exacted' [procedure]."

Mishna 3 *Ona'a* is four silver [pieces] in twenty-four silver [pieces], a *sela*, the sixth of a purchase. How long is one allowed to return it? As long as it takes to show to a merchant or to one's relative. R. Tarphon proposed in Lydda that *ona'a* be eight silver [pieces] in twenty-four silver [pieces], a *sela*, the third of a purchase. And the merchants were pleased. He said to them: The whole day be allowed for retracting. They said to him: Let R. Tarphon leave us where we were. And they went back to the words of the Sages.

Be he a buyer or a seller, they have *ona'a*. Just as a private individual has *ona'a*, so has the merchant *ona'a*. And R. Judah said: The merchant has no *ona'a*. He who suffered, he has the upper hand. If he wishes, he says: Give me my money, or: Give me that by which you have wronged me.

Gemara 3 Rav said: "[The four pieces of silver mentioned in the Mishna] is the [lowest] limit [of defrauding]." R. Johanan said: "It is not a limit."

Rav said: "Anyone who negotiates [a price] on condition that he is not

---

4 The mistaken reading was corrected by the commentators. This correct reading is found in Ms. Escorial.

5 The corrected reading agrees with that of Ms. Escorial.

6 So in Ms. Escorial, p. 57, line 50.

subject to [the rules of] defrauding, he is [nonetheless] subject to the rules of defrauding."

R. Levi taught: Defrauding must be worth [not less than] a *peruta*, and <defrauding> [an admission of indebtedness][7] must be worth [not less than] a *peruta*.

But what happens [in the case of] defrauding itself? We have learned: "The purchase is acquired [and] the [money] defrauded is returned to him"; these are the words of R. Judah ha-Nasi. R. <Johanan> [Nathan][8] said: "His purchase is cancelled."

Kahana asked Rav: "When the vendor is defrauded, he is defrauded of a fifth. When the purchaser is defrauded, he is defrauded of a sixth!" He said to him: "The real price of the sale and the defrauding,[9] (i.e. the losses of either the vendor or the purchaser) join together [in being calculated] to a sixth."

He sold him [something] worth five or six, [why] can [not the seller] tell him: "You have been cheated of one *denarius*. Take back your *denarius*."? Said R. Zera (Zeura): "He (the buyer) may say to him: "It is not befitting my honour that people say of [me], 'That fellow made a laughing-stock of you'." And others wish to explain: "He can say, 'It is not befitting my honour to wear [a garment] worth [only] five *denarii*'. R. Johanan, R. Eleazar and R. Hoshaya said: 'What is the reason for that <Tannaim> [Tanna]?' He can say: 'I knew that that was not worth but five *denarii*. [However,] since he (= you) was pressed[10] [for money], I gave [him] (= you) six *denarii*. Take back yours, and give me back mine'."

He was selling him [something] worth five for six, [but], before they completed negotiating, it went up to seven — R. Jacob b. Idi, R. Abahu in the name of R. Johanan: "Just as it [may] be cancelled by him (i.e. the buyer), so it [may] be cancelled by him (i.e. the seller)."

We learned there (in a *beraitha*): Four rules apply to them that sell: A man sold wheat to another as good wheat, and it was found to be bad, the purchaser can retract. If he sold it as bad wheat, and it was found to be good, the vendor can retract. Surely then, the purchaser cannot retract.[11] Said R. Jose b. R. Bun: "It is in accordance with that [*beraitha*] which

---

7 This is the reading in Ms. Escorial (p. 57, line 54).
8 J.N. Epstein, *Mavo le-Nusah ha-Mishna* (Jerusalem, 1948), p. 300, note 5, emends: יונתן 'ר, R. Jonathan = Nathan. See also Lieberman, *Tosefta ki-fshutah* 9 (New York, 1988), p. 179, note 21.
9 So according to Ms. Escorial, p. 57, line 57.
10 Ms. Escorial reads: Since you were needy, I gave etc.: ... יהבת צריך דהוית את.
11 Absent in printed editions, but found in Ms. Escorial, p. 57, line 64, and in early authorities (*Rishonim*). See Lieberman, p. 151 to line 64.

teaches: He who negotiates [merely] verbally, one does not subject him to the 'He that exacted' [procedure, should he retract]."

Mishna 4   By how much is a *sela* to be deficient, yet there shall be no *ona'a* on it? R. Meir said: Four *issars,* an *issar* to a *dinar.* And R. Judah said: Four *pundions,* a *pundion* to a *dinar.* And R. Simeon said: eight *pundions,* two *pundions* to a *dinar.*

Gemara 4   We have learned [in a *beraitha*]: By how much is a *sela* to be deficient, and yet there shall be no *ona'a* in it? R. Meir says: Four *issars,* an *issar* to a *dinar.* R. Judah says: Four *pundions,* a *pundion* to a *dinar.* R. Simeon says: Eight *pundions,* two *pundions* to a *dinar.* From here [onwards (i.e. more than this)] he may use it at [its] value. A *sela* up to a *shekel*; a *dinar* up to a quarter [*shekel*]. Less than this, even if it is like an *issar,* he must not use it. If it was valued at a *sela* as *asemon* (uncoined metal) and at a *shekel* as a coin, [or] at a *shekel* as *asemon* (uncoined metal), and a *sela* as a coin, it is not [valued] other than at its coin marking alone. He must not give it to a tax-officer or to a murderer, because they cheat others with it. But he may pierce it and hang it round his son's neck.

When do we say so? With regard to [silver] *denarii* and *sela'im*; but a gold *denarius* and coins of <silver> [bronze][12] are used at their value. Just as one may use them for profane matters, so also one may use them for the Second Tithe, as long as one does not calculate to use them [for that].

Mishna 5   How long is one allowed to return it? In towns, as long as it takes to show to a money-changer; in villages, until the Sabbath eve. If he recognises it, even after twelve months, he accepts it from him, and he has against him only resentment. And he may give it for Second Tithe and have no scruple — for it is only ill-will.

Four pieces of silver count as defrauding; two pieces of silver suffice in a claim [for repayment]. Five [cases of] *perutot* are [prescribed]: an admission of indebtedness [must be worth no less than] a *peruta,* and a woman may be betrothed with a *peruta*'s worth, and he who derives a *peruta*'s worth of benefit from *Hekdesh* (Temple property) is subject to the law of sacrilege, and he who finds something worth a *peruta* must announce [the find], and he who robs from his fellow a *peruta*'s worth and swears [falsely that he will make restitution] must bring it to him even as far as Media.

---

12 Ms. Escorial here reads: But coins of silver and *denarii* of gold are used at their face value.

There are five [cases where added] fifths [is prescribed]: He who eats heave-offering (*Teruma*), heave-offering of Tithe (*Terumat Ma'aser*), heave-offering of *Demai*, dough-offering (*Halla*), or first-fruits (*Bikkurim*), must add a fifth [when he makes restitution]. He who redeems [the fruit] of a fourth-year planting (*Neta Revai*), or his Second Tithe (*Ma'aser Sheni*) adds a fifth. He that redeems that which he has dedicated (to the Temple) adds a fifth. He who derives a *peruta*'s worth of benefit from Temple property (*hekdesh*) adds a fifth. If a man robs his fellow a *peruta*'s worth and swears [falsely] to him, he must add a fifth.

Gemara 5 Hezekiah said: "[If he wishes] to change it <in Jerusalem> [outside Jerusalem] he changes it at a full rate. If he wishes to redeem it <outside Jerusalem> [in Jerusalem] he may redeem it at a bad rate." "But have we not learned in a Mishna (Ma'aser Sheni 2.6): 'He should then choose out the finer of them and exchange it [again] for them'? Let him choose out the less fine one and make it [Second Tithe] as though it were the finer!"[13] We may answer[14]: "It is different here, for already it was certain that there was Second Tithe in it."

One may give it as Second Tithe money without scruple, for he is but an evil-souled person [that would refuse it].

R. Jacob b. Zavdi, R. Johanan[15] in the name of R. Simon: "And [in the case of] anything of Second Tithe that is not worth a *peruta*, one does not add a fifth." R. Johanan in the name of R. Jannai[16]: "[With regard] anything of Second Tithe, [whose worth is such] that an added fifth is not worth a *peruta*, one does not add a fifth." There are some teachers who support this [one view], and there are some teachers who support this [other view].

As we have learned in a *beraitha*: "from his tithe" (Lev. 27.31) — [This is] to exclude less than a *peruta*'s worth. That is as you said: only if the Second Tithe itself is worth a *peruta*. Another *beraitha* teaches: "from his tithe a fifth" (Lev. ibid.), — [This is] to exclude less than a *peruta*'s worth. That is as you said: only if a fifth of its value is worth a *peruta*.

Said R. Ba b. Memel[17]: "Our Mishna is neither in accordance with the

---

13 So in Ms. Escorial, parallel in Y. Ma'aser Sheni 2.7, 53c, and Ramban to Bava Mezia 52b: כיפה.
14 אימר as in Ms. Escorial, as opposed to אמר, he answered in the standard editions.
15 Jonathan in Ms. Escorial.
16 Sinai in Ms. Escorial and Y. Ma'aser Sheni, ibid. Sinai is the more correct reading. See Lieberman, p. 152, line 79.
17 In the printed editions Ravin b. Memel, which is incorrect. Ms. Escorial preserves the correct reading R. Ba (= Aba) b. Memel, as does the parallel in Y. Ma'aser Sheni. In Ms. Leiden R. Aba b. Memel's statement is missing, and has been supplied in the margin,

one, nor with the other. For we learn [in it] 'five *perutot*', and we do not learn [among them] 'only if it (i.e. the Second Tithe) is worth a *peruta*'. And we learn 'five fifths'[18] and we do not learn [among them] 'only if a fifth of its value is worth a *peruta*'."

Mishna 6 These are the things to which the law of defrauding does not apply: slaves, bills of indebtedness, immovable properties, that which is Temple property; they have no twofold restitution, nor fourfold or fivefold restitution. An unpaid guardian need not take an oath, and a paid guardian need not make restitution. R. Simeon says: Hallowed things (*Kodeshim*) which must be replaced (if damaged or lost) are subject to the law of defrauding, but those things which do not need to be replaced are not subject to the law of defrauding.

R. Judah says: The law against defrauding does not apply to [the sale of] a Torah scroll, or cattle, or pearls. But they answered him: They only said these [are not subject to the law of defrauding] (intending to include no more in their list).

Gemara 6 We have learned in a *beraitha*: R. Judah says: "Also to Torah scroll, cattle or a precious stone the law of defrauding does not apply. A Torah scroll has no maximum price; cattle and precious stones, people wish to find them a double." They said to him: "Surely [for] everything a person wants [to find] a double?"

We have learned in a *beraitha*: R. Judah b. Bathyra says: "A horse, sword and a shield, in [times of] war the law of defrauding does not apply to them."

Mishna 7 Just as the law of defrauding applies to buying and selling, so it applies to spoken words. A man should not say: "How much is this thing?" when he does not want to buy [it]. If a man was a repentant sinner, one should not say to him: "Remember your former deeds." If a man was descended from proselytes, one should not say to him: Remember what were the deeds of your forefathers." For it is written, "And a stranger thou shalt not wrong, nor shalt thou oppress him for ye were strangers in the Land of Egypt" (Exod. 22.21).

One sort of produce must not be mixed up with another sort of produce,

perhaps not in the right place. For in Ms. Escorial this section appears straight after the statement of R. Johanan in the name of R. Jannai, ending "....one does not add a fifth."

18 Some commentators have suggested emending here to "five *perutot*". However, this is not borne out by Ms. Escorial, which reads "five fifths".

even fresh [produce] with fresh [produce], and, needless to say, fresh with old. However, verily, with regards wine, they permitted strong to be mixed with weak, since this improves it. One may not mix wine lees with wine, but he (the vendor) may give him (the purchaser) his lees (i.e. the lees that come from the same wine he bought). He who mixed water with his wine may not sell it in a shop, unless he has informed (the purchaser), and not to a merchant, even if he does inform him, since he would [only buy it to] deceive with it. A place where they are accustomed to put water in wine, they may do so.[19]

A merchant may take from five threshing-floors and place [it] into a single store-chamber; or from five wine-presses and put [the wine] into a single storage-jar, provided he does not intend to mix [for purposes of fraud]. R. Judah says: A shop-keeper may not distribute parched corn or nuts to children, because [in this way] he accustoms them to come [only] to him. But the Sages permit [it]. And he may not lower the price. And the Sages say: [If he does] let him be remembered with gratitude. He may not sift crushed beans, according to the view of Aba Saul. But the Sages permit [it]. But they agree that he should not sift them at the entry of the store-chamber, since [in this way] he is merely deceiving the eye. And one does not bedizen [for purposes of sale] neither people nor animals nor utensils.

Gemara 7   R. Avdima Malha used to soak his nets (?). R. Jacob b. Aha said to him: "Surely we have learned in our Mishna: One should not bedizen?" His (R. Jacob b. Aha's) words teach us[20] that bedizening applies to food.

R. Zera[21] was engaged with this flax. He came to R. Abahu and asked him: "May I beautify the work (or merchandise)?" He answered him: "Go do as [best] you know how."

R. Abahu was engaged with these veils. He came and asked R. Josa b. Hanina: "What may we do with these veils?" He answered him: "Go do as [best] you know how."

Rabbah used to paint [and] shine [his merchandise].

R. Jacob Amsoniah[22] taught: "What does it mean. 'One may not bedizen [a person]'?" He should not say to him: "Go make yourself up."

---

19 At this point Ms. Escorial (p. 58, lines 93-97), includes *beraithot* from Tosefta Bava Mezia 3.27-28, ed. Lieberman, p.80. See *Tosefta ki-fshutah 9 (New York, 1988), p. 188.*

20 Printed editions have: מילתיה אמרה, while Ms. Escorial has: ואהין הוא = ואהינו, "and this is [what we have learned in the Mishna]," that one must not bedizen, including food too.

21 Zeura in Ms. Escorial.

22 Omsaiah in Ms. Escorial.

COMMENTARY

Mishna 1 The Mishna in the Yerushalmi is identical to that in the Bavli in all but the first line. For while the Bavli reads: Gold acquires silver, but silver does not acquire gold, the Yerushalmi records exactly the opposite. Both the Bavli and the Yerushalmi Talmudim know of *both* versions of the Mishna, explaining that the "gold" version (Bavli—Mishna) is that of Rabbi (= R. Judah ha-Nasi), while the "silver" one (Yerushalmi version) is that of R. Simeon, his son. Rabbi himself, the Talmud relates, in his youth, held the opinion expressed in R. Simeon's Mishna, i.e. that silver acquires gold, etc. But in his later years, he changed his mind and taught that gold acquires silver. R. Simeon, his son, however, continued to teach the other Mishna version. We have a parallel example of this phenomenon in Avoda Zara 4.4; see Bavli 52b, and Yerushalmi 4.4, ibid. It should, however, be noted that the Escorial Ms. of Yerushalmi Nezikim here preserves the Babylonian reading ("Gold acquires...") in the Mishna. However, Lieberman rightly corrects this reading in accordance with the Yerushalmi *sugya* below (see his commentary, p. 145, and his comments in *Tosefta ki-fshutah 9* [New York, 1988], p. 176).

Gemara 1 The *sugya* in the Gemara here is fairly similar to that of the Bavli (44a-b), except that, as is usually the case, the Bavli's *sugya* is far more fully developed, entering into greater detail of argumentation, exploring more avenues of counter-argumentation, and pursuing each issue to its logical conclusion. The Yerushalmi, though including much the same material as is found in the Palestinian stratum of the Bavli *sugya*, is more terse and abbreviated. We are left with more working out to do for ourselves, and reference to the Bavli is of considerable aid to understanding the Yerushalmi *sugya*.

(See above Chapter XI, pp. 69 *et seq.* for a full discussion of this passage.)

The *sugya* opens with a general statement that everything — meaning here, every kind of coin — which is of lower value than its counterpart is considered less current (*harif*, in the Bavli), and hence less "coin"-like and

346

more "fruit" — (*pere-*) like. (*Pere* may also be translated as "commodity" or "produce" .) Now the *meshikha* — drawing or acquisition — of coin (*kesef* or *matbe'a*) does not effect a transfer of property in the object purchased (i.e. the *pere* — fruit). The *meshikha* of the *pere* on the part of the purchaser, on the other hand, does make the "coin" pass over into the property of the vendor, even without his actually handling it. Thus, that which is halachically defined as *pere* — and this includes less current coins when placed alongside more current coins — may effect a transfer of property upon a *matbe'a*. This principle, that things of lesser value may acquire things of greater value, can only be stated in connection with our Yerushalmi Mishna version. For it is this version which states that silver acquires gold, and copper silver, i.e. the metal of lower value acquires that of higher value. The Yerushalmi's opening principle is then an abstract formulation based on our Mishna version.

However, it would not be correct according to the other version of the Mishna, which the Yerushalmi (and Bavli 44a) attributes to Rabbi in his later years. For, according to that version, gold — the more valuable metal — acquires silver, but also copper — the *less* valuable metal — acquires silver. Rabbi wished that R. Simeon, his son, would change his mind, and teach that "Gold acquires silver", but he adamantly refused to concur.

Thus we find ourselves with a conflict of opinion (*mahloket*) between Rabbi and R. Simeon, his son, as to whether gold is "coin" (R. Simeon's view) or "produce" — *pere* — (Rabbi's view). Significantly, it is a Babylonian, R. Hiyya (b. Ashi), who introduces the Babylonian element, a text in which Rabbi attempts unsuccessfully to sway his son over to his own view. And, indeed, the Yerushalmi states (in a line omitted by reason of homeoioteleuton from the printed editions but found in the Escorial Ms.) that R. Hiyya himself disagrees with his own *beraitha* cited above, "Gold acquires silver", and concurs with Rabbi's early view that silver is like fruit (see Lieberman's commentary, p. 145.)

The Gemara now tries to demonstrate that R. Hiyya Rabba (or Rubbah in the printed editions), too, was of the opinion that gold is "coin", and not "produce". For, we are told, it once happened that his daughter lent Rav gold *denarii*, and, as we know from the parallel version in the Bavli 44b, they went up in value. She was unsure whether she was permitted to be repaid in full-weight coins, i.e. the same number of coins of the same weight as she had lent out. For, in doing so, surely she would be receiving back more than she gave out, as the price of the coins had risen. In other words she would be making a profit out of her loan, and this would constitute an infringement of the law of usury (*ribit*), which rules that it is forbidden to make profit on a loan made out to a fellow Jew. Nevertheless, her father ruled that she might receive back full-weight coins, and this would not constitute usury, since they are "coin". The reasoning is as follows: "Coin" is completely stable; it does not change value; it constitutes a fixed standard. "Produce", on the other hand, rises and falls in value in relationship to the "coin". Or, in other words, when the purchasing power of a coin changes, it is not that the value of the coin alters but that the price of the "produce" has risen or fallen relative to it. For this reason, one may not lend out a measure of produce on the understanding that one get back that same measure of the same produce (se'ah be-se'ah, Bavli 44b), since any change in the price of the produce may lead to the making of a profit on the part of the lender, i.e. to usury. But one may lend out a sum of money on the understanding that one get back that self-same sum, since its price is stable and unchanging. From the above episode we learn that R. Hiyya was of the opinion — as was R. Simeon — that gold is "coin", stable and unchanging in value. Hence, his daughter could be repaid in full-weight coin without infringing the laws of ribit. (See further Leiberman's comments, pp. 145-146.)

Some commentators read this last line as a question: Can we really learn from the above tale of R. Hiyya's daughter [that he was of the opinion that gold is "coin"]? Surely he might have made his decision on the basis of other, quite different and unstated, considerations. This latter interpretation is not altogether convincing, and was probably influenced by the knowledge of the Bavli sugya, which indeed offers plausible alternative explanations for R. Hiyya's ruling (44b).

The Gemara next tells us that Samuel's father asked Rabbi whether it be permitted to borrow [gold] denarii for [gold] denarii. (Unspecified denarii during the Tannaitic period are usually silver ones. But, during the Amoraic period, unspecified denarii are almost always gold ones. See above, p. 87.) Rabbi did not permit it. This means that Rabbi, too, regarded gold denarii as "coin". One might suggest that this was his view during his youth. However, this is very unlikely in view of chronological considerations. Samuel's father must have been considerably younger than Rabbi, and could hardly have spoken to him in his youth. It is more plausible that in his latter years Rabbi was repersuaded to share the opinion of his son, R. Simeon; that is to say, to revert to the position of his own youth. Thus understood, the point of this whole passage is to teach us that even Rabbi in the end ruled according to our Mishna version.

Finally, R. Jacob b. Aha relates that both R. Johanan and R. Simeon b. Lakish (Resh Lakish in the printed versions), those two giants of third-century C.E. Palestinian learning, stated that one may lend out gold *denarii* for gold *denarii*, i.e. that they are "coin".

Now all these above statements — of R. Hiyya, Rabbi, R. Johanan and Resh Lakish —, which posit that gold is "coin", are consistent with the Yerushalmi's Mishna version. However, we have already pointed out that the Bavli's version of our Mishna reads "Gold acquires silver", making gold "produce" and not "coin". Consequently, the Bavli *sugya*, which follows its Mishna version, must be of the opinion that one may *not* lend out gold *denarii* for gold *denarii*. This indeed is what we find there. For a statement of R. Johanan, ruling that "one may not lend out *denarii* for *denarii*" is explicitly explained as referring to *gold denarii* (45a). Now, it may well be that the original statement of R. Johanan referred to silver *denarii*. Silver, being regarded by him as "produce", could not thus be loaned out. The Bavli, however, consistent with its version of the Mishna, interpreted this statement as referring to gold coins, thus harmonising all the views, and obviating possible objections.

(For a discussion of the next section; see above, pp. 92-94.)

The next part of R. Jacob b. Aha's statement is his own addition, and not a continuation of the words of R. Johanan and Resh Lakish. One may even note the change in style, for while their words were in Hebrew מותר ללוות — his continuation is in Aramaic — קרט בקרט שרי. He is here referring to new monetary denominations which did not as yet exist in the time of R. Johanan and Resh Lakish (died *c.* 279). The *karat* was a silver coin, introduced by Diocletian, *c.* 300, which was linked in its value to the gold *denarius* (called an *aureus*). Since its value was linked to a halachically stable coin — i.e. fixed as a constant and unchangeable fraction of a larger denomination — its value was as stable as the gold to which it was linked, and not subject to price fluctuations. Therefore, ruled R. Jacob b. Aha, in the same way as we know one may lend out a gold *denarius* for a gold *denarius*, so also one must be permitted to lend out a *karat* for a *karat*. The *leukon*, however, also a Diocletianic coin, was of quite a different nature. It was basically a bronze coin, very lightly silvered over. *Leukon* is the Greek for white, describing the pale appearance of the coin. It is generally called a *follis*. This coin was subject to constant depreciation in value (see above, p. 94). Being basically copper, unlinked in value to the stable gold and silver denominations, highly fluctuating in value, it is hardly surprising that R. Jacob b. Aha should have regarded it as "produce", and thus ruled that one may not lend out a *leukon* for a *leukon*.

We now enter upon a new *sugya*, one which is only loosely connected to the preceding one. It is an attempt further to clarify the nature and

349

limitation of "coin". Here in Bava Mezia it is found in a fragmentary and corrupt form. A fuller, more readily understandable, version of it is to be found in Yerushalmi Kiddushin 1.6, and we shall draw upon this parallel source to explain, emend, fill out lacunae and make sense of, the problematic passages in our own *sugya*.

We begin with the citation of a Mishna in Kiddushin (1.6) which reads as follows:

> If one thing was assessed as full value in exchange for another thing, the other party becomes answerable for what was given in exchange. How so? If a man bartered an ox for a cow, or an ass for an ox, as soon as one party has acquired the one thing, the other party is answerable for what is given in exchange.

In other words, this Mishna comes to teach us that in a case where two people wish to barter or exchange two objects, and the one is assessed against the value of the other (so that each is, as it were, in lieu of monetary payment of the other), as soon as one party acquires (by *meshikha*, etc.) the one object, its counterpart automatically passes over into the possession of the opposite number — this by virtue of the act of barter, *halifin*. Thus, even if the opposite number has not touched his acquisition and, from a physical point of view, it has not yet entered into his property, nonetheless it is his, and he is responsible for it. Hence, if, for example, it should subsequently be stolen or destroyed, the loss is his own, and not his donor's, though it may still be in the donor's house. This method of acquisition by barter is possible for any two objects exchanged one for the other, provided their values were assessed against one another. Money, on the other hand, cannot be bartered, since it is not assessed against the value of the "produce" purchased. It, in itself, constitutes the standard and measure of value. Hence, the passing over of a coin cannot cause the "counter-acquisition" of produce. The produce itself has to have a *meshikha* of its own.

The next passage is very problematic and has been interpreted in a number of different ways. According to one explanation, R. Johanan now goes one stage further, saying that such acquisition by barter is only effective when the two objects to be exchanged have *actually* been assessed in value, one against the other — like a donkey for an ox, etc. However, where the two objects to be exchanged have not undergone a real assessment prior to the proposed contract, even though it is well known that their value is approximately equal — as, for example, with two piles of fruit that people wish to barter from one another — in such a case the *meshikha* upon the one object does not effect the transfer of the other. Or, in other words, *halifin* does not apply in such a case. Thus, R. Johanan's statement is actually an interpretation of the Mishna. He wishes to show that the second part of the Mishna (beginning, "How so? ... etc.") is more than merely a concrete exemplification of the first part, which was an abstract legal formulation. It also comes to teach us something new and explicit, namely, that objects of not-clearly defined value cannot be bartered one for the other.

A different interpretation is that this process of *halifin* is only effective when two *kelim* (literally: vessels) are exchanged. The legal concept of *kelim* includes live animals too. Fruit, however, are not considered *kelim* and can, therefore, not be exchanged by barter: the "piles" that R. Johanan speaks of are taken to be "piles of fruit" (as indeed they were in our first explanation).

Yet a third approach to our text assumes that the "piles" spoken of are "piles of coins". One might have thought that though one cannot barter an object for a coin, or two coins for one another, one might be able to exchange two money-bags that have to be weighed and assessed against one another. No, says R. Johanan; even in such a case the barter is ineffective. The term ציבור, though most usually applied to fruit (see Jastrow, 1274a, s.v.) can also apply to money; e.g. ציבורי מעות, Mishna Bava Mezia 2.2.

All these suggestions explain the (deduced) view of R. Johanan. However, says Rav Jeremiah, Rav was of the opinion that barter of "piles of piles" *is* effective. And R. Aba b. Bina (short for Avina, also found in the printed editions in the form: Mina) adds to this another ruling of Rav's, namely that the barter of one bag of coins (*involucrum*, see above, p. 207, note 6, and Lieberman, p. 146) for another is also effective. If we understand the "piles" mentioned above as referring to "piles of fruit", then R. Aba b. Bina is here teaching us a complete *novum,* a new ruling of Rav's that we could not have derived from the previous one, talking of piles of fruit. But if we take "piles" to be "piles of coins", then he is just recording another, differently formulated, tradition in the name of Rav, one that in effect bears out R. Jeremiah's previous statement.

We are left, then, with a divergence of opinion between Rav and R. Johanan — one that can be variously interpreted — as to the extent and efficacy of *halifin.*

Having introduced the issue of barter, in order to clarify its relationship with "coin", we now go off on something of a tangent, discussing other aspects of barter far from relevant to the essential coin issue. The case put

351

before us by R. Zera (Zeura, a more Palestinian form of the name, in the Escorial Ms.) (in the name of Rav Judah in the name of Samuel) is one where two people agree to exchange a cow for a donkey. One party, the donkey-owner, "drew" to himself the cow. In the light of what we have just learned above, we may assume that his *meshikha* of the cow caused the donkey automatically to pass over into the legal possession of the cow-owner, without any further action on his part. However, when the (former) cow-owner actually comes to take away his (acquired) donkey, he finds it is damaged. He therefore wishes to annul the transaction and get back his cow. Now, normally, the rule is that if one person is claiming from another something of which the other is in possession, it is incumbent upon the claimant to bring proof of the validity of his claim. The defendant, for his part, has only to rebut the claim. So also in our case, one might assume that since the (former) donkey-owner is now in possession of the cow, it is the (former) cow-owner who has to prove that the donkey was injured while yet in the donkey-owner's possession, i.e. before the transaction took place. The donkey-owner, for his part, will argue: "The donkey was damaged after it already has passed over into your possession," and the burden of proof to demonstrate otherwise is now upon the cow-owner.

This argument is, however, fallacious, says R. Zera. For it is based on the assumption that through his act of *meshikha* upon the cow, the donkey-owner has already gained possession of the cow. Yet our uncertainty as to when exactly the damage took place calls into doubt the very validity of the transaction itself. For, if it could be shown that the damage to the donkey took place *before* the *meshikha* was carried out, the *meshikha* itself would be meaningless and ineffectual. Thus the donkey-owner's very claim to be in possession of the cow has been undermined and cast into doubt. If he is not in possession of the cow, obviously there has been no exchange and he has only his own donkey — this is a truism. In fact, the main point of certainty in the whole case is that the donkey did belong to him, and at some time or other it was damaged. The onus of proof has now shifted onto his shoulders. It is he who must prove that any damage took place *after* the act of *meshikha* upon the cow, and that prior to that act the donkey was healthy and whole. As a consequence, his act of *meshikha* was an effective one, causing the donkey, willy-nilly, to pass over into the possession of the (former) cow-owner. While in the cow-owner's possession it was damaged, argues the donkey-owner, and this is, of course, wholly his own loss, and need be reimbursed by no one. This is what the donkey-owner must prove, and this, in fact, is fairly obvious. "If you cannot understand the logic in this argument, you'll never understand anything in the Tractate Nezikim (or in the laws of damages)," says R. Zera.

Our text gives the above passage in the name of R. Zera or Zeura (in the name of Rav Judah in the name of Samuel). However, the Yerushalmi continues that R. Zera said: "I am not of this opinion, and do I understand nothing in matters of damages?" This was obviously not said by the same person who made the preceding statement. It is a fact that there were two R. Zeras, who both lived in Palestine about a generation apart (see above, p. 58, and see below, commentary to Gemara 2), but rather than attribute the two statements to two different R. Zeras, it seems more plausible to read with the parallel *sugya* in Kiddushin, R. Ba (= R. Aba). (We shall see that this emendation is borne out by further readings below.) In fact, the Kiddushin *sugya* when explaining the above passage does so with far greater clarity, formulating the reasoning thus: For all who raise a claim against their neighbour have to bring evidence (to back it up), except in the case of *halifin* (barter).

R. Zera (or Zeira as he is called in Kiddushin) disagrees with R. Ba (according to our emendation on the basis of Kiddushin), citing in argument the Mishna in Ketubot 7.8. Our Yerushalmi here merely hints at the Mishna, apparently relying upon our whole-hearted acquaintance therewith. The Mishna teaches that if a man betrothed a woman, and defects were found in her while yet she was in her father's house, the father must bring proof that these defects arose in her *after* she was betrothed. That is to say, should the father wish to claim from the husband the *ketuba* (marriage-settlement), arguing that it is he (the husband) who has broken off the betrothal — and the breaking of a betrothal obligates such payment — he, the father, must first prove that the defects in the betrothed (which are the cause of the annulment) arose after his daughter was already affianced. Thus, responsibility for the annulment devolves upon the husband, and he has to make good the settlement. The Mishna is saying that, since the father is the claimant, he has to substantiate his claim in order to get anything out of the husband, who is *in possession of* the sum claimed. But have we not just learned above — to make a rather formal and somewhat superficial comparison — that, according to Samuel, he who is in possession — in that case, the donkey-owner — has himself to substantiate his claim. And carrying this view over to our case, the husband should have to prove that the defects were there before the betrothal, in order to free himself from the money-settlement.

The Gemara goes on to relate that three scholars, R. Huna, R. Pinhas and R. Hezekiah, went to visit R. Josa at Gadfa(?)[23] and repeated before him this argument brought to refute Samuel. His retort to them was to refer them to the continuation of the self-same Mishna, which reads as follows: However, if she had entered into the control of the husband, the husband must bring proof that these defects were in her before she was betrothed, and that the bargain [with the father] was a bargain made in error. "Now," argues R. Josa, "in this case too the father is still suing the husband for the *ketuba*, yet it is the husband who here has to prove his claim. According to you, who state that the Mishna is in conflict with Samuel's view," says R. Josa, "should it not be the father who has to prove his claim? Yet the Mishna clearly states otherwise." (It may also be that the last part of R. Josa's statement is not a question, but a statement of fact.... "and [according to this part of the Mishna] it is not the husband who must bring proof.") Does this then mean that the first part of the Mishna is in conflict with Samuel's view, while the latter is in accordance with it? Obviously not...!!

Here, the text of our *sugya* becomes highly fragmentary, and can only be at all understood by reference to the Kiddushin version. According to that version, R. Josa then proceeded to demonstrate that Samuel's view is in complete accordance with our Mishna. For, he argues, even though in the case we sketched above, the donkey-owner had to prove that his donkey was whole before he had sold it, that was only because the cow-owner had not yet actually taken the donkey over into his possession, into his property. Had he done so (and had the exchange been *physically* completed), and only afterwards raised this claim, that he found in the donkey injuries which were there prior to the exchange, *he* would have to prove this conclusively; he would have to bring evidence that the damage was not incurred while in his possession. Similarly, as long as the woman was in her father's house, there was a doubt as to the very fact of any legally binding betrothal having taken place. For the husband claims that the defects cancel the validity of the betrothal. Clearly, then, the father must prove that there had been a valid betrothal, before he can make the next move of claiming the *ketuba*. However, after the husband has taken the woman into his care and safe-keeping, it now becomes his task to prove that any subsequently-discovered defects were there prior to the

---

23 See Lieberman's comments, p. 146, that Ms. Escorial has a reading לגרפה, which he suggests may be a dialectical form of לגגרפה, which he suggests is λογογραφος, he that writes out the legal rulings. In other words, they went to R. Josa, the court scribe. See my additional comments on this suggestion in *Alei Sefer* 15 (1989), pp. 127-128.

betrothal. Only in this way can he annul the betrothal and free himself of the monetary obligations. Hence, there is a case where it is the husband who has to bring proof, i.e. after he has taken the woman into his control. So, also, there is a case where it is the (former) [cow-]owner who has to bring the proof — if he has already physically taken possession of the donkey.

The final part of this passage "so also here it is the owner ... who must bring proof" appears in a different version in the Escorial Ms., but with much the same meaning. There (p. 55, line 18), we read: אף הדא דמייה לה, so this, too, is similar to it, i.e. it is a comparable situation where the owner must bring proof.

If the previous part of our *sugya* was fragmentary and difficult to make out, how much more so the next section. For here the text as it stands is so corrupt (in the words of Ramban, to BM 46b) that it makes virtually no sense at all and has to be radically reconstructed again by a close comparison with the Kiddushin version. Firstly, the opening six words — ר' בא רב יהודה בשם שמואל — should be deleted. They are, in fact, a mistaken repetition of an earlier line, which prefaced a statement of the traditionary R. Ba. We saw above, that though our text actually reads R. Zera, it has to be corrected to R. Ba on the basis of the Kiddushin parallel. Thus, we are back to the earlier R. Ba in the name of Rav Judah in the name of Samuel ... etc. Since both cases, i.e. the earlier one and the one to follow, discuss the exchange of a cow for a donkey, and both are introduced by R. Ba, they were confused with one another and the confusion developed into our present garbled version.[24]

In place of what we have just deleted, we should now supply the following (from Kiddushin):

R. Ba, Rav Hamnuna, R. Ada b. Ahva, in the name of Rav: One [man] sold [another] a cow for money. He pressed him[25] [for

---

24 The strange וכי בא in some modern editions is an obvious corruption of ר' בא. In the *editio princeps* and the Escorial Ms., as well as other early authorities, the reading is correct: רבי בא, and so too in Kiddushin.

25 Our readings have ... אזל סמכיה, he went and deposited it. But Ms. Escorial (p. 55, line 22) has: ... אזל רחקיה, which Lieberman (p. 147) rightly corrects to: אזל דחקיה, סמכיה..., which we have translated: He (the vendor) went and pressured him and he (the purchaser) deposited.... As to the amount of money involved, the printed version reads: בשמונה דינרין, while the Escorial Ms. has: בחמשה דינ'. Presumably the בחמשה — five — was abbreviated to בח', which was later interpreted to mean eight, the numerical value of the letter *het*. For a similar such corruption see above, pp. 32-33.

payment], saying to him: "Give me the money". The other answered him: "What do you want it for?". "To buy myself a donkey", he replied. [Now the man who owed money for the cow offered his own donkey instead.]

And here we return to our text, which has laconically paraphrased the latter part of the above passage, stating that: The one had a cow, the other a donkey, and they exchanged [them]. — "If the cow-owner (= original vendor) 'drew' the donkey, the cow does not [thereby] pass over into the possession [of the original purchaser]. The donkey — can it cause acquisition?"

The Gemara here teaches that if the cow-owner "drew" the donkey *after* the original purchaser had taken possession of his cow, obviously one cannot say that there is here, in effect, a regular exchange of a cow for a donkey, and that therefore *meshikha* upon the one should bring about the completed acquisition of the other. This is patently absurd since the cow is already in the purchaser's possession. Furthermore, the purchaser of the cow still owes the vendor money for it. It is true that in the meanwhile the vendor has acquired the purchaser's donkey, but this is a separate contract and requires its own unrelated act of acquisition (*kinyan*). It is equally true that the cow-vendor will now almost certainly cancel the purchaser's debt — is that not what the vendor wants? — but this is actually yet a third contractual stage. Thus, the cancellation of the debt is not an *automatic* result of the acquisition of the donkey, and there has been no barter, *halifin*, of a donkey for a debt. This then, though possibly an exchange *de facto*, is very different from a *halifin*-exchange, where both acts of acquisition take place at one and the same time.

However, asks the Gemara, what would be the case if the purchaser had not yet taken possession of the cow, and he then agreed to give his donkey to the vendor? Would the vendor's "drawing" of the donkey automatically cause the cow to pass over into the purchaser's possession, since, in point of fact, an exchange was agreed upon? Or should we rather argue: The agreement began as a regular sale for money. The further acquisition of a donkey on the part of the vendor, even though it is from the purchaser, does not alter the terms of the original contract. Hence, the *meshikha* of the donkey can have no effect upon the legal position of the cow? According to R. Ba, such a case is like *halifin*, i.e. he follows the first line of argument, while according to R. Josa it is not, i.e. he accepts the second argument.

The next line should be emended from (אית הכא מילי)

356

דיודי ר' בא לר' יוסי to דיודי בה ר' יוסי ..., as becomes evident from a glance at the Kiddushin version.[26] For there we are told — and this is missing in our text — that R. Josa said, there are certain cases, superficially similar to the last one mentioned, in which each party has to make a separate act of acquisition. And, though R. Ba held the previous case to be like one of *halifin*, he too would agree that the following one is not like *halifin*. The case brought as an example, the final one in this *sugya*, is as follows: A man purchased a cow from his friend and paid him for it in full. He did not actually hand the money over to him, but placed it for him in his bank account.[27] The next day he happened to see his friend on the point of drawing the money out of his account, and asked him what he wanted it for. "To buy a donkey," replied the other. "You can have my donkey, if you want," says the first. Now the first man has not yet actually taken possession of his cow, even though he had paid for it. And, as we know, the receipt of a monetary payment on the part of the vendor does not make the article sold pass over into the purchaser's hands. This requires a separate act of acquisition on the part of the purchaser. (See above, Bavli Bava Mezia 47b *et seq.*) If the purchaser were now to "draw" the cow, the donkey would not automatically pass over into the hands of the vendor. For the purchaser has already paid for the cow, and is not exchanging the donkey for it. On the contrary, he will demand payment for this donkey, even if it is not of the same sum of money he himself placed into the other's bank account. Conversely, and for exactly the same reasons, should the other "draw" the donkey, the cow will not automatically pass over into the purchaser's possession. Thus, even R. Ba would here agree that we have in this case no *halifin* and that each party has to make his own separate act of acquisition.

Mishna 2   The Mishna in the Yerushalmi is identical to that of the Bavli in all but the version of *Mi she-para'* ("He that exacted...") formula. The Bavli Mishna (in the modern printed editions) reads: "He that exacted punishment from the generation of the Flood *and the generation of the Dispersion* (cf. Gen. 11.9) will exact punishment...," etc. The Yerushalmi here omits all mention of the "generation of the Dispersion", as does also

---

26   The reading in Ms. Escorial (p. 55, line 21) is: .... ‹יוסי› אית הכה מילה חורי דמודה בה ר'. The word יוסי is added in the margin. Trans.: There is here something else that R. Yosi agrees with...

27   Printed ed.: טרפוניטיה, Ms. Escorial: טרפי זיטא. Read: טרפזיטא, with Ramban, etc.: τραπεξιτης, banker, money-changer (Lieberman, p. 147).

the Tosefta (Bava Mezia 3.14). (So indeed do manuscript versions of the Mishna of the Bavli.) The Bavli (48a) brings yet another version in the name of R. Simeon: "He that exacted punishment from the generation of the Flood, and the generation of the Dispersion, and the men of Sodom and Gomorrah, and the Egyptians on the [Red] Sea...," etc. It appears, then, that there were several different versions of this formula, varying in length and detail. (See further, below, where we have shown that the Yerushalmi apparently knew of yet another version.)

Gemara 2 The Gemara opens with an Aggadic *derasha* (exegesis) which is also to be found (in the name of a different traditionary) in *Genesis Rabba* 31.5 (ed. Theodor-Albeck, p. 279). The *derasha* seeks to determine the nature of the sins of the Flood-generation, which has been singled out in the Mishna's *Mi she-para'* formula. Indeed, what is the connection between the "generation of the Flood" and the man who backs out of a deal after making a down payment on it? R. Aha answers that the "violence" mentioned in the Scriptural verse (Gen. 6.13), describing the doings of that generation, was of a very specific nature. People of that time would do evil deeds in such a manner that they could not be litigated against in court. For example, a group of them would band together to rob a passing salesman. But each of them would carefully take less than a *peruta's* worth. Now, less than this amount is so little that it is not considered real theft and can, therefore, not be reclaimed in the courts. (A *peruta* was the minimum size denomination in Rabbinic times.) Of course, since they all did it together, the net result was to leave the poor salesman totally bereft of all. And though he knew who it was who had stolen from him, and exactly what, he could still do nothing about it. His loss was complete and irremediable. Similarly, someone who backs out of a deal which has already been agreed upon and where, furthermore, a down payment has been made, obviously can cause the other party considerable embarrassment, trouble and even monetary loss. However, he is not actually punishable for this, and if he does decide to change his mind and break a contract there is nothing anyone can really do about it, even in a court. He can only be warned that it is "not fair play" or decent behaviour, or be cursed with the *Mi she-para'* formula (see Bavli 48b).

R. Hiyya b. Ba (-Va) (= Aba) now goes on to draw a parallel between the "generation of the Flood" and the people of Sodom and Gomorrah. He does so by pointing out that the identical word "great" — רבה — appears in two different contexts, (a) in Gen. 6.5, describing the "generation of the Flood"; "And the Lord saw that the wickedness of men was *great* on the earth," and (b), Gen. 18.20: "And the Lord said, 'Verily the cry of Sodom and Gomorrah is *great'.*" The appearance of these identical terms in their respective verses is intended to teach that there was an analogous element in both these generations, namely, their behaviour. It would appear that R. Hiyya b. Ba had before him a version of the *Mi she-para'* formula, which mentioned both the "generation of the Flood" and the people of Sodom and Gomorrah. (Cf. R. Simeon's version in the Bavli 48a, and our comment on the Mishna, above.) He wished to demonstrate that the same characteristics, which R. Aha had proved to be prevalent in the Flood-generation, were also present among the people of Sodom and Gomorrah, and that, therefore, the two generations were rightly coupled together in the *Mi she-para'* formula. He did so by this method of linking homiletically identical words, an exegetical technique called *gezerah shava.* (For related Midrashim, see *Genesis Rabba* 27.3; Theodor-Albeck, p. 257; =ibid. 49.4; Theodor-Albeck, p. 503.)

Next, the Gemara tells us that R. Hanina [b. Hama] ruled that the *halacha* (law) is according to R. Simeon, namely, that he who has the money — whether it be the seller who has received the payment or the buyer who has not yet parted with his money — has the upper hand, i.e. can back out of the deal. However, adds R. Hanina, we do not always go according to this rule. Presumably he wishes here to say that R. Simeon himself does not rigidly and unvaryingly follow his own principle, but that he too would admit that it has its limitations. For even according to R.Simeon, it is only if the purchase *and* the money are in the hands of the vendor that he can change his mind. But should the money be in the hands of the vendor and the "fruit" in the hands of the purchaser, the vendor cannot withdraw from the agreement. Not because the purchaser has already "drawn" the "fruit" — for that would mean that the transaction had been completed, and, obviously, by then no party could back down — but because the purchaser had rented out his store-room to the vendor and the vendor had kept his fruit in it, so that, in fact the fruit was on the purchaser's premises; in such a case the vendor cannot withdraw from the agreement. This, indeed, we learn from a *beraitha* in R. Simeon's name quoted in the Bavli 49b. (See further Lieberman's comments in *Tosefta ki-fshutah* 9 [New York, 1988], p. 177, to T. Bava Mezia 3.14, lines 47-48.)

We now come to a *sugya* which (with some differences) has its parallels in the Bavli 48b, and part of which also appears in Yerushalmi Kiddushin 2.1. We are first told that R. Hiyya b. Josef gave someone a [gold] *denarius* for a consignment of salt. In the meanwhile, the price of salt rose (according to an addition in the Bavli) and the seller decided to break the contract. (In the Bavli the roles are reversed, and R. Hiyya b. Josef is the vendor.) R. Hiyya b. Josef then warned him of the punishments that would be visited upon him — heavenly ones — should he really go through with breaking the contract. "Do you not know," he asked him rhetorically, "that as soon as you decided to change your mind, a sickle was, as it were, wielded in readiness across your legs, to cut them off, or break them, should you go through with breaking the contract?" This was a contemporary mode used by the Romans for punishment and torture. (See e.g., Krauss, *Dvir* 1 [1923], p. 93; Eusebins, *Hist. Eccles.,* VIII, 12, etc., and cf. M. Sota 8.7, and Lieberman, p. 147, note 8.) Using it metaphorically, R. Hiyya b. Josef attempted to frighten the vendor into reversing his negative decision.

The reading in Ms. Escorial is slightly different, perhaps reflecting an attempt to bring it more closely into line with its Bavli counterpart. The reading there is as follows: "R. Hiyya bar Josef was given a *dinar* for salt. His brother changed his mind. He (R. Hiyya bar Josef) said to him: Know that the Rabbis have already wielded the sickle across that man's legs...." The meaning seems to be that R. Hiyya bar Josef was in partnership with his brother. He received a gold *denarius* to sell someone salt. But his brother wanted to back out of the deal. So R. Hiyya Bar Josef chastised him, warning him of the punishment awaiting those who behave in such fashion. (See Lieberman, p. 147.)

In the next case we are told of a man who, wishing to buy a (large) amount of silk, made a (part) payment for it. (That he paid only part of the total sum initially becomes evident from the continuation of the passage, although this point is not explicitly stated here.) Again, one would presume, the silk went up in price, and therefore the vendor wished to withdraw from the deal. The two parties came before R. Hiyya b. Josef and R. Johanan. The former ruled that the vendor was obliged to sell the purchaser at least that amount of silk covered by the down payment. The rest, which had not yet been paid for, he could decide against selling and retain for himself. If, however, he refused to sell anything, he would be handed over for the *Mi she-para'* procedure. R. Johanan, however, ruled that the vendor had to supply the *whole* sale or submit himself to the *Mi she-para'*. For, according to R. Johanan, the handing over of even a part of a total payment commits the vendor to the total sale. (The reading we have noted above in Ms. Escorial probably has the same meaning, though slightly differently formulated. See also Lieberman's comment, p. 147, note 9.)

Now, continues the Gemara, R. [I]la[i] and R. Zera differed as to the exact interpretation of the above passage. What precisely had happened in that case? R. Ilai says that the [gold] *denarii* which the purchaser had given were meant to serve as a pledge or security (earnest money), rather than a portion of the actual payment. Therefore, according to R. Hiyya b. Josef, this pledge did not actually finalise the contract. Its point was primarily to obligate the *purchaser* to keep to his part of the deal. On the other hand, the pledge did have clear monetary value, and, therefore, the vendor's receipt thereof committed him at least to the amount equalling the value of the pledge. R. Johanan, however, considers that even a pledge, if it is of this nature — i.e. basically money — commits both parties to the *whole* sale. R. Zera, for his part, explains the controversy as dealing with a case where the *denarii* had been given as a part payment. They therefore committed the vendor either to the partial amount (R. Hiyya b. Josef's view) or to the full amount (R. Johanan's view). But in a case where only a pledge, or money meant as a pledge and not a payment, has been given, perhaps both R. Johanan and R. Hiyya b. Josef would agree that the vendor may completely withdraw from the whole sale without suffering the *Mi she-para'!*

Furthermore, the Gemara argues, whichever way we may interpret this controversy between R. Hiyya b. Josef and R. Johanan, on one point they would both agree, or, more correctly, R. Hiyya b. Josef would agree with R. Johanan. And that is if what was involved in the sale is something that cannot be divided up, such as, for example, a live cow or a cloak. Here R. Hiyya too would agree that the vendor must supply the whole article, as it cannot be cut up, even though he has not yet received the full payment.

R. Jacob B. Idi (in the name of R. Abahu) now adds that according to R. Johanan a ring is not a pledge. This statement as it stands is not very clear. When, however, we see it in the fuller context in which it is found in the parallel text of our *sugya* (Yerushalmi Shavi'it 10.9),[28] its meaning becomes perfectly evident. The full text there runs as follows:

> R. Zeira, R. Abahu in the name of R. Johanan [said]: "He who gives his friend a ring as a pledge (that he would honour a contract agreed upon), if he wished to change his mind he may do so". R. Zeira asked R. Abahu: "[Is this true also of] a gold coin?" "[No]", he

---

28 See S. Lieberman(n), *Talmudah shel Kisarin* (Jerusalem, 1931), pp. 54-55. Further parallels referred to in Lieberman, p. 147. The order of the following statements is different in Ms. Escorial, see Lieberman, pp. 147-148.

replied, "[only] a ring". And what is the difference between a ring and a gold coin? A gold coin changes (i.e. changes hands, is used and paid out as currency). A ring does not change.

The Gemara then tells us that if one gives a coin as a pledge, this coin will be used by the vendor, even before he receives the complete payment. And, when the purchaser brings him the full sum, even if he returns the pledge it will not be the same coin. For he will certainly have spent it in the meantime, and will, therefore, have to return a different one. And since he makes use of the coin immediately on receipt thereof, one may regard it as already a part of the real payment and, hence, committing him to the whole sale. A ring, for its part, is a pledge of quite a different nature. The vendor cannot make any real use of it. He has to return the self-same ring to its owner. "A ring does not change." Thus the ring can never be thought of as part of the actual payment, but only as a sign of goodwill on the purchaser's part. However, such a sign does not commit to a sale, and the vendor can therefore withdraw.

We see here that R. Zeira (= R. Zera) knows full well that R. Johanan holds a coin-pledge to be total committal. Why then, one may ask, did he explain above R. Johanan's view (in opposition to that of R. Hiyya b. Josef), specifically with reference to a part payment? This suggested to us (above) that in his view a coin-pledge might, according to R. Johanan, not be committal. The answer to this apparent contradiction is simple. Two different R. Zeras are being spoken of. The first one, above, was a direct pupil of R. Johanan and boon companion of R. Ilai (= La). However, the one mentioned in the Yerushalmi Shevi'it passage just quoted is the second R. Zera of the following generation, who was a pupil of R. Abahu (d. 309, who, in turn, was a pupil of R. Johanan, d. 279). In our version we have only the bare statement, here transmitted by another pupil of R. Johanan, R. Jacob b. Idi, that a ring given as a pledge cannot serve as a part payment and obligate the vendor to the sale. In fact, what we have here is a clear Caesarean tradition — R. Abahu was the leading Caesarean scholar of the later third century — that R. Johanan held a coin-pledge to be committal.[29]

Thus far we have discussed the degree to which the handing over of money, either a complete or partial payment, or the giving of a pledge,

---

29 Lieberman, p. 148 suggests a reason for the difference between the Caesarean tradition and that of Y. Shevi'it — presumably a Tiberian tradition — referring us to B. M. Lewin, *Ozar Hilluf Minhagim...* (Jerusalem, 1942), p. 52, note 2.

obligates the two parties to complete the sale. The Gemara now goes on to tell us that purely verbal negotiations are in no way committal, and that if someone breaks such an agreement he is not subject to the *Mi she-para'* procedure. And therefore, says R. Jacob b. Zavdi (in the name of R. Abahu) in the name of R. Johanan, if someone promised to give his friend a present and then wished to change his mind, he may do so, since merely the verbal statement did not legally commit him. There is now a short section in the Yerushalmi Shevi'it version which has been omitted in our version (for the sake of brevity), but is found (partially) in the Escorial Ms. (p. 56, line 38), which adds clarity and understanding to the passage. There it is related that on hearing this statement R. Jose rose and asked: "Can this really be so? Surely one must tell the truth and keep one's word?" To which R. Jacob b. Zavdi replied that at the time the man made his promise and said he would give a present, he fully intended doing so. Thus, at the time of making the statement he was being completely honest and truthful. But he is nonetheless not bound by his word, and may subsequently retract it.[30]

To this the Gemara now adds a proviso, that what has just been said is true of a poor man, who cannot always afford to fulfil his promises. Thus, his word is not one hundred per cent whole-hearted, and even though consciously he may have whole-hearted intentions of carrying it out, subconsciously he probably has his doubts as to whether he would be able to. Furthermore, the proposed recipient is probably equally dubious of the whole affair and does not completely believe he will really receive the present. And so, in fact, he too does not make a full mental claim upon it. If, however, a rich man should make a promise, he must fulfil it. For he never doubted his ability to fulfil his promise, and the recipient forthwith made a complete mental claim upon the present. Thus, the rich man's promise gains the authority of a vow, and cannot be retracted.

This above explanation is according to the text as we have it in our printed editions (and in Ms. Escorial). However, a number of early Talmudic commentators quote our text with a different reading, the reverse in fact: This you [can] say [is true] of a rich man, but with a poor man, [his word] becomes a vow. They understand it as follows: If one promises a present to a rich man, one may retract. But to a poor man, one may not. For a promise to give charity — and a present to a poor man is regarded as belonging to the halachic category of charity — acquires the

30 See Lieberman's comments, p. 148.

force of a vow which cannot be readily retracted. (Compare the *sugya* in Bavli 49a.)

This latter explanation (based on variant readings)[31] makes good sense in terms of the continuation of the *sugya*. For there we are told that Rav would not reconsider a promise to give a present to a poor man, while he would reconsider the promise of a present to a rich man.

In the next case we are told that R. Johanan paid his relatives some money for oil which subsequently went up in price. He then went to R. Jannai (an older contemporary) who told him that, according to Biblical law, payment of money actually makes acquisition, and that only Rabbinic ruling decreed otherwise. This indeed is R. Johanan's view in Bavli 46b. The difficulties in the above passage are clear. Could it be that R. Johanan did not know the ruling explicitly set out in our Mishna, that (both according to the Sages and R. Simeon) the vendor can break the contract, but that he will (according to the Sages) be subject to the *Mi she-para'* formula? Have we not seen him (earlier in our own *sugya*) giving rulings on this very subject? And when R. Jannai gave his answer, why did he not mention the matter of the *Mi she-para'*? The explanation of this passage, and answer to these questions, seems to be as follows: We know that strictly speaking, according to Biblical law, payment of money makes acquisition (cf. Bavli 46b). The Sages decreed, for the benefit of the purchaser, that it should not do so. For what could happen is the following: the purchaser buys wheat and pays for it, and it forthwith belongs to him. Nevertheless, it is still on the vendor's property, in his attic or storeroom. Then suddenly a fire breaks out and the wheat begins to burn. The vendor does not trouble himself unduly over this fire, since it is no longer his wheat that is being burned. Why should he disturb himself over someone else's property? The loss sustained would be the purchaser's. To obviate any such possibility, the Sages decreed that the wheat continue belonging to the vendor, and that he bear responsibility for it, until such time as it *physically* pass into the purchaser's possession (Bavli 46b). Thus, the Rabbinic decree was introduced to act in the purchaser's interest and to his advantage. Now, should he decide to waive the advantages granted him by the Sages, and make it conditional with the vendor that the money he gives completes the sale, is this condition valid and effective? Can he forgo the benefits decreed him? This is what R. Johanan apparently asked R. Jannai: And R. Jannai answered him in the affirmative. The Rabbinic decree was intended only to benefit him. If

31 See Lieberman(n), *Talmudah shel Kisarin*, p. 54, note 88 for sources of this variant.

he judges it to be to his advantage to revert to the primary Biblical law, he is within his rights to do so. This, then, is quite a different case from any mentioned in the Mishna, or by R. Johanan himself above, and one in which the *Mi she-para'* issue has no place (and, therefore, does not figure in R. Jannai's reply).

Lieberman(n), however, offers a different explanation for this text to answer the questions we raised above (see pp. 148-149). He suggests that R. Johanan's relative wished to give him the oil, but, since the oil had in the meanwhile appreciated in price, R. Johanan thought that there might be a question of *ribit,* usury, involved, and perhaps the sanction of *Mi she-para'* only applies when there has been no price change in either direction, or when the price of the produce has gone down and the purchaser wishes to back out of the deal. It is for this reason that R. Johanan approached R. Jannai, asking him if he be permitted to receive the oil. R. Jannai answered that according to Biblical law transfer of monies create a sale, and he would be receiving that which is his own. The sanction of *Mi she-para'* is not applicable in such a case. Lieberman adduces further proof of his interpretation from Y. Kiddushin 2.5.62d, and from further on in this *sugya* (see his comments, p. 149, to lines 46-47). See further below.

The next passage has also caused the Yerushalmi commentators considerable difficulties and some even thought to emend it radically. However, this seems unnecessary, as we shall presently see. R. Samuel b. Sosartai states in the name of R. Abahu that if a vendor said to a purchaser: "Your wheat has been burned in my attic," he is believed. To this simple statement R. Isaac asks: "What sort of case are we speaking of? If by paying for the wheat it immediately belongs to the purchaser (in accordance to Biblical law), then, of course, it was the purchaser's loss." Now, as soon as the purchaser paid for the wheat and it became his property, since it nonetheless remained on the vendor's premises, he, the vendor, became an unpaid guardian (*shomer hinnam*). It is true that he would be free of any responsibility if the wheat were indeed to have been destroyed by a fire, so long as there was no negligence on his part. But he must first take an oath (of Biblical authority), the "oath of the guardians", that this indeed was the case. Or he may bring witnesses rather than take an oath. But he certainly is not "believed" outright. If, on the other hand, payment of money does not effect a transfer of property — this according to Rabbinic law — then obviously the wheat still belongs to the vendor. Why should he not be believed when he claims that his own wheat has been consumed by fire? R. Isaac offers no answer to resolve the objections he raised.

What R. Abahu may possibly have meant is the following: He would agree that payment of money does not effect a transfer of property. Therefore, if the vendor claims that the wheat has been burned up, he is talking about his own wheat, and, of course, he would have to return to the purchaser his money. But should we take his word at its face value? Should we not, rather, suspect him of duplicity and falsehood? Perhaps the price of wheat went up and he found himself another better customer! In such a case, he would be only too pleased to give back the purchaser his money and cancel the original deal in order to make the sale to a higher bidder. Surely, then, he should not be automatically believed, but should be required to take an oath (of Rabbinic authority) — or to bring witnesses — that the wheat has really been destroyed. R. Abahu ruled that we do not view him with these suspicions, but that he is to be believed.

The next passage in our Yerushalmi is also very hard to make out, and the text which appears before us in the printed editions makes very little apparent sense. However, most of the *Rishonim* (classical commentators of the Talmud) bring a variant reading of our text, and one which makes much better sense. The *Ittur* — R. Isaac b. Aba Mari, a major French codifier, *c.* 1122-93 — explains our Yerushalmi as follows. He reads: גלבין בחמרא — bottles of wine — in place of the second דינרין — *denarii* — in our test, and this indeed is the reading in Ms. Escorial: If a man pays ten *denarii* for a hundred bottles of wine, and the wine is in a house, the payment of the money causes an immediate transfer of property. For the Rabbinic decree ruling otherwise was only intended to apply in the case where damage by fire, or some similar course, was a likely eventuality. However, where it is unlikely — as in a house which does not normally fall down, or burn down, for only attics are susceptible to fire — they did not intend their decree to apply. Hence, in the above case the payment of money effected an immediate acquisition on the purchaser's part. But if the wine was still in a vineyard, where there is every possibility that it catch alight — in the dry baking heat of a Palestinian summer this is an all too common occurrence[32] — the Rabbinic decree comes into play, delaying

---

32 Incidentally, we have noted above in the translation that we should read: a vineyard is likely to <fall> [be burned down], in accordance with Ms. Escorial; i.e. כרם מצוי הוא לישרף, as opposed to כרם מצוי הוא ליפול. However, Lieberman (p. 149) is not certain that this is a simple scribal error, influenced by the preceding בית אינו מצוי ליפול, a house is unlikely to fall. For it may be that we should read a vineyard is likely לישדף, to be blasted, struck by blight. The reading לישרף was, in that case, influenced by the preceding discussion on wheat burned in the attic. And if לישדף — blighted, is correct, ליפול might well have meant to droop with blight, be spoiled (perhaps similar to נבל, shrivel, dry up).

the legal transfer of the property, until the goods have been physically transferred to the purchaser's property.

If that were the whole explanation of the above passage, why, one might justly ask, the use of the terms "permitted" and "forbidden"? All the Gemara need say was: in the one case (of a house) the money effected a *kinyan* (acquisition); in the other (of the vineyard), it did not. There is, however, yet another element to be grafted onto our explanation which will complete our understanding of the text. For, if we say that the handing over of money does not effect a transfer of property, then until such time as the vendor hand over the wine, he is, one might say, merely a guardian of the money. But we have already seen above that when he receives money — even pledge-money — he immediately makes use of it. How much more so a real payment! And in so doing he becomes a borrower. In other words, he has been advanced the money for the sale as a loan. The benefit he will get from this "loan" will put pressure on him and obligate him to complete the deal. (See above, where we saw that a part payment creates obligations, etc.) He will not easily be able to back out of it — and this without any relation to the *Mi she-para'* issue. Thus, the buyer will be getting his purchase (for its true value) to a certain extent as the result of his having advanced the payment. He will be gaining benefit in excess of the loan — the purchase as opposed to the return of the money — because of the time he allowed it to be in the vendor's (borrower's) hands. This is forbidden under the laws of *ribit*, usury, or here technically called *agar natar* (literally "compensation for waiting"), see Bavli Bava Mezia 63b. If, however, the money does effect an immediate transfer of property, as in the case where the wine is in a house, then this is a straightforward sale, with no time-lag during which the vendor enjoys borrowed (or advanced) money. This, of course, is permitted.

It follows from this, learns R. Jose in the following passage, that if one person gave another ten *denarii* so that he supply him with one hundred bottles of wine, as soon as the supplier starts spending the money he cannot back out of the deal. R. Jose reasons as follows: The supplier has not yet received the wine — he has yet to find it — so the receipt of the money in itself does not now create a commitment and does not effect a sale. One might say that it is only a pledge. However, as soon as he starts using it, it ceases to be a pledge and takes on the nature of payment — or

---

In this passage the same word would be used with slightly different meanings in the two parts of the statement, a phenomenon not unusual in the Yerushalmi.

loan — which creates obligation (see above). But, you may argue, it cannot become a payment until the supplier has the wine in his hands. Indeed, this is correct. We are dealing here with a case where he finally received the wine, and probably, because it went up in price, wished to withdraw from the deal, and sell it elsewhere for more. This he may not do; for we say that in such a case, as soon as he receives the wine, the money he has already received immediately effects a real transfer of property, according to Biblical law, if the wine is in a house (as above). And if it is in a vineyard, it at least obligates him to fulfil his contract. And then if he still wishes to get out of the deal he is subject to the *Mi she-para'* procedure. For, in the previous case, the only reason why the enjoyment of an advance payment was forbidden was because it created an obligation. Had it not made the agreement in any way binding, it could not even have been viewed as an advance payment, since the payment had not yet been determined and fixed. Following this line of reasoning, R. Jose derived from the preceding passage that in our case he is obliged to supply the wine, be it in the house or in the vineyard. (See above, where we have cited Lieberman's view on whether *Mi she-para'* is applicable in a case when *ribit* is involved, and his comments, p. 149, to lines 46-47, and his discussion in *Tosefta ki-fshutah* 9 [New York, 1988], pp. 189-191.)

So far, the discussion of the Gemara has followed the view of R. Johanan, that according to Biblical law it is money that makes acquisition. Rabbinic law decreed otherwise (for reasons outlined above), and substituted an alternative form of *kinyan,* namely *meshikha,* or actual "drawing" of the purchase into the buyer's possession. However, Resh Lakish, R. Johanan's great friend and halachic counterpart, is of the opinion that *meshikha* makes acquisition according to Biblical, and not merely Rabbinic law (cf. Bavli 47b). Money, however, does not. And he learns the law of *meshikha* from the Scriptural verse (Lev. 25.14): "[If thou shall sell ought unto thy neighbour,] or buy out of thy neighbour's hand...," which teaches us that the actual purchase is made by receiving, or "drawing" the object "out of thy neighbour's hand." And, he further adds, the word "thy neighbour" informs us that when one buys from one who is not a "neighbour", i.e. not a Jew, one need not make *meshikha*. In such a case, payment of money alone is sufficient to complete acquisition.

The next part of the Gemara is paralleled by the *sugya* in the Bavli (47b-48a). The Gemara asks: According to Resh Lakish, who holds that money does not effect a transfer of property according to Biblical law, why should a man not be permitted to break a contract even after receiving money? Surely, if the money element is in no way binding, this is little more than a verbal agreement from a legal point of view. And, in that case, why would he ever be subjected to the *Mi she-para'* procedure. For if money does not effect a transaction by either Biblical or Rabbinic law, why should one not change one's mind? To which R. Jose b. R. Bun (= Avin) answers that Resh Lakish follows the *beraitha* which states that one who made a verbal negotiation alone, and then wishes to back down, is not subjected to the *Mi she-para'* procedure (cf. Tosefta Bava Mezi'a 3.14, ed. Lieberman, p. 76, where a very similar version is recorded). That is to say, only if he negotiated verbally *and no more* is he free of the *Mi she-para'*. (See Lieberman, p. 150 to line 50, according to Ms. Escorial.) However, where the verbal agreement was coupled with the handing over of money, even though that money may not have effected a *kinyan*, he is nevertheless subject to the *Mi she-para'* procedure. (See Bavli 48a for a fuller exposition of the reasoning. See also Lieberman's comments, p. 150, to line 51.)

Mishna 3   For the monetary system employed in this Mishna, see above, p. 29, Tables A and B. There are six *ma'ahs* in a *dinar*, the *ma'ah* being the smallest silver denomination, and hence called "a silver". There are four *dinars (denarii)* in a *sela (tetradrachm)*. Hence, there are twenty-four *ma'ahs* in a *sela*.

Gemara 3   The Mishna states that an overcharge of four pieces of silver in a *sela,* which is one-sixth of the purchase price, counts as defrauding.[33] Does the Mishna wish to say that any sixth of a purchase price counts as defrauding, and the mention of the four bits of silver in the *sela* is no more than an example of how one reckons the calculation? Or does the Mishna wish to teach that four bits of silver is the smallest sum that can count as defrauding? Less than that is so little that people would not normally bother about it, and the purchaser would forgo his loss. This is the subject of a controversy between Rav and R. Johanan, with which our Gemara opens. Rav holds that the Mishna's purpose in stating this sum of four bits of silver is to teach that this is the smallest amount that counts as defrauding. R. Johanan, for his part, regards it merely as an example of how one is to calculate one-sixth of the purchase price, and it is not intended as a lowest limit of defrauding. Interestingly enough, this same

---

33 Further on the law of *ona'a,* see my *Roman Palestine 200-400: The Land* (Ramat-Gan, 1978), Chapter VII, pp.136 *et seq.*

sum is again mentioned in Mishna 5, and this fact would seem to bear out, to a certain extent, Rav's view. See the discussion in Bavli 45a.

The Gemara now passes on to a different issue, namely, the question of whether a person can make a sale on condition that he is not subject to the rules of defrauding. Rav says he cannot. The whole matter is discussed in much greater detail in Bavli 41ab. Here it is merely cited as a second statement of Rav's in connection with the laws of defrauding.

We have just seen above that, according to R. Johanan, sums smaller then four bits of silver also count as defrauding. Rav Levi — here Levi bar Sissi (see Lieberman, p. 150, note 22) — is of the same view, holding that sums of as little as a *peruta* — the smallest denomination in Talmudic times — also count as defrauding. This statement of his occurs in Bavli 45a, and here we have emended the text — which makes little sense as it stands — in accordance with that text, and with the reading in Ms. Escorial.

The next passage is again a new and independent issue. It is somewhat abbreviated, and can best be understood by comparison with Bavli 50b. There it is stated that an overcharge of less than one-sixth is not considered "defrauding" and does not bring about the complete cancellation of the sale. Overcharge of more than a sixth does bring about the complete cancellation of the sale. What happens in a case where the amount overcharged is exactly one-sixth, asks our Gemara? (The Yerushalmi calls this sixth of overcharge "defrauding itself", cf. Rashi in Bavli 49b after the Mishna.) (This question was probably raised in relation to our Mishna [Lieberman, p. 150].) And the Gemara answers that, according to R. Judah ha-Nasi, the sale stands and the sum defrauded has to be returned. R. Jonathan or Nathan, on the other hand, is of the opinion that the whole sale is cancelled. Our printed text has R. Johanan; but a comparison with the Bavli (ibid.) will show that this is simply a scribal error for R. Nathan or for Jonathan = Nathan. It is, in fact, most unlikely that R. Johanan would have disagreed with R. Judah ha-Nasi, the great teacher, unless he did so basing himself on R. Nathan's view. Either way, the basic controversy must have been between the two Tannaim, and not between a Tanna and an Amora.

Interestingly enough, in the Bavli (ibid.) the views appear to be reversed. For there we read that it is R. Nathan who says of a case where the sum defrauded was exactly one-sixth that the sale stands, and the money overcharged is returned. While R. Judah ha-Nasi says that the defrauded person, in this case, is given the choice either of keeping the purchase and getting back the overcharge, or cancelling the whole sale.

(Cf. Bavli 51a, and Tosefta Bava Mezia 3.16, ed. Leiberman, pp. 76-77, which seems to bear out the Bavli's version of the controversy and Lieberman, p. 150, and in *Tosefta ki-fshuta* 9 [New York, 1988], p. 179.) This phenomenon of reversed views between the Bavli and the Yerushalmi is by no means uncommon.

Having introduced the issue of the "sixth" of defrauding, the Gemara now goes on to relate that Kahana questioned Rav more closely concerning the ways of calculating this sixth. His question seems to have been based on the Mishna, which states that an overcharge of four bits of silver in a *sela, which is a sixth of the purchase,* is considered defrauding. On this Kahana asks: Surely that depends on who exactly is being defrauded? For example, when the vendor is defrauded four bits of silver in the *sela*, that means he sells something worth six units for five, and therefore is losing a *fifth* of the sum received. Or, to put it slightly differently, he should have received one-fifth more than he did receive. But when a purchaser is overcharged four bits of silver in a *sela,* i.e. by buying something worth five units for six, he is losing one-sixth of the money he paid out.

To this Rav answers that when the Mishna talks of four bits of silver on the *sela,* this is only to teach that such is the minimum amount regarded as defrauding (see above). However, as to the actual reckoning of the sixth, this is always calculated as one-sixth of the "true" price of the purchase, i.e. either the selling of an object worth six units for seven — where the buyer loses one-sixth of the true price — or the selling of one worth six for five where the seller loses a sixth of the true price. Thus, the different combinations of loss, that of the purchaser and that of the vendor, can be treated in one and the same joint manner and calculated at one-sixth of the true price (otherwise known as the "purchase" price). (See Lieberman note, p.151 to line 57, that the reading in Ms. Escorial is the correct one, and that the explanations based on the corrupt reading in the printed editions are forced.)

This view is indeed consistent with what the Bavli has to say on this matter, and in point of fact our Yerushalmi can cast some light on the varying Bavli readings. For, according to the Bavli 49b, Rav holds that one reckons a sixth of the "purchase" price, differing in his view from Samuel. This is the reading in the printed editions of the Bavli. However, most of the manuscript readings, early commentators and codifiers read R. Kahana in place of Rav (see *Diqduke Soferim* ad loc.). This is consistent with the Yerushalmi's text, which reads Kahana. What presumably happened in the Bavli was that the name Kahana dropped out through a scribal error, leaving just Rav. This omission went unnoticed, since the new reading, Rav, made good sense in the context, Rav (alone) being most commonly found in a context with Samuel as his counterpart. We may go yet a stage further. For a number of manuscript readings in the She'iltot have "R. Kahana in the name of Rav" (see She'iltot, Lev., ed. Mirsky, p. 255). In view of our Yerushalmi passage, this reading becomes quite clear. For Rav Kahana (consistently called Kahana in the Yerushalmi, without the honorific "Rav"), asked Rav his opinion on this matter, and received an answer. When later he heard that Samuel held quite a different view, he objected to Samuel's view, but not on his own authority, but rather on the basis of what he had heard from his teacher Rav.

The Gemara now continues to ask as follows: If someone sells his friend something worth five units for six, we know that the defrauded purchaser has the upper hand, and may cancel the whole sale, should he so wish. But why, asks the Gemara, cannot the vendor say to the purchaser: "Indeed, it is true that you have been cheated[34] of one *denarius*. Here then, take your *denarius*, but do not cancel the whole sale, just because of a single *denarius* overcharge." In other words, since the vendor can easily correct the wrong he had done, and in a case where he will do so willingly, why does the purchaser nonetheless have the right to cancel the sale?

Three different solutions are offered to this question:

(a) R. Zera (Zeura, in Ms. Escorial) suggests that the reimbursement of the amount overcharged does not make full amends for the wrong done the purchaser. People will still say of him that he was made to look foolish. He, therefore, prefers to cancel the sale and terminate all dealings with the defrauding vendor.

(b) Others reject R. Zera's reasoning, arguing that people will, in any case, know that he was cheated and made a laughing-stock. There must, then, be another reason why he may cancel the sale. They suggest that it is the fact that he may claim that the cheaper cloak does not befit his honour. He would, rather, prefer another more expensive one, one really worth six *denarii*.

(c) R. Johanan, R. Eleazar and R. Hoshaya offer yet a third explanation.[35] They contend that the purchaser can claim that he never really intended buying the article in the first place. For he knew

---

34 The standard editions have א' גרבת, from גרב, to rob, i.e. you have been robbed. Ms. Escorial has: אי גחכת, from גחך, to laugh, jest, i.e. you have been fooled, made to look a fool. See below.

35 In Ms. Escorial part of this section is missing.

full well that it was worth far less than the vendor was asking. But he thought that, since he was obviously pressed for money, he would give him what he wanted for it. Now that he sees the vendor has money, he can say to him: "Here, take your article back and give me back my money."

The following passage appears with some variations in Bavli Bava Batra 83b-84c. The case is as follows: Someone tries to sell his friend a certain article worth five units for six. According to all we have learned above, this is more than one-sixth of the "true" price — it is, in fact, an overcharge of one-fifth — and under such circumstances the purchaser can cancel the whole sale. However, in the meanwhile, before the sale has been finally closed, the price of the article rises to seven units (eight in the Bavli).[36] Now this would mean a defrauding of exactly one-sixth of the "true" price, and we have seen that the vendor has the right either to cancel the sale or to demand reimbursement of the excess charge. In our case, the purchaser would prefer to receive the article and get back the excess charge, while the vendor, for his part, wishes to cancel the deal. (Probably both of them think that the value of the article will go on rising.) Do we say, that, since at the beginning of the transaction the purchaser who was being defrauded had the upper hand, he continues to retain the right of choice? Or should we, rather, say that, since now it is the vendor who is losing, it is he now who gains the upper hand? R. Jacob b. Idi, R. Abahu in the name of R. Johanan answers that, in such a case, the vendor has the right to cancel the deal. For he can say to the purchaser: "Since initially I defrauded you of more than a sixth, I already then could have cancelled the sale, even against your will. For in such a case (of an overcharge of *more* than a sixth), the defrauder has as much right to cancel the sale as does the defrauded. Hence, from the very beginning I had the right to cancel the deal. Why should I lose it now that I myself have become the defrauded?" (R. Johanan here differs from R. Hisda in the Bavli, ibid., who argues that had the purchaser not questioned the deal initially, undoubtedly it would have gone through. The Sages decreed him the right to cancel a sale to his own advantage. Now that it turns out to be more to his benefit to keep the sale, why should he lose his advantage?

---

36 Lieberman, p. 151, explains that "he had not completed the negotiation when it went up in price" means that the price went up before the purchaser managed to claim the overcharge. But if he had already done so, he cannot back out of the deal. (This is the view of the Ramban [Milhamot, Bava Batra, Chapter V, section 787].) He rejects alternative explanations.

And why should the sinful defrauder come off on top in this deal?)

The Gemara now asks, is not R. Johanan's view contrary to a Mishna (Bava Batra 4.6), which states quite clearly that if a man sold his neighbour wheat as good wheat and it was found to be bad wheat, the buyer can retract? This surely means that *only* the defrauded, and not the defrauder, may retract (even though this is a case where the sale should be cancelled as a "mistaken purchase"). Yet R. Johanan has just stated that both parties have the right to do so!

The Gemara answers, making a distinction between the case of the Mishna in Bava Batra and our own. In Bava Batra, the vendor had already paid out money; hence the defrauded has the sole right to retract. But in our case both parties had thus far only dealt with verbal negotiations, which are binding upon neither of them; there has as yet been no transfer of money. In such a case both parties have the right to retract. But is this not too obvious to bear saying? No. For one might have thought that the person who retracts should be subject to the *Mi she-para'* procedure. To correct any such mistaken presumption, R. Johanan teaches us (in accordance with a *beraitha* quoted above at the end of the last *halacha*), that, in the case of verbal negotiations, either party may retract without subjection to the *Mi she-para'*. Hence, here the vendor may retract, and cancel the sale, with clear conscience. (See also Lieberman, p. 152 to line 65.)

Mishna 4 For the name of denominations used in the Mishna see above p. 29, Table B. There are twenty-four *issars* in a *dinar*, and twelve *pundions* in a *dinar*.

Gemara 4 The Gemara here quotes a *beraitha* (found with slight differences in the Tosefta, Bava Mezia 3.17-18, ed. Lieberman, p. 27) which is likewise quoted and discussed in the Bavli 52ab. It begins (in the Tosefta) much as does our Mishna: How defective must a *sela* be and *not* fall within the rule of defrauding?... This is the reading in the *editio princeps* of the Tosefta and the Vienna manuscript. However, the Erfurt manuscript reads, with the Bavli (52a): How defective must the *sela* be and — without the word "not" — fall within the rule of defrauding?... Though the standard editions of the Yerushalmi do not quote the first part of the *beraitha*, the Escorial Ms. does, reading like the *editio princeps* with the word "not". Since the Tosefta's reading is so close to that of our Mishna, some of the Manuscripts abbreviated the text, omitting what appeared to them to be merely repetitious and unnecessary.

The *beraitha* (= Tosefta, ibid. 17) ends: *More than* this, he may use it at its value... (The Bavli reads: He *sells* it at its value — see above.) In the Bavli, we see that the Amoraim R. Ami and R. Huna differed in their explanations of this passage. We, for our part, will follow the explanation of the Palestinian R. Ami, rather than the Babylonian R. Huna. According to R. Ami, the *beraitha* is stating that, if the degree of defectiveness in the *sela* is more than the amounts specified above by the various Tannaim, he may use it at its present market value, that is, at the value of its metallic content, irrespective of what its official value once was. The reasoning is as follows: If it has become so defective, no swindler will ever be able to sell it at its (former) official value; it will always be weighed and assessed in accordance with its current defective condition. (See Lieberman, *Tosefta ki-fshutah* 9 [New York, 1988], p. 180, and ibid., 2 [New York, 1955], pp. 753-755.)

The continuation of the *beraitha* (Tosefta, ibid. 18) has a somewhat amplified reading in the Bavli: [How much may it be defective, and may one still keep it? — adds the Bavli.] In a *sela*, up to a *shekel* (= half a *sela*); in a *denarius* up to a quarter [*shekel*] (= half a *denarius*). The reasoning here is simple. A coin that is defective to half its original value will never be mistakenly bought for its original value. Therefore, there is no danger of its being used for purposes of swindling. However, when it becomes worth slightly less than half its original value, it would easily be passed off as worth the *full* value of another denomination worth half the value of the original coin. Thus, *less* than half a *sela* (*tetradrachm*) might be mistakenly taken to be a *shekel* (= half *sela* = *didrachm*). Hence, the danger that swindles may be perpetrated with such coins. And the *beraitha* adds here: Less than that, even *if it is like* an *issar*, he may not use it: meaning that, even if it has become so defective that it is worth as little as an *issar* (= 1/24 *denarius*), it may still not be used. The Bavli's reading in this *beraitha* is slightly different: "Less than this, even as an *issar*..." which might be explained as meaning that the degree of defectiveness was greater even by only an *issar* (see Bavli, ibid. 52a). However, this explanation cannot easily be read into the Yerushalmi's text. Nonetheless, the explanation we have given for the Yerushalmi's reading is somewhat perplexing. For the smallest silver coin in the Greco-Roman monetary system was the *ma'ah (obol* = 1/12 *denarius,* see above p. 29). Coins of lesser denominations were of *orichalcum,* a silver-bronze alloy, or copper or bronze (above pp. 29-30). Thus, a coin so defective as to be equal in value to an *issar* (= 1/24 *denarius*) could not easily be mistaken for any other coin, since any comparable denomination would be of a different metal. The answer to this may possibly lie in the fact that Roman *provincial tetradrachms* and *tridrachms* (= four and three *denarii*, respectively), which were in use in Palestine during the later Tannaitic period were of a much more debased silver content than were Roman *imperial* silver coins, the *denarius* and *quinarius* (= 1/2 *denarius,* called a *tarapik* in Rabbinic literature). Therefore, a defective *provincial* coin might possibly be passed off as an imperial coin of *orichalcum.* However, this is highly conjectural.

The next section of the *beraitha* is found neither in our Tosefta nor in the Bavli ibid. It is, however, found (with slight differences) in a very similar *beraitha* in Tosefta Ma'aser Sheni 3.6, ed. Lieberman, p. 258. In it is discussed a situation where the value of a minted coin differs considerably from that of an uncoined piece of metal of the same size or weight (called אסימון — Greek ἄσημον, meaning uncoined, literally: without sign, and usually applied to silver).[37] For example, when coins are of pure silver their value is worth more than that of their equivalent weight in uncoined silver of the same purity, since the mint adds a minting-charge to the metallic value of the coin. Conversely, if a coin is debased with a high admixture of low-grade metal, clearly the equivalent amount of *pure* silver would be worth much more. Thus, for example, if a person had a defective *sela* which he wished to change in the market, and he could get either one *sela's* worth of uncoined silver for it, or a *shekel* (= half *sela*) in actual coin; or, conversely, in a time of monetary depreciation, if he had a very defective (clipped), but metallically pure, *sela,* he might be given half a *sela* of pure silver, but a full *sela* in debased coinage. In all such cases, one goes by what he can get for it in actual money.

The examples here are somewhat formalised for didactic purposes, and are not necessarily indicative of contemporary monetary conditions. They are given in the very easily calculated ratios of 2:1, or 1:2, and it is difficult to imagine a situation during the Tannaitic period where coins could be overvalued by 100% in relation to their metallic content, i.e. that their metallic content was worth one *shekel* but as coins they were worth a *sela.* However, if we reduce the degree of overvaluation roughly by a half, we have a situation which truly obtained during Rabbi Judah ha-Nasi's time. For the *denarius* during his period was debased by some 25%,

---

37 See Lieberman, *Tosefta ki-fshutah* 2 (New York, 1955), pp. 715-716, citing also (note 19) "Sefer ha-Ma'asim li-Vnei Erez Yisrael", *Tarbiz* 1/1 (1929), p. 95. See above, index sv. *asemon.*

though its official value, *vis-à-vis* earlier and purer *denarii*, had not officially altered. (See above, p. 39.) Thus, the coins were being overvalued by some 30% over their metallic value. That would mean that, in his time, an older pure silver *denarius*, worn down some 25% of its original weight, would be more or less equal in value to a contemporary *denarius* from the point of view of its metallic content (*asemon*)— discounting the minting-charge for the moment—, but officially it would be valued at 25% less than a contemporary *denarius*. Thus, the examples given above in our *beraitha*, though exaggerated in degree (for didactic purposes), are sound in principle.

The *beraitha* now goes on to teach that such defective coins should not be given to tax-officers and "murderers", since they are likely to use them for swindling others. This, according to our reading הרג — murderer. However, Lieberman (*Tosefta ki-fshutah* 8 [New York, 1967], p. 419, and again in vol.9 [New York, 1988], pp. 180-181) has demonstrated that one should read here חרג (with a *het*). The two terms חרם and חרג often appear together (even in a Nabatean inscription from Petra, referred to ibid., note 43), and are types of government officials concerned with taxation or customs dues. These types of officialdom were generally open to bribery and corruption (e.g. Midrach Psalms 118.18, ed. Buber, p. 486), and one was well advised to steer a wide berth of them. Certainly, opportunities for swindling should not be put in their path. (The reading in the Yerushalmi differs slightly from that of the Bavli and Tosefta.)

All the above rules, continues the *beraitha*, refer only to silver coins, *sela'im* (= *tetradrachms*) or [silver] *denarii*, since these are usually accepted at their nominal value and it would be easy to swindle with defective ones. (We have pointed out above that unqualified *denarii* in Tannaitic literature are *silver* ones.) However, coins of gold (*aurei* = gold *denarius*) are not included in these rules, since they were always carefully checked, weighed and valued accordingly. Likewise, copper (or bronze) coins. So we must read, with the Tosefta (ibid. 19, ed. Leiberman, p. 78), and not "silver", as in our text, since silver coin, *sela'im* and [silver] *denarii* have already been included in these rules above. But copper coins are excluded for a different reason from that which we gave for the gold ones. Not because they were always checked and valued according to their weight, but, on the contrary, because in Palestine the value accorded the locally-produced copper coins bore no clear relationship to their metallic value. Normally, their metallic value was far lower than the value officially assigned them. Furthermore, weights in coins nominally of the same value, i.e. of the same denomination, vary most erratically. People knew the official value of such a copper coin, even if it had no mark of value (and they rarely did), either roughly by its size category (very large, medium, very small), and/or by the images and legends on its obverse and reverse dies. Thus, since the local mints produced coins of greater and lesser weights priced at one and the same value, one could not really cheat with a defective copper coin (any more than one can nowadays with a much fingered, dog-eared, bank-note). Hence, the above-stated laws do not apply to this category of coinage.

However, Lieberman (p. 152, line 73) argues in favour of the Yerushalmi reading, "but a gold *denarius* and coins of *silver* are used at their value." Furthermore, this is the reading in Ms. Escorial, albeit in a different order: but coins of silver and *denarii* of gold are used at their value. He explains his position in *Tosefta ki-fshutah* 9 (New York, 1988), pp. 181-182. Firstly he argues that this passage refers to the ruling that one must not give such coins to the tax authorities mentioned above, because they will cheat with them. But, he asks, who would bother to cheat with copper coins, which are of very limited value. Consequently, we should prefer the Yerushalmi reading, "coins of silver". This, he suggests, refers to silver coins which are not *denarii* and *selaim* — *tetradrachms*, "but to large silver coins, which were not current in Palestine, and therefore were not valued according to their designated value, but according to their weight, and hence could not be used for cheating (p. 181, where his formulation is a little confusing). He finds further support for this interpretation of the unemended Yerushalmi reading in R. Yeruham (Sefer Mesharim 9.3), who writes that: "any *dinar* of gold or *silver* that one weighs ... even if it is slightly defective, or even very much so, may be kept ... for whoever will purchase it will weigh it." The Gaon R. Elijah of Vilna already noted that this was based on the Yerushalmi.

While it is true that Lieberman has made some sort of sense of this Yerushalmi version, and has demonstrated that it was so understood by early authorities, this, in itself, is as yet no proof of the correctness of the reading. The notion of the use of non-current, rare, large-size silver coins in Tannaitic Palestine, is somewhat unlikely. And what sort of denominations would be larger than *denarii* — *drachms* and *tetradrachms*. We may further note that *didrachms* and *tridrachms* — if he was thinking of them — were about as uncommon as *tetradrachms* in Palestine of those times. We, therefore, prefer our earlier interpretation, based on the emended reading.

The *beraitha* ends by telling us that the same rules that apply to the use of defective coins for ordinary and profane purposes, apply also with reference to the Second Tithe. The law of the Second Tithe is that a person must take a tithe of his fruit and bring it up to Jerusalem, and eat it there. However, if he should live very far from the Holy City, and to bring actual fruit would be a great hardship for him, he may substitute the fruit by money of the value and with this money purchase fruit in Jerusalem and eat it there. Money set aside for such a purpose takes on a certain degree of sanctity, though it could be redeemed with other money and again "secularized". One can redeem the Second Tithe or Second Tithe money with defective coins, in accordance with the rules set out above. However, one must not wilfully and intentionally keep defective coins for the sole purpose of redeeming the Second Tithe with them. And this is not because there is any loss to the Second Tithe, as it were, but because such practice smacks of disrespect in matters of sanctity. The parallel Tosefta text (ibid. 19, ed. Leiberman, pp. 77-78) reads here "... as long as he does not calculate to put it (or the *sela*) on the Second." It would appear that the text should be (slightly) emended to read "...as long as he does not calculate to put it on (meaning, keep it for redeeming) the Second [Tithe]." (Cf. T. Ma'aser Sheni 3.6, ed. Leiberman, p. 258, and his discussion in *Tosefta ki-fshutah* 2 [New York, 1955], pp. 753-754.)

Gemara 5 The opening passage of our Gemara is found in similar but not identical form in Yerushalmi Ma'aser Sheni 2.7 (cf. also Bavli 52b). Hezekiah here tells us that if a person outside Jerusalem has small coins of the Second Tithe and he wishes to change them into one larger coin, he may do so, even changing them into a defective *sela*, reckoning it as though it were complete and of full value. (לצרף means to change, literally combine, small money into larger units.) However, when he gets to Jerusalem and he wishes to redeem it for food, i.e. to buy with it fruit to eat within the City walls, he uses it at its defective rate. For, clearly, buying with it as though it were a non-defective coin would be to defraud the seller. Thus, according to Hezekiah, initially one may exchange Second Tithe coins for a defective *sela*.

Against this the Gemara raises an objection, basing itself upon a Mishna in Ma'aser Sheni 2.6. The Mishna there reads as follows: If a *sela* of Second Tithe was confused with a *sela* of common money, [and the owner wished to spend the common money outside Jerusalem], he should bring a *sela's* worth of [copper] coins, and say: "Let the *sela* of the Second Tithe, wherever it may be, be exchanged for these coins." He should then choose the finer of the two *sela'im* and exchange it [again] for the copper coins; for they have said: "At need silver may be substituted by copper, not that it should remain thus, but that [the copper coins] should again be substituted by silver." Thus, the Mishna here teaches that in such a case one substitutes whichever *sela* be the Second Tithe by the copper coins. Now that neither of the two *sela'im* are Second Tithe, one takes the better of the two and exchanges it back into Second Tithe, while the less fine *sela* is ordinary and profane. However, asks the Gemara, according to Hezekiah one may change Second Tithe money for defective coins outside Jerusalem! Why then does the Mishna demand that the copper coins be exchanged for the *finer* of the two *sela'im?* "Let him rather choose out the less fine one and make it [Second Tithe] as though it were complete." (The last five words, though missing in our version, are present in the Ma'aser Sheni text: כיפה.)

To this the Gemara answers that the two cases are not comparable. For, in Hezekiah's case, he initially starts with copper coins, and his first substitution is to the *sela.* However, in the Mishna's case, we know that originally one of the two *sela'im* was Second Tithe money, and it may possibly have been the finer of the two. If we now take the less fine of the two, we may be causing a loss to the Second Tithe. However, if we take the more valuable of them we obviate any such possibility.

The Yerushalmi in Ma'aser Sheni gives a somewhat fuller and more closely reasoned answer, explaining the Mishna as follows: R. Jona said: "I say she (the finer *sela*) was the [original] Second Tithe [*sela*]." However, did it not become common money? (— by being substituted by copper coins. And in that case, it is of no interest to us what it *once* was. All that matters is that *now* it is common money, and should we choose to exchange the copper coins for a completely different *sela*, this one will remain common money.) R. Jona said [in answer]: "He should (or—did) not intend it to become [absolute and] certain common money, [when he exchanged it for copper coins]. You may know that this is so, from what we have learned (above) in the Mishna: '... not that it should remain thus, but that [the copper coins] should [again] be substituted by silver'." In other words, says R. Jona, his original intention when exchanging the Second Tithe *sela* was not really to make it fully and wholly profane, but to reconvert it shortly afterwards to the Second Tithe. Hence, we suspect that it may have been the finer of the two coins that was originally the Second Tithe one, and by "reconsecrating" it to the Second Tithe ensure that there was no loss involved. Apparently, substitution involving loss to the Second Tithe would, in this case, not be considered a whole-hearted substitution, but one which was to its gain (that is from the less fine to the finer *sela*) would be considered whole-hearted substitution.

(One may ask, why did the Mishna have to present such a complex procedure? Why could one not merely take out the finer of the two, as a first stage, and declare: "If this is the common coin, may the Second Tithe be substituted by it. And if it is itself the Second Tithe one, may it so remain"? Surely this would satisfy all our requirements in a far simpler fashion? The answer lies in the fact that there is a certain rule which states that silver Second Tithe coins may not be substituted by other silver ones. Hence, in our case, the process of substitution and resubstitution has to go through a copper-coin stage.)

The Gemara continues by quoting a passage from the Mishna which stated that one may use such defective coins as Second Tithe money without any scruples, since only an evil-minded person would refuse it. This quotation may be intended to give the basis for Hezekiah's statement cited above, that one may substitute copper Second Tithe coins for defective ones, etc. However, it may equally well be an independent statement, unrelated to the previous discussion. Indeed, this would not be the first time we have come across exact repetition of parts of the Mishna in the Gemara text.

The next passage in the Yerushalmi is to be compared with Yerushalmi Ma'aser Sheni 4.3, which, though differing considerably from our *sugya*, contains much parallel and related material. (See also above Bavli 53b.) R. Jacob b. Zavdi (Idi, in Ma'aser Sheni), R. Johanan (lacking in Ma'aser Sheni), in the name of R. Simon (Simai in Ma'aser Sheni, the more correct reading on chronological grounds) teaches that Second Tithe worth less than a *peruta* — the minimum denomination of Rabbinic times — is not subject to the law of the added fifth. Or, more correctly, it may not be substituted; hence, the law of the added fifth is not applicable to it. For, normally, when a man redeems his Second Tithe he must add one fifth more (Mishna Ma'aser Sheni 4.3). In this case, however, it is not considered redeemable. It is only considered redeemable when, if redeemed, a fifth of its value *can* be added according to Biblical prescription. When this is not possible — as in our case — it may not be redeemed. According to a second tradition, that of R. Johanan in the name of R. Jannai (or R. Jose b. R. Simon in the name of R. Johanan, as in Ma'aser Sheni), even if the actual Second Tithe is worth more than a *peruta*, but a fifth of its value would not equal a *peruta*, then, too, it is not deemed redeemable. (See Bavli 53b.)

The Gemara goes on to say that both these views have their support in Tannaitic sources, and their own exegetical derivations. They are both derived from the same Scriptural verse in Lev. 27.31: "And if a man

381

redeem aught of his tithe, the fifth part of it he shall add unto it." Some learn from the word ממעשרו "of his tithe" — "*of* his tithe" and not just "his tithe". This "of" is to exclude that tithe which is worth less than a *peruta*. Others apparently derive their view from the proximity of the two words in the verse: ממעשרו חמישיתו, proposing that the "of" relating to "his tithe" may be exegetically applied to the following adjacent word, "the fifth part thereof", as if to say "*of* the fifth part thereof" — מחמישית — some and not all fifths, to exclude the case where the fifth is worth less than a *peruta*. The whole controversy appears in Bavli 53b, in the names of R. Ami and R. Ashi.

The *sugya* winds up with R. Ba (= Aba) b. Memel (as in Ms. Escorial and in Ma'aser Sheni, the more correct reading) telling us that our Mishna appears to hold neither of the above views. For, among the "five *perutot*" enumerated there, there is no mention made of a *peruta* which is the minimum value of Second Tithe for it to be redeemable, and among the "five fifths" no mention of a *peruta* which is the minimum value of the added fifth thereof, for it (the Second Tithe) to be redeemable. Thus according to the reading in our printed editions.

However, Ms. Escorial reads somewhat differently and has this passage in a different position, following on the statement of R. Johanan in the name of R. Jannai. The text there reads as follows:

> Said R. Ba bar Memel: Our Mishna is neither like this one nor like this one. For we have learned in our Mishna, "There are five [cases where added] fifth [are prescribed], and we did not learn 'except where a fifth part of it is worth a *peruta*.' And we learned (i.e. listed among them) 'Five [cases of] *perutot* [are prescribed], and we have not learned (i.e. listed among them)' except when it is worth a *peruta*."

The meaning is much the same, and R. Aba bar Memel is stating that neither section of our Mishna, neither that which speaks of "five *perutot*" nor that which speaks of "five fifths" seem to reflect the views of R. Simai or R. Johanan. For R. Simai spoke of the Second Tithe having to be worth at least a *peruta,* and R. Jannai that a fifth of the Second Tithe must be worth at least a *peruta*. Our Mishna seems to reflect neither view, says R. Memel. Finally, in the order preserved in Ms. Escorial, we are told that there are some exegetes bearing out the one view, and others bearing out the other (see above). The order in Ms. Escorial seems preferable. Indeed (as noted above), R. Aba bar Memel's statement is absent in Ms. Leiden and was supplied in the margin by the editor, perhaps out of order.

Gemara 6 The whole Gemara appears with some variations in Bavli 58b. The *beraithot* quoted are to be found in Tosefta Bava Mezia 3.24, ed. Leiberman, p. 78. The Bavli adds to them some brief explanatory notes, as, for example, the reason why the laws of defrauding do not apply to horse and arms during times of battle, "because they are matters of life [and death]." We are reminded of the famous line in Shakespeare's Richard III (IV.7): "A horse! a horse! my kingdom for a horse." See also Lieberman's comment in *HaYerushalmi Kipshuto* (Jerusalem, 1934), p. 437, that we are talking of a mare and not a stallion.

As to the following word תריס, shield, the parallel Tosefta text has in its different reading: והטיאוב, והטיטוס, והסיטום. I discussed this in detail in my "Essays on Greek and Latin in the Mishna", *Talmud and Midrashic Literature* (Jerusalem, 1982), pp. 87-93, suggesting that this is the Homeric word καταῖτοξ, helmet. However, Lieberman, in his *Tosefta ki-fshutah* 9 (New York, 1988), p. 183, prefers (tentatively) to identify it with ἴτυς, a round shield, which would make it closely parallel our Yerushalmi's תרים, shield. Ms. Escorial (p. 58, line 89) reads: טומטום, which is surely a clear corruption from והסיטום or והטיטוס.

Gemara 7 The opening passage of the Gemara is fraught with difficulties. According to the text, in the form it now is found before us, it appears that R. Avdima Malha steeped his nets (סרדוותא; סרדוותא in Ms. Escorial) in water. Malha is a part of his name, and has nothing whatsoever to do with salt. It may well be Midgal Malhia, mentioned in Yerushalmi Demai 2.6 (see M. Avi-Yonah, *Geographia Historit shel Eretz-Yisrael*, p. 110; but cf. S. Klein, *Sefer ha-Yishuv*, vol.1, p. 105). Aramaic מפתר = Hebrew פשר, to soak, and סרדוותי׳ may be compared with Hebrew סרד, net, web, etc. (see Jastrow, *Dictionary*, p. 1023; S. Krauss, *Additamenta and Aruch Completum*, p. 304). He apparently did this to improve their appearance, and in seeing him do so R. Jacob b. Aha remarked in surprise: "Surely we have learned in the Mishna that one is not permitted deceptively to improve appearances thus?"

The first difficulty in this interpretation is encountered in the next line. For the Gemara now goes on to say that from R. Jacob b. Aha's question we may learn that the prohibition of the Mishna applies not merely to persons, live animals and vessels (the three categories enumerated in the Mishna), but also to foodstuffs. However, according to our understanding of the text thus far, no mention has been made of food, only of "nets".

And so some commentators explain the passage as meaning that

R. Avdima soaked lean meat in water so that it might look whiter and fatter. They suggest that we read סרדוותא (rather than סרדוותא), from the Greek σάρξ — σαρκός — meat, flesh (see A. Kohut, *Aruch Completum*, vol.6, p. 132). However, the difficulty here lies in the fact that there is a *beraitha* in the Tosefta (Bava Mezia 3.29, ed. Lieberman, p. 80, cited in the Bavli 60b) which states quite unequivocally that one may not soak meat in water. Thus, R. Jacob b. Aha should have cited the Tosefta in support of his objection, rather than the Mishna, which in fact makes no mention of food. Furthermore, even if we were to assume that R. Jacob b. Aha was not aware of this *beraitha*, and therefore did not quote it, surely the Gemara should have cited it in his support, concluding that the laws against improving appearance deceptively apply to foodstuffs too. The Tosefta is surely better authority for such a ruling than an Amora's objection! (See Lieberman, *Tosefta ki-fshutah* 9 [New York, 1988], p. 189.)

Jastrow in his *Dictionary* sought to solve the problem in a different fashion. On p. 1023 he explains our text as meaning that R. Avdima "steeped his sails in water (to improve their appearance)." You might ask: "But what has this to do with food?" However, we find that on p. 1171 of his *Dictionary*, Jastrow corrects יש פרכוס באוכלים to בכלים — "giving a deceptive appearance to *garments* is forbidden." In this way he makes this statement refer below to the following cases of R. Zera and his flax, R. Abahu and his veils, rather than to the preceding passage. However, his emended statement is quite superfluous, since it is mentioned already in the Mishna. And should one suggest that this is just another example of the repetition of a Mishnaic line in the Gemara, how does one explain the word מלתיה — his (R. Jacob b. Aha's) word (or question). One would have to emend this to מתניתא — our Mishna. Thus, all in all, Jastrow's explanation falls far short of being convincing. (See also Lieberman's comment, p. 153, note 29, that Jastrow's suggestion makes little sense. Indeed, why would anyone want to soak his sails?!)

In fact, we do not even know the meaning of the words we are dealing with. For example, פתר could mean "to make lean or thin," as well as to soak (*Aruch Completum*, vol. 8, p. 468). However, even without knowing the exact meaning of all the words in the passage, we may, nevertheless, still make an intelligent attempt at deducing the general gist of the argument. And the first point of importance seems to be that the Mishna and the Tosefta are *not* teaching the same thing. Thus, the Mishna says "one must not bedizen ... a live animal," presumably meaning one may not cover it with make-up, while the Tosefta says that one may not cause a live animal to have a deceptive appearance of stoutness, and the Gemara explains the Tosefta by stating that one may not feed it with bran-water which bloats it up. Likewise, one may not bloat the innards (of an animal), or soak meat in water so that it be heavier and fatter-looking. For, when selling things thus treated, one is selling, in fact, a certain amount of water under the guise of meat, since the meat is not really as heavy as it seems, nor the animal as stout as it looks. The extra is water, not meat. The Mishna, however, teaches that one may not superficially decorate, ornament or paint things, so that they appear to be nicer, newer, etc. than they really are. Here one would be deceiving the eye, rather than actually cheating and defrauding.

Apparently, R. Avdima did something which changed the outward appearance of what he was selling, though not its weight or inner form. Such an activity had not been dealt with by the Tosefta. R. Jacob b. Aha pointed out that the Mishna forbids such activity too. This was in the nature of a *novum,* since the Mishna had not actually mentioned food, only live animals, as the Gemara rightly points out.

According to this, it follows that R. Avdima did something in the nature of superficial or surface decoration of some kind of food item. Further than that we cannot go, and the exact meaning remains shrouded in uncertainty. (Perhaps, he did indeed soak meat, but in a coloured sauce that affected its colour. Cf. *Scriptores Historia Augusta,* Elegalus 24.1, where it is related that he would cook fish in a bluish sauce that preserved their natural colour, as though they were still in sea-water.)

See further Lieberman, p. 153, who understands סרדוותא — סדרוותא as nets or sieves. He suggests that R. Avdima, who has a shop (cf. Y.Sukka 2.5, 53a), used to soak perforated (wicker-work?) baskets full of foodstuffs in water. The water would drain off, and the foodstuffs would look better and fresher.

In the next two episodes related, we are told that one is allowed to decorate merchandise, and improve its appearance. We learn from the Bavli (60b) that this is not considered fraudulent practice, since people willingly pay more for an attractive product.

However the text of R. Abahu's question is a little problematic. He apparently manufactured and/or sold veils. He asked R. Jose (Josa) b. Hanina what he might do to beautify them. So according to the printed edition: מנן באילין לסוטיא (=מה אנן), what may I do with these veils [to make them more beautiful]. But Ms. Escorial (p. 59, lines 105-106) here reads מה פסיפסין באילין לסוטייה. Lieberman (p. 153) corrects: [נן מעבד] מה, פסיפסין באילין לסוטייה, may I make [coloured] spots (checks, square or striped) on these veils. He refers us to the Mishna in Nega'im 11.7: קייטא שיש בה פספסים צבועים ולבנים, a summer garment which has checkers coloured and white (the signs of leprosy)... It seems somewhat strange that he should have asked whether he was allowed to decorate, dye, his veils. What kind of deceit is here involved? Perhaps he was just creating an impression of colour, without really colouring them, such as, for example, by placing them on a multi-coloured background(?).

Then we come across three words (or, at least, three groups of three letters) רבה שקר[38] טהר, which appear to make little sense. Numerous interpretations have been offered, but none are really convincing. It is by no means clear whether this sentence belongs with what came before it, or with what follows after it. It seems clear that it requires emendation. Should we wish to harmonise it with the Bavli, we should bear in mind that there (60b) we read of Rabba's permitting the preparation of certain coarse threads of material. We might here correct our text, to harmonise it with the Bavli's tradition, to read רבה שרק טרד'. שרק (for שקר)=(סרק, to comb out. טרד' (for טהר; the די combined into a ה, and then there was a metathesis) = the Bavli's צרדי — coarse threads. (צ' and ט' frequently interchange in Semitic languages.) However, this is all complete conjecture, and only one of many such possibilities. Furthermore, the Leiden manuscript of the Yerushalmi reads here: רבה ר' שקר טהר — which, if anything, makes even less sense. Lieberman (p. 153, line 107) suggests that Rabba used to paint (סקר = שקר) (with red paint סיקרא?) and shine (טהר) his merchandise to make it look attractive.

Finally, the Gemara concludes by telling us that the beautification of a man (or slave) consists in painting him with make-up (see Bavli ibid.).

---

38 Ms. Escorial has: השקר.

INFLATION AND LINKAGE (INDEXATION) IN ROMAN PALESTINE: A STUDY IN REACTIONS TO INFLATION*

The Problem

We have seen that the third century C.E. was one of great inflations and devaluations. The precise details of the story may not be altogether clear, and may be subject to conflicting views. However, the general picture is fairly well known, and the scale and extent of monetary deterioration has been plotted with a fair degree of accuracy. We have shown that, during the first half of the century, the inflationary process was relatively slow, while during the 'sixties and' seventies of that century, the value of the *denarius* — whether as a coin or unit of reckoning is immaterial at this point — rocked and plummeted downwards in a somewhat irregular series of dives. Similarly for the fourth century, there is evidence of monetary deterioration and spiralling prices.

It is clear that people in all walks of life had to find techniques to protect themselves against such disturbing monetary instability. How did people lend out money, and assure themselves of getting the full value back? How were long-term payments in instalments calculated? Did landlords renegotiate the terms of their rent every few months? We know that the army paid an ever-increasing portion of the soldiers' salary in kind, food, drink, clothing and equipment. Likewise, during this period, land taxes tended more and more to be claimed in kind, grain, flour and other kinds of agricultural produce. The fourth-century taxes were claimed largely in the form of pure gold ingots of standard weight, stamped by the local

---

* First appeared in a volume entitled *Les "Dévaluations" à Rome Epoque Républicaine et Impériale*. École Française de Rome, Palais Farnèse, Collection de L'École Française de Rome, 1978, 181–191. (This version has slight changes.) References to "this volume" cited in the notes below refer to this book.

387

authorities.[1] Such techniques had the added effect of simplifying what might otherwise have been very complex operations both for soldiers, civilians and the authorities. Is there evidence of such protective measures in other sectors of society? Drawing upon Rabbinic sources — hitherto somewhat unforgivably ignored by classical historians —, the following study will try to show some of the attempts to find solutions to these problems. It purports to do no more than isolate a few solitary examples, but examples which demonstrate the solution of linking to some kind of stable "standard".

Linkage to Gold Coins

We begin with a text already partially discussed in our recent book on Roman Palestine.[2] The text appears in the Palestinian Talmud (hereafter designated Y. = Yerushalmi = Jerusalem Talmud), Ketubot 11.2. In it R. Abbahu (died 309), quoting his teacher R. Johanan (died 279), cites the following example to illustrate a legal point:

> If he borrowed from her twelve thousand for a year, on condition that he repay her one gold dinar (= *aureus*) a month.[3]

From this text we may deduce the following three things:

(a)   Since Jewish law does not permit one Jew to take from his fellow Jew interest on a loan, the sum returned cannot exceed the sum borrowed. Hence 12,000 [*denarii*] = 12 *aurei*, which means that at the time the statement was made there were 1000 *denarii* to the *aureus*. On the basis of this evidence we have dated the text to *circa* 268–74.

(b)   During this period, the *denarius* was so debased that it was no longer called by its name, but merely left as an unspecified unit. This becomes even clearer when we compare texts from this period with earlier ones where the *denarius* is always specifically mentioned.[4]

(c)   The third point, and the one of most significance for our present purposes, is that a person lending out money, in whatever denomination, makes it a prior condition that the money be repaid to him in gold coins,

---

1   On the effect of inflation on the army, see J.M. Carrié's communication in this volume (second part). On taxation problems see M. Corbier's remarks in her paper in this volume (sect. III. 3). See also my *Roman Palestine 200–400: The Land* (Ramat-Gan, 1978), *passim*.

2   Above, pp. 38–39.

3   The text is cited in its original form p. 302, text M.

4   Cf. above, pp. 91, 164–65.

aurei. In this way he guarantees himself that he get back the full value of the sum he lent out.[5]

Probably it became quite unprofitable to borrow in anything other than gold currency. The public had largely lost confidence in the debased silver coins which flooded the market, so much so that on the evidence of the famous P.O. 1411 (260) banks were loth to accept "the devine money of the emperors", and had to be forced to do so by special edict.[6] For this reason it became more common for the borrower to take out his loan in gold coins. We note, for example, the following text in the Palestinian Talmud, probably of a slightly later date than the one previously cited.[7]

Y. Ketubot 12.1: ... He undertook to give her twelve gold *dinars*, at [the rate of] one gold *dinar* per month for a year...

And still more explicit is the text in *Deuteronomy Rabba* 4.10,[8] which may be dated to the third quarter of the third century:

Said R. Levi: Just as one who said to his friend: "Lend me a gold piece (*zahuv*)". He answered him: "I do not know your account", (i.e., whether you are reliable and will be able to pay up). "Check up on me", he said. And he checked up on him, lent him [the money], and he repaid immediately. On a different occasion he said to him: "If you require even thirty gold pieces, take whatever you want... since you made a good account with me."

For much the same reason securities are given in gold coin during this period, as we may see from a text in Y. Sheviit 10.4. There, in a late third- or early fourth-century discussion between R. Zeira and R. Abbahu (which latter died 309), the *zahuv*, gold coin, is mentioned as the security par excellence, though gold rings also figure in this capacity.[9]

---

5 Cf. above, p. 85. Here it should further be noted that according to the nominalistic theory of money found in the Talmud, sums borrowed in coin must be repaid in coin, and not, for example, in gold bullion which was regarded as "produce" as opposed to "coin". And this in order not to transgress the laws of usury (*ribit*). See above, general index, s.v. "coin". On payment in gold, see also H.C. Pflaum's communication in this volume on the famous *Marbre de Thorigny*. See, however, further M. Corbier's remarks in her paper in this volume (section III.5).

6 Above, pp. 87, 231, n. 11. Cf. J. Schwartz's communication in this volume.

7 Later, because it is part of a discussion on a statement made by R. Simeon b. Lakish, who died *c.* 275.

8 Ed. Lieberman, p. 95, cited above, p. 87.

9 One may perhaps point out here that those fourth-century texts which speak of lending and borrowing 100 *myriad*, or 200 or 300 *myriads* (above, p. 165), obviously give no indication in which kind of currency these sums were borrowed.

Linkage to Gold Bullion

We have just seen that people would make it a prior condition that money they lent out be repayed to them in gold coins, or that someone undertaking to pay out a large sum in instalments would (be required to) do so in gold coin. And by gold coin we mean *aurei* primarily. Now we know that during the period under discussion the *aureus* was by no means of a standard weight. Indeed, there was a distinct tendency during the third quarter of the third century for its weight to be diminished. It has been suggested that this diminution was, as it were, in sympathy with the debasement of the *antoninianus*, in order to keep a more stable ratio between them.[10] It may also be that some of the small gold pieces, minted for example during Gallienus' later period, represent a different denomination, a *quinarius aureus*, or something of that nature. Even accepting this possibility, in the latter part of the third century large quantities of *aurei* of varying weights were circulating on the market. When people undertook to pay out in *aurei*, presumably they knew more or less what they meant by the term, larger ones and not smaller ones, and so forth. Nonetheless, one can easily see how this too could become a source of conflict and contention. The instability in the weight of the *aureus* made this a term of ambiguous value. The whole point of linkage is to make clear and safe one's investment, and to diminish elements of uncertainty and ambiguity. Hence, for example, a judge dealing out fines which he well knew might not be paid in the most immediate future, would seek to use terms unambiguous and stable with which to formulate the amounts he wished to specify. Against this background we may now appreciate more fully the meaning of a text found in Y. Bava Kama 8.6:

> A certain fellow angered R. Judah b. Ḥanina. The case came up before Resh (= R. Simeon) b. Lakish, and he fined him a *litra* (= *libra*) of gold.

R. Simeon b. Lakish died *circa* 275. Here we find him fining someone not the sum of x *denarii* or even y *aurei*, but a fixed weight of gold bullion. In this way his judgement is freed of all ambiguity, obviating the possibility of further argument as to the exact value of the fine. Here, then, the move is away from linking to gold coin towards linking to gold bullion.

Obviously this greater emphasis on the use of gold coin and even of gold

---

10   Above, p. 44.

bullion[11] brought increased hardship upon the poorer classes. During the time of grave economic difficulties, when the "underprivileged" were in great need of loans to tide them over the lean years, they were incapable of getting them, since they clearly could not guarantee return payment in gold specie. Hence, it is from the later third century that we hear (in Y. Pe'a 1.6) that "a poor man cannot borrow" (i.e. cannot get credit).[12]

Linkage to the Tyrian Standard (Holy Shekel)

The devaluation of the silver coinage had, of course, numerous and varying effects, both socio-economic and legal. One of these effects was to lower the real value of such obligations that the law had earlier stipulated in terms of a fixed sum of *denarii*. Thus, for example, the minimum sum for a (virgin's) *ketuba* (marriage-settlement)[13] was fixed at two hundred *denarii*. It is not yet known exactly when this sum was determined. However, in the first and second centuries of the common era, two hundred *denarii* constituted a significant amount of money, probably over two-thirds of an ordinary farmhand's annual wage.[14] Throughout the third century the real purchasing-power of this sum progressively decreased. Admittedly, prices did not change radically till probably some time around the 'sixties of that century.[15] Nonetheless, it is probable that already in the first half of the third century poor people were benefiting and enjoying the gradual decrease in their *ketuba*-obligations. Indeed, some authorities saw this as an acceptable development. Their fellow-Rabbis, on the other hand, regarded this as a progressive infringement upon the woman's legal rights, something the law obviously could not brook but was obliged to rectify.

Hence, during the first half of the third century we find the Rabbis discussing this issue. Couched in their own parlance, they formulated the problem as follows: Does the two hundred *denarii* of the *ketuba* represent a fixed and unwavering amount of silver to be reckoned in terms of the

---

11 Cf. above, pp. 85, 228–29, notes 1–5.
12 Above, p. 86, text on p. 306, text AB.
13 On the *ketuba*, see the article in the *Encyclopaedia Judaica* (Jerusalem, 1964), vol. 10, pp. 927–28. "The 'main' *ketubbah* is the amount determined by law as the minimum that a wife is entitled to receive from her husband or his estate on the dissolution of the marriage" (ibid., p. 927). To this may be added the increment, *tosefet ketuba*, which a couple may choose to add to the basic minimum.
14 Above, pp. 101–102.
15 Above, p. 132.

Holy *Shekel* (= Tyrian Standard)?[16] Or are they two hundred *denarii* of current usage, whatever the weight, metallic-content and purchasing power of the *denarius* happen to be?[17] In Y. Ketubot 1.2 we read that Huna in the name of Samuel (d. Babylonia 254) said: We reckon in the holy *shekel* standard while R. Ba (= Abba) b. Bina (= Avina) (*floruit circa* 240–270) says: *Matbe'a yoẓei*, i.e. whatever coin is circulating. The Talmud continues to tell that: All those Rabbis, R. Ḥanania, R. Jonathan,... R. Joshua b. Levi (*floruit circa* mid-third century) say: *Matbe'a yoẓei*. So also R. Jacob b. Aḥa[18] (late third century), R. Imi (= Ammi) (died early fourth century) and R. Simeon b. Lakish (died *circa* 275) in the name of R. Judan Nesiah say: *Matbe'a yoẓei*... And even R. Johanan (d. 279), (who apparently had earlier held otherwise) changed his mind to follow their opinion. It seems, then, that the majority of Rabbinic authorities through the third century saw this as quite an acceptable interpretation (viz. situation). It answered the needs of the poor who probably found it difficult, at this stage, to undertake a monetary obligation of the order of two hundred full-weight Tyrian *drachmae* (or the silver equivalent).

16 On the Tyrian standard see above, p. 270, note 6, with bibliography, from which it will be seen that this standard continued to be used in Palestine and in Syria long after Tyre had ceased to mint the full-weight *tetradrachmas*, etc. (around the mid-first century C.E.). The holy *shekel*, which basically means that money which the Bible is referring to (according to Rabbinic understanding) or money paid in accordance with a Biblical injunction, is always equated in Talmudic literature with the *shekel* (or *mana*) Ẓori = Tyrian *shekel* or standard. See, for example, Tosefta Ketubot ad fin., and further Lieberman's comments thereon in *Tosefta ki-fshuṭah*, ibid., pp. 391–92, with full references. The basic problem of whether the *ketuba* is of Biblical or Rabbinic authority formed the subject of extensive discussion and conflict of opinion in subsequent Jewish legal literature. See, for example, B.M. Lewin, *Otzar ha-Geonim*, 8, Ketubot (Jerusalem, 1938), Teshuvot pp. 38–43, and M. Margulies, *The Differences between Babylonian and Palestinian Jews* (Ha-Ḥillukim...), (Jerusalem, 1938), pp. 102–107.

17 This controversy is usually linked up with another even more basic one, namely, whether the *ketuba* obligation is of Biblical or of Rabbinic authority. If of Biblical authority, it should be paid in the holy *shekel* standard, but if Rabbinic in current coin. Indeed, this manner of explaining the source of a controversy is borne out by a text in Yerushalmi Ketubot ad fin. according to readings in some mediaeval commentators of the Talmud. The passage reads: R. Simeon b. Gamliel says: A woman's *ketuba* is only of Rabbinic authority (*mi-divrei soferim*). [This helps to bear out the view of him that said: *matbe'a yoẓei*.]... The section in square brackets is found in the Ittur, Shita Mekubeẓet (citing the disciples of R. Jona) and Hagahot Mordechai. See S. Lieberman, *Tosefta ki-fshuṭah*, 6 (New York, 1967), pp. 389–90 for an extensive discussion of this issue.

18 Perhaps we should amend to read R. Jacob b. Aba, of the mid-third century.

On the other hand, it is clear that when there were already as many as a thousand *denarii* to the *aureus*, a *ketuba* reckoned in current coin would be worth as little as a fifth of an *aureus*, a patently absurd situation. For what measure of security did such a sum guarantee to the wife in the event of her being divorced or widowed? Even more so in the fourth century, when there were many thousands and even tens of thousands of *denarii* to the *aureus* (or *solidus*).[19] With this in mind the bride, or more probably her parents or guardian, would, no doubt, demand additions to the basic *ketuba* (called in Rabbinic terminology *tosefet ketuba*),[20] which might even take the form of gold ornaments, etc. Such additions were recorded in writing in a *document* called the *(shetar) ketuba*, (to be distinguished from the *ketuba obligation*), and were contractually binding.

The Talmud (ibid.) continues:

A case came up before R. Ḥanina (second half of fourth century) of a woman whose *ketuba* was less than two hundred *zuz* (= *denarii*) and he said: She should take what he (the husband) wrote her (i.e. what is written in the *ketuba*). He said to R. Mana: Sit and sign (that you confirm my judgement). Said he (R. Mana) to him: On the

---

19 Above, pp. 164–168. I think my suggestion that the fourth-century inflationary condition known so well from Egypt obtained in Palestine and Syria too has been generally accepted. See, for example, J.-P. Callu's communication in this volume (section V), and his careful assessment of the epigraphic evidence from Syria. Perhaps it is in place here to point to yet another piece of possible evidence in this direction. A text in *Canticles Zuta* to Cant. 8.14 (ed. Buber, p. 37; ed. Schechter, p. 46, line 1377, and p. 95) states that Rabbenu ha-Gaddol(?) said: At that hour Amalek sent and took all the leaders (*alufei*) of Edom and gave each of them a thousand thousands (*elef-alafim*) of *denarii* (= 1,000,000 d.)... (In the parallel in Yalkut ha-Machiri to Isaiah 9.11 [ed. Schapira, p. 74]: he gave a *dinar* to each of them... The "thousand thousands" has apparently been deleted as being an unreasonable exaggeration. However, this is a secondary text, and the reading in Cant. Zuta should be preferred.) Obviously we have here a word-play on *alafim* and *elef-alafim*. Nonetheless, the resultant total of one million *denarii*, even if it be an exaggerated round number, must have made some kind of sense to the audience of this homily. The attribution of this text to Rabbenu ha-Gaddol (usually R. Judah ha-Nasi, died *c.* 220 C.E.) is most likely pseudo-epigraphic. Certainly the text as it stands could not have been formulated in the late second or early third century. It would, therefore, appear that we have here a text of the mid- or later fourth century, one which speaks in sums of money the order of which made good sense at that time. Such a dating of the text fits the general literary character of *Canticles Zuta*. The use of the term *denarius* in the mid-fourth century is well attested (see Callu's paper in this volume, section V).

20 E.g. Y. Ketubot 12.1; also called *tenai [ketuba]*, literally "the [additional] condition [of the *ketuba*]", e.g. Y. Ketubot 9.10, 12.2.

contrary, you change your opinion to conform with mine, and sign thus. Did not R. Ḥiyya[21] say in the name of Samuel: In holy *shekel* standard, we reckon.

The *sugya* (= Talmudic unit of argumentation) goes on to tell:

R. Avduma of Sepphoris (third quarter of fourth century) in the name of R. Ḥuna[22] (mid-fourth century) says: Because she has forgone (i.e. if there was less than two hundred *denarii* written in her *ketuba*, obviously she was willing to forgo the full amount, and receives no more than what appears in the *ketuba* document, and this in current coin).[23] If so,[24] let a woman whose *ketuba* is less than two hundred *denarii* hide it (i.e. the document) and claim according to the holy *shekel* (rate).[25] They[26] (i.e. the students of the Academy) said in the name of R. Ḥuna: This is in a place where they do not write out the *ketuba*. But in a place where they do write out the *ketuba*, whatever she can get (according to her *ketuba*) is all she can get.[27]

---

21 Note that above the reading was Huna.

22 Or according to another reading: Yoḥana. But Ḥuna seems more acceptable.

23 So, according to the interpretation of Z.W. Rabinovitz, *Sha'are Torath Eretz Israel* (Jerusalem, 5700–1940), pp. 376–77, basing himself on the reading as found in Naḥmanides' commentary to Ketubot ad fin. On the permissibility of stipulating a *ketuba* of less than two hundred *denarii*, see M (= Mishna) Ketubot 4.9, 5.1; B (= Babylonian Talmud) Ketubot 56b. Cf. also Y. Ketubot 4.12 ad fin.

24 So according to Rabinovitz, ibid., the printed editions read: *mishum vitur me'ona*, which the classical commentaries to the Yerushalmi (Pnei Moshe and Korban ha-'Edah) explain as being the name of a scholar. (Most unlikely!) Rabinovitz (basing himself on the Ramban) convincingly emends to: *mishum vitur. Me'ata...* (= If so...). The different explanations vary in accordance with the readings, but this point in no way affects our argument.

25 It is not altogether clear whether the Yerushalmi means to say that under such circumstances a woman will be able to hide her *ketuba*, etc., even though this is not legal, or that she has the legitimate right to do so. We have followed the latter interpretation, with the commentators, which argues that if the *ketuba* is to her disadvantage she may suppress it, whereas, if it is to her advantage she may claim according to its terms. The difficulty in this interpretation lies in the wording of the Talmud. Why does she have to hide it? If it is invalid because it runs counter to an established ruling, she should not have to hide it, but just to demonstrate its legal invalidity. This whole problem need, however, not be discussed in this context, since the differences in interpretation do not affect our argument.

26 The printed edd. have "He said", but Rabinovitz (ibid.), following Naḥmanides (above, note 23), reads "They said", which makes better sense. Naḥmanides see this as the beginning of a new issue, while according to our interpretation it is a natural continuation of the preceding argument.

27 Cf. Y. Ketubot 9.9.

The commentators (ad loc.) explain that in such places where the *ketuba document* was not actually written out, people relied upon local practice. The local authorities presumably fixed the amount according to certain agreed criteria, and this amount was accepted as authoritative and binding, and constituted local practice. Now we have seen from the above text that local practice reckoned the *ketuba*, not in terms of *matbe'a yozei* — current coin — but in terms of the holy *shekel*, full-weight silver *denarii*. Why should this be so? Was not the view of the Rabbis of the third century overwhelmingly in favour of reckoning in "current coin"? Why then this sudden change of view, which expresses itself in the opinions of R. Mana and R. Avduma of Sepphoris and the anonymous students of the Academy of the later fourth century?

The answer to this anomaly would appear to be as follows: In those places where local practice was to write out the *ketuba*, each couple came to their own individual contractual arrangement. In doing so, they used the traditional two hundred *denarii* as the basic minimum, and added to it the increment (*tosefet*) at will, in accordance with their individual requirements and understanding. However, where local custom was *not* to write out the *ketuba*, this must surely have been because the resident authorities had fixed a standard rate for everyone to follow. In such a case where the couple nonetheless decided to write out their *ketuba*, despite the fact they were not required to do so, this was because they wished to deviate from the local norm, either adding to it in the case of the wealthy, or subtracting from it, in the case of the poor. The Talmud appears to rule that if someone wrote out a *ketuba* which obligated him to less than what local practice required, the wife nonetheless retained the right to the full amount, counselling that she suppress the written document and claim in accordance with the local norm.[28]

Now it seems reasonable to assume that in those places where the *ketuba* was not written out and the authorities (periodically?) decided upon a fixed rate, they based their decisions upon the traditional sum of two hundred *denarii*. However, were they to follow that (third-century) view which interpreted this sum as being reckoned in local currency, they would reach the absurd situation where a woman's marriage settlement would be worth virtually nothing. For, in the fourth century, two hundred *denarii* equalled a mere fraction of a *solidus*. The *ketuba* would be valueless and meaningless. Such a situation was obviously quite untenable and had to be rectified. The Rabbis had to find a way to restore real value to the *ketuba*.

---

28 Cf. above, note 22.

They could have done so by adding to the now worthless *ketuba* an increment (*tosefet*) of real worth. But this would result in a peculiar legal situation, where the real (*ikkar*) *ketuba* was worthless and, practically speaking, the increment formed the real *ketuba*. Rather than suggest such an anomalous and illogical solution, the local Rabbis of the fourth century simply reverted to an interpretation of the *denarius* as being of the holy *shekel* type. In other words, they now linked the traditional sum of the *ketuba* to the Tyrian standard, and, according to this reckoning, the *ketuba* would be worth a little over eight *solidi*.[29] In point of fact, in doing this they were not ruling against the opinion of the earlier third-century Rabbis,[30] but merely exercising their legitimate right to fix the value of the *ketuba* for local use according to the holy *shekel* standard.[31] Of course, poor people who felt they could not afford such amounts would try to reduce them by writing out their own private contractual documents and stipulating lesser sums. The phenomenon of the *ketuba* of less than two hundred *denarii* remains an eloquent testimony to the poverty of certain strata of society.

Conclusion

These few examples, which merely whet the appetite for further research, may serve to give some kind of insight into the sort of problems encountered as a result of inflation, devaluation and monetary instability. Such major economic and monetary disturbances made their impact on people in all walks of life. They raised problems which were for them

29 There are twenty-five Tyrian *drachmae* to the *aureus*; hence two hundred *denarii* (= Tyrian *drachmae*) = eight *aurei*, and slightly more *solidi*. The Tyrian *drachma* was approximately comparable with the fourth-century *argenteus* (see above, pp. 61–62). This sum is also not really of significant value, and in all probability additional increments were required, increments whose value were periodically determined. However, the *ikkar ketuba* did not have to be periodically revalued since it was linked to a stable silver standard. This further avoided the problem of "retroactive" revaluation. For the *ketuba* should be of realistic value at the time of divorce or decease and not merely at the time of marriage. In the intervening period between marriage and divorce or decease a given sum of money, which was in no way linked to anything stable, would (and usually did) decrease considerably in value. Retroactive revaluation can be legally a complex issue.

30 It is most unlikely that the Rabbis of the fourth century would decide directly against the rulings of their predecessors of the third century, most especially when these predecessors included such outstanding personalities as R. Johanan (first and foremost) and (then) R. Simeon b. Lakish.

largely new and hitherto unencountered. To us these problems sound strangely topical and the solutions have a contemporary ring to them. Nowadays gold indexes, cost-of-living indexes and the numerous other forms of indexing are a commonplace, by-words in every house and home. In antiquity the problems were basically similar, but the means of dealing with them were far less sophisticated.[32] Our knowledge of these various attempts to grapple with such fundamental economic phenomena adds a further dimension to our understanding of the times.

31   One might well ask why this legal innovation is only first attested in the middle or later fourth century and not earlier. Surely the monetary situation already in the earlier part of that century would have justified such a change? One can only reply that legal thinking is traditionally conservative, and there is often quite a time-lag between the social cause and the legal reaction or reply. In addition, a careful perusal of J.-P. Callu's paper in this volume suggests that probably the period when the situation became truly acute was during the 'forties. If so, our Rabbis' legislation may not have been so tardy in coming.

32   See P.O. 2587 from the year 289, for an arrangement in which a creditor was repaid in "new coin" for a loan that was made in old "Ptolemaic" coin. The editor writes (pp. 145–146): "By way of an explanation I suggest that some old coin, which still retained a value as bullion, was adopted as a standard so that no loss would be incurred by a businessman who put his capital into a transaction that covered a period of time. That is, in the case of an interest-free loan, a man could lend current money equivalent to a certain number of 'Ptolemaic' *drachmae* on condition that the debtor repaid the value of the same amount of this coinage at the rate current at the time of the repayment. If the value of the new *tetradrachm* fell, more of them would have to be paid back at the end of the term." See also A. Segré, *Chronique d'Egypte*, 40 (Jan. 1965), pp. 204–205 (cf. above, pp. 311–12, which latter requires slight correction). This late third-century text fits well into the economic context described in the former part of this paper, but the technique involved is remarkably reminiscent of that discussed in the latter part of this paper. There is, indeed, a considerable amount of papyrological material mentioning coins of παλαιοῦ πτολεμαιχοῦ νομίσματος and χαινὸν νόμισμα (much of which is referred to in the above-mentioned articles), all from the later third century. These show a deep involvement in and concern with this problem of coin battling the effect of inflation upon private contractual arrangements. Indeed, the system was used in local banking, and "the bankers must have been familiar enough with them (i.e. the Ptolemaic coins, or the standard they represented — my own addition) to have a constantly revised exchange rate for them" (ibid., p. 146). The use of an older, better value coin as an exchange standard is paralleled by the use of coins "of the old kings" in Rabbinic Palestine (above, pp. 136–67, 253, n. 27).

'MEHAGINOT' = TRAJANIC *TETRADRACHMS**

A passage in the Palestinian Talmud which has troubled scholars for over a century is that which speaks of *Mehaginot tetradrachms*. In the following study we shall analyse explanations hitherto offered, point out their weaknesses, and suggest a new interpretation for the text.

In Y. Ketubot 1.2 we read the following: "...Said R. Johanan (d. C.E. 279): Sela'im [= *tetradrachms*] Severiniyot, Mehaginot, Yerushalmiyot, some say so and some say so..."[1]

The legal context is as follows: Some authorities are of the opinion that a woman's marriage settlement (*ketuba*) must be paid in a given sum, 200 *drachmae* for a virgin and 100 *drachmae* for a widow, as reckoned according to the Tyrian standard. (This was believed to be the full-weight standard to which the Bible referred.[2]) Others stated that it could be paid in current coin, i.e. with 100 or 200 current *denarii* (= *drachmae*), whatever their weight or standard be. R. Johanan now entered the discussion by adding that three types of *tetradrachms* were considered by some to be suitable for the payment of the *ketuba* and by others unsuitable. Presumably this is because these three classes of coins did not satisfy the requirements of the Tyrian standard. Hence, those that required payment according to the full Tyrian standard ruled out their use, while those who permitted the sum to be reckoned as 100 or 200 current *drachmae* or *denarii* admitted their use.

---

* First appeared in Numismatic Chronicle 1977, pp. 153-55.

1 The Hebrew text reads: א״ר יוחנן: סלעים סביריניות מהגינות ירושלמיות אילין אמרין אכן ואילין אמרין אכן. (So according to Ms. Leiden, edn. *princeps*, etc.) I have been unable to find any significant variants to this reading.

2 See, e.g., M. Bechorot 8.7 = B. Bechorot 50b = B. Kiddushin 11a = B. Bava Kama 36b. (See also Y. Kiddushin 1.3 and parallels, and my remarks on this text in *Tarbiz* XLII/1–2 [1973], 55–9.) The whole halachic context of our passage is extremely complex. See, e.g., S. Lieberman, *Tosefta ki-fshuṭah*, 7 (New York, 1967), p. 389f.

The first and the last class of *tetradrachms* are easily identifiable. "Severan *tetradrachms*" are those from the (late?) period of the Severan dynasty, when the coinage was already considerably debased, and well below the Tyrian standard. "Jerusalem *tetradrachms*" are those issued during the first Palestinian revolt (68–70), bearing the legend "Jerusalem the Holy". These, though perhaps of full weight, were considered "revolt money" and hence were not legal tender. As such, their value could be reckoned only according to the weight in bullion, which, of course, would be slightly below their professed value.[3] But what is 'Mehaginot'? Zuckermann, already in 1862,[4] suggested that we correct מהגינות to מהנינות — *Mehaninot* — 'ist eine Dyrrhachiner Münze des königs Monunios'. However, such an explanation is extremely far-fetched, since Monunios lived far from Palestine, several hundred years before R. Johanan, and there is no reason that R. Johanan should ever have known of this obscure coinage.[5]

Levy, in the same year,[6] suggested emending the whole text to: סלעים נרוניות מהגמונות ירושלמיות — "Neronian *tetradrachms* from Jerusalemite leaders." However, this emendation makes little sense, and was rightly rejected by Herzfeld,[7] whose own tentative suggestion (relating it to a Persian word) is, however, hardly an improvement. Jastrow[8] unnecessarily emends Severan to Tiberian,[9] and creates a new verb הגן — "to balance, make corresponding," hence reaching the following translation of our text: "The Tiberian Selaim are of the same weight as etc." [i.e. the Jerusalem ones]. The emendation has no basis; the conclusion is numismatically meaningless — Tiberias never produced *tetradrachms*[10] — and the lexicographic innovation is fanciful, to put it mildly.

---

3   See above, p. 223, note 19; also p. 136 f., 253, note 27. On "revolt money", see ibid., p. 136 f.

4   B. Zuckermann, "Über talmudische Münzen und Gewichte", *Jahresbericht des jüdisch-theologischen Seminars Breslau* (1862), p. 15f.

5   On Monunios see *PWRE*, 1/31, p. 231 f., s.v.

6   M. A. Levy, *Geschichte der jüdischen Münzen gemeinfasslich dargestellt* (Leipzig, 1862), p. 125, note 2.

7   L. Herzfeld, "Metrologische Voruntersuchungen zu einer Geschichte des ibräischen resp. altjudischen Handels, III," *Jahrbuch für die Geschichte des Juden und des Judenthums*, 3 (Leipzig, 1863), p. 160. (It is strange that this very valuable study received no mention in B. Kanael's otherwise excellent bibliography in *JNG* [1967] 158–298.)

8   Jastrow, *Dictionary*, 331b, s.v. הגן.

9   See my remarks above, p. 223, note 19.

10 See, e.g., A. Kindler, *The Coins of Tiberias* (Tiberias, 1961), *passim*.

Other attempts, for example that of N. Brüll,[11] to read מונוגיניות =
Μονογένης,referring to Bar-Kochba, or S. Krauss,[12] who explains it as
coming from the Latin *mango* = false(?), are in the final analysis
unconvincing.

What is required is a coin, a *tetradrachm*, current in Palestine and (still?)
well known in the third century C.E., a coin prior to the year 279
(R. Johanan's decease). This *tetradrachm* was, for some reason or other,
worth less than a Tyrian *tetradrachm*. It may well lie chronologically
between the Severan ones, of the late second and/or early third centuries
C.E. and the Jerusalem ones of the years 68–70.

Tentatively I would offer the following suggestion to satisfy the
requirements we have set for a solution to our problem. The Hebrew letter
with which the *mem* (M) is most regularly interchanged through scribal
miscopying is the *tet* (T)–this in view of their great similarity in form,
most especially in handwritten manuscripts. The *heh* (H) could well have
come about through a *waw* (V) entering into the space underneath a *resh* (R).
Admitting this (conjectural) development, we reach an original reading of
טרוגינות. Now the emperor Trajan is, in Rabbinic sources, variously called
טרגינוס, טורגינוס, טרוגיונוס.[13] Hence טרוגינות could very possibly refer to
Trajanic *tetradrachms*. (This fits chronologically well in between the
Jerusalem and the Severan *tetradrachms*; see above.) It is well known that
during Trajan's reign there was a change in coin standards and that he
minted new *denarii* of a slightly lower standard than those of Domitian
and Nerva, debasing them around 15 per cent.[14]

It would seem not implausible that during this period, i.e. some time
after *c.* 100, the approximate date of Trajan's monetary reform, certain
authorities ruled that such coins of reduced weight and metallic content
could no longer be regarded as equalling the Tyrian standard, and
therefore could not be used as a standard for reckoning the payment of a
ketuba, etc. Or, to formulate it slightly differently, one could no longer

---

11 In his *Jarbücher für Judische Geschichte und Literatur*, 1 (Frankfurt-am-Main, 1874),
    p. 183f.
12 *Griechische und Lateinische Lebnwörter im Talmud, Midrasch und Targum*, ii (Berlin, 1899),
    323b, s.v. מהגן. See also I. Löw's remarks thereto, ibid., 323b–324a. (H. Y. Scheftel, in
    his *Erech Millin*² [Berditschev, 1907], 100a, s.v. מהגינית סלע, seems to have
    misunderstood Krauss, or more precisely Löw.) See further L. Hamburger, *Die
    Münzprägungen während des letzten Aufstandes der Israeliten gegen Rom* (Berlin, 1892),
    p. 104, whose suggestion is also highly unlikely. (Our explanation follows that of Löw.)
13 See Krauss, *Lehnwörter II*, p. 273a, s.v. טרייגוס.
14 See my article, *NC* 1970, p. 111, bibliography, ibid., note 1.

reckon a virgin's *ketuba* as 200 Trajanic *denarii*. It would now be somewhat more.

This leads us on to a further point. It is obvious that R. Johanan, in the later third century, did not make a ruling on the status of Trajanic *tetradrachms*. From his (halachic) point of view, the same is true of all coins subsequent to this period, since the process of debasement was progressive and constant. Indeed, he is quoting the opinions of others, not his own. Furthermore, he is quoting these traditions in something like their original form. For basically there is no real difference between the halachic position of the Trajanic *tetradrachms* and that of the Severans. Yet R. Johanan cites them as separate cases. This clearly suggests that he was basing himself on earlier traditions, presumably *beraithot*, which he collected, collated and (partially) reformulated. The *beraitha* dealing with Jerusalem revolt money was probably first formulated in the later first century C.E., the ruling on Trajanic reduced coinage in the early second century, and that of Severan coins in the late second or early third century. R. Johanan linked them together in one sentence.

However, while some of the coins discussed belong to the first and early second centuries, these coins were still known in R. Johanan's time, and even current within his lifetime. They were used as a partially stabilizing element alongside the official debased currency of the mid-third century.[15] This continued to be the case until their demonetization some time between *c.* 250 and 260.[16] Hence, R. Johanan's statement, which was formulated some time before *c.* 260, was not totally abstract, but had practical contemporary meaning.

15 See above, pp. 135–40.
16 Ibid., and *NC* 1970, pp. 113–15.